IS THE CHINESE ECONOMY A MIRACLE OR A BUBBLE?

IS THE CHINESE ECONOMY A MIRACLE OR A BUBBLE?

Lawrence J. Lau

World Scientific

NEW JERSEY • LONDON • SINGAPORE • BEIJING • SHANGHAI • HONG KONG • TAIPEI • CHENNAI • TOKYO

Published by

World Scientific Publishing Co. Pte. Ltd.
5 Toh Tuck Link, Singapore 596224
USA office: 27 Warren Street, Suite 401-402, Hackensack, NJ 07601
UK office: 57 Shelton Street, Covent Garden, London WC2H 9HE

British Library Cataloguing-in-Publication Data
A catalogue record for this book is available from the British Library.

Originally published by The Chinese University of Hong Kong Press

ISBN 9789819807055 (hardcover)
ISBN 9789819807291 (softcover)

For any available supplementary material, please visit
https://www.worldscientific.com/worldscibooks/10.1142/14154#t=suppl

Printed in Singapore

To Ayesha, my muse, my love, and my life

Contents

Section II: The Strategies of Economic Development: China and East Asia

Section III: The Chinese Economy in the New Era

Foreword

Dale W. Jorgenson[*]

This volume of Lawrence Lau's collected papers on the Chinese economy provides a comprehensive and detailed discussion of the remarkable growth of the Chinese economy at nearly double-digit rates in the four decades since the reforms begun by Deng Xiaoping in 1978. The book begins with an analysis of the sources of Chinese economic growth, including the accumulation of tangible assets, increases in education levels, economies of scale, and improvements in technology. Surprisingly, improvements in technology play a very minor role as sources of Chinese economic growth.

The introduction to the sources of Chinese economic growth concludes with a forward-looking view of the future of the Chinese economy in the "new era" of President Xi Jinping. Although the growth rate of the Chinese economy is beginning to slow, China will continue to grow more rapidly than advanced economies in Europe, North America, and Asia. The book presents an analysis of the Asian currency crisis of the late 1990s and the Chinese response to the United States economic crisis that followed the Lehman bankruptcy in 2008.

The volume continues with an analysis of the economic strategies adopted by the Chinese government to promote the transition of the Chinese economy from a centrally-planned economy to a market-based economy by means of a "dual-track" approach. The key to this strategy is to preserve the central planning mechanism, while developing a wider and wider range of markets. An important component of this strategy is the opening of the Chinese economy

---

* Prof. Dale W. Jorgenson (1933–2022) was Samuel W. Morris University Professor at Harvard University.

to international trade and carefully controlled foreign investment. The volume concludes with projections of the long-term development of the Chinese economy and provides an up-to-date discussion of the consequences of a trade war between China and the United States.

The book provides an answer to the question posed by the title, *Is the Chinese Economy a Miracle or a Bubble?* The exceptional performance of the Chinese economy is unexpected, but its persistence rules out the possibility of a bubble. The growth of the Chinese economy can be explained by fundamental principles of economics: capital accumulation, improvement of labour quality, and economies of scale. Chinese economic growth, though very impressive, is not a miracle. This volume will be an indispensable reference to the development of the Chinese economy—past, present, and future.

December 2018

Preface

I was born in 1944, near the end of the Sino-Japanese War (1937–1945), in Zunyi, Guizhou Province, China, while my parents, fleeing from the invading Japanese army, were en route from Guilin to Chongqing, the wartime capital of China. Guizhou was then, and still is now, one of the poorest provinces in China. Our family moved back to Hong Kong from Chongqing when I was two. I received my kindergarten, primary school, and secondary school education in Hong Kong, before enrolling at Stanford University as a freshman in 1961. It would be more than 40 years later before I would become a resident of Hong Kong again. Stanford was my home from 1966 to 2004, when I returned to Hong Kong to assume the position of Vice-Chancellor (President) of The Chinese University of Hong Kong.

In my freshman year at Stanford, I took an introductory course in economics from Prof. John G. Gurley (then the Managing Editor of *American Economic Review*), using Prof. Paul A. Samuelson's *Principles of Economics* as a textbook. Prof. Gurley was such a great teacher and Prof. Samuelson's textbook was so lucid and logical that I decided to switch from physics to economics for my graduate studies. I was recruited by Prof. Dale W. Jorgenson, who later became my Ph. D. dissertation adviser, and enrolled in the Department of Economics of the University of California at Berkeley as a graduate student in 1964.

Sometime in 1965, I received a telephone call from Prof. Edward S. Shaw, then the head of the Department of Economics at Stanford University. I had taken a course on money and banking from him when I was an undergraduate student. He offered me a position as Acting Assistant Professor in the Department of Economics, specialising in the Chinese economy, but without any teaching responsibility in the first year. Not fully realising what I would be getting into, I accepted, and wound up spending the next almost forty years at Stanford. Because of the Stanford assignment, as well as my own background, I was particularly interested in the economic development of China and began to do research in the subject area. In 1966, I constructed what was probably the first econometric model of Mainland China, a purely supply-side model, using whatever fragmentary data that I could find at the time.

My first visit to China as an adult was in 1979, soon after China decided to undertake economic reform and open its economy to the world, as a member of the first U.S. delegation of economists to China, under the auspices of the American Economic Association. There were ten of us, led by the late Prof. Lawrence R. Klein, the 1980 Nobel Laureate in Economic Sciences. Also in our delegation was the late Prof. Kenneth J. Arrow, the 1972 Nobel Laureate in Economic Sciences, and Prof. Dwight H. Perkins, an expert on the Chinese economy at Harvard University. The Chinese Academy of Social Sciences was our host. We visited Beijing, Changsha, Nanjing, Shanghai, Wuhan, and Xi'an. We had an audience with Chinese Vice-Premier Gu Mu. We also met with quite a few Chinese economists such as Prof. Chen Daisun of Peking University, Prof. Chen Xikang of the Chinese Academy of Sciences, and Prof. Xu Dixin, Vice-President of the Chinese Academy of Social Sciences. At that time, the roads in the major cities had almost no cars, but many bicycles; the few shops had little to sell; and everyone wore more or less the same blue outer jacket. At the end of our visit, we were asked to forecast the future rate of growth of the Chinese economy. Using my simple supply-side econometric model, I forecast 8 percent, the highest in our delegation; the lowest forecast of my fellow delegation members was 1 percent. As it turned out, the average annual rate of growth of the Chinese economy over the past 45 years was over 9 percent!

In the summer of 1980, I visited China again, as one of the faculty members of a seven-week Econometrics Workshop in Beijing organised by Prof. Lawrence Klein in conjunction with the Chinese Academy of Social Sciences. The other faculty members of the workshop were Prof. T. W. Anderson of Stanford University, Prof. Albert Ando of the University of Pennsylvania, Prof. Gregory Chow of Princeton University, Prof. Cheng Hsiao, then of the University of Toronto, and Prof. Vincent Su of the City University of New York. The workshop was held in Longwangmiao (the Temple of the Dragon

King) on an island in the middle of Kunming Lake inside the Summer Palace. We had one hundred students drawn from all over China, many of whom (for example, Mr. Wang Chunzheng and Ms. Li Boxi) became important contributors to the success of the Chinese economic reform. We also had an audience with Chinese Vice-Premier Yao Yilin. One outcome of our visit was the decision of the Chinese Academy of Social Sciences to establish an Institute of Econometrics, which became the Institute of Technical and Quantitative Economics.

Then in 1986, Prof. Gregory Chow arranged for four U.S. economists of Chinese descent, all members of the Academia Sinica in Taipei—Prof. John C. H. Fei, Prof. Anthony Y. C. Koo, Prof. Chow himself and me—to visit Beijing and advise the Commission for Restructuring the Economic System, which was chaired concurrently by the then Chinese Premier Zhao Ziyang. We introduced to the Commission and its Vice-Chairman, Mr. An Zhiwen, the development experience of the Taiwan economy, including, in particular, the foreign exchange certificate trading system adopted in the process of liberalisation of its current account. We were also assigned the task of developing a plan for the adjustment mechanism of the renminbi (the Chinese currency) exchange rate. Thus began my many subsequent visits to China, advising various organs of the Chinese government on the economy.

In 1988, I was introduced by Prof. Lü Yingzhong, a Visiting Scholar at Stanford from Tsinghua University, to Prof. Zhu Rongji, then the Dean of the School of Economics and Management of Tsinghua University. Prof. Zhu invited me to become an honorary professor of his school and I readily accepted. Prof. Zhu would later become first the Executive Vice-Premier and then the Premier of the People's Republic of China.

In 1992, macroeconomic stabilisation became a pressing issue. The Commission for the Restructuring of the Economic System, with the support of the then Executive Vice-Premier Zhu Rongji, convened an international conference on the subject in Dalian in 1993. I participated in the planning of the conference and, with the cooperation of the World Bank, Mr. Lou Jiwei, Prof. Qian Yingyi and Ms. Alice Yu, succeeded in inviting Dr. Li Kwoh-Ting, widely acknowledged as the "Father of the Taiwan Economic Miracle," to attend the conference and to visit Beijing. At the time, Dr. Li was the highest-ranked official from Taiwan to visit the Mainland since 1949. While in the Mainland, he was received by both President Jiang Zemin and Executive

Vice-Premier Zhu Rongji, who consulted with him on economic, financial and exchange rate matters. Much of Dr. Li's advice was incorporated in subsequent Chinese economic policies and measures. With the macroeconomy stabilised, in 1994, China undertook three important reforms: the unification of the multiple exchange rates and the adoption of current-account convertibility of the renminbi, reform of the financial sector, and the introduction of the value-added taxation system.

In the aftermath of the Mexican currency crisis in 1994, I began to think about the detection of early warning signals of currency crises to come. In September 1995, in a paper jointly authored with Prof. Jungsoo Park of Sogang University, Seoul, presented at the Project LINK world meeting in Pretoria, South Africa, I identified Thailand, South Korea and the Philippines as the economies most vulnerable to a currency crisis, and that the Chinese economy would be relatively safe. The East Asian currency crisis actually erupted in Thailand on 1 July 1997 and soon spread to other East Asian economies. I then made a series of specific recommendations to the Chinese government as to the appropriate response, including the maintenance of the renminbi exchange rate vis-a-vis the U.S. dollar, the expansion of public infrastructural investment, the full rebate of the domestic value-added tax paid for exports, etc. These recommendations were adopted by the Chinese government, enabling the Chinese economy to maintain its steady growth and survive the crisis relatively unscathed. By not devaluing the renminbi, the Chinese government also facilitated the recovery of the other East Asian economies from the East Asian currency crisis, earning their praise and gratitude.

Chinese accession to the World Trade Organization in 2001 was pivotal to its economic growth in the new millennium. It enabled the massive movement of the surplus labour from the primary (agricultural) sector to the secondary (manufacturing, construction and mining) sector, in response to the rising demand for Chinese manufactured exports from the rest of the world. In 2018, a trade, investment and eventually technology war broke out between the U.S. and China. However, by this time, China is no longer dependent on rising net exports for its growth and instead relies on its own internal demands for consumption and investment. The priority of the Chinese Government has also shifted to enhancing the quality of growth rather than the quantity of growth. The prospects for continued Chinese economic growth at an average annual rate of around 6 percent for the coming decade look quite promising.

The focus of this collection of my published papers on the Chinese economy is economic growth and macroeconomic strategies, policies, and measures. I have therefore not included other papers either authored or co-authored by me that deal with Chinese economic phenomena at the microeconomic or sectoral levels, such as agriculture and international trade (except for one article on the China-U.S. trade war [Chapter 13 of this volume]). For example, I have not included the value-added-based estimations of the China-U.S. bilateral trade balances. Hopefully, these articles will be included in future collected volumes.

Hong Kong, China
November 2023

Acknowledgments

I wish to thank my wife, Ayesha Macpherson Lau, for her constant encouragement as well as her insightful comments on many successive drafts of this collected volume. I am also most grateful to the late Prof. Dale W. Jorgenson, my mentor, Ph. D. dissertation adviser, and collaborator for more than half a century. What I know about economic research I have learnt from him. And I particularly want to thank him for writing the Foreword for this volume in 2018. I thank my my co-authors, Jong-Il Kim, Yingyi Qian, Gerard Roland, and Huanhuan Zheng, for the privilege of collaborating with them, and for allowing me to reprint our joint articles in this volume.

My very first visit to China as an adult was in 1979, soon after the late Mr. Deng Xiaoping steered China down the road of economic reform and opening. I was privileged to have had a ring-side seat for the entire process of the Chinese transition from a centrally-planned to a market economy. I also had the good fortune of knowing personally Premiers Zhu Rongji and Wen Jiabao, Vice-Premiers Li Lanqing, Zeng Peiyan, Wang Qishan and Liu He, Vice-Chairman Chen Zhili, Chen Yuan, and Zhou Xiaochuan, and many other Chinese economists and government officials such as An Zhiwen, Chen Xikang, Dai Xianglong, Du Runsheng, Guo Shuqing, Huang Da, Jiang Mianheng, Li Jiange, Li Kemu, Li Yining, Lin Yifu (Justin), Liu Guoguang, Liu Mingkang, Lou Jiwei, Lu Mai, Peng Xiaomeng, Wu Jiapei, Wu Jinglian, Wu Xiaoling, Xie Ping, and Xu Guanhua. I am most grateful to all of them for their friendship and for educating me about the Chinese economy over all these years.

I am also indebted to Prof. Chen-Ning Yang, Michael Boskin, Kwok-Chiu Fung, Ambrose Y. C. King, Pak-Wai Liu, Peter Nolan, Jungsoo Park, Dwight Perkins, Myron Scholes, Michael Spence, Joseph Stiglitz, Lawrence Summers, Junjie Tang, Suping Wu, Yanyan Xiong, and Ting-Hin Yan for their invaluable advice, assistance, encouragement and support, without which this book would not have been possible. Credit should also go to my colleagues at The Chinese University of Hong Kong Press—Gan Qi, Lin Ying, Ye Minlei, Justin Wai Hin Cheung, and Angelina Wong—for their strong commitment and persistent efforts in publishing this volume. Finally, I also wish to express my heartfelt thanks to Claudia Chui, my long-time personal assistant, for her loyal and unfailing support. Of course, I retain sole responsibility for any remaining errors and for all opinions expressed herein, which do not necessarily reflect the views of any of the organisations with which I am or have been affiliated.

Introduction

The economic growth of China, since it undertook economic reform and opened its economy to the world 45 years ago, in late 1978, was historically unprecedented in terms of both its speed and longevity. The Chinese economy has been growing without interruption at an average annual real rate of over 9 percent for more than four decades, even though it has slowed down to an average rate of growth of around 6 percent in more recent years. Chinese GDP grew from US$389 billion in 1978 to US$17.37 trillion in 2022 (all in 2022 prices and exchange rate), almost 45 times, to become the second largest economy in the world, with 68.2 percent of the GDP of the largest economy, the United States. What is most remarkable is that during the 45 years between 1978 and 2023, there was not a single year in which the level of Chinese real GDP declined (or equivalently the rate of growth turned negative), despite the many crises that occurred both inside and outside of China. However, due to the outbreak of the COVID-19 epidemic in the city of Wuhan in late 2019, and its subsequent resurgence in Shanghai in 2022, the rates of growth declined to 2.2 percent in 2020 and 3.0 percent in 2022, the lowest and second lowest since the beginning of economic reform.

This is also in great contrast to China's economic performance in the three decades, 1949–1978, before its economic reform and opening to the world, during which its annual rate of growth fluctuated unpredictably and wildly, with a high of 22.3 percent in 1952, the year before the launch of China's First Five-Year Plan, and a low of –27.3 percent in 1961, the last year of the great famine of 1959–1961. Even then, the average annual rate of growth during this pre-reform period was a very respectable 7.5 percent. This high average annual rate was due in part to the rapid economic recovery after the

Communist victory in the Chinese Civil War in 1949.[1] If the period of recovery and rehabilitation of 1949–1952 is excluded, the Chinese pre-reform average annual real rate of growth still stood at 6 percent, higher than those of most developing economies. The annual levels and rates of growth of the Chinese real GDP in 2022 U.S. dollars from 1949 to 2022 are presented in Chart 0.1.

As the Chinese population has been growing continuously between 1978 and 2022, when it declined for the first time, the rate of growth of real GDP per capita has been lower than the rate of growth of real GDP, but by not quite 2 percent. Chinese real GDP per capita grew from US$404 in 1978 to US$12,309 in 2022 (also in 2022 prices) at an average annual rate of 8.1 percent, without any interruption, achieving a more than 30-fold increase (see Chart 0.2). China went from being a very poor country, with a GDP per capita barely above the subsistence level of one U.S. dollar a day, to being a middle-income country,[2] in just a little more than a generation.[3] Even then, the Chinese economy still only ranks below 70th in terms of real GDP per capita in the world. During the pre-reform period of 1949–1978, the average annual rate of growth of Chinese real GDP per capita was 5.2 percent. The rate would drop to 4.0 percent if the recovery and rehabilitation period of 1949–1952 is excluded. The more than doubling of the average annual rate of growth of real GDP per capita in the post-reform period, from 4.0 percent to 8.1 percent, is mostly attributable to the economic reform and opening that was undertaken, with perhaps around 1 percentage point attributable to the decline in the rate of growth of the Chinese population as a result of the adoption of the "one-child" policy in 1979 in China.[4]

---

1 There are also some questions with regard to the reliability of the Chinese economic statistics during the Great Leap Forward period of 1958–1959.

2 The threshold for a middle-income country is often taken to be an annual GDP per capita of US$12,000.

3 A generation is usually taken to be between 25 and 30 years.

4 The "one-child" policy resulted in a lower population and a lower level of household consumption, hence a higher rate of national saving and a higher rate of national investment, resulting in a higher rate of growth of real GDP per capita.

Chart 0.1. Chinese Real GDP and Its Annual Rate of Growth (Trillion 2022 US$ and percent)

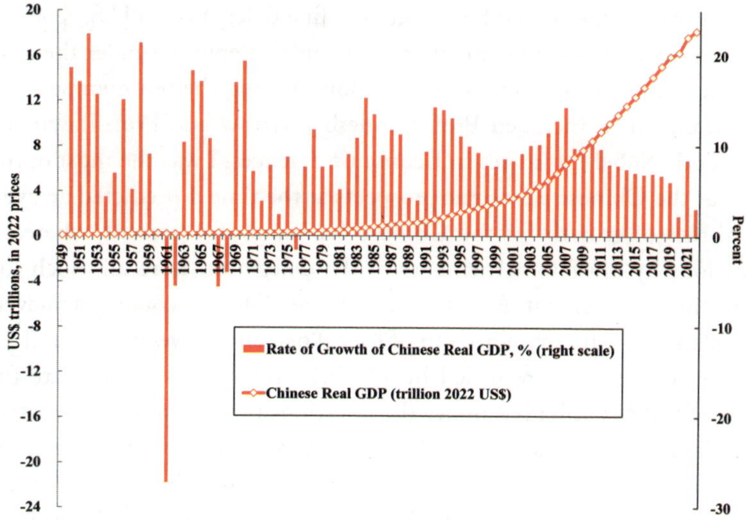

Source: National Bureau of Statistics of China, converted to 2022 U.S. dollars by the author.

Chart 0.2. Chinese Real GDP per Capita and Its Annual Rate of Growth (Thousand 2022 US$ and percent)

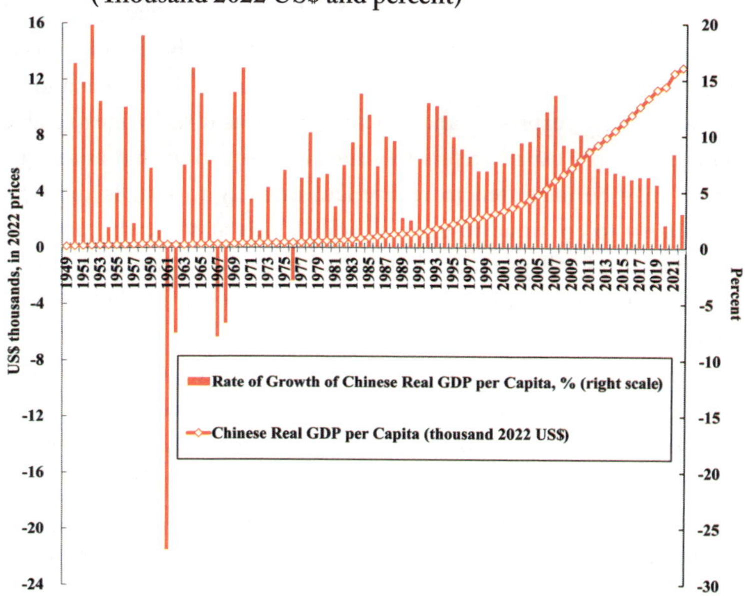

Source: National Bureau of Statistics of China, converted to 2022 U.S. dollars by the author.

The Chinese development experience since 1978 has been most unexpectedly and spectacularly successful. The first time I visited China as an adult was in 1979, as a member of the very first delegation of U.S. economists to China since the establishment of the People's Republic, under the auspices of the American Economic Association. Among the ten members of the delegation, which included Prof. Kenneth J. Arrow and Prof. Lawrence R. Klein, both Nobel Laureates in Economic Sciences, I was the most optimistic about the Chinese economic prospects at the time. I predicted an average annual rate of growth for the Chinese economy of 8 percent, whereas the predictions by my fellow members of the delegation were all much lower, some as low as 1 percent. As it turned out, the Chinese economy achieved an average annual real rate of growth of over 9 percent between 1978 and 2022. No other economy in recorded history has grown at as high a rate for as long a period as China has done. The questions that naturally arise are: Was the Chinese economy a miracle? Or was it a mere bubble? Will the Chinese economy begin to stagnate like the Japanese economy did in the 1990s, and perhaps even go into decline? Will it be able to escape the "middle-income trap"? If it is not a miracle, can the Chinese development experience be replicated elsewhere?

A miracle is defined in the dictionary as "a surprising and welcome event that is not explicable by natural or scientific laws and is therefore sometimes considered to be the work of supernatural power." The highly successful Chinese economic development performance over the past four and a half decades was clearly surprising and welcome, but was it really inexplicable? In economics, a bubble usually refers to a fortunate situation that arises quickly, but which may be unrelated to reality and unlikely to last. Is the Chinese economy likely to continue to grow steadily, albeit at somewhat lower rates, or will it burst and collapse like a bubble? I hope to convince readers that the growth of the Chinese economy is neither a miracle nor a bubble and that it will continue its solid and steady growth.

Section I and the chapters included therein are concerned with the following questions: What are the sources of this unprecedentedly high and sustained rate of economic growth? Can the Chinese economic growth of the past 45 years be understood in conventional economic terms?

Of course, one obvious explanation for the high rate of growth of real output is the high rates of growth of the primary inputs—tangible capital, labour, and human capital. Their rates of growth have indeed been high for China, both before and after the economic reform of 1978. The establishment of free markets and the introduction of conditional autonomy for the producers under the economic reform begun in 1978 obviously had a large and positive impact. But there were also other factors at work as well in the Chinese economy: for example, the growth of intangible capital such as human and Research and Development (R&D) capital, the existence and realisation of significant economies of scale and "learning by doing," the initial slack in the economy prior to the economic reform in 1978, and technical progress (or equivalently the growth of total factor productivity [TFP]). What are the relative contributions of these different sources of economic growth since 1978? How much of the Chinese economic growth is due to the growth in inputs, and how much is due to increases in efficiency (or equivalently technical progress or the growth of TFP)? How much is due to "working harder"? And how much is due to "working smarter"?

However, high rates of growth of inputs alone do not always guarantee success in achieving a sustained high rate of growth of real output, in the absence of appropriate facilitating and supporting government economic policies. Many developing economies have had high rates of growth of inputs but nevertheless have not been able to grow in a sustained and sustainable manner. The economy of the former Soviet Union was such an example. The economic strategies adopted and the economic policies and measures implemented can and do make a difference. The chapters included in Section II review and analyse the economic strategies, policies, and measures employed by China in its process of economic reform and opening to the world since 1978. Choosing economic strategies and policies that were appropriate to the unique Chinese domestic conditions and environment was critical to the success of Chinese economic reform. These include export promotion, maintenance of a stable exchange rate coupled with capital control, development of basic infrastructure, macroeconomic stabilisation, and implementation of the "grandfathering" principle and the "dual-track" system. However, it also turned out that many of the Chinese policies and measures were similar to those used in other East Asian economies, beginning with Japan, during the early stages of their economic development. Some pre-existing economic policies were already in place before 1978, and they were not significantly modified under the economic reform. One such policy is the low-wage policy in the non-agricultural sector. Prior to 1978, all workers in the non-agricultural sector were employed, directly and indirectly, by the state, which could unilaterally dictate the wage rate and other conditions of employment.[5] A low-wage policy would minimise aggregate household consumption and maximise the profits of state-owned enterprises (SOEs), which would in turn help to keep the national savings rate high. Moreover, a continuing low wage rate in the non-agricultural sector would enhance its capacity to absorb the continuing inflow of the surplus labour from the agricultural sector and put it to much higher productivity use in the non-agricultural sector.

A low-wage policy also supports a high national savings rate,[6] which in turn enables a high domestic investment rate, without having to rely on the more fickle inflows of foreign investments, foreign loans, or foreign aid. And to the extent that the savings are under the control of the central government, they can be used to finance investment in basic infrastructure, such as communication and transportation networks, ports and airports, and power plants, which are absolutely essential in the early stage of economic development.[7] Moreover, with the availability of fresh domestic savings for new investments every year, there is no pressure to restructure or privatise the existing, almost all state-owned, enterprises, which would have been both economically and socially disruptive. It is interesting to note that in neither China nor the economies of Taiwan and South Korea in earlier times, was there any systemic privatisation of state-owned enterprises, as in the former Soviet Union and the formerly socialist Eastern European countries during their transitions to market economies. This was possible, in part, because of their respective high domestic savings rates. In the Chinese case, many state-owned enterprises eventually became publicly listed companies on stock exchanges in Hong Kong, Shanghai, and Shenzhen. However, in almost all such cases, the

5 These would include all the employees of the central and local governments, their affiliated service units, as well as all the state-owned enterprises. They were all paid according to the same wage and salary scales.

6 Of course, Chinese households, like other East Asian households, are already high voluntary savers.

7 For example, in China's First Five-Year Plan (1953–1957), approximately 55.8 percent of total investment was devoted to investment in basic infrastructure.

government retains a majority stake and management control. There was no privatisation of control.[8] The Chinese government wants to retain state-owned enterprises as one of its instruments for the control of the economy and the implementation of social policies, such as environmental preservation, protection and restoration, and poverty alleviation. Despite this, the private sector in China has grown rapidly since the economic reform in 1978 to account for 88 percent of its urban employment[9] and 95 percent of its total profits in 2021.[10]

Another such policy, which was adopted almost concurrently with the beginning of the economic reform, was the "one-child" policy, a population planning policy of China introduced in 1979 and implemented in September 1980. The policy remained in force until the beginning of 2016. It has had a large impact on the population trajectory of China. Without the "one-child" policy, the Chinese population would have been at least a couple of hundred million people larger today, implying much higher aggregate household consumption, a lower national savings rate, a greater demand for social services, slower GDP growth, higher unemployment, lower real GDP per capita, higher prices for food and other necessities, and much greater damage to the environment. However, the demise of the "one-child" policy was also timely, perhaps even slightly overdue, as the Chinese working-age population[11] had begun to decline, the Chinese society had begun to age, and the Chinese dependency ratio had begun to rise.

---

8 The same is true of the more recent "mixed ownership system reform" (混合所有制改革), under which SOEs partially privatise some of their subsidiaries but retain a majority ownership and management control. In principle, the SOEs can also acquire a majority stake and management of control of existing privately owned enterprises.

9 According to data from the National Population Census.

10 According to data from the National Bureau of Statistics of China. Unfortunately, there are no reliable statistics on the share of the private sector in GDP.

11 However, the Chinese definition of its working-age population is different from those of other countries. In China, the mandatory retirement age for a woman is 50 (55 if she is a cadre) and for a man, 60. Thus, the size of its working-age population is significantly smaller than that of another country with similar demographics.

One of the major new economic initiatives adopted by the Chinese government in 1978 was opening the economy to both international trade and direct investment. Machinery, equipment, and raw materials which could not be produced in China at the time would be imported. In order to pay for these imports, China would promote exports as well as inbound foreign direct investment. The promotion of exports required the setting of an internationally competitive exchange rate for the renminbi. From the early 1950s to late 1971, the renminbi exchange rate stood at a constant 2.46 yuan per U.S. dollar (see Chart 0.3). The international embargo against China that began with the Korean War continued even after the fighting ended with an armistice in 1953. There was little international trade between China and the rest of the world, except for the essentially barter trade between China and the former Soviet Union and the formerly socialist Eastern European countries.[12] In the 1960s, even the limited barter trade dwindled because of the then Sino-Soviet dispute. The only country in Europe that had any economic exchange with China at the time was Albania. However, with the secret visit of U.S. Secretary of State Henry Kissinger to China in July 1971 and the subsequent visit of U.S. President Richard Nixon in February 1972, international trade between China and the U.S. and other Western countries began to grow again.

During the period 1971–1978, the renminbi exchange rate actually appreciated, reaching its highest level vis-a-vis the U.S. dollar of 1.46 yuan in 1980, partially driven by capital inflows. Then China began to undertake a series of explicit and implicit devaluations of the renminbi, which reached 8.7 yuan per U.S. dollar at the beginning of 1994, when China unified its multiple exchange rates and adopted current-account convertibility. The renminbi then appreciated slightly to 8.3 yuan per U.S. dollar until the East Asian currency crisis of 1997–1998, during which the renminbi exchange rate held steady and remained unchanged with respect to the U.S. dollar even as all of the other East Asian currencies with the exception of the Hong Kong dollar and the Japanese yen underwent significant devaluations.

---

12 There were significant imports of machinery and equipment from the Soviet Union during the First Five-Year (1953–1957) Plan period, financed by a combination of Soviet aid and loans.

Then beginning in mid-2005, because of China's large and growing current-account surpluses, the renminbi began to appreciate significantly. However, this appreciation came to a halt in late 2008 because of the global financial crisis triggered by the collapse of the Lehman Brothers in the United States and did not resume until 2010. Since then, the renminbi exchange rate has fluctuated within a relatively narrow band between 6.3 and 7.3 yuan per U.S. dollar. The renminbi no longer follows the U.S. dollar but appears to adjust with reference to the value of a trade-weighted basket of the currencies of its major trading partner countries, in effect keeping its exchange rate relatively stable vis-a-vis the average trading partner country and maintaining the average purchasing power of the renminbi abroad.

Chart 0.3. Nominal Exchange Rate of the Renminbi since 1957 (Yuan per US$, end of month)

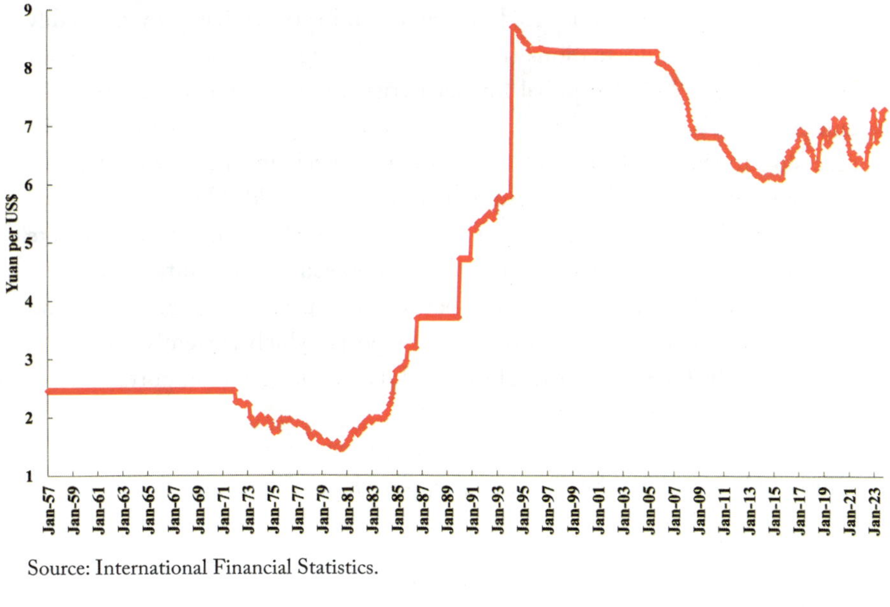

Source: International Financial Statistics.

In addition to setting a competitive exchange rate and making the renminbi current-account convertible, China also applied to join the World Trade Organization (WTO) as part of its export promotion strategy. It finally acceded to the WTO in 2001, after prolonged negotiations with the U.S. and other countries. The growth of Chinese international trade in both goods and services since the visit of U.S. President Richard Nixon in 1972 has been phenomenal, especially after its accession to the WTO in 2001, with an average annual compound rate of 15.2 percent. This is in great contrast to what happened in the period 1950–1971, with an average annual rate of growth of only 7.4 percent (see Chart 0.4). As mentioned above, in the 1950s and continuing through the 1960s, there was a trade embargo against China by the U.S. and the West. There was also the great famine of 1959–1961 and the Great Proletarian Cultural Revolution of 1966–1967. All of the above were not favourable to either the economy or international trade. However, since 1972, Chinese international trade in goods and services has grown steadily despite significant fluctuations (for example, during the East Asian currency crisis in 1997–1998, the global financial crisis in 2008, and the COVID-19 epidemic in 2020–2022). In particular, it grew by leaps and bounds after its accession to the WTO in 2001. China is now neck and neck with the U.S. for the position of the largest trading nation in the world.[13] In terms of international trade in goods only, China is the undisputed champion. But the rate of growth of Chinese international trade has slowed down significantly in the past few years. A tariff war broke out between China and the U.S. in 2018 and appears to be continuing. However, net exports, which currently constitute approximately 2 percent of the Chinese GDP, is no longer an important driver of the Chinese economy.

In its transition from a centrally-planned economy to a market economy, China did not adopt the "big bang" approach, as the former Soviet Union

---

13 In 2022, the total value of international trade in goods and services was US$ 6.86 trillion for China, according to the State Administration of Foreign Exchange of China, and US$ 6.99 trillion for the U.S., according to the U.S. Bureau of Economic Analysis.

Chart 0.4. Chinese International Trade in Goods and Services and Its Annual Rate of Growth since 1950 (Trillion US$ and percent)

Source: National Bureau of Statistics of China.

did. Instead, it employed the "dual-track" approach, that is, with the mandatory central plan continuing in force and the establishment of free markets in parallel. Every individual, collective, and enterprise was free to participate in the free markets provided that he/she/it had fulfilled all the obligations under the mandatory central plan. One of the most important consequences of the "dual-track" approach is that no losers were created by the introduction of the free markets since everyone's rights (and obligations) under the mandatory central plan continued to be enforced. In fact, a distinguishing characteristic of Chinese economic reform is its emphasis on ensuring that there are no losers. Indeed, "reform without losers" is what made Chinese economic reform so successful and the economic transition so smooth. It maximises public support and minimises opposition. In the jargon of economics, Chinese economic reform is always Pareto-improving, meaning everyone is better off. Moreover, the "dual-track" approach, with full enforcement of the pre-existing mandatory central plan, also results in full economic efficiency.[14] As a result, China had a very smooth transition without experiencing any decline in GDP in either aggregate or per capita terms or hyperinflation, as almost all of the former Soviet Union and Eastern European socialist countries did.

The Chinese government has also maintained appropriate macroeconomic and exchange rate policies throughout the post-reform period of 1978 to the present. We note that there has been no real recession—the rate of growth has never gone negative. There is careful aggregate demand management. Inflation has been kept under control. The renminbi exchange rate has been basically maintained at a relatively stable level appropriate for its current-account conditions since the foreign exchange reform of 1994. In particular, it held steady during the East Asian currency crisis of 1997–1998, facilitating the recovery of the affected East Asian economies. There have been difficult economic problems, but they have all been reasonably well managed if not completely solved.

However, it would be wrong to think that there was an overall comprehensive blueprint for Chinese economic reform from the very beginning. As Mr. Deng Xiaoping, the late Chinese paramount leader, famously said, the process of Chinese economic reform was like "crossing the river by feeling the stones underneath" (摸著石頭過河). There was a great deal of uncertainty as to the right path. Trial and error was the norm, pragmatism was the guide, and adaptability would be widely practised. It was also not at all clear what would be found on the other side of the river. What was clear was that staying on the existing side was not a viable option.

But the Chinese government has shown itself to be willing to experiment with new approaches. There are many pilot schemes being tested in different localities. If they prove successful, they will be extended to the entire country; if not, they will be abandoned. The large size of the Chinese economy also makes it uniquely possible to conduct pilot experiments on specific policies in isolation. For example, the introduction of the household responsibility system started with only one village in Anhui Province with 18 households. One notable example of a failed experiment was the introduction of multi-province district branches of the People's Bank of China, emulating the U.S. Federal

---

14 See Lau, Qian and Roland (1997) and Lau, Qian and Roland (2000), included in this volume as Chapter 11.

Reserve System, with the objective of reducing the potential influence of the officials of individual provinces on the local regulation of money supply and credit. In principle, the heads of these multi-province district branches were not beholden to the secretaries of the individual provincial branches of the Communist Party of China. In practice, the system turned out not to work well, and the multi-province district branches were replaced by individual provincial and municipal branches within a few years.

Chinese accession to the WTO in 2001 is a pivotal decision. Since then, the Chinese economy underwent a significant transformation, driven by the growth of net exports, which in turn enabled the massive movement of surplus labour from the agricultural sector to the non-agricultural sector. However, by 2020, the export promotion strategy has basically run its course, and the Chinese economy is once again largely dependent on its own domestic aggregate demand. Section III reviews the more recent developments and the future prospects of the Chinese economy. Actually, beginning in the 2010s, the external environment facing the Chinese economy has also begun to change. The China-U.S. strategic competition has become more intense, leading to wars on trade and technology, and restrictions on exports and investments. There have also been various attempts at economic de-globalisation, de-coupling, and de-risking around the world.

However, as a large, continental economy just like the U.S., the Chinese economy today is not significantly affected by external disturbances. The economic fundamentals of China still look favourable. Even though its population has begun to decline, the Chinese economy will not suffer from a labour shortage for at least a couple of decades. China continues to be committed to economic reform and opening to the world, policies it has followed since 1978. Domestically, China has shifted its emphasis from the quantity of growth to the quality of growth, in part through the expansion of the supply of public goods. This has led to sustained improvements in education, the environment, public health, and poverty alleviation.[15] While investments in the quality of growth may lower the measured rate of growth of the real GDP somewhat, the overall outlook remains positive.

---

15 See Lau (2022), included in this volume as Chapter 15.

What about the prospects for the future? In Chapters 5, 14, and 16,[16] there are projections of the future levels and rates of growth of Chinese real GDP, based on the then most current data. All the projections show that the Chinese real GDP will reach parity with the U.S. real GDP sometime in the early 2030s. There are, however, many other potential factors, including the renminbi-U.S. dollar exchange rate, at work that may shift this date in either direction. A revised set of projections of the future levels and rates of growth of Chinese and U.S. real GDPs, which shows the Chinese real GDP reaching parity with the U.S. real GDP in 2033, is presented in the Conclusion. We note that in purchasing power parity (PPP) terms, the Chinese real GDP already caught up with the U.S. real GDP in 2015, a finding supported by both the International Monetary Fund and the World Bank.

In the Conclusion, a brief answer to the question raised in the title of this volume is also provided. While the Chinese economy is unique and exceptional in many ways, its development experience can be explained and attributed, and thus it cannot be said to be a miracle. Is it surprising? Yes. Welcome? Definitely. Miraculous? Not quite. It has also grown rapidly during the past four and a half decades and is forecast to continue growing at average annual rates of between 5 and 6 percent going forward. It has durability and is therefore definitely not a bubble. Moreover, its model has also been adopted, and its success has been replicated, in other formerly centrally-planned economies such as Vietnam, Cambodia, and Laos. The Chinese model for economic reform, which allows a smooth economic transition and rapid economic growth while maintaining political control and social stability, may also turn out to be potentially suitable for Cuba, North Korea, or other centrally-planned economies if it wishes to transform into a market economy.

---

16 Lau (2023).

References

Lau, Lawrence J. "Public Goods Provision and Chinese Economic Development." *China and the World: Ancient and Modern Silk Road*, 5, no, 1, (2022), pp. 1–34.

———. "The Prospects for the Chinese Economy in 2023 and Beyond." *China-U.S. Focus*, January 24, 2023, https://www.chinausfocus.com/finance-economy/the-prospects-for-the-chinese-economy-in-2023-and-beyond.

Lau, Lawrence J., Yingyi Qian, and Gerard Roland. "Pareto-Improving Economic Reforms through Dual-Track Liberalization." *Economics Letters* 55, no. 2 (1997), pp. 285–292.

Lau, Lawrence J., Yingyi Qian, and Gerard Roland. "Reform without Losers: An Interpretation of China's Dual-Track Approach to Transition." *The Journal of Political Economy* 108, no. 1 (February 2000), pp. 120–143.

Section I
Economic Growth: China and East Asia

Commentary

Section I consists of my articles on the sources of economic growth of China and East Asian countries and regions, either singly or with co-authors Prof. Jong-Il Kim of Dongguk University, Seoul, and Prof. Huanhuan Zheng of the National University of Singapore. The main focus of Section I is on the relative importance of the different sources of growth for the Chinese economy during the past four and a half decades.

Chapter 1, co-authored with Prof. Jong-Il Kim in 1994,[1] and published in 1994, is an empirical analysis of the sources of growth of the four East Asian "Newly Industrialised Economies" (NIEs)—Hong Kong, South Korea, Singapore, and Taiwan—during their early stages of economic development (starting from the 1950s and 1960s and ending with 1990). It employs the framework of an aggregate meta-production function,[2] which is econometrically estimated by pooling time-series and cross-section data across countries, but without having to impose the restrictive assumption that the production functions of different countries and regions are identical. Moreover, the pooling of time-series and cross-section data enables the separate identification of the

1 This paper was first presented at a conference in Taipei in 1992 and subsequently published as a journal article (Kim and Lau [1994a] and also in the conference proceedings as Kim and Lau [1994b]).

2 The meta-production function approach was introduced by Lau and Yotopoulos (1989). It has quite a few advantages over the conventional growth accounting approach. It requires fewer assumptions in that it is not necessary to assume constant returns to scale and profit maximisation under competitive factor markets, which are not likely to be true in general or in particular for the Chinese economy.

magnitudes and biases of economies of scale and technical progress, if any.[3] Chapter 1 concludes that "the hypothesis that there has been no technical progress during the postwar period cannot be rejected for the four East Asian newly industrialized countries," even though they all had high average annual real rates of growth of between 7.8 and 8.9 percent. The growth in their outputs may be mostly attributed to the growth of their inputs, and the overwhelmingly important source of growth turns out to be the accumulation of tangible or physical capital, that is, structures and equipment, accounting for between 68 and 85 percent, "in contrast to the case of the Group-of-Five (G-5) industrialised countries,[4] in which technical progress has played the most important role."

The absence of measured technical progress in the East Asian NIEs may at first glance seem rather puzzling, as there was significant importation of machinery and equipment into these NIEs from the developed economies of North America and Western Europe, and hence there was an implied technology transfer during this period. However, the effects of this implied technology transfer did not show up in the measurement of the rates of technical progress, or, equivalently, the growth of total factor productivity (TFP) in the four NIEs. Our explanation is that while the technology transfer indeed took place, it was not free and was already fairly and fully priced in the markets and embodied in the cost of the imported machinery and equipment and their maintenance contracts, and in licensing fees and royalty payments. There was therefore no additional return to be captured or explained in the form of technical progress. The economic growth of the four East Asian NIEs during this period was achieved entirely by working harder, not smarter.

---

3 This is notwithstanding the Diamond-McFadden Impossibility Theorem. See Diamond and McFadden (1965) and Diamond, McFadden and Rodriguez (1978).

4 The Group-of-Five (G-5) countries consist of France, (West) Germany, Japan, the United Kingdom, and the United States.

Chapter 1, along with an article by Prof. Alwyn Young,[5] was cited by Prof. Paul Krugman[6] in his influential article in *Foreign Affairs*, "The Myth of Asia's Miracle,"[7] as empirical evidence of the non-sustainability of the high rates of economic growth of the East Asian NIEs.[8] The empirical analysis in Chapter 1 does not include the Chinese economy; however, Chapter 1 is included in this volume for two reasons. First, it provides the underlying analytical framework for the empirical analysis of Chapter 2, also co-authored with Prof. Jong-Il Kim, which includes the Chinese economy. Second, it enables us to show that the experiences of the economic growth of China and those of the ASEAN countries of Indonesia, Malaysia, the Philippines, and Thailand are not that different from those of the East Asian NIEs at their respective comparable stages of economic development.

Chapter 2, based on data from a similar period as Chapter 1, also finds that tangible capital accumulation was the most important source of growth for the Asian Pacific economies, including Japan, accounting for between 55 (Hong Kong) and 116 (Indonesia) percent[9] of the growth in real output, whereas technical progress was the most important source of economic growth for the Group-of-Five (G-5) industrialised countries (except Japan), accounting for between 41 and 64 percent of their economic growth. For the Chinese economy, 92 percent of the economic growth (up to that time) may be attributed to the growth of tangible capital, 9 percent to the growth of labour,

---

5 See Young (1992). However, the findings of Kim and Lau (1994a, 1994b) differ from those of Young (1992): Kim and Lau found that there was no technical progress in all four of the newly industrialised economies of Hong Kong, South Korea, Singapore, and Taiwan, whereas Young found technical progress in Hong Kong but not in Singapore.

6 Nobel Laureate in Economic Sciences (2008).

7 See Krugman (1994).

8 "Among the first to notice this surprising fact (of the lack of productivity growth in East Asia NIEs) was Stanford University's Lawrence Lau, a careful, reserved researcher who had spent many years developing sophisticated techniques for the estimation of total factor productivity." See Krugman (1999), p. 31.

9 The contribution of the growth of tangible capital can be over 100 percent if the combined contributions of the other sources of growth are negative.

and –1 percent to technical progress.[10]

Chapter 3, co-authored with Prof. Huanhuan Zheng, addresses a different but related question. From 1953 to 1978, China was a completely centrally-planned economy with mandatory sector-, industry-, enterprise-, village-, farm-, and household-specific production targets and was essentially closed to the rest of the world, except for the former Soviet Union and the Eastern European socialist countries before the Sino-Soviet break around 1960. It is well known that there can be significant inefficiencies in centrally-planned economies, with the economy operating well within the interior of its set of production possibilities—that is, far away from the frontier. As economic reform and opening proceeded successfully in China, the economy became progressively more efficient, and the point of operation of the economy began to move from the interior of the set of production possibilities to its frontier. During this process, in principle, the real output of the economy could be increased without any increase in its inputs. This increase in economic efficiency should show up as measured technical progress or growth in total factor productivity, even in the absence of any expansion of the set of production possibilities or outward movement of its frontier. How much slack was actually there in the Chinese economy before its economic reform in 1978?

It was in Xiaogang Village, Anhui Province, that the contract responsibility system in the Chinese agricultural sector was first introduced, spontaneously, in December 1978, setting in motion the agricultural economic reform in first Anhui Province and then the rest of China. Xiaogang Village reported that its total grain output increased from 15,000 kilograms per year before the reform to 90,000 kilograms in 1979, a fivefold increase.[11] Since the economic reform in the Chinese industrial sector did not start until a few years later in the 1980s, it can be safely assumed that Xiaogang Village had no additional inputs in 1979 beyond what were or could have been available before the reform. This would imply that the slack could be as much as five-sixths ([90,000–15,000]/90,000)! Without doubting the reliability of the Xiaogang

10 See Kim and Lau (1996), p. S452, Table 3. This article is included in this volume as Chapter 2.

11 The Xiaogang Village Story, http://www.china.org.cn/china/features/content_11778487.htm, accessed 14 July 2017.

figures, the grain output data of Anhui Province as a whole before and after the reform of 1978 cannot support the existence of such a large slack in the entire province. I have found, and reported elsewhere, that the transition of Chinese agriculture from a collective system to an essentially private individual household system resulted in large gains in efficiency of the order of between 30 and 40 percent from 1979 to 1985, holding inputs constant.[12]

Chapter 3 employs an original yet simple method to estimate the degree of economic inefficiency, or equivalently, the slack that might have existed in the Chinese economy before its reform in 1978, taking advantage of the fact that different municipalities and provinces in China began their respective agricultural and industrial economic reforms at different times. It is found that the real output of the Chinese economy as a whole in 1978 could have been 50 percent higher if it were operating efficiently—that is, on the frontier rather than in the interior of its set of production possibilities. This implies that the Chinese economy operated a third of the way from the frontier of its set of production possibilities in 1978. In other words, even if there were no increases in production inputs after 1978, the Chinese GDP would have been able to increase 50 percent, from US$389 billion in 1978 to US$584 billion (all in 2022 prices), solely as a result of the economic reform.[13] This seems like a reasonable estimate of the degree of the Chinese economic slack pre-reform.

Chapter 4 was written for an academic conference honouring Prof. Joseph E. Stiglitz, the 2001 Nobel Laureate in Economic Sciences, held at Columbia University in 2015. Prof. Joseph Stiglitz has always been an ardent supporter of Chinese economic reform as well as Chinese economic development. Whether in or out of the U.S. government or the World Bank, he has always been an important adviser to and a true friend of China. Chapter 4 takes a detailed look at the then most recently available data on the growth of inputs and outputs in the Chinese economy and attempts to estimate the relative contributions of the different sources of growth since 1978, taking into account the pre-existing economic inefficiency, or equivalently, economic slack, estimated by Lau and Zheng (2017).[14] It is found that Chinese economic growth since 1978 may be

12 Lau (1997), p. 49. Lau (1997) is included in this volume as Chapter 7.

13 But it would take some time.

14 See Lau and Zheng (2017). This article is included in this volume as Chapter 3.

attributed to the following sources: (1) The realisation of the potential surplus output from the initial economic slack that existed before the economic reform (12.7%); (2) The growth of tangible capital (55.7%) and labour (9.7%) inputs; (3) Technical progress (or equivalently the growth of total factor productivity [TFP]) (8.0%); and (4) The effect of economies of scale (14.0%). Thus, the growth of tangible capital is still the most important source of economic growth, and technical progress—or the increase in efficiency, other than the elimination of the initial slack—is still not yet an important source of growth for the Chinese economy, as it is in the developed industrialised economies. Economies of scale are found to be a more important source of growth than either the elimination of the pre-existing economic slack or technical progress.

Chapter 5, titled "What Makes China Grow?", was written for an academic conference commemorating the life and work of the late Prof. Lawrence R. Klein, the 1980 Nobel Laureate in Economic Sciences, held in Toronto in 2015. Prof. Klein led the first delegation of U.S. economists to China since the establishment of the People's Republic, under the auspices of the American Economic Association, in 1979, and organised the very first econometrics workshop in China in 1980, introducing the field to Chinese economists. I was fortunate enough to have been a member of both. Prof. Klein went on to become an adviser to the State Planning Commission of China, the predecessor to the National Development and Reform Commission of today, for one U.S. dollar a year. In 2010, at the 30th anniversary of the first econometrics workshop in China, he challenged the economists present, via a pre-recorded video speech, to explain Chinese economic growth. I hope Chapter 5 together with the other chapters in this volume constitute a small step towards this goal. Chapter 5 examines the entire process of development and growth of the Chinese economy since it began its economic reform and opened to the world in 1978, and identifies its economic fundamentals, its initial conditions, as well as the economic reform policies and measures responsible for its achieving a historically unprecedented high and sustained rate of growth. Chapter 5 also compares and contrasts the experience of the Chinese transition from a centrally-planned to a market economy, using the "dual-track" approach,[15] with those of the former Soviet Union and the formerly socialist Eastern European

15 The "dual-track" approach is discussed in Chapters 9 and 11 of this volume.

countries, using the "big bang" approach. The Chinese transition proved to be much more successful not only in terms of having a much higher rate of economic growth, but also because the Chinese people did not have to suffer any decline in their standard of living or the consequences of hyperinflation. Chapter 5 contains a projection that the Chinese real GDP will reach parity with the U.S. real GDP in the early 2030s.

Chapter 6, titled "The Great Transformation—East," was a lecture delivered at the Lamfalussy Lectures Conference in Budapest, organised by Magyar Nemzeti Bank (the central bank of Hungary) in 2018.[16] It identifies the commonalities in the development experiences of East Asian economies. Beginning with Japan, then Hong Kong, then Taiwan, then Singapore and South Korea, and then the ASEAN economies, and then Mainland China, industrialisation spread from economy to economy in East Asia successively. This process was first observed by Prof. Kaname Akamatsu in 1962,[17] who introduced the metaphor of the "wild-geese-flying pattern" of East Asian economic development to describe how within East Asia, the initially fast-growing economies, beginning with Japan, would slow down as surplus labour ran out, real wage rates rose, and exports began to be restricted by the quota imposed by the importing country, and a lower-cost economy would take over as the fastest-growing economy.

Thus, East Asian industrialisation spread from Japan to first Hong Kong and then Taiwan in the 1950s, and then Singapore and South Korea in the 1960s, and then the ASEAN economies of Thailand, Malaysia and Indonesia in the 1970s, and then to the Provinces and Municipalities of Guangdong, Shanghai, Jiangsu, and Zhejiang in Mainland China as China undertook economic reform and opened to the world beginning in late 1978. All of these economies had similar characteristics (such as high national savings rate and surplus agricultural labour[18]) and initial conditions, adopted similar strategies, policies, and measures, such as export promotion, and experienced similar development paths. And they have all benefitted from economic globalisation, with quite a few of them—for example, Japan, Hong Kong, and Singapore—achieving developed economy status. In 2022, China also achieved a real

16 Lau (2018a).

17 Akamatsu (1962).

18 Except in Hong Kong and Singapore.

GDP per capita of US$12,309, exceeding the middle-income threshold of US$12,000.

References

Akamatsu, Kaname. "A Historical Pattern of Economic Growth in Developing Countries." *Journal of Developing Economies* 1, no. 1, (1962), pp. 3–25.

Diamond, Peter A., and Daniel L. McFadden. "Identification of the Elasticity of Substitution and the Bias of Technical Change: An Impossibility Theorem." Working Paper No. 62, Department of Economics, University of California, Berkeley, 1965.

Diamond, Peter A., Daniel L. McFadden, and Miguel Rodriguez. "Measurement of the Elasticity of Factor Substitution and Bias of Technical Change." In Melvyn A. Fuss and Daniel L. McFadden, eds., *Production Economics: A Dual Approach to Theory and Applications*, vol. 2. Amsterdam: North-Holland Publishing Company, 1978, pp. 125–147.

Kim, Jong-Il, and Lawrence J. Lau. "The Sources of Economic Growth of the East Asian Newly Industrialized Countries." *Journal of the Japanese and International Economies* 8, no. 3 (September 1994a), pp. 235–271.

———. "The Sources of Economic Growth of the Newly Industrialized Countries on the Pacific Rim." In L. R. Klein and C. T. Yu, eds., *The Economic Development of ROC and the Pacific Rim in the 1990s and Beyond.* Singapore: World Scientific Publishing Co., 1994b, pp. 65–103.

———. "The Sources of Asian Pacific Economic Growth." *Canadian Journal of Economics* 29 (April 1996), pp. S448–S454.

Krugman, Paul. "The Myth of Asia's Miracle." *Foreign Affairs* 73, no. 6 (November/December 1994), pp. 62–78.

———. *The Return of Depression Economics.* New York: W.W. Norton & Company, 1999.

Lau, Lawrence J. "The Role of Government in Economic Development: Some Observations from the Experience of China, Hong Kong, and Taiwan." In Masahiko Aoki, Hyung-Ki Kim, and Masahiro Okuno-Fujiwara, eds., *The Role of Government in East Asian Economic Development: Comparative Institutional Analysis*. Oxford: Clarendon Press, 1997, pp. 41–73.

———. "The Great Transformation—East." In *Great Transformations: East and West, The Lamfalussy Lectures Conference 2018 Logbook*. Budapest: Magyar Nemzeti Bank (Central Bank of Hungary), 2018a, pp. 53–80.

———. "The Sources of Chinese Economic Growth since 1978." In Martin Guzman, ed., *Towards a Just Society: Joseph Stiglitz and 21st Century Economics.* New York: Columbia University Press, 2018b, pp. 323–352.

———. "What Makes China Grow?" In Peter Pauly, ed., *Global Economic Modeling: A Volume in Honor of Lawrence R. Klein*. Singapore: World Scientific Publishing Company, 2018c, pp. 182–233.

Lau, Lawrence J., and Pan A. Yotopoulos. "The Meta-Production Function Approach to Technological Change in World Agriculture." *Journal of Development Economics* 31, no. 2 (October 1989), pp. 241–269.

Lau, Lawrence J., and Huanhuan Zheng. "How Much Slack Was There in the Chinese Economy Prior to Its Economic Reform of 1978?" *China Economic Review* 45 (September 2017), pp. 124–142.

Young, Alwyn. "A Tale of Two Cities: Factor Accumulation and Technical Change in Hong Kong and Singapore." In Olivier J. Blanchard and Stanley Fischer, eds., *National Bureau of Economic Research Macroeconomics Annual.* Cambridge, MA: The MIT Press, 1992, pp. 13–54.

Chapter 1.

The Sources of Economic Growth of the East Asian Newly Industrialised Countries*

Co-authored with Jong-Il Kim

1. Introduction

In Lau and Yotopoulos (1989) and Boskin and Lau (1990), a new empirical methodology for estimating the relationship between aggregate output and inputs, including technical progress, from inter-country data, called the "meta-production function" approach after Hayami and Ruttan (1970, 1985), is introduced. One advantage of this approach is that it enables the separate identification of the scale and technical progress effects, which in general would be confounded if time-series data from only a single country is used. A second advantage of this approach is the possibility of identifying the biases in the directions of the scale and technical progress effects, provided that a sufficiently flexible functional form is used for the aggregate production

---

* This chapter was originally published in *Journal of the Japanese and International Economies* 8, no. 3 (September 1994), pp. 235–271. An earlier version of this paper, based on preliminary data, was presented at the Conference on the "Economic Development of the Republic of China and the Pacific Rim in the 1990s and Beyond," Taipei, Taiwan, Republic of China, 25–28 May 1992. The authors are grateful to Masahiko Aoki, Tein-Chen Chou, Win-Lin Chou, Paul David, Steven Durlauf, John Fei, Yujiro Hayami, Bert Hickman, Lawrence Klein, Anjini Kochar, Lee Tsao Yuan, Tzong-Biau Lin, Joan Lo, Ronald McKinnon, Kenichi Ohno, Mitsuo Saito, Julie Schaffner, Samuel Shieh, Robert Staiger, Joseph Stiglitz, Vincent Su, An-Chi Tung, Jean Waelbroeck, John Weyant, and Tzong-Shian Yu for their helpful comments; Shu-Cheng Liu for his invaluable research assistance; and the Ford Foundation, the Pine Tree Charitable Trust, the Asia/Pacific Research Center, and the Center for Economic Policy Research, Stanford University, for financial support. Responsibility for errors is solely the authors'.

function. A third advantage of this approach is the possibility of identifying the relative efficiencies or qualities of the outputs and inputs of the different nations and their changes over time. For example, using this approach, it is possible to obtain annual estimates of the "efficiency-equivalent" conversion factors between Japanese and U.S. labour in the postwar period.

Boskin and Lau (1990) obtain striking results from their analysis of the data on the outputs and inputs of the Group-of-Five (G-5) countries—France, West Germany, Japan, the U.K. and the U.S.—in the postwar period. They find, under the maintained hypothesis that the aggregate production functions of the individual countries are of the transcendental logarithmic form,[1] for the G-5 countries in the postwar period, that:[2]

(1) The maintained hypotheses of the meta-production function approach, i.e., (i) the aggregate production functions of all countries are identical in terms of efficiency-equivalent units of output and inputs, and (ii) technical progress in all countries can be represented in the commodity-augmentation form, with constant geometric augmentation factors, cannot be rejected. These two hypotheses in turn imply that the aggregate meta-production function can be written in the form

$$A_{i0}(1 + c_{i0})^t Y_{it} = F(A_{iK}(1 + c_{iK})^t K_{it}, A_{iL}(1 + c_{iL})^t L_{it}),$$

where Y_{it}, K_{it}, and L_{it} are the measured quantities of aggregate real output, capital, and labour, respectively, of the ith country in the tth period, t is an index of chronological time, and $A_{ij}(1+c_{ij})^t$ is the country-specific and time-varying constant-geometric commodity-augmentation factor for the ith country and the jth commodity in the tth period, where j = output (0), capital (K), and labour (L).

(2) The maintained hypotheses of traditional growth accounting, i.e., (i) constant returns to scale, (ii) neutrality of technical progress, and (iii) profit maximisation, all of which are assumed in almost all growth accounting exercises, can all be rejected.[3]

---

1 The transcendental logarithmic production function was introduced by Christensen, Jorgenson and Lau (1973).

2 See Appendix, Tables A1.1 and A1.2.

3 In fact, locally decreasing returns to scale are found for the Group-of-Five countries.

(3) Given that technical progress in the G-5 countries can be represented in the commodity-augmentation form, the hypothesis of purely capital-augmenting technical progress cannot be rejected,[4] which implies that the aggregate meta-production function can be written in the form

$$Y_{it} = A_{i0}^{-1}F(A_{iK}(1 + c_{iK})^t K_{it}, L_{it}).$$

There are significant differences in both the *levels* of output-augmentation factors, A_{i0}'s, and the *rates* of growth of capital-augmentation factors, c_{iK}'s, across countries. The rates of capital augmentation are significantly higher for France, West Germany, and Japan than for the U.K. and the U.S. However, in the base period (1970), France, West Germany, and Japan achieved only approximately 60 percent of the productive efficiency of the U.S.; i.e., given the same measured inputs of capital and labour, these countries could produce approximately 60 percent of what the U.S. produced in the base period.

(5) Technical progress is by far the most important source of economic growth in the G-5 countries, accounting for between one-half and three-quarters of the growth of aggregate real output in the postwar period, followed by capital, which accounts for between 25 and 40 percent.

The objective of this study is to extend the Boskin and Lau (1990) study to include the four East Asian newly industrialised economies (NIEs)—Hong Kong, Singapore, South Korea, and Taiwan. The questions of interest include:

1. Does the same aggregate meta-production function that applies to the Group-of-Five countries also apply to the East Asian NIEs?
2. Has there been more, or less, technical progress in the NIEs than in the industrialised countries?
3. How important are the different sources of economic growth for the NIEs and the G-5 countries?
4. Is there any evidence of convergence in technology between the G-5 countries and the East Asian NIEs? (In other words, is there any

---

4 It is important to note that purely capital-augmenting technical progress does not necessarily mean that the quality of capital per se has improved or that labour per se has not improved. (For example, an increase in the computer literacy of workers may be represented as an increase in the *effective* number of computers.)

catching-up in technology on the part of the East Asian NIEs?) Do countries with a lower level of technology exhibit a higher rate of technical progress?

In part 2 of this chapter, a concise presentation of the meta-production function approach is given. In parts 3 and 4, we discuss briefly the data and the statistical method, respectively. In part 5, the empirical results of applying the meta-production function model to the sample consisting of only the four East Asian NIEs are presented. In part 6, the empirical results for the pooled sample of East Asian NIEs and G-5 countries are presented. In part 7, a growth accounting exercise is carried out, based on our estimates of the aggregate meta-production function, and the results are compared with those obtained by using the conventional approach. In part 8, an international and inter-temporal comparison of the levels of productivities of the East Asian newly industrialised economies and the Group-of-Five countries is undertaken. Finally, some concluding remarks are made in part 9.

2. The Meta-Production Function Model

We begin with a brief presentation of the meta-production function model. The basic assumptions are:

(1) All countries have the same underlying aggregate meta-production function $F(\cdot)$, which, however, applies to efficiency-equivalent quantities of outputs and inputs; i.e.,

$$Y^*_{it} = F(X^*_{i1t}, \ldots, X^*_{imt}), \qquad i = 1, \ldots, n, \tag{1}$$

where Y^*_{it} and X^*_{ijt} are the efficiency-equivalent quantities of output and inputs, respectively, of the ith country in the th period, m is the number of inputs, and n is the number of countries.[5]

5 The assumption of a meta-production function for all countries implies that the function $F(\cdot)$ does not depend on i (but may depend on t). It is further assumed in this study that $F(\cdot)$ depends on t only through the commodity-augmentation factors; in other words, $F(\cdot)$ does not depend directly on t.

(2) The efficiency-equivalent quantities of output and inputs of each country are not directly observable. They are, however, linked to the measured quantities of outputs, Y_{it}'s, and inputs, X_{ijt}'s, through time-varying, country- and commodity-specific augmentation factors $A_{ij}(t)$'s, $i = 1, \ldots, n, j = 0, \ldots, m$,

$$Y_{it}^{*} = A_{i0}(t)Y_{it}, \tag{2}$$

$$X_{ijt}^{*} = A_{ij}(t)X_{ijt}, \qquad j = 1, \ldots, m. \tag{3}$$

In terms of the *measured* quantities of outputs, the production function may be rewritten as

$$Y_{it} = A_{i0}(t)^{-1}F(X_{i1t}^{*}, \ldots, X_{imt}^{*}), \qquad i = 1, \ldots, n, \tag{4}$$

so that the reciprocal of the output-augmentation factor $A_{i0}(t)$ has the interpretation of the possibly time-varying level of the technical efficiency of production, also referred to as output efficiency, in the ith country in the tth period. There are many reasons why these commodity-augmentation factors are not likely to be identical across countries. Differences in climate, natural resources, topography, and infrastructure; in definitions and measurements; in quality; in the composition of outputs; and in the technical efficiencies of production are some examples. The commodity-augmentation factors are introduced precisely to capture these differences across countries. In this study, the commodity-augmentation factors are assumed to have the constant geometric form with respect to time. Thus

$$Y_{it}^{*} = A_{i0}(1 + c_{i0})^{t}Y_{it}, \tag{5}$$

$$X_{ijt}^{*} = A_{ij}(1 + c_{ij})^{t}X_{ijt}, \qquad j = 1, \ldots; m, i = 1, \ldots, n, \tag{6}$$

where the A_{i0}'s, A_{ij}'s, c_{i0}'s and c_{ij}'s are constants.[6] We shall refer to the A_{i0}'s and A_{ij}'s as *augmentation level* parameters and the c_{i0}'s and c_{ij}'s as *augmentation rate*

6 Constancy of the c_{i0}'s and c_{ij}'s is a maintained assumption in this study. These parameters may be interpreted as the average annual rates of augmentation of output and inputs, respectively, in the ith country over the same period. It is in principle possible to test whether these augmentation rate parameters remain the same over time.

parameters. For at least one country, say the *i*th, the constants A_{i0} and A_{ij} can be set identically at unity (or some other arbitrary constants), reflecting the fact that efficiency-equivalent outputs and inputs can be measured only relative to some standard.[7] Without loss of generality the A_{i0}'s and A_{ij}'s for the U.S. are taken to be identically unity. The most important observation, however, is that all of the augmentation level and rate parameters are potentially estimable subject to such a normalisation—there is thus no need to rely on arbitrary assumptions.

(3) In order to accommodate the wide ranges of variation of the quantities of inputs in the pooled inter-country data, a flexible functional form is chosen for $F(\cdot)$ above. A flexible functional form is also needed to allow the possibility of non-neutral returns of scale and technical progress.[8] In this study, the aggregate meta-production function is specified to be the transcendental logarithmic (translog) functional form. For a production function with two inputs, capital (K) and labour (L), the translog production function, in terms of efficiency-equivalent output and inputs, takes the form

$$\begin{aligned}\ln Y_{it}^{*} = \ln Y_0 + a_K \ln K_{it}^{*} + a_L \ln L_{it}^{*} \\ + B_{KK}(\ln K_{it}^{*})^2/2 + B_{LL}(\ln L_{it}^{*})^2/2 \\ + B_{KL}(\ln K_{it}^{*})(\ln L_{it}^{*}).\end{aligned} \tag{7}$$

Equation (7) is written in terms of the efficiency-equivalent quantities of output and inputs. By substituting Equations (5) and (6) into Equation (7), we obtain the translog production function in terms of measured quantities of output and inputs,

7 Econometrically this means that the constants A_{i0} and A_{ij} cannot be uniquely identified without some normalisation.

8 For example, if the meta-production function $F(\cdot)$ is chosen to be of the Cobb-Douglas form, then the returns to scale will be neutral with respect to the inputs. Moreover, the commodity-augmentation factors cannot be separately identified and thus the technology will be indistinguishable from one with neutral technical progress. On this last point, see, for example, Lau (1980).

$$
\begin{aligned}
\ln Y_{it} = \ln Y_0 &- \ln A_{i0} + a_K \ln A_{iK} + a_L \ln A_{iL} \qquad (8)\\
&+ B_{KK}(\ln A_{iK})^2/2 + B_{LL}(\ln A_{iL})^2/2 + B_{KL}(\ln A_{iK})(\ln A_{iL})\\
&+ (a_K + B_{KK} \ln A_{iK} + B_{K\dot{L}} \ln A_{iL}) \ln K_{it}\\
&+ (a_L + B_{KL} \ln A_{iK} + B_{LL} \ln A_{iL}) \ln L_{it}\\
&+ B_{KK}(\ln K_{it})^2/2 + B_{LL}(\ln L_{it})^2/2 + B_{KL}(\ln K_{it})(\ln L_{it})\\
&+ (-c_{i0} + a_K \ln(1 + c_{iK}) + a_L \ln(1 + c_{iL})\\
&+ B_{KK}(\ln A_{iK}) \ln(1 + c_{iK})\\
&+ B_{KL}(\ln A_{iL}) \ln(1 + c_{iK}) + B_{LL}(\ln A_{iL}) \ln(1 + c_{iL})\\
&+ B_{KL}(\ln A_{iK}) \ln(1 + c_{iL}))t\\
&+ (B_{KK} \ln(1 + c_{iK}) + B_{KL} \ln(1 + c_{iL}))(\ln K_{it})t\\
&+ (B_{KL} \ln(1 + c_{iK}) + B_{LL} \ln(1 + c_{iL}))(\ln L_{it})t\\
&+ (B_{KK}(\ln(1 + c_{iK}))^2 + 2B_{KL}(\ln(1 + c_{iK}))(\ln(1 + c_{iL}))\\
&+ B_{LL}(\ln(1 + c_{iL}))^2)t^2/2,
\end{aligned}
$$

which simplifies into

$$
\begin{aligned}
\ln Y_{it} = \ln Y_0 &+ \ln A^*_{i0} \qquad (9)\\
&+ a^*_{Ki} \ln K_{it} + a^*_{Li} \ln L_{it}\\
&+ B_{KK}(\ln K_{it})^2/2 + B_{LL}(\ln L_{it})^2/2 + B_{KL}(\ln K_{it})(\ln L_{it})\\
&+ c^*_{i0}\, t\\
&+ (B_{KK} \ln(1 + c_{iK}) + B_{KL} \ln(1 + c_{iL}))(\ln K_{it})t\\
&+ (B_{KL} \ln(1 + c_{iK}) + B_{LL} \ln(1 + c_{iL}))(\ln L_{it})t\\
&+ (B_{KK} (\ln(1 + c_{iK}))^2 + 2B_{KL} (\ln(1 + c_{iK}))(\ln(1 + c_{iL}))\\
&+ B_{LL} (\ln(1 + c_{iL}))^2)t^2/2,
\end{aligned}
$$

where A^*_{i0}, c_{i0}, a^*_{Ki}, and a^*_{Li} are country-specific constants. Note that the only parameters that are independent of *i*, i.e., of the particular individual country, are B_{KK}, B_{LL}, and B_{KL}. They must be identical across countries. This provides a basis for testing the hypothesis that there is a single meta-production function for all the countries. The number of restrictions is $3(n - 1)$, where *n* is the number of countries. Note further that the parameter corresponding to the $t^2/2$ term for each country is not independent but is completely determined given B_{KK}, B_{KL}, B_{LL}, c_{iK}, and c_{iL}. All the other parameters, conditional on the hypothesis of a single meta-production function, are unrestricted. This provides a basis for testing the hypothesis of commodity-augmentation representation of technical progress. The number of restrictions is *n*, where *n* is the number of countries.

In addition to the aggregate meta-production function, we also consider the behaviour of the share of labour costs in the value of output, $w_{it}L_{it}/p_{it}Y_{it}$ where w_{it} is the nominal wage rate and p_{it} is the price of output in the *i*th country in the *t*th period, as a function of measured capital and labour inputs:

$$\frac{w_{it}L_{it}}{p_{it}Y_{it}} = a^{**}_{Li} + B_{KLi}\ln K_{it} + B_{LLi}\ln L_{it} + B_{Lti}\,t. \tag{10}$$

Under the hypothesis of profit maximisation, the parameters in Equation (10) are identical with the corresponding ones in Equation (9). This provides a basis for testing the hypothesis of profit maximisation. Equations (9) and (10) constitute the estimating equations for this study.

It is the essence of the meta-production function approach that countries may differ in their factor inputs and intensities and possibly in terms of the qualities and efficiencies of their inputs and outputs, but they do not differ with regard to the technological opportunities, i.e., they are assumed to have equal access to technology.

3. The Data

We use data from the four "Little Dragons"—the East Asian newly industrialised economies of Hong Kong, Singapore, South Korea, and Taiwan—and five Organisation for Economic Cooperation and Development (OECD) countries—the Group-of-Five countries of France, West Germany, Japan, the U.K., and the U.S.—for the post-war period. The precise period covered varies from

Table 1.1. Average Annual Rates of Growth of Real GDP, Capital, and Labour (Percent)

Economy	Period	GDP	Capital Stock	Utilised Capital	Employment	Labour Hours
Hong Kong	1966–1990	7.8	9.0	8.7	2.9	2.6
Singapore	1964–1990	8.9	10.4	11.0	4.4	4.4
South Korea	1960–1990	8.6	12.4	12.4	3.1	3.5
Taiwan	1953–1990	8.7	12.1	12.1	2.8	2.5
France	1957–1990	3.7	4.4	4.6	0.4	–0.1
West Germany	1960–1990	3.2	4.4	4.5	0.1	–0.4
Japan	1957–1990	6.7	10.1	10.4	1.2	0.7
UK	1957–1990	2.5	3.2	3.2	0.4	0.2
U.S.	1948–1990	3.1	2.9	3.2	1.8	1.6

country to country, depending on the availability of data, and is generally shorter for the East Asian NIEs than for the G-5 countries (see Table 1.1).

The aggregate real output (Y) of the economy is measured as the real Gross Domestic Product (GDP) in 1980 prices, converted, with the exception of the U.S., into 1980 U.S. dollars using the period average market exchange rates between the currencies of the respective countries and the U.S. dollar prevailing in 1980.[9] Labour (L) is measured as the number of person hours worked. The share of labour in the value of output is estimated by dividing the current labour income (compensation of employees paid by resident producers) by the current GDP of each country. The capital input (K) is measured as the *gross* total (public and private) non-residential fixed capital stock[10] at the beginning

9 The exchange rates in 1980 for France, West Germany, Japan, and the U.K. were 4.225, 1.818, 227.206, and 0.448, respectively; the exchange rates for Hong Kong, Singapore, South Korea, and Taiwan were 5.13, 2.1412, 607.43, and 36.01, respectively.

10 The capital stock is derived as an accumulation of gross fixed investments of different vintages less retirements (but not depreciation). Gross fixed investment is measured as gross fixed capital formation in non-residential assets (equipment and structure) in 1980 prices. Residential assets are not included because the measured gross domestic products of the countries in the sample, with the possible exception of the U.S., do not appear to reflect adequately the outputs produced from owner-occupied housing.

of the period, multiplied by the average capacity utilisation rate of the period. However, for the East Asian NIEs, data on the benchmark capital stocks are either unavailable or unreliable and must be estimated separately. Time (t) is measured chronologically in years with the year 1970 being set equal to zero. A detailed discussion of the construction of the variables used in this study, including the sources of the primary data, is given in Boskin and Lau (1994) and Kim and Lau (1994).

The instrumental variables used in the estimation include real output lagged one and two periods; lagged labour force; country dummies; world population; female life expectancy; male life expectancy; female population; male population; arable land; land under permanent crops; world prices of cotton, oil, and iron ore relative to the world price of wheat; lagged relative prices of cotton, oil, and iron ore; and time. For the first-differenced model, the actual instrumental variables employed consist of first differences of the natural logarithms of the continuous variables listed above as well as the dummy variables listed above.[11]

A summary of the data on output and the inputs is presented in Table 1.1. The most striking features of Table 1.1 are: (1) the significantly higher rates of economic growth of the East Asian NIEs compared to the G-5 countries over the periods of analysis; (2) the significantly higher rates of growth of the capital input in the East Asian NIEs (and Japan); and (3) the significantly higher rates of growth of the labour input in the East Asian NIEs. Since the rates of growth of both inputs have been more rapid in the East Asian NIEs, it is not surprising that the rate of growth of output has also been more rapid. The interesting questions are first, how much of the economic growth of the East Asian NIEs can be attributed to the growth in inputs and how much, if any, can be attributed to technical progress (or increase in efficiency), and second, whether there is any evidence of catching-up in technology, i.e., whether countries with lower initial levels of technology have experienced higher rates of technical progress.

---

11 The sources of the data on the instrumental variables are given in Boskin and Lau (1994).

4. The Statistical Method

Under the assumption of joint normality of the stochastic disturbance terms, we can estimate the system of two equations consisting of the production function and the labour share equation (both first-differenced)[12] and its various specialisations by the method of nonlinear instrumental variables.[13] By using the first-differenced form, the stochastic disturbance terms are assumed to be permanent shocks. Since the economies and their real GDPs range in size from Singapore to the U.S., the stochastic disturbance terms of the aggregate production function are further adjusted for possible heteroscedasticity across countries.

For testing hypotheses, we use as our criterion function the weighted sum of squares of residuals of the system of two equations projected in the space spanned by the instrumental variables. Asymptotically, the difference between the weighted sum of squares with and without the restrictions implied by the null hypothesis is distributed as the χ^2 distribution with the appropriate degrees of freedom under the null hypothesis.[14] These are the test statistics used in this study.

5. The Empirical Results for the East Asian Newly Industrialised Economies

The meta-production function model is first applied to the data of the East Asian NIEs only. The objective is to ascertain whether the meta-production function model is empirically valid for the East Asian NIEs.

Tests of Hypotheses

First, a series of hypotheses, analogous to those in Boskin and Lau (1990), are tested. We choose as the overall level of significance for this series of tests a = 0.10. We assign different levels of significance to the different (groups of)

---

12 The un-differenced model yields Durbin-Watson statistics that are close to unity for both equations, indicating significant first-order autocorrelation of the stochastic disturbance terms.

13 See, e.g., Gallant and Jorgenson (1979).

14 See Gallant and Jorgenson (1979).

hypotheses of interest so that their sum is less than or equal to 0.10, which ensures that the overall level of significance of this series of tests is at least 0.10. The test statistics for the different null hypotheses are presented in Table 1.2. The critical values at different levels of significance are presented in Table 1.3 for the convenience of readers who may wish to assign alternative levels of significance to some of the tests.

(1) The maintained hypotheses of the meta-production function approach are: (i) the aggregate production functions of all countries are identical in terms of efficiency-equivalent units of output and inputs; and (ii) technical progress in all countries can be represented in the commodity-augmentation form, with constant geometric augmentation factors. Neither hypothesis can be rejected at the assigned level of significance of 0.01. We conclude that the meta-production function approach is also appropriate for the NIEs.

Conditional on the validity of the maintained hypotheses of the meta-production function approach, additional hypotheses on the nature of the technology are tested.

The hypotheses of identical augmentation level parameters are (i) identical capital-augmentation level parameters across countries; and (ii) identical labour-augmentation level parameters across countries. Neither hypothesis can be rejected at the assigned level of significance of 0.01. We conclude that the augmentation level parameters do not differ across countries. (This means that in the base period, 1970, the measured inputs are of approximately equivalent efficiency in all of the NIEs.)

(2) The hypothesis of zero technical progress cannot be rejected, which implies that the technology of the NIEs has been approximately stationary.

The hypothesis of purely capital-augmenting technical progress means zero output and zero labour-augmentation rates. This hypothesis cannot be rejected. We conclude that technical progress can be represented as purely capital-augmenting for the NIEs.[15]

---

15 In view of the non-rejection of zero technical progress under (3) above, the hypothesis of purely capital-augmenting technical progress must necessarily not be rejected. The test of this hypothesis is reported here only for the purpose of reference.

Table 1.2. Tests of Hypotheses for Four Newly Industrialised Economies

Tested Hypothesis	Maintained Hypothesis	Assigned Level of Significance	Number of Restrictions	Test statistic χ^2/ Degrees of Freedom
I. Single meta-production function	Unrestricted	0.01	9	1.38
II. Commodity augmentation	I	0.01	4	0.15
III. Identical augmentation levels of				
(1) Capital	I + II	0.01	3	0.21
(2) Labour	I + II	0.01	3	0.22
IV. Zero technical progress	I + II	0.01	12	1.30
V. Purely capital-augmenting technical progress	I + II	0.01	8	1.36
VI. Cobb-Douglas production function	I + II	0.01	3	6.26

Table 1.3. Critical Values of χ^2 Divided by Degrees of Freedom

Degrees of Freedom	Levels of Significance			
	0.05	0.01	0.005	0.001
1	3.84	6.64	7.88	10.83
2	3.00	4.61	5.30	6.91
3	2.61	3.78	4.28	5.42
4	2.37	3.32	3.72	4.62
5	2.21	3.02	3.35	4.10
8	1.94	2.61	2.74	3.27
9	1.88	2.34	2.62	3.10
10	1.83	2.32	2.52	2.96
12	1.75	2.18	2.36	2.74
15	1.67	2.04	2.19	2.51
18	1.60	1.93	2.06	2.35
24	1.52	1.79	1.90	2.13
27	1.49	1.74	1.84	2.05

The hypothesis of the Cobb-Douglas production function can be rejected.[16]

Our test results confirm the validity of the meta-production function approach for the East Asian NIEs. Moreover, they also confirm that, similar

---

16 The rejection of the hypothesis of the Cobb-Douglas production function indicates that there is actually some power to our tests.

Table 1.4. Estimated Parameters of the Aggregate Production Function for Four Newly Industrialised Economies

Parameter	Restrictions	
	I + II + III + IV	I +II + III + V
Y_0	0.304	0.145
	(109.761)	(127.167)
a_K	0.789	0.599
	(8.846)	(5.791)
a_L	0.360	0.266
	(2.260)	(1.385)
B_{KK}	0.041	0.030
	(1.944)	(1.815)
B_{LL}	–0.011	0.032
	(–0.102)	(0.296)
B_{KL}	–0.018	–0.049
	(–0.493)	(–1.020)
A_{i0}		
Hong Kong	1.123	1.098
	(63.344)	(148.356)
Singapore	1.136	1.089
	(92.306)	(128.147)
South Korea	0.889	0.959
	(53.251)	(109.097)
Taiwan	1.000	1.000
C_{iK}		
Hong Kong	0.000	0.038
		(2.130)
Singapore	0.000	0.018
		(1.089)
South Korea	0.000	0.032
		(1.014)
Taiwan	0.000	0.043
		(1.859)
$\overline{R}^2$	0.727	0.744
D.W.	0.754	0.999

Note: Numbers in parentheses are *t* ratios. Y_0 and A_{i0} are estimated indirectly.

to the case of the G-5 countries, technical progress can also be represented as purely capital-augmenting for the NIEs. However, they also indicate that the hypothesis of no technical progress cannot be rejected for the NIEs.

The Empirical Estimates

Synthesising the results of our tests of hypotheses, we obtain estimates on which the restrictions corresponding to hypotheses that are not rejected are imposed. These parameter estimates are presented in Table 1.4. For reference, estimates of the purely capital-augmenting technical progress specification are also presented. As expected on the basis of the test results, the estimated rates of capital augmentation of the NIEs are not statistically significantly different from zero. In any case, in terms of magnitude, they are distinctly lower than the estimated rates of capital augmentation for the G-5 countries (see Appendix, Table A1.2).

6. The Empirical Results for the East Asian Newly Industrialised Economies and the Group-of-Five Countries

The meta-production function model is next applied to the pooled data of the East Asian NIEs and the G-5 countries.

Tests of Hypotheses

An almost identical series of tests of hypotheses are carried out with the pooled sample. Again, we choose as the overall level of significance for our series of tests $\alpha = 0.10$. We assign different levels of significance to the different (groups of) hypotheses of interest so that their sum is 0.10, which ensures that the overall level of significance of our series of tests is at least 0.10. The test statistics for the different null hypotheses are presented in Table 1.5.

(1) In order to justify the pooling of the data from the two groups of countries, the maintained hypotheses of the meta-production function approach of (i) identical aggregate production functions and (ii) commodity-augmenting representation of technical progress are tested. Neither hypothesis can be rejected at the assigned level of significance of 0.01 (or in fact, at any level of significance). We conclude that the meta-production function approach is appropriate for both the East Asian NIEs and the G-5 countries. In particular, all nine countries share the same aggregate meta-production function.

Table 1.5. Tests of Hypotheses for Nine Industrialised and Newly Industrialised Economies

Tested Hypothesis	Maintained Hypothesis	Assigned Level of Significance	Number of Restrictions	Test Statistic ^{2}/ Degrees of Freedom
I. Single meta-production function	Unrestricted	0.01	24	1.11
II. Factor augmentation	I	0.01	9	0.67
III.				
(1) Homogeneity	I + II	0.005	2	19.97
(2) Constant returns to scale	1 + 11	0.005	3	16.02
(3) Neutrality	I + II	0.01	18	4.30
(4) Profit maximisation	I + II	0.01	27	1.96
IV. Identical augmentation levels of				
(1) capital	I + II	0.01	8	1.83
(2) labour	I + II	0.01	8	1.16
V. Zero technical progress				
(1) G-5	I + II	0.01	15	18.10
(2) NIEs	I + 11	0.01	12	1.23
VI. Purely capital-augmenting technical progress	I + 11	0.01	18	1.80

(2) Conditional on the validity of the maintained hypotheses of the meta-production function approach, the traditional maintained hypotheses of growth accounting exercises, which include (i) homogeneity of the production function in capital and labour (0.005), (ii) constant returns to scale in capital and labour (0.005),[17] (iii) neutrality of technical progress (0.01), and (iv) profit maximisation (0.01), are tested for the pooled sample. All of these hypotheses can be rejected at the assigned levels of significance in parentheses. We conclude that the traditional maintained hypotheses of growth accounting are false for the East Asian NIEs and for the G-5 countries.

(3) Conditional on the validity of the maintained hypotheses of the meta-production function approach, the hypotheses of identical augmentation level parameters, which include (i) identical capital-augmentation level

17 Constant returns to scale implies homogeneity but not vice versa. Thus, if the hypothesis of homogeneity is rejected, there is actually no need to test the hypothesis of constant returns to scale. The test statistic is reported for reference only.

parameters across all nine countries and (ii) identical labour-augmentation level parameters across all nine countries, are tested. Neither hypothesis can be rejected at the assigned level of significance of 0.01. We conclude that the augmentation level parameters do not differ across countries.

(4) Conditional on the validity of the maintained hypotheses of the meta-production function approach, the hypothesis of zero technical progress, i.e., zero rates of output, capital, and labour augmentation, are separately tested for the East Asian NIEs and for the G-5 countries. It can be rejected for the G-5 countries but not for the East Asian NIEs at the assigned level of significance of 0.01.[18]

(5) Conditional on the validity of the maintained hypotheses of the meta-production function approach, the hypothesis of purely capital-augmenting technical progress in all nine countries is tested. It cannot be rejected at the assigned level of significance of 0.01. We conclude that technical progress can be represented as purely capital-augmenting in all nine countries.[19]

These test results confirm the general validity of the maintained hypotheses of the meta-production function approach. However, the conventional assumptions of growth accounting—constant returns to scale, neutrality of technical progress, and profit maximisation—continue to be rejected, as in Boskin and Lau (1990). The test results also confirm that technical progress can be represented as purely capital-augmenting for both the East Asian NIEs and the G-5 countries. The hypothesis of zero technical progress can be decisively rejected for the G-5 countries but not for the East Asian NIEs as a group.[20]

---

18 In fact, for the G-5 countries, the hypothesis of zero technical progress can be rejected at almost any reasonable level of significance.

19 For reference, the test statistic for the hypothesis of purely labour-augmenting technical progress is 3.96 and that for the hypothesis of purely output-augmenting technical progress (equivalent to Hicksian neutrality of technical progress) is 4.30, both with 18 degrees of freedom. Thus both hypotheses would have been rejected at a level of significance equal to 0.01.

20 If the hypothesis of zero technical progress is tested for the NIEs, conditional on the hypotheses of the meta-production function approach (I + II), identical capital- and labour-augmentation level parameters (IV), and purely capital-augmenting technical progress (VI), the x^2 test-statistic is 3.32 with four degrees of freedom, which is exactly on the borderline of acceptance/rejection at a level of significance of 0.01. Moreover, if a separate test of this hypothesis is carried out for each of the four East Asian NIEs at a level of significance of 0.0025 (so that the levels of significance sum to 0.01), it cannot be rejected for all of the NIEs.

Table 1.6. Estimated Parameters of the Aggregate Production Function for Nine Industrialised and Newly Industrialised Countries

Parameter	I + II + IV + V(2) + VI	I + II + IV + VI
Y_0	0.293	0.331
	(399.295)	(318.414)
a_K	0.265	0.245
	(8.103)	(7.929)
a_L	0.639	0.524
	(6.666)	(5.077)
B_{KK}	–0.074	–0.058
	(–7.445)	(–4.919)
B_{LL}	–0.073	–0.012
	(–1.101)	(–0.178)
B_{KL}	0.032	0.025
	(1.324)	(1.103)
A_{i0}		
Hong Kong	0.420	0.241
	(33.347)	(71.629)
Singapore	0.440	0.221
	(111.065)	(131.180)
South Korea	0.295	0.228
	(102.036)	(106.386)
Taiwan	0.338	0.242
	(74.817)	(69.337)
France	0.723	0.699
	(250.234)	(243.813)
West Germany	0.747	0.736
	(411.306)	(397.599)
Japan	0.648	0.622
	(194.785)	(193.810)
U.K.	0.543	0.534
	(448.787)	(434.764)
U.S.	1.000	1.000
C_{iK}		
Hong Kong	0.000	0.062
		(2.443)
Singapore	0.000	0.045
		(1.702)
South Korea	0.000	0.026
		(1.197)
Taiwan	0.000	0.024
		(1.523)
France	0.083	0.100
	(8.735)	(6.394)
West Germany	0.074	0.089
	(6.761)	(5.465)
Japan	0.072	0.098
	(3.927)	(3.483)
U.K.	0.046	0.056
	(5.794)	(5.045)
U.S.	0.061	0.067
	(7.592)	(6.321)
$\overline{R}^2$	0.753	0.753
$D.W.$	1.448	1.473

Note: Numbers in parentheses are t ratios. Y_0 and A_{i0} are estimated indirectly.

The Empirical Estimates

Synthesising the results of our tests of hypotheses, we obtain estimates on which the restrictions corresponding to hypotheses that are not rejected—that is, identical augmentation level parameters, purely capital-augmenting technical progress, and zero technical progress for the East Asian NIEs—are imposed. The parameter estimates are presented in Table 1.6. For reference, estimates without the restriction of zero technical progress for the East Asian NIEs are also presented. Based on the estimated rates of capital augmentation, the nine countries may be classified into three distinct groups—the East Asian NIEs, which have zero (or in any case low and statistically insignificant[21]) rates of capital augmentation; France, West Germany, and Japan, which show robust rates of between 8 and 10 per cent per annum; and the U.K. and the U.S., with intermediate and statistically significant rates of between 5 and 7 percent per annum.

However, in the ensuing analysis, in order to be conservative and give the East Asian NIEs the benefit of the doubt, we use the parameter estimates in the second column of Table 1.6 (i.e., *without* imposing the restrictions implied by zero rates of capital augmentation in the East Asian NIEs). Thus, the effect of technical progress in the East Asian NIEs may have been overstated—a fact that should be taken into account in the interpretation of the results.

In Table 1.7, some parameters of interest—the elasticities of output with respect to capital and labour and the degree of local returns to scale (equal to the sum of the capital and labour elasticities)—evaluated at the 1970 values of the inputs, are presented.[22] They reveal that (1) the capital elasticities are significantly higher in the East Asian NIEs than in the G-5 countries; (2) the labour elasticities are significantly lower in the East Asian NIEs than in the G-5 countries; and (3) there are generally decreasing returns to scale but the degrees of returns to scale exhibited by the East Asian NIEs are significantly higher than those of the other G-5 countries.

21 The critical value for a one-tailed t test at a level of significance of 0.0025 is approximately 2.9.

22 For a definition of the degree of local returns of scale, see Lau (1987).

Table 1.7. Estimated Parameters of the Aggregate Production Function (at 1970 values of the Independent Variables)

	Capital Elasticity	Labour Elasticity	Local Degree of Returns to Scale
Hong Kong	0.463	0.432	0.895
	(9.144)	(3.455)	(7.278)
Singapore	0.496	0.420	0.915
	(8.226)	(2.577)	(5.809)
South Korea	0.493	0.417	0.910
	(8.553)	(4.092)	(10.988)
Taiwan	0.505	0.413	0.918
	(9.074)	(4.103)	(9.870)
France	0.308	0.495	0.803
	(10.772)	(7.687)	(15.052)
West Germany	0.282	0.506	0.788
	(10.834)	(7.968)	(15.185)
Japan	0.324	0.487	0.811
	(7.776)	(4.934)	(11.222)
U.K.	0.289	0.503	0.792
	(10.853)	(7.927)	(15.207)
U.S.	0.227	0.528	0.755
	(7.583)	(6.024)	(10.906)

Note: Numbers in parentheses are *t* ratios.

In Chart 1.1, the annual estimates of the production elasticity of capital of each of the nine countries are plotted against time. It is clear that the production elasticities of capital in the East Asian NIEs are distinctly higher than those in the G-5 countries, although a generally declining trend is evident for both groups of countries. In Chart 1.2, the annual estimates of the production elasticity of labour of each of the nine countries are plotted against time. It is clear that the production elasticities of labour in the East Asian NIEs are distinctly lower than those in the G-5 countries, although a general rising trend is also evident for both groups of countries. In Chart 1.3, the annual estimates of the degree of local returns to scale in each of the nine countries are plotted against time.[23] The

23 Since the hypothesis of homogeneity is rejected and is therefore not imposed on the translog production function, the degree of local returns to scale changes with the quantities of capital and labour.

Chart 1.1. Production Elasticity of Capital

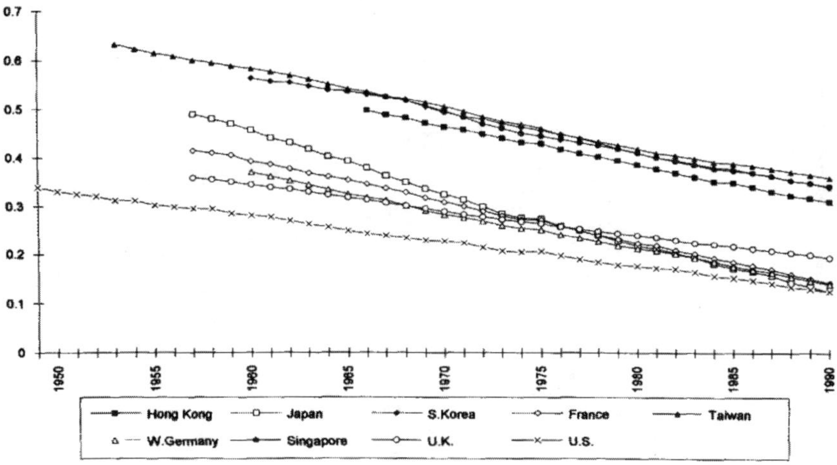

Chart 1.2. Production Elasticity of Labour

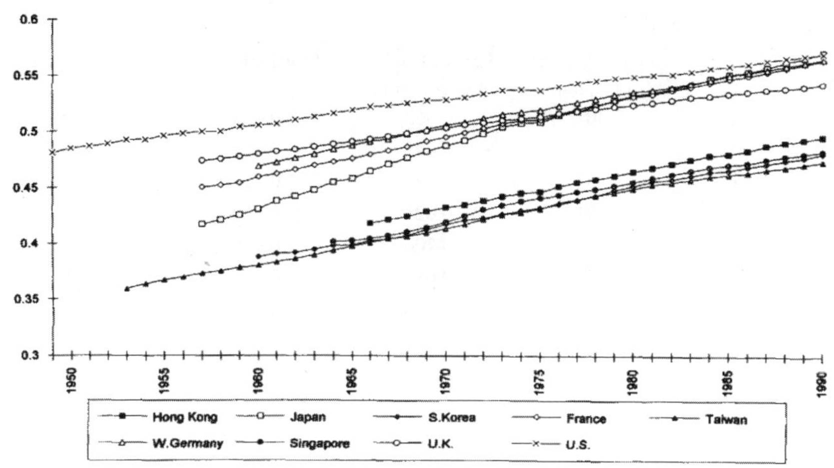

Chart 1.3. Local Returns to Scale

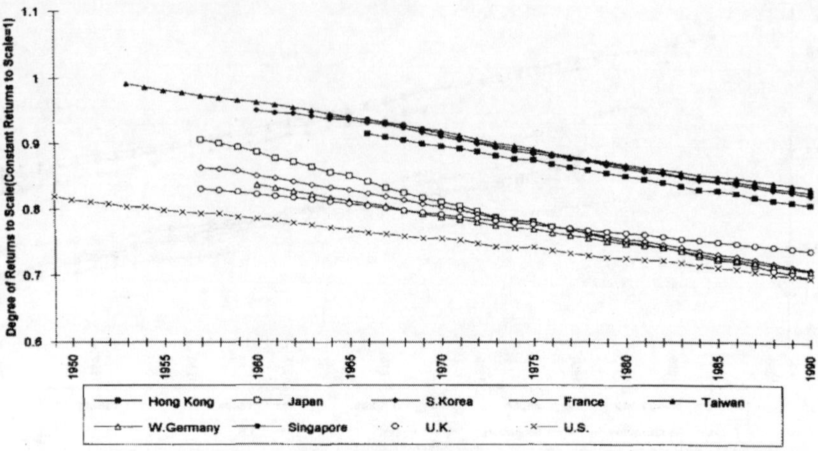

Table 1.8. Alternative Estimates of Average Annual Rates of Technical Progress

Country	Average Elasticity of Capital	Rate of Capital Augmentation	Our Estimates	Conventional Estimates
Hong Kong	0.401	0.062	0.024	0.020
Singapore	0.437	0.045	0.019	0.004
South Korea	0.454	0.026	0.012	-0.005
Taiwan	0.491	0.024	0.012	0.008
France	0.280	0.100	0.026	0.015
West Germany	0.250	0.089	0.022	0.012
Japan	0.296	0.098	0.029	0.010
U.K.	0.273	0.056	0.015	0.011
U.S.	0.230	0.067	0.015	0.008

degree is unity if there are constant returns to scale. It is evident that the estimated degrees of returns to scale are decreasing and moreover have been declining over time, mostly because of expansion in the inputs and diminishing returns. The East Asian NIEs, as well as Japan prior to 1970, have higher, albeit still decreasing, returns to scale than the other countries. By 1990, the estimated degrees of returns to scale range between 0.7 (U.S.) and 0.85 (Taiwan).

Why are returns to scale observed to be decreasing? The most obvious reason for finding decreasing returns to scale is the omission of other important factors of production. For example, land is not explicitly included as a factor of production in our empirical analysis.[24] Thus, even if returns to scale were constant or increasing with respect to capital, labour, *and* land, they would not necessarily be constant or increasing with respect to only capital and labour. Since land is fixed over time, to the extent that it is an important factor of production, one should not expect that simply doubling capital and labour will double real output. The same argument applies to the natural resource base, which may actually be declining in some countries. Another potentially important omitted factor of production is R&D or knowledge capital, which must have been growing over time, especially in the G-5 countries.

One implication of the finding of decreasing returns to scale is that the measured rate of technical progress will be higher than if constant returns were assumed—more of the growth in real output will be attributed to technical progress. Thus, if one were to assume constant returns, the measured rates of technical progress of the East Asian NIEs would have been even lower than those reported here.

7. Sources of Economic Growth

The economic growth of a nation can in general be attributed to three factors: growth in capital, growth in labour, and technical progress (including increases in efficiency). An interesting question is the relative importance of each of the three factors. First, we estimate the average annual rates of technical progress, defined as the average annual rate of growth of output holding measured inputs constant, for each of the nine countries in our sample. Two sets of estimates are derived—the first is based on our estimated aggregate meta-production function for the pooled sample, reported in column 2 of Table 1.6, and the second is based on the conventional "growth in the total factor productivity formula," which assumes constant returns to scale, neutrality of technical progress, and profit maximisation. The results are presented in Table 1.8.

---

24 To the extent that the land input is fixed over time for each country, its omission does not affect the validity of the econometric analysis.

For all nine economies, our estimated average annual rates of technical progress are uniformly higher than the conventional estimates, primarily because (local) returns to scale have been found to be rather significantly decreasing rather than constant, as assumed in the derivation of the conventional estimates, in all nine economies. For the East Asian NIEs, our estimated average annual rates of technical progress are all positive, ranging between 1.2 (South Korea and Taiwan) and 2.4 percent (Hong Kong) per annum, whereas the conventional estimates are negative for South Korea and small (0.4 percent) for Singapore. For the G-5 countries, our estimates are considerably higher than the conventional estimates. It may be thought paradoxical to find in East Asian NIEs average annual rates of technical progress that are comparable in magnitude to those of the G-5 countries even though their estimated rates of capital augmentation are distinctly lower. This is due, given the purely capital-augmenting nature of technical progress, primarily to the higher estimated capital elasticities of the East Asian NIEs in the sample period.

In Table 1.9, we present three alternative sets of estimates of the relative contributions of the different sources of growth for each of the nine economies, first, using the parameters of our estimated aggregate meta-production function in column 1 of Table 1.6, second, using the parameters in column 2 of Table 1.6 (which allows the rates of capital augmentation in the East Asian NIEs to be nonzero), and third, using the conventional total factor productivity formula.

According to our first set of estimates, which are based on zero rates of capital augmentation in the East Asian NIEs, capital accumulation is the most important source of growth for the NIEs (and Japan), whereas technical progress is the most important source of growth for the G-5 countries.

According to our second set of estimates, capital is still the most important source of growth for the NIEs (and Japan), accounting for between 48 and 72 percent of the growth in real output. Technical progress is still the most important source of economic growth for the G-5 countries,[25] accounting for between 46 and 71 percent of the economic growth in these countries. Capital is the second most important source of economic growth for the G-5 countries (except for the U.S.), whereas technical progress is the second most important source for the East Asian NIEs (except for South Korea). Finally,

25 Capital is marginally more important than technical progress for Japan.

Table 1.9. Relative Contributions of the Sources of Growth

	Capital	Labour	Technical Progress	Capital + Technical Progress
	Estimates Based on I + II + IV + V(2) + VI			
Hong Kong	74	26	0	74
Singapore	68	32	0	68
South Korea	80	20	0	80
Taiwan	85	15	0	85
France	37	−1	65	102
West Germany	40	−7	66	106
Japan	56	5	39	95
U.K.	39	4	57	96
U.S.	26	26	49	75
	Estimates Based on I+ II + IV + VI			
Hong Kong	48	17	35	83
Singapore	55	23	23	77
South Korea	67	19	14	81
Taiwan	72	13	15	87
France	33	−1	69	102
West Germany	36	−7	71	107
Japan	49	6	46	95
U.K.	35	4	61	96
U.S.	24	28	49	73
	Conventional Estimates			
Hong Kong	55	18	27	82
Singapore	77	18	5	82
South Korea	92	14	−6	88
Taiwan	78	13	9	87
France	62	−2	40	102
West Germany	66	−7	41	107
Japan	79	5	15	94
U.K.	52	4	44	96
U.S.	43	31	26	69

labour accounts for less than 6 percent of the economic growth in the G-5 countries (except for the U.S.) and between 13 and 23 percent of the economic growth in the East Asian NIEs. The contrast between the East Asian NIEs and the G-5 countries in the relative importance of the contributions of capital and technical progress is most striking.

Our results may be compared to those of the conventional approach, which identify capital as the most important source of economic growth of all countries (accounting for between 43 and 92 percent). Capital is followed, for the G-5 countries, by technical progress (accounting for between 15 and 44 percent), with labour an unimportant factor except for the U.S.

For the East Asian NIEs, the conventional estimates of technical progress are negative for South Korea and small for Singapore, with Hong Kong the only country where technical progress is relatively important.[26] Labour accounts for between 13 and 18 percent of economic growth of the East Asian NIEs.

By any approach, capital and technical progress combined account for more than 68 percent of the economic growth of both the industrialised and the newly industrialised countries. However, it is interesting to note that, according to the conventional estimates, technical progress is even less important as a source of growth for the East Asian NIEs than our second set of estimates. These results raise the intriguing and important question of why technical progress (or increase in efficiency) has been relatively unimportant in the East Asian NIEs compared to that in the G-5 countries.

8. International and Intertemporal Comparison of Productive Efficiency

In order to compare productive efficiencies across countries and over time, we must net out the effects of differences in capital intensity and scale. We note that within our framework, in terms of efficiency-equivalent quantities of output and inputs, the production functions of the different countries are, by definition, identical. In terms of the measured quantities of output and inputs, however, they are not identical. We therefore pose the hypothetical question, if all countries have the *same quantities of measured inputs* of capital and labour as the U.S., what would have been the quantities of their real outputs and how would they evolve over time? In other words, we compare their productive efficiencies holding inputs constant.

We answer the question of relative productive efficiency by projecting the time series of hypothetical real outputs that would have been produced by each country in each period if it had the measured inputs of the U.S. in that period. For this purpose, we use the estimates presented in column 2 of

26 This is consistent with the finding of Young (1992) that Hong Kong has had a higher rate of growth of total factor productivity (technical progress) than Singapore. Young's approach is based on assumptions similar to the conventional approach.

Table 1.6. Thus, to the extent the projections are biased, they will be in the direction of overstating the contribution of technical progress in the East Asian NIEs.

Before making the projections, however, we need to estimate the country-specific output-augmentation level parameters, which do not appear in the first-differenced estimating equations. The output-augmentation level parameters are estimated indirectly.[27] These indirect estimates of $ln\ A_{i0}$'s have been presented in Table 1.6. They reflect the technical efficiencies of production of the different countries relative to the U.S. in the base year (1970), as well as possible differences in definitions and measurements of the variables. We find that in the base year, the U.S. had the highest output efficiency, followed by West Germany and France, with an output efficiency of approximately 70 percent of the U.S., and then by Japan and the U.K., which had output efficiencies of approximately 65 and 55 percent of that of the U.S., respectively. The output-augmentation level parameters of the East Asian NIEs are, as expected, much lower as a group and are very closely clustered together at approximately 25 percent of that of the U.S.

The time series of hypothetical outputs are plotted for each economy in Chart 1.4. Chart 1.4 shows that in 1949 the U.S. had the highest level of overall productive efficiency and West Germany the second highest (but considerably lower than the U.S.), followed by the U.K., France, and Japan, and then by the cluster of East Asian NIEs—Taiwan, South Korea, Singapore, and Hong Kong—further behind. By the late 1950s, France and Japan had overtaken the U.K., which continued to fall behind the rest of the G-5 countries. As of 1990, the U.S. remained in first place and the U.K. in last place among the G-5 countries, with West Germany and France, which were closely clustered together, and Japan taking the intermediate positions. The East Asian NIEs remained clustered together as a group but fell behind in terms of relative productive efficiency.

In Chart 1.5 we plot the relative productive efficiency of each of the eight economies against time, using the U.S. level as the reference (i.e., with U.S. productive efficiency normalised at unity). Chart 1.5 provides the same picture

---

27 See Boskin and Lau (1990) for a description of the procedure for estimating the output-augmentation level parameters.

Chart 1.4. Hypothetical Output Levels of Economies with Measured Inputs of the U.S.

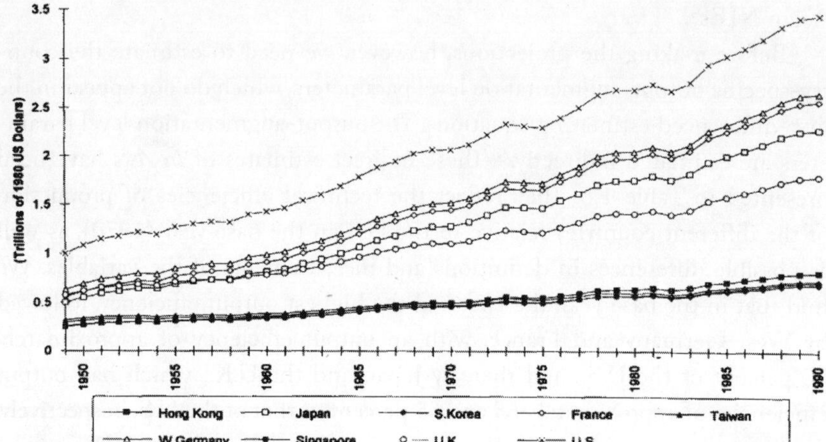

Chart 1.5. Production Efficiency Relative to the U.S.

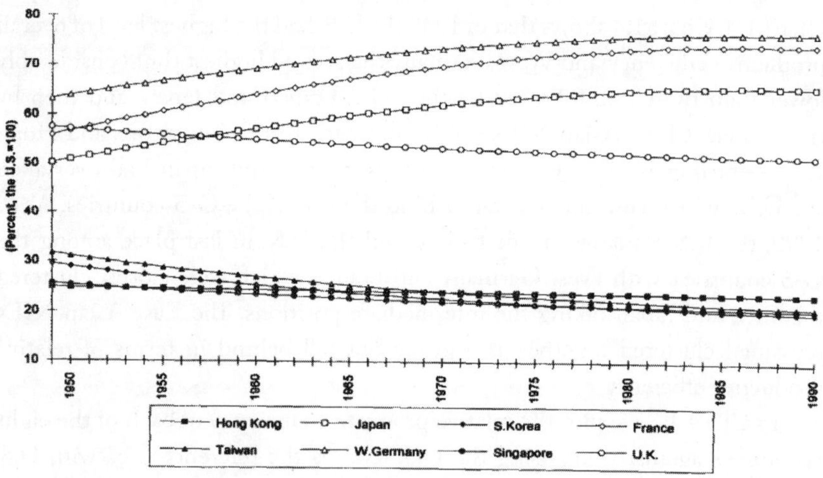

as Chart 1.4, namely, that West Germany, France, and Japan have closed the productive efficiency gap with the U.S. significantly but not completely, with the U.K. falling behind. The surprising finding is that the gap between the U.S. and the East Asian NIEs as a group has in fact widened. This is consistent with the fact that economic growth in the East Asian NIEs, unlike the economic growth in the G-5 countries, is due mostly to the increases in the inputs, especially the capital input, rather than to technical progress or increase in efficiency. For the nine economies as a whole, the empirical evidence does not appear to support the hypothesis of *convergence in technology*, i.e., given the same inputs, different economies will over time produce increasingly similar levels of real output. There is also little evidence that countries with a lower technological level have a higher rate of technical progress.

9. Concluding Remarks

It is gratifying to find that the meta-production function approach works for both the industrialised and newly industrialised economies—that both groups operate on the same aggregate meta-production function. Yet the estimated values of the production elasticities of the two groups of economies differ significantly, in accordance with the relative factor scarcities—higher capital elasticity and lower labour elasticity in the East Asian NIEs than in the G-5 countries.[28] It is also gratifying that our results reaffirm that technical progress can be represented as purely capital-augmenting. It is, however, somewhat surprising to find that technical progress (or increase in efficiency) has played an insignificant role in the postwar aggregate economic growth of the East Asian NIEs. By far the most important source of economic growth of the East Asian NIEs is capital accumulation, accounting for between 48 and 72 percent of their economic growth, in contrast to the case of the industrialised G-5 countries, in which technical progress has played the most important role.

---

28 This is the advantage of using a flexible functional form such as the transcendental logarithmic production function, introduced by Christensen, Jorgenson and Lau (1973), which allows the production elasticities to change with differing relative factor proportions.

Why is technical progress unimportant as a source of growth in the East Asian NIEs? Obviously this is a most worthy topic for further research. But here are some plausible explanations. First, it may be argued that since the gross capital stock rather than the net capital stock is used as a factor in the production function in this study, allowance has been made only for retirement, but not physical depreciation, of capital. To the extent that physical depreciation is significant, the measured capital stock will overstate the "true" capital stock and the estimated capital-augmentation rate may be an underestimate of the true capital-augmentation rate. Thus, an estimated capital-augmentation rate of zero may not necessarily imply a zero rate of capital augmentation. It is also consistent with the interpretation that the true rate of capital augmentation is precisely equal to, and hence offset by, the true rate of depreciation, resulting in an estimate of zero for the measured capital-augmentation rate. However, since the same concept of the gross capital stock is also used in the production function for the industrialised countries, the above argument cannot explain the fact that the estimated rates of capital augmentation are positive and statistically significant for the industrialised countries but low and statistically insignificant for the East Asian NIEs.[29]

Second, the effect of technical progress in this study is essentially being captured by the time trend, which is supposed to reflect the influence of omitted variables, such as human capital and R&D capital. However, it is possible that such omitted variables are actually not important in the East Asian NIEs. For example, for the East Asian NIEs, there has been, until very recently, very little investment in research and development, especially in basic research. Thus the *indigenously* generated improvements in technology must be quite scarce. Third, while it is true that there has been very rapid capital deepening in the East Asian NIEs, their industries are, at least until recently, by and large

---

29 Unless one were to assume, in addition, that the true depreciation rate is higher in the East Asian NIEs than in the G-5 countries, because of various factors such as the composition of outputs. However, we may also note that Japan, which is well known to have a high 'depreciation' rate, also has a high estimated rate of capital augmentation. In any case, given the magnitudes of the estimated capital-augmentation rates of the G-5 countries, the implied true depreciation rates will have to be implausibly high.

not knowledge or technology intensive. Moreover, these industries typically employ mature technologies, the capital equipment for which, being mostly imported, has been fully priced (i.e., the acquisition as well as royalty costs fully reflect the possible efficiency gains and the amortisation of R&D and other developmental costs) in the international market. Fourth, and related to the above, the East Asian NIEs have been playing "catch-up" in technology—the capital goods installed are likely to be the on-the-shelf variety and the possibility for indigenous improvement is limited. They are also likely to be new capital goods of older vintages, which have become appropriate for their then current factor endowments. Fifth, it is possible that whatever technical progress there is in the world is mostly embodied in the capital goods used in the high-technology industries and thus the newly industrialised economies would not have been able to take advantage of it to the same extent as the industrialised countries. Sixth, it is also possible that the growth of the "software" component of investments, broadly defined to include managerial methods, institutional environment, as well as supporting infrastructure, lags behind the "hardware" component in the East Asian NIEs and hence the capital goods have not been able to realise their full potential productivity. Seventh, the constraints on economic development imposed by poor natural and human resource endowment (in terms of advanced scientific manpower) may work in a way so as to nullify the potential gains resulting from technical progress in the world. Finally, it is also possible that improvements in the quality of life, brought about by increased inputs of both capital and labour, may not be fully reflected in measured real GDP. In other words, not all of the output resulting from the inputs, and its growth over time, is captured by measured real GDP.

It is, however, also well known that the labour forces in these East Asian NIEs are among the best educated in the world outside of the OECD countries and both the average level and the quality of education have been rising rapidly in the East Asian NIEs. It is therefore somewhat puzzling why there is so little measured growth in productive efficiency over time. Is it possible that there is an excess supply of human capital relative to physical capital, or that there is complementarity of the fixed-coefficients variety between human capital and physical capital? Further research, incorporating data on human capital, is needed to shed light on this important question.

What policy implications do these empirical findings have for the East Asian NIEs? It is troubling to find that despite their high rates of economic growth and rapid capital accumulation, the East Asian NIEs have actually experienced a significant decline in productive efficiency relative to the U.S. As their capital stocks continue to grow, the capital elasticities will continue to decline, and increases in the capital input alone will not be sufficient for the East Asian NIEs to maintain their current rate of economic growth. It will be necessary for the East Asian NIEs to devote greater proportions of their resources to research and development and to innovation in order to attain a positive rate of growth in productive efficiency (technical progress). Otherwise it is unlikely that they will ever be able to catch up with the industrialised countries. It may also be necessary for the East Asian NIEs to upgrade further the quality of their investment in human capital and in the software necessary to realise the full productive potential of technology.

Appendix

Table A1.1. Tests of Hypotheses for Five Industrialised Countries

Tested Hypothesis	Maintained Hypothesis	Assigned Level of Significance	Number of Restrictions	Test Statistic χ^2/ Degrees of Freedom
I. Single meta-production function	Unrestricted	0.01	12	1.01
II. Factor augmentation	I	0.01	5	0.59
III.				
(1) Homogeneity	I + II	0.005	2	20.89
(2) Constant returns to scale	I + II	0.005	3	18.57
(3) Neutrality	I + II	0.01	10	5.13
(4) Profit maximisation	I + II	0.01	15	2.42
IV. Identical augmentation levels of				
(1) capital	I + II	0.01	4	1.29
(2) labour	I + II	0.01	4	3.01
V. Zero technical progress	I + II	0.01	15	20.42
VI. Purely capital-augmenting technical progress	I + II	0.01	10	1.99

Table A1.2. Estimated Parameters of the Aggregate Production Function for Five Industrialised Countries

Parameter	Restrictions I + II + IV + VI
Y_0	0.291
	(245.061)
a_K	0.122
	(2.825)
a_L	0.927
	(3.641)
B_{KK}	–0.046
	(–3.859)
B_{LL}	–0.241
	(–1.737)
B_{KL}	0.068
	(2.328)
A_{i0}	
France	0.559
	(440.502)
West Germany	0.614
	(431.755)
Japan	0.583
	(149.991)
U.K.	0.447
	(434.206)
U.S.	1.000
C_{iK}	
France	0.137
	(5.299)
West Germany	0.112
	(4.493)
Japan	0.093
	(3.524)
U.K.	0.071
	(4.501)
U.S.	0.063
	(4.816)
$\overline{R}^2$	0.792
D.W.	1.796

Note: Numbers in parentheses are *t* ratios. Y_0 and A_{i0} are estimated indirectly.

References

Abramovitz, Moses. "The Catch-up Factor in Postwar Economic Growth." *Economic Inquiry* 1 (1990), pp. 1–18.

Arrow, Kenneth J. "The Economic Implications of Learning by Doing." *The Review of Economic Studies* 29, no. 3 (June 1962), pp. 155–173.

Baily, Martin N. "Productivity and the Services of Capital and Labour." *Brookings Papers on Economic Activity* 4 (1981), pp. 1–50.

Barro, Robert J. "Economic Growth in a Cross Section of Countries." National Bureau of Economic Research Working Paper 3120, 1989.

Baumol, William J. "Productivity Growth, Convergence, and Welfare: What the Long-Run Data Show." *American Economic Review* 76 (1986), pp. 1072–1085.

Baumol, William J. and Edward N. Wolff. "Productivity Growth, Convergence, and Welfare: Reply." *American Economic Review* 78 (1988), pp. 1155–1159.

Boskin, Michael J. "Tax Policy and Economic Growth: Lessons from the 1980s." *Journal of Economic Perspectives* 2 (1988), pp. 71–97.

Boskin, Michael J. and Lawrence J. Lau. "Post-War Economic Growth of the Group-of-Five Countries: A New Analysis." Technical Paper 217, Center for Economic Policy Research, Stanford University, 1990.

———. "Capital Formation and Economic Growth." In *Technology and Economics: A Volume Commemorating Ralph Landau's Service to the National Academy of Engineering*. Washington, D.C.: National Academy Press, 1991, pp. 47–56.

———. "Capital Technology, and Economic Growth." In Nathan Rosenberg, Ralph Landau and David Mowery, eds., *Technology and the Wealth of Nations*. Stanford: Stanford University Press, 1992a, pp. 17–55.

———. "International and Intertemporal Comparison of Productive Efficiency: An Application of the Meta-Production Function Approach to the Group-of-Five (G-5) Countries." *Economic Studies Quarterly* 43 (1992b), pp. 298–312.

Chen, Edward K. Y. *Hyper-Growth in Asian Economies: A Comparative Study of Hong Kong, Japan, Korea, Singapore and Taiwan*. London: Macmillan, 1979.

Christensen, Laurits R., Dale W. Jorgenson, and Lawrence J. Lau. "Transcendental Logarithmic Production Frontiers." *The Review of Economics* and *Statistics* 55 (1973), pp. 28–45.

Denison, Edward F. *Why Growth Rates Differ: Post-War Experience in Nine Western Countries.* Washington, D.C.: Brookings Institution, 1967.

———. *Accounting for United States Economic Growth, 1929–1969*. Washington, D.C.: Brookings Institution, 1974.

———. *Accounting for Slower Economic Growth: The United States in the 1970s.* Washington, D.C.: Brookings Institution, 1979.

———. *Trends in American Economic Growth, 1929–1982*. Washington, D.C.: Brookings Institution, 1985.

Denison, Edward F., and William K. Chung. *How Japan's Economy Grew So Fast.* Washington, D.C.: Brookings Institution, 1976.

Denison, Edward F., and R. P. Parker. "The National Income and Product Accounts of the United States: An Introduction to the Revised Estimates for 1929–80." *Survey of Current Business* 60, no. 12 (1980), pp. 1–26.

Gallant, A. Ronald, and Dale W. Jorgenson. "Statistical Inference for a System of Simultaneous, Nonlinear, Implicit Equations in the Context of Instrumental Variables Estimation." *Journal of Econometrics* 113 (1979), pp. 272–302.

Griliches, Zvi, and Dale W. Jorgenson. "Sources of Measured Productivity Change: Capital Input." *American Economic Review* 56 (1966), pp. 50–61.

Hall, Robert E. "Technical Change and Capital from the Point of View of the Dual." *The Review of Economic Studies* 35 (1968), pp. 35–46.

Hayami, Yujiro, and Vernon W. Ruttan. "Agricultural Productivity Differences Among Countries." *American Economic Review* 60 (1970), pp. 895–911.

———. *Agricultural Development: An International Perspective*, revised and expanded ed. Baltimore: Johns Hopkins University Press, 1985.

Jorgenson, Dale W., and Barbara M. Fraumeni. "The Accumulation of Human and Nonhuman Capital, 1948–1984." In Robert E. Lipsey and Helen Stone Tice, eds., *The Measurement of Saving, Investment and Wealth*. Chicago: University of Chicago Press, 1989a, pp. 227–282.

———. "Investment in Education," *Educational Researcher* 18 (1989b), pp. 35–44.

Jorgenson, Dale W., Frank M. Gollop and Barbara M. Fraumeni. *Productivity and U.S. Economic Growth*. Cambridge: Harvard University Press, 1987.

Jorgenson, Dale W., and Zvi Griliches. "The Explanation of Productivity Change." *The Review of Economic Studies* 34 (1967), pp. 249–283.

———. "Issues in Growth Accounting: A Reply to Edward F. Denison." *Survey of Current Business* 52, no. 5 (1972), pp. 65–94.

Jorgenson, Dale W., and Ralph Landau. *Technology and Capital Formation*. Cambridge: MIT Press, 1989.

Kendrick, John W. *Postwar Productivity Trends in the United States, 1948–1969*. New York: Columbia University Press, 1973.

Kim, Jong-Il, and Lawrence J. Lau. "The Importance of Embodied Technical Progress: Some Empirical Evidence from the Group-of-Five Countries." Working Paper, Department of Economics, Stanford University, 1992.

———. "The Sources of Economic Growth of the Newly Industrialized Countries on the Pacific Rim." In Lawrence R. Klein and Chuan-Tao Yu, eds., *The Economic Development of ROC and the Pacific Rim in the 1990s and Beyond*. Singapore: World Scientific Publishing Company, 1994, pp. 65–103.

Kravis, Irving B., Alan Heston, and Robert Summers. *International Comparisons of Real Gross Product*. Baltimore: Johns Hopkins University Press, 1982.

Kuznets, Simon S. *Economic Growth of Nations*. Cambridge: Harvard University Press, 1971.

Landau, Ralph. "Capital Investment: Key to Competitiveness of Growth." *Brookings Review* (Summer 1990), pp. 52–56.

Lau, Lawrence J. "On the Uniqueness of the Representation of Commodity-Augmenting Technical Change." In Lawrence R. Klein, Marc Nerlove and Sho-Chieh Tsiang, eds., *Quantitative Economics and Development: Essays in Memory of Ta-Chung Liu*. New York: Academic Press, 1980, pp. 281–290.

———. "Simple Measures of Local Returns to Scale and Local Rates of Technical Progress." Working Paper, Department of Economics, Stanford University, 1987.

Lau, Lawrence J., Dean T. Jamison, and Frederic. F. Louat. "Education and Productivity in Developing Countries: An Aggregate Production Function Approach." Working Paper WPS 612, The World Bank, 1990.

Lau, Lawrence J., and Pan A. Yotopoulos. "The Meta-Production Function Approach to Technological Change in World Agriculture." *Journal of Development Economics*, 31 (1989), pp. 241–269.

———. "Intercountry Differences in Agricultural Productivity: An Application of the Meta-Production Function." Working Paper, Department of Economics, Stanford University, 1990.

Levine, Ross, and David Renelt. "A Sensitivity Analysis of Cross-Country Growth Regression." Working Paper, The World Bank, 1990.

Liesner, Thelma. *One Hundred Years of Economic Statistics*. New York: The Economist Publications, 1990.

Maddison, Angus. *Phases of Capitalist Development*. Oxford: Oxford University Press, 1982.

Nelson, Richard R. "Aggregate Production Functions and Medium-range Growth Projections." *American Economic Review* 54 (1964), pp. 576–605.

Organisation for Economic Cooperation and Development. "Flows and Stocks of Fixed Capital, 1955–1980, 1960–1985, 1964–1989." Paris: Organisation for Economic Cooperation and Development.

———. "Labour Force Statistics, 1956–1967, 1958–1969, 1965–1985, 1970–1990." Paris: Organisation for Economic Cooperation and Development.

———. "Main Economic Indicators, 1986, 1992." Paris: Organisation for Economic Cooperation and Development.

———. "Main Economic Indicators: Historical Statistics, 1955–1971, 1960–1979, 1964–1983." Paris: Organisation for Economic Cooperation and Development.

———. "National Accounts, 1953–1982, 1960–1985, 1969–1990." Paris: Organisation for Economic Cooperation and Development.

Romer, Paul M. "Increasing Returns and Long-run Growth." *Journal of Political Economy* 94 (1986), pp. 1002–1037.

Solow, Robert M. "A Contribution to the Theory of Economic Growth." *Quarterly Journal of Economics* 70 (1956), pp. 65–94.

———. "Technical Change and the Aggregate Production Function." *Review of Economics and Statistics* 39 (1957), pp. 312–320.

———. "Technical Progress, Capital Formation, and Economic Growth." *American*

Economic Review 52 (1962), pp. 76–86.

Summers, Robert and Alan Heston. "A New Set of International Comparisons of Real Product and Price Levels: Estimates for 130 Countries, 1950–85." *Review of Income Wealth* 34 (1988), pp. 1–25.

———. "The Penn World Table (Mark 5): An Expanded Set of International Comparisons, 1950–1988." *Quarterly Journal of Economics* 106 (1991), pp. 327–368.

Tsao, Yuan. *Growth and Productivity in Singapore: A Supply Side Analysis*. Ph.D. dissertation. Cambridge: Harvard University, 1982.

———. "Growth Without Productivity: Singapore Manufacturing in the 1970s." *Journal of Development Studies* 18 (1985), pp. 25–38.

———. "Sources of Growth Accounting for the Singapore Economy." In Chong-Yah Lim and Peter J. Lloyd, eds., *Singapore: Resources and Growth*. Singapore: Oxford University Press, 1986, pp. 17–44.

United Nations. *Demographic Yearbook*, annual. New York: United Nations.

United Nations. *Statistical Yearbook*, annual. New York, United Nations.

U.S. Council of Economic Advisors. *Economic Report of the President, 1993*. Washington, D.C.

U.S. Department of Commerce. "Fixed Reproducible Tangible Wealth in the United States, 1925–1985." Washington, D.C., 1988.

U.S. Department of Commerce. "Historical Statistics of the United States: Colonial Times to 1970." Washington, D.C., 1975.

U.S. Department of Commerce. "National Income and Product Accounts of the United States." Washington, D.C., 1975.

U.S. Department of Commerce, Bureau of Economic Analysis. *Survey of Current Business* 60, no. 12 (1980).

Wong, K.-P. "Saving, Capital Flow and Capital Formation." In Chong-Yah Lim and Peter J. Lloyd, eds., *Singapore: Resources and Growth*. Singapore: Oxford University Press, 1986, pp. 45–78.

Young, Alwyn. "A Tale of Two Cities: Factor Accumulation and Technical Change in Hong Kong and Singapore." In Olivier J. Blanchard and Stanley Fischer, eds., *National Bureau of Economic Research Macroeconomics Annual*. Cambridge, MA: MIT Press, 1992, pp. 13–54.

Chapter 2.

The Sources of Asian Pacific Economic Growth*

Co-authored with Jong-Il Kim

1. Introduction

The objective of this study is to analyse the sources of economic growth of 10 Asian Pacific economies (APEs)—China, Hong Kong, Indonesia, Japan, Malaysia, the Philippines, Singapore, South Korea, Taiwan and Thailand—in conjunction with four industrialised Western countries (IWCs)—France, West Germany, the U.K. and the U.S.—in the postwar period. In previous studies, Boskin and Lau (1990) and Kim and Lau (1994b) find, for the Group-of-Five (G-5) and the East Asian newly industrialised economies (NIEs) respectively, that (1) all economies share the same aggregate meta-production function in terms of "efficiency-equivalent" units; and (2) technical progress can be represented in all economies as purely capital-augmenting. However, Kim and Lau (1994b) also find that there has been *no measured technical progress* in the East Asian NIEs, despite their much higher rates of economic growth. The questions of interest in this study are: (1) Does the same aggregate meta-production function that applies to the G-5 countries and the East Asian NIEs also apply to other APEs? (2) Does the finding of absence of technical progress hold for all the other APEs except Japan? (3) What is the relative importance of the different sources of economic growth for the APEs?

---

* This chapter was originally published in *Canadian Journal of Economics* 29 (April 1996), pp. S448–S454. This is an abridged version of a paper presented at the Annual Meeting of the Canadian Economic Association, Calgary, June 1994.

2. The Meta-Production Function Model

The basic assumptions of the meta-production function approach[1] are: (1) all economies have the same underlying aggregate meta-production function in terms of "efficiency-equivalent" quantities of outputs (Y^*_{it}) and inputs $(K^*_{it}$ and $L^*_{it})$; and (2) the unobservable "efficiency-equivalent" quantities of outputs and inputs of each country are linked to the measured quantities of outputs (Y_{it}) and inputs $(K_{it}$ and $L_{it})$ through time-varying, country- and commodity-specific augmentation factors $A_{ij}(t)$'s. In this study, the $A_{ij}(t)$'s are assumed to have the constant geometric form, where for $i = 1, \ldots,$ n, n the number of economies,

$$Y_{it}^* = A_{i0}(1+c_{i0})^t \, Y_{it}; \tag{1}$$

$$K_{it}^* = A_{iK}(1+c_{iK})^t \, K_{it}; \text{ and } L_{it}^* = A_{iL}(1+c_{iL})^t \, L_{it}. \tag{2}$$

In (1) and (2), the A_{ij}'s and c_{ij}'s are constants referred to as *augmentation level* and *augmentation rate* parameters respectively. The most important observation, however, is that all of the augmentation level and rate parameters are estimable subject to a normalisation.

To accommodate the wide ranges of variation in the quantities of inputs in the pooled inter-country data, a flexible functional form, the transcendental logarithmic (translog) functional form of Christensen, Jorgenson and Lau (1973), is chosen for the aggregate meta-production function. In addition to the production function, we also consider the behaviour of the share of labour costs in the value of output, which, under the hypothesis of profit maximisation, is equal to the elasticity of output with respect to labour. This allows us to test the hypothesis of profit maximisation.

3. The Data and the Statistical Method

The aggregate real output (Y) is measured as the real Gross Domestic Product (GDP) in 1980 prices, converted into 1980 U.S. Dollars using the period average market exchange rates in 1980. Labour (L) is measured as the number

---

1 Readers interested in the details of the meta-production function approach may consult either Boskin and Lau (1990) or Kim and Lau (1994b).

of person-hours worked. The share of labour in the value of output is estimated by dividing the current labour income (compensation of employees paid by resident producers) by the current GDP. The capital input (K) is measured as the *gross* total (public and private) non-residential fixed capital stock at the beginning of the period, multiplied by the average capacity utilisation rate of the period. Time (t) is measured in years chronologically with the year 1980 being set equal to zero. A detailed discussion of the construction of these as well as the instrumental variables used is given in Boskin and Lau (1990) and Kim and Lau (1994a, 1994b).

Under the assumption of joint normality of the stochastic disturbance terms, the system of two equations consisting of the production function and the labour share equation (both first-differenced) and its various specialisations are estimated by the method of nonlinear instrumental variables.[2] Since the economies and their real GDPs range in size from Singapore to the U.S., the stochastic disturbance terms of the aggregate production function are further adjusted for possible heteroscedasticity across economies. For testing hypotheses, we use as our criterion function the weighted sum of squares of residuals of the system of two equations projected in the space spanned by the instrumental variables.

4. The Empirical Results

First, a series of hypotheses are tested. The test statistics are presented in Table 2.1.[3] These tests confirm the general validity of the maintained hypotheses of the meta-production function approach. However, the conventional assumptions of growth accounting-constant returns to scale, neutrality of technical progress, and profit maximisation—continue to be rejected, as in Boskin and Lau (1990) and Kim and Lau (1994b). The tests also confirm that technical progress can be represented as purely capital-augmenting for both the APEs and for the IWCs. The hypothesis of zero technical progress against the alternative of positive technical progress can be decisively rejected for Japan and the IWCs but not for the APEs other than Japan on the basis of Bonferroni t-statistics.

---

2 See, e.g., Gallant and Jorgenson (1979).

3 The p-values for the test-statistics are also presented for the convenience of readers who may wish to assign alternative levels of significance for the different hypotheses.

Table 2.1. Tests of Hypotheses

Tested hypothesis	Maintained Hypothesis	Level of Significance	Number of Restrictions	Test Statistic	p-value
I. Maintained hypotheses of meta-production function analysis					
1. Single meta-production function	Unrestricted	0.01	39	0.18	1.00000
2. Commodity augmentation	I.1	0.01	14	0.22	0.99890
II. Maintained hypotheses of traditional growth accounting					
1. Homogeneity	I	0.005	2	26.09	0.00000
2. Constant returns to scale	I	0.005	3	18.70	0.00000
3. Neutrality	I	0.01	28	2.16	0.00051
4. Profit maximization	I	0.01	56	2.26	0.00000
III. Identical commodity augmentation levels					
1. Identical capital aug. levels	I	0.01	13	0.69	0.76699
2. Identical labour aug. levels	I	0.01	13	1.01	0.43416
IV. Purely capital-augmenting technical progress	I	0.01	28	1.13	0.29359

Synthesising the results of our tests of hypotheses, we obtain estimates on which the restrictions corresponding to hypotheses that are not rejected—that is, identical augmentation level parameters and purely capital-augmenting technical progress—are imposed. Using these estimated parameters, several parameters of economic interest—the production elasticities with respect to capital and labour and the local degree of returns to scale—are estimated and reported in Table 2.2. They show that the production elasticities of capital are higher and those of labour are lower in the APEs other than Japan compared to the IWCs and Japan, in accordance with the prevailing relative factor scarcities. In addition, the local returns to scale are slightly decreasing with the degree of returns of scale somewhat higher in the APEs other than Japan than those of the IWCs and Japan.

Table 2.2. Parameters of Interest (at 1980 values of the Independent Variables)

Country	Capital Elasticity	Labour Elasticity	Local Returns to Scale
APEs			
China	0.630	0.260	0.890
Hong Kong	0.443	0.432	0.875
Indonesia	0.673	0.234	0.907
Japan	0.325	0.514	0.840
Malaysia	0.525	0.363	0.888
Philippines	0.592	0.304	0.896
Singapore	0.448	0.431	0.880
South Korea	0.564	0.326	0.891
Taiwan	0.548	0.343	0.891
Thailand	0.584	0.309	0.893
IWCs			
France	0.268	0.564	0.833
West Germany	0.273	0.559	0.833
U.K.	0.327	0.516	0.843
U.S.	0.283	0.546	0.829

5. Sources of Economic Growth

In Table 2.3, we present our estimates of the relative contributions of the different sources of growth for each of the 14 economies, using our estimated meta-production function parameters. These estimates show that capital accumulation is the most important source of growth for the APEs, accounting for between 55 (Hong Kong) and 116 (Indonesia) percent of the growth in real output, whereas technical progress is the most important source of economic growth for the IWCs, accounting for between 41 and 64 percent of the economic growth in these countries. Labour is the second most important source of growth for the APEs other than Japan (except for Hong Kong and Thailand) whereas capital is the second most important source of growth for the IWCs. For both the APEs and the IWCs, capital and technical progress combined account for more than 70 percent of the economic growth. These results confirm our earlier similar

Table 2.3. The Contributions of the Sources of Growth (Percent)

Country	Capital	Labour	Technical Progress
APEs			
China	92.2	9.2	−1.4
Hong Kong	55.8	16.0	28.2
Indonesia	115.7	11.5	−27.2
Japan	62.9	4.7	32.4
Malaysia	70.9	18.7	10.5
Philippines	99.5	22.6	−17.5
Singapore	60.0	20.9	20.1
South Korea	86.3	12.7	1.0
Taiwan	88.9	8.6	2.5
Thailand	71.9	12.7	15.3
IWCs			
France	37.8	−1.3	63.5
West Germany	43.7	−6.3	62.6
U.K.	46.0	3.7	50.3
U.S.	32.9	26.2	41.0

findings for the East Asian NIEs.[4] However, they also raise the intriguing and important question of why technical progress (or increase in efficiency) has been relatively unimportant in the APEs other than Japan.[5]

6. Concluding Remarks

What policy implications do our empirical findings have? First, our findings imply that economic growth in the Asian Pacific developing economies is

---

4 These results reaffirm the findings of Kim and Lau (1994b) and are consistent with those of Tsao (1982, 1985) and Young (1992) for Singapore. They are at variance with those of the World Bank (1993). According to Moses Abramovitz, U.S. economic growth in the late 19th and early 20th centuries can also be mostly attributed to the growth in tangible (physical) capital.

5 See Kim and Lau (1994b) for a discussion of some plausible explanations for the relative unimportance of technical progress as a source of growth for the APEs other than Japan.

primarily attributable to the growth in the physical capital stock, which is in turn due mostly to domestic saving, with the possible exception of Hong Kong, South Korea in its early development phase, and Singapore. High levels of investment and saving are therefore essential for rapid economic growth. Second, in the long run simply having high levels of saving and investment is not enough. As the capital stocks of the APEs continue to grow, their production elasticities will continue to decline because of diminishing marginal productivity. Eventually increases in the capital input alone will not be sufficient for the APEs to maintain their current rate of economic growth. It is therefore necessary for the APEs to begin to devote greater proportions of their resources to indigenous research and development and other innovation activities in order to increase the contribution of technical progress to their economic growth in the future.

References

Boskin, Michael J., and Lawrence J. Lau. "Post-War Economic Growth of the Group-of-Five Countries: A New Analysis." Technical Paper 217, Center for Economic Policy Research, Stanford University, 1990.

Christensen, Laurits R., Dale W. Jorgenson, and Lawrence J. Lau. "Transcendental Logarithmic Production Frontiers." *Review of Economics and Statistics* 55 (1973), pp. 28–45.

Gallant, A. Ronald, and Dale W. Jorgenson. "Statistical Inference for a System of Simultaneous, Nonlinear, Implicit Equations in the Context of Instrumental Variables Estimation." *Journal of Econometrics* 113 (1979), pp. 272–302.

Kim, Jong-Il, and Lawrence J. Lau. "The Sources of Asian Pacific Economic Growth." Paper presented at the Annual Meeting of the Canadian Economic Association, Calgary, June 1994a.

———. "The Sources of Economic Growth in the East Asian Newly Industrialized Countries." *Journal of the Japanese and International Economies* 8 (1994b), pp. 235–271.

Tsao, Yuan. *Growth and Productivity in Singapore: A Supply Side Analysis*. Ph. D. dissertation. Cambridge: Harvard University, 1982.

———. "Growth Without Productivity: Singapore Manufacturing in the 1970s." *Journal of Development Studies* 18 (1985), pp. 25–38.

———. "Sources of Growth Accounting for the Singapore Economy." In Chong-Yah Lim and Peter J. Lloyd, eds., *Singapore: Resources and Growth*. Singapore: Oxford University Press, 1986, pp. 17–44.

The World Bank. *The East Asian Miracle: Economic Growth and Public Policy*. Oxford: Oxford University Press, 1993.

Young, Alwyn. "A Tale of Two Cities: Factor Accumulation and Technical Change in Hong Kong and Singapore?" In Olivier J. Blanchard and Stanley Fischer, eds., *National Bureau of Economic Research Macroeconomics Annual*, Cambridge, MA: MIT Press, 1992, pp. 13–54.

Chapter 3.

How Much Slack Was There in the Chinese Economy Prior to Its Economic Reform of 1978?*

Co-authored with Huanhuan Zheng

1. Introduction

China has made tremendous progress in its economic development since it began its economic reform and opened to the world in 1978. It is currently the fastest growing economy in the world—averaging 9.7 percent per annum over the past 36 years (even though its rate of growth has recently slowed down to around 7 percent). It is, however, historically unprecedented for an economy to grow at such a high rate over such a long period of time.

What are the sources of this Chinese economic growth? They include the growth in the conventional tangible inputs, physical capital and labour; the growth in intangible inputs, such as human capital and R&D capital; technical progress, also known as the growth of total factor productivity (TFP); and technology transfer from abroad. They include the effects of the realisation of economies of scale. But they should also include the reduction and elimination of the economic slack or inefficiency that existed in the Chinese economy prior to its economic reform and opening to the world in 1978.

---

* This chapter was originally published in *China Economic Review* 45 (September 2017), pp. 124–142. The authors wish to thank Ayesha Macpherson Lau, Xiaomeng Peng, Dwight Perkins, Yanyan Xiong, Feng Yao, and Junsen Zhang for their invaluable advice, comments and suggestions, and Ms. Sophia Lok for her able research assistance, but retain sole responsibility for any remaining errors. All opinions expressed herein are the authors' own and do not necessarily reflect the views of any of the organisations with which the authors are affiliated.

The existence of economic slack or inefficiency is a common phenomenon of economies that operate under mandatory central planning. It implies that the economy operates in the interior of its set of production possibilities and not on its frontier. The "distance" between where an economy operates and its frontier is then the economic slack. It also implies that output can be increased without any increase in the inputs if the constraints that prevent the economy from operating on the frontier in the first place are removed. Thus, there is "surplus potential output." The objective of this study is to attempt to identify and estimate the surplus potential output in the Chinese economy prior to its economic reform in 1978 and to help answer the question: How much of the Chinese economic growth since 1978 can be attributed to the reduction and elimination of the pre-existing economic slack? This question is important because the increase in output due to the reduction or elimination of the economic slack can only take effect once and cannot be continuing. When an economy already operates on its production possibilities frontier, there is no more surplus potential output and further increases in output will have to come from the outward movement of the production possibilities frontier, which requires increases in tangible and intangible inputs or technical progress. It will also affect the attribution of the sources of Chinese economic growth.

While many studies, including Bettelheim (1988), Hsueh and Liu (1980), Lin (1988, 1992), Rawski (1994, 1995, 1999) and Naughton (1995, 2007) have analysed the effects of Chinese reforms on the Chinese economy, there has not been any quantitative estimate of the size of the pre-existing economic slack that was reduced and eliminated through the economic reform. It is, however, in general difficult, if not impossible, to identify and distinguish from *aggregate time-series data of a single country or region* how much of a given increase in output is due to a movement from the interior of the set of production possibilities to its frontier and how much is due to a movement of the frontier itself. This is true regardless of whether the economy in question is a centrally-planned or a market one. Yet, it is well known that for an economy operating under mandatory central planning, there is inherent economic inefficiency, and hence economic slack, even though the size of the slack is not known.[1] Stochastic production frontier analysis has been proposed to identify and estimate the frontier of the set of production possibilities (see, for example, Aigner, Lovell and Schmidt [1977]). However, such an approach is not possible with aggregate time-series data of only a single economy. If cross-sectional or panel data are available within an economy, it may be possible to identify and estimate the frontier of the set of production possibilities under some assumptions. Yet in a centrally-planned economy, even cross-sectional data are of no help as all the production units in a centrally-planned economy are likely to operate in the interior of their sets of production possibilities.

But for economies transitioning from a centrally-planned system to a market system, as in the case of China, there is actually an opportunity to identify the pre-existing slack, by observing the economic performance before, during and after the implementation of the market-enabling economic reform.[2] Our objective here is to introduce two different simple methods to estimate the size of the surplus potential output, or its mirror image, the economic slack, in China before its economic reform in 1978. This possibility hinges on a number of observations and assumptions discussed below:

First, economic reform can remove the constraints in the economy that prevent it from operating on its production possibilities frontier in the first place. The effect of the economic reform on the reduction and elimination of the economic slack, if any, when it is fully implemented, is for one-time only and not continuing. Moreover, the effect is not instantaneous, as it takes time for the prior constraints in the economy to be removed so that the economic

---

1 With aggregate time-series data of more than one economy, it is in principle possible to identify and estimate the degree of relative economic inefficiency under suitable assumptions. Conventional methods that rely on inputs data to estimate production frontier/efficiency cannot identify slack because they ignore that the same input could be utilised in different intensity and thus has different impacts on outputs.

2 In the absence of a transition from a centrally-planned to a market economy, it would be difficult to identify and estimate the economic slack, as the slack may persist over time. It is only when the economic slack is reduced or eliminated over time because of economic reform that it has a chance of being identified and estimated.

slack can be reduced and eliminated and the surplus potential output realised. Thus, it is necessary to look beyond the first year(s) of the economic reform, although the effect will eventually dissipate. In this study, we make the working assumption that on average, it takes six years for the full effect of the economic reform to be realised.[3] We thus compare the economic performance of the pre-reform, reform, and post-reform periods to try to identify the effect of economic reform on the reduction or elimination of the pre-existing economic slack and the corresponding realisation of the surplus potential output.

Second, it is also necessary to try to control for the effects of additional inputs, if any, during the reform period, as they would have caused the production possibilities frontier to move outward and output to be increased. Even in the absence of economic reform, the set of production possibilities might still be expanding, although the economy could continue to operate in its interior rather than on its frontier. Thus, the increase in output during the reform period cannot be entirely attributed to the economic reform itself—the effects of the "usual and customary" increases in inputs during the same period must also be taken into account and deducted first. Since data on the quantities of the additional inputs during the reform period are not readily available, we make the assumption that the effects of the increased inputs during the reform period, if any, on the growth of output can be approximated by the trend rate of growth of output in the six years before the reform period.

Thus, the increase in output during the reform period is attributable to economic reform only after the subtraction of the increase in output that would have occurred if output had continued to grow at the pre-reform trend rate. While this assumption may seem arbitrary, it is actually quite realistic in the Chinese case, as throughout the reform period, say from 1979 to 1984 in the case of agricultural reform, the mandatory central plan continued to be enforced in China, so that additional supplies of inputs, beyond what was then

3 We also experimented with alternative assumptions on the duration of the economic reform period. However, our results are robust as to whether the reform period is assumed to be four, five or six years (see Appendix, Table A3.1). They are also robust with regard to the assumed durations of the pre-reform and post-reform periods (see Appendix, Table A3.2).

usual and customary, were unlikely.[4] Alternatively, one can also assume that the economic performance in the six years after the reform period represented the expected normal condition after all the prior constraints imposed by central planning in the economy were removed. Thus, one would attribute the excess of the growth of output in the reform period over the post-reform trend rate of growth to the reduction and elimination of the pre-existing economic slack.

China is a large country, and economic reform was implemented at different paces and to different degrees in different parts of the country, so it is difficult to identify from data on the Chinese economy as a whole the effects of economic reform and hence to estimate the magnitude of the surplus potential output that might have existed. We therefore focus on Anhui Province and Shanghai Municipality to estimate the magnitude of the surplus potential output. Anhui is chosen because that was where the Chinese agricultural reform was first proposed and implemented, in late 1978. Shanghai is chosen because it was the very last Chinese provincial-level administrative unit to undergo urban non-agricultural economic reform, in early 1992. Thus it is possible to identify and estimate from the economic performance of Anhui and Shanghai the effects of the introduction and implementation of the respective agricultural and non-agricultural economic reforms on the reduction and elimination of the economic slack there, which can then be used to obtain estimates for China as a whole. This study represents a first attempt to identify and estimate the pre-existing slack in a centrally-planned economy prior to its transition to a market economy.

In part 2 below, we explain briefly why there is inherent economic slack or inefficiency in a centrally-planned economy. In part 3, we give a brief chronology of the early Chinese economic reform. In parts 4 and 5, we examine the economic records of Anhui Province and Shanghai Municipality respectively and try to identify and estimate the surplus potential outputs that might have existed at the beginning of their respective agricultural and non-agricultural economic reforms. In part 6, we attempt to fit the data on China, Anhui and Shanghai in a simple piecewise linear econometric model of growth under

4 Moreover, Chinese economic reform first occurred in the agricultural sector. It would be quite a few years later that the industrial sector began to supply inputs such as chemical fertilizers and insecticides to the agricultural sector.

reform. In part 7, we estimate the magnitudes of the surplus potential outputs in China, Anhui and Shanghai that might have existed prior to the economic reform using the econometrically estimated parameters in part 6. Some brief concluding remarks are made in part 8.

2. The Inherent Economic Inefficiency under Central Planning

From 1953, when China adopted its First Five-Year (1953–1957) Plan, to the end of the last century, the Chinese economy operated under a series of mandatory five-year central plans, modelled after the former Soviet Union. However, in a centrally-planned economy, there is always inherent economic inefficiency, which in turn implies the continuing existence of economic slack or surplus potential but unrealised output in the economy. This surplus potential output can in principle be realised with the introduction of economic reforms granting autonomy to the producers and providing incentives for them through the free markets, which should then lead to a one-time spurt in the growth of real GDP, possibly phased in over several years, even in the absence of increases in inputs.

Why is there inherent economic inefficiency in a centrally-planned economy? A principal characteristic of a centrally-planned economy is the administrative allocation of resources. What goods and services to produce? How much to produce? Where to produce them? What raw materials and parts should be used to produce them? From which enterprises should the raw materials and parts be bought? To which enterprises should the outputs be sold? All of these decisions are made by the central planners and embodied in the mandatory central plan. Enterprises do not have any autonomy in these decisions. The prices of goods and services are also completely set in the central plan and are only used for accounting purposes. They do not necessarily reflect relative scarcities in the economy and do not play any role in the equilibration of market supply and demand. For reasons to be explained below, a centrally-planned economy always has slack, that is, it always operates in the interior and not on the frontier of its set of production possibilities. Thus, output can be increased by simply reducing the slack—by moving to the frontier from the interior of the set of production possibilities—in principle without having to increase any inputs. The existence of inherent inefficiency therefore also implies the existence of surplus potential output.

In order to understand why there always exists inefficiency in a centrally-planned economy, we consider the following simple example drawn from agriculture. There are two farm households, headed by two farmers, A and B. Each has a hectare of land. Both cotton and rice are needed by the economy. The central planner's problem is to decide which household should grow cotton and which household should grow rice, as well as how much of each crop to grow.

First of all, there may be a problem of insufficient or inaccurate information on the part of the central planner. The central planner may not know which one of the two plots is more suitable for growing cotton or rice. Moreover, the central planner may also not know whether Farmer A can grow cotton better than Farmer B or vice versa. If the central planner makes any mistake in the assignment of the production responsibilities, a simple rearrangement of the assignment can increase total output without having to increase any input.

Second, the central planner may fail to optimise, even if he or she has the complete information. Full optimisation may not be possible, for example, across all the farmers, because of the immense complexity of the problem or because of unforeseen constraints. Failure of optimisation again implies that for the economy as a whole there is room for increasing output without having to increase any input.

Third, there is also the problem of a lack of incentive on the part of the farmers to exceed the assigned production targets even if they are in principle able to do so. To the farmer, if he or she manages to produce an output that exceeds the assigned production target, not only would his or her income not increase under a mandatory central plan, so that the extra efforts would have gone un-rewarded, but also the assigned production responsibility for the following year might even be increased, now that the higher target has been shown to be feasible, making it more difficult for the farmer to fulfil his or her obligation. (This is sometimes referred to as the "ratchet" effect.) Thus, the optimal strategy for a farmer is to try to produce only the assigned target output as specified in the mandatory central plan, and not to try to exceed it, even if it is possible to do so. Once again there is surplus potential output that is not realised under mandatory central planning.

For these reasons, there is always economic slack, or surplus potential output, in a centrally-planned economy. However, if there is a way to remove the constraints on and provide the necessary incentives to the producers, then without having to increase the aggregate inputs assigned under the central plan, aggregate output can be increased. For example, the farmers can be given the autonomy to grow anything on their plots once they have fulfilled their obligations under the central plan, and to retain the resulting profits (and to bear the resulting losses), if any.

We shall try to identify and estimate the surplus potential output in the Chinese economy prior to its economic reform of 1978 by comparing the economic performance in the periods preceding the reform, during the reform, and following the reform.

3. A Brief Chronology of Early Chinese Economic Reform

Chinese economic reform first began in 1978 in the agricultural sector. The "household contract responsibility system" (家庭聯產承包責任制), also called the "household responsibility system," was introduced in the countryside of Anhui Province, at first almost spontaneously.[5] Under this system, each member household of a commune and its production brigades was individually responsible for its share of the commune or brigade output delivery quotas assigned under the central plan. Subject to the fulfilment of its individual share of these quotas first, each member household was free to grow whatever it wished, on plots under its own exclusive management, sell its extra output on the free market at prices determined in the market, and enjoy whatever gains and suffer whatever losses entirely on its own. Then the commune—which would wind up with almost no real function for agricultural production under this system—would establish township and village enterprises (T&V enterprises) to produce other goods and services, using its own surplus resources, and sell the outputs on the free market. Thus, the agricultural production assignment of the central plan to the commune continued to be enforced and fulfilled after the agricultural economic reform of 1978, at the same time that free markets were introduced on which output above and beyond the assigned production quota could be freely sold at market-determined prices.

5 The arrangement was first initiated by the 18 households in Xiaogang Village, Fengyang County, Anhui Province (安徽省鳳陽縣小崗村) in December 1978.

It should be clear that no one would be made economically worse off by the introduction of the "household contract responsibility system" in the agricultural sector. The commune and its officials would not be worse off, because they would still be able to deliver the required quota under the mandatory central plan to the government. The households would not be worse off, because they would not be required to produce any more output than before. In addition, the commune would be able to generate additional income through their T&V enterprises and the households would also be able to do so by growing more on their plots and selling the extra output on the free markets. So no one would lose, but anyone who would want to become a winner would be free to do so.

After the initial introduction of the "household contract responsibility system" in Xiaogang Village, Fengyang County, Anhui Province, in December 1978, it soon spread to other parts of Anhui Province and to Sichuan Province as well. Ultimately it was adopted almost everywhere nationwide in the early 1980s, supplanting the role of the people's commune as an organisation for production. Subsequently the "household contract responsibility system" was also extended to the urban areas, covering the industrial enterprises as well, making the entire Chinese economy a "dual-track" economy, with the free markets functioning alongside the mandatory central plan. Shanghai, which had been responsible for contributing much of the revenue of the central government, was among the last provinces, autonomous regions and municipalities to have conditional autonomy granted to their enterprises and parallel free markets established, in early 1992.

4. The Estimation of the Pre-Reform Surplus Potential Outputs by the Direct Comparison Method—Anhui Province

While there must have been slack in the Chinese economy, and in its agricultural sector in particular, before the introduction of economic reform in 1978, it is not straightforward to estimate how much slack there was. We define the pre-reform surplus potential output as the additional output that would have been produced relative to the actual pre-reform output if the economy had been operating efficiently, that is, on the frontier of its set of production possibilities. We note that in principle, this is the additional output that could have been realised without additional inputs. For the present purpose, we do not consider the additional labour services performed by a grossly under-employed rural labour force as additional inputs.

However, since it takes time for the effects of economic reform to be fully realised and for the economic slack to be reduced and eliminated, we would have to take into account that even in the absence of economic reform, inputs and therefore outputs would have grown too. It is assumed that, on average, the time required for the full elimination of the economic slack is six years. In what follows, we use a primitive but direct method to estimate the size of the surplus potential output—we simply compare the growth of real output during the six-year "pre-reform period" before the initiation of economic reform and for the two successive six-year periods after the initiation of economic reform (the "reform period" and "post-reform period" respectively). We assume that in the absence of economic reform, output would have grown during the "reform period" at the average rate of growth of the "pre-reform period," on the basis of the "usual and customary" growth of inputs. It is assumed that no new inputs, such as chemical fertilizers or insecticides that did not exist before the reform were introduced during the reform period. This is not an unreasonable first approximation as the agricultural sector was the very first to undergo reform and the industrial sector, still operating under mandatory central planning, was not in a position yet to provide the additional inputs such as chemical fertilizers to the agricultural sector. (In addition, Anhui was not particularly industrialised to start with.) The increase in output attributable to the elimination of the prior economic slack can therefore be estimated as the difference between the actual output realised at the end of the reform period and the hypothetical output at the end of the reform period assuming "business as usual" as in the pre-reform period. For example, if the actual realised output at the end of the reform period represents an average rate of growth of 9 percent per annum relative to the actual output at the end of the pre-reform period, and the average trend rate of growth for the pre-reform period is 3 percent per annum, then the growth of output attributable to the elimination of the economic slack is the difference between 9 percent and 3 percent, that is, 6 percent per annum compounded over six years, or 42 percent.

Alternatively, the average annual rate of growth over the "post-reform period" can be taken as a benchmark for the post-reform "normalised" (or "steady-state") growth under the new policies after the prior economic slack has been exhausted during the reform period. Thus, it would have reflected the increases in labour and other inputs in response to the economic reform. The increase in output attributable to the elimination of the economic slack can therefore be estimated as the difference between the hypothetical output at the end of the post-reform period assuming that the average annual rate of growth is the same as that of the reform period and the actual output realised at the end of the post-reform period.

One may question why we choose six years as opposed to five or even four years as the time required for the elimination of the economic slack. Clearly, any reform will take time to diffuse from the village where it first started to the entire province and then to the entire country. There are also local administrative and political problems to overcome. Moreover, the slack is likely to be reduced only gradually over time as both experimentation and learning are involved. After some preliminary examination of the data, in which the rates of growth of real output and other economic indicators generally experienced a significant decline between 1984 and 1985, we choose six years (1979–1984) as the period over which the pre-existing economic slack is likely to be entirely eliminated or exhausted in the province/autonomous region/municipality in question in response to the economic reform.[6]

We look at Anhui Province as well as China as a whole. The agricultural reform was first started in Anhui in December 1978, and soon spread to the rest of the province, and then to China as a whole. By the end of 1982, the "household contract responsibility system" was introduced in almost all of the rural areas of China. So for agricultural reform (in Anhui), the six-year pre-reform period would be 1973–1978; the actual reform period would be 1979–1984; and the normalised post-reform period would be 1985–1990.

In Chart 3.1, the rates of growth of grain output in Anhui Province and in China are presented for the 18-year period from 1973 through 1990. It is clear that for both Anhui Province and China, the rates of growth of grain output were higher during the agricultural reform period than either the pre-reform or the post-reform period. For Anhui Province, the average annual rate of growth of grain output during the pre-reform period of 1973–1978 was 1.35

---

6 The results of our econometric analysis in part 7 are also quite robust with regard to whether the reform period is assumed to be four, five or six years (see Appendix, Table A3.1).

percent, compared to 6.83 percent during the reform period (1979–1984), and 1.84 percent for the post-reform period (1985–1990). The surplus potential grain output in Anhui Province may therefore be estimated as either the difference in output resulting from the difference between the average annual rates of growth of the reform and pre-reform period, 5.48 percent per year, or that resulting from the difference between the average annual rates of growth of the reform and post-reform period, 4.99 percent per year. Over a six-year period, the cumulative surplus potential output may be estimated to be between 33.93 percent and 37.73 percent for Anhui Province.[7] For China as a whole, the average annual rate of growth of grain output during the pre-reform period was 4.03 percent, compared to 4.95 percent during the reform period, and 1.53 percent for the post-reform period. The surplus potential output in China may therefore be estimated as either the difference in output resulting from the difference between the average annual rates of growth of the reform and pre-reform period, 0.92 per year, or between the reform and post-reform period, 3.42 percent per year. Over a six-year period, the cumulative surplus potential output may be estimated to be between 5.68 percent and 22.35 percent for China as a whole. However, this would be an under-estimate of the size of the pre-existing potential surplus grain output for China as a whole, as the agricultural reform was introduced in some of the Chinese provinces only in 1982.

The agricultural sector cannot be represented by grain output alone. We next examine the data on the rates of growth of the gross value of agricultural production, adjusted for inflation, for both Anhui Province and China. These rates of growth are presented in Chart 3.2. It is also clear that for both Anhui and China, the rates of growth were similarly higher during the reform period than either the pre-reform or the post-reform period. For Anhui Province, the average annual real rate of growth of the gross value of agricultural production during the pre-reform period was –0.02 percent, compared to 8.55 percent during the reform period and 3.23 percent for the post-reform period. Thus, the size of the surplus potential agricultural output in Anhui may be estimated at between 5.32 percent and 8.57 percent per year, or somewhere between

7 The six-year cumulative effect is estimated with annual compounding. The same is true of all other estimates of cumulative effects in this paper.

Chart 3.1. The Rate of Growth of Grain Output: China and Anhui Province (Percent per annum, 1973–1990)

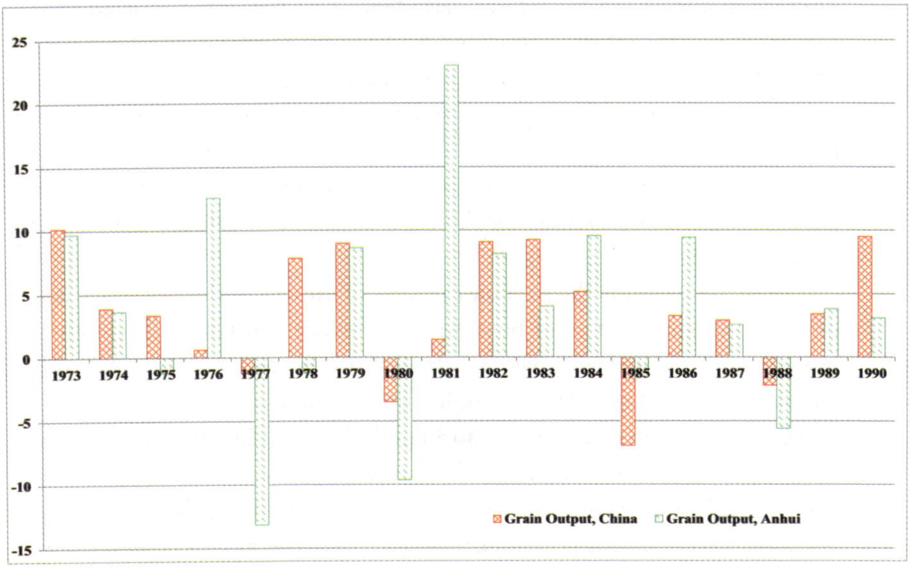

Chart 3.2. The Real Rate of Growth of the Gross Value of Agricultural Production: China and Anhui Province (Percent per annum, 1973–1990)

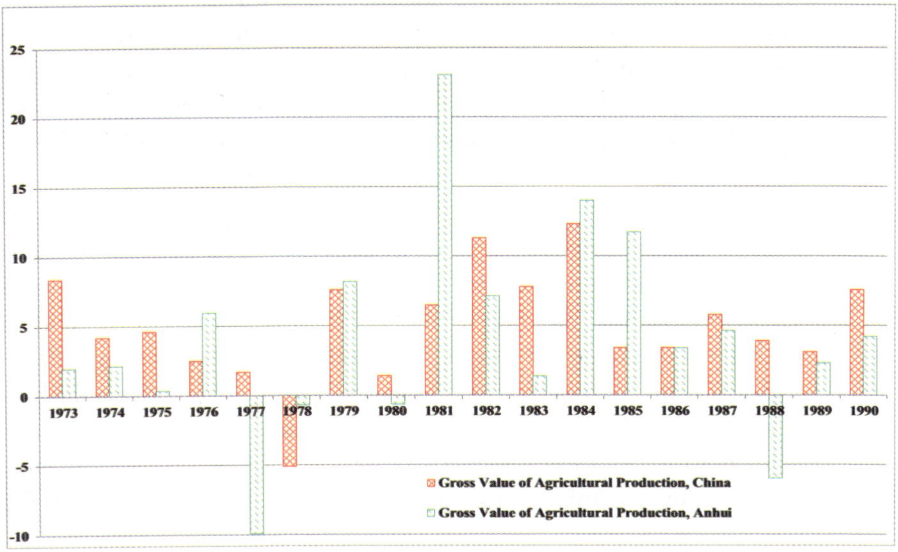

36.47 percent and 65.10 percent cumulatively over six years. For China as a whole, the average annual real rate of growth of the gross value of agricultural production during the pre-reform period was 2.63 percent, compared to 7.76 percent during the reform period and 4.52 percent for the post-reform period. Thus, the size of the surplus potential agricultural output for China may be estimated at between 3.24 percent and 5.13 percent per year, or somewhere between 21.06 percent and 34.96 percent cumulatively over six years. For similar reasons as in the case of grain output, we believe the estimated surplus potential agricultural output for Anhui is much more reliable than that for China as a whole.

Third, we examine the data on the rates of growth of the real value-added of the agricultural sector for both Anhui Province and China. These rates of growth are presented in Chart 3.3. It is also clear that for both Anhui and China, the rates of growth were higher during the reform period than for either the pre-reform or the post-reform period. For Anhui, the average annual rate of growth of the real value-added in agriculture during the pre-reform period was 0.16 percent, compared to 8.03 percent during the reform period and 2.84 percent for the post-reform period. Thus, the surplus potential output in Anhui may be estimated at between 5.19 percent and 7.87 percent per year, or somewhere between 35.46 percent and 57.52 percent cumulatively over six years. For China as a whole, the average annual rate of growth of the real value-added in agriculture during the pre-reform period was 2.46 percent, compared to 7.28 percent during the reform period and 3.77 percent for the post-reform period. Thus, the surplus potential output may be estimated at between 3.51 percent and 4.82 percent per year, or somewhere between 23.02 percent and 32.63 percent cumulatively over six years. We should note, however, that during the post-reform period, additional inputs for agriculture such as chemical fertilizers began to be more generally available, contributing to the continued increase in agricultural output. Thus, the surplus potential output is probably more accurately reflected by the actual additional output produced in the reform period over what would have been produced if there were no economic reform and by the data on Anhui rather than China as a whole.

In 1978, the distribution of Chinese GDP by sector originating was primary (agriculture), 27.90 percent, secondary (manufacturing, mining and construction), 47.56 percent, and tertiary (services), 24.54 percent. If we multiply the estimated Anhui potential surplus output of 57.52 percent in the

Chart 3.3. The Rate of Growth of Real Value-Added in the Agricultural Sector: China and Anhui Province (Percent per annum, 1973–1990)

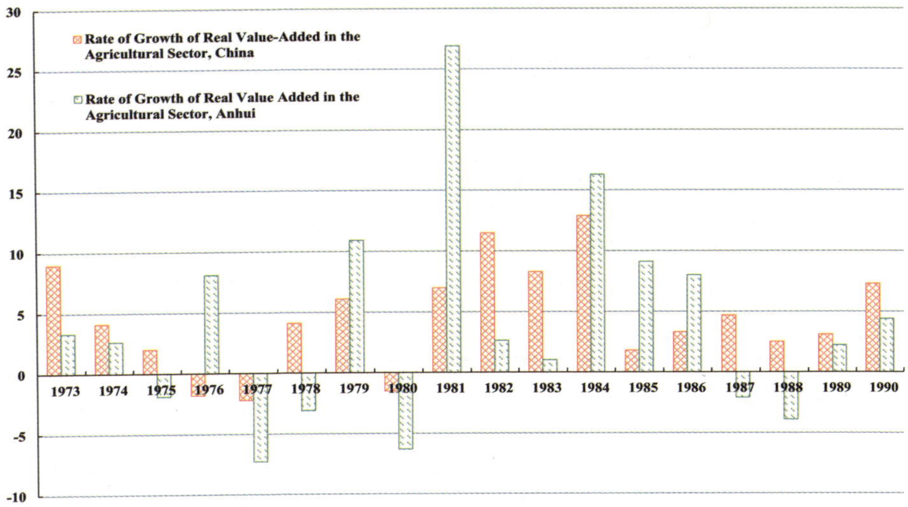

primary sector, estimated above, to the share of the primary sector in GDP, we obtain 16.05 percent, which, on the assumption that similar slacks existed in the primary sectors of all Chinese provinces, regions and municipalities, can be used as an estimate of the pre-existing potential surplus output in terms of GDP in the primary sector of China.

Fourth, we examine the data on real disposable income per capita in the rural areas for both Anhui Province and China. The data, which are only available for the years after 1978, are presented in Chart 3.4, which shows that the rate of growth of rural real disposable income per capita was the highest for both Anhui and China during the reform period. The average annual rate of growth during the reform period was 19.07 percent for Anhui and 16.46 percent for China, compared to average annual rates of 8.91 percent and 3.75 percent respectively in the post-reform period. The implied surplus potential output was 78.69 percent for Anhui and 105.00 percent for China. However, the increase in rural real disposable income per capita did not come solely from agriculture; it also came from the secondary sector, through the township and village enterprises, through the homeward remittances of migrant labourers, and through the service sector.

Chart 3.4. The Rate of Growth of Real Disposable Income per Capita in Rural Areas: China and Anhui Province (Percent per annum, 1973–1990)

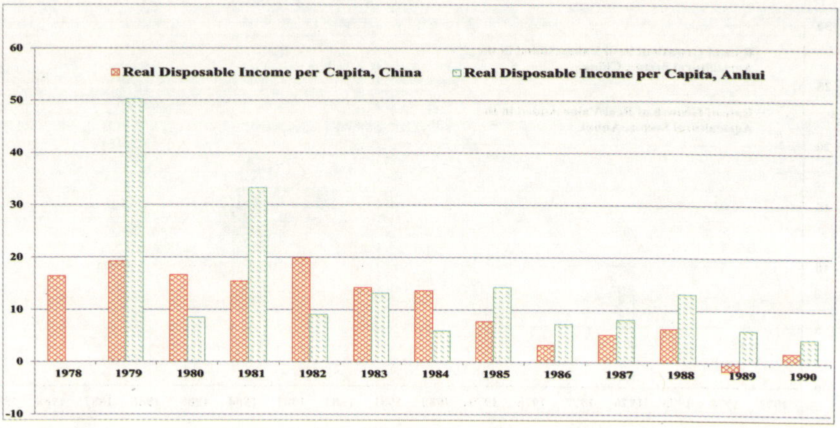

Finally, we examine the data on the rate of growth of real GDP for both Anhui Province and China. The data are presented in Chart 3.5. For Anhui, the rate of growth of real GDP increased from 2.58 percent in the pre-reform period to 11.24 percent in the reform period, an increase of 8.66 percent, or 64.65 percent cumulatively over a six-year period. In the post-reform period, the real GDP of Anhui grew at 7.38 percent. However, we believe the increase in real GDP during the post-reform period should be attributed to the economic reform measures implemented in the urban areas subsequent to the agricultural reform and not to the agricultural reform per se. For China as a whole, the rate of growth of real GDP increased from 5.97 percent in the pre-reform period to 9.22 percent in the reform period, an increase of 3.25 percent, or 21.14 percent over a six-year period. It then fell back to 8.85 percent in the post-reform period. However, we believe the increase in real GDP during the post-reform period should be attributed to the non-agricultural reform measures implemented in the urban areas subsequent to the agricultural reform and not to the agricultural reform per se.

It is clear from the data presented above that the economic reform implemented in late 1978 did have a highly significant one-time effect on the economic performance of both Anhui Province and China. This one-time effect can be attributed to the reduction and/or elimination of the economic slack that had existed prior to the economic reform. We summarise our estimates of the surplus potential output in Table 3.1.

Chart 3.5. The Rate of Growth of Real GDP: China and Anhui Province (Percent per annum, 1973–1990)

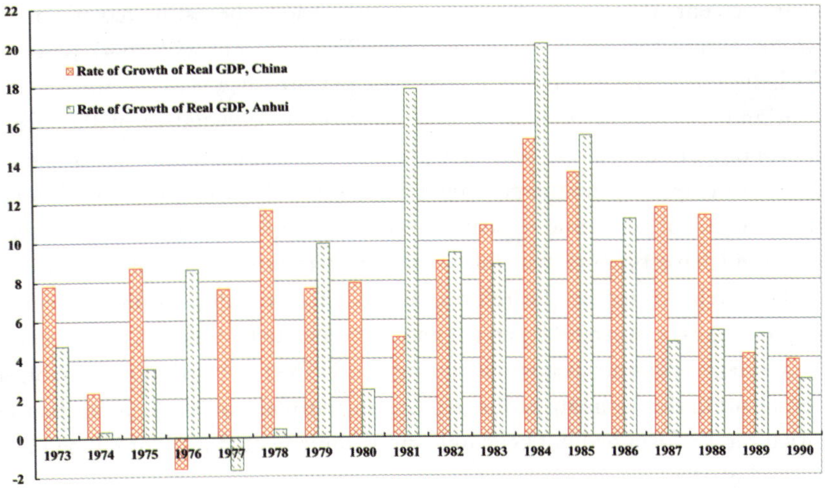

Table 3.1. A Summary of Estimated Pre-Reform Surplus Potential Outputs in China and Anhui Province (Percent)

	Anhui			China		
	Relative to Pre-Reform	Relative to Post-Reform	Average	Relative to Pre-Reform	Relative to Post-Reform	Average
Real GDP	64.65%	25.53%	45.09%	21.14%	2.23%	11.69%
Grain Output	37.73%	33.93%	35.83%	5.68%	22.35%	14.02%
Real Gross Value of Agricultural Production	65.10%	36.47%	50.79%	34.96%	21.06%	28.01%
Real Value-Added, Agricultural Sector	57.52%	35.46%	46.49%	32.63%	23.02%	27.83%
Real Income per Capita of Rural Population	/	78.69%	78.69%	/	105.00%	105.00%
Average	56.25%	42.02%	49.13%	23.60%	34.73%	29.17%

Notes: The surplus potential outputs relative to pre-reform (post-reform) period is calculated as the difference between the average growth rate over the reform period and the average growth rate over the pre-reform (post-reform) period, compounded over six years. The average surplus potential output is the mean of surplus potential outputs relative to pre-reform and that relative to post-reform.

As we can see from Table 3.1, relative to the pre-reform period, the estimated surplus potential output for Anhui ranges between 37.73 percent and 65.10 percent. Relative to the post-reform period, the estimated potential surplus output for Anhui ranges between 25.53 percent and 36.47 percent. We believe that the difference in economic performance between the pre-reform and the reform periods is probably more representative of the effect of economic reform alone, and that the difference in economic performance between the reform and the post-reform periods only provides a lower bound for the effect of economic reform since more inputs from the industrial sector would have become available in the post-reform period. For China as a whole, relative to the pre-reform period, the estimated surplus potential output ranges between 5.68 percent and 34.96 percent. However, the effect on the Chinese economy as a whole during the 1979–1984 period is probably a significant under-estimate of the pre-existing surplus potential output, as the agricultural reform had not been uniformly implemented in all of China until the end of 1982.

Taking all of these considerations into account, we believe that an estimate of the existence of a pre-reform potential surplus output in the agricultural sector on the order of 50 percent for Anhui, and by extension for the agricultural sector of the Chinese economy as a whole, is not unreasonable.

5. The Estimation of the Pre-Reform Surplus Potential Outputs by the Direct Comparison Method—Shanghai Municipality

We next examine the economic record of Shanghai. Economic reform came very late to Shanghai. Shanghai had the responsibility of providing much of the revenue of the Chinese central government and was not allowed to undertake new investment projects until early 1992, after the famous "Southern Inspection Tour" of Deng Xiaoping. It is precisely because Shanghai was not allowed to fully develop its economy until 1992 that it provides an opportunity for us to estimate the pre-reform economic slack in the secondary and tertiary sectors in China, using Shanghai as a typical case. Thus, for Shanghai, instead of focusing on the period immediately after the beginning of economic reform in 1978, we look at the six-year period from 1992 to 1997, and compare the economic performance to those during the preceding seven-year pre-reform period of 1985–1991, and the following six-year post-reform period of

1998–2003. We choose 1985–1991 to be the pre-reform period rather than 1986–1991 because the latter half of 1989 and 1990–1991 were abnormally slow-growth years for China because of the June 4 incident in 1989. In addition, since agriculture is not important in Shanghai, we shall restrict our attention to the growth of its real GDP and the real value-added of its secondary and tertiary sectors.

In Chart 3.6, the rates of growth of real GDP of Shanghai Municipality and China as a whole are presented for the 19-year period from 1985 through 2003. It is clear that for both Shanghai and China, the rates of growth were higher during the Shanghai reform period of 1992–1997 than either the pre-reform or the post-reform period. For Shanghai, the average annual rate of growth of real GDP more than doubled from the pre-reform period of 7.00 percent to 14.10 percent during the reform period, dropping back to 10.97 percent in the post-reform period. The fact that the rate of growth in Shanghai in the post-reform period fell significantly from 14.10 per cent to 10.97 percent supports the interpretation that the growth spurt during the reform period was due to the one-off effect of the elimination of the pre-existing economic slack and the realisation of the surplus potential output. Cumulatively, the growth spurt during the reform period accounted for an additional 50.92 percent increase in the real GDP of Shanghai over the pre-reform period. For China as a whole, the average annual rate of growth of real GDP during the pre-Shanghai reform period was 8.97 percent, compared to 11.90 percent during the reform period, and 8.54 percent for the post-reform period. Cumulatively, the surplus potential output for China may be estimated to be between 18.91 percent and 21.95 percent over the six-year Shanghai reform period (bear in mind that economic reform had been on-going for the rest of the country for more than 10 years by 1992).

In Chart 3.7, the rates of growth of real value-added in the secondary sector (which includes manufacturing, mining and construction) in Shanghai and China are presented for the 19-year period from 1985 through 2003. It is also clear that for both Shanghai and China, the rates of growth were similarly higher during the reform period than either the pre-reform or the post-reform period. For Shanghai, the average annual rate of growth also more than doubled from 6.71 percent in its pre-reform period to 14.10 percent in its reform period, and then dropped back to 11.20 percent in its post-reform period. The growth spurt in Shanghai during its reform period accounted for an additional cumulative increase in its real value-added in the secondary

Chart 3.6. The Rate of Growth of Real GDP: China and Shanghai Municipality (Percent per annum, 1985–2003)

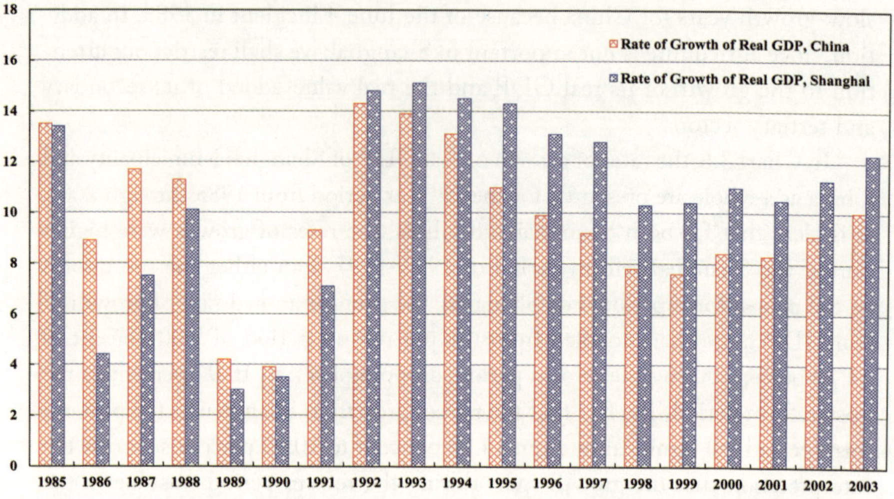

Chart 3.7. The Rate of Growth of Real Value-Added in the Secondary Sector: China and Shanghai Municipality (Percent per annum, 1985–2003)

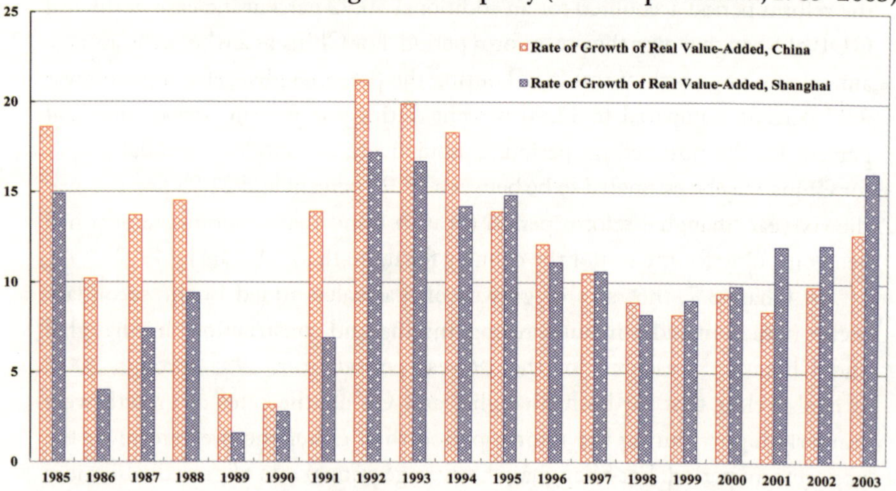

sector of 53.35 percent, which may also be attributed to the elimination of the pre-existing economic slack in the secondary sector in Shanghai. Again, the significant decline in the rate of growth in the post-reform period supports the interpretation that the growth during the Shanghai reform period was due to the one-off elimination of the pre-existing economic slack. For China as a whole, the average annual rate of growth of real value-added in the secondary sector during the pre-reform period was 11.11 percent, compared to 15.98 percent during the reform period, and 9.57 percent for the post-reform period.[8] The growth spurt in China as a whole during its reform period accounted for an additional cumulative increase in its real value-added in the secondary sector of 33.01 percent, which may also be attributed to the elimination of the pre-existing economic slack in the secondary sector.

In Chart 3.8, the rates of growth of real value-add in the tertiary (service) sector in Shanghai and China are presented for the 19-year period from 1985 through 2003. The pattern for Shanghai is similar to those in the cases of real GDP and real value-added in the secondary sector: the rates of growth were also higher during its reform period than either the pre-reform or the post-reform period. The average annual rate of growth increased from 9.03 percent in its pre-reform period to 15.27 percent in its reform period, and then dropped back to 11.83 percent in its post-reform period. The growth spurt in value-added in the tertiary sector in Shanghai during its reform period, which accounted for an additional cumulative increase in the real value-added in its tertiary sector of 43.77 percent may also be similarly attributed to the reduction/elimination of the pre-existing economic slack in Shanghai.

It is clear from the data presented above that the urban non-agricultural economic reform implemented in Shanghai beginning in early 1992 did have a highly significant positive impact on the economic performance of Shanghai Municipality, especially when compared with the its pre-reform period. We summarise our estimates of the surplus potential outputs in Table 3.2 below.

As we can see from Table 3.2, the estimated surplus potential outputs for

---

8 However, the rate of growth during the post-reform period might have been affected negatively by the East Asian Currency Crisis of 1997–1998 and positively affected by the Chinese accession to the World Trade Organization (WTO).

Chart 3.8. The Rate of Growth of Real Value-Added in the Tertiary Sector, China and Shanghai Municipality (Percent per annum, 1985–2003)

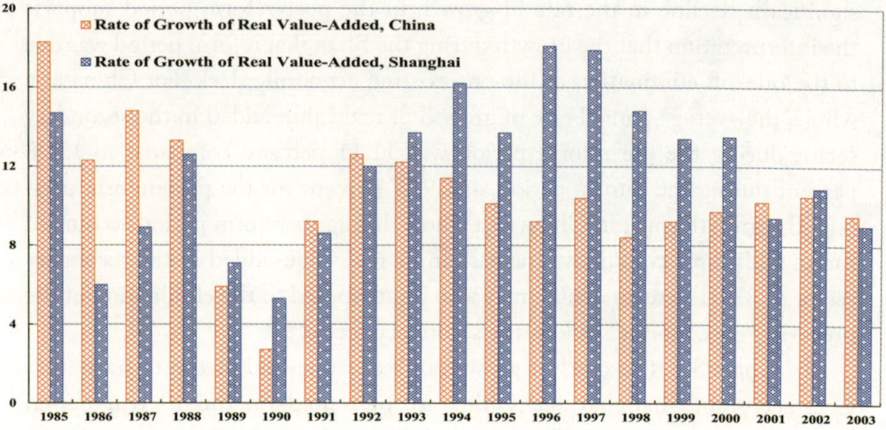

Shanghai Municipality were between 43.77 percent and 53.35 percent when compared with the pre-reform period. Taking into account the fact that the difference in economic performance between the pre-1992 and the 1992–1997 periods is probably more representative of the effect of the economic reform in the non-agricultural sectors (with the post-1997 period negatively affected by the East Asian currency crisis and positively affected by the accession of China to the WTO), we believe that an estimate of the existence of a pre-reform non-agricultural economic slack on the order of approximately 50 percent in Shanghai and by extension in China is not an unreasonable one.

In 1978, the distribution of Chinese GDP by sector originating was primary (agriculture), 27.90 percent, secondary (manufacturing, mining and construction), 47.56 percent, and tertiary (services), 24.54 percent. If we multiply the estimated Shanghai surplus potential outputs of 53.35 percent in the secondary sector and 43.77 percent in the tertiary sector to their respective shares in GDP and add them together, we obtain 36.11 percent, which can be used as an estimate of the pre-reform surplus potential outputs in terms of GDP in the secondary and tertiary sectors of China as a whole.

The average estimated surplus potential outputs for the Chinese economy as a whole in Table 3.2 are also on the order of 20 percent. However, we believe that this is not a reliable estimate of the pre-existing surplus potential output for the Chinese economy as a whole because by 1992 the rest of China had already undergone significant agricultural and non-agricultural economic reforms.

Table 3.2. A Summary of the Estimated Pre-1992 Surplus Potential Outputs in China and Shanghai Municipality (Percent)

	Shanghai			China		
	Relative to Pre-Reform	Relative to Post-Reform	Average	Relative to Pre-Reform	Relative to Post-Reform	Average
Real GDP	50.92%	20.34%	35.63%	18.91%	21.95%	20.43%
Real Value-Added, Secondary Sector	53.35%	18.71%	36.03%	33.01%	45.23%	39.12%
Real Value-Added, Tertiary Sector	43.77%	22.45%	33.11%	0.33%	8.70%	4.51%
Average	49.35%	20.50%	34.92%	17.42%	25.29%	21.35%

Notes: The surplus potential outputs relative to the pre-reform (post-reform) period is calculated as the difference between the average growth rate over the reform period and the average growth rate over the pre-reform (post-reform) period, compounded over six years. The average surplus potential outputs are the mean of surplus potential outputs relative to pre-reform and that relative to post-reform.

6. The Econometric Estimation of a Piece-Wise Linear Model of Economic Growth—Anhui Province and Shanghai Municipality

An alternative and more systematic method for estimating the size of the surplus potential output (or its mirror image, the pre-existing economic slack) is to assume that the natural logarithm of real output grows in accordance with a piecewise linear functional form with respect to time.[9] Prior to the reform, the natural logarithm of the real output is assumed to take the form:

$$\ln Y_t = \alpha_0 + \gamma_0 t, \; 0 \le t < t_0,$$

9 Still another alternative is to estimate a production function, relating the real output to the primary inputs of tangible capital and labour as well as technical progress econometrically. The estimated production function then allows us to test whether the economic performance during the reform period is different from those during both the pre-reform and post-reform periods, and if so, to provide an estimate of the magnitude of the difference, which can then be attributed to the pre-existing slack before the reform. However, the necessary data are not readily available to carry out this exercise.

where t is a time trend variable taking the value 0 at the beginning of the pre-reform period, say 1973 in the case of Anhui (or 1985 in the case of Shanghai), t_0 is the first year of the reform period, say, 1979 for the agricultural sector in Anhui (or 1992 for the secondary and tertiary sectors in Shanghai), and γ_0 is the trend rate of growth in the pre-reform period.

During the reform, the natural logarithm of the real output can be specified as:

$$\ln Y_t = \alpha_0 + \alpha_1 + \gamma_0 t + \gamma_1 (t - t_0),\ t_0 \leq t < t_1,$$

where t_1 is the first year after the end of the reform period, say 1985 in the case of Anhui (or 1998 in the case of Shanghai)[10], α_1 represents a possible jump and γ_1 represents a possible increase in the trend rate of growth at the beginning of the reform period. The above equation simplifies into:

$$\ln Y_t = (\alpha_0 + \alpha_1 - \gamma_1 t_0) + (\gamma_0 + \gamma_1)t.$$

During the post-reform period, the natural logarithm of the real output is

$$\ln Y_t = (\alpha_0 + \alpha_1 + \alpha_2 + \gamma_1 (t_1 - t_0) - \gamma_2 t_1) + (\gamma_0 + \gamma_2)t,\ \geq t_1,$$

where α_2 represents a possible jump (up or down) and γ_2 represents a possible change in the trend rate of growth at the beginning of the post-reform period. Taken together, we have:

$$\ln Y_t = \alpha_0 + \gamma_0 t + \alpha_1 D1 + (\alpha_1 + \gamma_1 (t_1 - t_0) + \alpha_2) D2 \qquad (1)$$
$$+ \gamma_1 D1.\ (t - t_0) + \gamma_2 D2.\ (t - t_1),$$

where $D1 = 1$, during the reform period, $t_1, > t \geq t_0$ and 0 otherwise;
$D2 = 1$, during the post-reform period, $t \geq t_1$, and 0 otherwise.

10 Recall the assumption that it takes six years to fully realise the effect of the economic reform. For Anhui, the reform started in 1979; the pre-reform, reform and post-reform period are, respectively, 1973–1978, 1979–1984 and 1985–1990. For Shanghai, the reform started in 1992; the pre-reform, reform and post-reform period are, respectively, 1985–1991, 1992–1997, 1998–2003.

Chart 3.9. The Hypothetical Path of Growth of the Natural Logarithm of Real Output Pre-, During- and Post-Reform

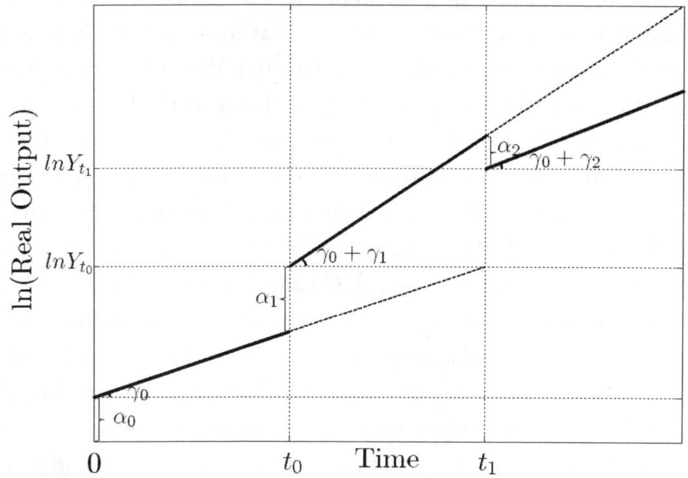

In Chart 3.9 we present a chart of such a typical piecewise linear function representing the growth path of the natural logarithm of real output during the pre-reform, reform and post-reform periods.

If we now take first differences of Equation (1) above, we obtain:

$$\ln Y_t - \ln Y_{t-1} = \gamma_0 + \alpha_1 d_1 + \alpha_2 d_2 + \gamma_1 (D1 - d_1 + d_2) + \gamma_2 (D2 - d_2),$$

where $d_1 = 1$ when $t = t_0$, 0 otherwise; and

$d_2 = 1$ when $t = t_1$, 0 otherwise.

This is then our basic estimating equation after appending a stochastic disturbance term ε_t with the usual assumed properties:

$$\ln Y_t - \ln Y_{t-1} = \gamma_0 + \alpha_1 d_1 + \alpha_2 d_2 + \gamma_1 (D1 - d_1 + d_2) + \gamma_2 (D2 - d_2) + \varepsilon_t. \quad (2)$$

The econometric model is applied to the real value-added in the primary (agricultural) sector and the real GDP of Anhui Province and China, with the reform period set to 1979–1984, and to the real value-added in the secondary and tertiary sectors and the real GDP of China and Shanghai Municipality, with the reform period set to 1992–1997.

We note that α_1 and α_2 are possible jumps (up or down) in the constant term. It is reasonable to expect a positive jump at the beginning of the reform period. A jump (up or down) at the end of the reform period is also possible. The expectation is that a negative jump is likely at the end of the reform period as the pre-existing economic slack is exhausted. We first test the hypothesis that $\alpha_2 = 0$, that is, there is no jump, up or down, at the beginning of the post-reform period. We next test the hypothesis of no reform effect, that is, there is no jump at the beginning of the reform period, and no change in the slope of the growth path during the reform period. This amounts to the joint hypothesis that $\alpha_1 = \gamma_1 = 0$. The *p*-values of the tests of these two hypotheses are presented in Table 3.3. Columns (1), (3) and (5) report the *p*-values from testing the null hypothesis of no jump between the reform and post-reform periods for China, Anhui and Shanghai, respectively. The *p*-value is less than 5 percent for different measures of output in China, and for real GDP and real value-added of the secondary sector in Shanghai. Therefore, we cannot reject the hypothesis that there is no jump between the reform and post-reform period in China and Shanghai (for real GDP and real value-added of the secondary sector). The p-value is more than 10 percent for real GDP and real value-added of the primary sector in Anhui, and for the tertiary sector in Shanghai, which provides no evidence of growth jump after the end of reform. Columns (2), (4) and (6) report the *p*-values from testing the null hypothesis of no reform effect for China, Anhui and Shanghai, respectively. The p-value is less than 1 percent for different measures of output in both Anhui and Shanghai, which rejects the null hypotheses of no reform effect at 1 percent significance level. We find similar evidence of reform effect in China during the urban non-agricultural economic reform period from 1992 to 1997. No such evidence is found in China for the first agricultural reform period from 1979 to 1984. We believe this is due to the relatively slow diffusion of the reform effects across the entire Chinese economy, especially at the beginning of the economic reform.

The estimated coefficients of the piecewise linear functions are presented in Table 3.4. First of all, we note that the estimates of the α_1's, the jumps at the beginning of the reform period, are consistently positive and are statistically significant except for the real GDP of China in 1979 (column 1) and the tertiary sector of China in 1992 (column 7). The real GDPs of both Anhui and Shanghai jumped around 7 percent at the beginning of their respective reform

Table 3.3. *p*-values of the Tests of Hypotheses

	China		Anhui		Shanghai	
	(1)	(2)	(3)	(4)	(5)	(6)
	$\alpha_2 = 0$	$\alpha_1 = \gamma_1 = 0$	$\alpha_2 = 0$	$\alpha_1 = \gamma_1 = 0$	$\alpha_2 = 0$	$\alpha_1 = \gamma_1 = 0$
Real GDP (1973–1990)	0.01	0.43	0.28	0.00	N.A	N.A
Real GDP (1985–2003)	0.02	0.00	N.A	N.A	0.00	0.00
Real Value-Added, Primary Sector (1973–1990)	0.05	0.17	0.80	0.00	N.A	N.A
Real Value-Added, Secondary Sector (1985–2003)	0.01	0.00	N.A	N.A	0.00	0.00
Real Value-Added, Tertiary Sector (1985–2003)	0.00	0.01	N.A	N.A	0.29	0.00

Table 3.4. Estimated Parameters

	Sample Period: 1973–1990				Sample Period: 1985–2003					
	China		Anhui		China			Shanghai		
	(1)	(2)	(3)	(4)	(5)	(6)	(7)	(8)	(9)	(10)
	Real GDP	VA Primary	Real GDP	VA Primary	Real GDP	VA Secondary	VA Tertiary	Real GDP	VA Secondary	VA Tertiary
α_1	0.02	0.03*	0.07***	0.10***	0.05***	0.09***	0.02	0.07***	0.09***	0.03*
	(0.02)	(0.02)	(0.02)	(0.02)	(0.01)	(0.02)	(0.02)	(0.01)	(0.02)	(0.01)
α_2	0.04**	–0.05**	0.03	0.02	–0.03***	–0.05***	–0.02***	–0.03***	–0.05***	–0.01
	(0.02)	(0.03)	(0.03)	(0.06)	(0.01)	(0.02)	(0.00)	(0.00)	(0.01)	(0.01)
γ_1	0.03	0.05	0.08**	0.07	0.02	0.03	–0.00	0.06***	0.06***	0.06***
	(0.03)	(0.03)	(0.03)	(0.06)	(0.02)	(0.03)	(0.02)	(0.01)	(0.02)	(0.02)
γ_2	0.02	0.02	0.03	0.01	–0.00	–0.01	–0.01	0.04**	0.05**	0.02
	(0.03)	(0.02)	(0.02)	(0.03)	(0.01)	(0.02)	(0.02)	(0.01)	(0.02)	(0.02)
γ_0	0.06**	0.02	0.03	0.00	0.09***	0.10***	0.10***	0.07***	0.06***	0.09***
	(0.02)	(0.02)	(0.02)	(0.02)	(0.01)	(0.02)	(0.02)	(0.01)	(0.02)	(0.01)
Observations	18	18	18	18	19	19	19	19	19	19
R-squared	0.22	0.26	0.50	0.22	0.32	0.37	0.06	0.64	0.53	0.57

Notes: The table reports estimation results from the regression based on Equation (2). The dependent variables are the first differences of the the natural logarithms of real GDP, real value-added in the primary sector (VA Primary), the secondary sector (VA Secondary), and the tertiary sector (VA Tertiary). The real outputs are measured in 2014 yuan. Numbers in parentheses are estimated standard errors calculated using the Huber/White (1980)/sandwich estimator. The symbols ***, **, * denote significance at 1 percent, 5 percent and 10 percent respectively.

periods. Second, the estimates of the α_1's are all greater than the corresponding estimates of the α_2's, the jumps at the end of the reform period, except for the real GDP of China. In particular, the estimates of the α_2's for the post-reform period of 1998–2003 are all negative and statistically significant (except for the value-added of tertiary sector in Shanghai), which suggests the presence of a negative jump at the end of the reform period. Such a finding lends support to the interpretation that the high rates of growth during the reform period were one-off in nature, reflecting the elimination of the pre-existing economic slacks. Third, the estimates of the γ_1's, the increases in the rates of growth during the reform periods, are all positive, except for the tertiary sector of China (column 7). Moreover, estimates of the γ_1's are all greater than the estimates of the γ_2's, the increases in the rates of growth during the post-reform periods. These results are actually quite robust with extending the pre-reform period back to 1952 and the post-reform period forward to 2014, the results of which are reported in the Appendix, Table A3.2.

7. The Estimation of the Pre-Reform Surplus Potential Outputs by the Econometric Method—Anhui Province and Shanghai Municipality

Using the estimated parameters in Table 3.4 above, we proceed to estimate the surplus potential outputs that might have existed at the beginning of the reform periods. At the very end of the pre-reform period, the natural logarithm of real output (Y_{t0-}) is given by:

$$\ln Y_{t0-} = \alpha_0 + \gamma_0 t_0. \tag{3}$$

If there were no prior economic slack, then the change in natural logarithm of real output at the end of the reform period (compared to the end of the pre-reform period would have been given by:

$$\ln Y_{t1-} - \ln Y_{t0-} = \gamma_0 (t_1 - t_0). \tag{4}$$

If there were slack, then the change in natural logarithm of real output would be given by:

$$\ln Y_{t1-} - \ln Y_{t0-} = \alpha_1 + (\gamma_0 + \gamma_1)(t_1 - t_0). \tag{5}$$

The natural logarithm of the surplus potential output may therefore be estimated as the difference between Equation (5) and Equation (4):

$$\alpha_1 + \gamma_1(t_1 - t_0) = \alpha_1 + 6\gamma_1. \tag{6}$$

The surplus potential output is then given by the exponential of Equation (6):

$$\text{Exp}\,(\alpha_1 + 6\gamma_1). \tag{7}$$

Equation (7) is the formula used to estimate the pre-reform surplus potential output based on econometric method. Table 3.5 summarised the estimated surplus potential output compared to the pre-reform period based on visual and econometric method. The estimated surplus potential outputs, whether derived by the direct comparison method (columns 1, 3, and 5) or the econometric method (columns 2, 4, and 6), are broadly similar for China, Anhui and Shanghai. For example, for China as a whole, the pre-reform surplus potential real GDP calculated based on Equation (7) is 23.74 percent (see column 2), which is very close to the value obtained by the visual method discussed in part 4 (see column 1). Similar evidence is found for other measures of outputs and in Anhui and Shanghai. Based on the experiences of Anhui and Shanghai, an estimate of a pre-reform surplus potential output in a range between 49.03 percent to 77.36 percent may be supported.

An alternative approach would be to extrapolate the growth path of real output during the reform period for a further six years beyond the end of the reform period, which would be given by:

$$\ln Y_{t1+6} - \ln Y_{t1-} = 6(\gamma_0 + \gamma_1); \tag{8}$$

and compare it with the estimated growth path during the post-reform period based on actual data, which would be given by:

$$\ln Y_{t1+6} - \ln Y_{t1-} = \alpha_2 + 6(\gamma_0 + \gamma_2). \tag{9}$$

The estimate of the difference in real output, or the (foregone) surplus potential output, is given by:

$$\text{Exp}\,(-\alpha_2 + 6(\gamma_1 - \gamma_2)). \tag{10}$$

Table 3.5. Estimated Surplus Potential Outputs Compared to the Pre-Reform Period (Percent)

	China		Anhui		Shanghai	
	(1) Visual Method	(2) Econometric Method	(3) Visual Method	(4) Econometric Method	(5) Visual Method	(6) Econometric Method
Real GDP (1973–1990)	21.14%	23.74%	64.65%	77.36%	N.A	N.A
Real GDP (1985–2003)	18.91%	20.44%	N.A	N.A	50.92%	57.62%
Real Value-Added, Primary Sector (1973–1990)	32.63%	38.13%	57.52%	68.54%	N.A	N.A
Real Value-Added, Secondary Sector (1985–2003)	33.01%	34.72%	N.A	N.A	53.35%	59.36%
Real Value-Added, Tertiary Sector (1985–2003)	0.33%	1.01%	N.A	N.A	43.77%	49.03%

Table 3.5A. Estimated Surplus Potential Outputs Compared to the Post-Reform Period (Percent)

	China		Anhui		Shanghai	
	Visual Method	Econometric Method	Visual Method	Econometric Method	Visual Method	Econometric Method
Real GDP (1973–1990)	2.23%	5.65%	25.53%	32.84%	N.A	N.A
Real GDP (1985–2003)	21.95%	20.08%	N.A	N.A	20.34%	20.80%
Real Value-Added, Primary Sector (1973–1990)	23.02%	28.02%	35.46%	37.03%	N.A	N.A
Real Value-Added, Secondary Sector (1985–2003)	45.23%	39.79%	N.A	N.A	18.71%	14.68%
Real Value-Added, Tertiary Sector (1985–2003)	8.70%	7.14%	N.A	N.A	22.45%	29.95%

We calculate the surplus potential output compared to the post-reform period based on Equation (10). The results are presented in Table 3.5A. When economic performance during post-reform period is treated as the benchmark, the estimated surplus potential outputs based on visual and econometric methods are broadly similar. These estimates are however somewhat smaller than those presented in Table 3.5, when the benchmark for comparison is the economic performance during the pre-reform period. In particular, the pre-reform surplus potential real GDP for Anhui is 32.84 percent when compared with the post-reform period (column 4 in Table 3.5A), which is about half of the estimates when compared with the pre-reform period (column 4 in Table 3.5). We believe the estimates in Table 3.5 to be more reliable and representative, as the economic performance of the post-reform periods are influenced by many other factors and in particular by the growth in inputs.

8. Concluding Remarks

One of our estimates of the magnitude of the surplus potential output of China on the eve of its economic reform in 1978 is 52.16 percent of Chinese GDP (16.05 percent from the primary sector [see part 4] and 36.11 percent from the secondary and tertiary sectors combined [see part 5][11]). A similar conclusion of a surplus potential output of approximately 50 percent may also be reached on the basis of the results for Anhui and Shanghai in Table 3.5. This may seem like a large number, but it really is not.

The actual average annual growth rate of Chinese real GDP between 1978 and 2014 is 9.72 percent. On the assumption that the Chinese real GDP in 1978 was 50 percent higher than it actually was, the implied average annual rate of growth between 1978 and 2014 would have been 8.49 percent if there were no

11 It is calculated by multiplying the surplus potential output in each sector with their corresponding share in GDP.

economic slack before the reform.[12] Thus, the reduction of the economic slack existed before 1978 accounts for approximately 1.23 percentage points of the economic growth over the past 36 years, or approximately 12.5 percent of the post-1978 economic growth. The remaining economic growth of 8.49 percent per annum can be attributed to the growth of tangible capital and labour, technical progress or growth of total factor productivity, and economies of scale. Of course, most of the reduction and elimination of the economic slack would have occurred during the first decade after the initiation of economic reform (with the exception of Shanghai). But an average annual rate of growth of 8.49 percent over 36 years is still a most impressive economic achievement.

Another way of looking at the importance of this pre-existing economic slack is to imagine an economy growing at a rate under its potential by 1.23 percent per annum; then, over 36 years, the cumulative surplus potential output amounts to 56 percent. In other words, Chinese real GDP would have been less than half of what it is if there had been no economic slack in the economy prior to 1978. The existence of a surplus potential output of 50 percent implies a prior economic slack of one-third or 33.3 percent.

Since most of the economic slack would have been reduced/eliminated at a relatively early stage of the economic reform, it is likely that approximately 2 percentage points of Chinese economic growth per annum during the first two decades of Chinese economic reform can be attributed to the reduction in the economic slack alone.

---

12 The Chinese real GDP in 1978 and 2014 in 2014 prices are: 1978: RMB 2,259.34 billion yuan (US$369.23 billion); 2014: RMB 63,613.90 billion yuan (US$10,396.13 billion). Actual real GDP in 1978 was 2,259.34 billion yuan. If there were no slack, that is, if the utilisation of inputs in 1978 were efficient, it should have been 1.5 times that, or 3,389.01 billion yuan. Actual GDP in 2014 was 63,613.90 billion yuan, implying an actual average annual (geometric) compound real rate of growth of 9.72%. But if there were no slack in 1978, GDP would have grown from 3,389.01 billion yuan to 63,613.90 billion yuan, implying an average annual real rate of growth of only 8.49%. The difference between the actual average growth rate of 9.72% and the counterfactual average growth rate of 8.49% is 1.23% per year, which can be ascribed to the effect of the reduction of the economic slack that existed in 1978.

However, it is also important to note that the movement from the interior of the set of production possibilities to its frontier is a one-off phenomenon and cannot be replicated. It is therefore almost certain that by the late 1990s, the initial economic slack resulting from the inherent inefficiency of a centrally-planned economy would have been exhausted.

The same methodology used here may be applicable to the identification and estimation of the pre-reform potential surplus outputs of other reformed or reforming previously centrally-planned economies. It can also be extended to the estimation of the potential surplus output of every individual Chinese province, autonomous region and municipality before their respective reforms. We would need to identify the precise beginnings of the agricultural and non-agricultural reforms in each province, region and municipality. But if we can obtain estimates of the surplus potential output of each province, region and municipality in China, we shall be able to derive an even more reliable estimate of the size of the surplus potential output in 1978 for the Chinese economy as a whole.

Finally, an intriguing question has to do with the economies of the former Soviet Union and the formerly socialist countries of Eastern Europe. Clearly, there must have been significant slacks in these economies prior to the break-up of the Soviet Union in 1991. However, these slacks did not seem to have enabled any growth spurt in these economies during their transition from centrally-planned to market economies. The pre-existing surplus potential outputs did not seem to have been ever realised. Why? This is a question worthy of additional research.

Appendix

Table A3.1. Estimation Results Using Different Reform Periods

	China		Anhui	
	Real GDP	VA Primary	Real GDP	VA Primary
	Panel A: Sample Period: 1962–2000			
α_1	0.006	0.020*	0.039**	0.052**
	(0.019)	(0.011)	(0.016)	(0.021)
α_2	0.035**	–0.055**	0.034	0.015
	(0.015)	(0.023)	(0.028)	(0.052)
γ_1	0.023	0.033	0.053	0.020
	(0.024)	(0.026)	(0.032)	(0.056)
γ_2	0.024	–0.002	0.034	–0.015
	(0.021)	(0.012)	(0.021)	(0.034)
γ_0	0.068***	0.040***	0.056***	0.052**
	(0.019)	(0.011)	(0.016)	(0.021)
Observations	39	39	39	39
R-squared	0.062	0.110	0.142	0.028
Hypothesis Test: $\alpha_1 = \gamma_1 = 0$				
F statistics	0.798	1.611	2.901	3.072
p value	0.458	0.215	0.069	0.059
	Panel B: Sample Period: 1952–2014			
α_1	0.014	0.039***	0.060**	0.083***
	(0.021)	(0.014)	(0.023)	(0.026)
α_2	0.035**	–0.055**	0.034	0.015
	(0.014)	(0.022)	(0.027)	(0.051)
γ_1	0.032	0.052*	0.075**	0.052
	(0.025)	(0.026)	(0.036)	(0.057)
γ_2	0.033	0.019	0.066***	0.015
	(0.022)	(0.014)	(0.024)	(0.029)
γ_0	0.059***	0.020	0.034	0.020
	(0.021)	(0.014)	(0.023)	(0.026)
Observations	62	62	62	62
R-squared	0.058	0.093	0.154	0.031
Hypothesis Test: $\alpha_1 = \gamma_1 = 0$				
F statistics	1.014	4.057	3.474	5.379
p value	0.369	0.023	0.038	0.007

Notes: The table reports estimation results from the regression based on Equation (2), assuming the reform period to be five years (top two panels) and four years (bottom two panels). The dependent variables are the first differences of the the natural logarithms of real GDP, real

China			Shanghai		
Real GDP	VA Secondary	VA Tertiary	Real GDP	VA Secondary	VA Tertiary
Panel A: Sample Period: 1962–2008					
0.058***	0.095***	0.043***	0.069***	0.087***	0.047***
(0.012)	(0.020)	(0.012)	(0.017)	(0.020)	(0.014)
−0.033***	−0.053***	−0.021***	−0.033***	−0.047***	−0.010
(0.008)	(0.015)	(0.004)	(0.004)	(0.010)	(0.008)
0.032**	0.042*	0.026**	0.061***	0.054**	0.081***
(0.014)	(0.025)	(0.013)	(0.017)	(0.022)	(0.016)
0.020	0.007	0.031**	0.042**	0.037*	0.053***
(0.013)	(0.021)	(0.013)	(0.018)	(0.022)	(0.016)
0.076***	0.097***	0.075***	0.070***	0.072***	0.066***
(0.012)	(0.020)	(0.012)	(0.017)	(0.020)	(0.014)
47	47	47	47	47	47
0.072	0.045	0.079	0.105	0.067	0.214
17.748	17.948	14.506	10.301	14.831	15.070
0.000	0.000	0.000	0.000	0.000	0.000
Panel B: Sample Period: 1952–2014					
0.065***	0.091***	0.049***	0.058**	0.067**	0.051***
(0.015)	(0.026)	(0.014)	(0.023)	(0.030)	(0.014)
−0.033***	−0.053***	−0.021***	−0.033***	−0.047***	−0.010
(0.008)	(0.015)	(0.004)	(0.004)	(0.009)	(0.008)
0.039**	0.037	0.031**	0.051**	0.035	0.085***
(0.016)	(0.030)	(0.015)	(0.023)	(0.031)	(0.016)
0.023	−0.003	0.028*	0.019	0.000	0.046***
(0.015)	(0.027)	(0.015)	(0.024)	(0.032)	(0.016)
0.069***	0.102***	0.070***	0.080***	0.092***	0.062***
(0.015)	(0.026)	(0.014)	(0.023)	(0.030)	(0.014)
62	62	62	62	62	62
0.044	0.015	0.041	0.021	0.008	0.149
15.816	12.830	13.496	5.357	8.382	16.188
0.000	0.000	0.000	0.007	0.001	0.000

value-added in the primary sector (VA Primary), the secondary sector (VA Secondary), and the tertiary sector (VA Tertiary). Numbers in parentheses are estimated standard errors calculated using the Huber/White (1980) sandwich estimator. The symbols ***, **, * denote significance at the 1 percent, 5 percent and 10 percent respectively.

Table A3.2. Estimation Results Using Different Pre-Reform and Post-Reform Periods

	China		Anhui	
	Real GDP	VA Primary	Real GDP	VA Primary
	Panel A: Sample Period: 1974–1988 (Five-Year Reform Period)			
α_1	0.047**	0.019	0.108***	0.073***
	(0.015)	(0.025)	(0.029)	(0.019)
α_2	0.061*	0.063***	0.099	0.093**
	(0.028)	(0.012)	(0.069)	(0.030)
γ_1	0.048	0.024	0.057	0.069*
	(0.032)	(0.027)	(0.075)	(0.036)
γ_2	0.018	0.053*	0.030	0.066*
	(0.016)	(0.026)	(0.045)	(0.031)
γ_0	0.012	0.055*	–0.005	0.021
	(0.015)	(0.025)	(0.029)	(0.019)
Observations	15	15	15	15
R-squared	0.506	0.443	0.262	0.557
Hypothesis Test: $\alpha_1 = \gamma_1 = 0$				
F statistics	4.988	0.388	7.363	7.384
p value	0.031	0.688	0.011	0.011
	Panel B: Sample period: 1975–1986 (Four-Year Reform Period)			
α_1	0.054**	0.011	0.116**	0.068**
	(0.017)	(0.031)	(0.037)	(0.025)
α_2	0.026	0.032**	–0.056	–0.008
	(0.039)	(0.012)	(0.096)	(0.043)
γ_1	0.049	0.008	0.078	0.067
	(0.043)	(0.033)	(0.103)	(0.050)
γ_2	0.052	0.055	0.117**	0.118**
	(0.039)	(0.036)	(0.044)	(0.034)
γ_0	0.005	0.063*	–0.012	0.026
	(0.017)	(0.031)	(0.037)	(0.025)
Observations	12	12	12	12
R-squared	0.329	0.354	0.316	0.571
Hypothesis Test: $\alpha_1 = \gamma_1 = 0$				
F statistics	5.043	0.084	5.032	3.901
p value	0.044	0.920	0.044	0.073

Notes: The table reports estimation results from the regression based on Equation (2) with a six-year reform period, and various pre-reform and post-reform periods. The dependent variables are the first differences of the the natural logarithms of real GDP, real

China			Shanghai		
Real GDP	VA Secondary	VA Tertiary	Real GDP	VA Secondary	VA Tertiary
Panel A: Sample Period: 1987–2001 (Fiver-Year Reform Period)					
0.100***	0.032	0.056***	0.104***	0.032**	0.078***
(0.026)	(0.023)	(0.017)	(0.015)	(0.012)	(0.014)
–0.049**	–0.003	–0.025**	–0.032**	0.021*	–0.013***
(0.017)	(0.006)	(0.009)	(0.011)	(0.010)	(0.004)
0.056	0.015	0.036*	0.078***	0.062***	0.073***
(0.031)	(0.024)	(0.019)	(0.019)	(0.016)	(0.014)
–0.009	0.003	–0.000	0.039**	0.039**	0.040**
(0.026)	(0.023)	(0.017)	(0.017)	(0.016)	(0.014)
0.092***	0.087***	0.077***	0.054***	0.081***	0.060***
(0.026)	(0.023)	(0.017)	(0.015)	(0.012)	(0.014)
15	15	15	15	15	15
0.541	0.116	0.485	0.756	0.705	0.811
10.713	4.446	8.134	26.205	8.165	16.937
0.003	0.042	0.008	0.000	0.008	0.001
Panel B: Sample period: 1988–1999 (Four-Year Reform Period)					
0.109**	0.044	0.065**	0.109***	0.033*	0.081***
(0.032)	(0.024)	(0.020)	(0.019)	(0.016)	(0.018)
–0.046**	–0.018**	–0.025**	–0.036***	0.031***	–0.013***
(0.016)	(0.006)	(0.008)	(0.007)	(0.008)	(0.002)
0.077*	0.032	0.050**	0.092***	0.055**	0.079***
(0.036)	(0.025)	(0.021)	(0.021)	(0.018)	(0.018)
0.005	0.015	0.010	0.039	0.062**	0.049**
(0.033)	(0.025)	(0.020)	(0.021)	(0.020)	(0.019)
0.083**	0.074**	0.069***	0.050**	0.080***	0.057**
(0.032)	(0.024)	(0.020)	(0.019)	(0.016)	(0.018)
12	12	12	12	12	12
0.614	0.317	0.621	0.824	0.753	0.803
7.591	3.901	7.039	18.568	6.228	10.596
0.018	0.073	0.021	0.002	0.028	0.008

value added in the primary sector (VA Primary), the secondary sector (VA Secondary), and the tertiary sector (VA Tertiary). Numbers in parentheses are estimated standard errors calculated using the Huber/White (1980)/sandwich estimator. The symbols ***, **, * denote significance at the 1 percent, 5 percent and 10 percent respectively.

References

Aigner, Dennis J., C. A. Knox Lovell, and Peter Schmidt. "Formulation and Estimation of Stochastic Frontier Production Function Models." *Journal of Econometrics* 6 (1977), pp. 21–37.

Bettelheim, Charles. "Economic Reform in China." *The Journal of Development Studies* 24, no. 4 (1988), pp. 15–49.

Hsueh, Tien-Tung, and Pak-Wai Liu. "Collectivization of Chinese Agricultural Production, 1952–1957: A Land-Saving Organizational Change." *Journal of Comparative Economics* 4 (1980), pp. 378–398.

Lin, Justin Y. "The Household Responsibility System in China's Agricultural Reform: A Theoretical and Empirical Study." *Economic Development and Cultural Change* 36, no. 3 (April 1988), pp. S199–S224.

———. "Rural Reforms and Agricultural Growth in China." *The American Economic Review* 82 (1992), pp. 34–51.

Naughton, Barry. *Growing Out of the Plan: Chinese Economic Reform, 1978–1993.* Cambridge: Cambridge University Press, 1995.

———. *The Chinese Economy: Transitions and Growth.* Cambridge: The MIT Press, 2007.

Rawski, Thomas G. "Chinese Industrial Reform: Accomplishments, Prospects, and Implications." *The American Economic Review* 84 (1994), pp. 271–275.

———. "Implications of China's Reform Experience." *The China Quarterly* 144 (1995), pp. 1150–1173.

———. "Reforming China's Economy: What Have We Learned?" *The China Journal* 41 (1999), pp. 139–56.

White, Halbert L., Jr. "A Heteroskedasticity-Consistent Covariance Matrix Estimator and a Direct Test for Heteroskedasticity." *Econometrica* 48 (1980), pp. 817–838.

Chapter 4.

The Sources of Chinese Economic Growth since 1978*

1. Introduction

It is my great honour and pleasure to participate in this conference in honour of my old friend Prof. Joseph Stiglitz. Joe has made path-breaking contributions in almost all areas of economics: macroeconomics, microeconomics, monetary theory, public finance, international economics, economic development, economic growth, the economics of information, the economics of risk and uncertainty, you name it. His breadth and versatility are unique and unparalleled. He is interested in the most minute, some would almost say arcane, details of theory, but at the same time he has the most insightful and practical policy advice to offer. He is also most original—he always has something new and interesting to say on an old and supposedly tired subject.

I first met Joe when he joined the Department of Economics at Stanford in the early 1970s. Joe, Eytan Sheshinsky and I collabourated on an article together. We have since kept in touch—every time I meet Joe, I always

---

* This chapter was originally published as "The Sources of Chinese Economic Growth since 1978," in *Toward a Just Society: Joseph Stiglitz and Twenty-First Century Economics*, edited by Martin Guzman. This is a paper presented at the conference, "A Just Society: Honoring Joseph Stiglitz," held at the Columbia Business School, Columbia University, New York, 16–17 October 2015. The author wishes to thank Michael Boskin, Ayesha Macpherson Lau, Joseph Stiglitz, Yanyan Xiong, Huanhuan Zheng, and Wentong Zheng for their invaluable advice, comments and suggestions, but retains sole responsibility for any remaining errors.

learn something new. He became very interested in economic development in general and in China in particular, and involved me in a number of his projects on economic growth in East Asia and on Chinese economic reform. Joe was instrumental in China being granted the most-favoured-nation status in the mid-1990s, which was the forerunner to Chinese accession to the World Trade Organization (WTO) in 2001. Throughout the years, Joe has provided most helpful advice to the highest levels of the Chinese government. That is one reason I decided to contribute a paper on the Chinese economy to this conference in his honour.

China has made tremendous progress in its economic development since it began its economic reform and opened to the world in 1978. It is currently the fastest growing economy in the world—averaging 9.72% per annum over the past 36 years. It is historically unprecedented for an economy to grow at such a high rate over such a long period of time. However, the Chinese economy has begun to slow down, to an annual rate of growth of around 7%, in a process of transition to a "New Normal." Why has China been able to grow at such a high rate and for such a long period of time? What are the sources of Chinese economic growth since 1978? These are the questions explored in this paper.

It is interesting to compare the growth of Chinese and U.S. real GDP in both aggregate and per capita terms (Charts 4.1 and 4.2). The red and blue lines represent the levels of real GDP and real GDP per capita of China and the U.S. respectively. The red and blue columns represent the annual rates of growth of China and the U.S. respectively. Chart 4.1 shows that between 1978 and 2014, Chinese real GDP grew from US$369 billion to US$10.4 trillion (in 2014 prices), to become the second largest economy in the world, after the U.S. Chinese economic growth began to take off after China began its economic reform in 1978, and accelerated in 2001, when China acceded to the WTO. The rate of growth of Chinese real GDP has been higher than that of the U.S. in every single year since 1978, sometimes significantly so. By comparison, the U.S. GDP of approximately US$17.4 trillion was approximately 1.7 times Chinese GDP in 2014.

However, despite the rapid growth of the Chinese economy in the aggregate, in terms of its real GDP per capita, China is still very much a developing economy. Chart 4.2 shows that in 1978, the Chinese real GDP per capita was only US$383 (in 2014 prices), approximately 1.25% of the then U.S. real GDP per capita of US$30,472. By 2014, the Chinese real GDP per capita had

Chart 4.1. Chinese and U.S. Real GDPs and Their Rates of Growth since 1949 (2014 US$)

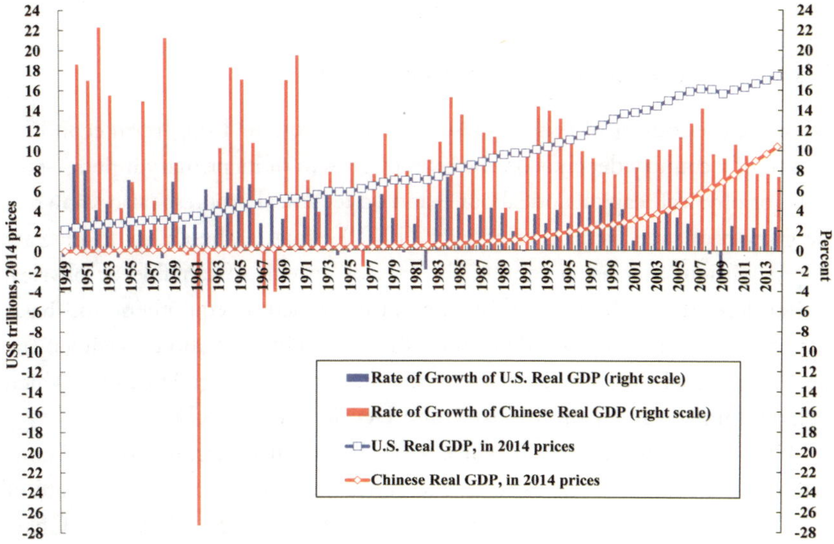

Chart 4.2. Chinese and U.S. Real GDPs per Capita and Their Rates of Growth since 1949 (2014 US$)

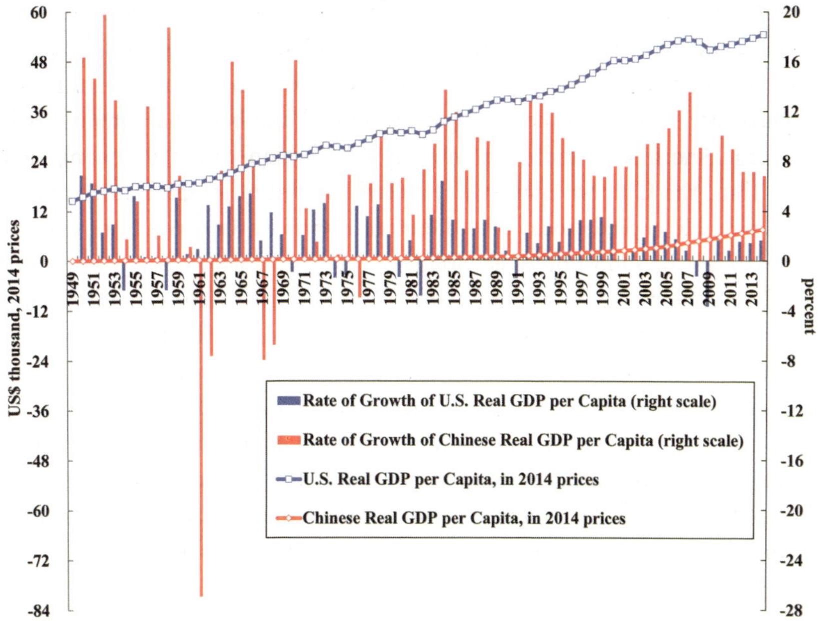

grown to US$7,604, still less than one-seventh of the U.S. GDP per capita of US$54,575.

2. The Chinese Economic Fundamentals

What are the sources of this Chinese economic growth? Long-term economic growth of a country depends on the rates of growth of its primary inputs—tangible (or physical) capital and labour—and on technical progress (also known as the growth of total factor productivity [TFP])—that is, the ability to increase output without increasing inputs. The rate of growth of tangible or physical capital depends on the rates of investment on structure, equipment and basic infrastructure, which in turn depend on the availability of national savings. The rate of technical progress depends on investment in intangible capital, which includes human capital and Research and Development (R&D) capital.

Chinese economic growth since 1978 has been underpinned by a consistently high domestic investment rate, enabled by a national saving rate of over 35% except for a brief start-up period in the early 1950s (see Chart 4.3). The Chinese national saving rate rose to around 40% in the early 1990s and at times approached or even exceeded 50% in more recent years. The high Chinese saving rate means that the Chinese economy can finance all of its domestic investment needs from its own domestic savings alone, without having to depend on the more fickle foreign capital inflows (including foreign direct investment, foreign portfolio investment, foreign aid, or foreign loans). In particular, it does not need to borrow abroad and bear the potential risks of a large, short-term and often interruptible foreign-currency-denominated debt. Thus, the Chinese economy is always assured of a high rate of growth of its tangible capital stock. It is therefore also more immune from external disturbances than most other economies.

China, like Japan, Taiwan, and South Korea in their respective early stages of economic development, has an unlimited supply of surplus labour—there is therefore no shortage of, and no upward pressure on, the real wage rate of unskilled, entry-level labour over an extended period of time. The distribution of Chinese GDP by production-originating sectors in 2014 was approximately: primary (agriculture), 9.2%; secondary (manufacturing, mining and construction), 42.6%; and tertiary (services), 48.2% (see Chart 4.4). (Note that mining is normally included in the primary sector in most other economies.)

Chart 4.3. Chinese National Saving and Gross Domestic Investment as a Percent of GDP

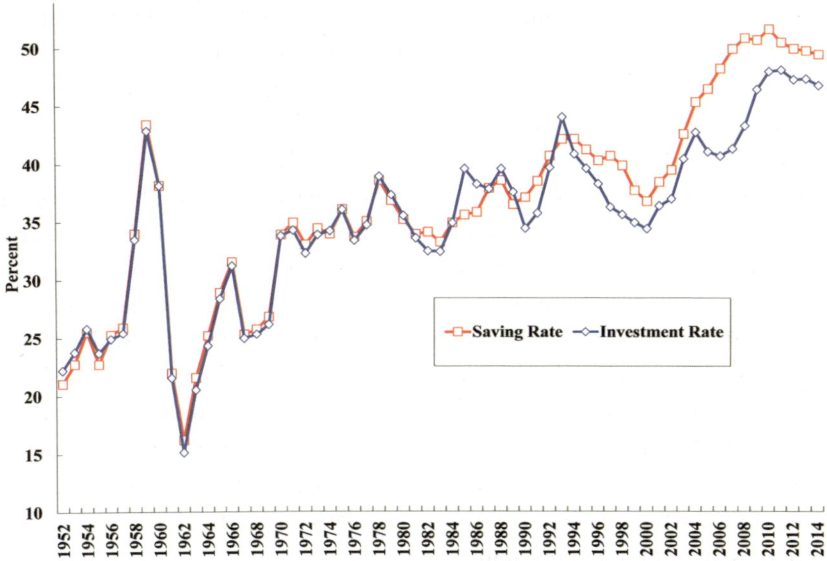

Chart 4.4. The Distribution of Chinese GDP by Sector since 1952

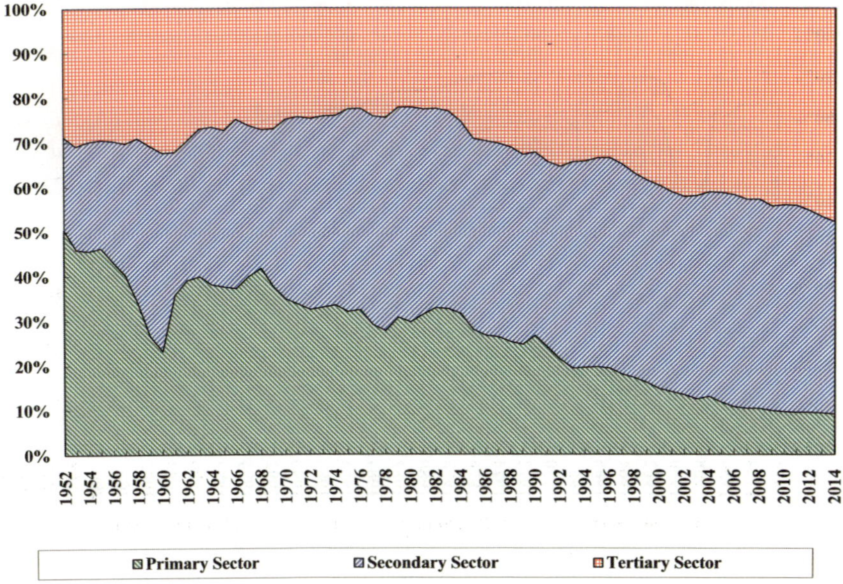

The distribution of employment by sector in 2014 was: primary, 29.5%; secondary, 29.9%; and tertiary, 40.6% (see Chart 4.5). The agricultural sector employed 29.5% of the Chinese labour force but produced only 9.2% of the Chinese GDP in 2014. Thus, labour can be productively transferred to the other two sectors where labour productivities and wage rates are higher as long as complementary capital and demand are available.

The huge size of the domestic market, with 1.37 billion consumers and their pent-up demands for housing and transportation and other consumer goods and services (e.g., education, health care, and more recently, elderly care), enables the realisation of significant economies of scale in production, based entirely on the domestic demand in China. The huge domestic market also greatly enhances the productivity of intangible capital (e.g. R&D capital and goodwill, including brand building) by allowing the fixed costs of the R&D for a new product or process or advertising and promotion in brand building to be more easily amortised and recovered. In addition, the huge domestic market also enables significant "learning-by-doing," so that the unit costs of production decline with rising cumulative outputs. This is yet another form of manifestation of economies of scale.

Chart 4.5. The Distribution of Chinese Employment by Sector since 1952

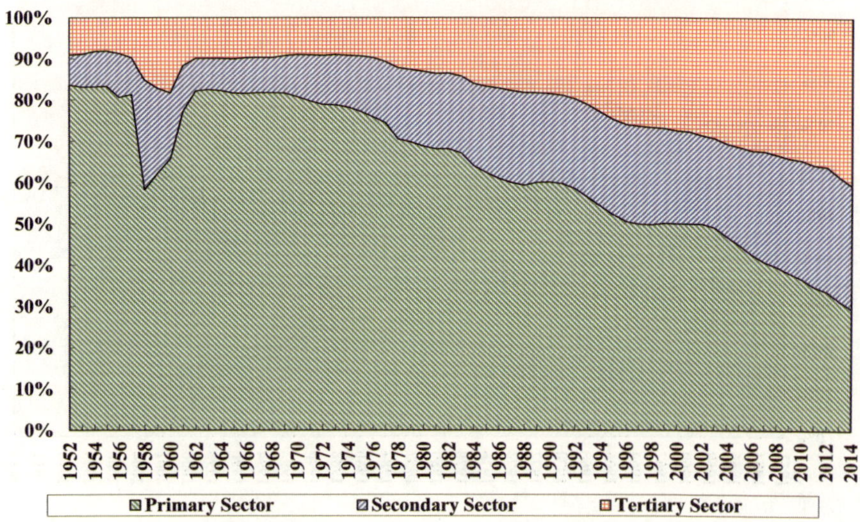

Another important implication of the huge size of the domestic economy is the relatively low external dependence. Thus, while the quarterly rates of growth of Chinese exports and imports fluctuate like any other economy (see Chart 4.6 for the rates of growth of exports, and Chart 4.7 for the rates of growth of imports, respectively, for China, represented by the red lines, and selected Asian economies). The quarterly rate of growth of the Chinese real GDP, represented by the red line in Chart 4.8, can be clearly seen to be relatively much more stable than those of other economies. It never turned negative whereas many of the other Asian economies would experience absolute declines in their real GDPs. This is of course also due in part to the fact that China does not have to depend on the inflow of foreign savings for its investment.

Chart 4.6. Quarterly Rates of Growth of Exports of Goods: China and Selected Asian Economies

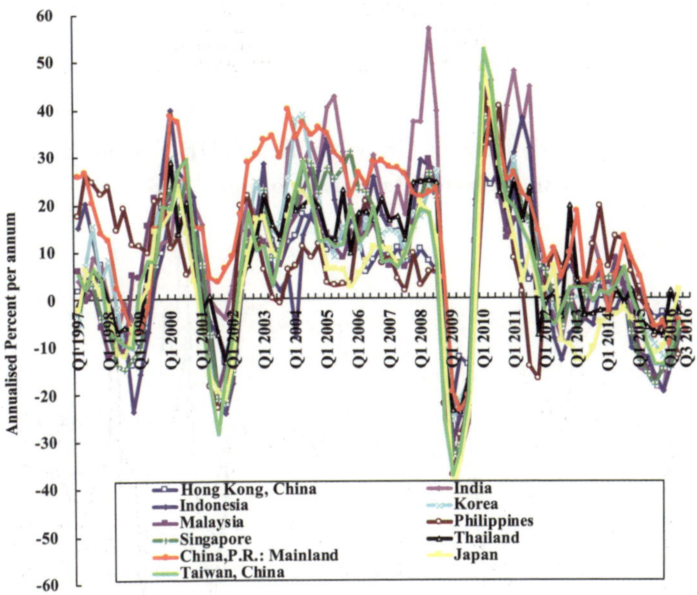

Chart 4.7. Quarterly Rates of Growth of Imports of Goods: China and Selected Asian Economies

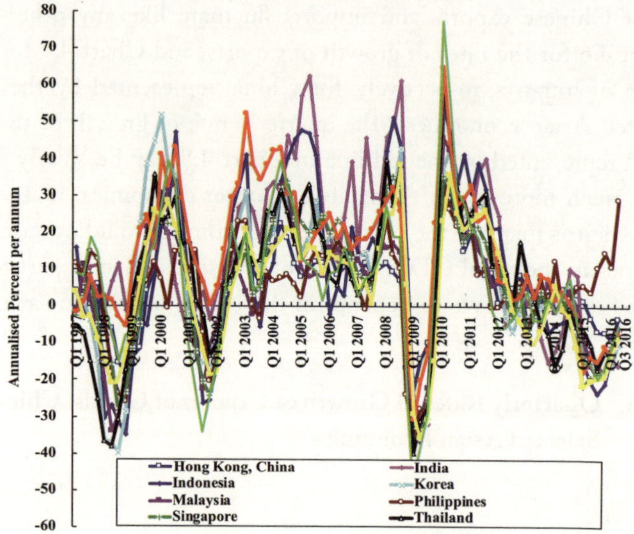

Chart 4.8. Quarterly Rates of Growth of Real GDP, Year-on-Year: China and Selected Asian Economies

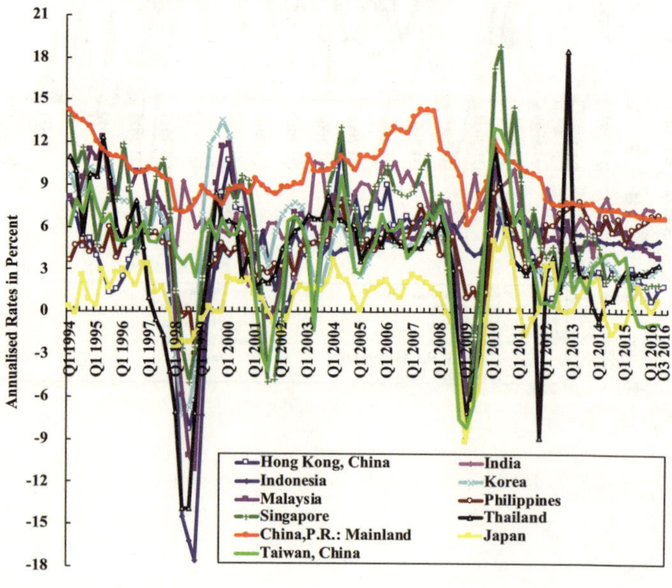

Finally, China also had the additional "advantage" of having been a centrally-planned economy for more than a quarter of a century before it undertook its economic reform and opened its economy to the world in 1978. A centrally-planned economy is well known to have inherent economic inefficiency, or equivalently, economic slack, which implies that China had surplus potential output prior to its economic reform, which could be realised under appropriate economic reform policies. This prior economic inefficiency or surplus potential output thus also constituted an additional source of Chinese economic growth since 1978.

3. The Monopsonistic Labour Market in China

Chart 4.3 above shows that China has an extraordinarily high national saving rate. This rate would be considered high even by the standards of East Asian economies.[1] Why is this the case, especially considering that the Chinese GDP per capita is still significantly below those of other East Asian economies? One explanation is that the Chinese government was and still is the largest single employer of non-agricultural workers in China and therefore has both the ability and the incentive to keep wage rates low. Before the economic reform of 1978, the Chinese government was the sole employer for all workers in the urban areas of China and set their wage rates. As the sole employer, the Chinese government could exercise its monopsonistic power and pursued a low (and egalitarian) wage policy, resulting in a low share of labour in GDP of less than 50% over the past several decades compared to a share of between 60 and 70% in the developed economies of the West.

The low-wage policy reflected three considerations: First, it was designed to increase national savings through higher profits of the enterprises, most of which are state-owned, so that the needed domestic investments could be readily financed. This objective of the low-wage policy is similar to the "price scissors" policy of maintaining a large gap between industrial and agricultural prices, practiced in the former Soviet Union in the early 20th century and in China in the 1950s. Second, a low wage policy helped to maximise employment, and

---

1 Among East Asian economies, only Singapore has a comparably high national saving rate.

in particular, the absorption of surplus labour from the agricultural sector into the industrial and service sectors. Third, it was compatible with the ideological preference of the Chinese Communist Party for thrift and egalitarianism in the distribution of income. Note that if the government is the sole employer, the wage and individual income tax policies can be de facto integrated—no separate individual income tax is necessary. In this context, a low-wage (and low or no tax) policy has a similar economic effect as a high-wage and high-tax policy but is politically easier to adopt, implement and sustain.

Even as recently as 2010, the share of Chinese public-sector employment, including the employees of central and local governments and their affiliated units, state-owned enterprises (SOEs), and publicly financed educational and health care institutions, was still over 50% of all urban employment (see Chart 4.9). The government could therefore exercise a decisive influence on not only the wage rates of the public-sector employees, but also the level of wage rates in the economy as a whole. Today, a government job is still the preferred choice for many Chinese workers because of the job and income security and the significant fringe benefits that it offers. Many married couples adopt the strategy of having one spouse working in the public sector and the other working in the private sector.

Chart 4.9. The Share of Public Sector Employment in Total Non-Agricultural Employment in China

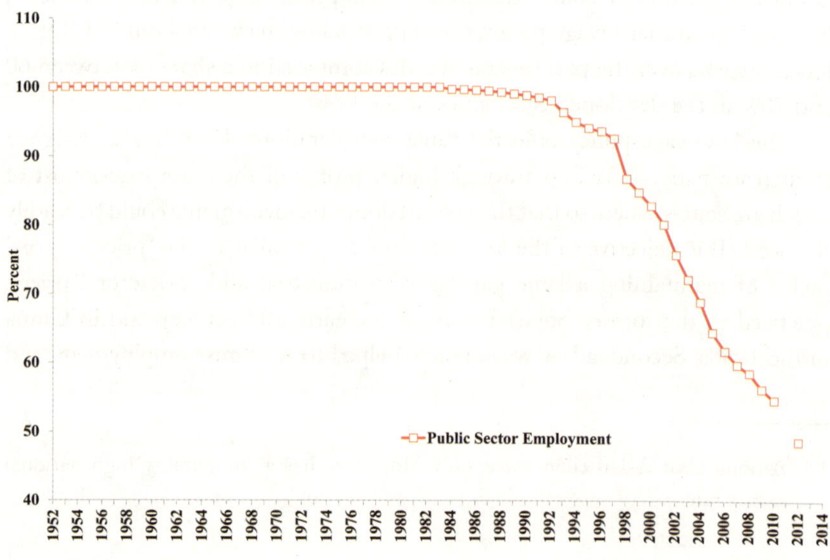

This low-wage policy has had two major effects: First, it has kept the labour share (and the household share) of GDP low; and secondly, it has created large profits for state-owned (and other) enterprises. The disposable household income share of GDP in China may be estimated at around 50% in 2014, much lower than the corresponding share in a developed economy, where it would typically be above 60%, and also lower than those of other developing economies with a comparable real GDP per capita. The Chinese share of labour is likely to be lower than the share of household disposable income, as the latter includes, in addition to wages and salaries, also net proprietor's income, net asset income and net transfers (which amounted to 43% of the total household disposable income), but excludes direct taxes and other mandatory charges such as social security contributions. As Chinese households have less disposable income to spend relative to Chinese GDP, China also has a lower household consumption to GDP ratio than others. This ratio, as well as the total final consumption (which is the sum of government consumption and household consumption) to GDP ratio, have been declining over time (see Chart 4.10). As of 2014, the total final consumption ratio was just over 50% and the household consumption ratio was approximately 38%, both significantly lower than most other economies with a comparable real GDP per capita. The Chinese household saving rate may be estimated at around 30% from survey data, comparable to those of ethnically Chinese households in Hong Kong and Taiwan. What all of this means is that the high Chinese saving rate is not due to a particularly high household saving rate but instead to high enterprise profits and reinvestment rates. Thus, Chinese household consumption cannot be expected to be a major source of growth of Chinese aggregate demand in the short or medium term, even though it has been growing in real terms at one and a half times the rate of growth of GDP, as long as household disposable income remains relatively low.

The high Chinese national saving rate of between 40% and 50% should therefore be attributed to the high propensity to save on the part of Chinese enterprises out of their profits, especially since they distribute very little in terms of cash dividends to their shareholders, which include the Chinese government (the majority shareholder of the SOEs) and the households. Household income and government revenue can both be increased if the SOEs are required to distribute a greater proportion of their profits as cash dividends to their shareholders, which may in turn lead to higher household and government consumption.

Chart 4.10. Total Chinese Final and Household Consumption as a Percent of China's GDP

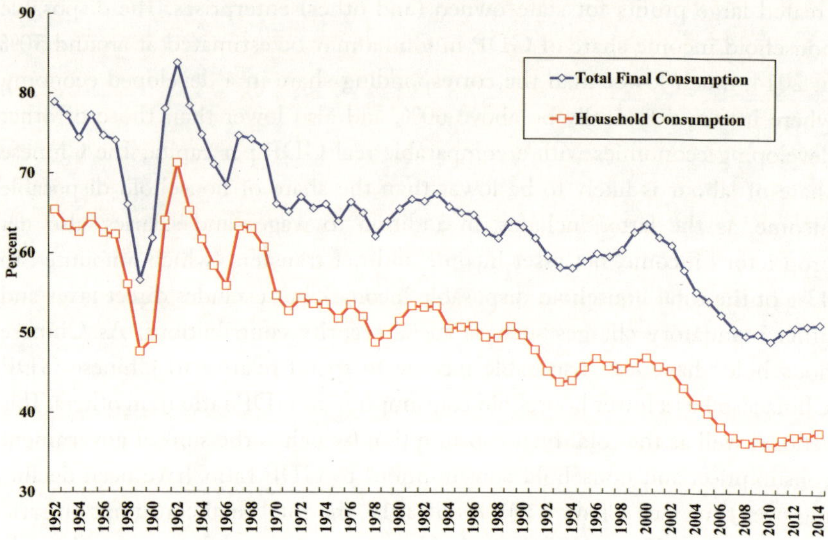

4. The Sources of Chinese Economic Growth

The rates of growth of Chinese real output, real tangible capital stock and labour (employment) over the past 36 years are presented in Table 4.1. It is clear that the tangible capital stock has grown much more rapidly than labour over the past 36 years.

Table 4.1. The Rates of Growth of Real Output, Tangible Capital Stock, and Labour

Rate of Growth of Real Output (1978–2014)	9.72%
Rates of Growth of Inputs (1978–2013)	
Tangible or Physical Capital	10.83%
Labour	1.88%

Chinese economic growth since 1978 could have come from several sources: (1) The realisation of the surplus potential output from the initial economic slack that resulted from mandatory central planning; (2) The growth of tangible capital and labour inputs (and the growth of the intangible inputs such as human capital and R&D capital[2]); (3) Technical progress (growth of TFP); and (4) The effect of economies of scale.

Lau and Zheng (2017), by comparing the economic performance of Anhui Province and Shanghai Municipality before and after the introduction of economic reform, found that the pre-existing slack in the Chinese economy before it undertook its economic reform and opened to the world in 1978 could be estimated to be 50% of the actual output in 1978. Based on the assumption that the Chinese real GDP in 1978 was 50% higher than it actually was, the implied average annual rate of growth of the Chinese economy between 1978 and 2014 would have been 8.49% instead of 9.72%. Thus, the reduction of the economic slack that existed before 1978 would account for approximately 1.23 percentage points of the economic growth over the past 36 years, or approximately 12.5% of the post-1978 economic growth. The remaining economic growth of 8.49% per annum can be attributed to the growth of the primary inputs, technical progress or growth of TFP, and economies of scale.

The degree of economies of scale cannot be estimated in a straightforward way. In fact, it is under-identified with time-series aggregate data from only a single country—the effects of economies of scale are confounded with the effects of technical progress. However, a meta-production function approach, first introduced by Lau and Yotopoulos (1989) and extended by Boskin and Lau (1992), based on the transcendental logarithmic production function introduced by Christensen, Jorgenson and Lau (1973), can be used to identify and separate the effects of economies of scale and technical progress under fairly general and testable assumptions. Boskin, Guo and Lau (2015) have recently estimated the degrees of returns to scale for the Group-of-Seven (G-7) Countries using the meta-production function approach. They found the degree of local returns to scale of the U.S. to be 1.20 in 1960 and 1.11 in 2007. The average degree of returns to scale for the U.S. over this period would be 1.155, almost the same as the 1.15 estimated by Denison (1974)[3]

---

2 In this paper, the contributions of the growth of human capital and R&D capital to Chinese economic growth are not estimated separately but subsumed in the contribution of technical progress or growth of TFP.

3 See Denison (1974), p. 75.

but somewhat larger than the assumption of 1.10 used by Denison (1961)[4]. Assuming that this estimate of the returns to scale also applies to the Chinese economy on average, it would mean that over a 36-year period, from 1978 to 2014, the average rate of growth would have been 8.36% if there were only constant returns to scale, instead of the actual 9.72%. This difference would have accounted for 36.1% of the Chinese real GDP in 2014. It also means that out of the rate of growth of 9.72%, economies of scale account for 1.36 percentage points, or 13.99% of the measured economic growth over this period.

As pointed out in part 3 above, the actual share of labour in GDP in China is low relative to other economies. It may be estimated to be around 50%[5]. However, it is believed that the production elasticity of labour is probably higher than the labour share, somewhere between 0.55 and 0.6, as labour has been systematically underpaid due to the low-wage policy maintained by the Chinese government. Since there exist increasing returns to scale, capital, as the residual claimant, cannot in general be paid its marginal product; but because labour is actually underpaid, capital can be either underpaid or overpaid relative to its marginal product. With returns to scale assumed to be 1.155, and the production elasticity of labour estimated as between 0.55 and 0.6, the production elasticity of capital may be estimated as (1.155–0.55) or (1.155–0.6), or between 0.555 and 0.605, as the capital and labour elasticities should sum to the degree of returns to scale. Thus, the relative weights of capital and labour may be estimated as 0.48 versus 0.52, or vice versa. Since they are almost equal, we shall use 0.5 as the relative weights of capital and labour for the purpose of the growth-accounting exercise.

---

4 See Denison (1961), p. 175.

5 One possible estimate of the share of household disposable income in Chinese GDP is 43% in 2014, based on officially published data. However, the labour share can differ from the above because of net proprietor's income, net household asset income and direct taxes and transfers. The data on the household consumption share of GDP, which are probably less prone to errors, indicate a share of around 38% in 2014 (see Chart 4.10). However, a household consumption share of 38% does not seem to be consistent with a household income share of 43%, which would imply an exceptionally low household saving rate out of disposable income. A more reasonable estimate of the household disposable income share or labour share in GDP in 2014 is probably around 50% or even a little higher.

The results of the growth-accounting exercise are presented in Table 4.2. We note that the elimination of the pre-existing economic slack and economies of scale account for respectively 1.23 and 1.36 percentage points, or a total of 2.59 percentage points, of the Chinese economic growth of 9.72% between 1978 and 2014. If we subtract 2.59% from 9.72%, we obtain 7.13%. This average annual rate of growth has been achieved by quite a few other economies over a couple of decades in the past. We also note that the growth of tangible capital accounts for more than half of the growth in real output, whereas the growth of labour and technical progress each account for less than 10% of the economic growth. If we take out the contributions of the elimination of the prior economic slack and economies of scale, the growth of tangible capital accounts for the bulk of the remaining economic growth, 5.42% out of 7.13%, or 76%. This is similar to the findings of Kim and Lau (1994) on the sources of economic growth of the East Asian Newly Industrialised Economies (NIEs). If a more conventional growth accounting exercise is done under the assumption of constant returns to scale, the effects of the elimination of the pre-existing economic slack and economies of scale would have been captured as part of technical progress or the growth of TFP. If that is done, technical progress or growth of TFP would have accounted for 34.61% of Chinese economic growth since 1978.

Table 4.2. The Sources of Chinese Economic Growth

Monopsonistic Labour Market Case		
Sources of Chinese Economic Growth, 1978–2014	**Percentage Points**	**Percent**
Elimination of Pre-Existing Economic Slack	1.23	12.65
Growth of Tangible Capital	5.42	55.71
Growth of Labour	0.94	9.67
Technical Progress	0.78	7.97
Economies of Scale	1.36	13.99
Total	9.72	100.00

5. The Role of Expectations

Expectations of the future are important determinants of the behaviour of enterprises and households, which in turn determines whether and how much they invest and consume respectively. For a large economy such as China, the domestic investment and consumption together determine the level of aggregate demand and ultimately whether the economy grows or stagnates, not net exports. There are many ways in which expectations about the future may be formed. Expectations may be based on past experience, such as "tomorrow will be the same as today," but they may also not be based solely on past experience; for example, they may be based on the views of so-called opinion leaders. Expectations may also be affected by the occurrence of some important event, such as the breakout of a war, the election of a new government, the rise of an epidemic, or some specific government pronouncement or action, which can credibly cause changes in the public expectations of the future. Moreover, expectations can often, but not always, and certainly not consistently, be self-fulfilling, if they are sufficiently strongly held by a sufficiently large number of people.

One well-known manifestation of self-fulfilling expectations is in the asset markets. If investors expect the price of an asset, for example, real estate or stock, to go up, and act accordingly by buying real estate or stock, the price of real estate or stock will indeed be driven up by the concerted buying, because the increase in demand in real estate or stock is not and cannot be immediately met by an increase in supply. Thus, the expectations of the investors can be self-fulfilling. There are many such examples in which asset price bubbles are created around the world.

The run-up in the price of Chinese residential real estate between October 2012 and October 2013 was an example of self-fulfilling expectations. The more recent Chinese stock price run-up between November 2014 and July 2015 may also be considered as another such example. But self-fulfilling expectations do not always have to be bullish. If all investors believe that the price of residential real estate is likely to be stable, and act accordingly—that is, they do not try to out-bid one another since they know they can always buy a similar property later—then the price of residential real estate will indeed be quite stable. This was what occurred in Singapore, where the government was believed by the public to adjust the rate of release of new lots for residential construction upwards and downwards in the same direction as the price of residential real estate, thus dampening the price changes.

However, the prices of assets cannot continue to go up forever. All asset price bubbles are sustained by new investors with new buying power coming into the market. At some point, the available potential new buying power will be exhausted with the price levels significantly exceeding what can reasonably be supported by the underlying economic fundamentals in steady state. When that happens, the asset prices will begin to fall and fall precipitously. So ultimately, the rosy expectations may fail to be fulfilled. And this will lead to a collective downward revision of the expectations.

In the context of China, an important way in which self-fulfilling expectations can be created and changed is through the signalling by the Chinese government. A government with credibility can use its pronouncement of policy changes and actual actions as instruments for changing the macroeconomic expectations of the public about the future of the economy. In fact, Keynesian countercyclical fiscal policies often work because they have the ability to change expectations. In a country such as China, expectations are often formed not only from directly experienced market outcomes but also from the pronouncements and actions of its senior government leaders. The government, because of the many potential instruments at its disposal, is widely believed to have the power to turn around the economy, and is thus a credible authority that can play the coordinating role. The following examples drawn from the Chinese experience show how the Chinese government was able to change negative expectations credibly through its pronouncements and actions.

In 1989, in the aftermath of the June 4 incident, the Chinese economy became quite depressed, in part because of foreign sanctions, but mostly because of generally negative expectations about the future on the parts of enterprises and households. As a result, enterprises did not invest and households did not consume. 1990 and 1991 were similarly slow years, despite an abundance of liquidity. The rates of growth of real GDP in 1989 and 1990 were the lowest since economic reform began in 1978 (see Chart 4.11) and the rates of growth of fixed asset investment in 1989 and 1990 were negative—the only years with a negative rate of growth of fixed asset investment since 1978 (see Chart 4.12), which showed how negative expectations were.

Then in early 1992, Deng Xiaoping, the paramount Chinese leader at the time, undertook his famous southern inspection tour. Everywhere he went, he urged the people to seize the moment and grasp opportunities. His words changed expectations in the entire country almost overnight. Enterprises began investing and households began consuming once again. As a result, the rest of 1992, as well as 1993 and 1994, were boom years with double-digit rates of economic growth (and relatively high rates of inflation) and high rates of growth of fixed asset investment (see Charts 4.11, 4.12 and 4.13).

In mid-1997, the East Asian Currency Crisis broke out, first in Thailand, and then in South Korea, until it engulfed almost all of the East Asian economics, with the exception of Japan. Almost all of the East Asian currencies, with the exception of the Hong Kong dollar, which was (and still is) pegged to the U.S. dollar, devalued significantly. The quarterly rates of growth of exports and imports of all East Asian economies fell precipitously (see Charts 4.6 and 4.7). Chinese Premier Zhu Rongji decided to hold the renminbi/US$ exchange rate steady amidst the chaos of the East Asian currency crisis, and thus managed to maintain the confidence of the domestic investors and consumers about China's economic future, keeping the Chinese economy growing (see Chart 4.14). In so doing, he also helped to stabilise the exchange rates of the other East Asian currencies and facilitated the recovery of the other East Asian economics. Had China also devalued at that time, it would have led to another cycle of competitive devaluation among the East Asian economies, with unimaginably negative economic and social consequences.

In 2000, the whole world was suffering from the burst of the internet bubble in the U.S., and China was no exception (the negative expectations then were reflected in the exceptionally low rates of growth of fixed asset investment). Then in December 2001, China became a member of the WTO. The Chinese accession to the WTO also changed expectations in a dramatic way, which also reflected the expected expiration of the Multi-Fibre Agreement that governed global trade in textiles in 2005. It had a significant effect on the rates of growth of both real GDP (see Chart 4.13) and fixed asset investment (see Chart 4.14). In 2005, the renminbi began to be allowed to appreciate relative to the U.S. dollar, which adversely affected the growth of exports, and the rate of growth of fixed asset investment fell back to more normal levels.

In 2008, in the immediate aftermath of the collapse of Lehman Brothers in the U.S., all credit dried up in the U.S. as well as the other developed economies. Overnight, importers in the U.S. and other developed economies could no longer place their import orders with China and other trading

Chart 4.11. Annual Rates of Growth of Chinese Real GDP

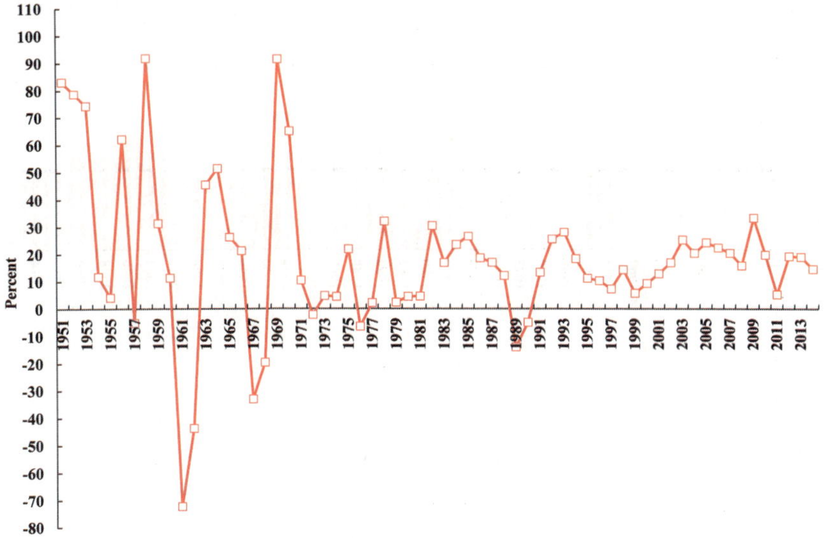

Chart 4.12. Annual Rate of Growth of Chinese Fixed Assets Investment (Percent per annum)

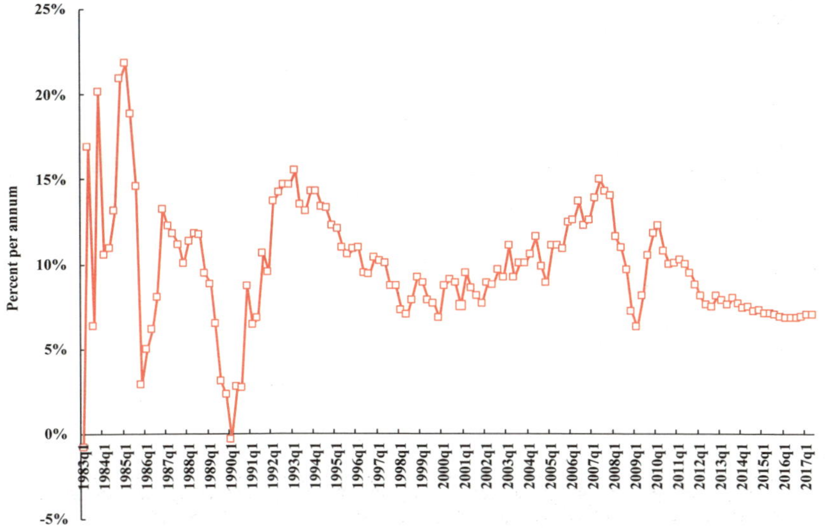

Chart 4.13. Quarterly Rates of Growth of Chinese Real GDP, Year-on-Year

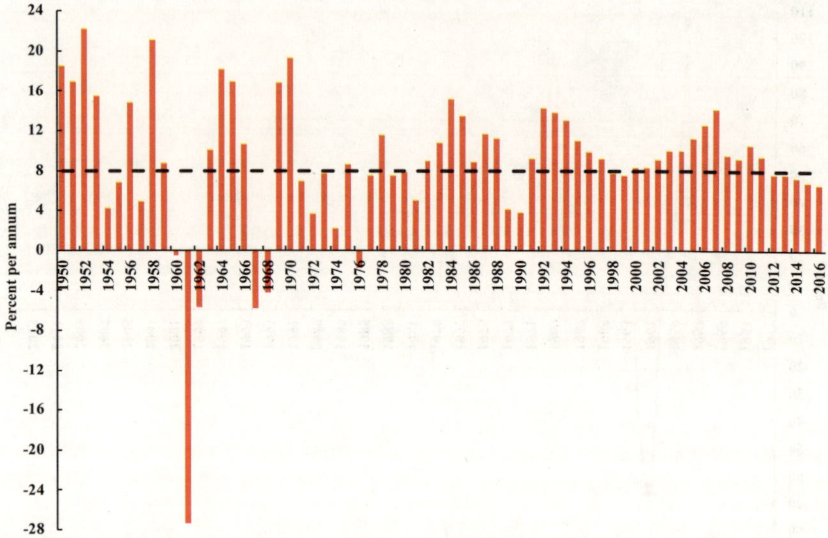

Chart 4.14. Monthly Rates of Growth of Chinese Fixed Assets Investment, Year-on-Year

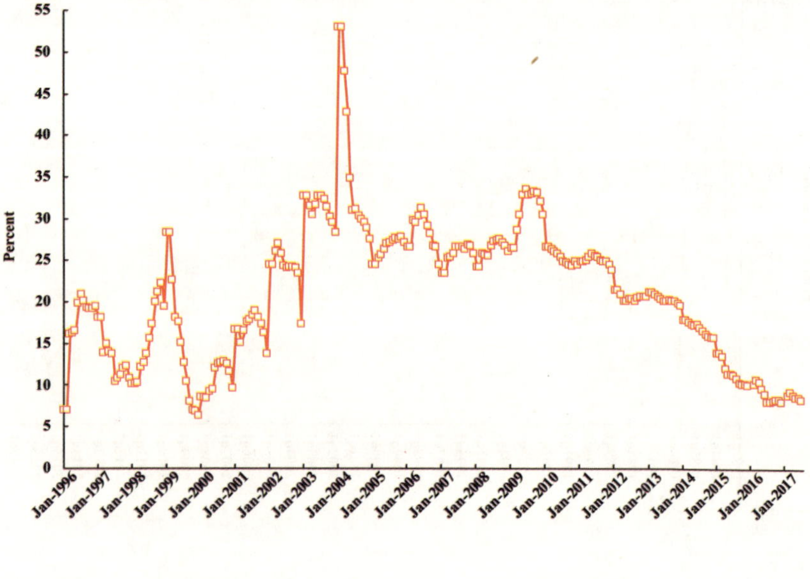

partner countries because their banks were not in a position to issue acceptable letters of credit. As a result, export orders received by Chinese enterprises declined by approximately 50% (see Charts 4.6 and 4.7). There was real panic in the air. Fortunately, barely six weeks later, Chinese Premier Wen Jiabao unveiled the four trillion yuan (approximately 6% of the then Chinese GDP) economic stimulus programme, which once again managed to maintain the confidence of Chinese enterprises and households in their economy. Actually, the economic stimulus programme did not really take effect until at least a year later, but the announcement of the programme itself alone managed to restore positive expectations among the Chinese public (see Charts 4.14 and 4.15).

Chart 4.15. Monthly Rates of Growth of Real Value-Added of Chinese Industry, Year-on-Year

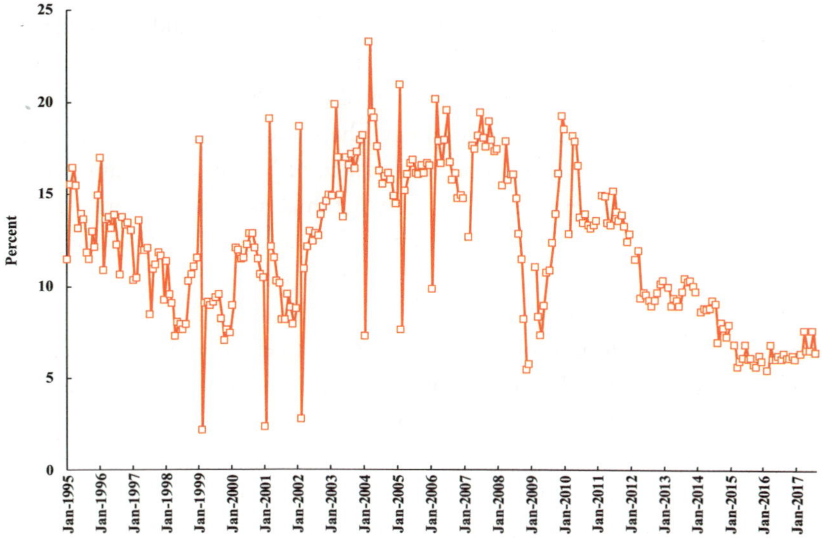

In all of these cases, the Chinese government was able to turn around the very negative domestic expectations about the future of the Chinese economy into positive ones, and in so doing greatly reduced the uncertainty pertaining to the future and increased general business as well as consumer confidence. These changes, in turn, fueled investment booms that resulted in the subsequent economic growth.

However, with the bursting of the Chinese stock market bubble in July 2015 and the slight but unexpected devaluation of the renminbi of approximately 4% in August 2015, the confidence of the Chinese enterprises and households has been somewhat shaken. At the same time, reacting to these developments in China, the world markets have also panicked and doomsayers have been coming out in droves, predicting the imminent collapse of the Chinese economy. Perhaps this is the time for the Chinese government to take more decisive and visible actions to increase domestic aggregate demand so as to reduce uncertainty, shore up confidence and change expectations of the Chinese public about the future.

6. Concluding Remarks

Chinese economic growth during the past 36 years can be attributed to the growth of tangible inputs—tangible capital and labour, and in particular, tangible capital—rather than the growth in intangible capital or technical progress, just as the past economic growth of other East Asian economies at a similar stage of economic development. The successful Chinese experience strongly reaffirms the fundamental importance of having and maintaining a high investment rate, enabled by a high national savings rate, and surplus labour. A low-wage policy was instrumental in a high national saving rate and a rapid rate of absorption of surplus labour. In addition, the size of the Chinese domestic economy is a favourable factor allowing the ready realisation of economies of scale and reducing vulnerability to external disturbances. The prior economic slack, inherent in any previously centrally-planned economy, has also been a significant source of economic growth upon Chinese transition to a market economy.

Expectations will continue to play an important role in the Chinese economy. A strong Chinese central government with the unique power to mobilise domestic aggregate demand can credibly change expectations from negative to positive at critical junctures to keep the economy growing.

References

Arrow, Kenneth J. "The Economic Implications of Learning by Doing." *The Review of Economic Studies* 29, no. 3 (1962), pp. 155–173.

Boskin, Michael J., Haiqiu Guo and Lawrence J. Lau. "Technical Progress and G-7 Economic Growth." Working Paper, The Institute of Global Economics and Finance, The Chinese University of Hong Kong, Hong Kong, 2015.

Boskin, Michael J. and Lawrence J. Lau. "International and Intertemporal Comparison of Productive Efficiency: An Application of the Meta-Production Function Approach to the Group-of-Five (G-5) Countries." *Economic Studies Quarterly* 43, no. 4 (1992), pp. 298–312.

Christensen, Laurits R., Dale W. Jorgenson and Lawrence J. Lau. "Transcendental Logarithmic Production Frontiers." *The Review of Economics and Statistics* 55, no. 1 (1973), pp. 28–45.

Denison, Edward F. *The Sources of Economic Growth in the United States and the Alternatives Before Us.* Committee for Economic Development, New York, 1961.

———. *Accounting for United States Economic Growth, 1929–1969*. Washington, D.C.: Brookings Institution, 1974.

Kim, Jong-II and Lawrence J. Lau. "The Sources of Economic Growth of the East Asian Newly Industrialized Countries." *Journal of the Japanese and International Economies* 8, no. 3, (1994), pp. 235–271.

Lau, Lawrence J. and Pan A. Yotopoulos. "The Meta-Production Function Approach to Technological Change in World Agriculture." *Journal of Development Economics* 31, no. 2 (October 1989), pp. 241–269.

Lau, Lawrence J. and Huanhuan Zheng. "How Much Slack Was There in the Chinese Economy Prior to Its Economic Reform of 1978?" *China Economic Review* 45 (2017), pp. 124–142.

Chapter 5.

What Makes China Grow?*

1. Professor Lawrence R. Klein and China

It is my honour and privilege to participate in this Conference in Memory of Prof. Lawrence R. Klein. Professor Klein was an intellectual giant. He was a pioneering econometrician, having constructed the first econometric model of the United States, the Klein Model I, and followed it with a succession of increasingly larger and more sophisticated econometric models, including the Wharton Econometric Model. He not only founded Project LINK, a global project linking national econometric models together for joint prediction and simulation, as one country's exports must be the imports of other countries, with Robert Aaron Gordon, Bert G. Hickman, and Rudolf R. Rhomberg, but also acted as the patriarch of the extended Project LINK family. To me personally, he was a selfless mentor, an exemplary role model, and a most respected and dear friend.

In the late 1960s, through the introduction of Professor Bert Hickman, my colleague at Stanford, Professor Klein invited me to construct the first

---

* This chapter was originally published in *Global Economic Modeling: A Volume in Honor of Lawrence R. Klein*, edited by Peter Pauly. Copyright © 2018 World Scientific Publishing Company. This paper was presented at "Global Economic Modeling: A Conference in Honor of Lawrence Klein," held at the Institute for International Business, Rotman School of Management, University of Toronto, Toronto, Canada, on 11 June 2015. The author is grateful to Ayesha Macpherson Lau for her valuable comments but remains solely responsible for any errors. All opinions expressed herein are the author's own and do not necessarily reflect the views of any of the organisations with which the author is affiliated.

econometric model of China and contribute it as one of the national models in Project LINK. Thus began my long association with Professor Klein and Project LINK. Professor Hickman and I also constructed aggregated and disaggregated trade matrix models that were used in the linkage of the national econometric models. In 1979, Professor Klein invited me to join the first delegation of the American Economic Association to the People's Republic of China, led by him and hosted by the Chinese Academy of Social Sciences. This was the first time I had visited China as an adult. We were received by Vice-Premier Gu Mu. Professor Klein then followed up with organising "The Summer Palace Workshop on Econometrics" in 1980, with 100 participants drawn from all over China. This was the first introduction of econometrics in China. In addition to Professor Klein, there were six faculty members in the workshop: Professors Theodore Anderson, Albert Ando, Gregory Chow, Cheng Hsiao, Vincent Su and me. We were received by Vice-Premier Yao Yilin. Our workshop eventually led to the establishment of the Institute of Quantitative and Technical Economics at the Chinese Academy of Social Sciences. Later, Professor Klein also served as an adviser to the State Planning Commission of the People's Republic of China for one U.S. dollar a year.

In 2010, at the 30th Anniversary Celebration of the Summer Palace Workshop on Econometrics, Professor Klein, who was not able to attend but sent a pre-recorded videotape, laid down the challenge: Can the highly successful Chinese economic growth since its economic reform and opening in 1978 be explained? What are the factors common to all economies that have been able to grow successfully? And what are the factors unique to the Chinese economy due to its own history and circumstances? This study is an attempt to provide a preliminary answer.[1]

2. Introduction

China has made tremendous progress in its economic development since it began its economic reform and opened to the world in 1978. It is currently the fastest growing economy in the world—averaging 9.6% per annum compounded over

1 See also Perkins (2015). For a different perspective, from the point of view of a foreign entrepreneur in China, see Beardson (2013).

the past 37 years. It is historically unprecedented for an economy to grow at such a high rate over such a long period of time. Between 1978 and 2015, Chinese real GDP grew more than thirtyfold, from US$346 billion to US$10.4 trillion (in 2015 prices), to become the second largest economy in the world, after the U.S. (see Chart 5.1, in which the levels and the rates of growth of Chinese real GDP are presented). By comparison, the U.S. real GDP of approximately US$17.9 trillion was a little less than 1.7 times the Chinese real GDP in 2015. However, the Chinese economy has recently begun to slow down, to an average annual rate of growth of around 6.5%, in a process of transition to a "New Normal." In 2016, the Chinese economy grew 6.7% in real terms.

Why has China been able to grow at such a high rate and for such a long period of time? What makes China grow? Will China be able to continue to grow at such a high rate in the future? Of course, the adoption and implementation of the correct economic policies and measures by the Chinese government, led by the Chinese Communist Party, and their uninterrupted continuity since 1978, are important reasons for China's highly successful record of economic growth. However, we shall also examine the Chinese economic fundamentals as well as the Chinese initial conditions in 1978 to

Chart 5.1. Chinese Real GDP (2015 US$) and Its Rate of Growth since 1949

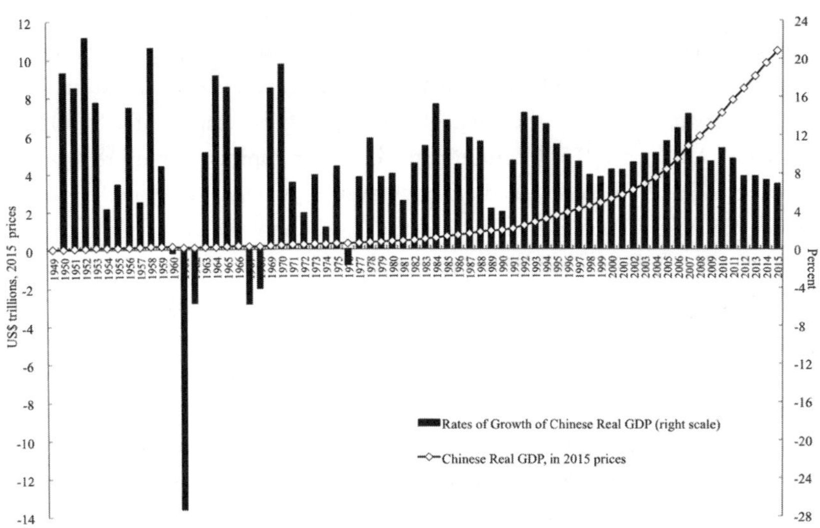

analyse why the adopted and implemented economic reform policies and measures were so effective in China.

During this same period, China also had to face many domestic and international challenges and several financial crises, such as the East Asian currency crisis of 1997–1998, the bursting of the internet bubble in 2000, the global financial crisis of 2007–2009, as well as the European sovereign debt crisis. China was able to survive all of these crises relatively unscathed, even maintaining a healthy rate of real economic growth. The Chinese government leaders have demonstrated their ability to confront these challenges and solve difficult problems. The Chinese economy has recently begun a process of transition to a "New Normal," with a lower average annual rate of growth of between 6.5% and 7%, a cleaner environment, and a greater contribution from innovation than from the growth of tangible inputs.

In Table 5.1, the performance of the Chinese economy before and after its economic reform began in 1978 is compared. It is clear that the Chinese economy has done significantly better in almost every dimension—real GDP, real consumption, exports and imports—under the economic reform, on both an aggregate and a per capita basis. The only economic indicator that has performed worse is the rate of inflation, which rose from 0.6% per annum in the pre-reform period to 5.1% per annum in the post-reform period.

However, despite its rapid economic growth in the aggregate, in terms of the level of its real GDP per capita, China is still very much a developing economy because of its large population. China is the most populous country in the world. In 1978, the Chinese real GDP per capita was US$360 (in 2015 prices), less than 1.2% of the then U.S. real GDP per capita of US$30,886. Between 1978 and 2015, Chinese real GDP per capita grew more than 21 times, to US$7,584, still less than one-seventh of U.S. GDP per capita of US$55,759 (see Chart 5.2, in which the levels and the rates of growth of Chinese real GDP per capita are presented).

While many problems have arisen in the Chinese economy within the past decade—for example, increasing income disparity at both the inter-regional and intra-regional levels, uneven access to basic education and health care, environmental degradation, inadequate infrastructure and corruption—it is fair to say that every Chinese citizen has benefitted from the economic reform and opening to the world since 1978, albeit to varying degrees, and few want to return to the central planning days.

Table 5.1. Key Performance Indicators before and after the Chinese Economic Reform of 1978

	Growth Rates % per Annum	
	Pre-Reform Period (1952–1978)	Post-Reform Period (1978–2015)
Real GDP	6.1	9.6
Real GDP per Capita	4.0	8.5
Real Consumption	5.0	9.2
Real Consumption per Capita	2.9	8.2
Exports	10.0	15.9
Imports	9.1	14.6
Inflation Rate (GDP deflator)	0.6	5.1

Chinese international trade in goods and services has also grown very rapidly since the beginning of economic reform in 1978, and the rate of growth accelerated after Chinese accession to the World Trade Organization (WTO) in 2001. Chinese total international trade grew from US$20.3 billion in 1978 to US$4.67 trillion in 2015, making China the second largest trading nation in the world, just after the U.S. with its total international trade of US$5.21 trillion. (See Chart 5.3, in which the black lines and black columns represent the levels and rates of growth of Chinese international trade respectively, and the open-square lines and grey columns represent the levels and rates of growth of U.S. international trade respectively). While China is the largest exporting nation in terms of goods and services (US$2.56 trillion in 2015), followed by the U.S. (US$2.22 trillion), the U.S. is the largest importing nation in terms of goods and services (US$2.76 trillion), followed by China (US$2.11 trillion). China is also the largest exporting nation in terms of goods alone, followed by the U.S. The U.S. is the largest exporting as well as importing nation in terms of services, followed by the United Kingdom and Germany respectively.

3. China in the Global Economy

The most important development in the global economy during the past 37 years is the reform and opening of the Chinese economy and its participation in the world. As a result, the centre of gravity of the global economy, in terms of both GDP and international trade, has been gradually shifting from North America and Western Europe to East Asia, and within East Asia from Japan to China. In 1970, the United States and Western Europe together accounted for almost 60% of world GDP. By comparison, East Asia[2] accounted for approximately 10% of world GDP. By 2014, the share of the United States and Western Europe in world GDP declined to approximately 40%, whereas the share of East Asia rose to around 25% (see Chart 5.4 and Chart 5.5). The Japanese share of world GDP declined from a peak of almost 18% in the mid-1990s to 5.6% in 2015, while the Chinese share of world GDP rose from 3.1% in 1970 and less than 4% in 2000 to over 14.8% in 2015 (see Chart 5.6).

Chart 5.2. Chinese Real GDP per Capita and Its Rate of Growth (2015 Prices) since 1949

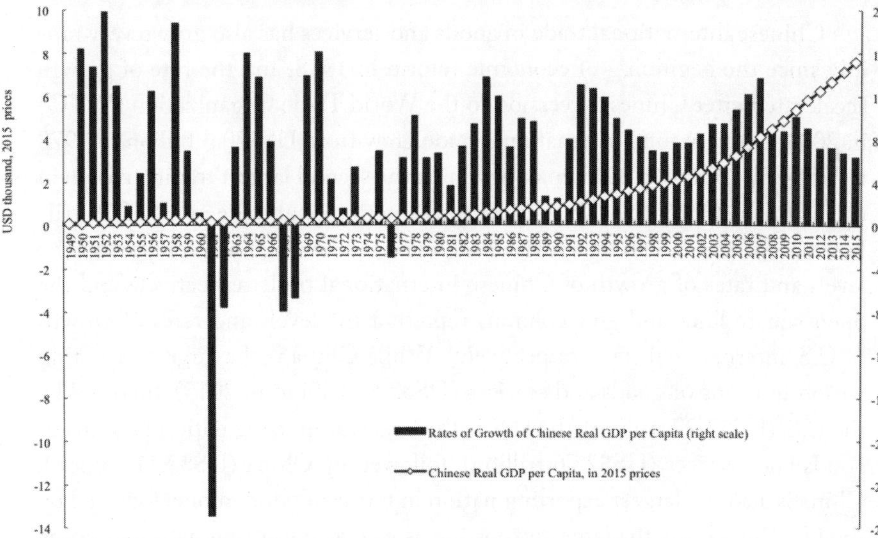

---

2 Defined as the 10 ASEAN countries (Brunei, Cambodia, Indonesia, Laos, Malaysia, Myanmar, the Philippines, Singapore, Thailand, and Vietnam) plus China (including Hong Kong, Macau, and Taiwan), Japan and the Republic of Korea. Hong Kong, the Republic of Korea, Singapore, and Taiwan are also known collectively as the East Asian Newly Industrialised Economies (NIEs).

Chart 5.3. Chinese and U.S. International Trade (US$) and Their Rates of Growth since 1970

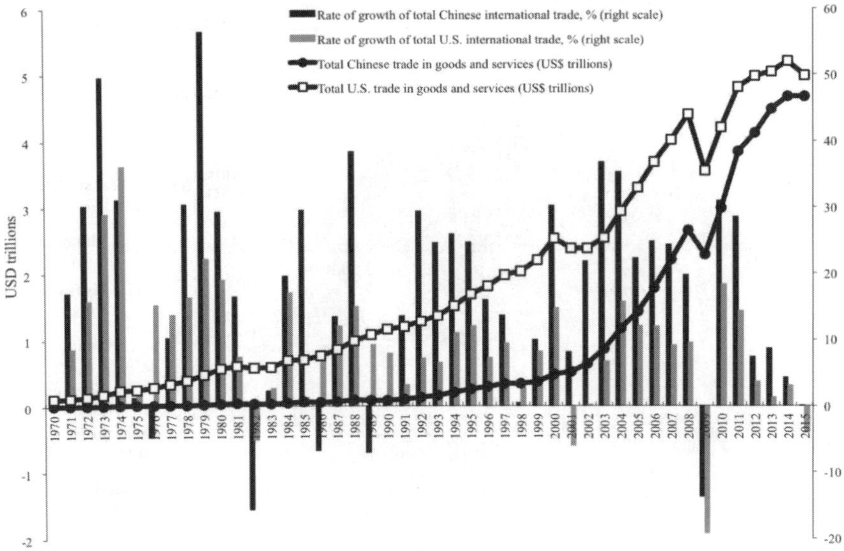

Chart 5.4. The Distribution of World GDP in 1970 (1970 US$)

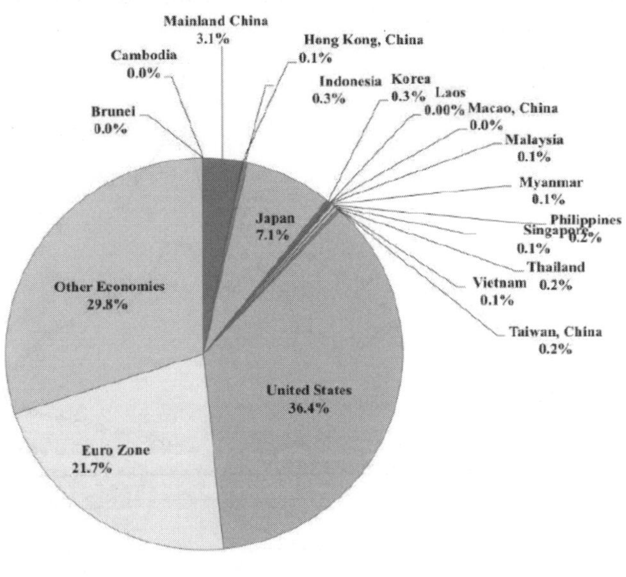

Chart 5.5. The Distribution of World GDP in 2014 (2014 US$)

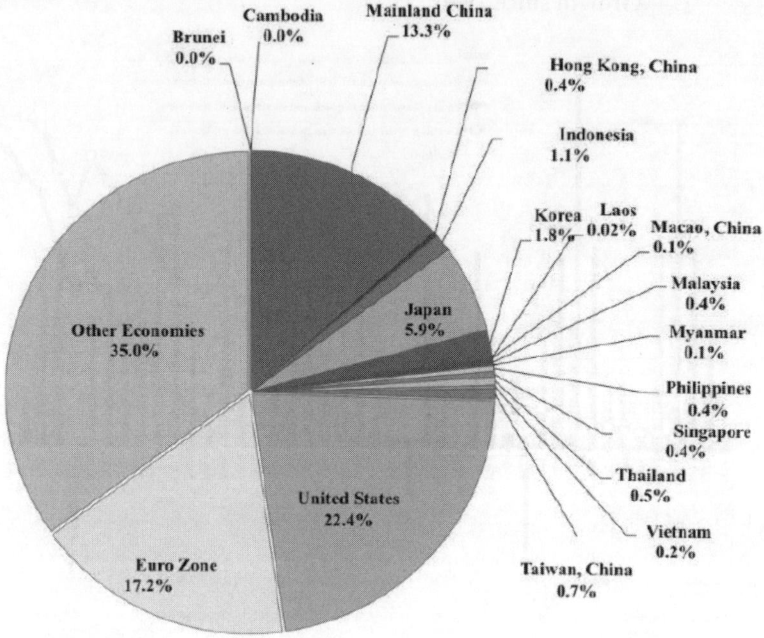

Chart 5.6. The Shares of East Asia, China, Japan, and South Korea in World GDP, 1960–2015

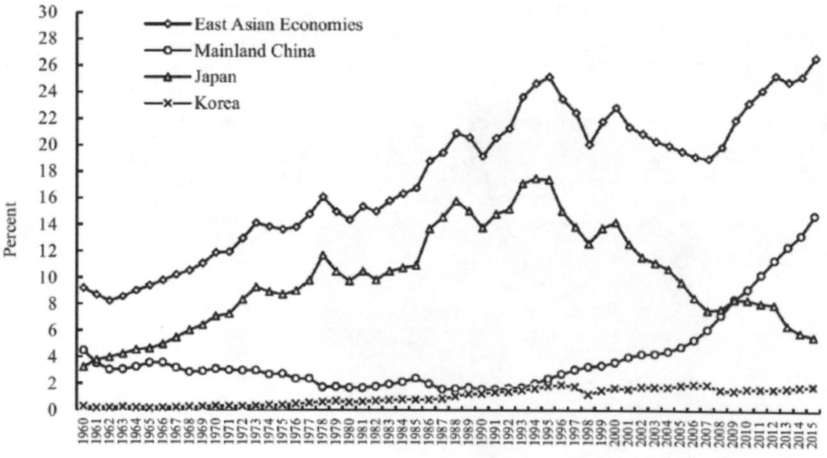

A similar shift occurred in the distribution of world trade. In 1970, the United States and Western Europe together accounted for almost 60% of world trade in goods and services. By comparison, East Asia accounted for 9.5% of world trade. By 2014, the share of United States and Western Europe in world trade declined to 41%, whereas the share of East Asia rose to almost 28% (see Charts 5.7 and 5.8).

Chart 5.7. The Distribution of Total International Trade in Goods and Services, 1970

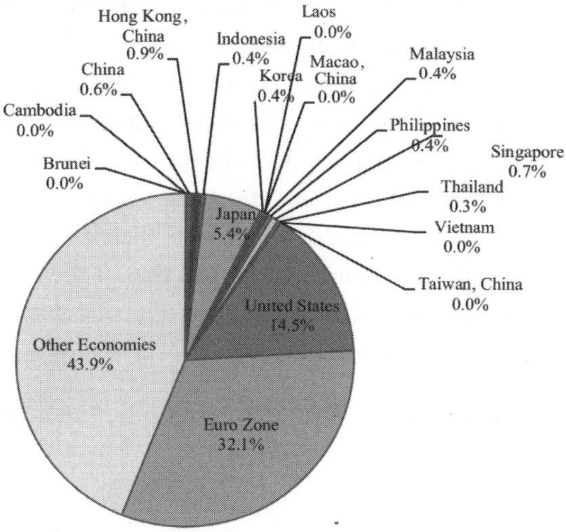

Chart 5.8. The Distribution of Total International Trade in Goods and Services, 2014

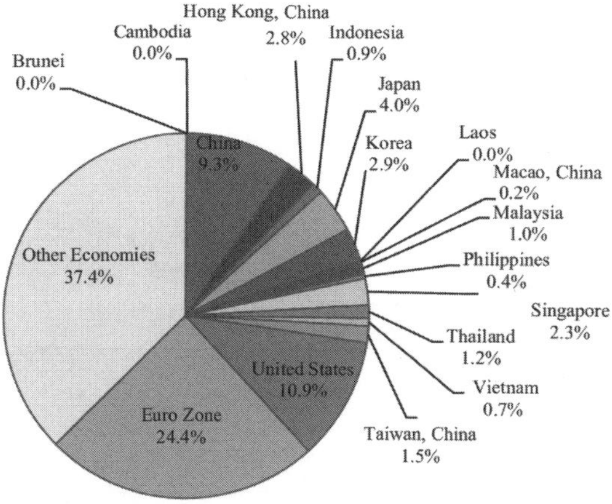

The Chinese share of world trade rose from 0.6% in 1970 to 12.2% in 2015 (see Chart 5.9). The growth in Chinese international trade may be attributed in part to the reform of the Chinese exchange rate system in the early 1990s, accompanied by a significant devaluation, to Chinese accession to the WTO in 2001, and to the expiration of the Multi-Fibre Agreement governing world trade in textiles. China has also become either the most important or the second most important trading partner of almost all of the economies in the Asia-Pacific region (see Table 5.2).

Contrary to the public impression, the ratio of Chinese exports of goods and services to GDP is actually relatively low compared with other economies (see Chart 5.10). Among large economies, only Japan and the U.S. have a lower share of exports in GDP than China. This is a reflection of the fact that China is a large continental economy, with relatively abundant diversified natural resources and a huge domestic market. Most of the other East Asian economies (except Japan) are either export-oriented or were export-oriented when they began their processes of economic development. Their exports to GDP ratios have been and continue to be much higher than that of the Chinese economy. The same is true of the ratio of Chinese imports of goods and services to GDP (see Chart 5.11) and for the same reasons.

Chart 5.9. The Chinese Share of Total World Trade, 1950–2015

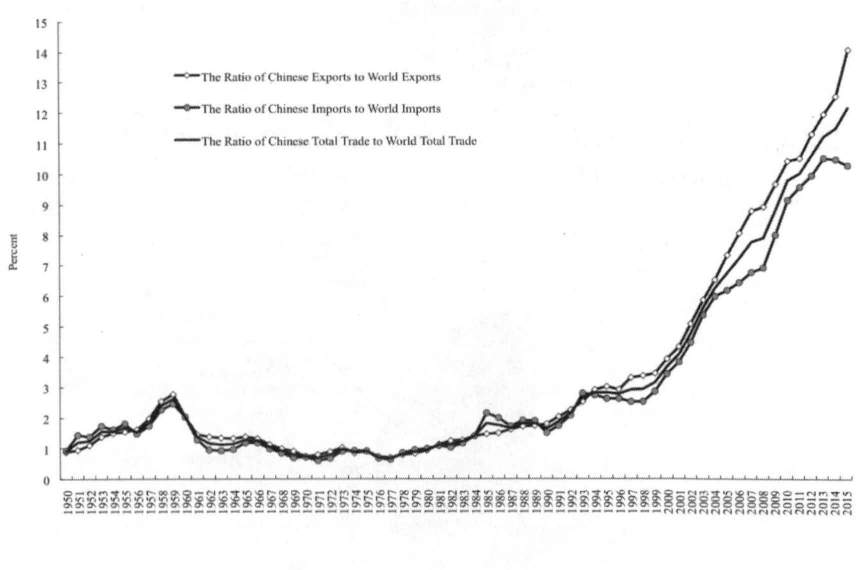

Table 5.2. The Ranks of China as Trading Partner of Asia-Pacific Countries/Regions and Vice Versa, 2014

Country/Region	Chinese rank as trading partner of country/region	Rank of country/region as trading partner of China
Australia	1	9
Brunei	3	107
Cambodia	2	87
Hong Kong, China	1	4
Indonesia	1	20
Japan	1	5
Korea	1	6
Laos	2	90
Macau, China	1	84
Malaysia	1	10
Myanmar	1	36
New Zealand	1	45
Philippines	2	27
Singapore	1	15
Taiwan, China	1	7
Thailand	1	17
United States	2	2
Vietnam	1	13

In Chart 5.12, Chinese exports and imports as a share of its GDP over time are presented. It is clear that these shares peaked in 2006 and have been declining steadily since then. Moreover, the Chinese trade surplus as a % of its GDP has also begun to decline as well. This trend is expected to continue in the future.

China has also opened its economy to inbound foreign direct investment (FDI). China imported from abroad capital goods as well as advanced technology that enhanced its domestic production capacity. Foreign direct investment also enabled the surplus resources of the Chinese economy, principally labour, to be productively employed.

As a result of the accumulated trade surpluses and, to a lesser extent, the net capital inflows since the mid-1990s, the Chinese official foreign exchange reserves have also risen steadily, reaching a peak of approximately US$4 trillion in mid-2014, and becoming the largest official foreign exchange reserves held by any central bank in the world (see Chart 5.13).

Chart 5.10. Exports of Goods and Services as a Share of GDP: Selected Economies

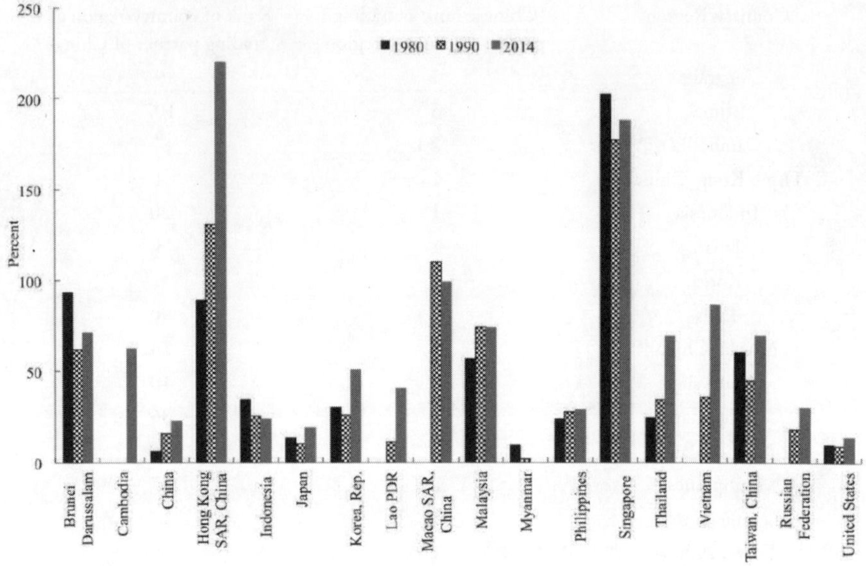

Chart 5.11. Imports of Goods and Services as a Percent of GDP: Selected Economies

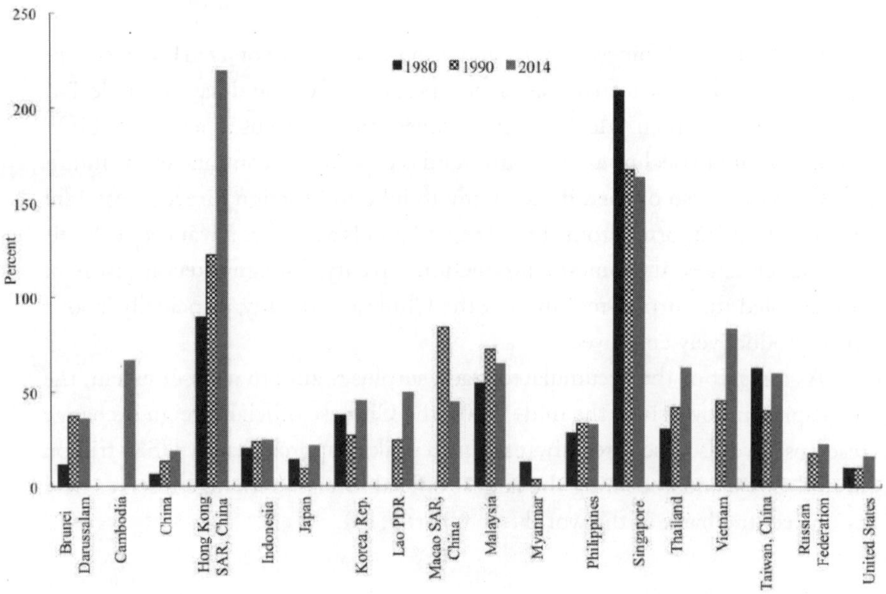

Chart 5.12. Exports and Imports of Goods and Services as a Percent of Chinese GDP, 1982–2015

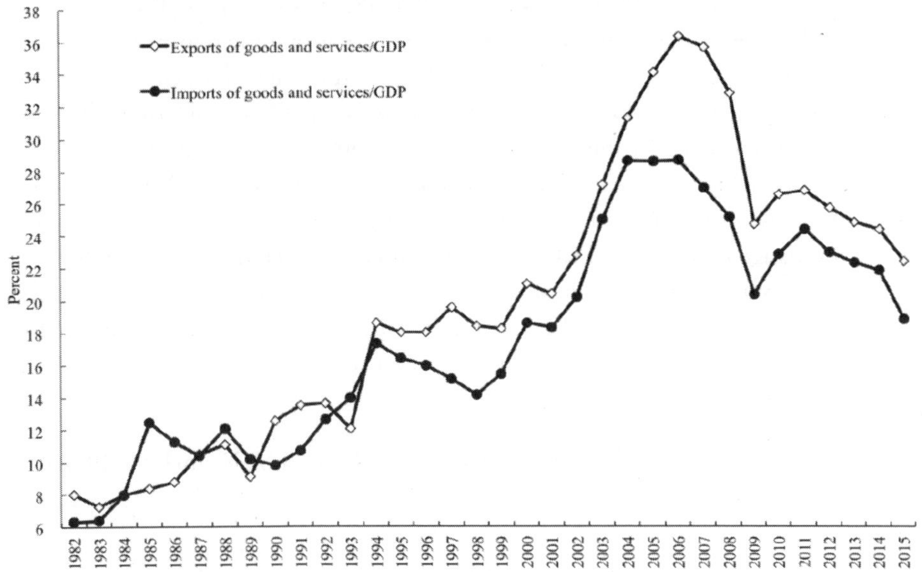

Chart 5.13. Chinese Foreign Exchange Reserves and the Yuan/US$ Exchange Rate

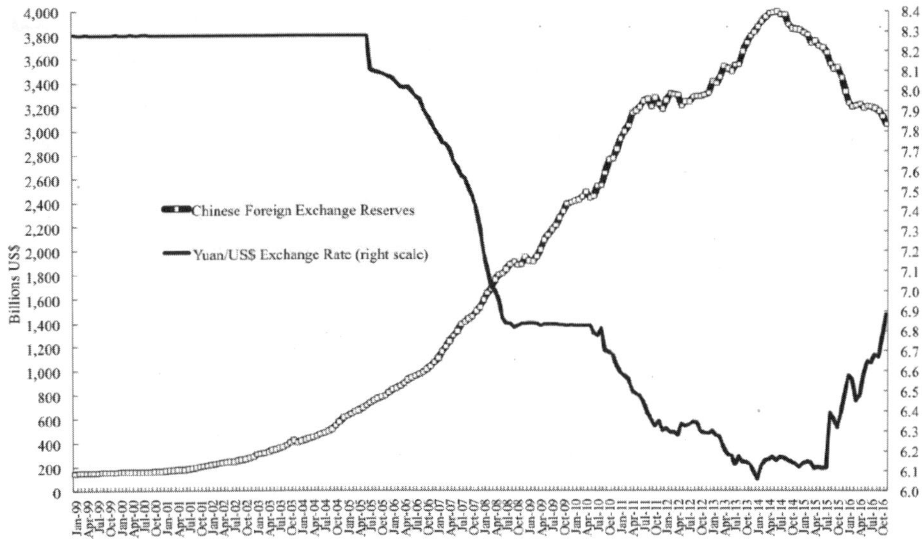

In the meantime, the exchange rate of the Chinese currency, the renminbi or yuan, vis-à-vis the U.S. dollar, has also undergone huge changes during the past 37 years (see Chart 5.14). In 1978, US$1 was worth less than 2 yuan. In order to maximise the benefits of the policy of economic reform and opening, the Chinese government began to devalue the renminbi significantly with respect to the US dollar in 1980, to a more competitive and sustainable level. For a few years in the early 1990s, China maintained dual exchange rates: an official rate and an "adjustment" rate determined in a market restricted to Chinese exporters and importers with import licenses. At the time, foreign exchange certificates (FECs) were also used by foreign visitors to China instead of the renminbi. China implemented full current-accounts convertibility in 1994. In both nominal and real terms, the renminbi has been appreciating relative to the U.S. dollar since 1994, but especially after 2005 (see Chart 5.15), until the past couple of years.

Chart 5.14. Nominal Exchange Rate of the Renminbi, Yuan/US$, 1978–2016

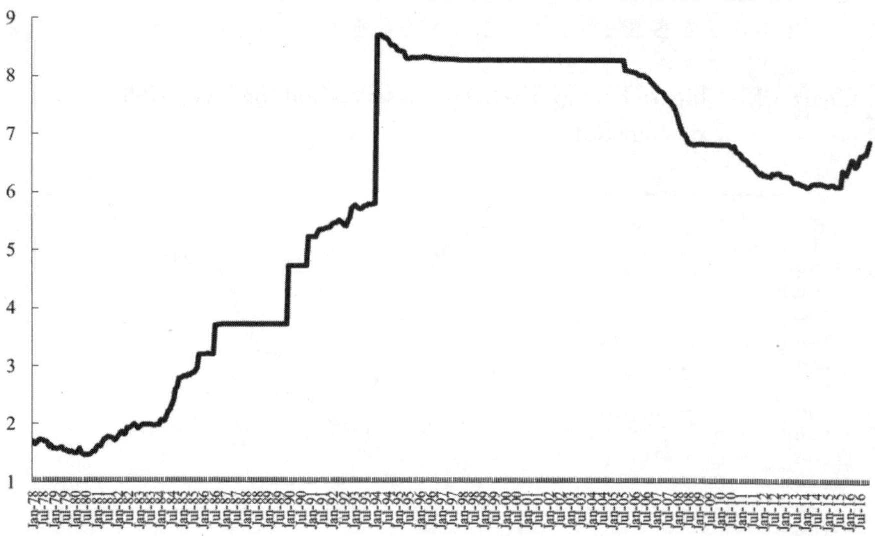

Chart 5.15. The Nominal and Real Yuan/US$ Exchange Rates

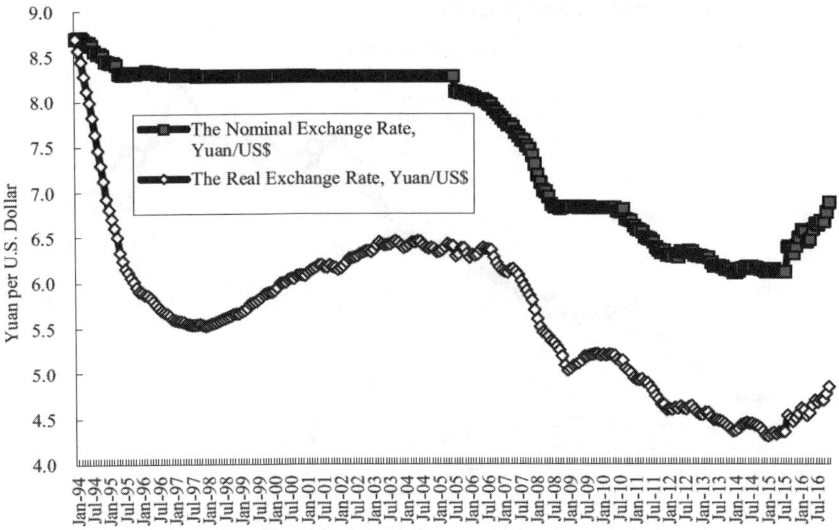

Since 2010, the renminbi has been increasingly used as an invoicing and settlement currency for cross-border transactions, especially those involving Chinese enterprises as transacting parties. The proportion of Chinese international trade settled in renminbi has grown rapidly, from almost nothing in the first quarter of 2010 to 32.5% of the total value of Chinese international trade in goods in the third quarter of 2015, equivalent to US$334 billion (see Chart 5.16). However, the proportion has since declined to just over 20%, with an approximate total value of US$800 billion of Chinese international trade settled in renminbi annually.

The renminbi is also used for foreign direct investment and portfolio investment both inbound and outbound, but its use can be further expanded. The central banks and monetary authorities of many countries and regions have entered into swap agreements with the People's Bank of China, the central bank of China, which facilitates the use of renminbi as an invoicing, clearing and settlement currency. In Charts 5.17 and 5.18, the share of each currency used in world trade settlement and the share of the issuing country or region in world trade are compared in 2010 and in November 2016 respectively. In 2010, the renminbi was not even within the top 20 currencies

Chart 5.16. Renminbi Settlement of Chinese Cross-Border Trade (US$ billion and percent)

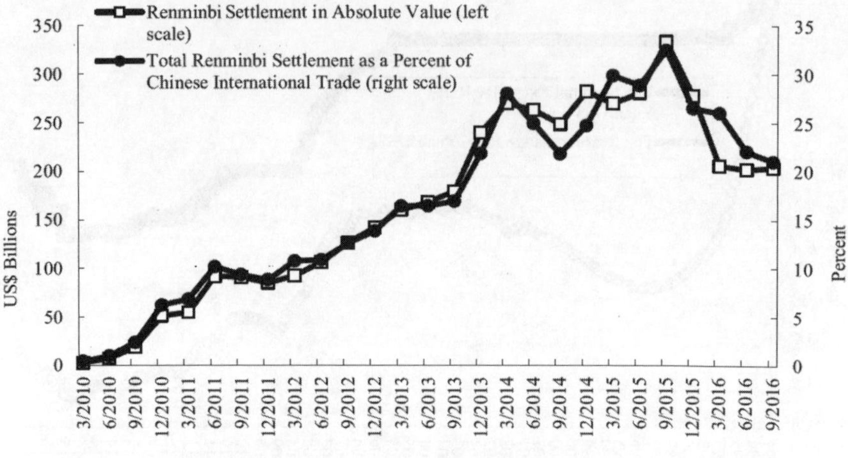

Chart 5.17. Distribution of World Trade Settlement Currencies versus World Trade, 2010

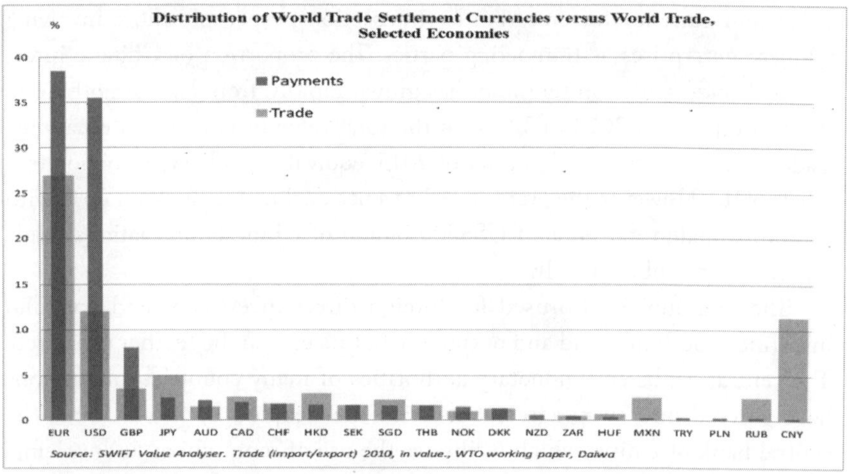

Chart 5.18. Distribution of World Trade Settlement Currencies Versus World Trade, November 2016

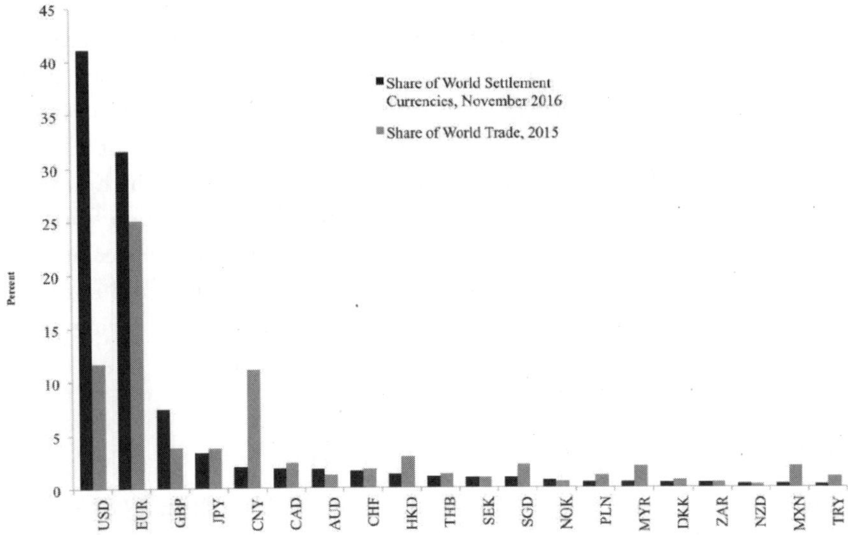

used in world trade settlement. By November 2016, it became the fifth most used currency in world trade settlement. However, even though China accounted for approximately 11% of world trade, the renminbi accounted for only 2% of world trade settlement in November 2016; and while the U.S. had a similar share of world trade as China, the U.S. dollar accounted for 41.1% of world trade settlement in November 2016. By comparison, Japan accounted for 3.8% of world trade and its currency, the yen, accounted for 3.4% of world trade settlement in November 2016. There is still plenty of room for the expansion of the use of renminbi for cross-border trade settlement in the future. If the Japanese experience is any guide, the use of the renminbi for world trade settlement should triple or even quadruple over the next few years.

The exchange rate of the renminbi relative to the U.S. dollar is likely to hold steady over the next few years. This should facilitate the further expansion of the use of the renminbi for the invoicing, clearing and settlement of international transactions. Capital account convertibility is expected to be achieved for the renminbi before 2020. It can occur sooner if short-term capital flows, both outbound and inbound, can be appropriately regulated or "discouraged," for example, with the imposition of a "Tobin tax"[3] on capital account inflows and outflows.

One reason the Chinese economy has been able to survive the successive financial crises—beginning with the 1997–1998 East Asian currency crisis, followed by the global financial crisis of 2007–2009, the European sovereign debt crisis, as well as the successive quantitative easing on the part of the U.S. Federal Reserve Board (QEI, II, and III), the Bank of Japan and the European Central Bank (ECB), relatively unscathed—is its relative insulation from the financial disturbances in the world economy through its maintenance of controls on both inflows and outflows of capital. Moreover, China did not have to depend on foreign capital because of its own high domestic saving rates. Potential contagion from abroad has therefore been minimised.

4. The Chinese Economic Fundamentals

The long-term economic growth of a country depends on the rates of growth of its primary inputs—capital (tangible or physical) and labour—and on technical progress (or equivalently, the growth of total factor productivity) that is, the ability to increase output without increasing inputs. The rate of growth of tangible or physical capital depends on the rate of investment in structure, equipment and basic infrastructure, which in turn depends on the availability of national savings. The rate of technical progress depends on investment in intangible capital (including human capital and research and development [R&D] capital).

The most important source of Chinese economic growth over the past 37 years has been the growth of inputs, principally the growth of tangible capital (structure, equipment, and basic infrastructure), not technical progress. Thus, past Chinese economic growth was mainly due to "working harder, not working smarter." The growth of tangible capital accounts for the bulk, approximately 75%, of the measured economic growth in China. This experience

3 This is a financial transaction tax, first proposed by Prof. James Tobin, Nobel Laureate in Economic Sciences, which can be applied to currency conversion transactions.

Chart 5.19. Chinese National Saving and Gross Domestic Investment as a Percent of GDP

is not unlike those of other East Asian economies such as South Korea and Taiwan and even Japan, as well as that of the United States, at a similarly early stage of economic development. The growth of inputs, principally tangible capital, has always been found to be the most important source of growth at an early stage of development. This is especially true of economies with initially abundant supplies of surplus labour.

Chinese economic growth since 1978 has been underpinned by a consistently high domestic investment rate, enabled by a national savings rate on the order of 30% and above, except for a brief start-up period in the early 1950s (see Chart 5.19). Since the early 1990s, the Chinese national saving rate has stayed around 40% and has at times approached or even exceeded 50% in more recent years. This means, among other things, that the Chinese economy can finance all of its domestic investment needs from its own domestic savings alone, thus assuring a high rate of growth of the tangible capital stock without having to depend on the more fickle foreign capital inflows (including foreign direct investment, foreign portfolio investment, foreign aid, or foreign loans). In particular, it does not need to borrow abroad and bear the potential risks of a large, short-term and often interruptible, foreign-currency denominated debt. Hence the Chinese economy is also more immune from external disturbances than other economies. In addition, since new resources are made available each year from new savings, enabling new investments to be made, the necessity of restructuring, redeploying or privatising existing fixed assets is greatly diminished (thus making it more possible to avoid potentially politically divisive issues and the creation of "losers"). A high national saving rate also allows the normally more efficient non-state sector greater room and greater scope for development and expansion, as there is less likelihood of "crowding out."

The national saving rate in China will remain high in the foreseeable future even though it is expected to decline gradually, in part because the household or labour share of GDP is relatively low, below 50% (the household disposable income was approximately 43% of GDP in 2014), and because Chinese enterprises, especially the state-owned enterprises, distribute little or no cash dividends, reinvesting almost all of their profits.

However, tangible capital input-driven economic growth has its limitations, because as the stock of tangible capital relative to labour increases, the marginal productivity of tangible capital will begin to decline and will eventually reach a point where additional tangible capital is no longer productive. This is a point made by Prof. Paul Krugman.[4]

China, like Japan, Taiwan, and South Korea in their respective early stages of economic development, has an unlimited supply of surplus labour—there is therefore no shortage of and no upward pressure on the real wage rate of unskilled, entry-level labour. This means the Chinese economy can continue to grow without being constrained by the supply of labour or by rising real wage rates of unskilled, entry-level labour over an extended period of time. Investment in tangible or physical capital such as structure, equipment and physical infrastructure is very productive under conditions of surplus labour. As long as there is sufficient complementary domestic physical capital, the surplus labour can be gainfully employed and enable the real output of the economy to grow rapidly. This is exactly what the late Prof. W. Arthur

---

4 Krugman (1994) drew on the work of Kim and Lau (1994). See also Kim and Lau (1995), Lau and Park (2002) and Lau and Park (2007).

Lewis, Nobel Laureate in Economic Sciences, said in his celebrated paper on surplus labour 60 years ago.[5]

The distribution of Chinese GDP by originating sectors in 2015 was approximately: primary (agriculture), 9.0%; secondary (manufacturing, mining and construction), 40.5%; and tertiary (services), 50.5% (see Chart 5.20). (Note that mining is normally included in the primary sector in most other economies.)

By comparison, in 2015, the distribution of employment by sector was: primary 28.3%, secondary 29.3%, and tertiary 43.4% (see Chart 5.21). The agricultural sector employed 28.3% of the Chinese labour force but produced only 9% of the Chinese GDP in 2015. Thus, labour can be productively transferred to the other two sectors where labour productivities and wage rates are higher as long as complementary capital and demand are available. Hence, as long as the percentage of labour force employed in the primary sector significantly exceeds the percentage of GDP originating from the primary sector, there will be little or no upward pressure on the real wage rate of unskilled, entry-level labour in the secondary and tertiary sectors. Surplus labour will continue to exist in the Chinese economy.

Even with increases in the levels of minimum wage rates in the different provinces, regions and municipalities, the real wage rate of unskilled, entry-level labour for the country as a whole has basically remained stable and is expected to be stable for a long time because of the continuing existence of significant surplus labour in the Chinese economy. However, there is upward pressure on the real wage rates of skilled and experienced labour, which is actually in short supply, especially as Chinese enterprises move up the value-added chain. But given the trend of rapid expansion of Chinese tertiary education in recent years, with more than six million new graduates projected annually, the increase in the real wage rate of even skilled labour is likely to be relatively limited going forward.

---

5 See Lewis (1954). For an alternate model of the development of a dual economy, see Jorgenson (1961).

Chart 5.20. The Distribution of Chinese GDP by Originating Sector since 1952

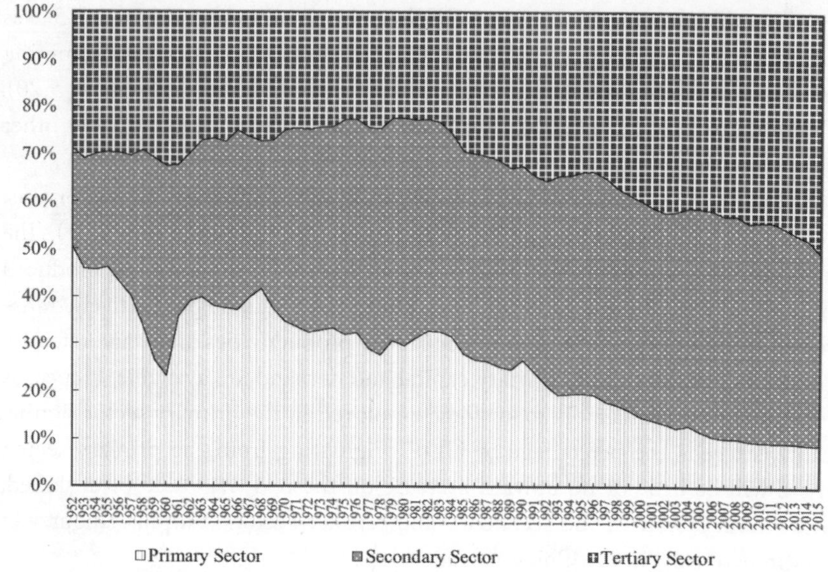

Chart 5.21. The Distribution of Chinese Employment by Sector since 1952

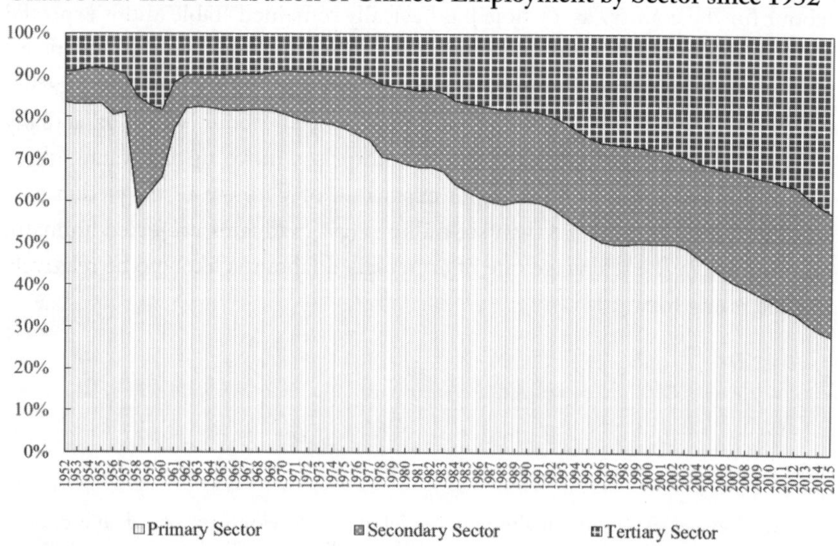

China has a long tradition of emphasis on education and learning (human capital) and will be increasing its investment in human capital. The enrolment rate of tertiary education has been rising rapidly and stands at approximately 30% today. It is expected to rise further over the next decades as private tertiary educational institutions become more numerous in response to demand and facilitated by government policy. China has also begun to increase its expenditure on Research and Development (R&D), with the goal of increasing it from 2.1% in 2015 to 2.5% of GDP by 2020. However, relative to many other economies, China lags behind in investment in both human capital and R&D capital. (This deficit and gap will be further discussed.)

The size of the Chinese economy is a natural advantage. The huge domestic market of 1.34 billion consumers with pent-up demand for housing and transportation and other consumer goods and services (e.g., education and health care) enables the realisation of significant economies of scale in production. The huge domestic market also greatly enhances the rate of return on investment in intangible capital (e.g., R&D capital and goodwill, including brand building) by allowing the fixed costs of the R&D for a new product or process, or advertising and promotion in brand building, to be more easily amortised and recovered. For intangible capital, once the initial fixed costs are recovered, any additional revenue is almost all pure profit. Brand-building enables the owners of brand names to have much more pricing power and higher profit margins than enterprises that do only OEM (original equipment manufacturing) business. The huge domestic market also facilitates active Chinese participation in the setting of product and technology standards, for example, in fourth-generation (4-G) standards for telecommunication, and sharing the economic benefits of such standard-setting.

An economy with significant economies of scale will grow faster than an economy with constant returns to scale given the same rates of growth of the measured inputs. The degree of returns to scale at the economy-wide level is not precisely known. The assumption used by Edward F. Denison for the degree of returns to scale for the U.S. is 1.1, that is, if all inputs are doubled, output will be increased by 1.1 times. On the assumption that this also holds for the Chinese economy, it implies that Chinese economic growth will be 10% higher each year than an economy with the same rates of growth of capital and labour inputs but without the economies of scale. Of course, the effects of economies of scale are sometimes confounded with those of technical progress or growth of total factor productivity (there is an identification problem).[6] However, if there were economies of scale at all, they should be manifested in the Chinese economy.

Suppose the annual rates of growth of the inputs in the economy are 7%. Under constant returns to scale, the economy will grow at 7% per annum. However, under increasing returns to scale of degree 1.1, the economy will grow at 7.7% per annum. In 10 years, the economy with economies of scale will be 7% larger than the one without; in 20 years, 14%; and in 40 years, 31%, a significant difference. Thus, the existence of economies of scale can make a huge difference in the level of GDP in a few decades. Moreover, economies of scale can increase the rates of return to investment and may lead to higher investment rates than otherwise.

Another important and favourable implication of a large domestic economy is the relatively low degree of external dependence and hence vulnerability. Large continental economies, such as China, Russia and the United States, are likely to be self-sufficient in many of the resources because of their large size and geographically diversified location. These economies are also mostly driven by their internal demands, not by international trade. For example, exports have never been very important to the U.S. economy, and the U.S. economy has never been dependent on international trade, except perhaps in the 19th century. The Chinese economy is similar—China has adequate supplies of most natural resources domestically (with the possible exception of oil). Chinese economic growth in the future decades will be mostly driven by internal demand rather than exports.

The powerful advantage of a large economy can be seen by an examination of Charts 5.22, 5.23, and 5.24 on the rates of growth of exports, imports and real GDP of selected Asian economies (with the solid black line representing China). The figures show that even though Chinese exports and imports fluctuate like those of all the other selected Asian economies, the rate of growth of Chinese real GDP has remained relatively stable compared to those of the other economies. It is relatively immune to external economic disturbances.

---

6 See Boskin and Lau (1992) for a method of identifying both the degree of returns to scale and the rate of technical progress by analysing the pooled time-series data of several economies simultaneously.

Chart 5.22. Quarterly Rates of Growth of Exports of Goods: Selected Asian Economies

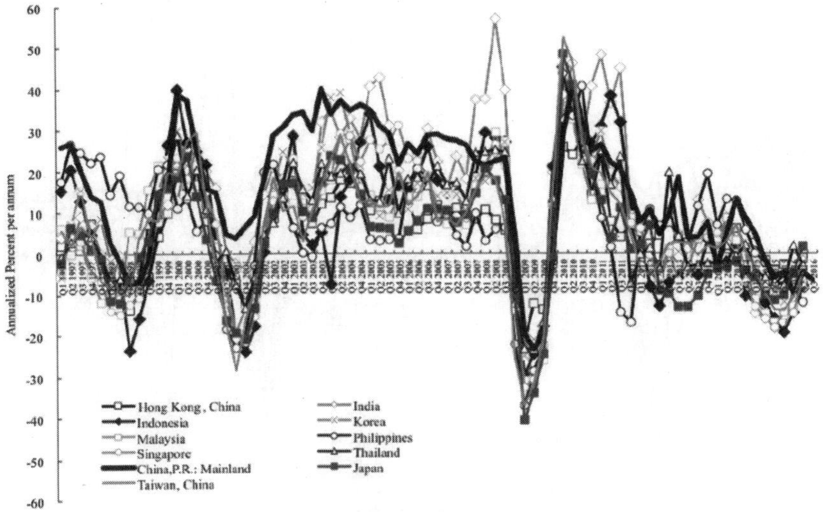

Chart 5.23. Quarterly Rates of Growth of Imports of Goods: Selected Asian Economies

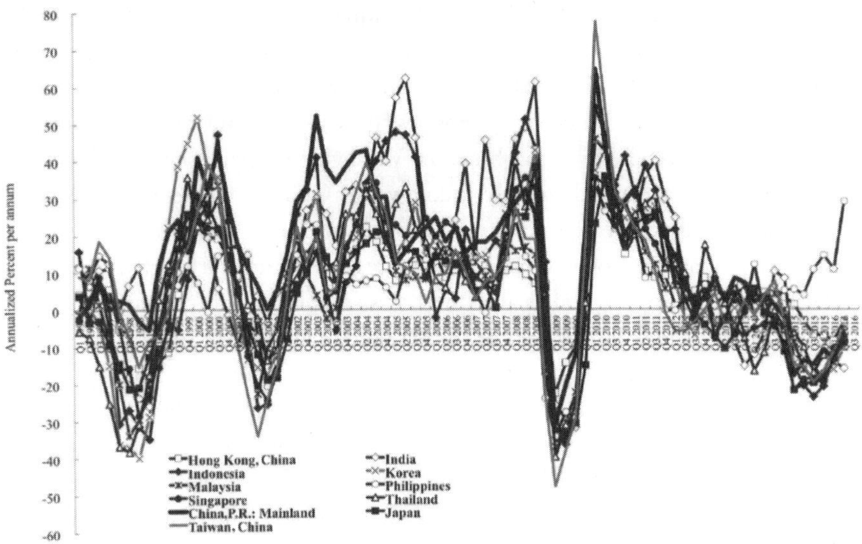

Chart 5.24. Quarterly Rates of Growth of Real GDP, Year-on-Year: Selected Asian Economies

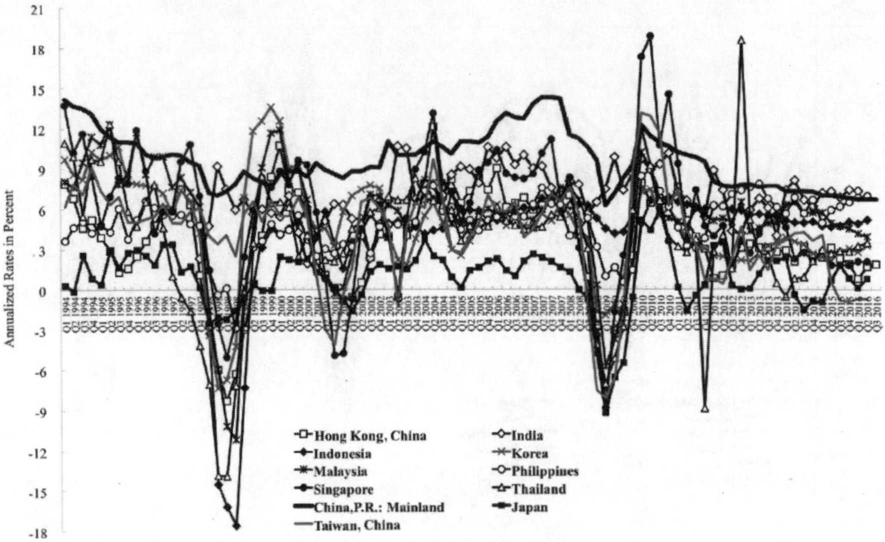

In addition to a high national savings rate, a large pool of surplus labour, rising investment in intangible capital (human capital and R&D capital), and the large size of its economy, China also has the advantage of relative backwardness, which has enabled the Chinese economy to learn from the successes and failures of other economies; to leap-frog and by-pass stages of development (e.g., the telex machine, the VHS video-tape player, and the fixed landline telephone are all mostly unknown in China); and to have creation without destruction (e.g., online virtual bookstores like Amazon.com do not have to destroy brick and mortar bookstores which do not exist in the first place; internet shopping takes away business from brick and mortar malls).

However, while good economic fundamentals are necessary for a sustained high rate of growth of an economy, they are by no means sufficient. In the 30 years between 1949, the year of the founding of the People's Republic of China, and 1978, the first year of the Chinese economic reform and opening to the world, China also had: (1) a high domestic saving rate; (2) an unlimited supply of surplus labour; and (3) a large domestic economy. But the Chinese economy did not experience a sustained high rate of growth during that period.

Similarly, the former Soviet Union also had a high rate of tangible capital accumulation as well as a large domestic economy, but did not experience a sustained high rate of economic growth either.

5. The Inherent Economic Inefficiency of Central Planning

Why didn't China and the former Soviet Union experience sustained high-rate economic growth despite favourable economic fundamentals? The short answer is that both the Chinese economy before its economic reform of 1978 and that of the former Soviet Union operated under central planning, with its inherent economic inefficiencies. From 1953, when China adopted its First Five-Year Plan, to the end of the last century, the Chinese economy operated under a series of mandatory central plans. Similarly, the former Soviet Union and the East European countries operated under central planning until 1989.

A principal characteristic of a centrally-planned economy is the administrative allocation, rather than market allocation, of scarce resources. What goods and services to produce? How much to produce? Where to produce them? What raw materials and parts should be used to produce them? From which enterprises should the raw materials and parts be bought? To which enterprises should the outputs be sold? All of these decisions are made by the central planners and embodied in the mandatory central plan. Enterprises do not have any autonomy in these decisions. The prices of goods and services are also completely determined in the central plan. They do not necessarily reflect relative scarcities in the economy, and do not play any role in the equilibration of market supply and demand. The prices are only used for accounting purposes.

Why is there inherent economic inefficiency in a centrally-planned economy? We begin by defining what economists mean by efficiency. A production allocation or plan for an economy is said to be efficient if for given aggregate quantities of inputs (the tangible capital stock and labour), no output of any good or service can be increased without decreasing the output of another good or service. In other words, there is no slack: the economy is operating on the frontier of its set of production possibilities. A production allocation or plan is said to be inefficient if it is possible to increase the output of any good or service without decreasing the output of any other good or service. In other words, the economy is operating in the interior of its set of production possibilities.

It is important to understand and distinguish between the two different ways in which the real output of an economy can be increased: either through an outward movement of the frontier of the set of production possibilities, or through a movement from the interior of the set of production possibilities set to its frontier. The first way can only occur either through an increase in the inputs, tangible and intangible, or from the adoption of a more efficient technology imported from abroad. The second way can occur even in the absence of any increase in the inputs or technology transfer. It can be regarded as a pure increase in domestic economic efficiency, resulting in an increase in actual output, but without an increase in potential output. In Chart 5.25, the expansion of the old production possibilities set (shaded in light grey) to include the area shaded in darker grey, is accompanied by the movement of the old production possibilities frontier (the line with black diamonds◆) to the new (the line with black squares ■). The movement from the old production point to the inner frontier line represents a movement from the interior of the old production possibilities set to the old frontier.

Chart 5.25. Movement of the Production Possibilities Frontier versus Movement to the Frontier

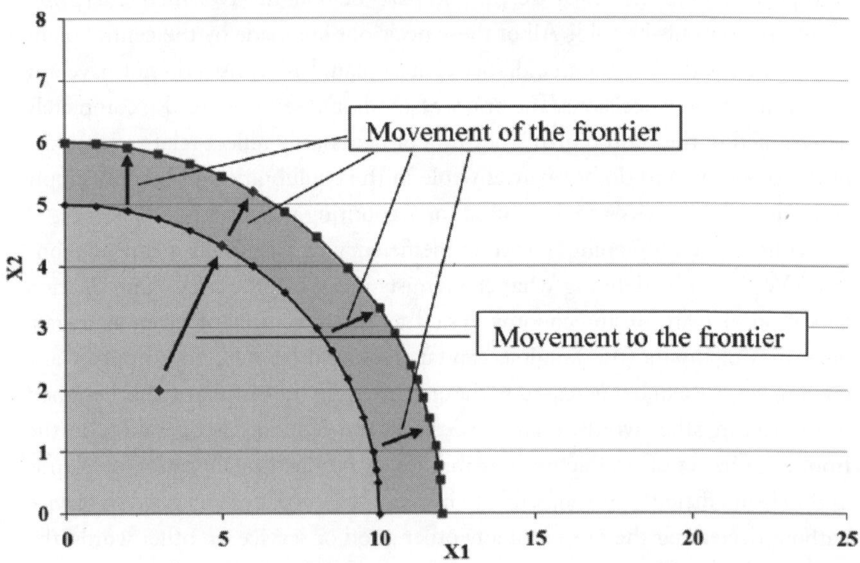

But for various reasons—incomplete information, failure to optimise and the lack of incentive—a centrally-planned economy always operates in the interior of its set of production possibilities. Thus, output can always be increased by simply moving to the frontier from the interior of the set of production possibilities, without any increase in inputs. The existence of this inherent inefficiency therefore also implies the existence of surplus potential output. In order to understand why there always exists inefficiency and hence surplus potential output in a centrally-planned economy, we consider the following simple example drawn from agriculture.

There are two farm households, A and B. Each has a hectare of land. Both cotton and rice are needed by the economy. The central planner's problem is to decide which household should grow cotton and which household should grow rice, as well as how much of each crop to grow. First of all, there may be a problem of insufficient or incorrect information. The central planner may not know which plot is more suitable for growing cotton and which plot is more suitable for growing rice. Moreover, the central planner may not know whether Farmer A can grow cotton better than Farmer B or vice versa. If the central planner makes any mistake in the assignment of production responsibilities, a simple exchange of the assignment can increase aggregate output without having to increase any input.

Second, even with full, complete and accurate information, it is still possible for the central planner to fail to optimise. The optimisation problem may be too large or too complex; or the problem may not be well behaved (for example, there may be non-convexities); or the problem may have multiple possible distinct solutions.

Third, there is also the problem of a lack of incentives on the part of the farmers to become more efficient—to try to move to their respective production possibilities frontiers. Under a centrally-planned system, the farmers are generally wary of exceeding the assigned production targets even if they are in principle able to do so. To them, if they manage to produce outputs that exceed the assigned production targets, not only would their income not increase, so that the extra efforts would have been in vain, but also the assigned production targets for the following year might be raised, making it more difficult for them to fulfil their obligations. (This is sometimes referred to as the "ratchet" effect.) Thus, under a centrally-planned system, the best strategy for the farmers is to each try to produce the respective assigned target output and not to exceed it.

However, if there is a way to provide the necessary incentives to the farmers without increasing the aggregate inputs assigned under the central plan, aggregate output can also be increased. For example, the farmers can be given the autonomy to grow anything on their plots once they have fulfilled their obligations under the central plan, and to retain the resulting profits and to bear the resulting losses, if any; or they can be allowed to exchange their assigned responsibilities with each other. The combined outputs of the two farmers will be higher than before without any increase in the aggregate inputs.

On the eve of the beginning of its reform and opening in 1978, the Chinese economy still operated under a mandatory central plan, and therefore had significant surplus potential output or slack. The countries of the former Soviet Union and Eastern Europe were all centrally-planned economies on the eves of their economic transitions and thus also had similarly significant surplus potential outputs. If the surplus potential outputs can be fully exploited and realised, the real rates of growth of these economies can become very high, even without any significant growth in their aggregate inputs, at least in the near term. With growth in aggregate inputs, the economies should be able to grow even faster.

We may therefore conclude that for an economy under central planning, there always exists inefficiency and hence surplus potential output. Moreover, the surplus potential output should and can be realised with the introduction of economic reforms granting autonomy to the producers and providing incentives for them through the free markets, even without an increase in the aggregate inputs.

6. The Benefits of an Open Economy

What are the benefits of an open economy? The theory of comparative advantage tells us that free and voluntary trade between two trading partner countries always benefits both (although the distribution of the gains between them and within them may not be uniform). Exporters and importers will tend to benefit, whereas import-competing industries and their workers may lose. An economy may also benefit from the ability to import and augment resources not sufficiently available domestically using its export revenues or relying on foreign direct investment, foreign portfolio investment, foreign loans and foreign aid. Technology transfer is another way in which an economy can benefit, resulting in an expansion of its set of production possibilities (equivalently the outward shifting of its production possibility frontier).

Chart 5.26 makes it clear how opening the economy to the rest of the world always improves aggregate social welfare. For an economy without international trade, the consumers can only consume what can be produced domestically. The consumption possibilities set is therefore the same as the production possibilities set (the area shaded in grey). With international trade, the consumption possibilities set becomes the entire area of the triangle bounded by the international price line (grey line) tangent to the production possibilities set and the vertical and horizontal axes, which properly contains the old consumption possibilities set in the absence of trade. Since every consumption plan (combination of good 1 and good 2) in the old consumption possibilities set is attainable with trade, but not every consumption plan in the new consumption possibilities set is attainable in the old consumption possibilities set, aggregate social welfare must be higher with trade, because more consumption choices are available. As shown in Chart 5.26, without trade, the economy operates at the old production point, which is the same as the old consumption point. With trade, the economy operates at the new production point but through exports and imports achieves the new consumption point, with the same quantity of good 1 as, and a higher quantity of good 2 than, the old consumption point. Aggregate social welfare must have increased.

Chart 5.26. Opening the Economy Enhances Domestic Economic Welfare

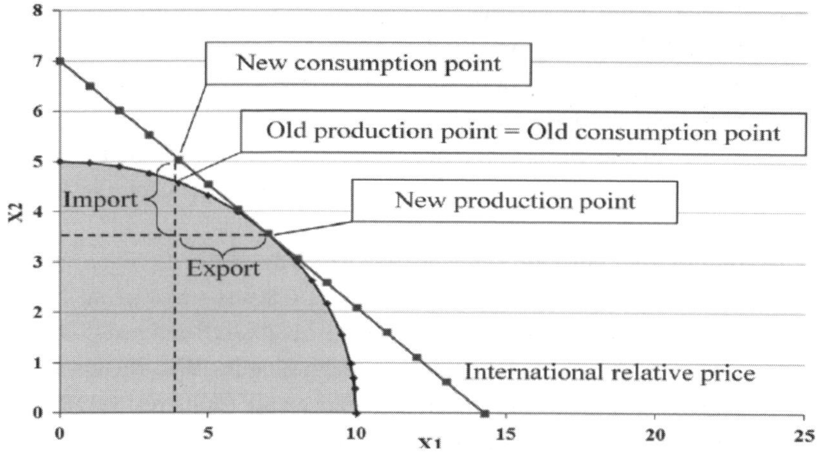

Even if the international relative price is the same as the domestic relative price in the absence of international trade, so that the optimal combination of the goods to be produced remains the same with or without international trade, given the possibility of exports and imports, every point on the international relative price line is a possible domestic consumption plan. The domestic consumption point can be different from the domestic production point, and since the set of consumption possibilities has expanded, the resulting aggregate social welfare must also be higher with international trade. Thus, it is possible for aggregate social welfare to increase even if the production possibilities set remains the same as the economy opens to the world.

It may be thought that with the inherent economic inefficiency of a centrally-planned economy, its real rate of growth must be very high as it makes its transition from a centrally-planned to a market economy. Similarly, one should expect aggregate social welfare to rise as an autarkic economy opens to the world. However, empirically, this turns out not to be true in general, except for the few rare cases such as the Chinese economy.

7. The Transition from a Closed Centrally-planned to an Open Market Economy

In the former Soviet Union and the formerly socialist Eastern European countries, the transition from a closed centrally-planned economy to an open market economy beginning in the late 1980s was both difficult and painful. Many of these countries experienced negative real rates of growth for approximately a full decade, from 1989 to 1999 (see Chart 5.27) and suffered from extremely high rates of domestic inflation (see Chart 5.28). Real GDPs per capita in these formerly centrally-planned economies took even longer to recover to the same levels of 1989, the year in which central planning was first abandoned (see Chart 5.29). For example, the real GDP per capita of Russia (solid grey line) did not recover to its 1989 level until 2007.

In contrast, the transition from a closed centrally-planned economy to an open market economy in China beginning in 1978 was smooth and highly successful (see Charts 5.1 and 5.3). Both Chinese real GDP and real GDP per capita have grown rapidly and continuously beginning in 1978. There was not even a single year of decline in either aggregate or per capita real GDP as in the other formerly centrally-planned economies.

Chart 5.27. The Rates of Growth of the Real GDP of Former Soviet Union and Formerly Socialist Eastern European Countries

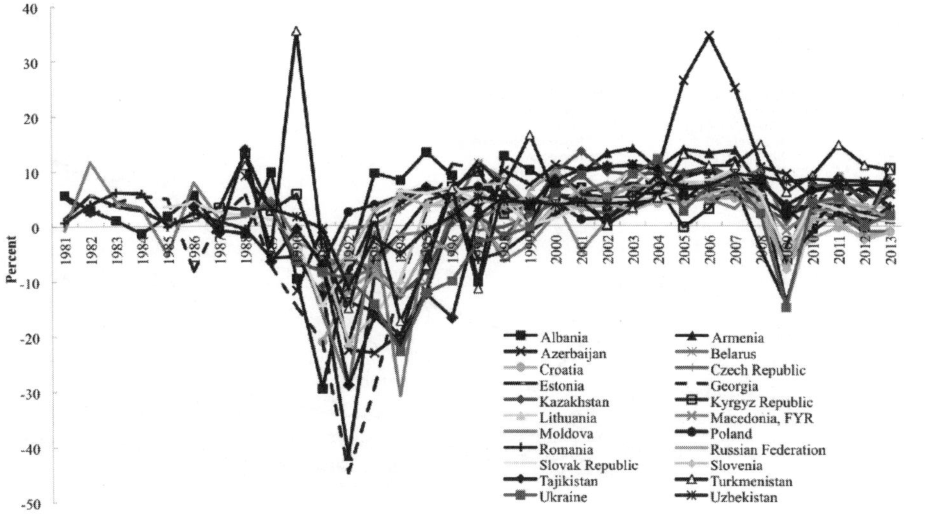

Chart 5.28. The Annual Rates of Inflation of Former Soviet Union and Formerly Socialist Eastern European Countries

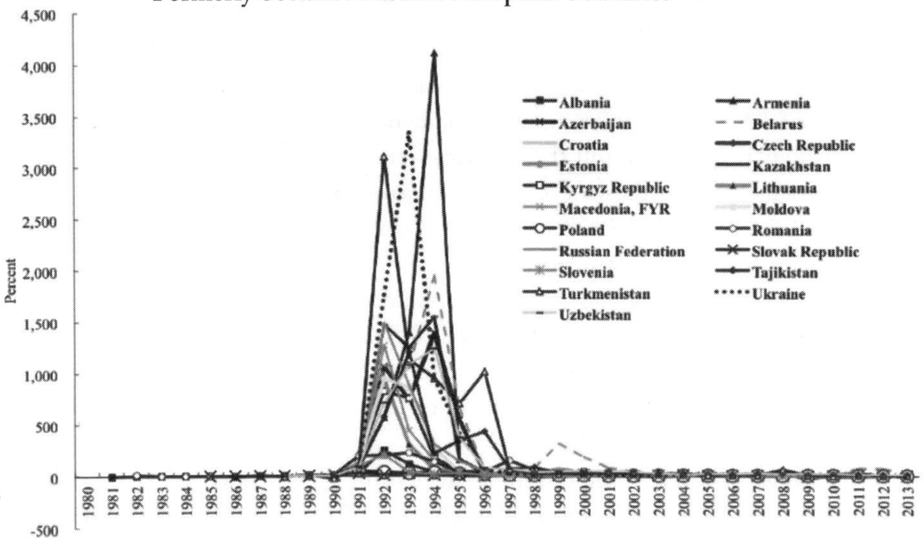

Note: Georgia is omitted because some of its data are off the scale of the figure.

Chart 5.29. The GDP per Capita of Former Soviet Union and Formerly Socialist Eastern European Countries (2005 US$)

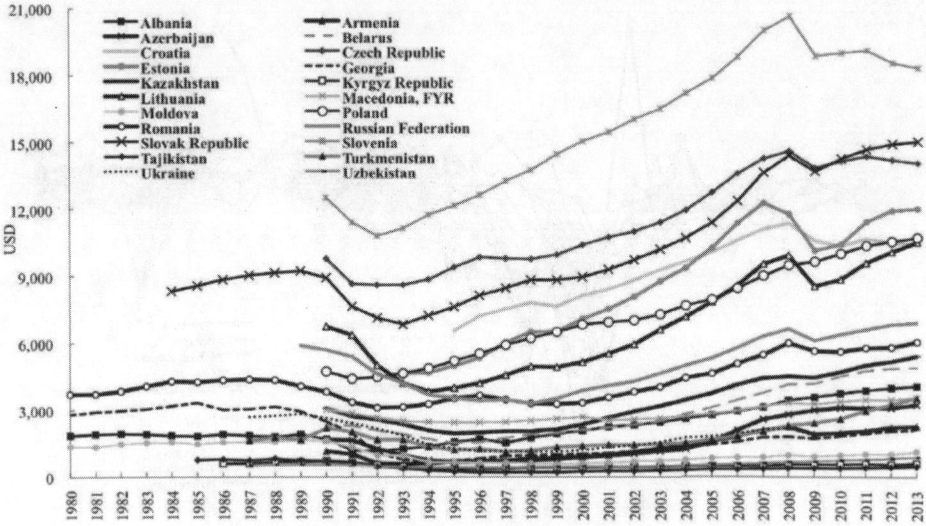

8. Reform without Losers—The Chinese Strategy for Economic Reform

We have identified two factors that contributed to Chinese economic success since 1978: favourable economic fundamentals and the prior existence of surplus potential output. But these factors were also common to other transition economies such as those of some of the former Soviet Union and the formerly socialist Eastern European countries. What part 7 above shows is that for a previously centrally-planned economy, even though there might have been good economic fundamentals and prior economic inefficiency (and hence surplus potential output), introduction of producer autonomy and the free market and opening to the world may not be sufficient to ensure a successful economic transition and a high rate of real economic growth. Only China was able to do so.

Why was the Chinese economic reform and opening to the world so successful? Why was China able to achieve a smooth and successful transition from a closed centrally-planned economy to an open market economy while some of the other countries attempting similar transitions failed so miserably? It turns out that the choice of strategy for the economic transition matters. In the former Soviet Union and the formerly socialist Eastern European countries, the strategy adopted for the transition was the so-called "shock therapy" or "big bang" strategy—that is, a strategy that calls for the immediate and full abolition of the mandatory central plan, relying completely and solely on the newly introduced and still relatively primitive free markets, which lacked the necessary facilitating and supporting institutions. In China, instead of dismantling the mandatory central plan all at once, the Chinese government adopted the "Dual-Track" approach: introducing "conditional" autonomy and free markets in goods and services on the margin while continuing to enforce the existing central plan. "Conditional" autonomy means that for a household, a village, a commune, a township, or an enterprise, as long as it has already fulfilled its assigned obligations under the mandatory central plan, it is free to engage in any other economic activity and sell the resulting goods and services produced on the free markets at market-determined prices if it wishes to do so.

There were therefore in the Chinese economy simultaneously a "Plan Track" and a "Market Track," which operated in parallel but separately from each other. As everyone—a commune, a township, a village, an enterprise, a household or even an individual—had the option of staying with the pre-reform arrangements under the mandatory central plan, with identical rights and obligations as before (both prices and quantities), no one would be worse off under the "Dual-Track" approach. Thus, there could not be any "losers"; in addition, everyone had the opportunity to "win." All the "vested interests" were "grandfathered," as they did not have to suffer any losses. This "Dual-Track" approach as implemented in China can be shown to be not only Pareto-improving, that is, making everyone better off (hence creating no losers), but also would enable the economy to achieve full economic efficiency.[7]

All economic reforms are supposed to generate a net increase in aggregate social welfare, if not in real GDP, of the entire economy. Economic reform requires government leadership; it cannot occur autonomously, otherwise it would have occurred on its own already. However, most economic reforms

---

7 See Lau, Qian, and Roland (2000).

create both winners and losers in the economy. While it is true that in the aggregate, the gains from economic reform should outweigh the losses, it is often difficult, if not impossible, to redistribute the gains so that no one is worse off. And the redistribution, if any, has to be implemented by a government with the authority, the power and the will.

The key to the success of the "Dual-Track" approach is that the production targets in the mandatory central plan are entirely fixed and must be fulfilled at the fixed plan prices before autonomy and participation in the free markets are allowed. Thus, profits and losses (taxes and subsidies) of enterprises under the central plan remain the same before and after the introduction of the "Dual-Track" approach. Differences between plan and free market prices of plan-assigned inputs and consumption goods constitute feasible lumpsum transfers among enterprises and households. The government, by continuing to enforce the plan, ensures that this de facto redistribution built into the plan continues to take place. Thus, the continued planned consumer goods deliveries enable the maintenance of the pre-reform standard of living for all people as a floor. Since no one has to lose and everyone can win, opposition to the economic reform is minimised, support for the reform is maximised, and social stability is preserved. Such a win-win strategy for economic reform has the best chance of success.

As a result of the "Dual-Track" approach, the Chinese economic reform proceeded smoothly and did not result in economic chaos or contraction as in the former Soviet Union and the formerly socialist Eastern European countries. The Chinese economy was able to continue to grow rapidly in the midst of its transition from a closed centrally-planned economy to an open market economy. Ultimately, in the late 1990s, the centrally-planned part of the Chinese economy, which had been contracting relative to the market part of the economy, became sufficiently insignificant so that the mandatory features of the central plan could be gradually phased out. The transition to an open market economy in goods and services (but not yet in factors) was thus completed.[8]

The feasibility of the dual-track approach depended critically on the continued enforcement of the rights and obligations under the existing central

8 See also the discussion in Naughton (1995) and Naughton (2007).

plan, which in turn depended on whether the central government had sufficient authority, credibility, power and will to do so. Credibility of state enforcement, and expectations thereof, affect the behaviour of enterprises and households, and hence their degree of compliance with the central plan (post-reform). The governments of the former Soviet Union and the formerly socialist Eastern European countries all became relatively weak around 1989, and did not really possess the ability to continue to enforce the pre-existing central plans. And after the former Soviet Union evolved into the Commonwealth of Independent States, what used to be domestic trade became international trade overnight, which became even more difficult for the successor governments to control and operate. It was therefore almost impossible for these countries to avoid the creation of losers.

The Chinese government, in the implementation of its economic reform, tried to minimise as much as possible the creation of losers and the impact of the reform on the existing economic system and the vested interests. At the same time, it also tried to allow new value and new winners to be created on the margin. Examples of reform measures that preserve pre-existing vested interests include the introduction of the "household responsibility system" in agriculture, the township and village enterprises in the rural areas, the special economic zones, the "processing and assembly" trade, the reforms of the foreign exchange system and the national taxation system. Related to the principle of "reform without losers" is the idea of treating existing people and new people differently even though they may be in identical situations. "New people, new way; old people, old way"[9] is the Chinese contribution to the method of implementing new economic reform. It embodies the idea of "grandfathering"—whatever rights and privileges (and obligations) a person had before the reform, he or she would have the option of retaining the same afterwards and thus would not have to lose anything. In a way, the two-tiered wage structure used in some enterprises and industries (e.g., the airline industry) in developed market economies also reflects the same underlying considerations—"grandfathering" minimises opposition to any reform by vested interests.

---

9 In Chinese, *xinren xinbanfa, jiuren jiubanfa* (新人新辦法，舊人舊辦法).

9. The Monopsonistic Labour Market in China

Before the economic reform of 1978, the Chinese government was the sole employer for workers in China and could set the wage rates for all workers in the urban areas. As the sole employer, the Chinese government exercised its monopsonistic power and pursued a low-wage policy, resulting in a low share of labour in GDP. The low-wage policy was designed to increase national savings so that the needed investments could be financed. The objective of the low-wage policy was similar to the "price scissors" policy of maintaining a large gap between industrial prices and agricultural prices adopted by the former Soviet Union.

Even after the economic reform of 1978, the Chinese central government, together with all the local governments, its affiliated units, and the state-owned enterprises, has remained the largest employer in China and continued to exercise its monopsonistic power to keep the wage rates low. Even in 2010, Chinese private employers still accounted for less than half of the total Chinese employment of workers. The low wage rate paid by the largest employer have kept the wage rates paid by the other employers low (see Chart 5.30).

This low-wage policy has had two effects: First, it has kept both the labour share (and the household share) of GDP low; and secondly, it has created large profits for state-owned as well as private enterprises. The low household share of GDP has in turn resulted in a lower Chinese household consumption to GDP ratio, currently around 40%, than in most other economies with a comparable real GDP per capita, because the Chinese households have less disposable income to spend. The saving rate of Chinese households out of their disposable income may be estimated at approximately 30%, comparable to ethnic Chinese households in the economies of Hong Kong and Taiwan. The large profits of the enterprises, both state-owned and private, have resulted in a higher national saving rate in China than in most other economies, because the enterprises, especially the state-owned enterprises, declare little cash dividends and save and re-invest almost 100% of their profits. It has been recently reported that the wages and salaries of civil servants will be raised by almost 60%. This is great news. It will not only lead to a significant increase in the consumption of their households but also to a general increase in wages and salaries across the board.

Chart 5.30. The Share of Public Sector Employment in Total Non-Agricultural Employment in China

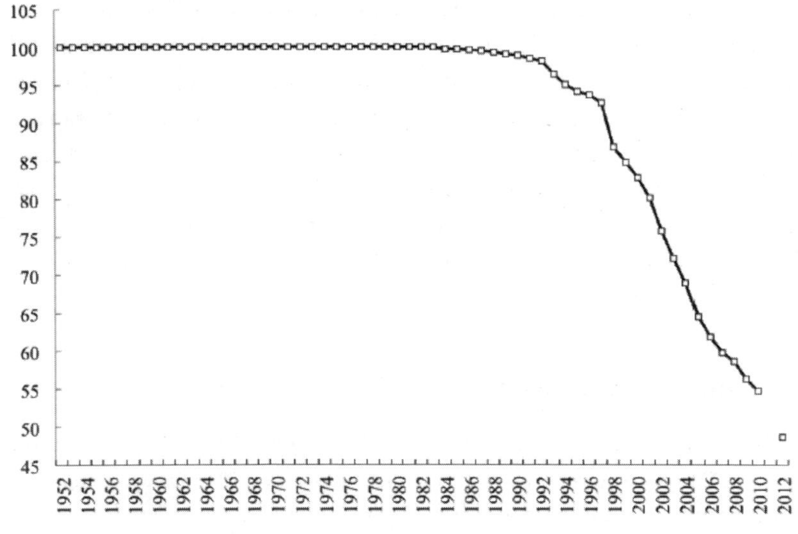

10. The "Wild Geese Flying Pattern"—The Further Advantage of China's Size

Prof. Kaname Akamatsu was the first to introduce the metaphor of the "wild-geese-flying pattern" of East Asian economic development, which suggests that industrialisation will spread from economy to economy within East Asia as the initially fast-growing economies, beginning with Japan, run out of surplus labour and face labour shortages, rising real wage rates, and quota restrictions on their exports, and need to relocate some of their industries to lower-cost economies. The fastest-growing economy will thus slow down, and a lower-cost economy will take over as the fastest-growing economy.

Thus, East Asian industrialisation spread from Japan to first Hong Kong in the mid-1950s, Taiwan in the late 1950s, South Korea and Singapore in the mid-1960s, Southeast Asia (Thailand, Malaysia, Indonesia) in the 1970s, and then to Guangdong, Shanghai, Jiangsu, and Zhejiang in China, as China undertook economic reform and opened to the world beginning in 1978. During this industrial migration, the large trading firms such as Mitsubishi, Mitsui, Marubeni and Sumitomo of Japan and Li and Fung of Hong Kong played an important role as financiers, intermediaries, quality assurers, and managers of logistics and supply chains.

However, this metaphor actually applies not only to East Asia but also to China itself because of its large size. Within China, industrialisation first started in the coastal regions and then would migrate and spread to other regions in the interior—to Chongqing, Henan, Hunan, Jiangxi, Shaanxi and Sichuan—as real wage rates rose on the coast. As the coastal regions began to slow down in their economic growth, the regions in the central and western regions of China would take their turns as the fastest growing regions in China. China as a whole will therefore be able to maintain a relatively high rate of growth for many more years to come.

11. China as a Surplus Economy

With a high domestic investment rate of over 40% of its GDP, China in the early 2000s has begun to evolve into not only a surplus labour economy but also a surplus capital economy. The high domestic investment rate, enabled by a high national saving rate, has resulted in massively excess manufacturing capacities almost everywhere—in coal, steel, cement, glass, ship-building, aluminium, solar panels, etc. The average capacity utilisation rate in many manufacturing industries is around 70%. Given the excess manufacturing capacities, Chinese real GDP going forward is actually not supply-constrained but aggregate demand-determined. As long as there is aggregate demand, there will be sufficient supply forthcoming to meet the demand. However, the growth of exports and fixed investment in manufacturing and residential housing can no longer be the principal drivers of the growth of Chinese aggregate demand.

How did the surplus economy come about? It came about because of massively excess fixed investment in manufacturing and in residential housing. Fixed investment in manufacturing was undertaken by both state-owned and private enterprises without regard to its potential rate of return, often supported by local government officials eager to increase local real GDP and employment. Fixed investment in residential housing was undertaken by developers at the local level, often also with the support of local governments.

Since the performance of Chinese local government officials are judged by key performance indicators, which include the growth of the local GDP and employment, they have a strong incentive to do whatever is possible during their term of office to increase both. Beginning in the early 2000s, the local government officials began to realise that they could make use of the land under their control to finance the development of local manufacturing industries, such as steel, cement and glass as well as residential housing. In order to protect the local manufacturing industries that were established with their support, the local governments imposed, illegally, effective bans on the use of competitive manufactured products of non-local origin within their respective jurisdictions. Moreover, since a local government official is usually promoted to a different locality at the end of his or her term, he or she is not too concerned with the longer-term viability of these fixed investments in manufacturing, leaving them for the successor to deal with. Private enterprises also participated in making fixed investment in manufacturing and in residential real estate development, either with the support of local government officials or with loans made possible by a loose credit culture. Furthermore, many residential real estate developments are financed by pre-sales of units yet to be constructed rather than by construction loans from commercial banks.

Thus, as long as there is growth in Chinese aggregate demand, the Chinese economy should be able to continue to grow at an average annual rate of between 6.5% and 7% for the next five to ten years, more or less independently of what happens in the rest of the world. The growth of Chinese aggregate demand will come principally from domestic demand, consisting of public infrastructural investment, public goods consumption, and household consumption. Public infrastructural investment will consist of high-speed railroads, urban mass-transit systems (China and the world cannot afford "a car in every garage"); facilities for the support of universal free or low-cost internet access in urban areas; and affordable housing through urban slum clearance and renewal. Other public infrastructural projects can include the construction of sea water desalination plants as an alternative source of fresh water supply in the coastal areas in northern China and storage facilities for a national strategic petroleum reserve. Continually rising urbanisation can not only increase the demand for public infrastructure and housing, but also promote the growth of the service sector, on both the supply and the demand sides. Public goods consumption (including the necessary related investments) can consist of education, health care, care for the elderly, and environment control, preservation and restoration—securing cleaner air, water and soil. Household consumption, especially from the fast expanding and rising middle class, has actually been growing quite rapidly since the first quarter of 2009. The rates of growth of real retail sales have been running at approximately one and a half times the rates of growth of real GDP. However, it will be a long time before Chinese household consumption can become the principal driver of Chinese economic growth. The share of disposable household income in Chinese GDP was approximately 43% in 2014. Even if the household saving rate declines to zero, household consumption cannot possibly exceed 50% of GDP, compared to between 65% and 70% for developed economies.

Both public infrastructural investment and public goods consumption require the leadership and support of the central and local governments. While expenditures on public goods consumption, including the necessary related investments, will count as GDP, much of the benefits of these expenditures may not be pecuniary—for example, cleaner air, water and soil, better education, and better national health—and may not be fully reflected in the conventional measurement of GDP. However, the increase in general social welfare as a result of these expenditures is definitely real. Moreover, increasing public goods consumption is an effective method of redistribution in kind. For example, since everyone breathes the same air, if the air is cleaner, both the wealthy and the poor benefit equally; and better access to health care may benefit the lower-income households more. Expansion of public goods consumption can thus also reduce the real income disparity.

In order to reduce the further growth of excess manufacturing capacity, one must reduce the moral hazard in borrowing and hence in investing. Vigorous enforcement of loan collection and bankruptcy laws and prosecution of bribery and financial fraud will help to reduce moral hazard. However, a change in the set of "key performance indicators" for the local government officials may also be necessary, so that the production and supply of public consumption goods such as the environmental enhancement (air, water and soil quality), education, health care, elderly care, and long-term economic viability and sustainability are also taken into account, in addition to short-term growth in real GDP and employment.

12. The Importance of Expectations

Expectations of the future are important determinants of enterprise and household behaviour, which in turn determines whether an economy grows or stagnates. Expectations often have the ability to be "self-fulfilling". If everyone believes that the economy will do well and acts accordingly, by investing and consuming, the economy will indeed turn out to do well, and vice versa. The Chinese central government has the proven credibility to change expectations through its plans and actions.

In 1989, there was the June 4 incident, as a result of which economic growth ground to a virtual halt in the years that followed. However, in early 1992, Mr. Deng Xiaoping undertook his famous southern tour, urging people everywhere to take advantage of the opportunity to invest, which changed expectations in the entire country overnight. Enterprises started investing and households started consuming. As a result, 1992, 1993 and 1994 were boom years. In 1997, at the height of the East Asian currency crisis, Premier Zhu Rongji held the renminbi/US$ exchange rate steady amidst the external chaos, and thus managed to maintain the confidence of the investors and consumers about China's economic future, and succeeded in keeping the economy growing. In 2008, after the collapse of the Lehman Brothers, the export orders received by Chinese enterprises declined by 50% overnight, because of the frozen banking sector in the U.S. and other developed economies, creating widespread panic. Barely six weeks later, Premier Wen Jiabao launched the four trillion yuan economic stimulus program, which once again helped to hold the confidence of Chinese enterprises and households in their economic future and changed their expectations. The Chinese economy has continued growing since.

In all of these cases, the Chinese government was able to turn around the very negative expectations about the future of the Chinese economy into positive ones, and in so doing greatly reduced the uncertainty pertaining to the future and increased general business confidence. These changes, in turn, fueled investment booms that resulted in the subsequent economic growth. Expectations will continue to play an important role in the Chinese economy. A strong central government with the power to mobilise aggregate demand can credibly change expectations in a positive direction to keep the economy growing.

13. The On-Going Economic Challenges

Despite its record of great success during the past 37 years, the Chinese economy still faces many significant on-going challenges: the rapidly aging population, corruption, rising income disparity, environmental degradation, excess manufacturing capacity, excess supply of residential real estate, shadow banking, local government debt, the deficit in human capital and the innovation gap, to name only a few. However, a hard landing of the Chinese economy seems unlikely. The principal challenge facing the Chinese economic policy makers is not so much the growth of real GDP but employment. In 2013, 13 million new jobs were created. In 2014, 10 million new jobs were created. The employment target is achievable because the service sector (50.5% by GDP and 43.4% by employment) is now larger and growing faster than the manufacturing sector (40.5% by GDP and 29.3% by employment). An expansion of the service-sector GDP creates 30% more employment than an expansion of the manufacturing-sector GDP by the same amount and requires much less fixed investment. Space does not allow a discussion of all of the economic challenges. We shall focus here on the two challenges that have the most significant implications for long-term economic growth: the deficit in human capital and the innovation gap.

First, we examine the Chinese deficit in human capital relative to other economies. One indicator of the level of human capital in an economy is the average number of years of schooling per person in the working-age population. In Chart 5.31, the average number of years of schooling of the working-age population is compared across selected economies. By this measure, the United States and Japan are clearly the global leaders. South Korea has been catching up fast. Most of the other East Asian economies also have quite rapidly increasing levels of human capital, but it will take a while before they can catch up with the levels of human capital in the developed economies. China, Indonesia and Thailand have lagged behind in terms of human capital, but China has been expanding its tertiary education sector rapidly and can be expected to catch up to the levels of the developed economies by 2020 or so.

Second, we examine the innovation gap between China and the developed economies. Investment in R&D capital is important for promoting innovation (technical progress). China has also begun to invest more heavily in R&D in recent years: Its R&D expenditure has been rising rapidly, both in absolute value, and as a percentage of GDP; but it still lags behind the developed economies as well as the newly industrialised economies of East Asia. (The Chinese R&D expenditure/GDP ratio is targeted to reach 2.5% in 2020, equal to the historical average for the U.S.) The Republic of Korea currently leads the world with the percentage of its GDP expended on R&D exceeding 4%, followed by Japan, with an average ratio of 3% over the past quarter of a century (see Chart 5.32).[10]

One indicator of the potential for innovation, or national innovative capacity, is the number of patents created each year. In Chart 5.33, the number of patents granted in the United States each year to the nationals of different countries, including the U.S. itself, over time, is presented. The U.S. is the undisputed champion over the past 40 years, with 140,969 patents granted in 2015, followed by Japan, with 52,409. (Since these are patents granted in the U.S., the U.S. may have a home advantage; however, for all the other countries and regions, the comparison across them should be fair.) The number of patents granted to Chinese applicants in the United States each year has increased from the single-digit levels prior to the mid-1980s to 8,166 in 2015. The number of domestic patents granted to domestic applicants in China reached 263,436 in 2015, exceeding those of Japan (225,571 in 2013 and 146,749 in 2014). China aims to increase the stock of Chinese patents in force held by Chinese nationals from four per 10,000 inhabitants in 2013 to 14 per 10,000 inhabitants by 2020. However, it is not clear whether these patents are all comparable in quality to those approved in the U.S.

The stock of R&D capital may be defined as the cumulative past real expenditure on R&D less depreciation of 10% per year. It should quite properly be treated as capital since R&D efforts generally take years to yield any results. Since China has had both a much lower R&D expenditure to GDP ratio and a much lower GDP than the United States and other developed economies in the past, it will take more than a couple of decades before the Chinese R&D capital stock can catch up to the level of U.S. R&D capital stock. In 2013, Chinese R&D capital stock was only US$727 billion (in 2013 prices) compared to the United States' US$3.7 trillion. On per capita terms, China would be even further behind.

The stock of R&D capital can be shown to have a direct causal relationship to the number of patents granted. (See Chart 5.34, in which the annual number of U.S. patents granted is plotted against the R&D capital stock of that year for each economy). Chart 5.34 shows clearly that the higher the stock of

---

10 The discussion on R&D is based on Lau and Xiong (2015) as well as their unpublished research.

R&D capital of an economy, the higher the number of patents granted to it by the U.S. It will take at least a couple of decades before the level of Chinese R&D capital stock can catch up to that of the U.S. and hence to the number of U.S. patents granted each year.

However, successful innovation also depends on the existence of competition and free entry to markets. Monopolies are generally not very good in innovation and not very good in making full use of their own discoveries and inventions. China must create and maintain a competitive market environment with free entry and exit so as to encourage innovation in addition to investing in human capital and R&D capital. Moreover, in order to encourage innovation, China also needs to protect intellectual property rights vigorously, a direction in which it has been moving.

Chart 5.31. Average Number of Years of Schooling of the Working-Age Population, Selected Economies (1948–2010)

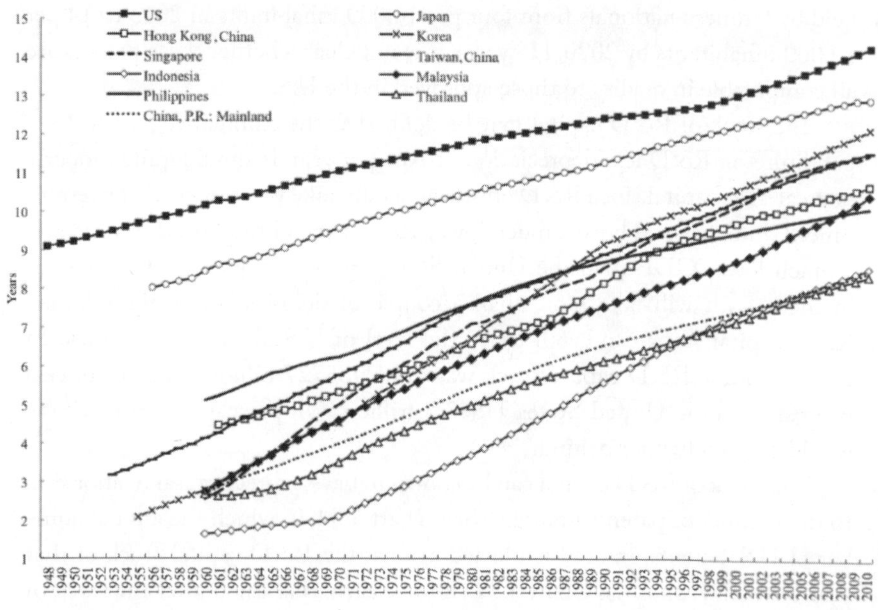

Chart 5.32. R&D Expenditures as a Ratio of GDP: G-7 Countries, 4 East Asian NIES & China

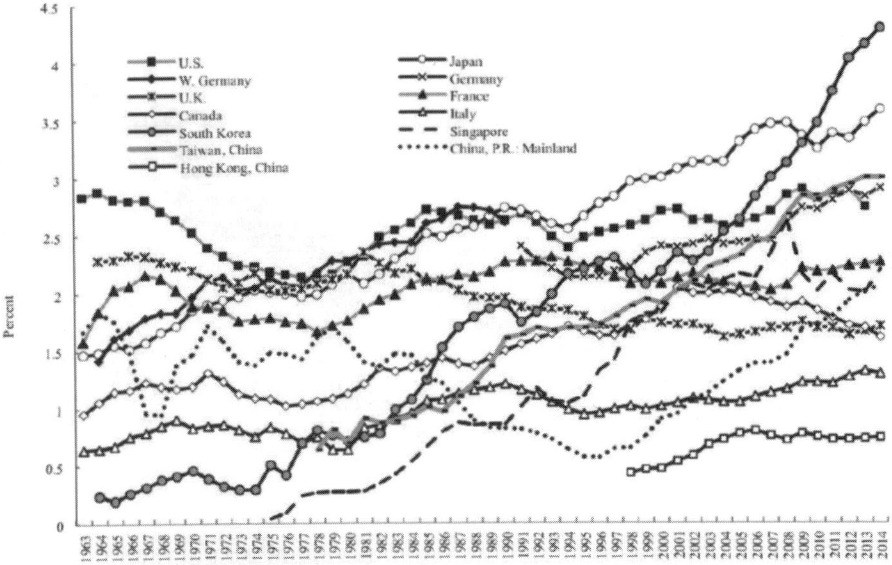

Chart 5.33. Patents Granted in the U.S.: G-7 Countries, 4 East Asian NIEs & China

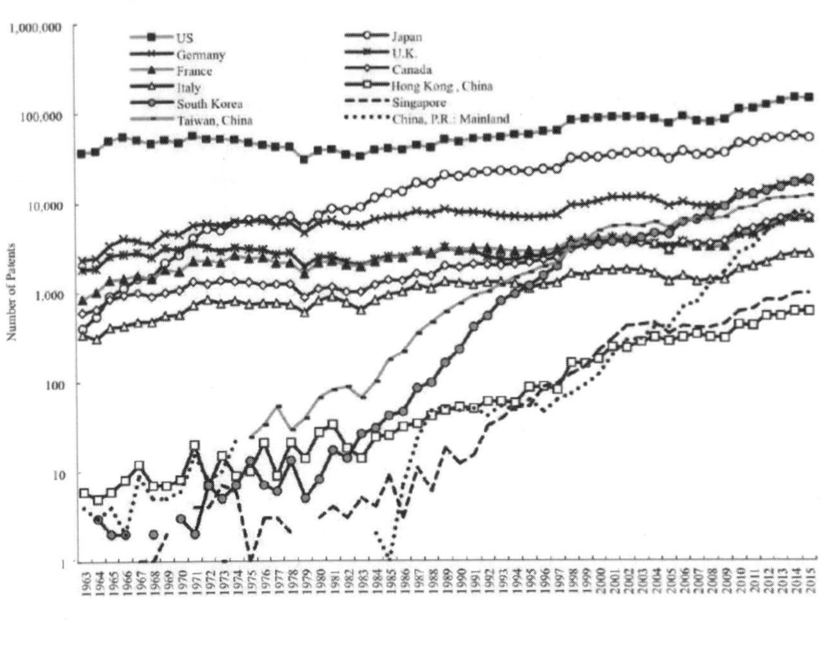

Chart 5.34. Patents Granted in the U.S. and R&D Capital Stocks, Selected Economies

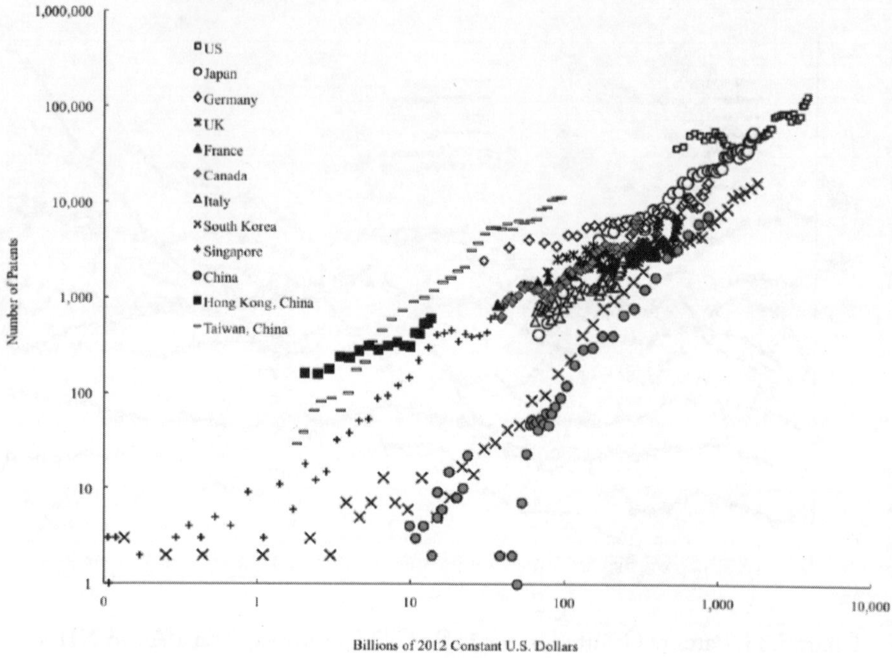

14. The Long-Term Economic Outlook

Going forward, will the Chinese economy continue to grow at close to 10% per annum in the future? The short answer is no, for many reasons. The target rate of growth under the "New Normal" is between 6.5% and 7% per annum. However, it is important to realise that because the Chinese economy is now much bigger—a 7% rate of growth today will generate an absolute increase in real GDP equivalent to what a 14% rate of growth would have done 10 years ago. On the supply side, the Chinese economy will still have strong economic fundamentals—a high domestic saving rate, abundant labour, and a huge domestic market that enables the realisation of economies of scale—for a couple of decades. Moreover, advances in the information and communication technology have enhanced the positive effects of economies of scale even further. On the demand side, Chinese economic growth will be driven by the growth of its own internal demand, consisting of public infrastructural investment, public goods consumption as well as household consumption, rather than the growth of exports, or fixed investment in the manufacturing sector, or high-priced residential real estate.

In the medium term, say three to five years from now, economic stimulus is unlikely to be inflationary because of the excess manufacturing capacities already in place, especially if the economic stimulus is carefully targeted. In the longer term, there is still a great deal of room for Chinese GDP to grow. There is still significant surplus labour. Both the tangible capital and the intangible capital per unit labour in China are still relatively low compared to the developed economies. Moreover, there is substantial scope for improvement in human capital and R&D capital. China has also been gradually changing from its role as the world's factory to the world's new growth market. It is already the world's largest exporting country and is on its way to becoming the largest importing country in goods and services combined in a couple of years.

It is projected that the Chinese and the U.S. economies will grow at average annual real rates of approximately 6.6% and 3.0% respectively between 2015 and 2030 (see Chart 5.35). Chinese real GDP is thus projected to catch up to U.S. real GDP in approximately 15 years' time, around 2030, at which time both Chinese and U.S. real GDP will be around US$28 trillion (in 2015 prices). This is almost three times the Chinese GDP and approximately one and a half times the U.S. GDP in 2015. By then, China and the U.S. will

Chart 5.35. Actual and Projected Chinese and U.S. Real GDPs and Their Rates of Growth

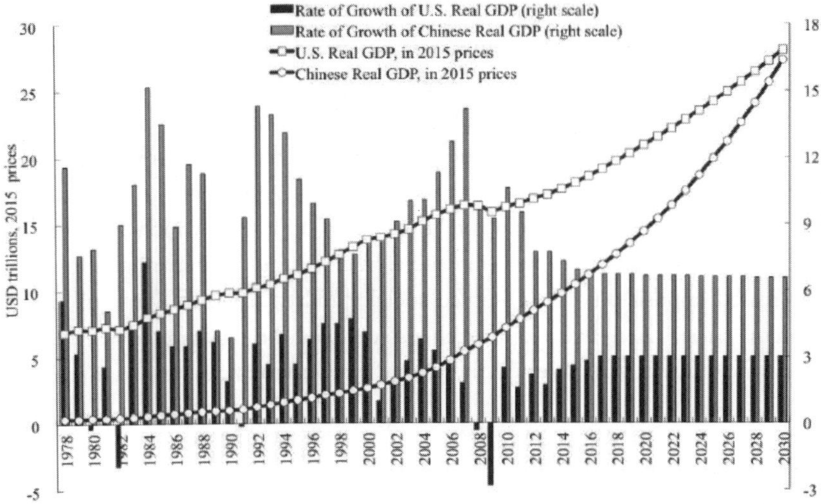

each account for approximately 15% of world GDP. One may consider that the projected rates of economic growth for China and the U.S. may be a little on the optimistic side. However, the year in which the two GDPs become approximately the same will not be too far off.

By 2030, the Chinese real GDP per capita is projected to reach 19,000 (in 2015 prices), which would still be less than a quarter of the projected then U.S. real GDP per capita of US$77,000. It will take around 40 years from now, till 2060, for China to catch up to the United States in terms of real GDP per capita. By that time, Chinese GDP is likely to be more than three times the U.S. GDP, and will account for perhaps 30% of world GDP (depending on the rates of growth of other economies, especially the developing economies of today), the same percentage of world GDP that China had in the early 19th century, according to an estimate made by Prof. Angus Maddison.

15. Concluding Remarks

The highly successful experience of Chinese economic growth over the past 37 years (as well as those of other East Asian economies) strongly reaffirm the fundamental importance of having and maintaining a high investment rate, enabled by a high national savings rate, and surplus labour. In addition, the size of the Chinese domestic economy is a favourable factor allowing the ready realisation of economies of scale and reducing vulnerability to external disturbances. However, these favourable factors alone were not sufficient, as the Chinese economy did not experience sustained economic growth between 1949 and 1978.

Economic reform and opening to the world in 1978 allowed the realisation of the surplus potential output, helped to enhance and assure the efficiency of the Chinese economy and facilitated technology transfer from abroad. It is the unique achievement of China that in its transition from a closed centrally-planned economy to an open market economy, it was able to use a “Dual-Track” rather than the “Big-Bang” approach, which ensured the success of reform without creating losers. Such a strategy maximised support, minimised opposition and preserved social stability. It led to win-win for all. Moreover, the “Dual-Track” approach also enabled the economy to achieve full economic efficiency. As a result, the Chinese economic transition was smooth, stable, successful and sustainable.

Chinese economic growth during the past 37 years can also be attributed to the growth of tangible inputs—tangible capital and labour, and in particular, tangible capital—rather than the growth in intangible capital or technical progress, just as the past economic growth of other East Asian economies at a similar stage of economic development. The speed of Chinese economic growth can be sustained longer than in other East Asian economies principally because of the size of the Chinese economy and its surplus labour and more recently its surplus capital.

Continuing economic growth going forward will depend mostly on the growth of internal demand (infrastructural investment, public goods consumption and household consumption), not on exports and not on fixed investment in manufacturing capacity in the existing industries or residential real estate. China is a large continental country like the United States and will similarly develop into a largely internal demand driven economy. International trade and international investment will not have a decisive impact on the Chinese economy in the future. Eventually, Chinese exports as a percentage of its GDP should be relatively low, in the teens. Chinese economic growth will be marginally, but not critically, affected by a large decline in its exports, as demonstrated by its experience in the past several years as well as during the 1997–1998 East Asian currency crisis. Thus, it will be able to survive even prolonged economic recessions or stagnation in the European and U.S. economies.

Given the huge excess capacities in the Chinese manufacturing industries, in the time frame of the next five to ten years, Chinese real GDP, as mentioned above, will not be supply-constrained but will be primarily determined by aggregate demand. China should have no problem achieving a rate of real economic growth of between 6.5% and 7%. Thus, the goal of doubling real GDP per capita by 2020, declared in 2013, should be readily achievable. The "New Normal" is neither a "boom" of close to double-digit rates of growth, nor a "bust" of negative or low single-digit real rates of growth. There will be both sufficient supply and demand in the Chinese economy to support continuing growth.

Beyond that, on the basis of its strong economic fundamentals, China should also be able to continue to grow at about the same average annual rate for the following decade, more or less independently of what happens in the rest of the world. In the longer run, Chinese economic growth will make a transition from being driven by the growth in tangible inputs to the growth in intangible inputs and innovation.

Is the Chinese economy a miracle or a bubble? A bubble is a transitory and unsustainable phenomenon that is ready to self-destruct any time. But the Chinese economy has been growing at a sustained high real rate of almost 10% per annum for the past 37 years and is expected to continue to grow between 6.5% and 7% per annum for another couple of decades. It cannot therefore possibly be a bubble. And the model of Chinese economic development has also been adopted and emulated, at least in part, by Vietnam, another economy in the process of transitioning from a centrally-planned to a market economic system, with some degree of success. It is also a model for other potential transition economies such as Cuba, Laos and North Korea. As the Chinese economic development experience can be replicated and reproduced elsewhere, it cannot be considered a miracle either. What is not replicable is its economies of scale. The only economy that has the potential of benefitting from economies of scale to the same degree as China is India.

References

Akamatsu, Kaname. "A Historical Pattern of Economic Growth in Developing Countries." *Journal of Developing Economies* 1, no. 1 (1962), pp. 3–25.

Beardson, T. *Stumbling Giant: The Threats to China's Future*. New Haven: Yale University Press, 2013.

Boskin, Michael J., and Lawrence J. Lau. "International and Intertemporal Comparison of Productive Efficiency: An Application of the Meta-Production Function Approach to the Group-of-Five (G-5) Countries." *Economic Studies Quarterly* 43, no. 4 (1992), pp. 298–312.

Denison, Edward F. *The Sources of Economic Growth in the United States and the Alternatives Before Us*. Committee for Economic Development, New York, 1961.

Jorgenson, D. W. "The Development of a Dual Economy. *The Economic Journal* 71, no. 282 (1961), pp. 309–334.

Kim, Jong-II, and Lawrence J. Lau. "The Sources of Economic Growth in the East Asian Newly Industrialized Countries." *Journal of the Japanese and International Economies* 8 (1994), pp. 235–71.

———. "The Role of Human Capital in the Economic Growth of the East Asian Newly Industrialised Countries." *Asia-Pacific Economic Review* 1, no. 3 (1995), pp. 3–22.

Krugman, Paul. "The Myth of Asia's Miracle." *Foreign Affairs* 73, no. 6, (1994), pp. 62–78.

Lau, Lawrence J., and J. S. Park. *Sources of East Asian Economic Growth Revisited.* Working Paper, Department of Economics, Stanford University, 2002.

———. *Sources of East Asian Economic Growth Revisited.* Working Paper, Department of Economics, The Chinese University of Hong Kong, 2007.

Lau, Lawrence J., and Y. Xiong. *Are There Laws of Innovation: Part I, Introduction.* Working Paper No. 39, The Institute of Global Economics and Finance, The Chinese University of Hong Kong, 2015.

Lau, Lawrence J., Y. Qian, and G. Roland. "Reform Without Losers: An Interpretation of China's Dual-Track Approach to Transition." *The Journal of Political Economy* 108, no. 1, (2000), pp. 120–143.

Lewis, W. A. "Economic Development with Unlimited Supplies of Labour." *Manchester School of Economic and Social Studies* 22 (1954), pp. 139–191.

Maddison, A. *The World Economy: Vol. 1: A Millennial Perspective and Vol. 2: Historical Statistics.* Paris: Development Centre of the Organization for Economic Co-operation and Development, 2006.

Naughton, Barry. *Growing Out of the Plan: Chinese Economic Reform, 1978–1993.* Cambridge: Cambridge University Press, 1995.

———. *The Chinese Economy: Transitions and Growth.* Cambridge: The MIT Press, 2007.

Perkins, D. H. *The Economic Transformation of China.* Singapore: World Scientific Publishing Company, 2015.

Tobin, J. *The New Economics One Decade Older.* Princeton, N. J.: Princeton University Press, 1974.

Chapter 6.

The Great Transformation—East*

1. Introduction

Today, East Asia as a whole accounts for close to 30% of world GDP. Angus Maddison (2006) estimated that China accounted for 30% of world GDP in the 18th century. In 1970, China accounted for approximately 3% of world GDP. In 2017, China accounted for approximately 15% of world GDP. Japan accounted for 18% of world GDP at its peak in the mid-1990s. China and India are the two fastest-growing large economies in the world today.

In the post-Second World War period, quite a few East Asian economies, beginning with Japan, reached developed status. They include the "newly industrialised economies" (NIEs) of Hong Kong, South Korea, Singapore, and Taiwan, also referred to as the "four little dragons." They were followed, in turn, by the other Association of Southeast Asian Nations (ASEAN) economies and by Mainland China,[1] which are still in the process of becoming developed. In the early 1950s, the Philippines was widely tipped to be the economy that was most likely to become developed. In fact, at the time, the Philippines had

---

* This chapter was originally published in *Financial and Economic Review: The Lamfalussy Lectures Conference Logbook 2018*, Vol. 17, No. 2, Budapest: Magyar Nemzeti Bank (Central Bank of Hungary). This is a revised version of a presentation made at the Lamfalussy Lectures Conference, Budapest, 12 February 2018. The author wishes to thank the Central Bank of Hungary for inviting him to the Conference and Mrs. Ayesha Macpherson Lau and Prof. Yanyan Xiong for their helpful comments and suggestions. All opinions expressed herein are the author's own and do not necessarily reflect the views of any of the organisations with which the author is affiliated.

1 In this paper, China and "Mainland China" are used interchangeably.

the highest GDP per capita in all of East Asia, higher than even that of Japan. Today, the Philippines still has the lowest GDP per capita among the five founding members of the ASEAN (the other four are Indonesia, Malaysia, Singapore, and Thailand).

The objective of this paper is to answer the question: How did the East grow rich? We begin by examining what successful East Asian economies have in common. All of these East Asian economies, beginning with Japan, adopted and implemented the economic development policy of export promotion. Export promotion turned out to be a successful policy for the then developing economies of East Asia because of the trade liberalisation around the world, beginning with the Kennedy Round (1964–1967) of trade negotiations under the General Agreement on Tariffs and Trade (GATT), the predecessor to the World Trade Organization (WTO).

Taiwan was one of the first, if not the very first, developing economies to explicitly adopt and implement the economic development policy of export promotion instead of import substitution. It proved to be highly successful in enhancing domestic savings and investment, attracting foreign direct investment, increasing employment, and stimulating economic development. Subsequently, these policies were also widely and successfully emulated by many other developing economies such as South Korea, the ASEAN, and Mainland China.

2. The Shifting Centre of Gravity of the Global Economy

In 1970, the United States and Western Europe together accounted for almost 60% of world GDP. By comparison, East Asia[2] accounted for only approximately 10% of world GDP. By 2016, the share of United States and Western Europe combined in world GDP has declined to approximately 41%, whereas the share of East Asia has risen to around 28%. The Japanese share of world GDP declined from a peak of almost 18% in the mid-1990s to 6.7% in 2016, while the Mainland Chinese share of world GDP rose from 3.1% in 1970 and less than 4% in 2000 to over 15.1% in 2016. See Charts 6.1 and 6.2.

---

2 Defined as the 10 ASEAN countries—Brunei, Cambodia, Indonesia, Laos, Malaysia, Myanmar, the Philippines, Singapore, Thailand, and Vietnam—plus three (China [including Hong Kong, Macau and Taiwan], Japan, and the Republic of Korea).

Chart 6.1. The Distribution of World GDP, 1970

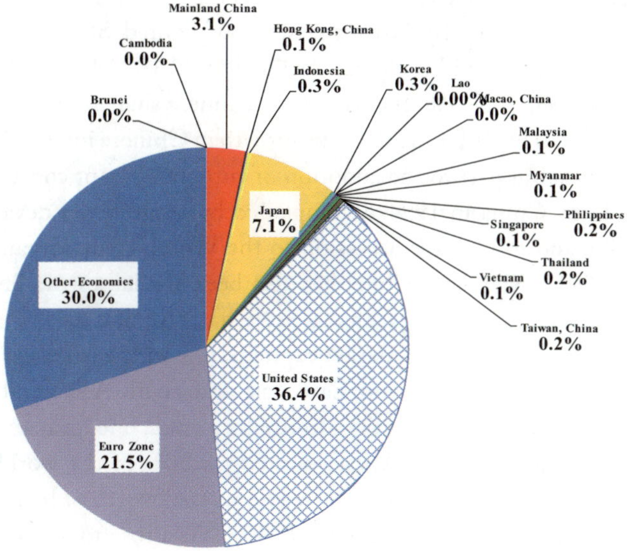

Chart 6.2. The Distribution of World GDP, 2016

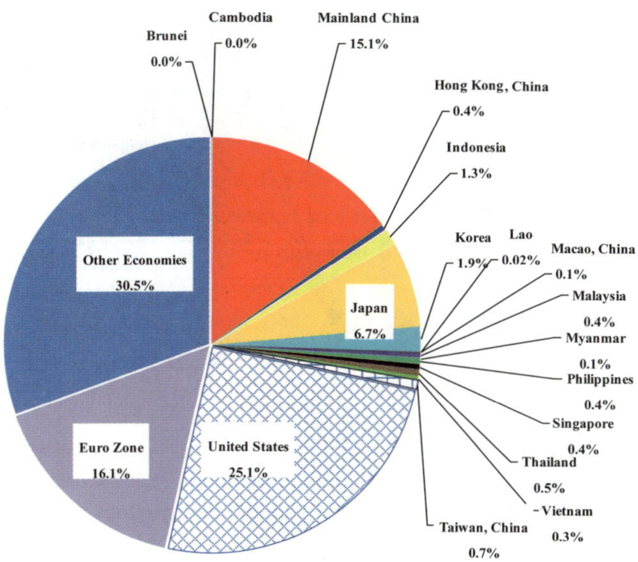

In 1970, the United States and Western Europe together accounted for 47% of world trade in goods and services. By comparison, East Asia accounted for 9.5% of world trade. By 2016, the share of United States and Western Europe combined in world trade has declined to 37.1%, whereas the share of East Asia has risen to 28.1%. The Mainland Chinese share of world trade rose from 0.6% in 1970 to 10.1% in 2016. The growth in Chinese international trade may be attributed in part to the adoption of current-account convertibility of the renminbi by China in 1994, accompanied by a significant devaluation of the renminbi, and to Chinese accession to the World Trade Organization in 2001. Since 2015, Mainland China has also been the largest trading partner country of the U.S., surpassing Canada. See Charts 6.3 and 6.4.

If we use the values of the market capitalisation of the stock exchanges of respectively the U.S., Europe, and East Asia and South Asia combined as a proxy for the values of their wealth (admittedly a crude one for many reasons), we can see that in 2001, the U.S. accounted for 50% of the world's wealth, Europe not quite 25% and Asia as a whole just above 10%. In 2016, while the U.S. still accounted for approximately 40%, Asia rose to almost 35% and Europe fell to less than 20%. See Chart 6.5.

Chart 6.3. The Distribution of International Trade in Goods and Services, 1970

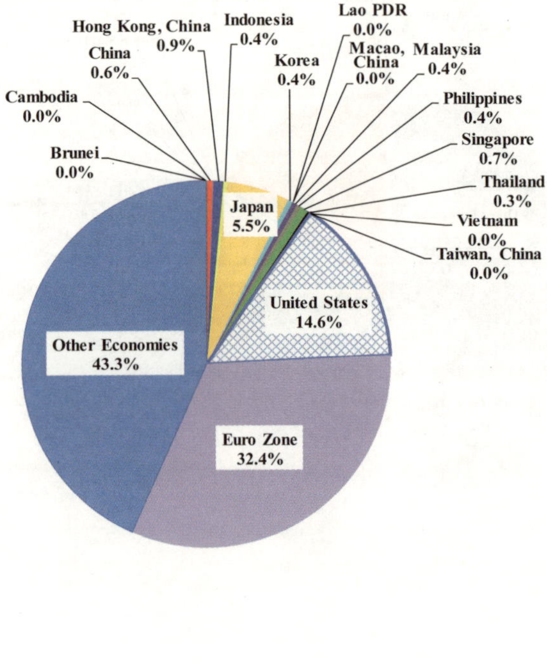

Chart 6.4. The Distribution of International Trade in Goods and Services, 2016

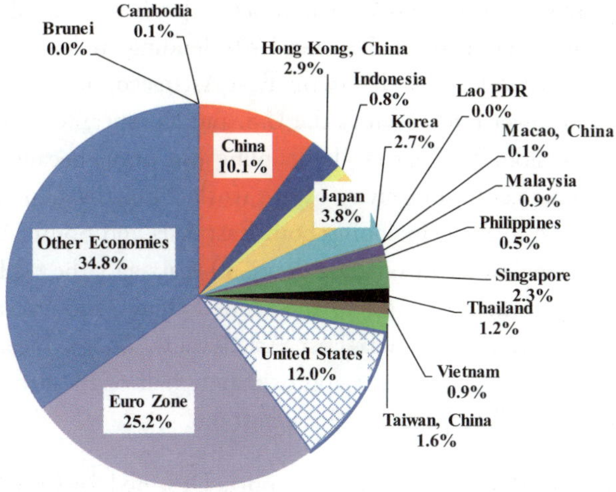

Chart 6.5. The Distribution of the Market Capitalisation of Stock Exchanges (%)

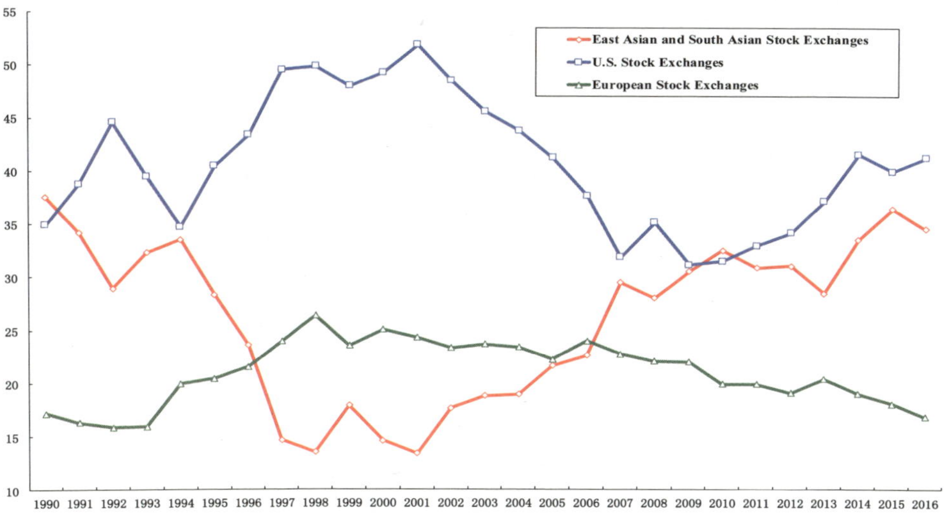

Throughout the 2007–2009 global financial crisis, as well as the subsequent European sovereign debt crisis, the East Asian economies continued to do reasonably well. Mainland China, in particular, has been able to maintain its real rate of growth above 6.5% since 2007, lending credence to the "Partial De-Coupling Hypothesis"—that is, the East Asian economies can continue to grow, albeit at lower rates, even as the U.S. and European economies go into economic recession. This partial de-coupling can occur because of the shift of the economic centre of gravity of the world from the United States and Western Europe to Asia (including both East Asia and South Asia) over the past four decades. In terms of trade flows, 30 years ago, the trade flows were predominantly from East Asia to the United States and Western Europe. There was relatively little intra-East Asian trade. Today, intra-East Asian exports and imports account for approximately half of the total exports and imports of East Asia respectively. See Chart 6.6.

Chart 6.6. The Share of East Asian Exports Destined for East Asia and the Share of East Asian Imports Originated from East Asia

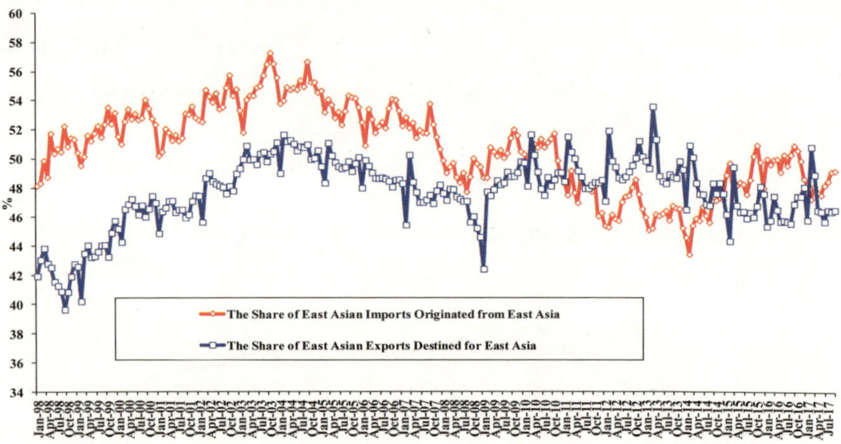

3. Economic Fundamentals

First, we consider the economic fundamentals of the East Asian economies. Most of them turn out to have a high domestic savings rate, abundant surplus labour, and significant cumulative investments in intangible capital such as human capital and research and development (R&D) capital.

Chart 6.7. The Savings Rates of Selected Economies and Groups of Economies

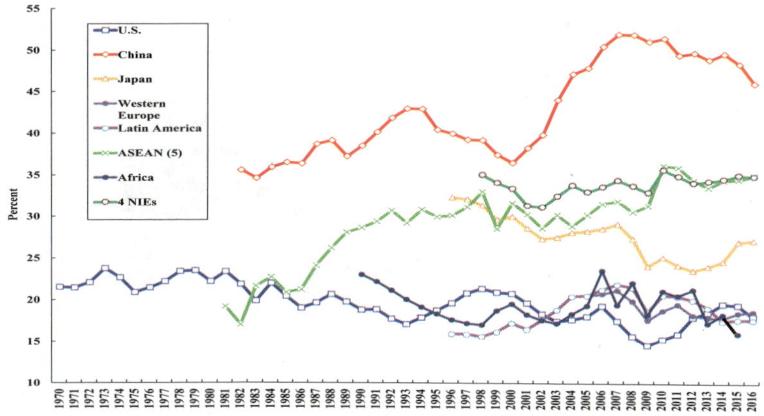

A High Domestic Savings Rate

The domestic savings rates of East Asian economies have been consistently high, with the possible exception of the Philippines. Chart 6.7 shows that the savings rates of China, Japan, the East Asian NIEs, and the ASEAN five are all significantly higher than those of not only African and Latin American economies, where the savings rates are typically low, but also those of the U S. and Western Europe (see Chart 6.7). A high domestic savings rate means that it is possible for the economy to maintain and sustain a high domestic investment rate without depending on the more fickle inflows of foreign aid, credits, loans, and direct and portfolio investment, enabling the tangible capital stock of the economy to grow consistently and continuously.

In Chart 6.8, the savings rates of each economy are plotted against its real GDP per capita. The savings rate of an East Asian economy typically started out low when its real GDP per capita was low and near the subsistence level. However, the savings rate rose quickly as real GDP per capita exceeded the subsistence threshold. It is, however, sometimes necessary for an economy to have a jump-start with an initial supply of savings to support the initial investment—from, for example, a good agricultural harvest, land reform, foreign aid, credit, or investment. The recent measured savings rates of Japan, Korea, Taiwan, and the U.S. may appear low because of the traditional statistical practice of expensing educational and R&D expenditures, which properly

Chart 6.8. The Relationship Between Savings Rate and Real GDP per Capita: East Asian Economies

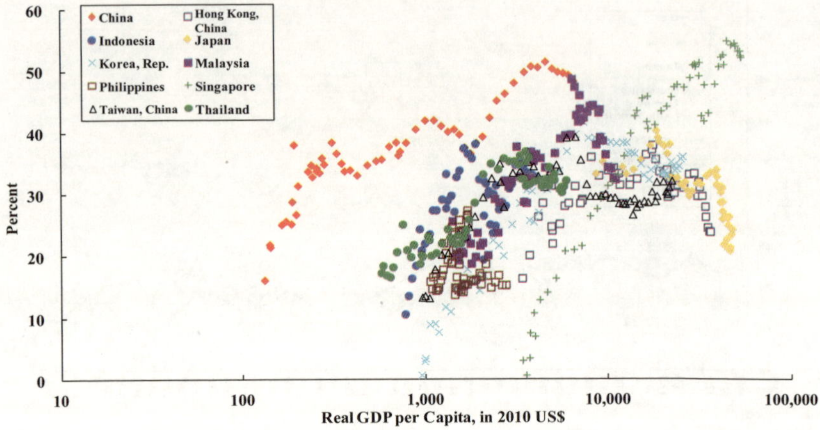

speaking should have been recognised as investment expenditures rather than current expenditures and appropriately accumulated as stocks of intangible capital such as human capital and R&D capital.

Abundant Surplus Labour

East Asian economies are also endowed with abundant surplus labour. Their economic development has proceeded along the lines of Prof. W. Arthur Lewis's celebrated model of surplus labour, first introduced in his 1954 article, "Economic Development with Unlimited Supplies of Labour." In almost every successfully developed East Asian economy, from Japan to Taiwan to South Korea to Mainland China and Southeast Asia, development began with the expanded employment of surplus labour from the agricultural sector in the non-agricultural sector, enabled by the continuing investment in tangible capital in the non-agricultural sector.[3] Initially, the bulk of the additional output is exported.

---

3 The city economies of Hong Kong and Singapore were different because they did not start with a large primary sector. However, even then, they had significant unemployed or underemployed labour.

During this surplus labour phase, tangible capital was accumulated in the non- agricultural sector, and surplus labour moved from the agricultural sector to the non-agricultural sector as complementary tangible capital became available in the non-agricultural sector. For such movement of labour to be sustainable, a relatively high domestic savings rate would be needed, both as a source of wage goods (food) and as a source of investable funds in the non-agricultural sector, unless they could be supplemented by imports and inflows of foreign capital. However, it is important to realise that the principal source of economic growth during this phase is not the surplus labour itself, but the accumulation of tangible capital in the non-agricultural sector, which made it possible for the surplus labour to move from the agricultural to the non-agricultural sector to be productively employed.

In the following series of charts (Charts 6.9–6.16), we show the changes in the distributions of GDP and employment by the three production sectors, primary (which includes agriculture and mining), secondary (which includes manufacturing), and tertiary (which includes services), over time in Japan, Taiwan, South Korea, and Mainland China. All of them started out with the primary sector accounting for the largest share of employment. With the growth of the economy and the secondary and tertiary sectors, the primary sector became progressively the sector accounting for first the smallest share of GDP and then the smallest share of employment.

Chart 6.9. The Distribution of Japanese GDP by Sector since 1970

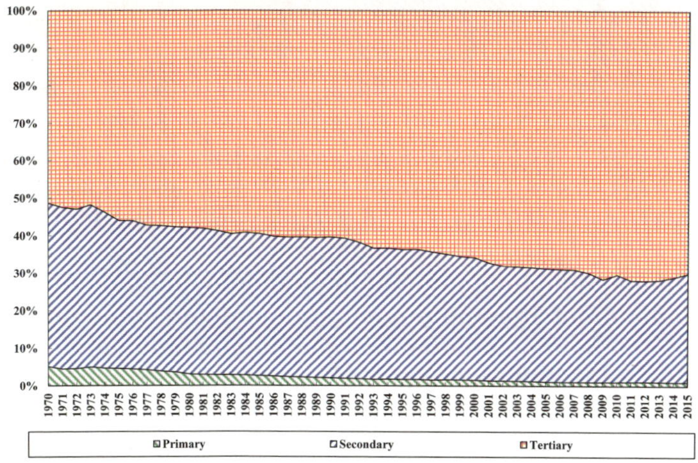

Chart 6.10. The Distribution of Japanese Employment by Sector since 1953

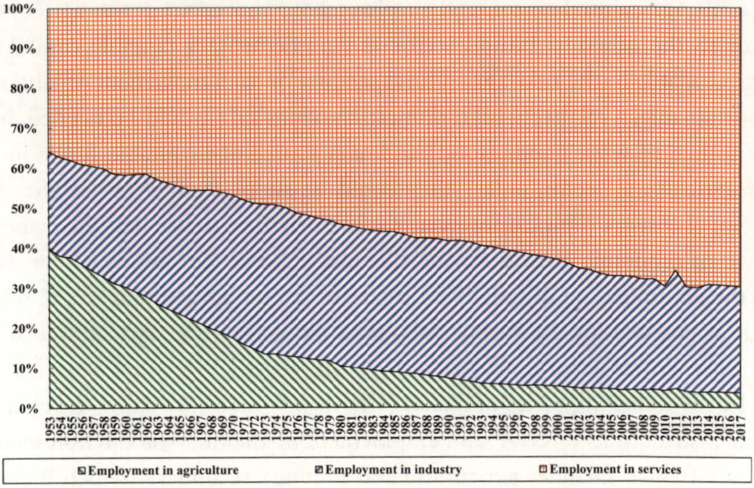

Chart 6.11. The Distribution of Taiwan GDP by Sector since 1951

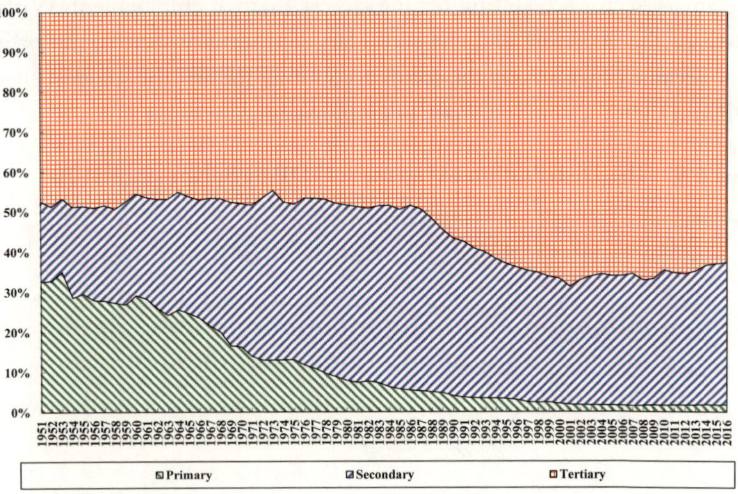

Chart 6.12. The Distribution of Taiwan Employment by Sector since 1951

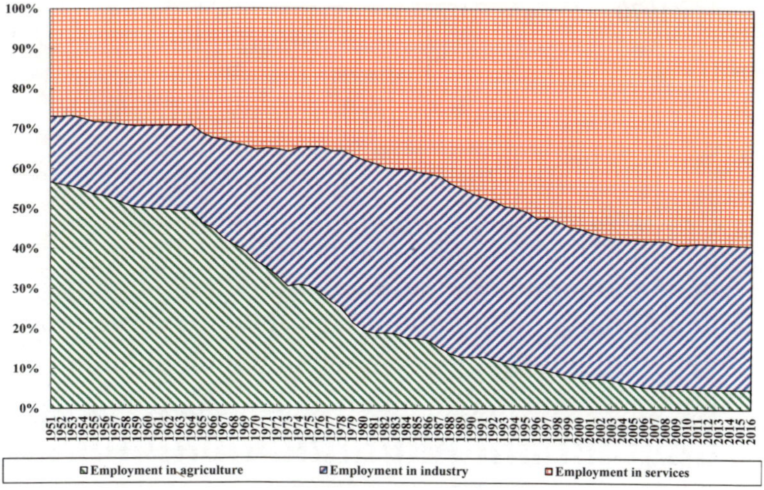

Chart 6.13. The Distribution of South Korean GDP by Sector since 1965

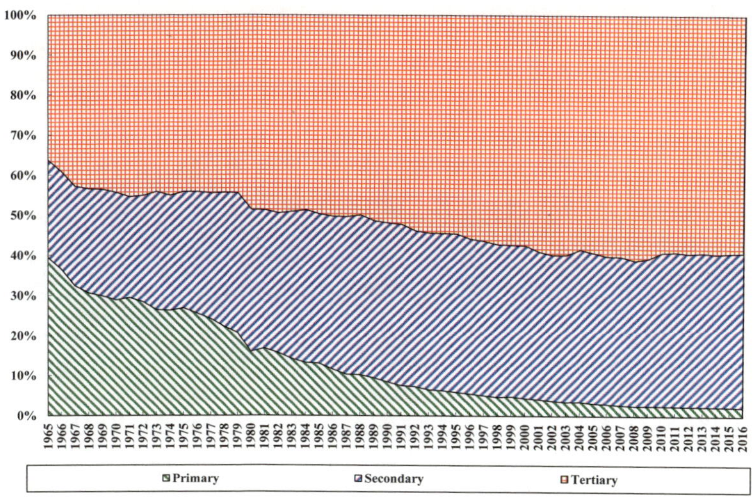

Chart 6.14. The Distribution of South Korean Employment by Sector since 1970

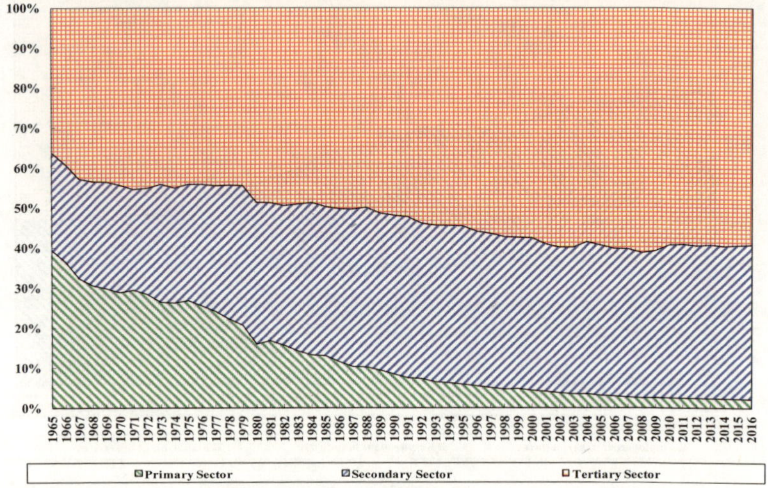

Chart 6.15. The Distribution of Chinese GDP by Sector since 1952

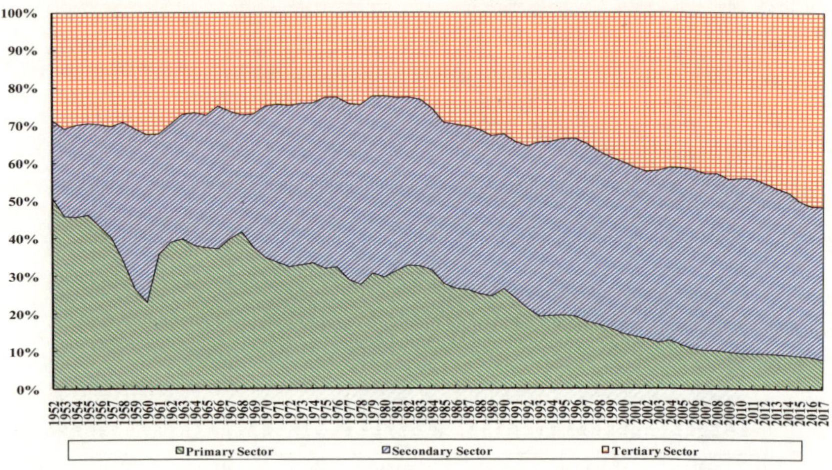

Chart 6.16. The Distribution of Chinese Employment by Sector since 1952

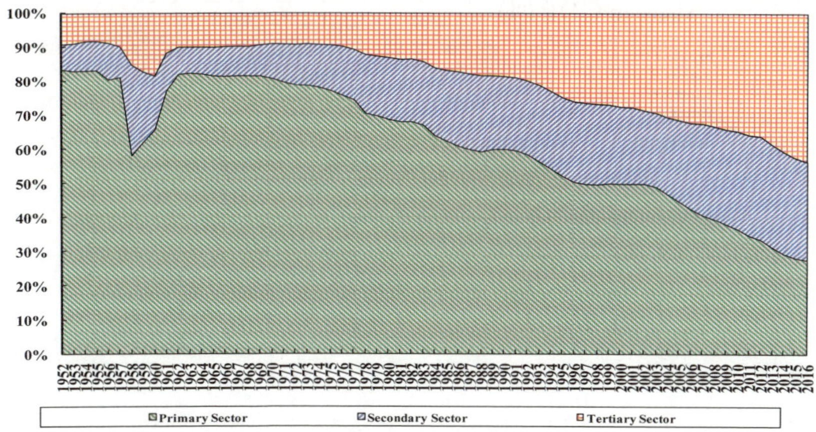

Several common features may be identified from these charts. First, as economic development proceeded, the share of GDP originating from the primary sector would decline continuously to below 10%. This has occurred in every single one of the economies of Japan, Taiwan, South Korea, and Mainland China. Second, the share of employment of the primary sector would also decline, but not to the same extent as the share of GDP. It has also fallen below 10% except in Mainland China, the economically least developed of the four economies. Third, the tertiary sector in all four economies, including even Mainland China, has grown to be the largest sector in terms of the share of GDP. Fourth, the tertiary sector has also become the largest sector by employment.

In Chart 6.17, the share of the primary sector in total employment is plotted against its share in GDP for the four economies: Japan, Taiwan, South Korea, and Mainland China. It is clear that there was much more surplus labour in Mainland China historically than in the other three economies. What this means is that Mainland China will be able to continue to benefit from its surplus labour for a while longer. The primary sectors of Japan, Taiwan, and South Korea have already reached a point with a very low share of employment and an even lower share of GDP originating. The primary sector of Mainland China still has some distance to go before its share of employment drops below 10%.

Chart 6.17. The Share of the Primary Sector in Total Employment Versus Its Share in GDP (%)

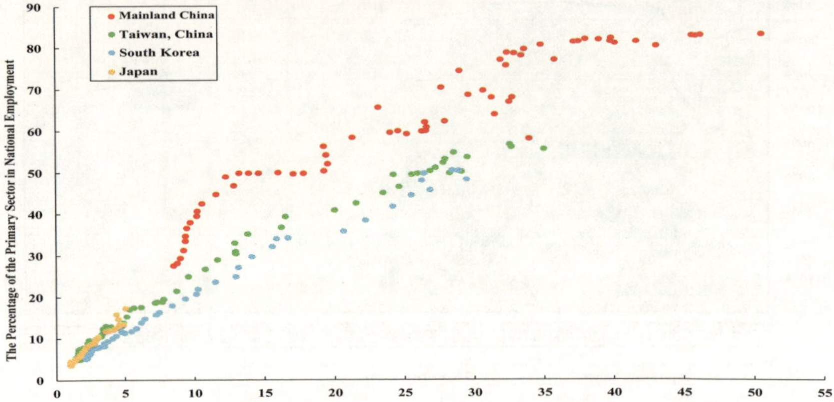

Investment in Intangible Capital

Innovation is the most important driving force of economic growth today, especially for mature developed economies with their already high capital-labour ratios and little, no, or even negative growth in the labour input measured in terms of labour hours. Sustained investment in intangible capital such as human capital and R&D is essential for the occurrence of economic innovation, reflected in measured technical progress or growth in total factor productivity in an economy. The East Asian economic development experience provides an example of created as opposed to natural comparative advantage. Japan, Hong Kong, South Korea, Singapore, Taiwan, and Mainland China all had little or no natural resources. However, they have all shown that human capital and R&D capital can substitute for natural resources.

East Asians have a long tradition of valuing education. One indicator of the level of human capital in an economy is the average number of years of schooling per person in the working-age population. In Chart 6.18, the average number of years of schooling is compared across selected economies. By this measure, the United States and Japan are clearly the global leaders. South Korea and Taiwan have also been catching up fast. Most of the other East Asian economies also have quite rapidly increasing levels of human capital but it will take a while before they can catch up with the levels of human capital in the developed economies.

The annual expenditure on R&D as a percentage of GDP is presented for selected economies in Chart 6.19. It shows that the U.S. has consistently invested a relatively high percentage of its GDP in R&D. The East Asian economies, including Mainland China, have been catching up fast, with the exception of Hong Kong.

Chart 6.18. The Average Number of Years of Schooling per Person in the Working-Age Population, Selected Economies

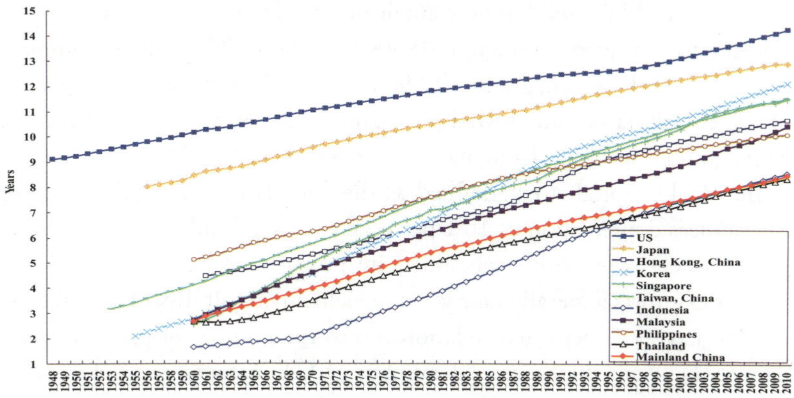

Chart 6.19. R&D Expenditure as a Percent of GDP: G-7 Countries, Four East Asian NIEs, China, and Israel

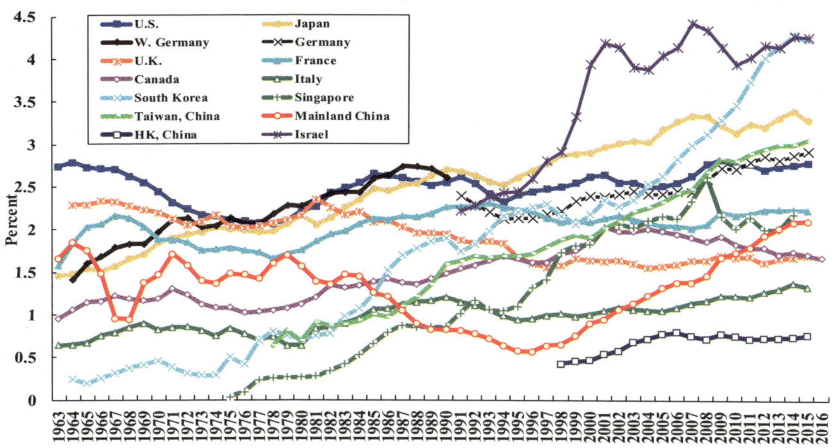

One indicator of the potential for technical progress (national innovative capacity) is the number of patents obtained each year. In Chart 6.20, the number of patents granted in the United States each year to the nationals of different countries, including the U.S. itself, over time is presented. The U.S. is the undisputed champion over the past 40 years, with 140,969 patents granted in 2015, followed by Japan, with 52,409. (Since these are patents granted in the U.S., the U.S. may have a home advantage; however, for all the other countries and regions, the comparison across them should be fair.) The number of patents granted to Mainland Chinese applicants each year has increased from the single-digit levels prior to the mid-1980s to 8,166 in 2015. The economies of South Korea and Taiwan, granted 17,924 and 11,690 U.S. patents respectively in 2015, are still far ahead of Mainland China. In contrast, the number of U.S. patents granted to Hong Kong nationals was only 601 in 2015.

The R&D capital stock, defined as the cumulative past real expenditure on R&D less depreciation of 10% per year, is a useful indicator of innovative capacity. R&D expenditures should quite properly be treated as investment since R&D efforts generally take years to yield any result. R&D capital can be shown to have a direct causal relationship to the number of patents granted. Chart 6.21, in which the annual number of U.S. patents granted is plotted against the R&D capital stock of that year for each economy, shows clearly that the higher the stock of R&D capital of an economy, the higher the number of patents granted to it by the U.S.

Chart 6.20. Patents Granted in the U.S.: G-7 Countries, Four East Asian NIEs, China, and Israel

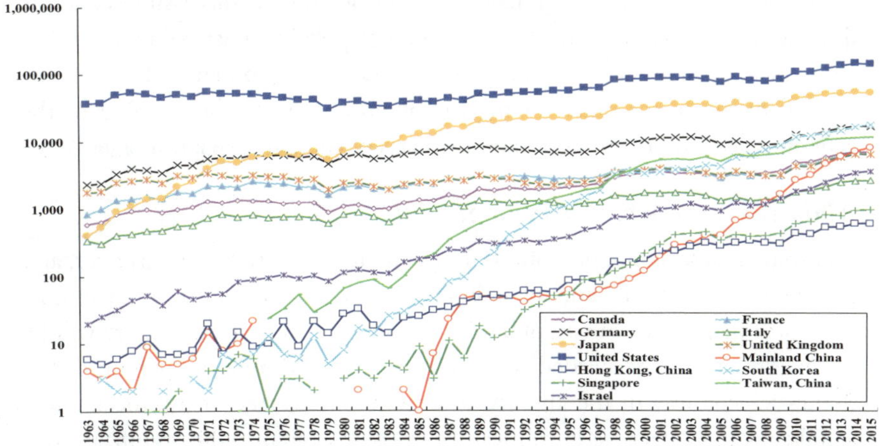

Chart 6.21. The Relationship between U.S. Patents Granted and R&D Capital Stocks: G-7 Countries, Four East Asian NIEs, China, and Israel

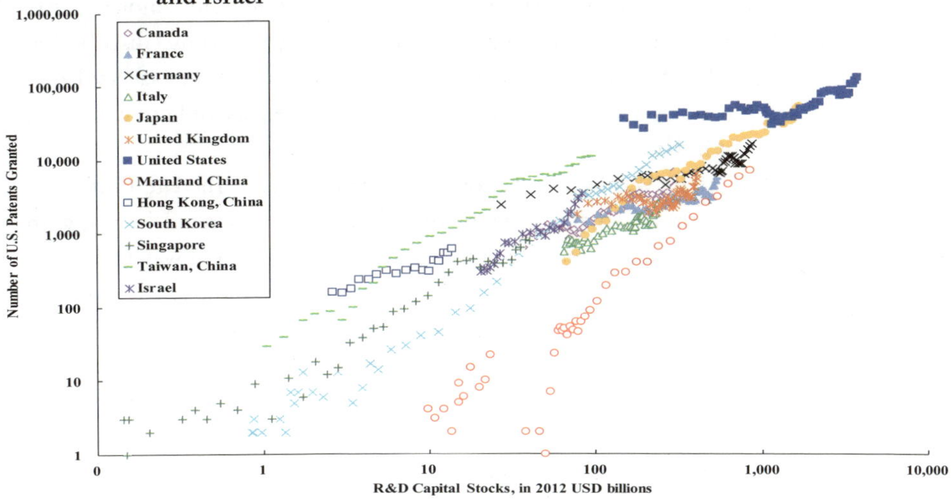

4. Economic Development Policies

Even sound economic fundamentals do not guarantee successful economic development. Correct economic development policies must be adopted. For East Asian economies, three common economic development policies can be identified: the maintenance of macroeconomic stability, the opening of the economy, and export promotion on the basis of comparative advantages.

Maintenance of Macroeconomic Stability

Domestic macroeconomic stability is crucial for households, enterprises, and governments to think and plan long-term. Without long-term planning, there will be no investment, public or private, and in particular, there will be no investment in the needed basic infrastructure. Moreover, opening of the domestic economy in the absence of a minimum degree of macroeconomic stability is risky because it will lead to massive capital flight, significant devaluation, and even more inflation. The control of inflation is thus an integral part of maintaining macroeconomic stability. It is also essential for the stabilisation of the exchange rate, which in turn makes it possible for the economic development policy of export promotion to be successfully implemented. Furthermore, a high rate of inflation often makes the income distribution more unequal. Inflation favours net borrowers and penalises net savers. Low-income individuals and retired individuals are also the least able to cope with the effects of inflation.

In 1947, there was hyperinflation in Mainland China. The late Prof. Sho-Chieh Tsiang proposed the issuance of inflation-indexed retail bonds, with both the principal and interest tied to the rate of inflation, as a way to tame it. The key is that if the commitment of the government to fight inflation is perceived by the public to be credible, inflationary expectations can be changed. Regrettably, this proposal was not adopted by the Nationalist government at the time. But when the Chinese Communists came to power in 1949, they adopted and implemented the indexing proposal, launching a kind of bank deposit, the principal and interest of which were indexed to the rates of change in the prices of a (weighted) basket of five goods—including rice, oil, salt, and cotton cloth. These indexed bank deposits helped bring down the rate of inflation on the Mainland very quickly.

Chart 6.22. The Monthly Rate of Inflation on the Mainland, 1946–1952 (Tianjin Wholesale Price Index)

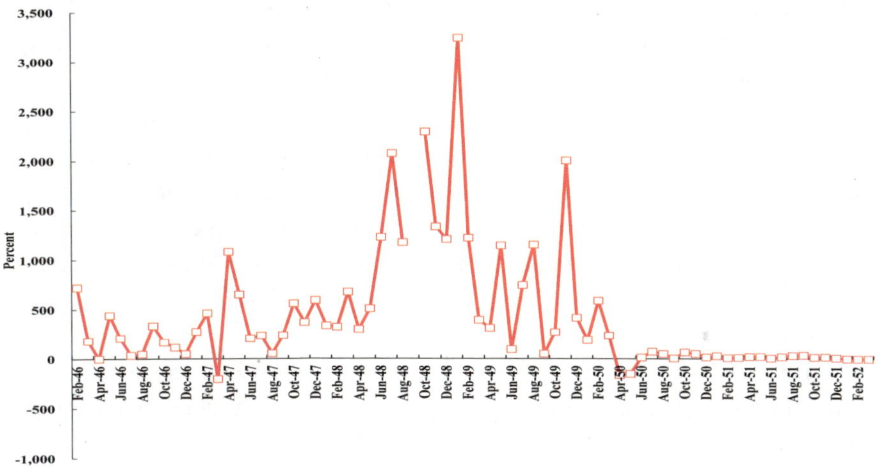

Chart 6.23. The Rates of Inflation of Taiwan, 1950–2017, as Measured by the Wholesale and Consumer Price Indices

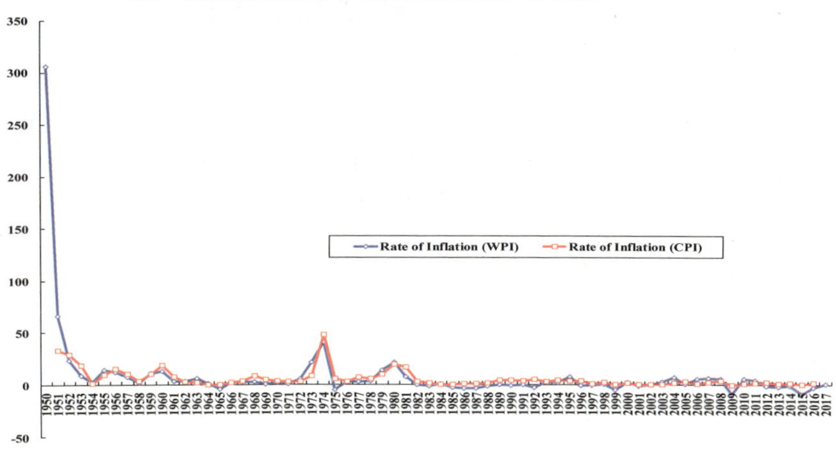

In January 1949, the rate of inflation on the Mainland was running at an annual rate of more than 3,000%! By June 1950, the rate of inflation fell to only 10%. By 1952, the price index began falling in absolute terms, at which point the Chinese government modified the rate of interest formula so that while it would go up with the rate of inflation, it would not go down when inflation turned negative. In Chart 6.22, the wholesale price index of the city of Tianjin between 1946 and 1952, compiled by Nankai University, is presented. No nationwide price indices were available for China during this period, but the price index of Tianjin is believed to be broadly representative of the rates of inflation in other urban areas in Mainland China at the time. Chart 6.22 shows how the introduction of indexed deposits brought down the rate of inflation very quickly on the Mainland.

Inflation was also very high in Taiwan in 1949–1950, and it was also brought down relatively quickly by the government by maintaining a nominal rate of interest higher than the actual rate of inflation so that the real rate of interest would almost always be positive.

Opening of the Economy

Japan, the East Asian NIEs, and Mainland China all had few natural resources. Capital equipment, oil, and raw materials such as cotton all had to be imported. Thus, an open economy is essential for their industrialisation. To finance these imports in a sustainable manner, there must be exports, and exports to the world must follow the principles of comparative advantage. In the case of these economies, they would begin with specialisation in the production of labour-intensive light-manufactured goods. Opening the economy also attracted foreign direct investment (FDI) to augment domestic savings and facilitated technology transfer.

The Promotion of Exports

First Japan, and then Hong Kong, and then Taiwan successively and successfully adopted and implemented the economic development policy of export promotion. This was accompanied by a significant devaluation of the respective currencies and the introduction of various direct and indirect incentives for exporters. However, import substitution, rather than export promotion, was the policy of choice of Western development economists in the 1950s. For example, India was advised to engage in import substitution as a strategy for its economic development. It proved to be a failed strategy.

Chart 6.24. Real World GDP and Trade in Goods and Services and Their Growth Rates (2016 prices)

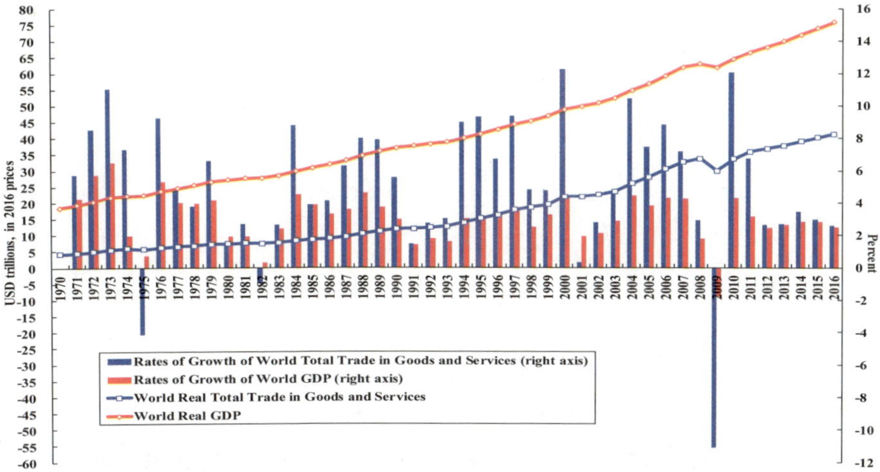

In Chart 6.24, the levels and the rates of growth of real world GDP and real world trade are presented. The red and blue lines in Chart 6.24 represent the levels of real world GDP and real world trade in 2016 prices respectively. The red and blue columns represent the rates of growth of real world GDP and real world trade respectively. It is clear that the blue columns are much higher than the red columns until the global financial crisis of 2008, showing that the growth of world trade led the growth of world GDP until recently.

Among the instruments used for the promotion of exports is the exchange rate. It should be set at a level that makes an economy's exports competitive in the world market, consistent with its comparative advantages. In Chart 6.25, the weighted average exchange rate of Taiwan and its share of exports in GDP are presented. After a series of significant devaluations, the multiple exchange rates were finally unified around 1959 at approximately NT$40 per U.S. dollar. These devaluations enabled exports to increase rapidly in both absolute terms and as a percentage of GDP. By the late 1980s, exports constituted over 50% of GDP. Subsequently, the New Taiwan dollar (NT$) appreciated as trade surpluses piled up. A further devaluation in 1996–1997, in response to the East Asian currency crisis, caused exports to rise further to approximately 70% of GDP. Currently, exports are approximately 65% of GDP in Taiwan.

Chart 6.25. The Nominal Exchange Rate and Exports as a Share of GDP: Taiwan

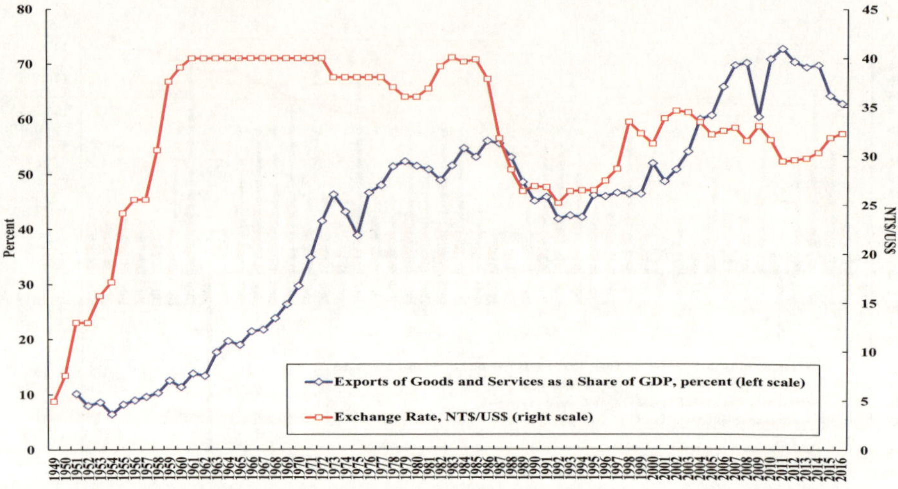

The patterns in South Korea, Mainland China, and Vietnam are basically similar—a devaluation of the domestic currency leads to an increase in the share of exports in GDP (see Charts 6.26–6.28).

Chart 6.26. The Nominal Exchange Rate and Exports as a Share of GDP: South Korea

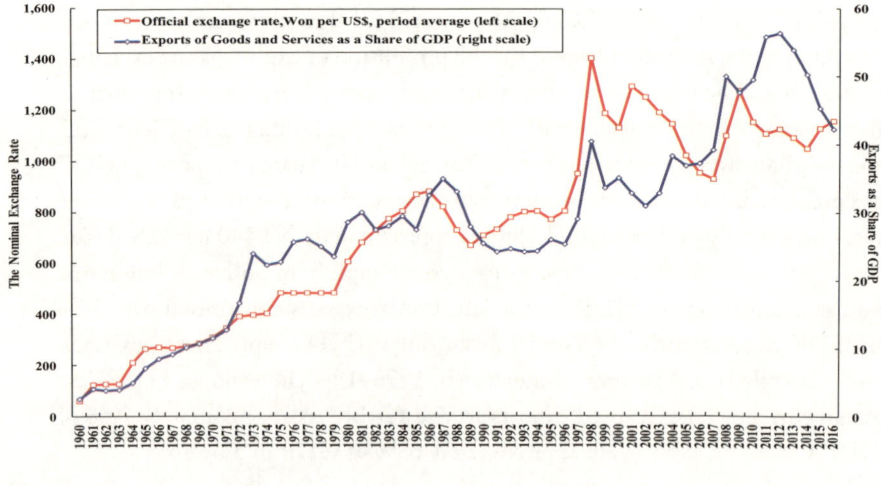

Chart 6.27. The Nominal Exchange Rate and Exports as a Share of GDP: Mainland China

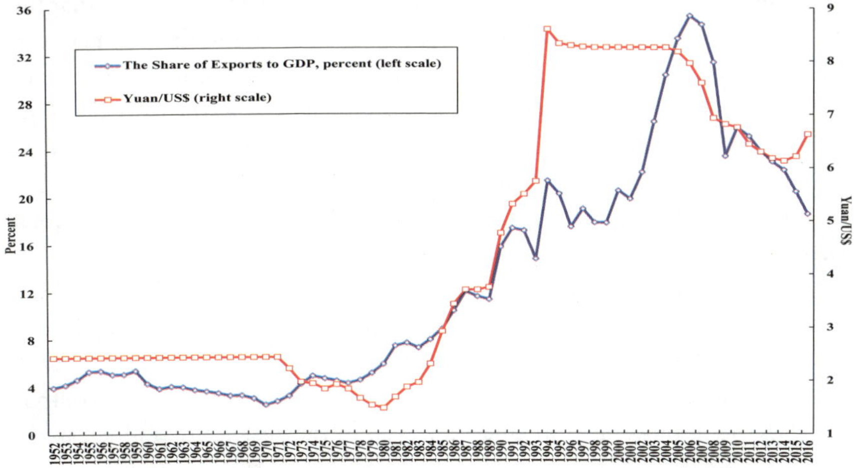

Chart 6.28. The Nominal Exchange Rate and Exports as a Share of GDP: Vietnam

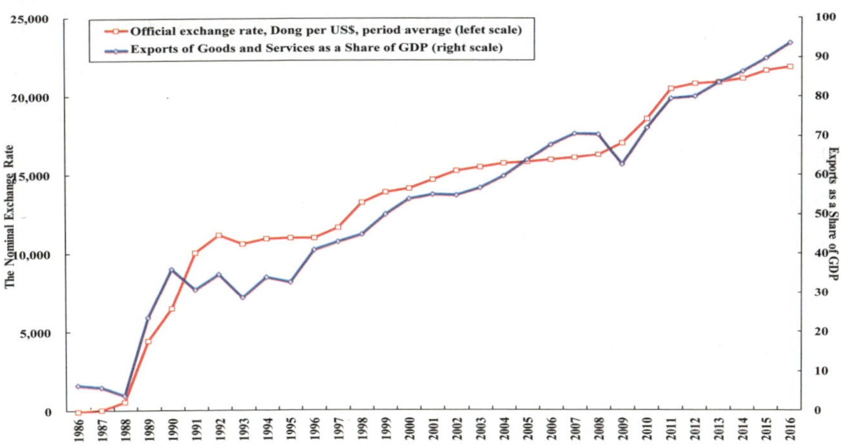

5. The Sources of Economic Growth

Our research, starting with Kim and Lau (1994, 1995, 1996), indicates that the bulk of economic growth at the beginning stage of economic development can be attributed to the accumulation of tangible capital. There is little evidence of technical progress or growth of total factor productivity at the early development stage.[4] It is only after these economies had made significant investments in intangible capital such as human capital and R&D capital over a period of time that they began to have measured technical progress or growth in total factor productivity.

The exception would be an economy such as Mainland China, which used to operate under a centrally-planned economic system, with significant inefficiency. With the launch of the economic reform in 1978, introducing producer autonomy and free markets, there was a significant increase in output through the improvement in efficiency, even in the absence of an increase in measured inputs. This increased efficiency in turn would be manifested in measured technical progress or growth in total factor productivity. Lau and Zheng (2017) attempted to estimate the degree of inefficiency on the eve of the Chinese economic reform in 1978. They conclude that Chinese output could have been approximately 50% higher if the Chinese economy were operating on its production possibilities frontier at the time.

6. Continuity of Governance

One common feature of the early development stages of the East Asian economies is that they were all characterised by continuous one-party rule, beginning with the Liberal Democratic Party in Japan, the British colonial government in Hong Kong, the Kuomintang (Nationalist Party) in Taiwan, President Park Chung-Hee in South Korea, Prime Minister Lee Kuan Yew of Singapore, and then Mainland China and Vietnam, just to name a few.

The advantages of continuous one-party rule are as follows: First, it is possible to plan long-term, without regard to the election cycle, as there is no need to settle for only short-term outcomes (basic infrastructure, so critical in the

4 See also Krugman (1994).

early development stage, can only be provided by a government with a long-term perspective); second, there is consistency, continuity, and predictability in economic policy; and third, the households and enterprises can share a common long-term vision and common expectations about the future, facilitating investment planning and coordination. Of course, this is not to say that there are no disadvantages to continuous one-party rule. Many countries governed by dictatorships are among the poorest in the world. But when one-party rule works well, it is better and more efficient than any other system.

7. Concluding Remarks

The development experiences of East Asian economies show that an open global economy can provide the environment for developing economies to grow and prosper through international trade. The East Asian economies have all benefitted significantly from the economic globalisation since the Second World War. The East Asian experiences also show that domestic macroeconomic stability is important. Without macroeconomic stability, no one will think or plan long-term, and investment will dry up. Moreover, opening of the domestic economy in the absence of a minimum degree of macroeconomic stability is risky because it will lead to massive capital flight, significant devaluation, and even more inflation. A low rate of inflation is also essential to the maintenance of a relatively stable exchange rate and the success of an export promotion policy.

The development experiences of East Asian economies also confirm the importance of sound economic fundamentals: A high domestic savings rate, the existence of abundant surplus labour, and investment in intangible capital provide the necessary domestic conditions for an economy to grow and prosper. However, a source of aggregate demand is also needed in order to be able to make full use of domestic resources, especially the surplus labour. Exports can provide the initial growth in aggregate demand. Today, no one argues seriously for import substitution as the sole policy to promote economic development. One important reason is the lack of sufficient domestic demand when the GDP per capita is still at a low level. Another important reason is that what needs to be imported can only be produced domestically at a very high cost, even if it is possible to do so at all. Most economies are better off exporting other things that they can more easily make themselves, capitalising on their comparative advantages.

Finally, the continuity of governance has been an important factor in the early stage of development of the East Asian economies, as it facilitates not only long-term planning but also faithful implementation of the plan once adopted. This affects in particular the investment in needed basic infrastructure, such as highways, ports, and power plants, which is especially critical at the early stage of economic development.

References

Kim, Jong-Il, and Lawrence J. Lau. "The Sources of Economic Growth of the East Asian Newly Industrialized Countries." *Journal of the Japanese and International Economies* 8, no. 3 (1994), pp. 235–271.

———. "The Role of Human Capital in the Economic Growth of the East Asian Newly Industrialised Countries." *Asia-Pacific Economic Review* 1, no. 3 (1995), pp. 3–22.

———. "The Sources of Asian Pacific Economic Growth." *Canadian Journal of Economics* 29 (April 1996), pp. S448–S454.

Krugman, Paul. "The Myth of Asia's Miracle." *Foreign Affairs* 73, no. 6 (1994), pp. 62–78.

Lau, Lawrence J., and Huanhuan Zheng. "How Much Slack Was There in the Chinese Economy Prior to Its Economic Reform of 1978?" *China Economic Review* 45 (2017), pp. 124–142.

Lewis, W. Arthur. "Economic Development with Unlimited Supplies of Labour." *Manchester School of Economic and Social Studies* 22 (1954), pp. 139–191.

Maddison, Angus. *The World Economy: Vol. 1: A Millennial Perspective and Vol. 2: Historical Statistics.* Paris: Development Centre of the Organisation for Economic Cooperation and Development, 2006.

Section II

The Strategies of Economic Development: China and East Asia

Commentary

Section II includes, in addition to my own articles, one article co-authored with Prof. Yingyi Qian of Tsinghua University, Beijing, and Prof. Gerard Roland of the University of California at Berkeley. The chapters in Section II deal with the economic strategies, policies, and measures adopted and implemented by the Chinese government during the past 45 years. These strategies, policies and measures include the "grandfathering" principle, the "dual-track" approach to the transition to a market economy, export promotion, maintenance of a stable exchange rate coupled with capital control, development of basic infrastructure, and macroeconomic stabilisation. They have mostly proved to be successful, as evidenced by the sustained high average annual rate of economic growth of over 9 percent during the period.

The Chinese economic reform was also characterised by numerous pilot (*shidian* 試點) experiments of different policies and measures, many of which were carried out locally first. If the experiment succeeded, such as the introduction of the "contract responsibility system" at Xiaogang Village, mentioned in the Commentary for Section I above, the policy would be extended to the entire country. When it did not succeed, the policy would be quietly folded. Another important point to note is that in the transition from a centrally-planned economy to a market economy, China employed a "dual-track" approach—keeping the mandatory central plan intact and simultaneously establishing free markets—which not only enabled full economic efficiency but also assured that everyone would be better off. There would be no losers.

Chapter 7 examines the economic policies adopted and implemented by the governments of Mainland China, Hong Kong, and Taiwan in their respective processes of economic development up to the mid-1990s. It presents a comprehensive list of policy instruments used by these governments in mobilising resource inputs, allocating them more efficiently, and shifting their production possibilities frontiers outwards. Chapter 7 goes on to emphasise the importance of developing basic infrastructure (social overhead capital) such as electric utilities, transportation and communication facilities and links, and industrial parks. Most basic infrastructure requires public investment, in part because it is often a public utility and has a large capital requirement and a long gestation period, and in part because it is frequently development-leading, that is, built in order to stimulate demand that does not yet exist. Moreover, it is also most likely a natural monopoly, which requires at least public regulation if not public ownership. In the case of China, enabling easy connectivity within the country through the development of basic infrastructure greatly facilitated the realisation of the benefits of the economies of scale inherent in the huge size of its own domestic market. Finally, because of the incompleteness of markets in the real world, it is sometimes necessary for the government to play a role in non-market coordination, especially with regard to changing public expectations, which can often be self-fulfilling.

Chapter 8, titled "The Sky Isn't Falling," was originally written in 1997 during the East Asian currency crisis. It basically suggests that there was no need for the Chinese people to panic because of the East Asian currency crisis, as the Chinese economy should be able to manage. It also explains why the renminbi should not be devalued at that time. A devaluation of the renminbi was neither necessary nor in the best interests of China itself. However, there were divided views within the Chinese government at the time. In the event, the sky didn't fall, the renminbi did not devalue, and the Chinese economy wound up with a real rate of growth of 7.8 percent in 1998. Two other papers, not included in this volume, were also written under similar titles in 2008 and 2015 respectively.[1] Chapter 13 in Section III, written in 2018, also has a similar title, "The Sky is Not Falling". This was done intentionally. The purpose of each of these papers was to reassure the readers that there was really no need to panic, and that whatever economic difficulties that had arisen in China at the time could be effectively managed.

1 Lau (2008) and Lau (2015).

The sudden collapse of the Lehman Brothers in the U.S. in 2008 triggered the Global Financial Crisis. "The Sky Is Not Falling (II),"[2] written in the immediate aftermath, was meant to reassure readers that once again there was no need for China to panic, similar to the time of the East Asian currency crisis 10 years earlier. In response to the new crisis, China launched a four-trillion-yuan economic stimulus programme, which enabled the Chinese economy to keep growing at an average annual rate of almost 8 percent in the immediately following decade. The economic stimulus programme managed to maintain public confidence and positive expectations about the future, thus preventing the Chinese economy from falling into a deep recession. It did lead to other problems subsequently, such as excess production capacity and heavy debt burden. However, it did what was needed at the time.

Chapter 9, titled "Gain without Pain: Why Economic Reform in China Worked," illustrates the use of the grandfathering principle[3] by the Chinese government in its economic reform so as to achieve "gain without pain."[4] "Gain without pain," or equivalently "reform without losers," is the dream of all economic reformers (and politicians) as it minimises political opposition to and maximises political support for the reform ex ante, as well as maximises political opposition to the reversal of the reform ex post (through the creation of new vested interests). The "grandfathering" of the vested interests assures that any economic reform measure must be Pareto-improving, that is, it improves the welfare of everyone—no one should be worse off than before. The "contract responsibility system," introduced in the Chinese agricultural sector in 1978, is an illustration of this principle. Under this reform, the commune's obligation to sell a fixed quantity of output at a fixed price and to pay a fixed amount of taxes to the government remained unchanged, so that the government was no worse off. The commune administration was also no worse off as individual households continued to be responsible for the deliveries of their allotted quotas of output deliveries and the payments of their pro-rata portions of the taxes to

---

2 Lau (2008).

3 This is known as the principle of *xinren xinbanfa, jiuren jiubanfa* (新人新辦法，舊人舊辦法), that is, "the new people follow the new system, and the old (existing) people follow the old system."

4 This phrase was suggested to me by Prof. Paul Krugman.

the commune. The households of the commune were also no worse off because after they fulfilled their same pre-existing obligations, they could do anything else they wanted to do and retain any income they managed to earn. They could also do nothing extra, but they would not be worse off. It was therefore a reform that no one should oppose.

Chapter 10, written in early 1999, can be regarded as a review of the developments in the Chinese economy at the time. This was right after the East Asian currency crisis. China did not devalue the renminbi while all the other East Asian economies except Hong Kong and Japan devalued their currencies significantly. Chinese exports had fallen significantly because of the decline in demands from not only the developed economies but also from the East Asian developing economies. The doomsayers and sceptics were out in droves, questioning the viability of the Chinese economy as well as the reliability of the Chinese economic statistics. Chapter 10 tries to answer some of the questions raised and reassure the public that the Chinese economy was basically in good shape and that the problems were manageable. It also proposes, in addition to investment in basic infrastructure, investment in residential housing as a source of additional aggregate demand for the Chinese economy. Subsequently, investment in residential housing has become a major component of Chinese aggregate demand. However, it now appears that residential housing units are in excess supply in all cities except for a few first-tier cities such as Beijing, Shanghai, and Shenzhen.

Economic reform in China since 1978 consists of two major components—the introduction of free markets for goods in the Chinese economy (coupled with conditional autonomy for the producers), and the opening of the Chinese economy to international trade and investment. Chapter 11, co-authored with Prof. Yingyi Qian and Prof. Gerard Roland, shows that the introduction of free markets in an originally centrally-planned economy, coupled with conditional autonomy for the producers, can make everyone better off and the economy efficient as well. It provides a rigorous proof that such a "dual-track" approach—keeping the mandatory central plan in force and simultaneously establishing free markets—is not only Pareto-improving but also achieves full economic efficiency.

This is a significant conclusion as economists have generally assumed that when the same good is sold at two different prices at the same time, there is inefficiency. The person who purchases the good at a lower price cannot use it as effectively as the person who is willing to pay a higher price. Everyone is better off if the purchaser of the good at the lower price sells it to the person who can better use it at a higher price. Thus, in equilibrium, there should only be a single (higher) price for the good. Chapter 11 shows that if the quantity of the good to be sold at the lower price is fixed and pre-allocated, then there is still efficiency overall, as long as there is a free market on which the price of the good is still determined by supply and demand on the margin. Consumers who are allocated the good at the lower price have simply been given a subsidy in the form of a lumpsum transfer: they can sell the same good at the higher price in the free market and pocket the difference if they choose to do so. Thus, in the transition from a centrally-planned economy to a market economy, if the central plan continues to be maintained and enforced at the same time that free markets are established, no losers are created and overall economic efficiency can still be attained if everyone is permitted to participate in the free markets. Economic efficiency is instantaneously achieved because, on the margin, everything is bought and sold at the free-market price. The absence of any losers is a major factor for the relatively smooth Chinese transition from a centrally-planned to a market economy.

Chapter 12, titled "The Chinese Economy: Myths and Realities," was originally written in 2010 and presented as the Inaugural Mok Hing-Yiu Lecture of the Oxford China Centre, St. Hugh's College, University of Oxford. It attempts to show that seven of the common myths that the Western press frequently entertained about the Chinese economy at the time were not true. The seven common myths were: (1) The renminbi (yuan) is under-valued; (2) The Chinese trade surpluses caused the global imbalances; (3) Chinese economic growth depends critically on exports; (4) The economies of China and East Asia cannot be de-coupled from the U.S. and Europe; (5) Chinese household savings rates are too high; (6) The Chinese economy faces labour shortages; and (7) Chinese economic power is comparable to that of the United States. In this chapter, all these myths are exposed as what they are—simply myths that are not supported by empirical evidence.

In the first half of 2015, there was a huge and rapid run-up in the Chinese stock market (see Chart 0.5). However, the stock market bubble burst in July, followed by an unexpected sudden devaluation of the renminbi vis-a-vis the U.S. dollar by approximately 4 percent in August. My article, "The Sky Is

Chart 0.5. The Shanghai Stock Exchange Composite Index

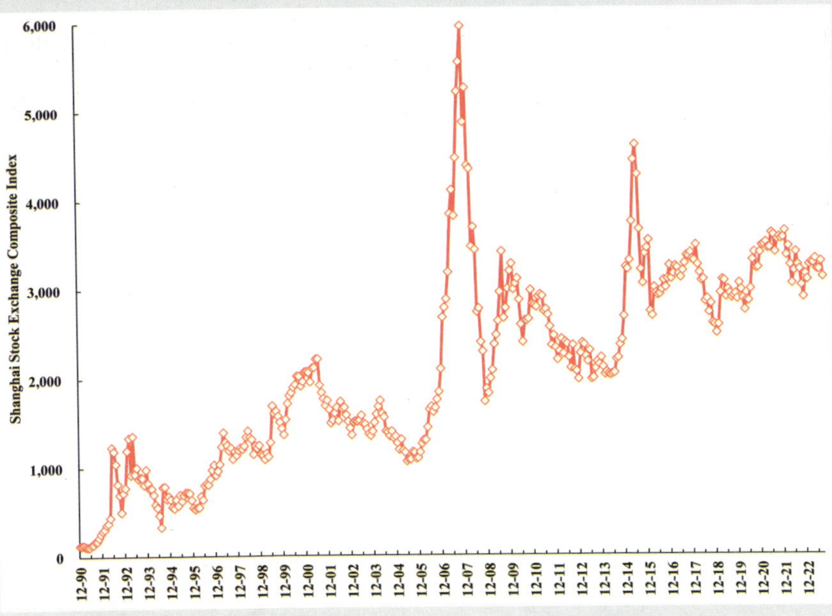

Source: The Shanghai Stock Exchange.

Not Falling on China's Economy," published in *China Daily*,[5] was meant to reassure readers that once again there was no need to panic. Indeed, since there was excess manufacturing production capacity in almost every industry in China at the time, aggregate supply was not a constraint. As long as there was aggregate demand, the supply would be forthcoming. The best sources of additional aggregate demand, given the size of the Chinese economy and the existing excess production capacities and surplus of residential housing, would be investment in basic infrastructure and in the provision of public consumption goods such as environmental preservation, protection, and restoration, the prevention of climate change, education, health care, and elderly care.[6] This continues to be the case at the present time.

---

5 Lau (2015).

6 For some reason, *China Daily* changed the term "public goods" to "public commodity" in the published article. I believe the term "public goods" conveys my intended sense much better—the provision of goods and services that everyone can enjoy at the same time.

References

Lau, Lawrence J. "The Sky Is Not Falling! (II)." Lecture presented at the Chinese Academy of Engineering, Beijing, 15 October 2008.

———. "The Sky Is Not Falling on China's Economy." *China Daily*, 30 September 2015.

Chapter 7.

The Role of Government in Economic Development: Some Observations from the Experiences of China, Hong Kong, and Taiwan*

1. Introduction

The role of the government in the highly successful development of the East Asian economies, including Japan, is an extremely broad subject with many different aspects. It is also a subject of considerable controversy. While all the governments, including the usually considered laissez-faire government of Hong Kong, have played important roles, there is in fact great diversity in their policies, actions, and outcomes.[1]

One can approach this subject in many ways. For example, one can take a "functional" approach and examine all of the functions that a government can or should fulfil in a developing economy, including the design and maintenance of the economic environment, the regulation of the economy, the enforcement of laws and contracts, and the provision of public goods such as infrastructure and education.[2] Another approach is the positive approach, which poses the

---

* This chapter was initially written in the mid-1990s, and originally published in *The Role of Government in East Asian Economic Development: Comparative Institutional Analysis*, edited by Masahiko Aoki, Hyung-Ki Kim, and Masahiro Okuno-Fujiwara. Copyright © 1997 Clarendon Press.

1 Even in Hong Kong, with its strong tradition of laissez-faire, the government has kept the exchange rate fixed relative to the U.S. dollar since the early 1980s, undertaken prudential supervision of the banking sector and the securities markets, and provided infrastructure such as public schools and hospitals, housing for low-income households, industrial estates as potential factory sites, and roads, subways, and airports.

2 See, for example, the remarks by Hyung-Ki Kim at the World Bank Workshop on the Role of Government in the Evolution of System Change, December 18–19, 1994, Tokyo, Japan.

questions: What have these governments actually done (or not done)? How have their policies worked? Under what circumstances? In this study, I mostly rely on the positive approach. Of course, it is taken as a given that at least one of the objectives of government is to promote the development of the economy.

More specifically, I focus on the policies adopted and implemented by the governments of China, Hong Kong, and Taiwan in the process of their economic development. I choose these three economies because of the strong economic linkages among them—they are already among the largest trading partners and foreign direct investors of one another; because of their shared cultural and historical heritage and ethnic affinity; and because of the demonstration effects of each economy on the others. I organise the discussion along the lines of how these governments have affected the growth of these economies.

Broadly speaking, three sources of growth of an economy can be identified: (1) increases in tangible inputs such as capital, labour, and human capital;[3] (2) increases in efficiency, both technical and allocative; and (3) increases in intangible inputs such as R&D capital, or adoption of new managerial methods or organisational forms for production.[4] The distinction between increases in efficiency and increases in intangible inputs is not particularly clear-cut, especially if the intangible input in question can only be measured indirectly, e.g., by the "residual" method. However, it is useful to maintain the hypothetical distinction between movements to the production possibility frontier, which is related to the efficient allocation and utilisation of available resources, and movements of the production possibility frontier, which is presumably due to intangible inputs (and luck). I examine the government policies adopted for augmenting each source of economic growth as well as their successes or failures. Along the way, I also identify the types of instruments used by the various governments in the implementation of their policies and evaluate their relative effectiveness. However, I am pragmatic in asking only whether a given policy has done some good, or is better in comparison with an alternative one, rather than whether it is optimal, recognising that in the real world there are so many constraints that we are in practice dealing with only the nth best policy.

---

3 For all three economies, the land input is virtually fixed over time.

4 Examples include the adoption of the just-in-time inventory method or quality-assurance circles.

In real terms, the gross domestic products (GDPs) of Hong Kong and Taiwan over the post-war period and China since it began its process of economic reform in 1979 grew at an average annual rate of approximately 9%. To put this performance in perspective, we may note that during the two decades of the most rapid economic growth in the history of the United States (approximately 1870–1890), real GDP grew at a rate of approximately 5% per annum.[5] Of all other countries, only Japan (1955–1976) and South Korea ever experienced a comparable rate of real economic growth over as long a period.[6]

A question mentioned earlier—under what circumstances?—turns out to be important. No policy, or sets of policies, no matter how brilliant, can work for all countries and at all times. Initial conditions as well as external circumstances influence the suitability and effectiveness of government policies and hence affect their choice. For example, if capital per unit of labour, or capital intensity, is low, then a policy that promotes saving and investment clearly makes sense. However, if capital intensity is already very high, then a policy that promotes R&D activities, or, in fact, invests in R&D activities, may be more necessary. The total amount of investable funds and the quality and quantity of human resources in the economy are also relevant considerations in determining the appropriate role of the government, especially if the capital requirements of minimum efficient scale (MES) plants are large relative to the total capital (physical as well as human) available. In the latter case, the government will have to make, whether consciously or by default, some choices that will have serious long-term consequences for the economy. Problems of this type are likely to be much more acute in the beginning phase of economic development when capital markets are small and underdeveloped. However, over time, there is also a tendency for the size of the MES plants to grow because of technological progress.

The potential size of the domestic market also makes a big difference. The size of the domestic market, relative to the MES plant, determines the nature of and the potential social benefits, if any, from any government intervention

---

5 See Abramovitz and David (1973), p. 431, Table 2.

6 See International Monetary Fund, *International Financial Statistics Yearbook* (Washington D.C.: International Monetary Fund), various issues.

and/or coordination.[7] In general, the larger the effective size of the economy, the less non-market coordination will be required. However, the size of the domestic economy should not be viewed as an unmitigated blessing. For a large economy, there is the question of controllability. The organisation of the flow of information and authority within the economy, which is in turn a function of the technology, becomes critical. There is an appropriate degree of decentralisation and devolution corresponding to the structure of information flows. Finally, the potential size of the domestic market also determines directly the amount of "rents" that can be created and/or distributed by the government through its policies.[8]

The initial size distribution of the enterprises also has a significant and lasting effect on the appropriate role of the government. For example, if the economy consists of a large number of small enterprises, as in Hong Kong and Taiwan, the government will have to take a more active role in the promotion of R&D—simply enacting an R&D investment tax credit will have very little effect because none of the small enterprises has the capital or is able to accept the long gestation period and risk inherent in R&D projects. However, for an economy dominated by a small number of large, well-capitalised enterprises, such as South Korea, an R&D tax credit may well be very effective.[9]

Other initial conditions that may matter include whether there is still surplus labour, the level of per capita income, the savings ratio, agriculture's share of GDP, whether the government budget is in surplus or deficit, the government's capacity to raise revenue, the private sector's share of GDP and capital stock, the extent of marketisation, the public's tolerance for inflation, and the degree of tax compliance.

---

7 For example, if the potential domestic market is not large enough, then the protection granted to an infant industry may have to become permanent, unless it becomes export oriented and internationally competitive.

8 For example, the values of import or monopoly franchises (such as cement or steel manufacturing) are directly related to the size of the domestic market.

9 It should be noted that the size distribution of enterprises can be substantially influenced by government ideologies and policies as well as by new technologies and can undergo significant changes over time.

2. Augmenting the Inputs

How do the governments of the three economies attempt to augment their inputs of production, such as capital, labour, and human capital? I discuss each of the inputs in turn.

Capital

In order for the fixed capital stock to increase, there must be fixed investment. Fixed investment is financed from saving, both domestic and foreign. However, except for Hong Kong, foreign saving is not quantitatively important, so that domestic saving is the principal source of investment funds in these economies.[10]

Increasing Savings

Saving behaviour can depend very much on past historical experiences as well as cultural factors. All three economies achieved very high saving rates, of between 35% and 40%, after a certain threshold of per capita real GDP was reached. Before 1979, this high saving rate was partially achieved in China through a restriction of consumption opportunities. However, more recent data show that Chinese household consumption is voluntarily restrained, perhaps in anticipation of future expenditures on big-value items such as consumer durables and housing, or for ceremonial needs such as birthday celebrations, weddings, and funerals. Consumer durables as well as residential housing are relatively expensive in all of these economies. Moreover, savings accounts in China, as well as those in Taiwan, are virtually free of bank default risk because of explicit and implicit deposit insurance.[11] In addition, the rate of interest has almost always been positive in real terms in Taiwan, providing additional

---

10 However, foreign resources can be pivotal in making possible the initial "big push." For example, in the 1950s, loans from the former Soviet Union to China were crucial in financing China's very successful First Five-Year Plan (1953–1957). Similarly, U.S. aid to Taiwan was very important from the early 1950s to 1965.

11 For example, postal savings in Taiwan are guaranteed by the government. In fact, no depositors have ever lost any money from the failure of formal financial institutions in Taiwan. Nor, for that matter, have depositors in China.

incentive to save. If there was any financial repression in Taiwan, it was probably quite mild. In China, the longer-term savings deposits are indexed to domestic inflation, thus guaranteeing a non-negative real rate of return.

Saving (and investment) is further encouraged by the macroeconomic stability maintained by the different governments in their respective economies (except for China, but it tries). This has been achieved, in both Hong Kong and Taiwan, by almost always, at least until recent years, adopting a conservative fiscal policy and running a budget surplus. Monetary policy in Taiwan is targeted on a positive real rate of interest. China has a negative real rate of interest on bank loans (but not on savings deposits), which has since the beginning of 1995 become slightly less negative. The saving graces for China are the indexation of longer-term savings deposits and the lack of competition for bank savings, as there is a dearth of alternative financial instruments available to households.

Real wages in all three economies are somewhat repressed—the labour unions have been, until recently, kept weak. It should be noted that wage repression has the same "beneficial" consequences as "mild" financial repression. In particular, it augments business, as opposed to household, savings.[12]

Inflation can sometimes be used as a means of forced saving as well as subsidising borrowers, mostly enterprises, in these economies. As a method of forced saving, it has not been important in all three economies. However, in China, it may be viewed as a method of subsidising the net borrowers, which are by and large the state-owned enterprises. The subsidy takes the form of a negative real rate of interest.[13]

Savings can be further augmented through the encouragement of foreign investment, both direct and portfolio. Foreign investment is facilitated by a stable exchange rate (achieved by both Hong Kong and Taiwan), by the freedom

---

12 The basic idea is that the marginal propensity to save out of profits by firms is higher than the marginal propensity to save out of incomes by households. A redistribution from the households to the firms therefore increases the aggregate saving rate of the economy.

13 The real rate of interest in Hong Kong has been negative for quite some years. However, this is not due to government control of the financial and money markets. Rather, a banking cartel in Hong Kong sets the nominal rate of interest on deposits.

of capital movements (always true in Hong Kong but gradually attained in Taiwan), and through special concessions such as tax holidays, capital and profit repatriation rights, and special rights to import equipment and material inputs. Because of its complete freedom of capital movements, Hong Kong has always functioned as a safe haven for capital from Southeast Asian countries, especially for the overseas Chinese residents there.

Increasing Investments

Aggregate saving is not necessarily equal to aggregate investment—there can be both inflows and outflows. In addition, investment is not necessarily translated into capital stock: only fixed investment is; change in stocks is not. Fixed investment, of both domestic and foreign origin, is promoted by special tax incentives, such as tax holidays, in Taiwan and in China, although China has traditionally had a large excess demand for fixed investment. In addition, special privileges are available in the Special Economic Zones in China, such as Shenzhen. Hong Kong provides industrial estates for the establishment of factories and offers complete freedom to export and import. Technical assistance is provided by the government in Taiwan to enterprises undertaking pioneering or new investment projects. A relatively pliant labour force and "wage repression" in these economies have also helped.

Fixed investment is also promoted by macroeconomic stability. When inflation rises, the ratio of fixed investment to total investment declines, indicating a rise in the change in stocks—that is, an increase in hoarding activities at the expense of fixed capital formation. Inflation and expectation of inflation also discourage long-term investments. The stable exchange rates maintained by Hong Kong and Taiwan also favour investment because they reduce one major risk for foreign as well as domestic producers for the export market. The export orientation of Hong Kong and Taiwan also facilitates foreign direct investment because it assures that the foreign exchange will be available when repatriation time arrives.

However, loans, with the exception of short-term loans for export financing, were until recently not generally available from government banks in Taiwan to private enterprises—so that in fact the commercial banking system is not used very much to promote fixed investment. This is left for development banks such as the China Development Corporation and the Chiao Tung Bank (formerly the Bank of Communications). Similarly, during the initial stage of the economic development of Hong Kong, commercial banks were unimportant as a source of loans for fixed investment although they were active in providing working capital loans.

Since 1984, commercial banks in China, almost all government owned, have become the principal source of finance for the fixed investment projects of state-owned enterprises, replacing direct budgetary allocations. Unfortunately, many of the fixed investment projects undertaken by the state-owned enterprises did not turn out well, resulting in massive non-performing loans on the books of the commercial banks in China. The Chinese banks provided virtually no financing to non-state-owned enterprises.

Labour

The rates of growth of the labour force in China, Hong Kong, and Taiwan have been quite rapid, but both Hong Kong and Taiwan have experienced labour shortages and rising wages since the 1980s. The use of foreign contract labour has become quite common in Hong Kong and Taiwan. All three economies have had substantial and successful family planning programmes.[14] According to long-term projections of the Chinese economy, in the year 2020, the proportion of the Chinese labour force employed in the agricultural sector will still be 33%, even though the agricultural sector will only account for 7% of the GDP then.[15] Thus, labour per se will continue to be in "surplus" in China for a long time to come. The challenge for China is to create employment for the new entrants to its rapidly growing labour force—approximately 16 million new jobs are needed every year. For China, the emphasis must be on augmenting the quality, rather than the quantity, of its labour force.

The female labour force participation rates in all three economies are already quite high, especially among the below-40 cohorts. Further significant increases are not very likely and the growth of the labour forces in these countries will mostly follow the growth of the working-age population.

---

14 Family planning programmes were less successful in the rural areas in China in recent years.

15 See Lau (1995).

Human Capital

Universal compulsory primary education, financed by the government, was achieved in Taiwan sometime in the early 1960s. It was subsequently extended to nine years and then to 12 years. The constitution of Taiwan actually mandates the spending of 15% of the annual government budget on education. Universal secondary education was also mostly achieved in Hong Kong, but with a greater reliance on the private sector. Private education has always been an important component of Hong Kong's educational system. Taiwan has a stronger tertiary educational system than Hong Kong—its enrolment rates have been much higher. But Hong Kong is in the process of catching up, with the government establishing several new universities recently.

In China there is a potential deficiency in the supply of human capital. As an unintended consequence of the new economic prosperity in China, which is mostly concentrated in the coastal regions, the poorer rural areas of China are short on funds for education and unable to attract teachers. The demand for labour in the rural areas further erodes the incentive for many rural parents to send their children to school. Illiteracy is still a serious and increasingly important problem in the poorer rural areas of China. Tertiary educational opportunities are still relatively scarce in China. In both Hong Kong and Taiwan, the public educational system is supplemented by private institutions. It may well be that China will have to allow a similar development, given the emphasis on the quality and not the quantity of labour.

3. Allocating Resources Efficiently

An allocation of resources is said to be efficient if no additional output can be produced without increasing at least one input, and no input can be decreased without decreasing at least one output. Under constant or decreasing returns to scale and competitive markets, and profit and utility maximisation, efficiency is assured by the well-known Welfare Theorem. However, the Welfare Theorem breaks down if there are increasing returns to scale, other nonconvexities, informational asymmetry, or other externalities, and/or significant market power on either the supply side or the demand side of the economy. In that case, neither the market nor a bargaining solution by economic agents acting in their own self-interest will necessarily assure the efficiency of the economy. The role of the government is to help achieve an efficient allocation of resources (and thereby increase aggregate output). It should therefore adopt policies and actions that will lead to an efficient outcome—for example, one that corresponds to a solution to the full-information cooperative game, with the government possibly lending credibility to the commitments through its power of enforcement of contracts or more generally as a potential dispenser of economic favours. By thus adding value, the government is also able to create rents and in the process distribute any such rents to support the efficient outcome. For example, the returns to the land input, assuming that it is fixed in supply, are all rent. The government can modify the distribution of rents through property and capital gain taxation so that land is allocated to its socially highest and best use (subject to incentive compatibility constraints). Similarly, royalties on natural resources are also a form of rent.

There is a distinction between a permanent (one-time) allocation of rent and a repeated allocation of rent. Under repeated allocation, some care has to be taken to assure that there will actually be competition in the market. Precisely because the government has the power of creating and allocating rents, it runs the risk of being co-opted by rent seekers and/or by current rent recipients.

I examine the role of the government in achieving economy-wide efficiency by separating it into two parts: achieving technical efficiency within each industry and enterprise, and achieving allocative efficiency across industries and enterprises. But first, I discuss several factors that have significant influence on the incentives and abilities of the economic agents to achieve efficiency.

The Structure of Ownership

In both Hong Kong and Taiwan, the predominant mode of ownership of enterprises is private—in fact, family owned. Almost all of the successful large enterprises in both Hong Kong and Taiwan, even the publicly listed ones, with the possible exception of the public utilities in Taiwan, are family controlled.[16] The only major exceptions that come to mind are the Hong Kong and Shanghai Banking Corporation in Hong Kong, and the China Steel Corporation, as

16 Even the largest non-Chinese owned enterprises in Hong Kong, Jardine Matheson and Swire, are controlled by the Keswick and the Swire families, respectively.

well as the government-owned banks and financial institutions in Taiwan. In China, it is the non-state sector (consisting of collective—including the township and village—enterprises, foreign-owned enterprises, joint-venture enterprises, and private, including individual, enterprises) that has been the most dynamic and successful over the past 15 years. Even though there has been no significant privatisation in China, the non-state sector now accounts for well over half of Chinese GDP, compared to less than 10% in 1979.[17] Hong Kong has always operated as a private-enterprise economy: its public utilities—electricity, gas, and transportation—have always been privately owned and operated but publicly regulated.

With Taiwan, the reliance on the private sector was by no means inevitable—the share of the public sector in terms of the value of industrial assets in the early 1950s was almost 90%![18] However, early in the economic development drive of Taiwan (the late 1950s), there was considerable internal debate within its government of the relative merits of public versus private ownership, and it was decided at the highest level of the government that the new investments (initially mostly in export-oriented industries) would be undertaken by private rather than state-owned enterprises, except in naturally monopolistic industries such as public utilities.[19] It is a remarkable testimony of the success of this policy that the more rapid growth of the private sector in Taiwan has resulted in the public sector's share of industrial assets declining to below 15% in the 1980s, again without any significant privatisation of public enterprises. Even in China, the managers of many township and village enterprises, whose legal ownership status is still not clearly defined, often manage the enterprises and dispose of assets as if they are the actual owners of these enterprises. In practice, these enterprises are like partnerships, with the original residents of

17 Perhaps it is not as important whether an enterprise is public or private, as whether it has a soft or a hard budget constraint, to use a terminology introduced by Janos Kornai (1980). Enterprises that have hard budget constraints seriously take into account the negative consequences of their actions on their profit; enterprises with soft budget constraints do not care about their losses or potential losses because they expect to be bailed out by the government at the end.

18 See Lau and Song (1992).

19 Apparently this debate also occurred in South Korea in the early 1960s and was also concluded in favour of private enterprise.

the township or village being the beneficial owners/partners. It is significant to note that workers from outside the township or village are typically put on finite-term contracts and have no tenure, pension, or other rights, as distinct from workers from the same township or village itself.[20]

The choice of private over public ownership for enterprises other than public utilities turned out to have enormous economic significance. First, the effectively family-owned nature of these private enterprises implies that they are owner-managed.[21] There is thus no "agency problem"—the interests of the owner and the manager are identical.[22] The owner-managers of these enterprises, who are interested in maximising their own profits in the long run (or equivalently, present value), have an incentive to be efficient in both their production and investment decisions. They know that they have to put their own equity capital at risk, because no one, including the government, is going to make good any losses that they may incur. They thus have the incentives to maximise profit, minimise loss, and most importantly pay careful attention to the consequences of their actions, especially with respect to their investments,

---

20 However, the rights, if any, of residents emigrating from the township and village remain to be determined.

21 At a later stage, when the family enterprises have expanded so much that they require nonfamily members as executives, there may be an "agency problem" to the extent that the objectives of the owners and the non-owner managers do not coincide. Unavoidable economic inefficiency may result from such incompatibility—resources must then be devoted to assure that the agents (the non-Lowner managers) behave in a way so as to advance the objectives of the principal (the owners).

22 Agency problems may arise if the managers are not themselves substantial owners. In a large private, but publicly owned corporation, the interests of the owners and the professional managers may diverge. Consequently, the managers may not be responsive to the needs of the owners (shareholders) and instead may pursue their own interests. Such conflicts of interest frequently lead to inefficiency. In many ways, large private corporations with many small shareholders in which the managers do not have a significant stake have an incentive structure not unlike that of state-owned enterprises. The losses are borne by the shareholders and any glory goes to the managers. There is thus a natural tendency, on the part of the managers, to overinvest and to take inordinate risks, not to mention elabourate perks and privileges, at the expense of the shareholders.

unlike the managers of state-owned enterprises.[23] Their investment plans are sensitive to the real rate of interest, whereas those of state-owned enterprises run by managers with few ownership interests typically are not.

Empirically, the transition of Chinese agriculture from a collective system to an essentially private individual household system (with land leases) resulted in large gains in efficiency of the order of between 30 and 40% from 1979 to 1985, holding inputs constant. Efficiency gains of such a magnitude are very, very significant. This early success of the Chinese agricultural reform laid the foundations of its subsequent success in the other (mostly non-state) sectors, including the township and village enterprises.

The Market Environment

Hong Kong has always been a private-enterprise, free-market economy, even though the government does intervene from time to time and most notably has maintained a fixed exchange rate vis-à-vis the U.S. dollar since 1984.[24] The government of Taiwan has been more activist or interventionist, but by and large it has been content to let the market work where it can. China is probably the least marketised of the three, but even there, very few commodities are currently still under price control or rationing, and the prices of most tradable goods in China, including energy and grains, are now at or near world market levels.

In order to make the market work, however, one needs more than private enterprise and a determination by the government not to intervene. The government must also assure that there is the transportation and communication

---

23 However, there are potential limits to the expansion of a family-owned enterprise with a highly centralised process of decision making. At some point, the efficiency gain resulting from the alignment of the interests of the owner and the manager may be offset by the diseconomies of scale associated with overcentralised decision making and by the inability to recruit the best talents. Thus, at some scale, an enterprise with diffused ownership and professional (non-owner) management may become more efficient than a similar enterprise under family ownership and management.

24 The exchange rate of the Hong Kong dollar has been maintained at a fixed parity to the U.S. dollar of HK$7.8 per US$ since 1984. Moreover, the rate itself appeared to have been simply pulled out of a hat just to head off a free fall of the Hong Kong dollar during a crisis of confidence in Hong Kong.

infrastructure to make the one market a reality; that is why infrastructural development is such an important task for the government. The government must also assure that there is sufficient meaningful competition. It can influence the degree of competition in a market by regulating entry, licensing capacity, restricting foreign equity, controlling imports of goods as well as imports of technology, and promoting the creation of indigenous technological capabilities. The government also needs to provide services for standardisation, inspection, and certification. One simple example of standardisation is traffic signals—it does not matter whether one goes on green and stops on red, or vice versa—but someone has to decide one way or the other and to enforce it. Actually, during the Cultural Revolution in China, for a brief period, it was decreed that one should go on red (the revolutionary colour) and stop on green. It also worked. In any case, setting standards and conventions is a highly important and socially productive activity of the government. (Setting the gauge of railroad tracks and the voltage of the household electricity supply are other examples.)

In Hong Kong, a free port, the market works the best of the three economies, although as I have already mentioned there is the fixed exchange rate, and the banking cartel has been able to set the ceiling on the rate of interest on savings deposits at a low level. The market in Taiwan is becoming more and more open. However, there are still monopolistic or oligopolistic elements in the distribution systems as well as in construction (basically the non-tradable sectors). China is still far from being a competitive market, both because of infrastructural bottlenecks and because of significant monopolistic elements in the economy. Wholesale trade is still monopolised. There are still foreign trade export and import and service monopolies established and maintained by the government. For example, despite the split-up of the former Civil Aviation Administration of China and the proliferation of new airline companies,[25] the airline industry in China is still dominated by regional monopolies. Overall, though, there has been impressive progress—exchange rates have been unified, as are many other prices. Trades are becoming more and more anonymous (the same price regardless of the parties). And regulations are becoming more transparent.

---

25 The number of airlines in China currently exceeds 30.

In the three economies, commercial banks are not relied upon as a primary source of equity capital—they specialise in providing working capital—except in China where since 1984 they have had to provide state-owned enterprises with loans to finance fixed investment in lieu of direct allocations from the government budget. The financial market in Hong Kong is one of the most competitive in the world. If there is any financial repression in Hong Kong, it is done by the Foreign Exchange Banks Association, headed by the Hong Kong and Shanghai Bank. This association functions as a deposit-rate-setting cartel. In Taiwan, financial repression is practically absent, but not credit rationing. However, all the commercial banks in Taiwan were government owned until the late 1980s, when a large number of new private commercial banks were allowed to be established. Bank loans are generally used for working capital rather than long-term investment purposes. For large enterprises, the development banks, including Chiao Tung Bank and the China Development Corporation, may be tapped. Small and medium-sized enterprises are financed by equity investment and loans from the informal credit market. China is the only economy with bank-lending rates significantly below the market. Even there, because of the existence of indexation for longer-term savings deposits, the degree of financial repression is not as severe as it might otherwise be. Instead, most of the "rents" result from credit rationing, with the state-owned enterprises most favoured. Financial repression and credit rationing may be viewed as a reallocation of rents between lenders and borrowers, savers and investors. In China the rents appear to have gone mostly to the loss-making state-owned enterprises.[26]

Finally, it is worth noting that the export orientation and more general participation in the world market through international trade provide the competitive pressure for the exporting enterprises in China, Hong Kong, and Taiwan to be efficient. The predominant export orientation of Hong Kong, Taiwan, and the coastal provinces of southern China, coupled with the commodity nature of their products, means that most of the enterprises have to compete internationally with the enterprises of other countries, in third-country markets, over which neither they nor their governments have much control. The discipline imposed by the fiercely competitive world market keeps the enterprises lean, mean, and honest.

26 Part of the rent is also skimmed by bank officers with the authority to approve loans.

With the increasing openness of the domestic markets, the enterprises will be subject to even more intense competitive pressure to be efficient and rent-seeking activities will be reduced. Perhaps the critical difference between the policies of import substitution and export promotion lies in the fact that under import substitution, there is little or no competitive pressure on the enterprises, whereas under export promotion, enterprises in one country have to compete with enterprises all over the world. While it is true that inefficient export enterprises can still be directly subsidised, an explicit, direct subsidy is much more noticeable and more difficult to sustain in the long run than an import tariff or restriction. There is also much less rent to be sought and appropriated on the open world market.

Coordination Externalities

Often, there may be efficient economic outcomes that are not supportable through the market or through bargaining, cooperatively or non-cooperatively, among economic agents acting in their own self-interests alone. This is especially important when there is the possibility of multiple economic equilibria. Multiple economic equilibria can arise from "non-convexities," complementarity, information asymmetry, or the lack of credible commitments. One useful role of the government is to create conditions that are conducive to the achievement of the efficient economic outcome that otherwise is not achievable and to guarantee its implementation through its powers of enforcement. This may be broadly referred to as "coordination."

At its most elementary level, coordination means using or sharing the same information among the economic agents, so that the adverse effects of information asymmetry can be overcome. Put in these terms, it always pays to coordinate—it cannot do any harm. However, coordination is necessary only insofar as the information to be used or shared does not consist solely of information available in the market; for example, the market may provide information about the price and quantity of a good, but not necessarily information about the (individual) supply and demand functions. Coordination makes it possible for the different economic agents to use and share such information and thereby reduce uncertainty.[27] Coordination is much more

---

27 For example, standardisation, setting of a fixed exchange rate, and setting the schedule for rotating power outages under conditions of chronic excess demand for electricity are all different forms of non-market coordination.

important for investment decisions than for current production decisions: this is especially so if investment is not readily reversible.

However, non-market coordination does not necessarily need to involve the government. For example, private signalling, which can be done without the intercession of the government, can be an effective form of coordination, or at least attempted coordination. Economic agents may also find it advantageous to reveal their response functions to one another, thus saving learning and testing time. Collusion among economic agents can also be viewed as a form of privately but not necessarily socially beneficial coordination. Coordination, whether private or public, can lead to either private or social benefit, or both. Nor is government coordination necessarily preferable to private coordination, but it is more credible because it can assure the credibility of commitments made not only by itself but also by other economic agents through its powers of enforcement. It also tends to remove the gaming aspects that make private information appear fuzzy and unreliable and thereby inhibit the achievement of an efficient economic outcome.

For example, banks can avoid over-investment in certain industries, or over-lending to certain enterprises, through an exchange of information. Such an exchange of information does not necessarily have to be organised by the government. It can be done through credit bureaus and rating agencies, and through the practice of loan syndication. But the government can help by imposing exposure limits for individual banks. It can also compel truthful reporting and use its audit and investigative powers to ensure compliance.

For another example, there may be benefits generated by simultaneous expansion of all industries, so that one industry's additional supply will be taken up as another industry's additional demand and altogether the additional earnings of the workers will increase the aggregate final demand. In other words, the incomes generated by the new economic activities created can in turn provide the demands, directly and indirectly, for the goods produced. Of course, the domestic market must be large enough. For example, it is not possible for manufacturers in Hong Kong to get rich by relying on sales to one another and their own workers only; the domestic market is simply too small. This is not true of China. Such a "bootstrap" strategy that does not work for much smaller economies may actually work in China. However, in order for these so-called coordination externalities to be realised, all industries must share the common knowledge or belief that a simultaneous expansion will be forthcoming. This is a coordination problem—for example, the announcement or formulation of an economic plan may provide the signal. Announced economic growth and money supply targets can also serve as coordinating signals, to the extent that they are credible.

More concretely, consider how the Chinese economy emerged from its recession of 1989–1991. Publicity about Deng Xiaoping's visit to southern China in early 1992, as well as statements attributed to him, provided precisely the signal for the convergence of public expectations of a resumption of economic expansion, stimulating the subsequent boom that continues today.[28] This experience shows how it is possible for concerted actions prompted by a common expectation to move the economy into fast forward again, provided that the economy is large enough. This is a good example of the importance of coordination when there are multiple equilibria—one low growth and one high growth. In the absence of Deng's southern visit, the recovery in China from the recession caused by the Tiananmen incident would not have occurred so soon—it might not have occurred at all. As it was, it also made the Chinese economic reform totally irreversible.[29]

An example of failure of coordination is the almost complete absence of inter-enterprise trade credit among non-state-owned enterprises in China. The famous inter-enterprise, or "triangular," debts in China are almost exclusively debts among state-owned enterprises. The non-state-owned enterprises typically neither extend trade credit to nor receive trade credit from other enterprises in China. Most transactions among these enterprises are done on a "cash-on-delivery" basis. The insistence on cash on delivery is a defensive measure on the part of these non-state-owned enterprises, reflecting serious information asymmetry, and cannot be consistent with efficiency. Total trades, and transactions, would rise if short-term trade credit were made available.

28 In fact, Deng's southern visit coordinated not only China but also Hong Kong and Taiwan, which stepped up their direct investments in China in response. I owe this point to K. C. Fung.

29 The declared commitment by the United States to win the race to send a man to the moon in the aftermath of the successful launch of the Sputnik satellite by the Soviet Union in 1957 also served as a coordinating signal to the military-industrial-scientific complex.

It would appear that if a credible credit bureau or rating agency, like a Dun and Bradstreet, backed by either the government or one or more government banks (so as to compel truthful revelation), can be organised to provide credit information in China, it would greatly increase the volume of transactions and hence the overall efficiency of the economy.

Another role for the government is to reduce transaction costs. When the number of economic agents is large, there can be tremendous economies in adopting a government-imposed solution to a bargaining game situation.

Achieving Technical Efficiency

What are some measures that can be undertaken by the government that will move the economy closer to its production possibility frontier?

There is no question that reducing red tape increases efficiency. "Red tape" is a relic of the days when the government had to provide employment to a large number of people and carve up or make work for them. Both China and Taiwan have made special provisions to expedite foreign investment applications. But if it is possible to streamline the procedure for foreign investors, it should be possible to reduce red tape for all, including domestic, enterprises. Also relevant is whether the style of government is discretion-based or rule-based. A discretion-based system is open to "rent-seeking" and corruption. Hong Kong has already put in place a rule-based system. Taiwan is moving in that direction. However, even in the early phase of Taiwan's economic development, rent-seeking was not particularly prevalent, partly because the central government was dominated by people from the Mainland, whereas the private sector, where most of the potential rent-seekers would be, was dominated by people whose families had been resident in Taiwan for a long time. Even China, where traditionally government regulation is stated "permissively" as opposed to "prohibitively," that is, one can only do what one is explicitly "permitted" to do, is under some pressure to increase the transparency of its decision processes. It may be noted that in the transition from a discretion-based system to a rule-based system, kinship and long-term friendship rooted in shared cultural norms can provide the bases for the implicit contracts necessary to support economic transactions in the absence of explicit rules and regulations or established customs. This is one of the reasons why the initial foreign investors in China have been almost exclusively members of overseas Chinese communities.

What one can say is that with increasing democratisation, turnover in the government has become a real possibility in Taiwan. Under these circumstances, when longevity of the government or the bureaucracy can no longer be assumed, it is better for enterprises to have a rule-based system rather than a discretion-based system. This is especially the case if the real power does not reside in the permanent bureaucracy as in Japan and the United Kingdom. A rule-based system is also preferable to a discretion-based system if there are many players in the economic system.

Creating New Institutions and Drafting New Laws

The government can make new laws and create new institutions that facilitate and support economic development. These can be laws with regard to property rights, which can provide for greatly variegated forms of ownership. For example, in most jurisdictions under the influence of English Common Law, the mineral rights in the ground are not the property of the owner of the land but belong to the state. Land in Hong Kong (the island itself), when it is initially sold by the government, is mostly covered by leases for 999 years. By contrast, the land in the New Territories of Hong Kong used to be covered by leases that would expire in 1997. The property sector, which is so important for the Hong Kong economy, owed its start to two developments in the 1950s. First, the government of Hong Kong abolished rent control on new residential buildings. Second, it perfected the laws governing the condominium ownership of separate units in a building, thus making it possible for individuals to own their own individual units. Real estate ownership in Hong Kong had previously been confined only to those who could purchase an entire building, which severely limited the demand. These two developments ushered in a great expansion in residential building. The same "condominiumisation" concept was later also adopted in Taiwan.[30] China also adopted a transferable land lease system with durations of 15 years and up.

---

30 It may be noted that even in the United States, "condominiumisation" is a relatively recent concept that did not gain currency until the 1970s. Previously, most non-rental multiple-residential-unit buildings were owned jointly by the individual unit-owners as a "cooperative," under which legal structure the buying, selling, and financing of the units were extremely complex and difficult.

Another piece of legislation that may seem draconian made writing bad cheques a criminal offence prosecutable by the government rather than a civil matter between the cheque issuer and recipient. This legislation helped enormously in popularising the use and acceptance of cheques, including even post-dated cheques as a form of collateral for credit. One cannot possibly imagine how one could operate with currency alone in today's Hong Kong and Taiwan.

Social Safety Net, Income Distribution, and Social Welfare Programmes

It is a responsibility of the government to provide a social safety net, defined broadly. A social safety net reduces risks to workers and the population in general. It is more efficient for the government to assume this responsibility both because of economies of scale and because it has lower transaction costs. An alternative system run by the enterprises individually, say, will face serious complications as workers change jobs, are between jobs, or simply become disabled and unemployable. The government should also pay attention to the distribution of income to make sure that the gap between the rich and poor does not become so excessive that it may breed social and political instability, and to the equality of access to opportunities to make sure that sufficient social mobility, and hence hope, exists in society.

Traditionally, social welfare programmes are provided only for very low-income households in Hong Kong and Taiwan. However, with increasing democratisation, the governments of both Hong Kong and Taiwan are faced with increasing demands for social welfare programmes. While some social welfare programmes can enhance productivity and efficiency, others detract from it. Thus, social welfare programmes must be carefully designed. One important aspect of these programmes is that in order for them to work, they must be compulsory for everyone. Thus, the government needs to be involved so that its coercive power can be invoked. Left on a voluntary basis, many such programmes cannot survive financially because of the possibilities of the free rider (moral hazard) and adverse selection problems.

For example, if contribution to and participation in a retirement programme is voluntary, then there will be people who may reason that even if they do not participate during their working years, society will ultimately still have to provide for them in their old age—it cannot possibly let them starve—so that they are better off not joining the programme now but they will still be able to benefit later. This means that those who do participate will wind up paying more than they would receive actuarially to keep the programme solvent. This removes the incentive for anyone to join the programme, unless he or she is certain that everyone will participate. This is why the government has to make it compulsory.[31]

Infrastructural Investment

The social overhead capital such as electric utilities, transportation and communication facilities, and industrial parks all require a huge amount of investment, which cannot be afforded by individual private enterprises, especially in the early stage of economic development. Moreover, many of these industries are natural monopolies because of the existence of significant economies of scale (relative to the size of the domestic market) and thus in any case need to be publicly regulated even if they are privately owned.[32] Infrastructural projects are usually undertaken by the government rather than by private investors because of factors such as non-appropriability, lack of sufficient capital, long gestation period, or inability to bear the risk given the capital position. In other words, the social benefits of the infrastructural investment (but not necessarily the privately appropriable benefits) exceed the social costs. Thus, infrastructure should be an area of primary, and some would argue exclusive, focus of government investment.

Examples of successful infrastructural projects include the Hsinchu Science-Based Industrial Park in Taiwan, which is modelled after the Stanford Industrial Park. The park now produces several billion U.S. dollars worth of output a year. China is trying to do the same thing in an area located adjacent to the Chinese Academy of Sciences in Zhongguancun, a suburb of Beijing.

Sometimes infrastructural investment projects also act as signals for coordinated expansion in an industry, a cluster of industries, or a geographical area as well as a tangible demonstration of a government commitment. When potential investors see that an infrastructural project is being developed, they

---

31 One partial remedy is to institute a "means test" to impose some non-pecuniary costs to the free riders.

32 If these infrastructural activities were to be priced at marginal cost, the enterprise would operate at a loss—this is a well-known proposition in public finance.

know that the benefits of a related private investment will be enhanced, and the costs lowered. In addition, they also know that other investors also know. This will set off a stampede to undertake complementary new investment projects, helping to realise the economies of agglomeration and simultaneous expansion.

The existence of complementarities is a major reason for coordination. The use of turnkey infrastructural projects, under which a consortium of investors is asked to deliver a finished, operating facility, can be viewed as a way of solving a complex coordination problem in a developing economy. The establishment of special geographical areas—such as the export-processing zone in Kaohsiung[33] and the Science-Based Industrial Park in Hsinchu, Taiwan, as well as the Special Economic Zones of China (Shenzhen, Zhuhai, Shantou, Xiamen and Hainan)[34] and the Suzhou project run by Singapore—represents an attempt by the respective governments to implement, in one place, a complete package of complementary policies in an administratively efficient manner as well as to signal publicly a credible commitment to do so. All these aforementioned projects have been very successful, with the exception of the Suzhou project, for which it is still too early to tell.

Consumer and Environmental Protection

The area of consumer and environmental protection is one where the government must take a leading role. The problem with consumer and environmental protection is that every individual has only a very small stake and except for the most dedicated does not have sufficient incentive to become actively involved. By contrast, the enterprises that victimise consumers and pollute the environment or have the potential of doing so have every incentive to resist any control or sanction. However, recently, both movements have been coming to the fore in Hong Kong and Taiwan and the politicians there are beginning to take notice. Unfortunately, China still lags far behind in both consumer and environmental protection. Note, however, that in standard national income and product accounts, consumer and environmental protection are all costs

33 Established in the late 1960s, the Kaohsiung Export-Processing Zone is the first export-processing zone of its kind in the world.

34 Twenty-six per cent of foreign direct investment in China is located in the special economic zones.

and not benefits. Thus, greater expenditures on consumer and environmental protection will be reflected in lower measured real GDP and economic efficiency. New measures of real GDP or GNP are required in order to reflect the benefits of a cleaner, healthier, and safer environment.

Efficient Allocation across Industries

A necessary condition for overall efficiency of the economy is an efficient allocation of resources, including fixed investment and capital, across industries. The selection, or targeting, of industries for favoured treatment in order to promote investment in them by the government is often referred to as an industrial policy.

There are many reasons why an industrial policy may be justified: for example, the differences between social and private risk and time preferences,[35] the need to accelerate learning and change (because of externalities), and the existence of complementarities. Moreover, industrial expertise is much more industry-specific than country-specific. A successful entrepreneur would much prefer to move to a different country to continue in the same industry than to engage in a new industry in the same country. The government may therefore have an important role in the promotion of new industries.

In China, prior to 1984, the entire industrial sector was state-owned. All the investments were planned by the State Planning Commission. More recently, with the growth of the non-state sector and the devolution of economic decision-making power, greater attention has been paid to industrial policy. Industrial policy in Hong Kong is rather limited, if it exists at all, although in recent years the government has greatly expanded tertiary educational institutions as well as its support for research and development. In Taiwan, credit rationing is definitely used to support industries that the government wants to start—these are referred to as pioneering industries. From time to time, lists of pioneering industries are published and bureaucrats scour the island for potential investors. In addition to credit rationing, industrial policy in Taiwan is often carried out through the support of industrial R&D at national research

35 The society as a whole should be close to being risk-neutral, whereas individuals and firms are risk-averse to various degrees. The social rate of discount is also likely to be lower than the private rate of discount.

labouratories such as the Industrial Technology Research Institute. Of course, protection, in the form of tariffs, quotas, and import permits, is also used to favour certain industries. For example, until recently, China Steel Corporation in Taiwan had long been allowed to approve all import permits for steel! One notable failure of industrial policy in Taiwan is an attempt to promote large Taiwanese trading firms along the lines of the Japanese firms of Marubeni, Mitsubishi, and Mitsui. Despite the many incentives provided, it has not been successful. Direct investment by the government, or by government development banks, in favoured industries in the form of a state-owned or state-controlled enterprises, is also done. For example, China Steel Corporation, established in the mid-1970s, was majority owned by the government of Taiwan.

The export industries and enterprises have been favoured in the early phase of Taiwan's industrialisation and China's economic reform. In Taiwan, this is done through preferential interest rates for the finance of production for exports. There are also other miscellaneous advantages such as the rebating of import duties on inputs used in production for exports and reduction of port fees, etc. Chinese export enterprises also receive preferential treatment, such as the rebating of import duties on inputs, and until January 1995 they were allowed to retain part of the foreign exchange they earned. In Hong Kong, there has been no explicit government support for exports, but export orders are often accompanied by letters of credit from foreign banks which can be used as "security" to finance production for exports at the Hong Kong banks. The export orientation of the three economies, one can say, is also a form of industrial policy.

Efficient Allocation across Enterprises

First, the government has to take into account the existence of increasing returns to scale, which render the usual market allocation inefficient. For example, if the size of the market will support it, it is better to have one enterprise build one MES plant than to have two build two sub-MES plants. This is where the government can and should intervene to prevent potentially inefficient and possibly ruinous competition. However, if the government then creates a monopoly, it must also take steps to ensure that the enterprise selected does not overuse its monopoly power to the detriment of the consumers of the output produced. (For example, the world price can be used as a benchmark and the government can approve imports if the price charged by the enterprise exceeds the world price by a significant amount.)

To implement its industrial policy, the government must also be able to identify and enlist promising entrepreneurs/enterprises to undertake selected industrial projects in the early stage of its industrial development. The story of how Y. C. Wang of Formosa Plastics was chosen, which may be apocryphal, is well known. After approaching a member of a prominent wealthy family about investing in a plastics project and being turned down, the government turned to the individual with the largest bank account balance in the Bank of Taiwan, who happened to be a Mr. Wang. Today, the Formosa Plastics Group is the largest private industrial group in Taiwan. In practice, the government has the ability to create as well as allocate rents, through taxation and subsidies, franchising, preferential loans, and land grants, especially in the early stage of economic development, when markets are small and underdeveloped (and hence non-competitive).

The selection of Formosa Plastics was a one-time choice. A one-time choice often has to be based on expectations, because there are, in fact, no performance data until the enterprise has been selected, although one can sometimes rely on the track record of related activities in the past. It is also possible to reward an enterprise ex post, such as awarding a government contract to the most profitable enterprise in an industry. However, sometimes it is necessary to select enterprises continually, based on performance, which must be appropriately defined. The government may in fact run a tournament among the participating enterprises and reward the winners with "rents" in accordance with the results.[36] Examples of rewards or "performance-based rents" may include export quotas, preferential loans, and monopoly franchises. Such rents share a common characteristic, that is, the value of the "rents" depends positively on the efficiency of the enterprises being awarded the "rents."

The allocation of textile import quotas imposed by the United States and the European Union is a good example of performance-based rents. In Hong Kong, the quotas are given to the exporters in the year in which the quota system is imposed. They then become the property of the initial quota-holders

36 In the 1960s, the U.S. Department of Defense actually ran a tournament between two aircraft manufacturers based on their prototypes to determine which one would receive the actual order for many more of the same model.

and can be bought, sold, and "leased." In effect, this is a one-time selection of enterprises and transfers all the rents from the potential manufacturers to the quota-holders. Many such quota-holders in Hong Kong are known to have closed their factories immediately and live on the "rentals" generated by their quotas. By contrast, in Taiwan, the quota-holders are allowed to retain only 80% of their initial quotas, with the remaining 20% being returned to the government, which then puts it into a pool to be awarded through open competition on the basis of the highest unit value achieved on bona fide new export orders. This competitive bidding system provides the incentive for manufacturers to innovate and to try to increase the added value of their products (and as a side benefit reduces the tendency for exporters to understate their export revenue in order to circumvent capital export control and tax laws). It also has the advantage of being transparent and independent of bureaucratic discretion, which in turn reduces "rents" as well as rent-seeking. The 80% annual quota retention also provides the incentive for investment in new manufacturing machinery.[37] In February 1994, a similar bidding system was introduced for the allocation of the quotas on some export commodities in China, replacing an administrative examination and approval system used heretofore. All enterprises—foreign, joint-venture, and domestic—are permitted to participate in the quota bidding in China.

Other examples of "performance-based rents" include investment tax credits, accelerated depreciation, and tax holidays for new enterprises. Essentially, all of these benefits and special privileges are of no value to the new enterprises and of no cost to the government unless the new enterprises turn out to be successful and have large and otherwise taxable profits.

In Hong Kong, the natural monopolies such as broadcasting, communication, electric power, mass transportation, etc. are awarded franchises for fixed durations based on a competitive bidding process. There is presumably not too much economic rent created. In Taiwan, the natural monopolies are state-owned enterprises. There are also informally sanctioned oligopolies, for example, the cement industry. In China, wholesale trade is completely monopolised.

However, not all rents are "performance-based." There is another type of

---

37 If the quotas turn over every year, it will be too uncertain for any manufacturer to want to invest in manufacturing equipment with a long life.

rent, which may be referred to as "transition-facilitating rent," that is used to compensate vested interests so as to obtain their support for reforms that enhance the overall efficiency of the economy. For example, a two-track price system for manufactured goods was introduced in China in 1984. It essentially allowed a parallel free market for the above plan-quota outputs of state-owned enterprises while the within plan-quota outputs continued to be sold at the lower official prices to authorised purchasers. The introduction of these parallel free markets, coupled with the expansion of producer autonomy, greatly stimulated supply and alleviated shortages of food products and other consumer goods in China. By 1986, only a handful of consumer goods, compared to hundreds in the late 1970s and early 1980s, still needed to be rationed. In the past several years, the prices of such basic goods and services as grains, energy, and transportation were also adjusted upward continually to reflect true scarcity costs. Today, the prices of more than 97% of consumer goods and 80% of producer goods in China are determined in the free market.

Similarly, dual markets have been permitted to exist for foreign exchange in China since the mid-1980s. Prior to 1994, there was an official exchange rate, available only for certain limited approved transactions, as well as an officially sanctioned swap rate that was determined in markets around the country among exporters and importers qualified to trade in those markets. The supply of foreign exchange in the swap markets was provided by the exporters through the foreign exchange earnings they were allowed to retain. The swap rate was, not surprisingly, significantly higher than the official rate. At the same time, foreign visitors to China were required to use foreign exchange certificates (FECs), which were available at the official exchange rate, rather than the renminbi, the domestic currency. The dual exchange rate system functioned until January 1, 1994, when the two exchange rates—the official rate and the swap rate—were merged into a single rate, with its level determined in a market consisting of exporters and importers, and the FECs were finally withdrawn from circulation. The best way to characterise the current exchange rate system is that it is "current-account convertible" but not "capital-account convertible." The exchange rate itself is not determined by a free float, but rather by a "dirty" float, which is, however, not uncommon among both developed and developing economies.

The two-track price system, with one price market-determined and the other one fixed, is a major factor in the relatively smooth transition of the

Chinese economy from a centrally-planned one to a mostly market one. Under this system, efficiency is immediately achieved because, on the margin, everything is bought and sold at the free-market price. Thus, the value of an additional unit of any good is the same to all potential users. However, users who used to be allocated a good at the low fixed official price are no worse off than before, because they are given the same old quantity allocation at the same old low price. In fact, they are better off because they can now sell the same good at the higher price in the free market and pocket the difference, if they wish. Thus, the rights of the pre-existing vested interests are fully protected—"grandfathered"—under the two-track price system, at least during the transitional period. Not only does this neutralise any potential opposition, but it actually creates a constituency for the free market, which is now perceived as a source of effortless instant profit. Of course, the two-track price system can also be viewed as a system of market prices under which some purchasers are given a subsidy equal to the difference between the market price and the initial fixed price per unit of the good times the quantity of the initial allocation. It is "rent," pure and simple, to the recipients of the "subsidy" because no social value is created. The two-track price system also potentially breeds corruption because whoever is granted a subsidy reaps an effortless instant profit and therefore has an incentive to try to influence the grantor. But it does not in itself cause a distortion in the allocation of resources.

It is, however, important to note that the quantity of the good under "subsidy" is frozen at the initial level and in many instances the "transition-facilitating rents" are phased out after a predetermined number of years, exploiting the difference between the rates of time preference of the central government on the one hand and the state-owned enterprises and their managers on the other. With rapid economic growth, the free market accounts for an increasingly greater proportion of the total sales of the good over time, until the proportion of fixed-price transactions becomes so small that it is no longer material and the two-track price system in effect becomes a single market-price system. This has indeed been the experience of China for both the market for goods and the market for foreign exchange.

Efficient Allocation through Government Coordination

One important role of the government is to enforce contracts and commitments that are not "self-enforcing." Let us consider the case of two investment projects—an upstream project and a downstream project in, say, the petrochemical industry—so that one would be the exclusive supplier and the other would be the exclusive customer. Neither investment project would proceed if the other one did not (if only one went forward, it would have either no market or no supplier and hence would not be viable). This is a version of the classic "prisoner's dilemma" two-person game with its well-known inefficient non-cooperative solution. One possibility is for a single enterprise to invest in both projects, thus internalising the efficiency gains. If there were no capital, or risk-bearing constraints, this might be a good solution, with the government auctioning off the rights or otherwise selecting an enterprise to invest in the bundled project. However, if no enterprise can be found that has the capacity to invest in the bundled project, then only a cooperative solution between two enterprises is possible. However, since the cooperative game has the structure of a bilateral monopoly, the distribution of the gain from trade (or allocation of rent) between the two parties is not determinate and must be agreed upon by both parties. The problem arises with the enforcement of such an agreement. If the two parties are not of approximately equal financial strength, predatory behaviour may arise on the part of the stronger party in the future after the investment projects are completed. The government would have a role to play, not so much as an arbitrator for the distribution of rent, but as a credible neutral guarantor of the rent distribution scheme agreed upon by both parties. What the government could do, for example, is to permit the downstream enterprise to import the intermediate input if the upstream enterprise overcharged and to impose an excise tax on the output of the downstream enterprise if it underpaid. It is clear that in the non-cooperative two-enterprise case, without some kind of government intervention, the projects would not go forward.[38]

On the whole, the governments of Hong Kong and Taiwan tend to be less interventionist than, say, those of Japan and South Korea. While this

---

38 Note that in this example there is no information asymmetry or imperfection. What we have is an ex post reopening of the negotiations after the capital costs are sunk. In this case, the party with the greater financial resources would have the upper hand, as it could outlast the other party in a stalemate. As long as this possibility is known, it would doom the agreement in the absence of the government assuming a guarantor's role to both sides.

difference may be due partly to ideology (more so for Hong Kong), it may also be due to the fact that Hong Kong and Taiwan are much smaller economies and their own domestic markets may be too small to create or support a great deal of rents. The fact that there are many relatively small (non-state-owned) enterprises in Hong Kong and Taiwan (and now China) also suggests fairly intense competition and therefore a low level of potential rents that can be distributed by the government. Overall, rents tend not to be so important in Hong Kong and Taiwan. Whatever rents exist are to be found in the non-tradable sectors, often associated with land and real estate ownership.

The key to successful government coordination lies in the credibility of its commitments, including the commitments to enforce explicit and implicit agreements among independent contracting parties. The government must therefore use its credibility wisely and in particular should avoid engaging in predatory behaviour that undermines its future credibility.

4. Shifting the Production Possibility Frontier

To the extent that technical progress is embodied,[39] any policy that increases the quantity of gross domestic fixed investment shifts the production possibility frontier upward. Other measures that shift the production possibility frontier include R&D investments and reorganisations.

R&D and Technology

In the 1970s, Taiwan, which had heretofore largely eschewed an industrial policy, set up a number of national research institutes and dramatically increased its funding of large-scale industrial R&D projects. One of the research institutes, the Industrial Technology Research Institute, has been responsible for initiating or reviving several major industries, including bicycles, sporting goods, computers and computer peripherals, and semiconductors. Hong Kong is relatively late to this game, although it recently set up a new Hong Kong University of Science and Technology, which has an R&D arm that works closely with industry. China has strong scientific and technological capabilities

39 Kim and Lau (1992a, 1994a) find that technical progress, to the extent that it exists, is mostly embodied in new capital goods.

in the Chinese Academy of Sciences and in its national defence establishment. However, it needs to become more market-oriented and cost-conscious in order to play an important role in economic development.

Industrial policy is not infrequently linked to R&D and science and technology policies. The personal computer industry in Taiwan provides a successful example of government-financed R&D and industrial policy. In the early 1980s, the personal computer industries in Hong Kong and Taiwan consisted mostly of "pirates" who simply copied foreign designs (frequently through reverse engineering) without licenses or payment of royalties. All that activity was stopped as a result of legal actions on the part of the United States and other computer manufacturers. Then the Industrial Technology Research Institute of Taiwan came along and developed its own BIOS chip for the personal computer, which enabled the personal computer industry in Taiwan to continue (under foreign licensing). In Hong Kong, where such R&D effort was lacking, the personal computer industry never recovered. The Industrial Technology Research Institute also went on to develop a version of the notebook computer for a consortium of small computer manufacturers in Taiwan. The very successful semiconductor industry in Taiwan was also incubated in the Industrial Technology Research Institute.

It has long been recognised that the basic issue in the financing of R&D is appropriability. To the extent that the gains from R&D cannot be captured by the enterprise engaging in the R&D itself, the social returns will be greater than private returns, and there will be circumstances under which the government should finance, organise, and support these activities. The situation is further complicated if an industry consists of only small and medium-sized enterprises. In this case, even if in principle the gains are appropriable, in practice, no one single enterprise will have sufficient resources to finance an investment with a large capital requirement, long gestation period, and uncertain outcome, and the ability to bear the risks to enable it to capture the appropriable gains eventually. This sets up a prima facie justification for government intervention in

R&D and for the support of pioneering industries.[40] Government investment in R&D, whether directly through government labouratories, or indirectly by financially supporting R&D projects at universities and in private industry, can also be viewed as an attempt to create comparative advantage. However, one also needs to take into account that the case for government-sponsored R&D is strongest when the direction for the research is more or less known. When the direction is not clear, there is a risk that government sponsorship may send the wrong signal—that is, may prematurely and unduly lead to a concentration of both private and public resources in a limited direction only, with the result that the cost of a mistake, when it occurs, may be large. In general, when the direction for the research is not clear, diversification is probably warranted regardless of whether the R&D effort is publicly or privately sponsored.[41]

Technology Transfer

Foreign direct investment can also bring in new technology, and in principle can shift the production possibility frontier. The use of imported new equipment should also have the same effect. However, Kim and Lau (1992a, 1992b, 1994b, 1994c, 1995) find that there is virtually no technical progress, that is, no shift in the production possibility frontier in the East Asian newly industrialised economies in the post-war period, and that all of their economic growth can be attributed to growth in inputs—physical capital, labour, and human capital, with physical capital the most important. This finding is most surprising and is at variance with one of the conclusions of the World Bank (1993). It is, however, supported by the earlier results of Tsao (1982, 1985, 1986) for Singapore even though the results of Young (1992) for Hong Kong and Singapore are mixed (see also the discussion in Krugman 1994). There are many possible explanations of why there has been no measured technical progress in the East Asian newly industrialised economies, in contrast to the experience of the industrialised economies of

---

40 It is interesting to compare South Korea and Taiwan in this regard. In South Korea, most of the industrial R&D is carried out in the large conglomerates such as Samsung, Hyundai, Daewoo, and Lucky-Goldstar (recently renamed the LG Group).

41 This was pointed out to me by Masahiko Aoki.

France, Germany, Japan, the United Kingdom, and the United States, two of which are the most convincing. First, the East Asian newly industrialised economies had not done much R&D until relatively recently, so one should not expect to be able to measure too much of an effect, given the long gestation period of R&D investments. Second, while foreign direct investment and the use of imported new capital equipment and technology increase gross output, they do not necessarily increase added value above a normal return to the capital, and thus there are no "excess" returns to be measured. Another way of putting this is that the transferer of the technology and the (foreign) manufacturer of the new capital equipment have been able to appropriate substantially all of the gains from the use of the new technology.

Strategic R&D

Sometimes R&D can be used strategically. It is the standard practice in the technology transfer world to cross-license. In order to cross-license, an enterprise must have an invention, a patent, or something to cross-license to another enterprise. This means that it is important to have done some R&D before one comes to the table. In addition, an indigenous R&D effort often has the effect of coaxing a reluctant technology transferer to transfer the technology. This is especially the case with regard to the technology of so-called "critical components." There have been many instances in which an enterprise in a developed country has initially refused to transfer a technology, but upon learning that an indigenous investment was about to be launched based on the results of an indigenous R&D effort, readily agrees to either establish a joint-venture or license. Frequently the purely indigenous venture would then fail. But from a social point of view, the R&D effort has actually paid off even if the directly related venture itself has failed.

Finally, as long as a country does R&D itself and is in the business of cross-licensing, it will have the incentive to enforce intellectual property rights. This is exactly what has happened in Taiwan. In time, this will happen in China also.

Reorganisation

Reorganisation and the introduction of new modes of production are also measures that can shift the production possibility frontier. For Hong Kong and

Taiwan, whatever changes there have been are more evolutionary. They include the gradual transformation of the family enterprise to an enterprise with professional managers, the adoption of new inventory management and quality control methods, and the use of computer equipment in not only finance and accounting but also design and manufacturing. For China, the changes have been more radical. A major component of the Chinese economic reform that began in 1979 consists of the devolution of economic decision-making power and the creation of new modes of economic organisation for production. The intent of such decentralisation was to raise the efficiency and productivity of the production units by increasing their autonomy and providing the proper incentives. The foundation of this decentralisation effort is the "contract responsibility system." In rural areas, the contract responsibility system was implemented at the farm household level. It gave the individual farm household the autonomy to farm the land allocated to it on a long-term lease as it saw fit, in return for a commitment to pay its pro-rata share of agricultural taxes and meet its pro-rata share of delivery quotas. For all practical purposes, the new system amounted to a return of individual private farming, except that the farm households did not (and most still do not) have legal title to the land, only a lease.

The contract responsibility system, coupled with the agricultural price and market reforms, was immediately and immensely successful, generating huge increases in productivity in agriculture of the order of 30–40% within a few years. In turn, the high productivity in agriculture assured the supply of food and financial resources that enabled the reallocation of the labour force from agriculture to industry. In addition, private and collective township and village enterprises (TVEs), as well as foreign and joint-venture enterprises, that engaged in industrial and service activities were permitted to be established. These TVEs turned out to be the fastest growing sector of the Chinese economy during the years of reform. As of 1993, the gross value of industrial production of the TVEs constituted almost 45% of the gross value of the entire Chinese industrial production.

In the urban areas, the planning authority that was at one time concentrated in the State Planning Commission in Beijing was devolved to the provincial and local government levels in 1984. It would probably have been better, from an economic point of view, if the authority had been devolved to the enterprise levels, but that was not to be. An attempt was made to extend the contract responsibility system to the state-owned manufacturing enterprises. However, the contract responsibility system failed to elicit the same improvement in efficiency and productivity there as in the rural areas, except in small service establishments, although it did increase the outputs of certain goods. The inefficiency of the state-owned enterprises and the resulting losses remain major problems in the Chinese economy. As part of the urban economic reform, small private and collective (non-government) enterprises were also allowed, especially in the service sector. Some of the successful ones went on to become relatively large private or collective enterprises.

It is important to note that it is mostly the new enterprises established since 1979 and/or the new economic activities initiated since then that are responsible for the phenomenal economic success of China during the past 15 years. Most of these new organisations face hard budget constraints and hence have a strong incentive to be efficient. For example, the TVEs, even though they are organised and run by the administration of the former communes, in practice operate very much like a private partnership under managing partners. They typically receive no subsidies from the central or provincial governments but thus enjoy a high degree of autonomy. Their advantage over their urban counterparts lies in the natural social safety net in rural areas—every rural resident has the right to a lease on agricultural land and to farm it—which in turn implies that the wage rates paid by the TVEs can be flexible downward and that little or no new social infrastructure is necessary.

As a result of the much faster growth of the more efficient non-state-owned, including collective, township and village, private, joint-venture, and foreign-owned sectors, the state-owned sector has been contracting relative to the other sectors. In fact, even without any significant privatisation, the state-owned sector now accounts for well under half of Chinese GDP, compared to more than 90% in 1979.

5. Concluding Remarks

The role of government in the economic development of China, Hong Kong, and Taiwan has been diverse and multi-faceted. However, one has to conclude that the role of the government has been important in the three economies, albeit in each in a different way. Yet the commonalities are also striking—many similar policies and measures have been adopted in the different economies, albeit at different times, reflecting the differences in their relative stages of economic development (e.g., the unification of the dual exchange rates, the use of special economic zones, and the textile quota allocation system). The similarities stem from the demonstration effects of each economy on the others and from mutual learning and emulation, reinforced by the strong economic linkages among China, Hong Kong, and Taiwan, as well as the cultural and ethnic affinity among their respective citizens.

There are, of course, also major differences across the three economies. On the one hand, the relative lack of support for tertiary education and for R&D by the government in Hong Kong has resulted in the superiority that Taiwan has in high-tech industries. On the other hand, the freedom of capital movements, the low tax rate, and the adherence to the rule of law, coupled with a relatively relaxed regulatory regime, have contributed to Hong Kong's success as a leading financial centre in East Asia. The free trade policy of Hong Kong has also resulted in a much more even development in Hong Kong, whereas the economies of both China and Taiwan are characterised by dualism—the existence, side by side, of an efficient, externally oriented sector and an inefficient, domestic non-tradable and service sector.

The differences among the three economies will probably never disappear. In a sense, they will specialise in accordance with their respective comparative advantages, even though, as noted, these comparative advantages arose partly in response to government policies and actions. But precisely because these comparative advantages are creatable, the economies that are currently ahead in their respective dimensions must continue to innovate. Taiwan today is producing and exporting what Japan was producing and exporting a decade ago. China today is producing what Taiwan was producing a decade ago. Shanghai will be looking to replace or at least supplant Hong Kong's role as a financial centre serving the Chinese economy within the next couple of decades. It is this continuous competitive pressure that makes it necessary for governments to plan ahead and pursue forward-looking policies.

More generally, what distinguishes China and Taiwan on the one hand and Hong Kong on the other is the role of ideology and the East Asian tradition of a high degree of personalisation of government. Both ideology—communism in China, the Three People's Principles in Taiwan—and the high degree of personalisation of government in these East Asian societies mandate activism, at least superficially, for the heads of the governments, at all levels, especially in response to a perceived need. Benign neglect is not a politically feasible option. It may be reasonably expected that the role of government will increase in Hong Kong after 1997, not so much because of its reversion to Chinese sovereignty, but because of the larger role its citizens, mostly of Chinese ethnic origin, will play in its own governance.

References

Abramovitz, Moses, and Paul A. David. "Reinterpreting Economic Growth: Parables and Realities." *American Economic Review* 63 (1973): pp. 428–439.

Kim, Jong-II, and Lawrence J. Lau. "The Importance of Embodied Technical Progress: Some Empirical Evidence from the Group-of-Five Countries." Working Paper, Department of Economics, Stanford University, 1992.

———. "The Sources of Economic Growth of the Newly Industrialized Countries on the Pacific Rim." Paper presented at the Conference on the Economic Development of the Republic of China and the Pacific Rim in the 1990s and Beyond. Taipei, May 25–28 (1992b).

———. "The Sources of East Asian Economic Growth Revisited." Working paper, Department of Economics, Stanford University, 1994a.

———. "The Sources of Economic Growth in the East Asian Newly Industrialized Countries." *Journal of the Japanese and International Economies* 8, no. 3 (1994b), pp. 235–271.

———. "The Sources of Economic Growth of the Newly Industrialized Countries on the Pacific Rim." In L. R. Klein and C. T. Yu, eds., *The Economic Development of ROC and the Pacific Rim in the 1990s and Beyond*. Singapore: World Scientific Publishing Co., 1994c, pp. 65–103.

———. "The Sources of Asian-Pacific Economic Growth." *The Canadian Journal of Economics* 29 (1996), pp. S448–S454.

Kornai, Janos. *Economics of Shortage*. Amsterdam: North Holland, 1980.

Krugman, Paul. "The Myth of Asia's Miracle." *Foreign Affairs* 73, no. 6 (1994), pp. 62–78.

Lau, Lawrence J. "Global Impacts of Chinese Economic Growth." Paper presented at the Aspen Strategy Group Conference, The Growth of Chinese Power and Implications for U.S. Policy. Aspen, Colorado, August 1995.

Lau, Lawrence J., and D. H. Song. "Growth versus Privatization—An Alternative Strategy to Reduce the Public Enterprise Sector: The Experiences of Taiwan and South Korea." Working paper, Department of Economics, Stanford University, 1992.

Tsao, Yuan "Growth and Productivity in Singapore: A Supply Side Analysis." Ph.D. diss., Harvard University, 1982.

———. "Growth Without Productivity: Singapore Manufacturing in the 1970s." *Journal of Development Studies* 18 (1985), pp. 25–38.

———. "Sources of Growth Accounting for the Singapore Economy." In C. Y. Lim and P. J. Lloyd, eds., *Singapore: Resources and Growth*. Singapore: Oxford University Press, 1986, pp. 17–44.

The World Bank. *The East Asian Miracle: Economic Growth and Public Policy*. Oxford: Oxford University Press, 1993.

Young, Alwyn (1992), "A Tale of Two Cities: Factor Accumulation and Technical Change in Hong Kong and Singapore," in O. J. Blanchard and S. Fischer, eds., *National Bureau of Economic Research Macroeconomics Annual*, The MIT Press, Cambridge, Mass., pp. 13–54.

Chapter 8.

The Sky Isn't Falling —The East Asian Currency Crisis (1997)*

1. Yen Devaluation Does Not Necessarily Lead to Lower U.S. Dollar Export Prices

First of all, it should be noted that just because the exchange rate of the Japanese yen is lower, it does not necessarily mean that the export prices of Japanese goods will be lower in U.S. dollar terms. The easiest way to see this is to look at the situation from the point of view of a Japanese exporter. An exporter of, say, the Lexus, a car made by Toyota and sold in the United States, realises that he is already competitive in the United States at the existing U.S. dollar price. There is therefore no particular reason for him to lower his U.S. dollar price pari passu with the decline in the Japanese yen. Instead he should take advantage of the situation to increase his profit margin in yen terms by maintaining his U.S. dollar price at the existing level. This is especially true in the automobile case because of the existence of the so-called voluntary export restraints (in fact, Japanese automobile manufacturers have already announced that they will hold their U.S. dollar prices) but is not limited to it. Under this scenario, the U.S. dollar prices of Japanese exports will not be significantly changed regardless of the decline in the exchange rate of the Japanese yen. Consequently, there will be little or no competitive price pressure on the exports of other economies, such as South Korea and Taiwan. Thus, it should not lead to another round of competitive devaluations. Crucial to this analysis is the recognition that the exports of Japan

---

* This chapter was originally written in response to the large devaluation of the Japanese yen in 1998, and published as "The Sky Isn't Falling," *ICBC Economic Review* 305 (September–October 1998), pp. 1–12.

are not mere "commodities" that are easily available and substitutable elsewhere; instead, many Japanese manufacturers and exporters, such as Sony, already have significant market shares and with it market power and the ability to set U.S. dollar prices. Empirically, the U.S. dollar prices of Japanese exports have been much more stable than the U.S. dollar value of the Japanese yen. Thus, the U.S. dollar price of Japanese exports did not increase much as the Japanese yen appreciated to 80 yen per U.S. dollar in 1995, and also did not decrease much as the yen depreciated first to the 120 yen range and more recently to 145 yen per U.S. dollar. Moreover, it is also the case that most Japanese international trade is still denominated in U.S. dollars.

2. Yen Devaluation Does Not Necessarily Lead to Less Japanese Imports

What about the effect of a decline in the exchange rate of the Japanese yen on Japanese imports? With a devaluation, Japanese imports will become more expensive in yen terms. In principle, this should result in a decline in the quantity of Japanese imports. Will this in turn hurt the exports of China, South Korea, Taiwan and other East Asian economies to Japan? The answer is, to a first approximation, no. The reason is the well-known fact that Japanese imports are not very sensitive to changes in relative prices, but are very sensitive to changes in Japanese real income. In general, the gap between the prices of domestically produced products and imported substitutes in Japan is very large. Japan is thus unlikely to import much more in the absence of a massive decline in the price of imports; by the same token, Japan is also not going to import much less even as the imports become somewhat more expensive. Within the range of potential variations of the exchange rate, the price effect is therefore not likely to be significant. The current slump in Japanese imports from other, including East Asian, economies is caused not so much by a weak yen but by the anemic growth—in fact, decline—of Japanese real GDP. Devaluations by other East Asian economies since July 1997 have had only very marginal effects on the quantities of their exports to Japan to date and further competitive devaluations in response to the yen devaluation are unlikely to help. One useful way to think about it is to consider that since July 1997, the Thai baht has devalued approximately 30% with respect to the Japanese yen, but there has been no surge of imports by Japan from Thailand. Why should another

10% (competitive) devaluation of the Thai baht be expected to make much of a difference now? For this reason, it is neither necessary nor effective for the East Asian economies to devalue competitively in response to a weakened yen.

3. Yen Devaluation May Slow Foreign Direct Investment and Loans from Japan

The only possible genuinely significant effect of a weak yen on other East Asian economies is the slowdown of Japanese outward foreign direct investment to these economies. However, the current macroeconomic conditions in these economies are probably not propitious for Japanese foreign direct investment in any case, no matter what the exchange rate is, especially given the Japanese reputation as being very conservative and deliberate foreign direct investors. "Plunging right in" is simply not the Japanese way.

There has also been a very significant reduction in the credit extended by Japanese banks to the East Asian economies. As most of this credit is denominated in U.S. dollar, a weak yen will accelerate the withdrawal of Japanese banks from these markets. However, this process of withdrawal began quite some time ago, for reasons mostly related to the financial conditions of the Japanese banks, and would have continued whether the yen further devalued or not.

Even if there is a real effect on foreign direct investment from Japan, it is not clear that any economy should resort to a devaluation of its currency solely for the purpose of attracting foreign direct investment, or that such a devaluation would in fact be effective. Such a devaluation may actually have an adverse long-term effect as potential foreign investors factor in the risks of exchange rate losses in the future. It may also have negative consequences on the rate of inflation. Moreover, for those economies with net outstanding debt to Japan denominated in yen terms, there may actually be a windfall, a benefit, resulting from a devaluation of the Japanese yen, if they do not attempt to match the Japanese devaluation.

4. Other East Asian Currencies Need Not Follow the Japanese Yen

We have already made a general case for why other East Asian currencies need not follow the recent Japanese devaluation. We shall now examine specific currencies.

The Renminbi

First, it will be argued that the renminbi, the Chinese currency, does not need to follow the devaluation of the Japanese yen. There has been continuing speculation since July 1997 that the renminbi may devalue, long before the latest decline in the Japanese yen. The Chinese yuan and the Hong Kong dollar are the only two East Asian currencies that have not devalued since 1 July 1997. Will the renminbi devalue?

It should be noted that the renminbi is not a freely convertible currency and is therefore difficult for international speculators to attack. Any devaluation will have to be an intentional policy decision on the part of the Chinese economic decision makers. However, all the senior Chinese leaders—President Jiang Zemin, former Premier Li Peng, current Premier Zhu Rongji and Governor Dai Xianglong of the Chinese central bank—have said that the renminbi will not be devalued. There are diplomatic and political benefits from maintaining the value of the renminbi on the part of China, providing a pillar of stability in East Asia—a concrete gesture of cooperation with and support for the other East Asian economies.

However, we should not place all of our hope on what government officials say they will or will not do. We should also examine the Chinese economic fundamentals and Chinese economic self-interest. The economic fundamentals are strong. The domestic savings rate has remained high (between 35 and 40% of GDP), perfectly adequate for Chinese investment needs—there is no savings-investment gap. There is a trade surplus of at least US$40 billion in 1997 and a large current-account surplus of US$22.6 billion even in the first half of 1998, almost a full year after the beginning of the East Asian currency crisis. The foreign capital utilised by China is mostly in the form of foreign direct investment (FDI), which cannot be easily withdrawn at short notice. The external debt of approximately US$130 billion has staggered, longer maturities, unlike those of the other East Asian economies such as South Korea and Thailand. The rate of inflation cannot be much lower—it has been slightly negative for nine consecutive months. The official foreign exchange reserves of US$140 billion are the second highest in the world (after Japan) and perfectly adequate if ever a defence of the Chinese yuan becomes necessary.

The East Asian currency crisis will have a negative impact on the growth of Chinese exports. Chinese exports grew 7.6% to US$87 billion in the first half of 1998 (compared to the same period of 1997), a significant slowdown compared to the full- year growth of 26.2% in 1997. However, this slowdown is almost entirely due to the decline in Chinese exports to the affected Southeast Asian economies. Chinese exports have continued their strong growth in other markets (Europe [25.5%], U.S. [18.1%], Africa [44.7%], Latin America [38.1%], and Oceania [15.2 %]). In other words, it has not lost market share to the Southeast Asian economies and in fact has gained market share. As the Southeast Asian economies recover, with more stable exchange and interest rates, they will pose some competition to China. However, it will not be a huge impact and can be managed. Exports constitute only 20% of Chinese GDP and the Chinese economy, with its own huge domestic market, is nowhere nearly as dependent on exports as some other East Asian economies. The competition faced by Chinese exports from Southeast Asian economies is mostly in such goods as apparel, electrical appliances, footwear, and toys. The cost structure of such light industrial manufactured exports is approximately distributed as 20% local costs (including labour), 60% imported raw material and intermediate inputs, and 20% financing costs. The competitive advantage of the devaluations in the Southeast Asian economies is therefore substantially offset by the increase in the costs of the imported inputs, as well as by the increase in financing costs (with nominal rates of interest of up to 30% per annum). That is why exports of Southeast Asian economies have not surged, particularly even with devaluations in excess of 40%, and are not expected to do so in the near future. Moreover, some categories of exports, e.g., apparel, are quota-constrained, and hence are even less sensitive to competitive pressure.

Chinese export competitiveness can in fact be significantly enhanced without a devaluation. Chinese prices have already been falling for nine months in a row. Through a variety of measures such as tariff reductions on imports of equipment and intermediate inputs, value-added tax (VAT) rebates, discounting of export letters of credit, reduction of port fees, and the devolution of direct trading privileges to the individual enterprises, the costs of exports can be lowered. Moreover, relocation of factories from the high-cost coastal areas into the interior of China, as some firms have already done, can also result in substantial cost savings. Chinese labour costs are currently still lower than many of the Southeast Asian economies even after their recent devaluations. With regard to South Korea, Japan and Taiwan, the Chinese exports by and large do not compete directly in the same markets. In fact, China runs a significant trade deficit vis-a-vis both Japan and Taiwan, mostly due to the imports of intermediate inputs, and therefore benefits, on balance, more from devaluations of the Japanese yen and the New Taiwan dollar, than it is harmed.

One other short-term problem faced by Chinese enterprises is the possibility of dumping by South Korea and Southeast Asian economies in China and in other competing markets. However, while a firm can sell from its pre-existing inventory at lower than the true cost to raise cash, no firm can afford to dump indefinitely—it must break even on its costs, which typically include a significant direct and indirect import component, priced in U.S. dollar, as well as financing costs. Once the pre-existing inventory is exhausted, it will face the same costs as firms in other countries, e.g. East Asian petrochemical firms face the same prices for feedstock and energy (oil or gas), which are denominated in U.S. dollar terms; East Asian steel firms face the same prices for iron ore and energy, which are also denominated in U.S. dollar terms. The sensible way for China to discourage dumping is not a devaluation but the imposition of antidumping duties, which have been applied very successfully by the United States.

The major pressure for a devaluation of the renminbi actually comes from Chinese exporters, many of whom are state-owned trading corporations, even though they have not been significantly affected by the East Asian currency crisis, as the export data described above demonstrate. Like exporters in other countries, they always prefer a lower renminbi to a higher one, no matter what the exchange rate is. This is because even if the actual quantity of exports does not increase as a result of a devaluation, their profits, in renminbi terms, will always be higher. It is therefore in their self- interest to advocate a devaluation, regardless of the overall merit of the case for the economy as a whole. There is, in addition, a short-term profit motive. Many of the Chinese exporters have purposely been keeping all of their export proceeds abroad, in U.S. dollar, rather than selling the bulk of it to the Chinese central bank for renminbi, as required, hoping to make a quick "yuan" in the event that they succeed in pressuring the Chinese government to devalue.

The impact of the East Asian currency crisis on foreign direct investment (FDI) into China is significant but not critical. First of all, FDI, including recycled Chinese investment (to be explained below), accounts for only 10% of total Chinese domestic gross fixed investment, so that even if FDI dries up altogether, the Chinese investment rate will only come down from close to 40% of GDP to the mid-30s, still a very impressive rate. Second, in terms of the impact, FDI originating from Southeast Asian economies such as Indonesia, Malaysia, Singapore and Thailand, and from South Korea, will be most affected. FDI motivated by low labour costs may be affected because of potential competition from the Southeast Asian economies, even though, as noted above, Chinese labour costs are still lower than those of South Korea and Southeast Asian countries. However, FDI aimed at access to the Chinese market will be unaffected. Thus, General Motors and Motorola will continue to push ahead on their investment plans in China. Moreover, a significant proportion of FDI, estimated to be a third of the total, is actually recycled Chinese investment. This is investment made by Chinese enterprises in China itself, but masquerading as foreign direct investment, so that the investment projects can qualify for favourable tariff and tax treatments in China. This type of investment will, of course, be largely unaffected by the East Asian currency crisis. In the first half of 1998, actual FDI arrivals in China totalled US$20.5 billion, a slight decline of 1.3% from the same period of 1997, principally because of the withdrawal of investors from Southeast Asian countries. During the same period, FDI commitments totalled US$24.2 billion, an increase of 5.5% over the previous year, reversing two consecutive years of decline. Actual FDI arrivals in 1998 are projected to decline to US$40 billion from US$45.3 billion in 1997.

The Chinese economy has, however, shown signs of slowing down. Exports will not be growing as robustly in the new international exchange rate and growth environment. Domestic macroeconomic stimulus is needed to make up for the slowdown in the growth of exports and the expected, albeit relatively modest, decline in FDI. This will take the forms of increase and acceleration of infrastructural investment projects and the encouragement and promotion of the development of affordable owner-occupied residential housing in Chinese urban areas, among other measures. We shall begin to see the early effects of these stimulative measures in the third and fourth quarters of 1998. An effective macroeconomic stimulus package will also reduce the pressure for a devaluation.

Finally, the most convincing argument against a renminbi devaluation is that it will, at best, have a very marginal effect on Chinese exports but a high probability of actually doing great harm, not only to other East Asian economies but also to the Chinese economy itself. Exports to all markets other than East Asia have continued their high rates of growth. Imports by Japan from China are not price-sensitive but are income-sensitive. Southeast Asian countries are not going to import more from China, no matter how inexpensive

Chinese exports become, because of their crisis-induced recessions. Nor are they likely to invest more in China no matter how low the renminbi exchange rate becomes. However, there is a definite probability that a devaluation of the renminbi may well trigger another round of competitive devaluation among the East Asian economies, thus nullifying any competitive advantage that a renminbi devaluation alone might have gained, and leaving everyone, including China itself, in a worse situation than before. In fact, it would increase the cost of imports of intermediate goods and capital equipment as well as the real burden of the external debt for China, without an increase in the quantity of exports (on account of the competitive devaluation of the other East Asian economies). It would rekindle domestic Chinese inflation, or worse, might even lead to stagflation. It might also undermine the confidence of the Chinese citizens in their government and in its currency.

Actually, the devaluation of the Japanese yen—from 80 yen per U.S. dollar to 145 yen per U.S. dollar—while the Japanese economy remains mired in recession, itself is living proof that devaluation is not a cure-all by any means. In this regard, we may add that the recent Japanese yen devaluation, if unmatched by China, will actually result in a windfall gain for China. China is a significant debtor to Japan (estimated to be approximately US$40 billion) and the loans are denominated in yen; a Japanese yen devaluation lowers the cost of repayment of both the principal and the interest to China. The current weakness in the Japanese yen presents a good opportunity for China to purchase Japanese yen for the purpose of prepaying its yen-denominated debt.

All of these considerations suggest that a devaluation of the renminbi is neither necessary nor in China's best self-interests.

The Hong Kong Dollar

Another frequent question is: Will Hong Kong maintain its U.S. dollar peg? The peg was adopted in response to a crisis of confidence in October 1983 and has remained ever since. It has provided an anchor of confidence through various crises and periods of stress faced by Hong Kong, such as the stock market crash in 1987, the Tiananmen incident in 1989, the reversion to Chinese sovereignty in 1997, and now the East Asian currency crisis. Will a devaluation do Hong Kong any good? We shall show that there is nothing that a devaluation of the Hong Kong dollar can achieve that cannot be achieved through other means that are more desirable on economic grounds.

As a free port with few natural resources, the prices of tradable goods in Hong Kong follow world price levels. For example, an orange, being a tradable good, will always cost US$1 in Hong Kong (as in California, ignoring transportation cost), regardless of the exchange rate. International competitiveness of Hong Kong depends only on the prices of the two non-tradable goods (labour and land), both of which are flexible downward, in U.S. dollar terms. The wage rate depends on the cost of living, which in turn depends on the prices of tradables and land, so the one price that is critical for the international competitiveness of Hong Kong, and that can also be influenced by Hong Kong, is the price of land.

The international competitiveness of Hong Kong can be enhanced without the necessity of a devaluation. Compare two alternative scenarios: In the first scenario, there is a devaluation of the HK dollar. Such a devaluation leaves the prices of tradable goods the same in U.S. dollar terms, but non-tradable goods, principally land, lower in U.S. dollar terms (but not necessarily lower in Hong Kong dollar terms). In the second scenario, the peg is maintained at its current level, but the price of land is allowed to decline. In this second case, the prices of tradable goods remain the same in U.S. dollar terms, and the price of land is lower in U.S. dollar terms. Thus, to an international investor or a multinational corporation, the two scenarios have identical implications. However, from the point of view of the citizens of Hong Kong, the impact is vastly different between the two scenarios. A devaluation of the Hong Kong dollar will lead to an immediate jump in the Hong Kong dollar prices of all tradable goods, and with a time lag, higher prices of labour and land, hence higher domestic inflation as well as a higher nominal rate of interest, with significant adverse distributional consequences. By maintaining the peg and letting the price of land come down, there is not only no inflation in Hong Kong dollar terms, but the cost of living should decline, led by housing costs, and eventually so would the nominal wage rate. There is therefore no good justification for a devaluation of the Hong Kong dollar. Instead, the price of land, which by mid-1997 has been driven to astronomical levels by a real estate bubble, has been adjusting downward, which is the way it should be.

An additional argument against changing the peg is that its whole value for maintaining confidence in Hong Kong lies in its absolute stability. Once a precedent is set that the peg can be changed, the expectation is that it can be changed again, no matter at what level the new peg is set. This will lead to increased volatility in the expectation of the Hong Kong dollar exchange rate and defeat the whole purpose of a peg. Increased volatility will also increase, rather than decrease, the interest rate risk premium. There are of course economists and others who advocate doing away with the peg altogether and simply floating the Hong Kong dollar. Given the huge global pools of foot-loose hot money and the relatively small size of the Hong Kong dollar market, it is inevitable that any monetary authority or central bank of Hong Kong will have to wind up being a market-maker to prevent the currency being in an extended over-bought or over-sold condition, which will tend to obstruct, rather than facilitate, international commerce and investment. It is not clear that such a "managed float" is easier to maintain than a peg; but it is clear that with a floating rate regime, the interest rate risk premium will definitely be higher than that of a credible "peg" regime.

With a low aggregate external debt of only approximately US$20 billion and the third highest official foreign exchange reserves (US$96 billion) in the world, equal to more than seven times the currency in circulation (which the Monetary Authority is committed to redeem in terms of U.S. dollars on demand), the peg can be and has been successfully defended. The devaluation of the Japanese yen will have only very marginal impact on the Hong Kong economy. Japanese tourists have not been traveling so much because of prices in Hong Kong, which have been coming down in any case, but because of the uncertainty in their incomes and more recently the security of their employment. A lower Hong Kong dollar is unlikely to lure too many of them to come at this time.

The South Korean Won and the New Taiwan Dollar

Neither the South Korean won nor the New Taiwan dollar need to follow the Japanese yen. A devaluation of the Japanese yen is actually potentially more beneficial than harmful. Japan has a huge trade surplus vis-a-vis South Korea and Taiwan. Many South Korean and Taiwanese firms rely on imported Japanese intermediate inputs and capital goods. A decline in the value of the Japanese yen, to the extent that it implies lower Japanese export prices in U.S. dollar terms, benefits such firms. Of course, this is potentially offset by possible lower exports to Japan, as exports from South Korea and Taiwan appear more expensive in yen terms. However, as already argued above, the quantity of imports into Japan is not very price-sensitive. But even if the quantity of exports from South Korea and Taiwan to Japan are price-sensitive, a yen devaluation, on balance, will result in a net benefit to South Korea and Taiwan because they both import so much more from Japan than Japan does from them. There is therefore no compelling reason for South Korea and Taiwan to try to offset such a yen devaluation. In fact, the experience of the past six weeks indicates that the Korean won has appreciated and the New Taiwan dollar has stabilised. It should be noted that a further devaluation is not helpful to either South Korea or Taiwan in the upgrading of its industrial level. The costs of inputs to high-technology industries—equipment, engineers and scientists, and components and parts—are at world prices.

A devaluation would raise not only revenues but also costs in terms of domestic prices, resulting in little or no net advantage. Finally, with large trade surpluses vis-a-vis China (especially on the part of Taiwan), it is definitely in the interest of South Korea and Taiwan to see a stable renminbi.

Southeast Asian Economies

The Southeast Asian economies do not need to react to the recent devaluation of the Japanese yen because on the one hand, they do not compete with Japan in their export markets, and on the other hand, their exports to Japan are on the whole not price-sensitive (but income-sensitive). In any case, given the market power that Japanese importers have, they can extract concessions from Southeast Asian exporters even in the absence of an explicit devaluation of the Southeast Asian currencies.

There is a short-term speculative fervour in the currency markets in East Asia. However, if one examines the economic fundamentals, the capital-out-flow-induced weakness in the Japanese yen does not require any adjustment in the exchange rates of most currencies vis-a-vis the U.S. dollar. This list includes the renminbi, the Hong Kong dollar, the South Korean won, the New Taiwan dollar and the other Southeast Asian currencies. This is not to say that the Japanese economy is irrelevant—a higher rate of growth of real GDP on the part of Japan will definitely be helpful. However, the Japanese devaluation per se should not lead to another round of competitive devaluation in East Asia. The sky isn't falling.

Chapter 9.

Gain Without Pain: Why Economic Reform in China Worked*

1. Introduction

Over the past two decades, East Asia has been the fastest-growing region in the world, and China has been the fastest-growing country in East Asia, with an average annual growth rate of approximately 10% since its economic reforms began in 1979. Between 1979 and 1996, Chinese real GDP has quintupled from US$150 billion to US$750 billion (all in 1990 prices).[1] During the same period, real GDP per capita has increased more than fourfold, from US$150 to US$610 (again, all in 1990 prices). China is one of the very few socialist countries that have made a successful transition from a centrally-planned economy to a market economy.

Why has China been successful in its economic reforms while others, such as the former Soviet Union, appeared to have failed? Two principal reasons may be identified. First, China has implemented economic reforms in such a way that there are no losers. In other words, no Chinese citizen is made worse off as a result of the Chinese economic reforms. Second, through its high

---

* This chapter was originally published in *China's Political Economy*, edited by Gung-Wu Wang and John Wong. Copyright © 1998 Singapore University Press and World Scientific Publishing Company. The author is grateful for discussions with Masahiko Aoki, K. C. Fung, Hyung-Ki Kim, Masahiro Okuno-Fujiwara, Ying-Yi Qian, Dani Rodrik and Gerard Roland. Responsibility for any errors remains with the author.

1 To put these statistics in perspective, it is useful to remember that real GDP and real GDP per capita in the United States are approximately US$7 trillion and US$25,000 respectively. Thus despite its rapid growth, it will probably take another four decades to half a century before Chinese real GDP and real GDP per capita approach U.S. levels.

saving rate—approaching 40% in some years—China has had an abundant supply of new resources, most of which it has invested efficiently. The resulting rapid economic growth also makes it much easier to assure that there are no losers.[2] The abundance of new resources also makes it far less urgent a matter to try to redeploy the old assets efficiently, which requires the more likely to be painful reform and restructuring of the state-owned enterprises. Our estimates show that almost 80% of the fixed capital stock in 1996 is due to gross fixed investments made since 1979. A "gain without pain" strategy might not have been possible if the saving rates were not as high as they were.

2. The Problem of Compensating the Losers

When an economy starts from a state of inefficiency, any efficiency-enhancing economic reform will result in a net *gain* in real output in the aggregate. Thus, in principle, it should be possible to make everyone better off, or at least make nobody worse off, as a result of the reform, by suitably taxing or otherwise redistributing from the winners to compensate the losers. If this can in fact be done, then "gain without pain" is achieved. "Gain without pain" is the dream of all economic reformers (and politicians) because it minimises political opposition to and maximises political support for, reforms *ex ante* as well as maximises political opposition to reversal of reforms *ex post* (because of the new vested interests created).

In practice, potential losers are seldom compensated, and even if they are, they are seldom fully compensated, for several reasons. First, there is imperfect information—it is difficult to identify the potential winners and losers as well as to ascertain the magnitudes of their individual potential gains and losses. Second, it is difficult to devise implementable general taxation and subsidy schemes that target the potential winners and losers specifically—that is, to tax only the winners and to compensate only the losers. Third, the only way to tax the winners and compensate the losers without introducing distortions in the economy is to use a system of fixed lumpsum taxes and subsidies, that is, taxes and subsidies whose values do not depend on and hence do not affect

2 With an economy growing at 10% per annum, there is no reason why anyone has to be worse off in absolute terms.

the actions of the economic agents. Unfortunately, explicit lumpsum taxes and subsidies require such detailed information on the individual economic agents that they are virtually impossible, and most general taxation schemes, based on either earnings, income, consumption or retail purchases, are distortionary—that is, they will affect the actions of the economic agents and thereby prevent full economic efficiency from being achieved. Fourth, there are costs of information and implementation—that is, in order to effect transfers from winners to losers, a system of taxation and subsidies with its necessary institutions, e.g. the Internal Revenue Service, may have to be devised and implemented. That is why in many reforming economies, there is frequently no attempt to compensate the losers, and state promises of compensation, when made, generally lack credibility because of the perceived difficulty of implementation. The type of economic reforms implemented in the former Soviet Union and Eastern Europe, sometimes described as "Big Bang" reforms, generally suffers from this inability to compensate the potential losers. Potential losers are therefore likely to oppose the economic reform, often causing the reform to fail before it is even begun, or at least drastically reducing its chance of success.

Unlike economic reforms elsewhere, the Chinese economic reforms have not aroused significant political opposition and have enjoyed widespread popular support.[3] This is because the Chinese economic reforms have implicitly adhered to the principle that no one should be made worse off as a result. Thus, there are no losers from the economic reforms, only winners, even though the distribution of the gains from the economic reforms may be highly uneven.

But can economic reforms without losers bring about an efficient economy? The answer is an unequivocal yes.[4] It can be shown that, by using a "dual-track" approach, Chinese economic reforms, in addition to being Pareto-improving—that is, having no losers—also simultaneously enable the economy to be fully efficient, in the sense that all resources have been put to their fullest and best use. Thus, Chinese economic reforms have not only achieved "gain without pain," but also actually *maximal* "gain without pain."

---

3 There is, of course, dissatisfaction with the relative distribution of the gains from economic reform. Some have benefited much more than others. But no one will deny that everyone has gained.

4 See Lau, Qian and Roland (1997).

In part 3 we briefly review the Chinese economic reforms and the resulting outcomes. In part 4, we show how the "dual track" approach can simultaneously permit the protection of the pre-reform rights and obligations and yet also enable full economic efficiency, thus achieving "gain without pain." In part 5, we give examples of the "dual-track" approach from the Chinese experience. In part 6, we present evidence of how marketisation proceeded under the "dual track" approach in the agricultural, industrial and retail sectors, and how the central plan has been gradually phased out. We conclude with some brief remarks in part 7.

3. The Chinese Economic Reforms (1979–Present)

Four essential elements of Chinese economic reforms since 1979 may be identified. They are:

(1) The "open door"—meaning opening the Chinese economy to international trade and foreign investment.
(2) Marketisation—the introduction of markets in goods, factors, and foreign exchange to initially supplement and eventually supplant the plan.
(3) The devolution of decision-making power on the basis of the "contract responsibility system"—the de-communisation of agriculture, empowering provincial and local governments, professionalisation of the management of enterprises, and the granting of autonomy and incentives to enterprises on the margin.
(4) The creation of new, non-state-owned modes of organisation for production. This includes, in agriculture, the return to a system of individual cultivators with fixed rents and taxes in 1979, and in industry, the emergence of "Township and Village" enterprises (TVEs) as well as (foreign) joint-venture, wholly foreign, and private enterprises since 1984. Some state-owned enterprises and/or their subsidiaries have become publicly traded joint stock companies since 1990, with many private citizens becoming shareholders and hence partial owners. The trend of corporatisation of state-owned enterprises (SOEs) is poised to accelerate this year.

The results of the Chinese economic reforms may be characterised overall as very successful, with two exceptions. First, the average annual rate of inflation over the post-reform period is approximately 7%, much higher than the pre-reform average of less than .5% per annum. Second, the "contract responsibility" system, so successful in agriculture, failed by and large to elicit improvement in efficiency in the state-owned enterprises in the industrial sector. We discuss each element of the economic reforms in turn.

The Open Door

The open door policy has been extremely successful. Chinese international trade has increased by leaps and bounds. With the inclusion of Hong Kong, the People's Republic of China is now the world's fourth largest trading nation. It is also by far the largest recipient of foreign direct investment among developing countries.[5] The official foreign exchange reserves of China now exceeds US$100 billion, far more than is necessary to support the requirements of her current-account transactions.

Marketisation

Marketisation has also been extremely successful. The prices of all consumer goods and more than 95% of the producer goods are determined in the market. The price of low-grade grain is controlled (subsidised), only for social welfare purposes. The price of energy is at world market levels. The dual exchange rates were unified in January 1994. Current-account convertibility was achieved in December 1996. The labour markets have also been liberalised. The state no longer has the responsibility of placing college and university graduates, who can now work wherever they wish. Stock and bond markets were also established in the 1990s.

The Devolution of Economic Decision Power

A great deal of power has been devolved to the provincial and local government levels. For example, foreign direct investment projects of below US$30

---

5 However, the inflow of foreign direct investment only began to be quantitatively significant after the 1990s. Even then, at its peak, it accounted for less than 15% of gross fixed investment in China.

million can be directly approved by the provincial authorities. The managers of enterprises have more autonomy and power than before.

The Growth of the Non-State Sector

The state-owned sector has continuously shrunk *relative* to the aggregate economy; it currently accounts for no more than 30% of the aggregate output. The proportion of aggregate economy-wide gross fixed investments accounted for by state-owned enterprises was 72% in 1979. It stood at just over 50% in 1996. Because of the de-communisation of the agricultural sector, the state-owned sector accounts for only a very insignificant proportion of aggregate agricultural output. In industry, the state-owned sector's share of gross value of production fell from almost 80% in 1979 to just above 30% in 1995 (see Chart 9.1). This decline was caused primarily because of the considerably faster growth of the non-state sector. The growth of the non-state sector has far outstripped the growth of the state sector, which has been largely propelled by the growth of the output of the TVEs. As of 1994, TVEs accounted for almost half of the aggregate industrial output and almost two-thirds of the aggregate industrial employment of China.

Chart 9.1. The Distribution of Gross Value of Industrial Production by Ownership (China)

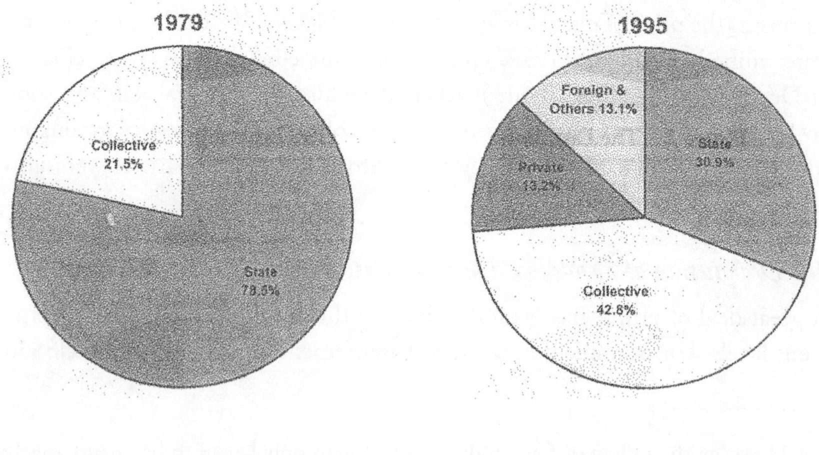

The distribution of retail sales by ownership shows a similar picture (see Chart 9.2). Here the rapid rise in prominence of the private sector in retail sales is clearly evident. From almost nothing in 1979, the private sector is now the largest sector in terms of retail sales.

Chart 9.2. The Distribution of Retail Sales by Ownership (China)

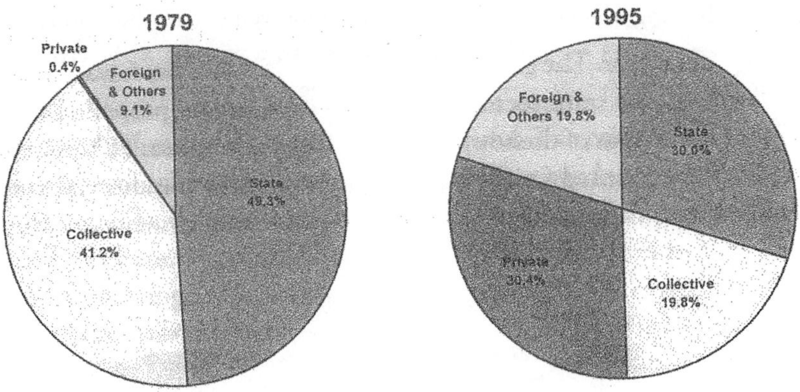

These trends in the transformation of ownership are not confined to the coastal or the more prosperous provinces. They are indeed nationwide. Even in Guizhou, the poorest province in China in terms of gross provincial product per capita, the distribution of retail sales by ownership is broadly similar to the national pattern (see Chart 9.3).

Chart 9.3. The Distribution of Retail Sales by Ownership (Guizhou Province)

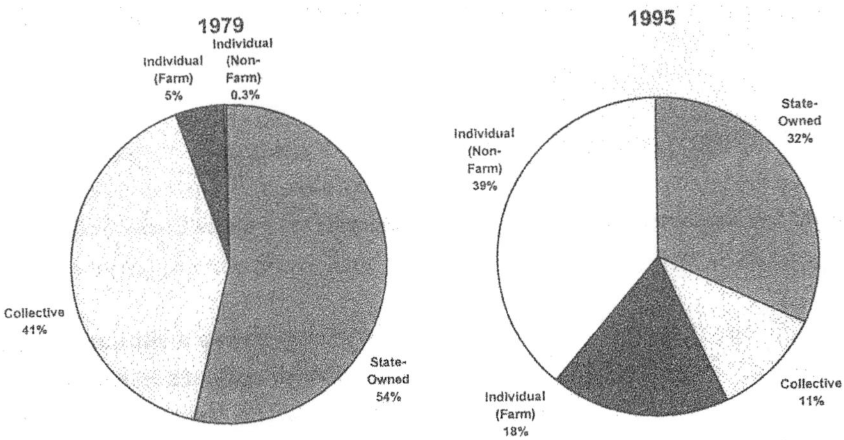

In Table 9.1, we present selected indicators of the economic performance of China before and after the commencement of economic reforms in 1979. Table 9.1 shows that in every dimension except one—the rate of inflation—the economic performance in the post-reform period is far superior to that before reform. Of particular interest is the rate of growth of real personal consumption per capita—it went from 2% per annum to over 7% per annum—indicating a genuine and significant improvement in the standard of living. That is one of the fundamental reasons why a reversal of the economic reforms is most unlikely—everyone in China benefited significantly from the economic reforms.

Table 9.1. Comparison of the Average Annual Rates of Growth of Selected Economic Indicators

	1954–1979 (Pre-Reform)	1979–1995 (Reform)
Real GDP	5.9	10.0
Real GDP/Capita	3.8	8.5
Real Gross Value of:		
Agricultural Production*	2.9	6.1
Light Industry*	8.7	16.5
Heavy Industry*	12.8	14.4
Real Personal Consumption*	4.0	8.6
Real Consumption/Capita*	2.0	7.1
Real Gross Fixed Investment	7.7	11.9
Capital Stock	5.3	9.1
Employment	2.5	2.6
GDP Deflator	0.4	7.4
Retail Price Index	0.7	8.1
Exports (in current U.S. dollars)	10.5	15.2
Imports (in current U.S. dollars)	9.9	13.7

4. Economic Reform Without Losers

The principle of Chinese economic reform is that no one loses as a result. This implies the "grandfathering" of the *status quo ante,* protection of "vested interests," and "discriminating" between the old and the new. For this reason, the availability of new resources and its efficient utilisation takes on additional importance, because they determine how fast a transition economic reforms without losers can be. We have already seen that new enterprises and the new activities have been primarily responsible for the phenomenal economic growth of China since 1979. The new resources come mostly from the high saving rates of between 35% and 40%. There has been little or no privatisation of existing enterprises as well as little or no successful restructuring of existing enterprises until recently.

Economic Reforms Without Losers: China's "Dual-Track" Approach

A dual-track strategy may be defined as follows:

(1) In one track, the "plan track," the existing (often inefficient) central economic plan, and the distribution of rents under it, are left intact; and
(2) In the other track, the "market track," liberalisation is carried out at the margin; that is, economic agents have both the right and the incentive to participate in the free market provided that the obligations under the original plan are fulfilled. In particular, market resales of plan-allocated inputs and consumption goods, and market purchases of outputs for redelivery, are allowed.

The dual-track approach combines the pre-existing plan and at the same time introduces the market; it grandfathers the "vested interests" through the enforcement of the rights and obligations under the pre-existing plan; it uses the "contract responsibility" system to stimulate participation in the market on the margin; it creates new, reform-oriented "vested interests"; and it is easy to implement because it relies solely on existing information and institutions, including enforcement. There is no doubt that because it is Pareto-improving, it must also be efficiency-enhancing. The question is: can the dual-track approach achieve full efficiency for the economy?

An Economist's Definition of Efficiency

An economy is said to be "efficient" if and only if no one output can be increased without decreasing another output. In other words, all resources in the economy have been put to their fullest and best use.

Comparison of the Big-Bang Strategy and the Dual-Track Strategy to Market Liberalisation

Under the big-bang strategy of market liberalisation, the central plan is completely abolished. All markets are instantaneously open. Producers are completely free to plan their production. Consumers are completely free to plan their consumption. The quantities and prices of all goods are determined through the equilibration between supply and demand in the market. Under the dual-track strategy, the central plan remains (and is frozen except for new increments of state-financed production capacity) but the rights and obligations under the central plan continue to be enforced. All markets are instantaneously open. Producers are completely free to plan their production and sales, provided output delivery obligations under the plan are fulfilled. Consumers are completely free to plan their consumption, given allocated consumption goods. Aggregate quantities and *market* prices of all goods are determined through the equilibration between supply and demand in the market with plan prices remaining fixed.

Making Economic Reforms Painless

The distinction between the big-bang and dual-track strategies lies in the role played by the pre-existing central plan. The sale and purchase obligations of the economic agents remain even after the economic reforms, but they are fixed at the pre-existing levels. In addition, all planned transactions take place at the pre-existing, fixed plan prices. Thus, planned profits and losses (taxes and subsidies) of economic agents remain precisely the same. If economic agents do not do anything outside the plan, they are precisely just as well off as before. If they choose to do anything outside the plan, after fulfilling their obligations under the plan, they must, by definition, expect that they will be better off. Moreover, since the economic agents are free to resell their plan-allocated goods and to purchase from the market goods for re-delivery under the plan, they face, at the margin, the market prices. Any differences between plan and market prices therefore represent implicit feasible lumpsum transfers. The values of these transfers depend on the market prices and are thus not fixed. However, they cannot be affected by the actions of the individual economic agents and hence their existence also does not affect the actions of the economic agents. Planned consumer goods deliveries to the government enable the maintenance of the pre-reform standard of living as a floor (e.g. in the urban areas).

Feasibility of the Pre-Existing Plan

It is reasonable to assume that the pre-existing central plan is feasible, that is, it can in fact be carried out. Otherwise, it may not be possible for all the obligations specified in the pre-existing central plan to be fulfilled and the central plan itself will fail to be a credible arrangement for the lumpsum transfers discussed above. Feasibility of the central plan implies the following conditions:

(1) The production plan for each producer is feasible;
(2) The consumption plan for each consumer is feasible;
(3) Material balance holds in the aggregate; and
(4) The consumption plan for each consumer is affordable at the plan prices.

The Openness of All Markets

Both the big-bang and the dual-track strategies require that all markets are open for economic efficiency. In particular, market resales of plan-allocated inputs and consumption goods, market purchases of outputs for redelivery under the plan, as well as subcontracting, are allowed. Under the dual-track approach, there are two prices for each good—q, the plan price, and p, the market price.

The Role of State Power

Under the dual-track approach, the state is required, even after market liberalisation, to enforce the rights and obligations under the pre-existing central plan (as well as any new contracts entered into through the market).[6] However, as soon as economic agents are allowed to participate in the market, the enforcement of the plan by necessity must shift to the enforcement of specific sales to and purchases from other economic agents as mandated in the pre-existing plan. Simple

6 It is important to point out that the enforcement required here is no different from the enforcement of contracts in a market economy.

enforcement of the planned aggregate production no longer suffices because an enterprise, for example, can fulfil its planned aggregate production target and yet at the same time fail to make any planned deliveries to other enterprises at the plan prices. Thus, even if the planned aggregate production target is fulfilled, the plan itself may not be fulfilled because the mandated sales and purchases are not made. But if enforcement is shifted to plan-mandated purchases and sales, it is most likely that enforcement actions are taken in response to complaints by other economic agents whose rights have not been honoured by specific enterprises. The potential recipients of the planned output deliveries must complain before the state planning commission will begin enforcement actions. The enforcement is not on total production, but on the actual delivery of goods as provided for in the plan. This also makes it likely that absent specific complaints, no enforcement actions are likely to be taken.

Whether the dual-track approach works depends on the credibility of state enforcement, and expectations thereof. If the state is not credible, then the economic agents will have no incentive to fulfil their obligations under the pre-existing plan. And if anyone thinks that the plan-mandated deliveries at plan prices are not going to be received by him or her, he or she will not make the plan-mandated sales at the fixed plan prices either. Thus, if the overall belief or expectation is that there will not be effective enforcement, no one will comply, and the dual-track approach reduces to the big-bang approach. Perceived credibility therefore affects enterprise (and household) behaviour, and hence compliance with the pre-existing plan (post reform). If economic agents do not comply with the pre-existing plan, it is no longer possible to assure that there are no losers.

In general, multiple equilibria (outcomes) are possible under a dual-track approach, depending on expectations of the credibility of state enforcement. If everyone thinks that the state will be able to enforce effectively, everyone will comply—then "gain without pain" can be achieved. If everyone does not expect that there will be credible state enforcement, the dual-track approach will degenerate into the big-bang approach. Thus, in technical terms, there are multiple "rational expectations" (or self-fulfilling) equilibria (a typical example is a bank run).

We have already shown that a dual-track approach assures that there are no losers. In other words, there is Pareto-improvement. In addition, under the above assumptions, a dual-track competitive equilibrium *is* efficient—that is, all resources are put to their fullest and best use. We note that the assumption allowing resales and purchases at market prices for redelivery is essential. Otherwise, the resulting outcome is not necessarily efficient.

Is Chinese Economic Reform Gradualist?

The dual-track approach of the Chinese economic reform is not gradualist because efficiency is instantaneously achieved as if under a big-bang reform. Efficiency is achieved because both the prices and quantities of goods allocated within the plan are *fixed,* and on the margin all economic agents face the market prices. Chinese economic reform *appears* gradualist because the population is protected from shock (pain). However, the pre-existing central plan is "phased out" gradually.

5. Examples from the Chinese Experience

We provide below nine examples of economic reforms implemented in China that utilise the dual-track approach since Chinese economic reforms began in 1979. Although different in each case, the economic reforms all share the common features described above. The examples are:

(1) The agricultural reform (the introduction of the "contract responsibility system" in agriculture);
(2) The industrial reform;
(3) The "dual-track" price system in urban consumer goods and services;
(4) The foreign exchange reform;
(5) Growth of economic activities outside the "plan";
(6) Special economic zones and foreign direct investment;
(7) The tax reforms;
(8) The rate of interest on household bank deposits; and
(9) The furloughing of the surplus labour of state-owned enterprises.

(1) The Agricultural Reform

The agricultural reform undertaken in China in 1979 may be regarded as the first successful application of the dual-track approach. Under this reform, the contract responsibility system was introduced in agriculture. The commune is assigned the responsibility to (1) sell a fixed quantity of grain (or other) output to the state procurement agency as previously mandated under the plan at predetermined (plan) prices, and (2) to pay a fixed amount of taxes to the state, as well as the right to (3) receive a fixed quantity of inputs, principally chemical fertilizers, from state-owned suppliers, again at predetermined (plan) prices. Subject to fulfilling these conditions, the commune is free to do whatever it wishes, e.g., it can produce whatever it considers more profitable, and sell any excess output on the free market, and retain any profit. In fact, under this system, the commune as well as its members are permitted to purchase grain or other output in the market to fulfil the delivery quota (an example of a "wash sale")—it is not required to actually produce the grain or other output itself.

In the implementation of the contract responsibility system, both the mandatory delivery quota and the taxes for the commune are fixed at their original planned levels. The commune in turn reassigns the collective responsibilities (and rights) to the individual farm households, allocating to them their shares of the commune's land and capital (and chemical fertilizers), and making them individually and directly responsible for the fulfilment of their shares of the delivery quota and taxes.

Thus, there is both a plan track and a free market track, each with different prices; however, the quantities of outputs and inputs under the plan track are fixed. It is therefore clear that under this system, only the market prices, and not the plan prices, are relevant for the allocation of resources. Note that both the commune (and its individual members) and the state cannot be worse off than before under this new arrangement. Moreover, as long as the state is not worse off in terms of the quantities of grain and other outputs and taxes delivered to the state, it will continue to be able to supply the urban consumers with food grains and industries with agricultural raw materials (such as cotton) at plan prices, with the consequence that even the urban consumers and industrial enterprises are no worse off as a result of the agricultural reform. Thus, the impact of the liberalisation at the margin must be Pareto-improving for all parties.

Since the agricultural reform is only partial, one cannot assert that the full efficiency of the entire economy is attained. However, since the agricultural reform is Pareto-improving for all parties, overall efficiency of the economy is unambiguously enhanced by the agricultural reform.

The dual-track price system has some historical antecedent. Even prior to the introduction of the contract responsibility system, there were two prices for grain—the plan price paid for mandated grain deliveries to the state and the negotiated (market) price for above-quota transactions.

(2) The Industrial Reform

There have been many studies on the Chinese industrial reform and its associated dual-track price system, which was introduced in 1984 (see, e.g., Byrd 1987, Wu and Zhao 1987, and Naughton 1995). The industrial reform represents, in part, an attempt to extend the contract responsibility system to the industrial sector, based on the successful experience of the agricultural reform. Under the reform, the mandatory delivery quotas as well as the quantities of plan-allocated inputs for each enterprise were frozen at their then-existing levels, and the enterprises are free to produce whatever they deem profitable and sell their output on the free market and retain any profit as long as they fulfil their delivery quota. At the same time, parallel free markets for the above-quota outputs of enterprises were introduced, while the within-quota outputs continued to be sold at the generally lower plan prices to authorised purchasers.

This example highlights the crucial elements in a dual-track approach. First, the "market track" must provide for full liberalisation (that is, no intervention of any kind), albeit only at the margin (but as we know, liberalisation at the margin is sufficient for efficiency); second, the enterprises must be allowed to reap the full marginal reward;[7] and third, input and output quotas on the plan track must be enforced, as outputs of some enterprises are needed as inputs of other enterprises. The ability of enterprises to meet their planned output quota may depend crucially on their timely receipt of the planned input delivery quotas.

(3) The Dual-Track Price System in Urban Consumer Goods and Services

Prior to the economic reforms of 1979, many essential consumer goods and services, such as grain, cooking oil, meat, electricity, housing, and monthly passes for mass transit, were rationed in the urban areas at lower than what

7 This is for reasons of both incentive and the avoidance of distortions.

would have been free market prices. With the introduction of the free markets and the dual-track price system, urban residents continued to be able to purchase grain, meat, electricity (lifeline rates), and housing (for those who had it) at the same pre-reform prices within the limits of the pre-reform rationed quantities, at the same time that they were able to purchase freely any quantity of any good at free market prices. They were thus no worse off than before. The state was also no worse off because the quantities of goods that it would be obligated to supply at the plan prices remained the same.

(4) The Foreign Exchange Reform

Dual markets were permitted to exist for foreign exchange in China from the mid-1980s to the end of 1993. Between 1985 and 1994, there was an official exchange rate, available only for certain limited approved transactions, as well as an officially sanctioned swap rate, that was determined in Foreign Exchange Adjustment Centres (more commonly referred to as "swap markets") in major cities around the country, among exporters and importers qualified to trade in those markets. The supply of foreign exchange in the swap markets was provided by the exporters through the foreign exchange they were allowed to retain from *net increases* in their export earnings relative to the base period.[8] The government did not control the transactions in the swap market, and the swap market exchange rate was mostly determined by supply and demand (see Khor 1994 for a detailed description). The swap rate was, not surprisingly, significantly higher than the official rate during this period.

At the same time, foreign visitors to China were required to use "foreign exchange certificates" (FECs), which were available at the official exchange rate, rather than the renminbi, the Chinese domestic currency, for their transactions.

The dual exchange rate system functioned until 1 January 1994, when the two exchange rates—the official rate and the swap rate—were merged into a single rate, with its level determined in a market consisting of exporters and importers, and the foreign exchange certificates were finally withdrawn from circulation. Under the new system, domestic exporters are required to sell all of

8 At the beginning, the enterprises were permitted to re-purchase part of their foreign exchange earnings at the official exchange rate.

their foreign exchange to the interbank market (thus, rights of retentions were abolished); in return, they are allowed to purchase foreign exchange as needed for legitimate business purposes.

At the time of this reform, the share of centrally allocated foreign exchange already fell to only 20% of the total. In this last step of the foreign exchange reform, central allocation of foreign exchange was completely abolished, but for those organisations that used to receive cheap foreign exchange, annual lumpsum subsidies in the domestic currency sufficient to enable the purchase of the pre-reform allocation of foreign exchange were offered for five years to assure a smooth transition (in other words, the state tried to maintain the same level of hithertofore implicit subsidies received by these organisations).

The exchange rate reform turned out to be a complete success: the exchange rate has remained stable and even appreciated slightly from 8.7 yuan per U.S. dollar to 8.3 yuan per U.S. dollar today. Since July 1 of this year, foreign and joint-venture enterprises, which hithertofore must use technically separate foreign exchange swap markets, have been permitted to use the same foreign exchange markets maintained by the banks for the domestic enterprises. The best way to characterise the current exchange rate system is that it is "current-account convertible," but not "capital-account convertible."

(5) Growth of Economic Activities Outside the "Plan"

A distinctive feature of Chinese economic reform is the growth of economic activities outside the state plan even before state-owned enterprises have begun to be privatised or shut down. These new economic activities are entirely market-oriented and are driven by new investments outside of the state plan (Qian and Xu 1993, Naughton 1995).[9] Two cases may be distinguished here. The first case is the entry and expansion of new unregulated enterprises, known collectively as "non-state-owned enterprises" in China, such as township and village enterprises, foreign-owned enterprises, joint-venture enterprises, and private enterprises, which face hard budget constraints. The second is the parallel development of new unregulated and market-oriented activities of state-owned enterprises, commonly described as "one-factory, two-systems."

---

9 The experience in Taiwan and South Korea showed a similar pattern (Lau and Song 1992).

For example, state-owned enterprises may set up subsidiaries as collective enterprises, universities may establish high-tech firms, and military hospitals may use slack resources to provide medical services to the public to augment their revenues.

The first case has worked extremely well. A crucial condition for the second case to work is that the regulated activities of the state-owned enterprises must be left to function at their previous level without disruption.[10] Under this condition, new activities can only increase welfare. Sufficient enforcement power of government is an essential condition here to prevent disruptive diversion of resources from the regulated to the unregulated activities of the state sector.

(6) Special Economic Zones and Foreign Direct Investment

This is not unlike the entry of new enterprises but takes place at the level of a country. The institution of special economic zones was chosen early as a reform measure in part to minimise its impact on and interaction with the rest of the economic system, which still operated under the state plan. Initially, special economic zones allowed only firms engaged in "material reprocessing" that imported all of their inputs, except labour, and exported all of their outputs—thus creating no disruption to the domestic aggregate supply and demand, labour being in surplus. The same rule applied to foreign and joint-venture firms operating in China but outside the special economic zones. The principal purpose of this approach is to minimise the impact of the new economic activities on the old-style domestic state-owned enterprises. Thus, once again, there were two tracks and the reform was Pareto-improving.

---

10 If entry of new firms reduces profits of SOEs through competition, why does the dual-track approach not hurt SOEs? As SOEs have plan-allocated inputs, they generally benefit from the lower plan prices, so competition does not seem to be an important factor. The dual-track system also protects producers of intermediate goods from competition because of the planned output deliveries. However, this may not be the case for the producers of final goods. Households are also not always protected by "input quotas," i.e. by rationing at lower than market prices. Thus enterprises in the final goods sector may be hurt by competition from non-state-owned enterprises. They may in the longer run lose their rents, if not fully compensated by the state. One has here an example in which reform does not necessarily leave everyone at least as well off as before. However, only a minority of firms can be hurt through this type of competition.

The initial success of the special economic zones and foreign direct investment was made possible through (1) the existence of overseas Chinese entrepreneurs willing to invest in China despite the uncertain economic, legal, political and social environment; and (2) the existence of slack and cheap labour in China. After a few years of experimentation, enterprises in the special economic zones as well as foreign and joint-venture enterprises were allowed to buy and sell on the domestic market at market prices.

(7) The Tax Reforms

We first discuss the fiscal contracting system introduced in the 1980s (see Bahl and Wallich 1992 for details). The experiment of the fiscal contracting system between the central and provincial governments started in 1980 and the system eventually covered all provinces by the mid-1980s. Under the fiscal contracting system, the province/municipality assumed the responsibility of collecting the taxes for the central government and were committed to deliver to the central government a fixed amount of revenue per year, and allowed to retain any excess. (Thus, this is similar to a tax-farming system.) Since the committed amount to be delivered to the central government would be based on historical experience, neither the central government nor the provinces/municipalities would be worse off under this arrangement.

Of course, it is possible that the provinces/municipalities may fail, or claim to fail, to collect even the fixed amount due the central government. In practice, this applied mostly to the poorer provinces—19 out of the 35 provinces/municipalities were able to retain 100% of the revenues they collected at the margin.

The 1994 tax reform introduced a nationwide value-added tax, abolished the fiscal contracting system and replaced it with a fiscal federalism, providing for revenue sharing as well as a separation of the national and local tax bases. Again, the reform ensured that all provinces were not made worse off. The provincial governments were guaranteed revenue no less than that of their 1993 actual expenditures for the three years between 1994 and 1996. As might be expected, the provinces/municipalities had a major spending spree in the last quarter of 1993, which also attested to their confidence that the central government would in fact be able to carry out their part of the commitment.

(8) The Rate of Interest on Household Bank Deposits

The dual-track approach also applies to the setting of the rate of interest for household bank deposits. During the two high-inflation periods (1988–1989 and 1993–1995), the Chinese government promptly indexed the household bank savings deposit rates for new long-term time deposits to the consumer price index in order to protect depositors from inflation (Qian 1994). Indexation of the rate of interest on the savings deposit to the rate of inflation is part of the strategy of "grandfathering" or "not making people worse off." This is in contrast to the rates for short-term deposits, which remained negative in real terms until very recently. Indexation of savings deposits was, however, once again abolished as of 1 April 1996, on the grounds that inflationary fears had abated.

A *de facto* dual-track credit market already exists in China, although it is not officially sanctioned. The market rate of interest for loans has remained significantly above the official bank lending rate. The practice of "re-lending" by state-owned enterprises with preferential access to credit is widespread.[11] As China moves to develop its money and capital markets, it is inevitable that a dual-track price system for money will eventually develop as a transitional device. Already, an inter-bank call money market has been introduced in January 1996. There is a reasonably active secondary market for government bonds. More recently, an auction of 10-year government bonds in the style of the U.S. Treasury Bond auction was successfully carried out in China. All of these developments suggest that in the not too distant future, on the margin, the rate of interest will be set in the market.

(9) The Furloughing of the Surplus Labour of State-Owned Enterprises

More recently, workers of state-owned enterprises have been furloughed at a percentage of their pre-existing wages and have been allowed to keep their enterprise-allocated housing. They are given the autonomy to seek alternative

---

11 But China has not officially adopted a dual-track approach to its lending activities in the banking sector. This would have guaranteed rollover to cheap old loans to SOEs while applying the free market rate to new loans. However, in reality, many credits were leaked from state banks to non-state-owned enterprises at market rates.

employment or to become self-employed. This has worked out quite well in Shanghai, where almost 900,000 of the one million workers furloughed have found alternative, gainful employment, possibly at lower marginal wages. The workers, who have been overpaid relative to the market, are no worse off than before, taking into account the subsidies received. The enterprises and the state are also better off. In fact, efficiency in the labour market can actually be attained with this type of partial subsidy.

6. Marketisation under the Dual-Track Approach

Under the dual-track approach, the central plan and the market coexisted at the commencement of economic reform. However, since the central plan has been essentially frozen at the original levels,[12] the output produced outside the plan has grown rapidly and the proportion of outputs that are sold and purchased at plan prices have declined continuously. In Tables 2, 3 and 4, we present the values of the transactions in each of the sectors of agriculture, industry and retail that are conducted at plan, guide and market prices respectively. It is clear that by the early 1990s, most of the transactions were conducted at market prices. The plan has been phased out for many goods. These tables demonstrate the effectiveness of the dual-track approach as a strategy of transition from a centrally-planned economy to a market economy. They also confirm the unmistakable importance of demand expansion due to the rapid economic growth, which takes place outside of the plan. The growth of the market (non-planned) portion of the output is largely due to the rise of new, non-state-owned enterprises established since 1984 whose sales and purchases are not included in the plan, even though a part of it may also be attributed to the participation of the state-owned enterprises in the market.

12 This is not true of all industries, however. The planned output was increased in certain limited industries in which the state-owned enterprises had undergone state-financed expansion, e.g., coal mining.

Table 9.2. Phasing Out the Plan Track: Agricultural Products (Percent of Output Value)

	1978	1985	1986	1987	1988	1989	1990	1991	1992	1993
Plan price	94.4	37.0	35.0	29.4	24.0	35.5	31.0	22.2	12.5	10.4
Guide price	0.0	23.0	21.0	16.8	19.0	24.3	27.0	20.0	5.7	2.1
Market price	5.6	40.0	43.7	53.8	57.0	40.4	42.0	57.8	81.8	87.5

Table 9.3. Phasing Out the Plan Track: Industrial Goods (Percent of Output Value)

	1978	1985	1986	1987	1988	1989	1990	1991	1992	1993
Plan price Guide price	100.0 0.0	64.0 23.0				60.0	44.6 19.0	36.0 18.3	18.7 7.5	13.8 5.1
Market price	0.0	13.0				40.0	36.5	45.7	73.8	81.1

Table 9.4. Phasing Out the Plan Track: Total Retail Sales (Percent of Sales)

	1978	1985	1986	1987	1988	1989	1990	1991	1992	1993
Plan price	97.0	47.0	35.0	33.7	28.9	31.3	30.0	20.9	5.9	4.8
Guide price	0.0	19.0	25.0	28.0	21.8	23.2	25.0	10.3	1.1	1.4
Market price	3.0	34.0	40.0	38.3	49.3	45.5	45.0	68.8	93.0	93.8

7. Concluding Remarks

The Chinese experience shows that by using a dual-track approach to economic reforms, one can achieve gain without pain. Economic reforms without losers are possible. Equity does not necessarily have to be sacrificed in order to achieve efficiency. The necessary conditions for the success of the dual-track approach to the transition from a centrally-planned economy to a market economy are: (1) Feasibility of the original plan; (2) Autonomy and incentive for the economic agents to participate in the market on the margin, including, in particular, the freedom of resale of plan-allocated goods, purchase of goods for redelivery under the plan, and subcontracting; and (3) Credibility of state enforcement of the plan-mandated sales and purchases of goods.

Looking ahead, it is most likely that China will still consider the maintenance of political and social stability a goal of the highest priority and will seek to achieve that by adopting economic policies with no or very few losers. For this reason, the creation of new jobs for the new entrants into the labour force (estimated to be approximately 16 million each year) and the preservation/replacement of existing jobs are of paramount importance. The control of inflation may also be viewed in part as an attempt to prevent the emergence of a large group of potential losers (after all, the *status quo ante* has shifted—the reference standard is no longer 1979 or 1984). Moreover, the political economy is such that it may be important to consider the question of "relative" rather than "absolute" losers. Even when no one loses absolutely, large segments of the population may lose relatively. Consistent relative losers can also become discontented. That is one reason why the Chinese government has recently begun to focus on the development of the interior, to prevent the population in the inland provinces from falling further behind—that is, continuing to be "relative losers," when compared to the coastal population.

References

Arrow, Kenneth J. "Toward a Theory of Price Adjustment." In Moses Abramovitz et. al., *The Allocation of Economic Resources: Essays in Honor of Bernard Francis Haley*. Stanford, Calif.: Stanford University Press, 1959.

Arrow, Kenneth J., and Frank H. Hahn. *General Competitive Analysis.* San Francisco: Holden-Day, 1971.

Bahl, Richard, and Christine Wallich. "Intergovernmental Fiscal Relations in China." Working Paper, Country Economics Department, WPS 863, World Bank, 1992.

Boycko, Maxim, Andrei Shleifer, and Robert Vishny. *Privatising Russia*. Cambridge, MA: MIT Press, 1995.

Byrd, William A. "The Impact of the Two-Tier Plan/Market System in Chinese Industry." *Journal of Comparative Economics* 11 (1987), pp. 295–308.

———. "Plan and Market in the Chinese Economy: A Simple General Equilibrium Model." *Journal of Comparative Economics* 13 (1989), pp. 177–204.

Diamond, Douglas and Philip Dybvig. "Bank Runs, Deposit Insurance and Liquidity." *Journal of Political Economy* 93 (1983), pp. 401–419.

Farmer, Roger. *The Macroeconomics of Self-Fulfilling Prophecies*. Cambridge, MA: MIT Press, 1993.

Hammond, Peter J., and Jaime Sempere. "Limits to the Potential Gains from Economic Integration and Other Supply Side Policies." *The Economic Journal* 105 (1995), pp. 1180–1204.

Khor, Hoe Ee. "China's Foreign Currency Swap Market." IMF Paper on Policy Analysis and Assessment, 94/1, International Monetary Fund, 1994.

Lau, Lawrence J., and Dae-Hee Song. "Growth Versus Privatisation—An Alternative Strategy to Reduce the Public Enterprise Sector: The Experience of Taiwan and South Korea." Working Paper, Department of Economics, Stanford University, 1992.

Lau, Lawrence J., Yingyi Qian and Gerard Roland. "Pareto-Improving Economic Reforms through Dual-Track Liberalisation." *Economics Letters* 55(2), 29 August 1997, pp. 285–292.

McMillan, John, and Barry Naughton. "How to Reform a Planned Economy: Lessons from China." *Oxford Review of Economic Policy* 8, no. 1 (1992), pp. 130–143.

Murphy, Kevin, Andrei Shleifer, and Robert W. Vishny. "The Transition to a Market Economy: Pitfalls of Partial Reform" *Quarterly Journal of Economics* 107, no. 3 (1992), pp. 889–906.

Naughton, Barry. *Growing Out of the Plan: Chinese Economic Reform, 1978–1993*. Cambridge: Cambridge University Press, 1995.

Qian, Yingyi. "Financial System Reform in China: Lessons from Japan's Main Bank System." In M. Aoki and H. Patrick, eds., *The Japanese Main-Bank System: Its Relevancy for Developing and Transforming Economies*. Oxford: Oxford University Press, 1994, pp. 552–591.

Qian, Yingyi, and Chenggang Xu. "Why China's Economic Reforms Differ: The M-form Hierarchy and Entry and Expansion of the Non-State Sector." Economics of Transition 1, no. 2 (1993), pp. 135–170.

Roland, Gerard. "The Role of Political Constraints in Transition Strategies." *Economics of Transition* 2 (1994), no. 1, pp. 27–41.

Sachs, Jeffery, and Wing Thye Woo. "Structural Factors in the Economic Reforms of China, Eastern Europe, and the Former Soviet Union." *Economic Policy* 18 (Spring 1994), pp. 101–145.

Wu, Jinglian, and Renwei Zhao. "The Dual Pricing System in China's Industry." *Journal of Comparative Economics* 11 (1987), pp. 309–318.

Chapter 10.

The Macroeconomy and Reform of the Banking Sector in China*

1. Introduction

First of all, it is useful to put the Chinese economy into the proper context. Chinese GDP and GDP per capita in 1998 were, at market exchange rates, US$960 billion and US$770 respectively. In comparison, the GDP and GDP per capita of the U.S. economy were approximately US$8.5 trillion and US$31,000 respectively. The Chinese economy, despite 20 years of phenomenal economic growth at approximately 10% per year, is still relatively small in both aggregate and per capita terms.

The Effects of the East Asian Currency Crisis

The Chinese economy has managed to remain relatively unscathed from the East Asian currency crisis, which has been ravaging most of the other East Asian economies since mid-1997. China and Hong Kong are the only two economies whose currencies have not devalued. The real rate of growth of the Chinese economy has remained the highest in East Asia and even the world (8.8% in 1997 and 7.8% in 1998), while almost all of the other East Asian economies, including Japan, had a negative real rate of growth in 1998,

---

* This chapter was originally published in "Strengthening the Banking System in China: Issues and Experience: A Joint BIS/ PBC Conference Held in Beijing, China, 1–2 March, 1999," Bank for International Settlements Policy Papers, No. 7 (October 1999), pp. 59–89. The author is grateful for discussions with Nicholas Hope, Nicholas Lardy, Yingyi Qian, Joseph Stiglitz, Philip Turner and Xiao-Chuan Zhou. Responsibility for any errors remains with the author.

except Singapore and Taiwan. The growth of Chinese exports, at US$183.8 billion in 1998, has, however, slowed down significantly to 0.5%, compared to 26.2% in 1997, mostly due to the decline in exports to the affected East Asian economies, including Japan. Otherwise, exports to European and North American markets have continued to grow at double-digit rates. In real terms, exports probably increased by 4.5% in 1998. Chinese imports declined for the first time in almost a decade, by 1.5%, to US$140.2 billion, compared to an increase of 2.5% for 1997. In real terms, imports probably increased 2.5%. There continued to be a healthy trade surplus of US$43.6 billion in 1998.

Foreign direct investment (FDI) arrivals in China totalled US$45.6 billion in 1998, an increase of 0.7% over 1997, with the reduction in investment from the East Asian economies offset by the increase in investment from Europe and the United States. FDI commitments totalled US$52.1 billion, 2.1% higher than in 1997.

The Chinese domestic price level has been falling for 15 consecutive months. For 1998, the retail price index (RPI) fell by 2.6% and the consumer price index (CPI) by 0.8%. However, much of the fall in the price level could be attributed to the worldwide decline in the price of commodities, especially that of oil, resulting from the East Asian crisis, and the decline in the domestic price of food, due in part to good harvests.

However, the East Asian currency crisis and the resulting turmoil in the financial sectors of the East Asian countries does focus attention on the banking and financial sectors of China and the need for their improved regulation.

2. The Macroeconomy

As mentioned above, the Chinese economy has remained relatively healthy—growing by 8.8% in 1997 and 7.8% in 1998. The rate of inflation has actually turned negative—prices have been falling for 15 consecutive months. The urban unemployment rates for 1997 and 1998 were 3.1 and 3.5% respectively. For 1999, the official government target rate of growth of real GDP is 7%. My own forecast is that it will be somewhere between 7% and 8%.

Two points are worth making here. First of all, for all practical purposes, the 8% target rate of growth for 1998, which was the focus of much discussion last year, was effectively achieved. For the entire year, the rate of growth of real GDP was 7.8%. However, the floods in the summer of 1998 reduced the rate of growth of real GDP by at least 0.5%. Thus, if it were not for the floods, 8% growth would have been comfortably achieved. My own estimate of the "core" rate of growth of the Chinese economy, based on its long-term fundamentals, is around 8%. Second, it is almost "dogma" among most financial journalists that the Chinese economy "requires" a real rate of growth of at least 8%, otherwise the social order will crumble and the economy will collapse. However, no theoretical argument or empirical evidence has ever been produced to support this often-expressed opinion. (There is also no other economy that is supposed to "require" an 8% or even 6% growth.) A simple calculation shows how fallacious this belief is. Chinese GDP and GDP per capita in 1998 were US$960 billion and US$770 respectively. The net new entrants into the Chinese labour force may be estimated to be approximately 10 million a year. If we assume that each new entrant into the labour force commands a wage rate of US$1,800 a year, which is on the generous side, the total cost of absorbing the net additions to the labour force comes to US$18 billion a year, which is less than 2% of GDP. Thus, in principle, a 2%, rather than an 8%, growth of the economy should suffice. I happen to think the Chinese economy has the potential of growing at approximately 8% per annum over the next two decades. However, the sky will not fall if the Chinese economy occasionally slows to a 4% or even 2% annual growth.

Are the Reported Rates of Growth of Real GDP Reliable?

One significant argument is, however, whether the official rates of growth of Chinese real GDP are reliable. There are many reasons why the real rates of growth may have been overstated at different times and for different reasons. For example, in the early to mid-1980s, it was quite possible that the rate of growth of real GDP might have simply reflected, in part, the effects of monetisation (or marketisation) of the economy. The eggs produced by a farmer for an in-kind exchange with another farmer for pork would not be included in the GDP figure. However, if both farmers sold their own outputs and purchased each other's output on the market, GDP would register an increase even though total output has not changed at all. In the late 1980s and early 1990s, the effects of land transactions on profits of enterprises and hence value added might have also caused GDP to be overstated. This is because land used to be carried on the books of Chinese enterprises at zero cost. When land was transferred from one enterprise to another, or to a foreign-invested firm (usually in the form of a long-term lease) at market, all the proceeds would be recorded as profit in the income statements and hence treated as value added in the national income accounts. In truth, many of the transfers were of raw, unimproved land, with little real "value added".[1] This was thus also a source of overstatement of GDP. However, over time, the importance of this source of overstatement would diminish as more and more land, especially the more valuable parcels, was marked to market on the books through the transfers. A possible source of understatement of real GDP comes from the upward bias in the measurement of the GDP deflator and generally the price indexes. The price indexes are likely to be overestimated because of the fixed weighting (changed only periodically), the lack of adjustments for quality improvements, and for the introduction of new products, among other things. The effects of the upward bias in the deflators should be higher in high inflation periods and lower in low inflation periods.

There is, however, no evidence of any deliberate falsification or change in the statistical methods on the part of the National Bureau of Statistics (NBS) of the People's Republic of China—although there may be discrepancies between the NBS data and reports made by provincial, regional, municipal and local governments. Moreover, the incentives for falsification work in both directions at the provincial and local levels. On the one hand, the provincial and local leaders may wish to appear to have done a good job, both to the central government and to their local constituencies. Thus, they may be tempted to inflate the statistics. (That is one reason why the central government statistics are likely to be more reliable.) On the other hand, they may also wish to minimise their liabilities for taxes and profit remittances to the central government.

By far the most convincing arguments that the official rates of growth figures are reasonably reliable are based on cross-validation using other methodological approaches for the measurement of GDP. In addition to the production approach—that is, the measurement of GDP by summing up the value added of the productive sectors, e.g. agriculture, industry and services—there is at least the expenditure approach and the factor incomes approach. These alternative approaches yield estimates for 1998 that are consistent with a rate of growth in the order of 7-8%, as we shall show below.

---

1 The transfer and sale of raw, unimproved land from one entity to another does not create value added per se even though it may create profit in the accounting sense.

The expenditure approach consists of looking at the rates of growth of the components constituting aggregate gross domestic expenditure (which in principle must be equal to gross domestic product). We begin with the gross domestic expenditure (*GDE*) equation, which is by definition equal to the sum of personal or household consumption expenditures (*C*), government consumption expenditures (*G*), gross domestic investment (*I*), and net exports of goods and services (*X-M*). Gross domestic investment or, equivalently, gross domestic capital formation, is in turn equal to the sum of gross domestic fixed investment (GDFI) and change in stocks or, equivalently, inventories ($\triangle$S). Thus,

$$
\begin{aligned}
GDE &= C + I + G + (X\text{-}M) \\
&= C + GDFI + \triangle S + G + (X\text{-}M).
\end{aligned}
$$

The rate of growth of real GDP can therefore be estimated from the expenditure side as the weighted sum of the real rates of growth of the components of gross domestic expenditure.

In 1998, the rate of growth of real retail sales was 9.7%. While the rate of growth of real retail sales alone does not translate directly into the rate of growth of real household consumption expenditures, the latter may be conservatively estimated to be 5%, or approximately half the rate of growth of real retail sales. On a per capita basis, this amounts to a 4% growth, which was quite consistent with the rates of growth of real per capita disposable income in 1998 of 5.8% in the urban areas and 4.3% in the rural areas. Since real household consumption has approximately a share of 40% in GDE, it contributes approximately 2% (= 0.4 times 5%) to the real rate of growth of GDE. The rate of growth of real government consumption was 6.5%. With a share in GDE of approximately 10%, real government consumption contributes 0.65% (= 0.1 times 6.5%) to the real rate of growth of GDE. The rate of growth of real gross domestic fixed investment was 14.1%. With a share of GDE of between 35 and 40%, real gross domestic fixed investment contributes at least 4.9% (= 0.35 times 14.1 %) to the real rate of growth of GDE. The real rates of growth of change in stocks and net exports were negligible in 1998. Thus, an approximate estimate of the rate of growth of real GDP may be obtained as the weighted sum of the real rates of growth of the components of GDE as 7.55% (2.0 + 0.65 + 4.9), which turns out to be very close to the official estimate of 7.8%.

The quantity theory of money provides another way of cross-validating the estimate of the rate of growth of real GDP. The quantity theory says that:

$$MV=PT,$$

where M is the nominal quantity of the money supply, V is the velocity of circulation of money, P is the price level, and T is the real quantity of transactions in the economy. Under the assumption that the velocity of money is constant, the rate of growth of the money supply is equal to the sum of the rate of growth of the price level (inflation) and the rate of growth of real GDP (identified with the real rate of growth of transactions). Thus, the rate of growth of real GDP may be estimated as the rate of growth of the money supply less the rate of inflation. In 1998, the rates of growth of the different measures of money supply were, respectively: MO, 10.1%; Ml, 11.9%; and M2, 15.3%. Given a negative rate of inflation (-2.6% for the retail price index and -0.8% for the consumer price index), the implied rate of growth of real GDP would be in excess of 10%, no matter which concept of money supply is used. In reality, V must have been declining. Thus, the rate of growth of the money supply in China was not inconsistent with a rate of growth of real GDP of between 7% and 8%.

Why Are the Rates of Growth of Electricity, Energy and Freight Traffic So Low?

One final question that needs to be addressed is the following: was it possible for real GDP to grow at 7.8% per annum while the rate of growth of electricity production was 2.8% and that of freight traffic was -1.3%? The answer is yes, mostly because the Chinese economy has been undergoing very rapid structural change. If China were a mature economy in a steady state like the U.S. economy, such large "discrepancies" in the rates of growth of real GDP compared to those of the production of energy, especially electricity and freight traffic, would have been impossible.

First, the rate of growth of electricity consumption has been lagging behind the changes in the real price of electricity, which has risen threefold since 1990. Thus, the ratio of electricity consumption to GDP was expected to decline over time—the rate of growth of electricity consumption should, based on consideration of the price effect alone, be lower than the rate of growth of

GDP. The same argument applies more generally to the energy consumption to GDP ratio. In addition, there were other forces at work to reduce the electricity consumption to GDP ratio. Second, the composition of the output of the Chinese economy has also undergone rapid change in recent years: the rate of growth of the manufacturing sector, which uses more electricity per unit value added, has slowed relative to the construction sector and the services sector, which uses much less electricity per unit value added. This results again in a decline in the electricity consumption to GDP ratio. The differential rate of growth between heavy and light industry also has an impact. Third, the effects of intra-industry changes in the composition of outputs can be very significant for a rapidly transforming economy. As the steel industry upgrades the quality of its products from ordinary steel to, say, stainless steel, the value added per metric ton doubles or triples, but the electricity consumption per ton increases much less. The same argument applies as the garment industry moves from making plain cotton shirts to silk shirts, with a significant increase in value added but almost negligible increase in electricity consumption. Thus, intra-industry changes in the composition of output by quality can result in a significant reduction in the electricity consumption to GDP ratio. Of course, in a mature economy, changes in the intra-industry composition of output are likely to be much smaller.

Fourth, there were genuine gains in efficiency, quite aside from the direct price effect, resulting from the replacement of old equipment with new equipment and from economies of scale of operation. Fifth, many of the arguments advanced above apply with equal force to the freight traffic to GDP ratio. A metric ton of steel is a metric ton of steel in terms of freight traffic even though the value added per metric ton can be vastly different. However, in the case of China, concern about pollution and environmental regulation had the additional effect of reducing the use of coal. But coal was responsible for 60% of Chinese freight traffic. Thus, a substitution of coal with oil, gas, hydro or nuclear electricity would result in a significant decline in freight traffic with no necessary corresponding effects on either total energy consumption or real GDP. This is the best and most plausible explanation for the observed contraction in freight traffic.

Sixth, more generally, changes in the loci of production and consumption would have the effects of reducing both electricity consumption and freight traffic. Suppose one power plant used to supply two cities 400 miles apart. Now suppose a new power plant closer to the second city becomes operational and takes over as the electricity provider for the second city. The overall electricity demand will come down because of the reduction in transmission losses; however, such contraction does not indicate a reduction in the economic activities in either city. The same argument works for freight traffic as well. A new plant opens in Chongqing, supplies the local area and replaces the "exports" from the old plant in Shanghai. Total GDP probably rises as the freight traffic declines. Of course, these effects would not have been important in a mature economy.

Seventh, technical improvements—new plants, better cables, higher voltages—over time could also have reduced transmission losses and hence overall electricity consumption in general.[2] Finally, as co-generation becomes more widespread in China, many industrial users have become marginal users. Thus, as their output level declines, they will not buy from the electric utilities. The output of the electric utilities is therefore especially sensitive to a slowdown in the rates of growth of industrial output. This will lead to a downward bias in the electricity consumption to GDP ratio if co-generated electricity is not fully included in the data on electricity production and consumption.

Is There Sufficient Aggregate Demand?

In order to answer this question, we should first examine what has happened to real GDP. Chart 10.1 presents the year-on-year quarterly rates of growth of Chinese real GDP. (There are no seasonally adjusted data available as yet; the measurement of quarterly rates of growth on a year-on-year basis is an attempt to control for the seasonal factors.) It shows that the rate of growth began to decline in the third quarter of 1992 until it reached bottom in the second quarter of 1998 (at 6.8%). It has been rising since. There is, however, a pronounced and readily apparent seasonality even in these year-on-year rates of growth. Thus, while the rate of growth appeared to have begun declining again from the fourth quarter of 1998, one should focus instead on the comparison of the rate of growth by the specific quarter—that is, for example, the fourth quarter with the previous fourth quarter (shown as similarly shaded columns). The resulting picture is actually one of a slow but steady rise in the rates of growth since the

2 Measures to reduce theft of electricity also result in a reduction in the "measured" rate of transmission loss.

Chart 10.1. Real GDP Year-on-Year Quarterly Rates of Growth

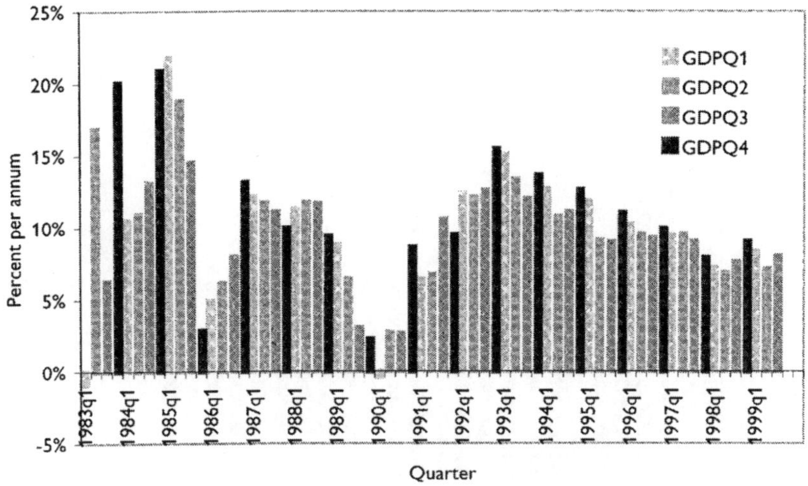

fourth quarter of 1998. Real GDP grew 7.6% in the third quarter of 1998, despite the floods that probably caused a reduction of 0.5% in real GDP, and 9.0% in the fourth quarter of 1998, representing a strong turnaround from a string of declining quarterly growth rates. We conclude that the declining trend in the growth rates so evident in the figure has finally been reversed. It is also useful to note that the year-on-year rates of growth tend to lag behind. Thus, when rates are rising on a year-on-year basis, the economy is actually doing better than the rates indicate (unfortunately, the reverse is also true, so that when the year-on-year rates are falling, things are worse than they appear).[3]

The rates of growth of industrial output, measured in terms of value added, are presented in Chart 10.2, and they tell a similar story. Ignoring the anomaly caused by the shifting of the Chinese (lunar) New Year between January and February, there was a readily discernible recovery in the rates of growth beginning in September 1998 and continuing through early 1999.[4] For 1998 as a whole, value added in industry grew 8.9%.

---

3 Developments subsequent to this conference have proven that our analysis is basically correct.

4 The recovery would probably have occurred in August had there not been the floods.

Chart 10.2. Value Added in Industry, Year-on-Year Monthly Rates of Growth

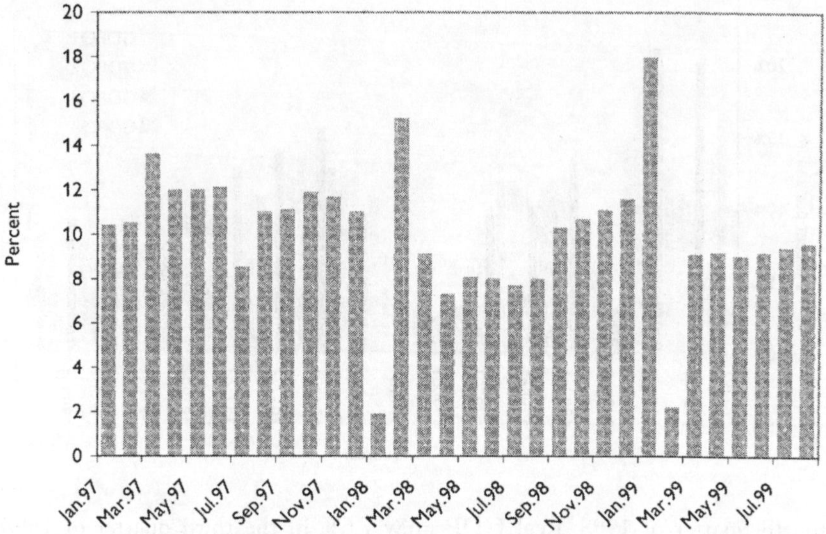

Beginning in the summer of 1998, the central government undertook a massive infrastructural investment programme. As a result, real gross domestic fixed investment grew by 14.1% in 1998. In the first two months of 1999, real gross domestic fixed investment of state-owned and other enterprises (excluding the collective and private enterprises) grew by 28.3% on a year-on-year basis, reflecting the continuing effects of the infrastructural investment initiative.

Prices have been falling for 15 consecutive months. However, much of the decline in the prices was caused by falls in the prices of energy, especially oil, and in the prices of food. The core rate of inflation—that is, the rate of inflation net of the changes in the prices of energy and food—may be estimated at between 1 and 2%, comparable to that of the United States. Thus, there is no empirical evidence of either a resurgence of inflation or of deflation. The rate of interest has been reduced four times since mid-1997. The yield on 10-year yuan-denominated bonds has fallen below 6%. Three-year yuan-denominated bonds issued in March/April 1999 carried an interest rate of 4.72%, whereas five-year bonds carried an interest rate of 5.13%. These long-term rates of interest are similar to the rates of U.S. Treasury securities of

Chart 10.3. Household Savings Deposits Year-end Stock, as a Percent of GDP

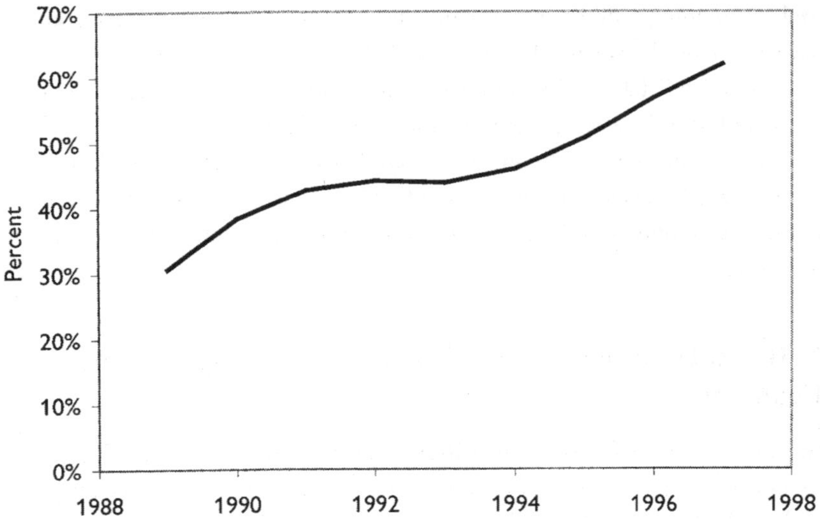

comparable maturity. They provide evidence of an absence of expectations of either long-term inflation or a devaluation of the renminbi.

The growth of household consumption has remained sluggish and lagged behind the growth of disposable income. This is because household consumption has been adversely affected by actual and expected furloughing of workers by the state-owned enterprises (SOEs); the reduction in the staff of the central government by almost 50%[5]; and the prospective reform of housing, health care, education, pension and other social services. It has also been affected by the East Asian currency crisis through its negative effects on consumer confidence, even though the direct effects of the crisis on the Chinese economy as a whole have remained relatively small. As a result, the national saving rate has remained high at approximately 40% and household savings deposits as a percentage of GDP have continued to rise, reaching over 70% in 1998 (see Chart 10.3). The enterprises, both state-owned and non-state-owned, faced with a weak consumer

---

5 The central government employees have been reduced by approximately 48% across the board (approximately four million in total).

market and excess capacity, have also reduced or even stopped their new investment altogether. Moreover, because of the East Asian crisis, exports to, as well as the foreign direct investment inflow from, certain East Asian countries have also slowed dramatically. This, coupled with the clampdown on smuggling since mid-1998, has resulted in pockets of economic recession, especially in the southern Chinese provinces of Guangdong and Fujian.

Overall, business and consumer confidence has remained weak. In order to continue to sustain a rate of growth that is close to the potential of the Chinese economy, additional economic stimulus by the central government is necessary.

3. The Roles of the Banking Sector in a Developing Market Economy

In this section, we consider the different possible roles of the banking sector in a developing market economy. First of all, a banking system is a payment and settlement system—it facilitates transactions and hence economic activities. Without a reliable banking system, all transactions will have to be conducted in the forms of barter, cash, or buyer- and seller-specific credits. The volume of economic activities that can be supported will be much smaller in the absence of a functioning banking system. Second, banks provide a safe depository for the money balances of households and enterprises, as a convenient and reliable alternative to mattresses and private vaults. Third, banks provide low-risk[6] investment vehicles for the savings of households and enterprises in the form of different types of savings deposits. Finally, by extending credit to enterprises and households, the banking system also performs financial intermediation, allocating savings to their highest and best use and pooling and hence diversifying the risks across investment projects on behalf of its depositors.

In terms of loans (and investments), the banking sector has many options. The safest loans for the banks are of course those to the central government,

---

6 In economies with either explicit or implicit deposit insurance, such investment vehicles are virtually risk-free.

and the safest investments are debt securities issued by the central government.[7] Next in the order of higher riskiness are short-term loans for international trade financing backed by letters of credit, followed by construction loans and short-term working capital loans. The biggest risk in construction loan and working capital financing is the diversion of the loan proceeds for unauthorised purposes. Construction loan financing, properly disbursed in accordance with verified progress, is relatively low-risk, but there may be some repayment risk to the extent that the structures constructed cannot be readily sold at completion. Short-term working capital is also relatively low-risk, provided that it is adequately monitored and collateralised (e.g. with warehouse receipts).[8] Banks can also provide loans for investment by government and enterprises. However, these loans are typically long-term in nature. While loans to the government are generally quite secure,[9] long-term loans to enterprises should properly be the province of specialised development, industrial and long-term credit banks. Ordinary commercial banks do not normally have the long-term funding base to make these long-term loan commitments because the bulk of their deposits are short-term in nature. Moreover, loans for financing long-term investment by enterprises are also inherently riskier because of both the long gestation period and consequently the long exposure period—the loans become much more like equity investment in terms of their risk characteristics. Finally, banks can also finance personal or household investment (e.g. residential mortgage loans) and consumption; however, non-collateralised consumption loans are probably quite risky in developing economies, and even collateralised loans such as mortgages may face the problem of potential maturity mismatch with respect to the liabilities (deposits).

It is, of course, not necessary that all financial institutions perform all of the roles discussed above. Division of labour is quite possible. For example, the

---

7 This also provides the central government with an alternative to the practice of printing money to finance budget deficits.

8 Working capital financing based on cash flows is riskier. In the East Asian developing economies, cash flow based lending is extremely rare among the local banks. Collateral is almost always required and most often takes the form of real estate.

9 Even then there may be a risk of maturity mismatch.

postal savings system in many countries essentially fulfils only the safe depository role. It does not typically support transactions other than those between the postal savings system and its depositors. It also does not typically make loans, except possibly to the central government, and purchases only central government securities. For another example, it is also possible to conceive of a system of narrow banking institutions that is specialised as a payments and transaction settlement system and does not otherwise make loans, except possibly to the central government, either directly or through the purchase of central government securities.[10]

How has the Chinese banking sector fulfilled these roles? As Chart 10.3 reveals, the savings deposits in Chinese banks have been growing much faster than Chinese GDP in recent years. The ratio of savings deposits to GDP has been rising rapidly, which demonstrates that the Chinese banking sector has done a great job in mobilising and collecting savings. The rising savings deposits also attest to the confidence of the average Chinese citizen in the ultimate ability of the Chinese banking system to pay its depositors upon demand. However, the Chinese banking sector does not seem to have done as good a job in terms of allocating the savings. The stock of non-performing loans in the Chinese banking sector is large and increasing. We shall discuss these problems in the next section.

4. The Conditions of the Banking Sector

In this section, we examine the conditions of the Chinese banking sector in some detail. We assess the capital adequacy of the state-owned commercial banks as well as the potential gravity of their non-performing loans problems.

Capital Adequacy of the State-Owned Banks

The "Big Four" state-owned commercial banks—Bank of China, Industrial and Commercial Bank of China, Construction Bank of China and Agricultural Bank of China—account for 90% of all bank assets. Recently, the People's Bank of China lowered the reserve requirement for the

10 Money market funds, common in Western countries, come closest to this type of narrow banking institution.

commercial banks. A special government bond issue in the amount of 270 billion yuan (US$32.5 billion), with an annual coupon rate of 7.2%, was then purchased by the commercial banks with funds freed up by the lowering of the reserve requirement. Using these proceeds, the government, in turn, purchased subordinated debt of the commercial banks, which counts as "capital," to enable them to satisfy the standard capital requirement of 8% of assets laid down by the Basel Committee on Banking Supervision. Further recapitalisation along these lines is possible. One possibility is the exchange of government bonds by either the Ministry of Finance or the People's Bank of China for the (non-performing) loan assets of the state-owned commercial banks. Such an asset swap would strengthen the balance sheets of the commercial banks by improving the average quality of the bank assets. Another possibility is the purchase of government bonds by the state-owned commercial banks from the Ministry of Finance or the People's Bank of China, which in turn would purchase preferred shares or subordinated debt of the commercial banks with the proceeds. The net result would be an increase in capital as well as an increase in good assets (government bonds) on the bank balance sheets. Thus, it should be clear that capital adequacy for balance sheet purposes per se is not an issue. There is no question that the state-owned commercial banks are capable of satisfying the capital requirements. The more important issue has to do with the non-performing loans of the state-owned commercial banks.

The Non-Performing "Loans" of the State-Owned Banks

The majority of the non-performing loans of the state-owned commercial banks in China are fundamentally different in nature from the non-performing loans of privately owned commercial banks in market economies. First of all, they are almost exclusively owed by state-owned enterprises to the state-owned banks. Until very recently, only SOEs had access to credit from the formal banking sector in China. Second, the fact that the loans have become "non-performing" is not in general a surprise to either the lenders or the borrowers—most of the lenders do not expect the loans to be collectible even at the time they are first made, and most of the borrowers know full well at the time that they will not be able to repay these loans. The truth of the matter is that most of these loans are actually government subsidies for loss-making SOEs disbursed in the form of bank loans.[11] These are, in fact, policy loans.

The non-performing loans to the SOEs at the state-owned banks can be approximately classified into three categories: loans to traditional old-line industrial enterprises; loans to enterprises established during the mid-1980s in lieu of a founding equity; and loans contracted during the overheated period in the early 1990s. On top of these three categories of loans, there were also the rollovers (appropriately disguised) of these non-performing loans since 1994. In terms of annual flows, the non-performing loans amount to between 2% and 3% of GDP, comparable to the government budget deficits in many countries. In terms of cumulative stocks, they amount to approximately US$200 billion. With a GDP of approximately US$960 billion in 1998, this implies a non-performing loan to GDP ratio of slightly over 20%, which is quite consistent with estimates of 20% by the People's Bank of China and 25% by international credit rating agencies. Ultimately unrecoverable non-performing loans have been estimated to be in the order of between one-third (by Chinese bank officials) and one-half (by rating agencies) of all outstanding non-performing loans. As mentioned above, these loans should be regarded as indirect loans by the state-owned banks to the state itself and thus should properly be included as part of the Chinese public debt. Official Chinese public debt outstanding was approximately 10% of GDP as of 1996. Adding in the estimated net new debts issued in 1997 and 1998, as well as the entire stock of outstanding non-performing loans, the public debt to GDP ratio will be somewhere between 35% and 40%, still considerably lower than that of many other countries (see the following section). Moreover, it is also clear that the Chinese banks will never be allowed to fail in a way that hurts the depositors—in other words, there is, in fact, universal implicit insurance for bank deposits.

Why Do State-Owned Enterprises Lose Money?

Since the majority of the non-performing loans are essentially government

---

11 If the fiscal condition of the Chinese central government were better, these subsidies could have come directly from the budget rather than indirectly through the state-owned commercial banks as loans.

subsidies for making up the losses of SOEs, it is useful to try to understand why SOEs lose money. Presumably, if and when these losses can be stopped, the subsidies will no longer be necessary, and the flow of new loans can be discontinued. The SOEs' losses can be attributed to many factors, most of which are unrelated to the profitability of the business operations of the enterprises. First, there is the burden of unfunded or under-funded pension and other social welfare liabilities such as housing, education and medical care. Second, there is the burden of the interest costs on loans incurred on the establishment of the enterprises in lieu of a founding equity. This applies to most SOEs established in the early 1980s. An enterprise otherwise breaking even on an operating basis may thus wind up in the red because of the payment of interest on the initial capital loan. Third, there are genuine operating losses due to antiquated equipment and technology and/or over-employment. Fourth, there may be losses due to diversion or re-lending of loan funds for other unauthorised purposes (e.g. from working capital to fixed asset investment, re-lending to third parties, or speculation in the real estate or stock markets) with or without the connivance of the loan officers, due to insufficient monitoring. These losses occurred mostly in the overheated period in the early 1990s. Fifth, there may be losses due to improper transfer pricing (e.g. selling low and buying high from related parties) and other irregular practices on the part of the SOEs—as long as the state or state-owned bank are ready to absorb them. Most of these losses are in the nature of accounting losses and imply only that the shareholders (the state), as opposed to the enterprises or the management, are losing money.[12] Finally, there may be losses due to the lack of incentives for efficient management or efficient allocation of new investment.

How can some of these losses be stopped? First, the burden of unfunded or under-funded pension and other social welfare liabilities such as housing, education, and medical care for the former and current SOEs must be assumed by the state in one way or another. Otherwise the haemorrhage will simply continue. Second, for an enterprise that did not have a founding equity, there

12 A government official was reported to have remarked that, if there were a regulation that any state-owned enterprise that loses money three years in a row would be shut down permanently, then many of the loss-making enterprises would report a small profit in the third year so as to avoid becoming closed.

should be a debt-equity swap, converting the initial capital loan into the equity of the enterprise, thus greatly reducing the burden of the continuing interest costs and hence the potential losses. Third, for an enterprise with antiquated equipment and technology and/or overstaffing, measures should be taken to close down the enterprise and/or reduce employment. To a certain extent, *xiagang* (literally, "stepping down from one's post")—the furloughing of the workers of the Chinese SOEs, which by the end of 1998 had already shrunk the workforce of the SOEs by some 20 million—is a major step in this direction. However, the speed with which the furloughing of workers can continue to be carried out may have to depend on the robustness of the rest of the economy, so that the majority of the redundant labour force thus released can be absorbed. Fourth, for loan losses due to diversion or unauthorised re-lending of loan funds, the obvious solution is increased monitoring. By adopting relatively simple controls on the disbursement of loan proceeds—e.g. the implementation of the "real bills" doctrine (collateralising the loans for financing inventories of materials, intermediate inputs and finished goods), using the construction loan method of disbursement (direct payment to vendors and contractors in accordance with verified progress), and more generally insisting on the direct transfer of funds to the authorised payees (including suppliers and workers). Fifth, improper transfer pricing and other irregular practices can be reduced with increased monitoring and better auditing. However, a more thorough solution will require a general hardening of the "budget constraint" and selective divestiture of some of the SOEs to the management so as to reduce the incentives for artificial loss creation. Finally, in order to reduce losses due to the lack of incentives for efficient management or efficient allocation of new investment, the system of governance of the SOEs has to be reformed both to solve the principal-agent problem and to reduce moral hazard through the hardening of the budget constraint.

However, it is clear from the discussion above that the SOEs losses do not necessarily reflect social inefficiency, as they may have been caused by fixed factors independent of the efficiency of the business operations of the enterprises and by unauthorised redistributions, both of which are basically infra-marginal in nature.

In principle, the solution of the non-performing loans problem is very simple. The liabilities can be simply assumed by the central government or the central bank, either directly or indirectly through another government-sponsored entity (like the Resolution Trust Corporation of the United States). In fact, China Construction Bank was the first of the four major Chinese commercial banks to undertake a restructuring of its non-performing loans by forming an asset management company. However, the real challenge of the non-performing loans problem is how to prevent its recurrence. A permanent solution of the problem of non-performing loans of the state-owned banks is only possible if the SOEs can be made viable so that new policy loans are no longer necessary. Thus, reform of the SOEs is essential for the long-term success of the reform of the banking sector. It is helpful that over time the state-owned sector has been shrinking. The percentage of GDP it accounts for has declined from almost 100% in 1979 to approximately 30% today. A growing GDP and a robust non-state-owned sector facilitates the reform of the SOEs and consequently the non-performing loans problem of the state-owned banks.

Other Issues Facing the Banking Sector

In addition to the non-performing loans problem, there are several other issues as well. First, in the current environment, the central government or the central bank must be prepared to guarantee the security of deposits of all individuals (perhaps up to a ceiling amount). In other words, the government must provide universal implicit deposit insurance to all commercial banks, and the central bank must act as the lender of last resort when necessary. The four major Chinese state-owned commercial banks are certainly "too big to fail." Implicit deposit insurance may, however, lead to moral hazard on the part of the depositors and the banks, and that is why a ceiling amount on the insurance may be desirable and financial regulation and supervision are necessary. For financial supervision and regulation to be effective, the management of the commercial banks must be made responsible for their banks' performance. Thus, there must be hierarchical and unitary control within the commercial banks. To enforce financial discipline, weak banks and non-bank financial institutions must be allowed to close or become bankrupt, or forced to consolidate and merge if necessary. To a certain extent, the government has already implemented this policy by the closure of non-bank financial institutions such as China Venturetech and Guangdong International Trust and Investment Corporation (GITIC).

The closure and bankruptcy of GITIC has significance for the banking sector well beyond the GITIC episode itself. It sets a precedent and sends a very strong signal that non-sovereign guaranteed debt is just that—non-sovereign guaranteed debt, and the lenders, both domestic and foreign, should beware. Thus, in one fell swoop, by not bailing out the institutional creditors of GITIC, both domestic and foreign, and otherwise not interfering in the workout process, moral hazard on the part of both potential lenders and borrowers is reduced. The GITIC bankruptcy provides for equal treatment for all creditors in accordance with the priority established by law. It leads directly to the downgrading of the credit ratings of the Chinese state-owned banks and investment companies. Standard and Poor's assigned a "junk" rating to China International Trust and Investment Company (CITIC), the Bank of China, China Construction Bank and the Industrial and Commercial Bank of China, but there was a strengthening in the sovereign credit rating of China. Indirectly the GITIC episode also strengthened central government control over the financial and banking sector.

Moral hazard can also be reduced through a reduction of "excess leverage." Asset price bubbles are frequently caused by over-leveraging. In any case, the damage from the bursting of the bubble can be minimised if the degree of leverage is controlled. Rules and regulations that reduce or limit leverage (e.g. by classification of assets) on the part of bank borrowers (enterprises and individuals) should be enacted—and they should cover loans collateralised by stocks and residential and non-residential properties as well. The swap of debt for equity by enterprises should also help to reduce leverage. Higher capital requirements on the banks also help to reduce the leverage of the lenders and hence their moral hazard. The overall credit quality of bank loans can be expected to improve with a reduction of moral hazard on the part of both lenders and borrowers.

Information asymmetry can also adversely affect both the quality and quantity of credit. Improvement of the accuracy and availability of credit-relevant information will lead to higher quality and quantity of loans. The information flow may be improved by imposing uniform accounting and auditing standards; encouraging the emergence of larger and more professional accounting and auditing firms with capital and reputation to protect; and promoting credit information collection, exchange and assessment organisations such as credit bureaus and rating agencies.

Mismatch of the maturities of assets and liabilities is a common problem for financial and banking sectors. The problem of the savings and loan associations in the United States in the early 1980s is a well-known example of such a mismatch—the savings and loan associations make long-term (30-year) fixed rate mortgage loans funded mostly by short-term deposits. The result, as the rate of interest rose in the early 1980s, was an unmitigated financial disaster that cost the U.S. taxpayers approximately US$600 billion. China will do well to try to avoid repeating the same mistake. As the demand for long-term fixed rate loans increases in the Chinese economy, for example for financing residential mortgages, the banks must make efforts to expand their long-term fixed rate deposits, or to issue long-term fixed rate bonds themselves, or to either directly or indirectly (by selling the loans to another organisation) securitize the loans, minimising the exposure to interest rate risk. The development of a long-term capital market, including secondary markets for debt securities, is absolutely essential to increasing the supply of long-term funds.

Political interference with banking and monetary policy decisions is potentially a problem. The recent institution of a system of district central banks in China similar to the U.S. Federal Reserve System is a first step to insulate the banking system from political influence at the provincial and local levels. Nine district branches of the People's Bank of China, each overseeing two or more provinces/municipalities/autonomous regions, have been established (Tianjin, Shenyang, Shanghai, Nanjing, Jinan, Wuhan, Guangzhou, Chengdu, and Xi'an). In addition, the original provincial-level branches have all been abolished. Eventually, perhaps even the central bank itself can become more independent of the executive branch of the government.

Finally, there needs to be more investment in human capital in the banking sector. More education, training and institution building are required. Efforts should be made to develop and nurture a modern bank "culture" with emphasis on credit analysis, risk control and efficient provision of banking services to customers.

5. The Fiscal Situation

We now turn to examine the Chinese fiscal situation to assess both the short-term viability and the long-term sustainability of the Chinese financial system. If the Chinese financial system were in imminent danger of collapse, it would place severe constraints on the set of feasible government policies, and in particular would limit the ability of the Chinese government to stimulate the economy through deficit spending. The viability and sustainability of the Chinese financial system depend on a number of factors, including: the size of the annual government total and current (or operating) deficit; the public demand for public debt; the fiscal capacity for servicing the public debt; the lending and bond-buying capacity of the banking system; and public confidence in the banking system and the currency.[13]

The Government Budget Deficit

In Chart 10.4, we present the central government budget revenue, expenditure and surplus as a percentage of GDP. It shows that the official Chinese government deficit has been quite low in recent years, less than 1.5% of GDP. However, it is also worth noting that total government revenue (expenditure) as a percentage of GDP has been falling continuously, from slightly over 30% in 1979 to below 15% in 1997. This ratio is actually among the lowest in the world.

Chart 10.4. Central Government Budget Revenue, Expenditure and Surplus/Deficit, as a Percent of GDP

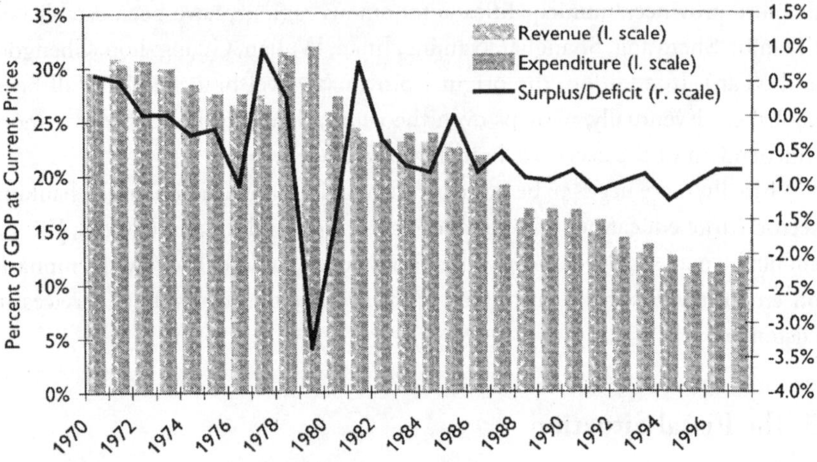

13 Since the renminbi is a non-convertible currency, only the confidence of the domestic citizens is relevant.

In Chart 10.5, we present the distribution between current (recurrent) and capital (non-recurrent) government expenditures. It is apparent that on a current (or recurrent) expenditure basis, the government budget has been in surplus in recent years. With the recent reduction in the size of the government, 48% of the central government employees have been laid off. This should result in a significant reduction in personnel and related costs in current expenditure in a couple of years. Thus, the surplus should become even larger in the future.

Chart 10.5. The Distribution Between Current and Capital Expenditure, as a Percent of GDP

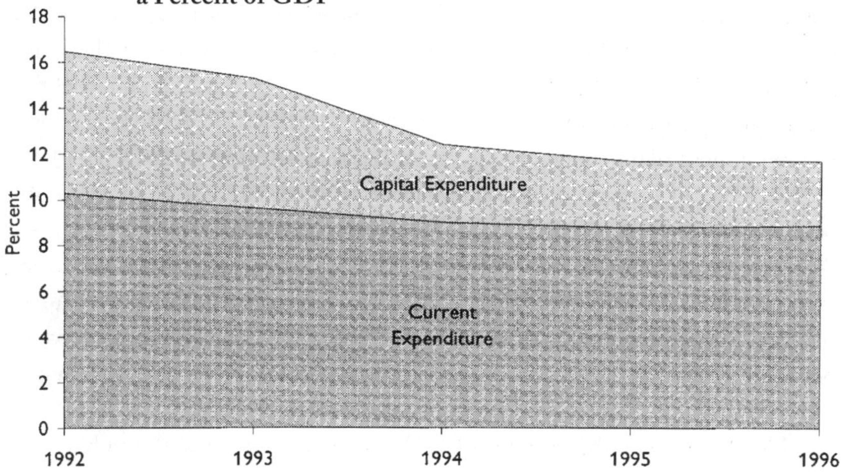

Chart 10.6. Government Deficit, Selected Countries, as a Percent of GDP

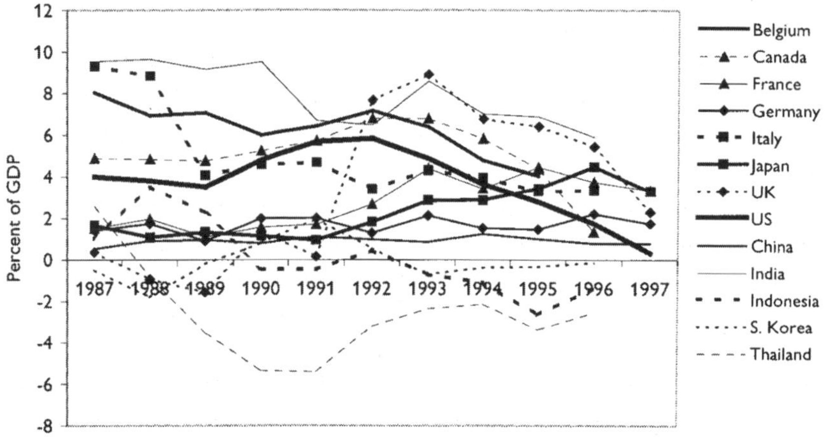

In Chart 10.6, as a comparison, we present the total government deficit as a percentage of GDP for selected countries. The Chinese government budget deficit has been rather modest compared to other countries, including India, Japan, the United Kingdom and the United States. The current level of official government budget deficit is completely sustainable in the long run.

The Stock of Public Debt

In Chart 10.7, we present data on the official Chinese stock of public debt as a percentage of Chinese GDP. In Chart 10.8, we present data on the stock of public debt as a percentage of GDP for selected countries. This shows that the public debt to GDP ratio of China is among the lowest. All the major industrialised countries, including Japan, have much higher public debt to GDP ratios. If we add the entire stock of the Chinese non-performing loans to the Chinese public debt (that is, assuming that nothing is recoverable), the public debt to GDP ratio of China will be approximately 40% in 1998, still below those of Belgium and Italy, which were above 100%, and the United States (70%), Japan (almost 100%), the United Kingdom, India and France. If we assume that approximately half of the non-performing loans can be recovered, then the public debt to GDP ratio of China will be somewhere between 25 and 30%, which is quite manageable. At 30% of GDP and at a rate of interest of, say, 5% (the current Chinese rate of interest is actually considerably lower), the amount of GDP required to service the public debt each year is approximately 1.5%. As a proportion of total government revenue, the debt service would amount to 10%.

If we assume that new non-performing loans add to this public debt to GDP ratio at the rate of 2.5% per year, and assume again that approximately half of these non-performing loans cannot be recovered, then, in 10 years time, we shall have added another 12.5% to the public debt to GDP ratio, bringing it to approximately 40%, still a manageable figure and nowhere near the danger zone.

We conclude that the Chinese economy is not in imminent danger of financial collapse, despite the existence of a significant stock of non-performing loans. Moreover, while the existence of the non-performing loans and their continual increase over time are not desirable, they do not yet pose a serious threat to the solvency of either the banking system or the central government. The system is sustainable for at least another decade or longer. It has already

Chart 10.7. The Stock of Public Debt at Year-end, as a Percent of GDP

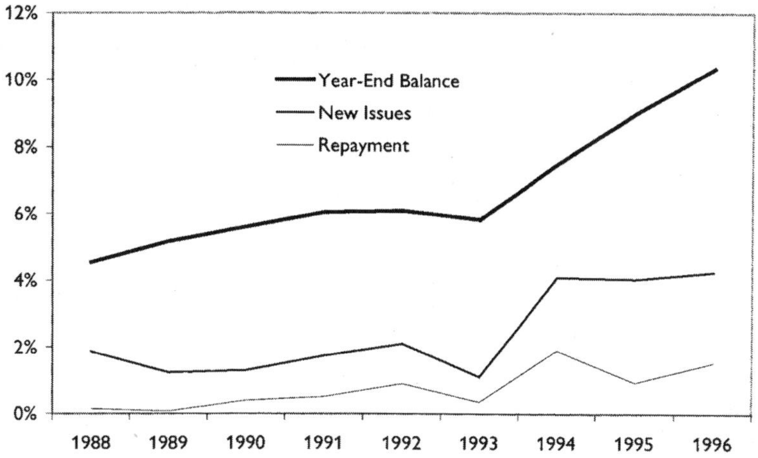

Chart 10.8. Public Debt, Selected Countries, as a Percent of GDP

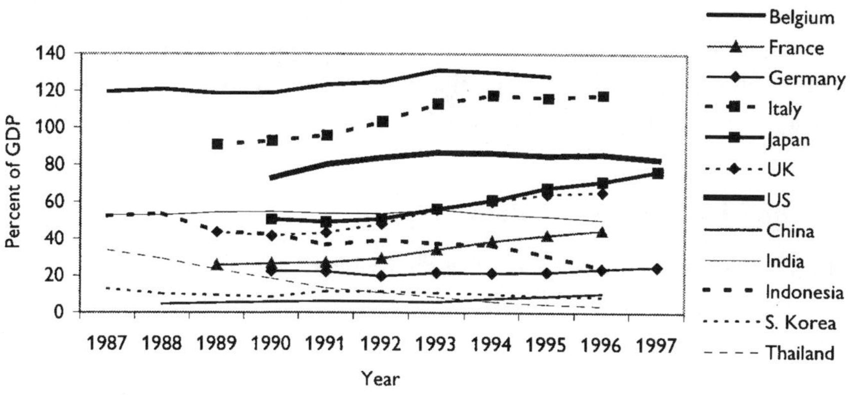

been pointed out that for a reform of the banking sector to be genuinely, as opposed to cosmetically, successful, it must await a successful reform of the SOEs. The present time, when the growth of the Chinese economy has slowed and public confidence in the economy, for a variety of reasons, is low, is definitely not the right time for hastening real reform of the SOEs, and hence there should be no rush to undertake a radical reform of the Chinese financial sector. Furthermore, the fiscal situation can certainly support a couple of years of deficit financing without significant adverse effects, especially given the low rate of growth of non-government aggregate demand and the low, indeed negative, rate of inflation currently prevailing in the economy.

While it is true that China's current capacity to expand tax collection is weak, it has been steadily improving. The reduction in the size of government should also result in real savings in a few years. For now, household deposits have been rising rapidly as a percentage of GDP and provide the wherewithal for the banks to continue financing the deficits of the SOEs either directly through bank loans or indirectly through the purchase of government bonds. Moreover, savings rates are expected to remain high and longer-term debt instruments can be used. Furthermore, the state-owned sector is relatively stagnant. It has already shrunk to 30% of GDP, and in another 10 years it will probably shrink to 15%. Its losses as a percentage of a growing GDP must also decline over time. Thus, while the annual flow of losses that need to be subsidised is unlikely to decrease without more genuine reform, its ratio to GDP should not be rising. The rate of interest has also remained low. Public confidence in the banking sector and in the renminbi has remained high, as shown by the continuing inflow of household savings deposits into the banking sector. All these considerations suggest that while the problem is serious, it is neither critical nor fatal, and that the current situation can be sustained for a decade or even two without causing a collapse of the Chinese economy.

6. The Macroeconomic Policy Options

In the previous section we show that the problem of non-performing loans in the state-owned banks does not impose a significant constraint on the ability of the central government to engage in the necessary fiscal and monetary policies to stimulate the economy. The near-term challenges that face the government include: maintaining aggregate demand (and hence economic growth and employment); stability of the Chinese yuan and the Hong Kong dollar; reform of the state-owned enterprises; reform of the banking system; and reform of the housing system.

First, we consider the external environment. The U.S. economy cannot be any better than it is now, with record low rates of interest, inflation and unemployment and a booming stock market. All of the risks are therefore downside risks. The Japanese economy will take a long time to turn around. The Southeast Asian countries (except Indonesia) and Korea will begin to recover in mid-1999 but the rates of growth for the entire year will be relatively low. Hong Kong is already in recession and the rate of growth of the economy of Taiwan has also begun to slow. Thus, China cannot rely on continued growth of its exports and must take the initiative on its own to maintain aggregate demand and to stimulate its domestic economy.

Second, domestically, neither household consumption nor enterprise investment (including foreign direct investment), state-owned or not, can be the engine of economic growth in the near term. In order to induce households to consume and enterprises to invest again, one must first try to turn around expectations.

Third, among the objectives of the Chinese policy-makers is the preservation of social stability—a policy of "no losers"—at least "no immediate losers." Thus, it is a high priority for the Chinese government to limit unemployment and create new jobs—approximately 10 million new workers enter the labour force each year.

Finally, economic growth and economic reform are actually complementary—neither one can run ahead of the other. On the one hand, if economic reform runs too fast, it will cause economic growth to slow (because of the furloughing of workers and the adverse expectations that it generates). On the other hand, if economic growth runs too fast without reform, it will run into bottlenecks. However, economic growth actually provides the environment in which genuine economic reform can be implemented. Economic growth and economic reform must therefore go hand-in-hand.

The Macroeconomic Policy Options

In the short run, increasing gross fixed investment through new and accelerated infrastructural investment projects is the only realistic macroeconomic policy option capable of providing immediate stimulus to the economy. This policy has already been implemented by the Chinese government. However, increasing infrastructural investment is only a transitional measure intended to maintain the rate of growth of GDP in the near term and to induce a change in expectations on the part of households and enterprises. Infrastructural investment alone cannot sustain the rate of economic growth for more than a couple of years. The promotion of affordable owner-occupied residential housing investment for and by the domestic population is therefore one of the few alternative promising sources of growth of aggregate demand. This also fits into the plan to marketise residential housing for employees of state-owned enterprises and the government by end-1998. The provision of long-term, preferably fixed rate, mortgages by the banking sector to households is critical to the success of this effort.

In the longer run, continued economic growth requires new investment by enterprises, which in turn requires new and increased lending to new enterprise (both state-owned and non-state-owned) investment projects. However, in recent months, the growth of loans has been very slow—both the demand for and the supply of loans have been low.

What are the reasons for the low demand for loans? First of all, the expectations of households and enterprises have to be turned around and their confidence in the economy restored. However, this will take both time and sustained economic stimulus on the part of the government. Second, the real rate of interest, at 8%, is still too high for borrowers. Third, the lack of clearly secure property rights (rights of transfer of property in addition to use rights) discourages investment by both non-state-owned enterprises and households.

What are the reasons for the low supply of loans? First of all, there is a general "reluctance to lend" on the part of loan officers at the banks, in part because of the introduction of "life-time" responsibility of the authorising loan officer for the repayment of the loan. As a result, many loan officers simply go into a defensive mode by simply not making any loans. Those loan officers with loan quotas to meet will make only "overnight loans," that is, he or she will "pretend" to lend to a customer who by pre-arrangement will borrow on one day and repay immediately on the next day, thus helping the loan officer fulfil the loan quotas but without the risk of any loss (this type of activity gives a new meaning to the term "overnight loans"). Second, the lack of clearly secure collateral, especially in the case of non-state borrowers, discourages lending. Third, information is both inadequate and unreliable for serious credit analysis. Finally, capital inadequacy and existing non-performing loans may limit a bank's ability to lend.

What Can the Government Do to Increase the Volume of Loans (Safely)?

First, the government will try to turn around the expectations of households and enterprises and restore their confidence in the economy by maintaining the growth in aggregate demand through undertaking infrastructural investment projects on a sustained basis. Recapitalisation of some of the enterprises through either a debt-equity swap, injection of new equity, or forgiveness of old debt will help enhance the borrowing capacity of enterprises. Second, the central bank can lower the nominal and hence the real rate of interest, which it has already done quite a few times. Third, laws should be enacted that guarantee the property rights of owners of residential housing units, including, in particular, the right of transfer to third parties (such rights can be completely analogous to the rights of the owners of rural housing units), thus solving the "lack of collateral" problem. In addition, the introduction of alternative modes of bankruptcy (e.g. reorganisation) in addition to liquidation will also help alleviate the "lack of collateral" problem.

Fourth, lending can be facilitated by drawing up "safe harbour" rules for loan officers so that they do not have to assume life-time responsibility for loans they make indefinitely if they follow all the rules.

Fifth, the incentive for commercial banks to lend can be increased by reducing or eliminating the payment of interest on excess reserves held by commercial banks at the People's Bank of China. Lending to non-state owned enterprises can be expanded by implementing a prime rate system—allowing the commercial banks to charge higher interest rates to less established borrowers (this has the advantage of also protecting the net spread of the commercial banks as they lend to small and medium-sized enterprises). Third, the information for credit analysis can be improved by promoting the establishment of credit rating and reporting agencies and by setting up a system of accreditation and regulation of accountants and auditors. Finally, the re-capitalisation of the banks and the transfer or sale of the non-performing loans to the government, or another entity set up by the government, should improve the ability of banks to lend.

References

Lardy, Nicholas. *China's Unfinished Economic Revolution*. Washington, DC: The Brookings Institution, 1998.

Lau, Lawrence J., and Yingyi Qian. "Financial Reorganisation of Banks and Enterprises in China: A Proposal." Working Paper, Stanford University, Department of Economics, 1994.

Qian, Yingyi. "The Institutional Foundations of China's Market Transition." Paper presented at the Annual World Bank Conference on Development Economics, Washington, DC, 28–30 April 1999.

Chapter 11.

Reform without Losers: An Interpretation of China's Dual-Track Approach to Transition*

Co-authored with Yingyi Qian and Gerard Roland

1. Introduction

Efficiency-enhancing economic reform should potentially allow winners to compensate losers, thereby making the reform Pareto-improving. However, in practice, it seems very difficult to find mechanisms that make economic reform Pareto-improving, and even more difficult for reform to be simultaneously Pareto-improving and efficient, because of distortionary costs of compensation or the lack of credibility of its implementation. We demonstrate in this paper that a simple mechanism of a "dual-track" approach, as used in China's economic reform, can serve to implement efficient Pareto-improving economic reform. The basic principle of the dual-track approach is as follows: Under the plan track, economic agents are assigned rights to and obligations for fixed quantities of goods at fixed plan prices as specified in the pre-existing

* This chapter was originally published in *The Journal of Political Economy* 108, no. 1 (February 2000), pp. 120–143. Lau and Qian gratefully acknowledge financial support from the Smith-Richardson Foundation, and Roland thanks the Center for Advanced Studies in the Behavioral Sciences in Stanford, where he was a fellow in 1998–1999 when the revision was completed. We wish to thank Masahiko Aoki, Kenneth Arrow, Coit Blacker, Ronald Findlay, Peter Hammond, Anne Krueger, Paul Krugman, Jean-Jacques Laffont, David D. Li, Ronald McKinnon, Roger Noll, John Riley, Dani Rodrik, Sherwin Rosen, T. N. Srinivasan, Ross Starr, Shang-Jin Wei, Ho-Mou Wu, and seminar participants at Département et Labouratoire d'Economie Théorique et Appliquée, the National Bureau of Economic Research, Stanford University, and the University of Michigan for helpful comments and discussions,@ and Shu-Cheng Liu and Li-An Zhou for excellent research assistance.

plan. In addition, a market track is introduced under which economic agents participate in the market at free-market prices, provided that they fulfil their obligations under the pre-existing plan.

We distinguish two types of market liberalisation in this context. We refer to it as "limited market liberalisation" if market resales of plan-allocated goods and market purchases by planned suppliers for fulfilling plan-mandated delivery quotas are not permitted. Thus, under limited market liberalisation, planned suppliers must physically produce all plan-mandated output deliveries and physically use all plan-allocated inputs themselves even though it might have been cheaper to sell the inputs on the market track and purchase the same output from the market track for redelivery. In contrast, we refer to it as "full market liberalisation" if market resales and market purchases for redelivery are all allowed by a planned supplier or a rationed user, as long as its obligations under the plan are all fulfilled.

Within the conventional supply and demand framework, we analyse various distributional and efficiency aspects of the dual-track mechanism.[1] We show that, independently of the initial conditions concerning supply and demand, as long as the pre-existing feasible plan continues to be enforced appropriately, the dual-track approach to market liberalisation is always Pareto-improving. In addition, it also achieves efficiency under full market liberalisation and other usual conditions such as profit maximisation and perfect competition.

The idea that the dual-track approach can provide a concrete mechanism for the implementation of efficient Pareto-improving reform is both simple and subtle. The introduction of the market track provides the opportunity for economic agents who participate in it to be better off, whereas the maintenance of the plan track provides implicit transfers to compensate potential losers from the market liberalisation by protecting the status quo rents under the pre-existing plan. Thus the dual-track approach is, by design, Pareto-improving. Moreover, as the compensatory transfers are inframarginal and thus lump sum[2] in nature, the dual-track approach can be efficient too. One

1 See Lau, Qian, and Roland (1997) for a general equilibrium analysis.

2 The term "lumpsum transfers" as used here simply means that the transfers are independent of the actions of the individual economic agents. The values of such transfers may depend on market prices.

desirable feature of the dual-track approach is its minimal *additional* informational and institutional requirements: it utilises the existing information contained in the original plan and enforces the plan through existing planning institutions. No new information and no new institutions are needed.

While the "single-track" (or "big-bang") full market liberalisation will lead to efficiency under the usual conditions such as profit maximisation and perfect competition, Pareto improvement cannot in general be assured. In contrast, the dual-track full market liberalisation provides a useful way to implement a reform without creating losers while simultaneously achieving efficiency under the same conditions. In transition economies under both democratic and non-democratic systems, there is a need to buy off bureaucrats, government employees, workers, and consumers accustomed to receiving implicit subsidies and to prevent reform reversal being pushed by coalitions hurt by the reform. Because of its Pareto-improving property, the dual-track approach minimises political opposition to reform ex ante and maximises political opposition to reversal of reform ex post. Enforcement of the plan track is crucial for preserving the pre-existing rents. Sufficient state enforcement power is needed here *not* to implement an unpopular reform, but to carry out a reform that creates no losers, only winners.

An implicit guiding principle underlying China's economic reform strategy since 1979 has been that reform should proceed without creating losers, and the dual-track approach has been a concrete mechanism to achieve that objective.[3] The agricultural market liberalisation illustrates that the dual-track approach can be both Pareto-improving and efficient. The commune (and later the household) is assigned the responsibility to sell a fixed quantity of output to the state procurement agency as previously mandated under the plan at predetermined plan prices and to pay a fixed tax (often in kind) to the

---

3 The principle of reform without losers has been perceived as common wisdom in the Chinese economic reform literature. Although economists inside China (e.g., Wu and Zhao 1987; Zhang and Yi 1995; Lin, Cai, and Li 1996) and experts on the Chinese economy outside China (e.g., McMillan and Naughton 1992; Naughton 1995) have made informal discussions on the issue, they have not presented formal analysis and systematic evidence. The only exceptions are Sicular (1988) and Byrd (1991), who analysed the dual-track pricing in China's agricultural and industrial reforms, respectively.

government. It also has the right (and obligation) to receive a fixed quantity of inputs, principally chemical fertilizers, from state-owned suppliers at pre-determined plan prices. Subject to fulfilling these conditions, the commune is free to produce and sell whatever it considers profitable and retain any profit. Moreover, the commune can purchase from the market grain (or other) output for resale to the state in fulfilment of its responsibility. There is thus full market liberalisation.

Beyond the Chinese experience, schemes involving various forms of "grandfathering" in the West resemble the dual-track approach. For example, the two-tier wage system with lower wages for newly hired personnel and higher wages for existing personnel has been used in some industries such as the U.S. airline industry. Discussions of pension reform involving the transition from "pay as you go" to funded pension schemes also feature similar considerations.

The rest of the paper is organised as follows. We present a theoretical analysis of the dual-track liberalisation in part 2. In part 3, we discuss the conditions for the success of the dual-track approach. In part 4, we examine to what extent these conditions were fulfilled in China and provide examples of its dual-track experience in product and labour markets. Part 5 presents concluding remarks.

2. The Theoretical Analysis

In order to understand fully the dual-track mechanism, we consider a variety of possible market situations concerning demand and supply. Since the plan price and quantity are fixed by the state, they need bear no particular relationship to the market equilibrium price and quantity and can be either below or above the market price and quantity, respectively. The plan prices of most normal producer and consumer goods are likely to be below the market prices; however, the pre-existing total compensation (wage plus housing, health, and pension benefits) of workers in state-owned enterprises (SOEs) under the plan may well be above the market wage rate. Similarly, while high-quality goods are often in short supply under the plan, the plan production of low-quality and unwanted goods may be greater than the total demand under full market liberalisation. Furthermore, in general, there is no reason to assume that the planned output is allocated to users with the highest willingness to

Chart 11.1. Efficient Rationed Demand and Efficient Planned Supply

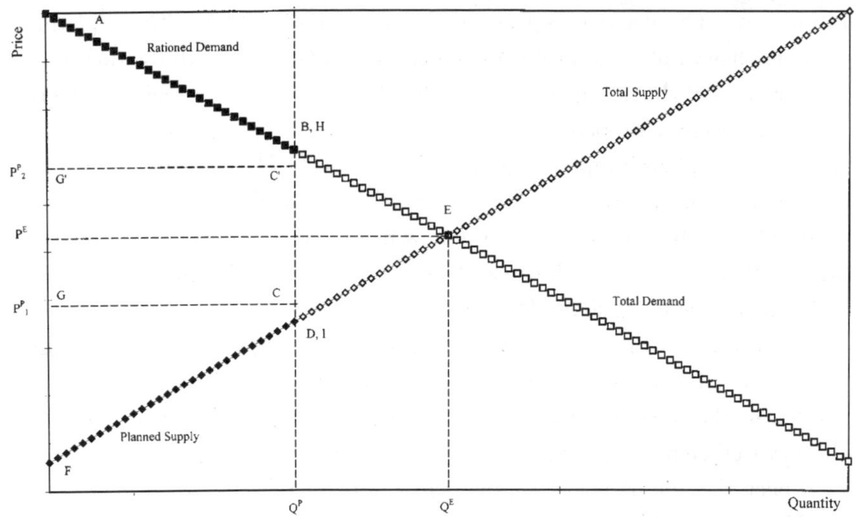

pay (efficient rationing) or that the planned supply is delivered by suppliers with the lowest marginal costs (efficient planned supply). In what follows, we denote by P^M and P^E (respectively, Q^M and Q^E) market equilibrium prices (quantities) under limited and full market liberalisation. We use Q^P to denote plan quantity and P^P_i $(i = 1, 2)$ to denote possible plan prices, with P^P_1 below P^E and P^P_2 above P^E.

The Plan Quantity Is Less than the Fully Liberalised Market Equilibrium Quantity

We begin with the special case of efficient rationing and efficient planned supply. Rationed demand and planned supply are therefore the top and bottom segments of the willingness to pay curve and the marginal cost curve, respectively (see Chart 11.1). Under the assumption of atomistic profit and utility maximisation, the willingness to pay and marginal cost curves turn out to be precisely the market supply and demand curves. Dual-track liberalisation means that Q^P continues to be delivered at plan price P^P_i but that any additional quantity can be sold freely in the market. The market track will thus provide an additional supply Q^E–Q^P at price P^E. The allocative outcome under dual-track liberalisation is just as efficient as that under single-track liberalisation. The difference between the two is entirely distributional.

Suppose first that the plan price is P^{P}_{1}, below P^{E}. Under the plan, the rationed users have a surplus given by the area bounded by *ABCG;* the planned suppliers have a planned profit/loss equal to area *GCDF.* With the dual track, the surpluses of the rationed users and the planned suppliers remain exactly the same, by design. Compared to the outcome of the single-track liberalisation, there is an implicit lump-sum transfer equal to $(P^{E}-P^{P}_{1})\ Q^{P}$ from the planned suppliers to the rationed users so that the latter and the former are both no worse off than before.[4] However, the new users and suppliers outside the plan are together better off by the area of the triangle *BED.* The analysis is similar if the plan price is P^{P}_{2}, above P^{E}.

Note that in this special case of efficient rationing and efficient planned supply, the introduction of the market track achieves efficiency even under limited market liberalisation. The reason is that the most deserving users and the most efficient suppliers are already under the plan track, and they would have been the first users and suppliers in a fully liberalised market in any case.

We next consider the general case in which Q^{P} is not necessarily allocated to users with the highest willingness to pay and some of the planned suppliers may have higher marginal costs than other potential suppliers. In Chart 11.2, we represent the willingness to pay curve of the rationed users by a generic curve *AH* and the marginal cost curve of the planned supply by a generic curve *FI.*

In contrast to the special case above, the allocative outcome now depends on whether there is limited or full liberalisation of the market track. Under limited liberalisation, the plan track and the market track are completely segregated; therefore, in our partial equilibrium framework the market track consists of only the *residual* demand and supply—that is, total demand and supply reduced, respectively, by the rationed demand and planned supply. Their intersection represents the limited market liberalisation equilibrium. While under limited liberalisation the dual-track approach is Pareto-improving, it cannot in general achieve efficiency because one cannot rule out the possibility that a rationed user may have a willingness to pay below P^{E}, or a

4 Note that in a general equilibrium framework, an equilibrium under a fully liberalised dual-track approach is generally not the same as that under a single-track approach because of differences in the distribution of income (see Lau et al. 1997). However, efficiency holds in either case.

Chart 11.2. Inefficient Rationed Demand and Inefficient Planned Supply: Planned Quantity Is Less Than the Fully Liberalised Market Equilibrium Quantity

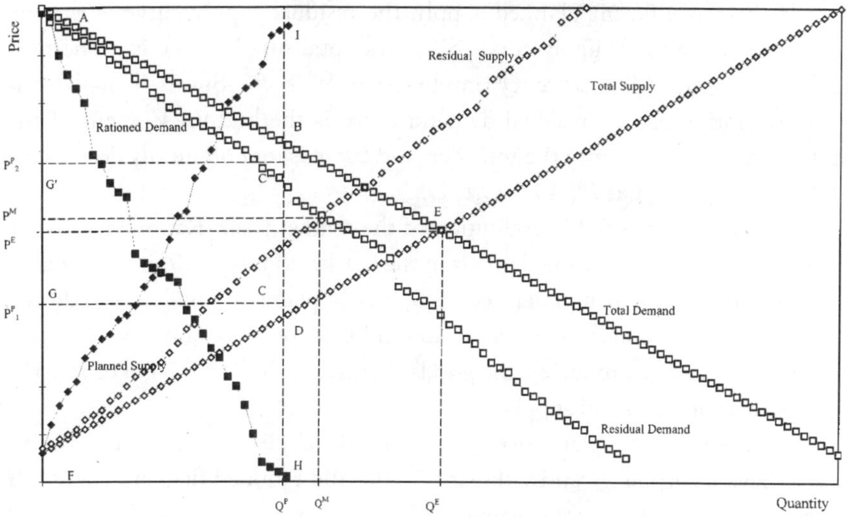

planned supplier may have their marginal cost above P^E. In fact, the following proposition shows that limited liberalisation of the market track always leads to inefficiency in the form of overproduction relative to the fully liberalised market equilibrium.

Proposition 1. If the plan quantity is less than the fully liberalised market equilibrium quantity, then (1) the combined output of the plan and market tracks under limited liberalisation of the market track is greater than or equal to the fully liberalised market equilibrium quantity, and (2) the market equilibrium price under limited liberalisation is greater (less) than or equal to the market equilibrium price under full liberalisation of the market track if planned supply (rationed demand) is efficient.

Proof. If $P^M \leq P^E$, then every potential user with a willingness to pay greater than or equal to P^E will be an actual user; moreover, since rationing is not necessarily efficient, there may also be actual users of planned supplies whose willingness to pay is below P^E. Thus total actual demand, $Q^P + Q^M$, must be greater than or equal to Q^E. If $P^M \geq P^E$, then every potential supplier with a marginal cost less than or equal to P^E will be an actual supplier; moreover, since supply planning is not necessarily efficient, there may also be one or more actual suppliers whose marginal costs are above P^E. Thus total actual supply, $Q^P + Q^M$, must also be greater than or equal to Q^E.

If there is efficient planned supply, the residual supply curve is the top segment of the total supply curve. Since the total supply curve is monotonically increasing, $Q^P + Q^M \geq Q^E$ implies that $P^M \geq P^E$. Similarly, if there is efficient rationing, the residual demand curve is the bottom segment of the total demand curve. Since the total demand curve is monotonically decreasing, $Q^P + Q^M \geq Q^E$ implies $P^M \leq P^E$. Q.E.D.

We now analyse full liberalisation of the market track. Rationed users are now allowed to resell rationed goods in the market as long as Q^P is delivered to and accepted by them at plan price P_i^P. Similarly, planned suppliers are allowed to purchase the goods in the market to fulfil their delivery obligations at plan price P_i^P instead of producing the goods themselves. Thus the market consists of the total demand and supply.

Suppose that the plan price P_i^P is below P^E. Under the plan, the rationed users have a surplus given by the area under the rationed demand curve *AH* less the rectangle $P_1^P \cdot Q^P$; the planned suppliers have a planned profit/loss equal to the difference between $P_1^P \cdot Q^P$ and the area under the planned supply curve *FI*. Compared to the outcome of the single-track liberalisation, the dual-track liberalisation entails an implicit lump-sum transfer equal to the rectangle $(P^E - P_1^P) \cdot Q^P$ from the planned suppliers to the rationed users. As a result, a rationed user whose willingness to pay is greater than or equal to P^E and a planned supplier whose marginal cost is less than or equal to P^E will have their pre-reform rents unchanged. A rationed user whose willingness to pay is less than P^E will still accept delivery from planned suppliers at the plan price but will resell the plan-allocated inputs on the market at price P^E, thereby obtaining a surplus equal to $P^E - P_1^P$. This corresponds to the common practice of "resale" of rationed goods. A planned supplier whose marginal cost is above P^E will still deliver to its rationed users their plan-mandated supplies at the plan price, but instead of producing them, he will try to purchase them on the market at price P^E for redelivery, thereby limiting his loss to only $P^E - P_1^P$. This corresponds to the common practice of "subcontracting" by inefficient planned suppliers to more efficient suppliers. Clearly, the rationed users and the planned suppliers are no worse off than before; and at least some of them are even better off. Thus Pareto improvement and efficiency are simultaneously attained.

A similar argument can be made for P_2^P above P^E, as, for example, in the context of a labour market. Under the dual-track approach, an enterprise whose marginal product of labour exceeds or equals P^E will also have its pre-reform rents unchanged. An enterprise whose marginal product of labour is below P^E will still pay the plan wage but will "resell" its labour on the market for P^E, thereby limiting its loss to the difference between P_2^P and P^E. This corresponds to the common practice of "labour reallocation." Reallocated workers preserve their pre-existing rents because they continue to receive a total compensation equal to the plan rather than the market wage rate. Similarly, those workers whose reservation wages are less than or equal to P^E will also have their pre-reform rents unchanged. Those workers whose reservation wages are above P^E will receive P_2^P–P^E and be replaced by workers whose reservation wage is below or equal to P^E at market wage P^E. This corresponds to the common practice of "labour substitution," which can take different forms. For example, a worker may be persuaded to take an early retirement package, or a worker may resign in exchange for a job for his or her child or relative, who may have a lower reservation wage. The rents received by existing workers under the plan are preserved in the form of (implicit) lump-sum transfers from the SOEs to the existing workers.

The discussion above is summarised by the following proposition.

Proposition 2. If the plan quantity is less than the fully liberalised market equilibrium quantity, then, independently of the initial conditions concerning the plan price and the degree of efficiency of rationed demand and planned supply, (1) the dual-track approach with either limited or full liberalisation of the market track is Pareto-improving and (2) the dual-track approach with full liberalisation of the market track achieves efficiency.

Now consider sequential dual-track liberalisation of the market in the following fashion: in a first stage, limited market liberalisation is implemented, and then in a second stage, full market liberalisation is implemented. By proposition 1, the first-stage limited market liberalisation leads to inefficient overproduction; by proposition 2, the second-stage full market liberalisation implies efficiency, and thus there must be production contraction. Furthermore, in the first stage, when one goes from a centrally-planned economy to limited market liberalisation, Pareto improvement is clearly attained, but efficiency cannot be guaranteed. In the second stage, when full liberalisation is introduced, compared with the terminal point of the first stage, the reform is still Pareto-improving for agents within the plan but is not necessarily Pareto-improving for agents outside the plan, although efficiency is attained.[5] Therefore, the sequential dual-track liberalisation may result in some opposition to further reforms (from some agents outside the plan) after the first and before the second stage, whereas the dual-track full market liberalisation implemented in one stroke will not. Nevertheless, it is also clear that even under the sequential dual-track liberalisation, there are no losers at the end of the second stage relative to the status quo before the reform.

It is useful to compare our results with those of the related literature. Murphy, Shleifer and Vishny (1992) study a "partial reform" scheme in a similar partial equilibrium model in which *(a)* suppliers are free to sell to all users (no quota delivery enforcement) and (*b*) private firms can freely purchase inputs at any price but state-owned firms (which are covered by the plan) are not allowed to purchase inputs above the plan price. They show that such a partial reform may lead to inefficient supply diversion, compared to the efficiency of the single-track liberalisation. In their model, there is no assurance that the partial reform is Pareto-improving since suppliers are freed from any prior delivery obligations. Moreover, inefficiency of the plan (e.g., inefficient planned supply) may persist under the partial reform. Our definition of dual-track liberalisation differs from that of their partial reform in two important respects: not only are plan delivery quotas enforced under the dual-track approach, but also SOEs, like private firms, in all sectors are allowed to buy and sell any inputs (and outputs) freely at the market price. In our model, the dual-track liberalisation is Pareto-improving, and with full liberalisation of the market track, it also achieves efficiency even if the original plan is inefficient.

Sachs and Woo (1994) observe that, in Eastern Europe and the former Soviet Union, a too high subsidised wage rate prevents employees of SOEs from moving to the more efficient non-SOEs, which pay the lower market rate of total compensation. They therefore argue that it is necessary to cut subsidies and close down SOEs in order to achieve an efficient labour reallocation. This is a situation of inefficient rationing in the labour market with the plan wage rate above the fully liberalised market equilibrium. Our results show

---

5 By the same argument, if there are black marketeers before the reform, they are likely to be made worse off by full market liberalisation.

that the dual-track approach with full liberalisation can provide a mechanism for achieving an efficient labour reallocation in a Pareto-improving way. For example, workers who benefit from subsidised wages in inefficient SOEs can be allowed to keep the housing provided by their enterprise while taking a new job in the more efficient but lower-paying non-state sector. Under this scheme, workers should have the incentive to leave the SOEs and accept the lower market wage rate because they would not be made worse off.

The Plan Quantity Is Greater than the Fully Liberalised Market Equilibrium Quantity

This case applies to the overproduction of goods such as tanks and other low-quality unwanted goods or to the overemployment of labour. The generic rationed demand and planned supply curves are depicted in Chart 11.3. Under limited market liberalisation, the plan track and the market track are completely segregated. By assumption, $Q^P \geq Q^E$. What is notable is that, generically, there is still positive demand and supply in the market track because among the residual users and suppliers there are still those with high willingness to pay and low marginal costs. Thus, once again, $Q^P + Q^M \geq Q^E$. Clearly, the dual-track approach is Pareto-improving but cannot achieve efficiency since the total quantity for the entire economy is greater than Q^E, the efficient quantity.

Chart 11.3. Inefficient Rationed Demand and Inefficient Planned Supply: Planned Quantity Is Greater Than the Fully Liberalised Market Equilibrium Quantity

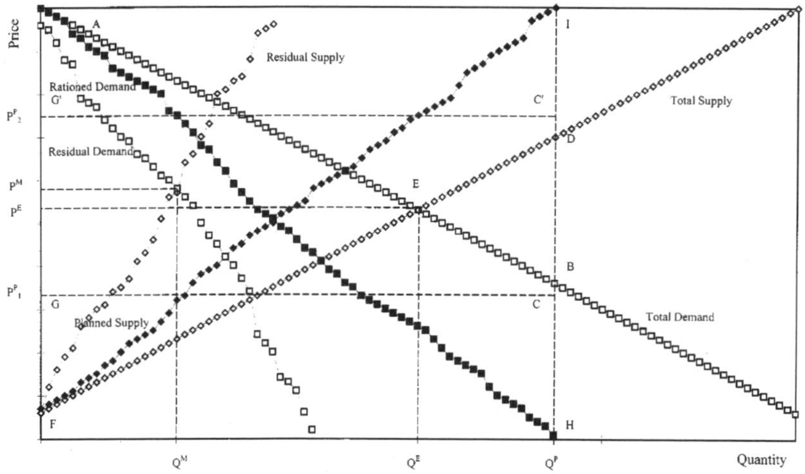

Under full liberalisation, the market consists of the total demand and supply. The important difference from the case above is that the physical fulfilment of the plan production target is incompatible with efficiency. However, Pareto improvement and efficiency can be achieved if the plan is enforced in terms of the rents that it generates rather than the physical output targets. With $P_1^P < P^E$, a planned supplier can buy back from the market, at equilibrium, delivery obligations (which may be interpreted as "call options" exercisable at P_1^P, held by the rationed users) in the good that it is supposed to deliver under the plan, at $P^E - P_1^P$, thus reducing or even eliminating the necessity of making physical deliveries (and actual production). A rationed user should be indifferent between accepting physical delivery and selling his delivery rights ("call options"), at a price $P^E - P_1^P$, since it is always possible to buy at the market price P^E. Profitable market exchanges of rights and obligations are possible because of the inefficiencies caused by the plan. Under this scenario, the net output of the good will be equal to Q^E, and yet there will be no complaints about the nonfulfillment of plan obligations from anyone. Indeed, the planned suppliers and rationed users have all received or given value for their plan rights and obligations and in fact are at their optimised levels of profits and utilities. Hence, we conclude that even when the plan quantity is greater than the market equilibrium quantity, the dual-track approach with full market liberalisation still results in the simultaneous attainment of Pareto improvement and efficiency as long as the plan is enforced in terms of the rents that they generate but not in terms of physical production.[6]

---

6 Another way to look at this case is to take into account the possibility of "recycling" of goods through the market. If the plan period, say a year, is subdivided into a sufficiently large number of sub-periods, say 365, then in each sub-period a planned supplier should produce $Q_i^P/365$ as planned output and be required to deliver $Q_i^P/365$ to rationed users. The planned supplier can meet his physical delivery obligations as follows: He produces and physically delivers $Q_i^P/365$ for the first sub-period at the plan price and then simultaneously repurchases from the market any available quantity at the market price P^E from rationed users whose willingness to pay is below P^E. In the second sub-period, the planned supplier produces to the point at which his marginal cost is equal to P^E, say $Q_i^P/365$, which he delivers together with his market purchases made in the previous subperiod, and just sufficient additional new current production if necessary so that his physical delivery

The case of P_2^P above P^E can be similarly analysed. A rationed user can buy back from the market acceptance obligations (which may be interpreted as "put options" exercisable at P_2^P, held by the planned suppliers) at price P_2^P–P^E in the good that it is supposed to receive under the plan. For the labour market, under full market liberalisation, enterprises allocated labour under the plan will "resell" labour at a loss of P_2^P–P^E per unit if its marginal product falls below P^E. This is equivalent to a subsidy scheme at the rate of P_2^P–P^E provided by the enterprise. Workers within the plan whose reservation wage is higher than P^E accept the subsidy and quit the job. Thus all enterprises will actually employ labour up to the point at which the value of the marginal product is equal to P^E. Any worker with a reservation wage below or equal to P^E will be actually employed. Efficiency is thus achieved. Moreover, the allocation is Pareto-improving. Before the reform, the workers within the plan have a surplus equal to Q^P less the area under the reservation wage curve *FI*. The enterprises within the plan have a surplus equal to the area under the curve *AH* less $P_2^P \cdot Q^P$. After the reform, all workers within the plan with a reservation wage above P^E are clearly better off since they no longer have to work at P^E and in addition receive a subsidy P_2^P–P^E. All enterprises with marginal products of labour below P^E are also clearly better off since they have to overpay their plan-allocated workers only by at most P_2^P–P^E. The remaining workers and enterprises within the plan are no worse off than before. Workers and enterprises outside the plan are also clearly better off because of the new opportunities offered by the market track.

The following proposition summarises the discussion above.

Proposition 3. If the plan quantity is greater than the fully liberalised market equilibrium quantity, then independently of the initial conditions concerning the plan prices and the degree of efficiency of rationed demand and planned supply, (1) the dual-track approach with limited or full liberalisation

---

obligations of $Q_i^P/365$ are fulfilled (Q_i^* can be zero). But simultaneously he repurchases again from the market a quantity equal to $(Q_i^P–Q_i^*)/365$ at the market price P^E from rationed users whose willingness to pay is below P^E. Every period, he continues this pattern of partial production cum purchases and resales until the end of the year. He would have produced approximately Q_i^*, which can be significantly less than the planned supply of Q_i^P, but he would have physically delivered exactly Q_i^P, as required by the plan. Thus total net production under full market liberalisation will not exceed Q^E but physical delivery is "fulfilled."

is always Pareto-improving and (2) the dual-track approach with full liberalisation achieves efficiency if the rights and obligations under the plan are enforced in terms of the rents.

3. Discussions on the Conditions for Pareto Improvement and Efficiency

Condition for Pareto Improvement: Enforcement of the Plan Track

The Pareto improvement property of the dual track requires enforcement of the rights and obligations under the plan track. Such enforcement, together with incremental autonomy on the market track, is also sufficient for Pareto improvement. No other conditions such as profit maximisation or perfect competition or full liberalisation are needed. By definition, enforcement of the plan track preserves existing rents whereas autonomy on the market track allows agents to exploit opportunities for trade. This also implies that enforcement of the plan track alone prevents any decline in aggregate output. This argument applies to the models that explain the output declines in central and Eastern Europe by the disruption effects from the single-track liberalisation under some types of market imperfection (Blanchard and Kremer 1997; Li 1999; Roland and Verdier 1999).

While Pareto improvement is always qualitatively valid under the enforcement of the plan track, how much scope for such improvement is there under limited market liberalisation? It depends on how many slack resources are available. As argued by Kornai (1980), there was always coexistence of shortages and slack in the planned economy. Furthermore, because of the very poor incentives of economic agents in the planned economy, the production was often organised deep inside the production possibility frontier. Therefore, even if the plan seemed taut, once some incentives are provided, new resources can be released for production and the scope for Pareto improvement can be substantial.

There are several reasons that make enforcement of the plan track possible. First, even if incentives to evade quotas may be stronger under reform than under central planning, these incentives would be the same in regard to the fulfilment of ex post unprofitable contracts in a conventional market economy. In either case, the government will have the responsibility for contract enforcement. Moreover, in a previously centrally-planned economy, such enforcement can be implemented by utilising the existing institutions, and no new institutions need to be created.

Second, enforcing the pre-existing plan is informationally much less demanding for the government than drawing up a new plan. Under central planning, the information requirement for drawing up a plan is huge because the market is not used. Enforcing a pre-existing plan is different. In fact, the dual-track approach uses minimal additional information as compared with other possible compensation schemes that may be used with other approaches to reform.

Third, under the dual track, the focus of plan enforcement shifts to the plan-mandated inter-enterprise deliveries as opposed to total enterprise productions. Under central planning, when an enterprise fulfils the production target, it will also fulfil the plan-mandated deliveries because there is no real incentive to do otherwise. In contrast, under the dual-track approach, an enterprise can fulfil its production target and yet at the same time fail to make or accept any planned deliveries (e.g., by selling the entire production or buying inputs on the market track). Therefore, the focus of enforcement must be shifted from physical production to deliveries, with the consequence that complaints from planned delivery recipients and planned suppliers become the most important source of information on plan compliance. Typically, enforcement actions will be undertaken only in response to complaints from the plan-mandated recipients or suppliers of the planned output deliveries.

Fourth, the rents of the economic agents under the pre-existing plan can be protected without the enforcement of *physical* deliveries. Physical deliveries are also difficult to enforce unless the state actively monitors the inter-enterprise material flows of the plan individually. Under the reform, the state needs to react only when delivery disputes arise, taking into account that there will be cases in which it is in the joint interests of the planned suppliers and the rationed users to evade the plan. In practice, the rights and obligations under the plan are likely to be enforced by the state only in terms of the rents that they generate. The plan-allocated delivery quotas can be viewed as the combination of a (put) option on the part of the planned suppliers to sell at price P_1^P to the rationed users and a (call) option on the part of the rationed users to buy from the planned suppliers also at price P_1^P.[7] Under full market liberalisation,

7 The values of these options are precisely the lumpsum transfers. Of course, the two options cannot simultaneously have positive value since they are exercisable at the same price.

enforcement of the rights and obligations under the plan amounts to enforcement of these options.

However, there are also reasons that may make enforcement of the plan track difficult. First, it is difficult, if not impossible, to enforce the allocation of consumer goods, especially when the plan price is above the market price. For example, low-quality consumer goods may become unwanted once the market is open to non-planned suppliers. According to the logic of the dual-track approach, the rationed users who no longer purchase planned quantities at the plan price must compensate the planned suppliers to maintain the latter's rents. This is clearly more difficult to enforce if the rationed users are individual consumers rather than enterprises.

Second, compliance with the plan by economic agents depends on their expectations of the credibility of state enforcement. If state enforcement is not credible, then the economic agents will have no incentive to fulfil their plan obligations. If anyone thinks that the plan-mandated deliveries at plan prices are not going to be received by him or her, he or she will not make the plan-mandated sales at the fixed plan prices either. In that case, dual-track liberalisation degenerates to single-track liberalisation. In general, multiple (self-fulfilling) equilibria (outcomes) are possible under a dual-track approach, depending on the expectations of the credibility of state enforcement.

Conditions for Efficiency

Additional conditions of profit and utility maximisation, perfect competition, and full liberalisation of the market track are required for efficiency of the dual-track liberalisation. But these conditions are also necessary for the efficiency of single-track liberalisation.

Our market supply and demand curves are assumed to reflect the marginal costs of suppliers and the willingness to pay of users. Behind these supply and demand curves, the enterprises are assumed to be atomistic (which implies perfect competition) and profit-maximising, and the households are assumed to be utility-maximising. Because the planned track represents lump-sum transfers, profit maximisation at the margin would be the same as total profit maximisation. The assumptions of utility and profit maximisation at the margin ensure that enterprises and households will have the right incentives. The efficiency of the dual-track approach relies on those incentives, which may depend on the ownership and governance structure.[8]

As we have shown, efficiency requires full market liberalisation under which market resales, subcontracting, and market purchases for redelivery are all allowed. Indeed, our distinction between limited and full market liberalisation is a major difference between our model and those of Byrd (1991) and others on the dual-track approach.

4. The Chinese Experience with Dual-Track Liberalisation

Applicability of the Model to China

To what extent are the conditions laid out in above fulfilled in China's implementation of dual-track liberalisation?

First, the credibility of continued enforcement of the rights and obligations under the plan seems not to be an issue in China.[9] Evidence of the credibility of continued enforcement is provided by the actual volume of transactions at plan prices, which, as we shall show below, remains large in absolute terms after a decade of reform. Moreover, it is also clear that until recently, SOEs in China could not lay off their pre-existing workers, nor could their pre-existing workers leave the enterprises without permission, which provides another example of the effective enforcement of the plan. With regard to consumer goods in the plan, it turns out that for China, almost all of them (cloth, grain, meat, oil, housing, etc.) were in excess demand at the beginning of the reform; thus they were not subject to the problem that plan quantity was greater than the fully liberalised market quantity.

Second, the validity of the profit-maximisation condition depends on circumstances. In the agricultural reform, the dual-track approach was introduced simultaneously with the household responsibility system, which essentially made farm households residual claimants (Lin 1992). Therefore, the assumption of profit

---

8 We do not consider the incentive problem resulting from the soft budget constraint. The soft budget constraints have the greatest impact on dynamic decisions concerning new investment, which are beyond the scope of this paper.

9 In contrast, the collapse of the Council for Mutual Economic Assistance and the breakup of the Soviet Union made unenforceable the cross-country planned deliveries in Eastern Europe and the former Soviet Union under the original plans.

maximisation is valid. In urban state-owned industrial enterprises, a "contract responsibility system" was introduced to expand autonomy and grant profit retention to enterprises. This reform also improved enterprise incentives and performance (Groves et al. 1994). However, in contrast to the agricultural reform, the contract responsibility system in industrial enterprises is not a good substitute for ownership reform. Indeed, the incentives of SOEs are much weaker than those of non-SOEs.

Third, the Chinese experience in the product market liberalisation is close to the case of full market liberalisation because resales, subcontracting, and purchases for redelivery were not prohibited. For example, farm households have been permitted to purchase grain or other output on the market to be redelivered to the state procurement agencies in fulfilment of their planned delivery quota since 1979. However, in the 1980s, there was only limited liberalisation of the market track in the labour market. Employers with plan-allocated workers were obliged to retain them at their pre-existing wage rates, and the market track applied only to new employment, with the market wage rate set by the equilibrium of the residual labour supply and demand. It is only in the mid 1990s that China has begun to deal with the problems of labour reallocation and layoffs on a significant scale.

Dual-Track Liberalisation in Product Markets

The agricultural reform undertaken in 1979 is the first successful application of the dual-track approach. Table 11.1 shows that the state procurement of domestically produced grains has remained essentially fixed over time, despite an almost one-third increase in grain output over the decade 1978–1988.[10] The data also demonstrate sufficiently effective enforcement by the state of the planned delivery obligations.

Table 11.2 shows that between 1978 and 1985, the share of transactions at plan prices in agricultural goods fell from 94% to 37%. Unfortunately, the absolute values of these transactions are not available. However, we do know that, between 1978 and 1990, the agricultural output of China doubled. Table 11.2, therefore, provides evidence of the huge supply response to the introduction of the market track in agriculture.

---

10 The years 1983 and 1984 were anomalies since there were bumper harvests and the state made additional purchases over and above the mandatory delivery quotas, partly because the market price was below the plan procurement price.

Table 11.1. Dual Tracks in Grain (Million Tons)

	1978	1979	1980	1981	1982	1983	1984	1985	1986	1987	1988
State procurement at plan price	47.8	54.0	50.2	52.1	56.2	91.2	102.4	59.6	53.3	56.9	50.5
State procurement at market price				10.6	17.5	7.6	9.3	19.6	32.3	42.3	43.8
Total domestic production	304.8	332.1	320.6	325.0	354.5	387.3	407.3	379.1	391.5	403.0	394.1
Plan procurement/ domestic production	.16	.16	.16	.16	.16	.24	.25	.16	.14	.14	.13

Source: Historic Materials for Grain Works in Contemporary China *(1989, pp. 1800–1805, 1838–1839). Domestic production:* China Statistical Yearbook, *various issues.*

Table 11.2. Dual Tracks in Agricultural Goods (Percent of Output Value)

	1978	1985	1986	1987	1988	1989	1990
Transactions at plan prices	94.4	37.0	35.0	29.4	24.0	35.5	31.0
Transactions at market prices	5.6	63.0	65.0	70.6	76.0	64.5	69.0

Source: *China Reform and Development Report (1992–1993), p. 54.*

Note: Transactions at market prices include transactions at so-called guide prices, which are government-set prices but with reference to market supply and demand.

Table 11.3. Dual Tracks in Industrial Goods (Million Tons)

	1981	1983	1985	1987	1988	1989	1990
				Coal			
Plan quota	328.94	365.31	400.25	402.58	407.98	426.66	455.19
Domestic production	621.64	714.53	872.28	928.08	979.88	1,055.14	1,079.88
Plan/production	.53	.51	.46	.43	.42	.40	.42
				Steel			
Plan quota	13.91	17.85	18.81	18.96	17.84	16.56	15.58
Domestic production	26.70	30.72	36.93	43.86	46.89	48.59	51.53
Plan/production	.52	.58	.51	.43	.38	.34	.30

Source: *China Statistical Yearbook* (1991, p. 482).

The most noticeable and often-cited application of the dual-track approach concerns industrial goods. Dual pricing in industry was first used for crude oil in 1981, when the government allowed the export of above-quota crude oil at a higher price. In 1984, the government permitted the market track for all industrial goods but with the market price range restricted to be within 20% of plan prices; such a restriction was removed in early 1985 (Wu and Zhao 1987). As a result, the share of transactions at plan prices, in terms of output value, fell from 100% before the reform to 64% in 1985 and further to 45% in 1990 (Xu 1988; *China Reform and Development Report (1992–1993)*). This provides evidence of the decline of the plan track relative to the market track but also of the relatively effective enforcement by the state of the plan delivery obligations (otherwise the share would have declined to zero).

Table 11.3 presents the cases of coal and steel, two of the most important industrial commodities, which were also the most tightly controlled under central planning. For coal, China's principal energy source, the planned delivery had some slight increases in absolute terms during the 1980s, but the market track increased much more. The increments came mainly from small rural non-state coal mines run by individuals and township and village enterprises. As a result, the share of the plan allocation declined from 53% in 1981 to 42% in 1990.[11] For steel, the plan track in absolute terms was quite stable (with a slight decline after 1987), but the share of plan allocation fell from 52% in 1981 to 30% in 1990. Unlike coal, steel came mainly from large SOEs rather

---

11 Outside the planned delivery, some local state-owned mines might be subject to a local plan. However, according to Byrd (1991), of the total incremental output between 1978 and 1984, 21.2% came from "unified allocation coal mines" (most of them were under the central plan), 8.4% from local state-owned mines, and 70.4% from non-state mines, which were under the market track. Similarly, Naughton (1995) figured that of the total increment between 1983 and 1987, the central government mines accounted for 27%, local state-owned mines 1%, and the non-state mines 72%. Therefore, the picture will not change even if we do not know exactly how local state-owned mines allocated coal.

than from small non-state firms (Byrd 1991).[12] In both the cases of coal and steel, because the plan track is essentially frozen, the economy is able to "grow out of the plan" on the basis of the market track expansion by state or non-state firms (Naughton 1995).

As for consumer goods, urban residents continued to have the right to purchase grain, meat, electricity, and housing at the same pre-reform prices and within the limits of the pre-reform rationed quantities. But at the same time, they were also free to buy the consumer goods from the free market at generally higher prices. Because we do not have data on the total retail sales of goods covered by the plan, we present in Table 4 available data on the share of transactions at plan prices in such retail sales. It shows that the proportion of transactions at plan prices declined from 97% in 1978 to only 30% in 1990. It has continued to decline since 1990.

Dual-Track Liberalisation in the Labour Market

China's labour market reform started with limited market liberalisation. China's high saving (investment) rate provides the potential for the rapid creation of new jobs in the market track without privatisation of the SOEs.[13] Table 5 shows that between 1978 and 1994, employment in the non-state sector increased by 318.8% (with the urban non-state sector increasing by 171.4% and the rural non-state sector by 426.4%), whereas employment in the state sector (including civil servants in government agencies and non-profit organisations) increased by only 50.5%. But within the state sector, there are two tracks. Beginning in 1980, while pre-existing employees maintained their permanent employment status, most new hires in the state sector were made

---

12 There might be some local government planned delivery outside the planned delivery figures here. We have data on enterprise direct sales of steel between 1987 and 1990, which are 9.53, 13.18, 14.57, and 18.23 million tons, respectively (*China Statistical Yearbook* 1988, p. 461; 1989, p. 379; 1990, p. 512; 1991, p. 478). If the difference between domestic production and plan quota together with enterprise direct sales is the local government planned delivery, then they represent 15.37, 16.31, 17.46, and 17.72 million tons, respectively, between 1987 and 1990, which are quite stable. Almost all increases in these years came from the market track.

13 The experience in Taiwan and South Korea showed a similar pattern (Lau and Song 1992).

under the more flexible contract system and often at lower wage rates. Table 5 shows that employment in the plan track has been virtually stationary: it went from 87.14 million in 1983, the eve of the introduction of economic reform in industry, to 83.61 million in 1994.[14]

Table 11.4. Dual Tracks in Retail Sales (Percent of Sales)

	1978	1985	1986	1987	1988	1989	1990
Transactions at plan prices	97.0	47.0	35.0	33.7	28.9	31.3	30.0
Transactions at market prices	3.0	53.0	65.0	66.3	71.1	69.7	70.0

Source: *China Reform and Development Report (1992–1993)*, p. 54.

Note: Transactions at market prices include transactions at so-called guide prices, which are government-set prices but with reference to market supply and demand.

A similar dual-track scheme is applied to senior government bureaucrats. In the early 1980s, the old revolutionaries who joined the government in 1949 were allowed to keep their benefits and ranks and were not forced to retire. But for all new appointments in the government, there have been strict age limits: 65 for ministers or provincial governors, 60 for vice ministers or vice provincial governors, and 55 for bureau directors. There are also term limits as well: two three- or five-year terms. Mandatory retirement has also been imposed.

As proposition 1 implies, limited labour market liberalisation had led to overemployment as compared with the full market liberalisation outcome. Mass labour furloughing and reallocation by SOEs have become a major nationwide phenomenon since 1994. In 1996, approximately 10 million factory workers lost their jobs (*China Daily,* April 5, 1997), but these furloughed workers are compensated. Two schemes used for protecting workers' pre-existing rents are *xiagang* ("stepping down from one's post") and *zaijiuye* ("re-employment"). *Xiagang* workers continue to receive a partial salary, housing, health care, and other benefits from their enterprises. Many furloughed workers were retrained through *zaijiuye* projects and later found jobs in the non-state sector. By the end of 1996, out of the 8.91 million *xiagang* workers, 3.57 million had found jobs, 2.34 million had decided to stay home, and three million were

14 If, in addition, we exclude civil servants in government agencies, employment in the plan track would not have risen at all.

still looking for jobs (Cao, Qian, and Weingast 1999). Although the interests of furloughed workers in the SOEs are protected, workers outside the state sector—say some migrant workers from rural areas—will suffer as a result of full market liberalisation because both the market equilibrium employment and wage rate are lowered. This is precisely the result of sequential dual-track liberalisation of the market as discussed in the paragraph after proposition 2.

Table 11.5. Dual Tracks in Non-Agricultural Employment (Million Employees)

	1978	1983	1985	1988	1989	1990	1991	1992	1993	1994
State	74.51	87.71	89.90	99.84	101.08	103.46	106.64	108.89	109.20	112.14
Permanent	74.51	87.14	86.58	89.76	89.18	89.74	90.75	88.31	85.24	83.61
Contract	.00	.57	3.32	10.08	11.90	13.72	15.89	20.58	23.96	28.53
Non-state	48.90	62.10	107.97	138.28	136.49	152.53	159.49	172.28	195.87	204.85
Urban	20.63	29.75	38.18	42.83	42.82	43.84	46.04	47.41	50.45	56.01
Rural	28.27	32.35	69.79	95.45	93.67	108.69	113.45	124.87	145.42	148.84
State permanent ÷ (state + non-state)	.60	.58	.44	.38	.38	.35	.34	.31	.28	.26

Source: *China Statistical Yearbook* (1994, pp. 84–85; 1995, p. 99).

5. Concluding Remarks

The tables in part 4 show the gradually declining trend of the plan track throughout the 1980s, providing evidence that, ex post, there is no "ratcheting up" of the plan. Moreover, recent data reveal that the plan track in product markets has been largely "phased out" in the 1990s, and this phasing out of the plan track was generally accompanied by explicit compensation. By 1996, the plan track was reduced to 16.6% in agricultural goods, 14.7% in industrial producer goods, and only 7.2% in total retail sales of consumer goods (*People's Daily,* August 22, 1997). Why was the implicit commitment on the part of the state to no ratcheting up or no phasing out without compensation credible? Without credible commitment, either the property of Pareto improvement is lost or economic agents would have diminished incentives to participate in the market track. Industrial enterprises may have found the no ratcheting up credible because of the earlier successful experience of dual-track reform in agriculture. Moreover, with rapid growth, the plan track becomes, in no time, a matter of little consequence to most potential losers, which in turn reduces the cost required for compensating them. The questions of credibility are beyond the scope of our paper because our model is essentially static and does not address the issues of investment and capacity expansion both within and outside of the plan. They will be pursued in future research.

References

Blanchard, Olivier, and Michael Kremer. "Disorganization." *The Quarterly Journal of Economics* 112 (November 1997), pp. 1091–1126.

Byrd, William A. *The Market Mechanism and Economic Reforms in China*. Armonk, N.Y.: Sharpe, 1991.

Cao, Yuanzheng, Yingyi Qian, and Barry R Weingast. "From Federalism, Chinese Style to Privatization, Chinese Style." *Economics of Transition* 7, no. 1 (1999), pp. 103–131.

China Daily, 5 April 1997.

China Reform and Development Report (1992–1993). Beijing: China Far East Publishing House, 1994.

China Statistical Yearbook. Beijing: China Statistical Press, various years.

Groves, Theodore, Yongmiao Hong, John McMillan, and Barry Naughton. "Autonomy and Incentives in Chinese State Enterprises." *The Quarterly Journal of Economics* 109 (1994), pp. 183–209.

Historic Materials for Grain Works in Contemporary China. Beijing: China Agriculture Press, 1989.

Kornai, Janos. *Economics of Shortage.* Amsterdam: North Holland, 1980.

Lau, Lawrence J., Yingyi Qian, and Gerard Roland. "Pareto-improving Economic Reforms through Dual-Track Liberalization." *Economics Letters* 55 (1997), pp. 285–292.

Lau, Lawrence J., and Dae-Hee Song. "Growth Versus Privatization—an Alternative Strategy to Reduce the Public Enterprise Sector: The Experiences of Taiwan and South Korea." Working paper, Department of Economics, Stanford University, 1992.

Li, Wei. "A Tale of Two Reforms." *The RAND Journal of Economics* 30 (1999), pp. 120–136.

Lin, Justin Yifu. "Rural Reforms and Agricultural Growth in China." *The American Economic Review* 82 (1992), pp. 34–51.

Lin, Justin Yifu, Fang Cai, and Zhou Li. "The Lessons of China's Transition to a Market Economy." *Cato Journal* 16 (1996), pp. 201–31.

McMillan, John, and Barry Naughton. "How to Reform a Planned Economy: Lessons from China." *Oxford Review of Economic Policy* 8 (1992), pp. ISO–43.

Murphy, Kevin M., Andrei Shleifer, and Robert W. Vishny. "The Transition to a Market Economy: Pitfalls of Partial Reform." *Quarterly Journal of Economics* 107 (1992), pp. 889–906.

Naughton, Barry. *Growing Out of the Plan: Chinese Economic Reform, 1978–1993.* Cambridge: Cambridge University *Press, 1995.*

Roland, Gerard, and Thierry Verdier. "Transition and the Output Fall." *Economics of Transition* 7, no. 1 (1999): pp. 1–28.

Sachs, Jeffrey D., and Wing Thye Woo. "Structural Factors in the Economic Reforms of China, Eastern Europe, and the Former Soviet Union." *Economic Policy* 9, no. 18 (1994), pp. 101–45.

Sicular, Terry. "Plan and Market in China's Agricultural Commerce." *Journal of Political Economy* 96 (1988), pp. 283–307.

Wu, Jinglian, and Renwei Zhao. "The Dual Pricing System in China's Industry." *Journal of Comparative Economics* 11 (1987), pp. 309–318.

Xu, Qingfei. *China's Economic System Reform.* Beijing: China Fiscal and Economic Publishing House, 1988.

Zhang, Weiying, and Gang Yi. "China's Gradual Reform: A Historical Perspective." Manuscript. Beijing: Peking University, 1995.

Chapter 12.

The Chinese Economy: Myths and Realities*

1. Introduction

There are many misunderstandings and myths about the Chinese economy. But repeated often enough, and by sufficiently respectable "authorities," they tend to become accepted as truths. However, accepting these misunderstandings and myths as truths has serious consequences: policy makers base their decisions on these assumed "truths." And their policies will not have the expected effects if these assumed "truths" turn out to be false. In this chapter I hope to help dispel some of the common myths about today's Chinese economy.

2. The Chinese Economy Today

China has made tremendous progress in its economic development since it began its economic reform and opened to the world in 1978. China is currently the fastest growing economy in the world—averaging approximately 10% per annum over the past 30 years. Between 1978 and 2009, Chinese real GDP grew 18 times, from US$277 billion to US$4.99 trillion (2009 prices) to become the third largest economy in the world, after the U.S. and Japan.

---

* This chapter was originally published in Working Paper No. 1, China Development Bank Financial Research Centre, Institute of Global Economics and Finance, The Chinese University of Hong Kong, July 2010. This is a slightly revised and updated version of the Inaugural Mok Hing-Yiu Lecture of the Oxford China Centre, St. Hugh's College, University of Oxford, that the author presented on May 13, 2010. He wishes to thank the Family of Dr. Hing-Yiu Mok for inviting him to deliver the Inaugural Mok Hing-Yiu Lecture and Mr. Andrew Dilnot, Prof. David Hendry, Mrs. Ayesha Lau, and Dr. Yanyan Xiong for their helpful comments.

During the same period, Chinese real GDP per capita grew more than 13 times, from US$288 to US$3,706. By comparison, the U.S. GDP (approximately US$14.12 trillion) and GDP per capita (approx. US$45,918) were 2.8 and 12.4 times the comparable Chinese figures in 2009, respectively.

The Chinese economy has survived the East Asian currency crisis of 1997–1998 as well as the global financial crisis of 2007–2009 reasonably unscathed. It will likewise survive the current financial crisis affecting some of the member countries of the European Union (Portugal, Ireland, Greece and Spain). If current trends continue, Chinese real GDP will approach the level of U.S. real GDP in less than 20 years' time—some time between 2025 and 2030.

However, despite its rapid growth, China is still a developing economy in terms of its real GDP per capita. An economy is generally considered to be developed if its GDP per capita exceeds US$10,000 (if we take into account inflation, this threshold should probably be much higher). It will probably take 20 years before China joins the ranks of developed economies, achieving a per capita real GDP of US$10,000, and another 20 to 25 years before China reaches the same level of real GDP per capita as the United States, some time past the middle of the 21st century (bearing in mind that in the meantime, the U.S. economy will also continue to grow, albeit at rates significantly lower than those of the Chinese economy, and that the Chinese population will reach a peak around 2035 and then begin to decline slowly).

Chart 12.1. Chinese Real GDP in US$ since 1952 (2009 Prices)

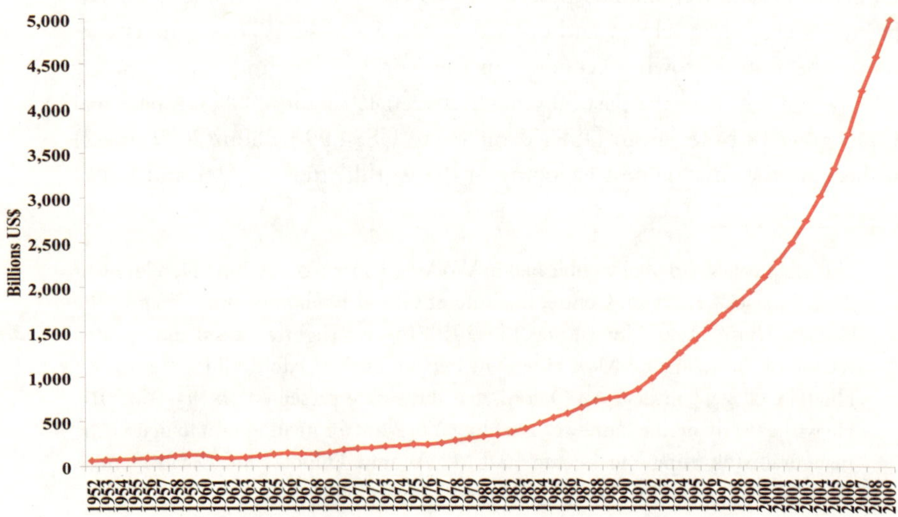

Chart 12.2. Chinese Real GDP per Capita in US$ since 1952 (2009 Prices)

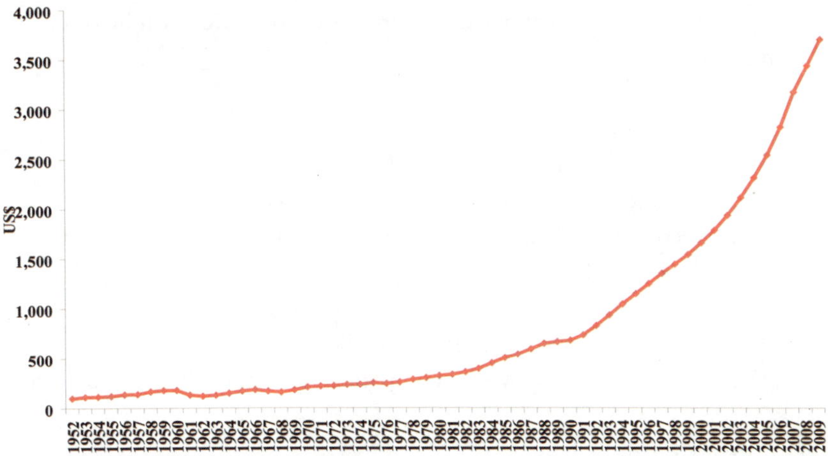

Table 12.1. Chinese Real GDP and Real GDP per Capita: Past, Present (2009) and Projected Future[1]

	1978	2009	2020
		US$ (2009 prices)	
Real GDP (trill.)	0.277	4.99	10.00
Real GDP/capita	288	3,706	7,100

And despite the many problems that have arisen in the Chinese economy within the past decade—for example, income disparity, environmental degradation, inadequate infrastructure and corruption—it is fair to say that everyone in China has benefited from the economic reform since 1978, albeit to varying degrees, and few want to return to the central planning days. China is one of the very few socialist countries that have managed to make a smooth transition from a centrally-planned to a market economy. It is a model for other transition economies (e.g., Vietnam) and potential transition economies (e.g., Cuba, North Korea, and Laos).

1 The projections for 2020 are derived from an econometric model of China of the author's.

3. The Seven Myths about the Chinese Economy

The seven common myths about the Chinese economy that will be discussed in turn in this lecture are:

(1) The renminbi (yuan) is under-valued;
(2) Chinese trade surpluses caused the global imbalances;
(3) Chinese economic growth depends critically on exports;
(4) The economies of China and East Asia cannot be de-coupled from the U.S. and Europe;
(5) Chinese household savings rates are too high;
(6) The Chinese economy faces labour shortages; and
(7) Chinese economic power is comparable to that of the United States.

(1) Is the Renminbi (Yuan) Under-valued?

A country's currency is considered under-valued if it runs persistent surpluses in trade in goods and services combined vis-à-vis the entire world. It is considered over-valued if it runs persistent trade deficits vis-à-vis the world. A bilateral trade surplus, even a persistent one, says nothing about whether a country's currency is under-valued because it may still have a near zero or even negative trade balance vis-à-vis the entire world. Most non-oil producing countries have persistent bilateral trade deficits with oil-exporting countries. And that does not necessarily mean the currencies of the oil-exporting countries are under-valued.

Chart 12.3. The Nominal and Real Yuan/US$ Exchange Rates

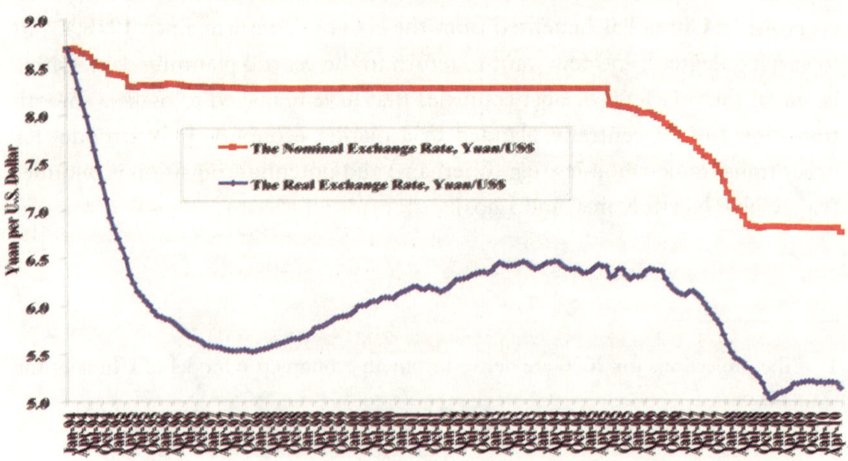

The statistics on Chinese trade balances over the past three decades indicate that China has had essentially balanced trade in goods and services combined with the world until 2005 and that its trade surplus has once again become relatively insignificant, especially relative to Chinese GDP, beginning in early 2010 (see the following chart).[2]

Chart 12.4. Chinese Monthly Exports, Imports and Trade Balance of Goods, US$

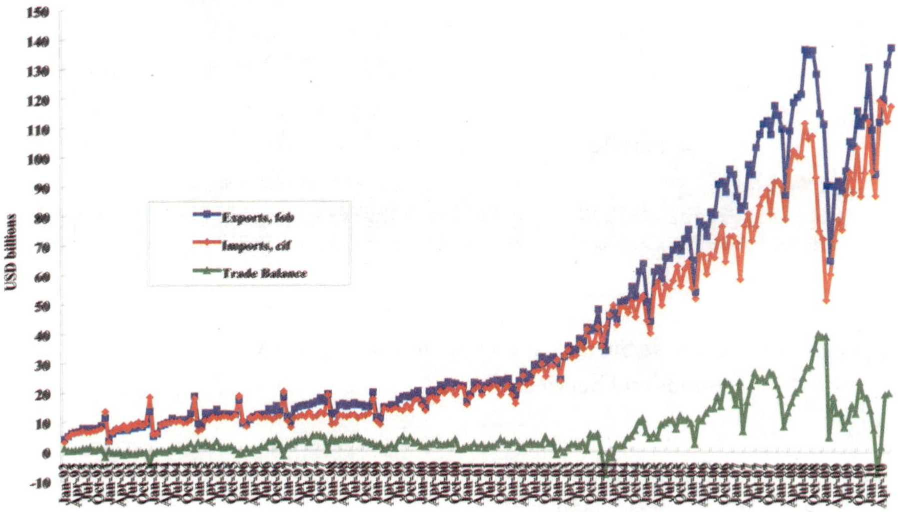

In contrast, the large U.S. trade deficit with the world existed since at least 1998, long before China began to have a trade surplus with the world, in 2005. What this means is that while there is evidence that the U.S. dollar might have been over-valued, there is no evidence that the renminbi was under-valued prior to 2005.

---

2 The Chinese exports and export surplus surged in June 2010, in part because exporters tried to beat the date for the expiration of value-added tax rebates on exports. However, it is believed that such a rate of growth of Chinese exports is only one-off and not sustainable.

Chart 12.5. Monthly Chinese Surplus and U.S. Deficit with the World, Trade in Goods (Billion US$)

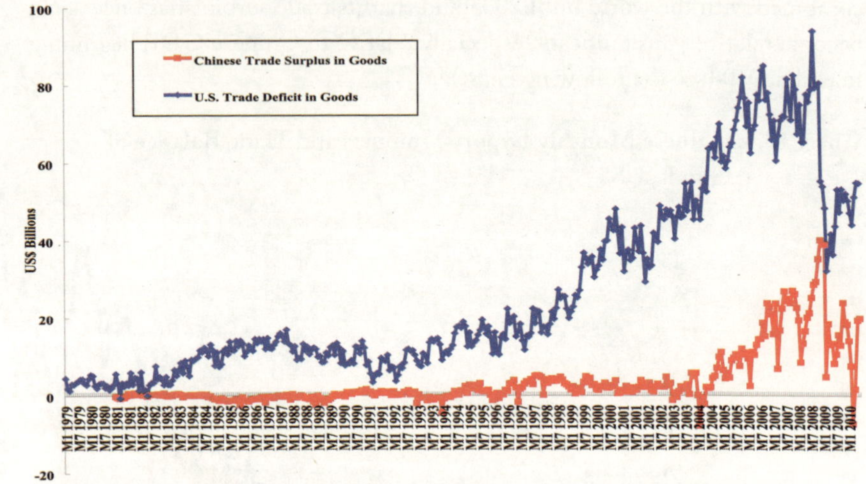

Chart 12.6. Chinese Surplus and U.S. Deficit with the World, Trade in Goods and Services

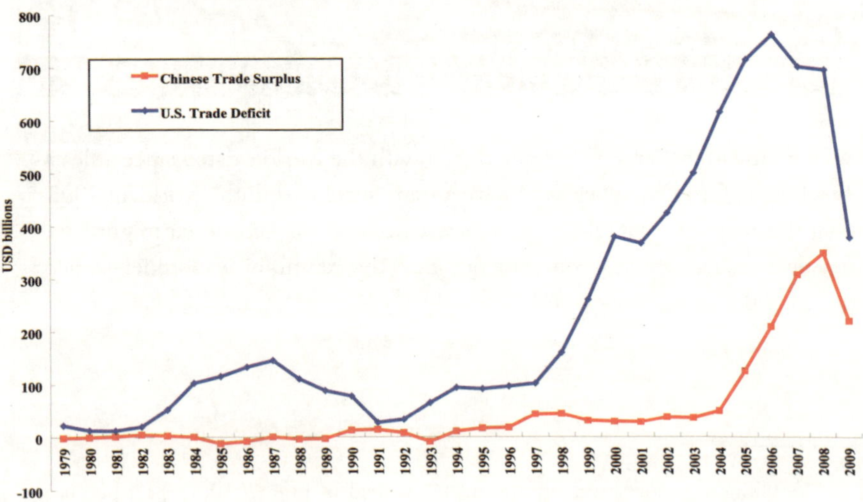

Partly in response to the rise in the Chinese trade surplus vis-à-vis the world, the renminbi was allowed to appreciate in July 2005, and rose 20% in nominal terms and 25% in real terms by the end of 2008. The Chinese trade surplus vis-à-vis the world reached a peak in 2008 when it began to decline. In 2009, it declined more than 30%. It has continued to fall and even turned negative in March 2010. The Chinese export surplus for the first half of 2010 represented a year-over-year decline of more than 42%. The long-term goal of the Chinese government is to reduce the Chinese trade surplus vis-à-vis the world to zero. If the current trend continues, the goal of zero annual trade balance can probably be achieved in a couple of years, without necessarily any large adjustment in the nominal yuan/U.S. dollar exchange rate.

(2) Did the Chinese Trade Surpluses Cause the Global Imbalances?

Global imbalances have been blamed as a major cause of the current global financial crisis. However, the large U.S. trade deficit with the world existed since 1998, long before China began to have a significant trade surplus vis-à-vis the world. In 2000, U.S. trade deficit was US$380 billion, whereas the Chinese trade surplus was only less than US$30 billion. Thus, the Chinese trade surpluses could not possibly have been the source of the global imbalances that supposedly fed the global liquidity that ultimately "enabled" the current global financial crisis.

In fact, the Case-Shiller U.S. Home Price Index, which can be taken as a proxy for the speculative asset price inflation caused by the growth of the sub-prime mortgage loans in the U.S., correlates almost perfectly with the U.S. trade deficit with the world but not with the Chinese trade surplus, demonstrating once again that the Chinese trade surpluses could not have been responsible for the global imbalances that caused the asset price bubble.

The oil-exporting countries and Japan accounted for most of the aggregate trade surpluses vis-à-vis the world,[3] and hence the resulting global imbalances, since 2000. Japan had the largest foreign exchange reserves in the world until it was overtaken by China in 2006,[4] and the Bank of Japan consistently held

3 The aggregate of trade surpluses in the world is by definition zero. What is meant by aggregate trade surpluses here is the sum over all countries of all their positive trade surpluses vis-à-vis the world.

4 A significant proportion of the increase in Chinese foreign exchange reserves is due to the inflow of hot money.

the largest amount of U.S. Treasury securities in the world until the last quarter of 2008, when holdings of the People's Bank of China exceeded the Bank of Japan's for the first time. If any country is to be blamed for the global imbalances since 2000, it should not be China.

Chart 12.7. Case-Shiller U.S. Home Price Index, Chinese Trade Surplus and U.S. Trade Deficit

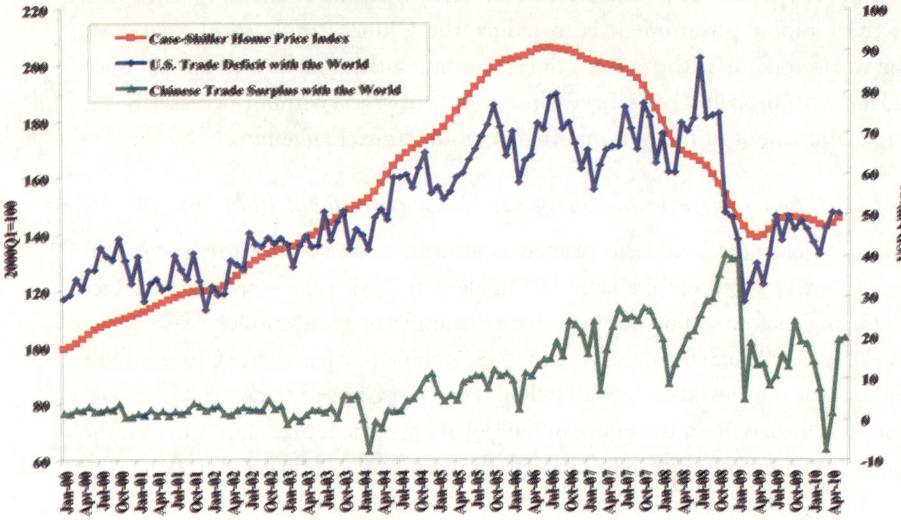

Chart 12.8. Foreign Exchange Reserves and U.S. Treasury Securities Held, China, and Japan

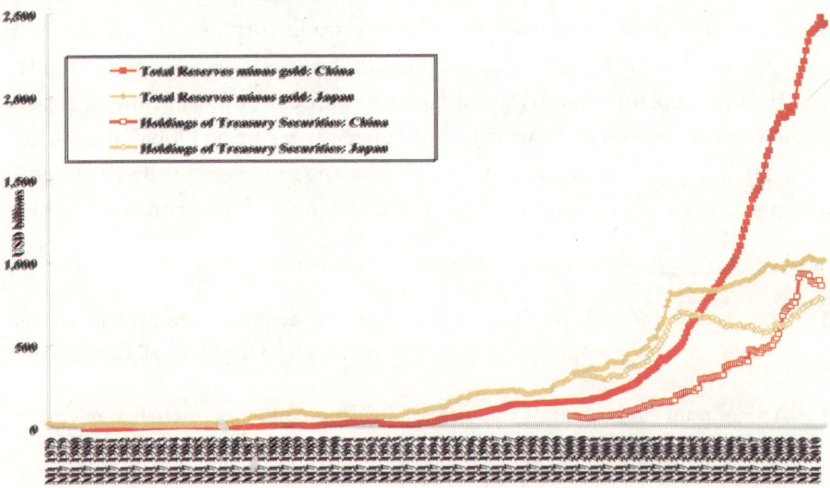

(3) Is Chinese Economic Growth Critically Dependent on Exports?

There is a common mis-impression that the Chinese economy is highly dependent on exports, and in particular, on its export surplus, as a source of growth. The fact is that China only began to have a significant trade surplus vis-à-vis the world in 2005, whereas the Chinese economy has been growing at an average annual real rate of growth of approximately 10% since 1978. It should therefore be obvious that the trade surplus per se could not have been an important source of growth for the Chinese economy during the past three decades. Chinese economic growth does not depend on Chinese trade surpluses.

Chinese trade surplus as a percentage of Chinese GDP fluctuated between –4.5% and 4.5% between 1982 and 2004, with an average of less than 2% of GDP. It then rose to almost 9% in 2007. It has since declined significantly and is expected to be below 2% once again in 2010.

Chart 12.9. Chinese Trade Balance of Goods and Services as a Percent of GDP, 1982–2009

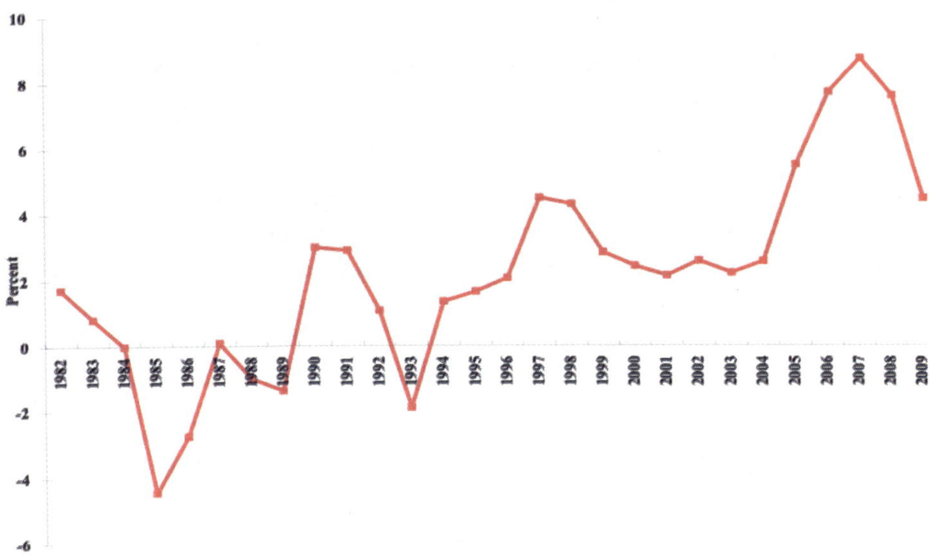

Chinese exports as a proportion of GDP rose steadily beginning in 1978 and reached a peak of almost 40% in 2006, and then began to decline to approximately 25% in 2009. While this ratio appears large, it is not when compared to Hong Kong, Singapore, South Korea and Taiwan, where exports are more than 100% of the respective GDPs. And the ratio of Chinese exports to GDP actually exaggerates the importance of exports in the Chinese economy because it fails to take into account the low domestic value-added content of Chinese exports.

Chart 12.10. Chinese Exports of Goods and Services as a Proportion of GDP, 1970–2009

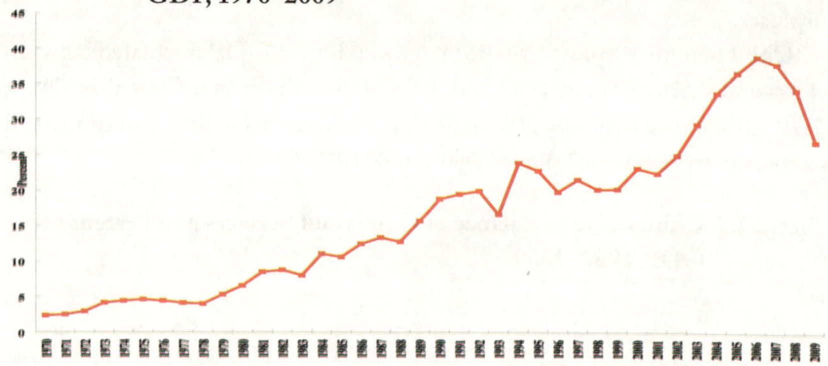

The domestic value-added content of Chinese exports is no more than 30%[5]—that is, for every dollar of goods exported, less than 30 cents, on average, consist of domestic value-added—the rest consists of imported raw materials, intermediate goods, components, parts, semi-finished goods, etc. The domestic value-added percentage is even less for the so-called "Processing and Assembly" exports, which at one time constituted more than half of Chinese exports. If we multiply the exports to GDP ratio of, say, 40% (it is currently much lower, at approximately 25%) to the domestic value-added content of

5 The domestic value-added content of Chinese exports was estimated as 20% in studies conducted by Chen et. al. (2009) and Lau et. al. (2007, 2010) several years ago. 30% is used here instead of 20% in order to make allowance for a possible increase in the domestic value-added content over the years. If the actual domestic value-added content is less than 30%, then the GDP generated by exports will be lower than 12%.

30%, we obtain 12%, which is the upper bound for the percentage of Chinese GDP (value-added) generated by exports.

Now, 12% of GDP is a large number, and no economy can afford to lose 12% of its GDP overnight. However, if 12% of GDP does not grow, or even declines by 25%, as long as the other 88% of the economy continues to grow, the economy as a whole should do all right, especially if appropriate compensatory economic stimulus measures are taken by the government. A 25% decline in Chinese exports should result in a 25% times 12% or 3% maximum decline in Chinese GDP, other things being equal. Thus, the reduction in exports caused by the global financial crisis should be expected to reduce the rate of real Chinese economic growth from 9% in 2008 by a maximum of three percentage points to no less than 6% in 2009, other things being equal. However, the two-year, four trillion yuan (equivalent to approximately 8% of GDP per year) economic stimulus programme launched by the Chinese government in November 2008 helped make up the shortfall in aggregate demand caused by the decline in exports. The Chinese economy actually managed to achieve a real rate of growth of 9.1% in 2009, even with its exports down by 25% from 2008 and the U.S. and European economies mired in recession.[6] If there were any lingering doubts on the degree of export-dependence of the Chinese economy, they should have been dispelled by this achievement alone. An 8% real rate of growth should be readily achievable for 2010 as well.

Moreover, even if Chinese exports manage to grow by 25% per year going forward (which is most unlikely), it will by itself lead to only 3% overall economic growth, which is hardly enough for the Chinese economy. That is why China cannot, and will not, rely on exports as a primary source of its future economic growth.

An important implication of the relatively low external dependence of the Chinese economy is that the rate of growth of Chinese real GDP is relatively stable even as Chinese exports and imports fluctuate as widely as the exports and imports of other East Asian economies. (See the following charts on the rates of growth of the exports, imports, and real GDP of selected East Asian economies.)

---

6 The actual year-on-year decline in Chinese exports in 2009 was 16%. 25% is an estimate of the decline from the peak value in 2008.

Chart 12.11. Quarterly Rates of Growth of Exports of Goods: Selected East Asian Economies

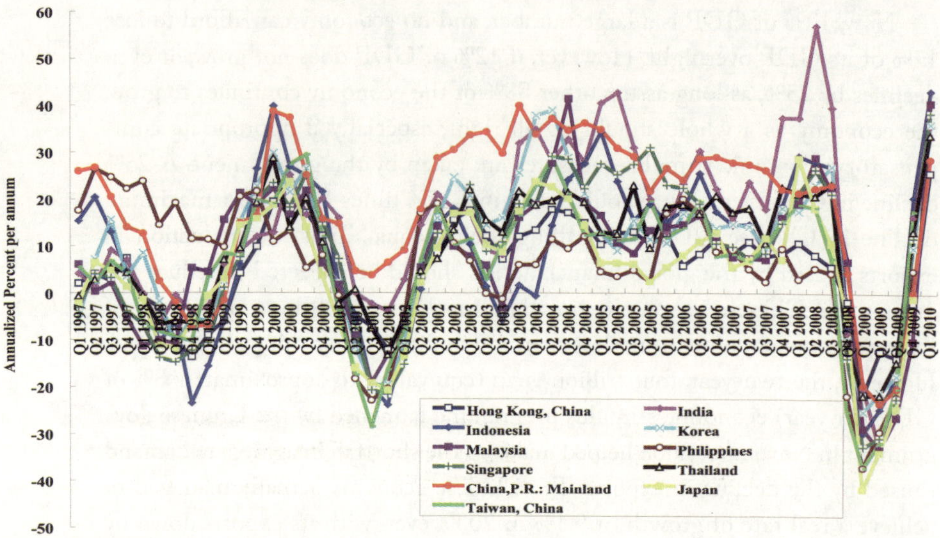

Chart 12.12. Quarterly Rates of Growth of Imports of Goods: Selected East Asian Economies

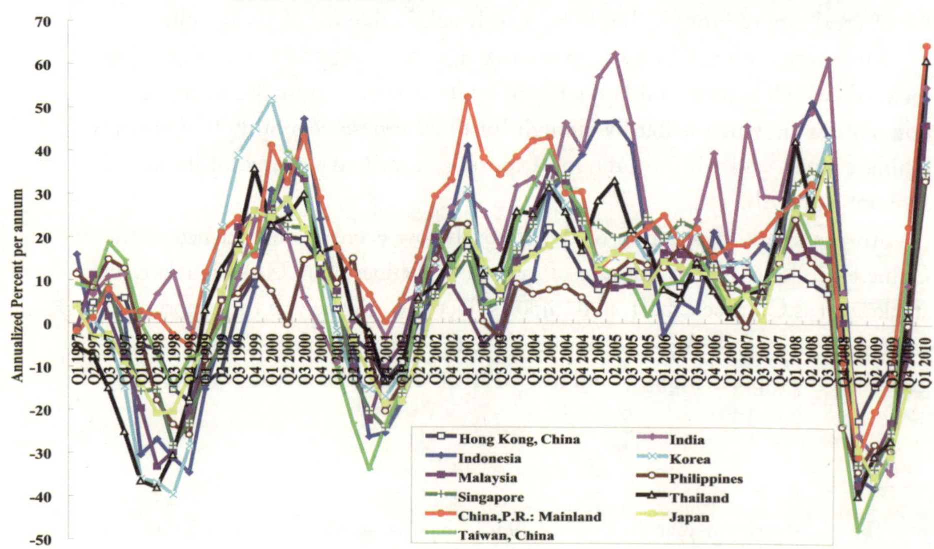

Chart 12.13. Quarterly Rates of Growth of Real GDP, Y-o-Y: Selected East Asian Economies

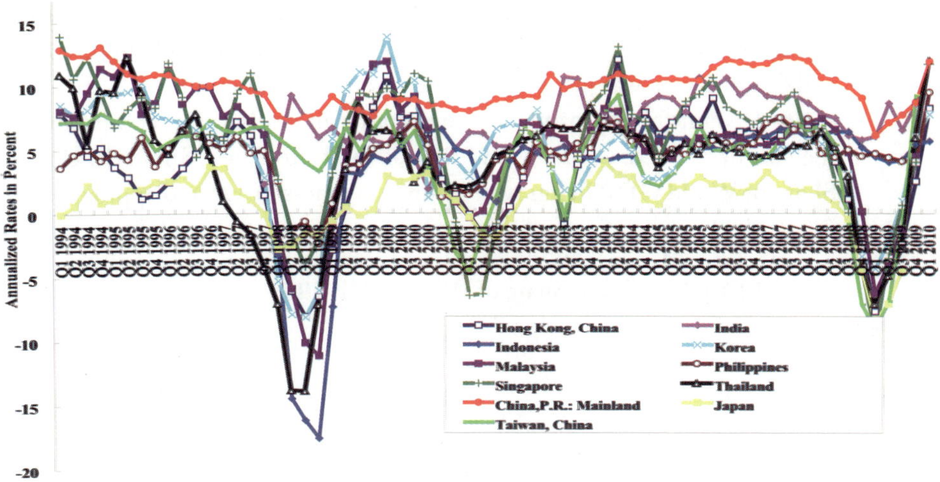

Large continental economies, such as the United States, are mostly driven by their internal demands, not by international trade. Exports have never been very important to the U.S. economy, and the U.S. economy has never been dependent on international trade, except perhaps in the 19th century. For the Chinese economy it is the same—Chinese economic growth in future decades will depend mostly on internal demand rather than exports.

(4) Can the Economies of China and East Asia be De-Coupled from the U.S. and Europe?

East Asia as used here is taken to mean the 10 ASEAN countries (Brunei, Cambodia, Indonesia, Laos, Malaysia, Myanmar, Philippines, Singapore, Thailand and Vietnam) plus three (China [including Hong Kong, Macau and Taiwan], Japan, and South Korea)—that is, approximately, everything east of Bangladesh and west of the Pacific Ocean. The "Partial De-Coupling Hypothesis" says that while East Asia is not immune from the effects of the economic recession in the United States and Europe, it can nevertheless continue growing, albeit at somewhat lower rates. Partial de-coupling is a consequence of the economic centre of gravity of the world gradually shifting to East Asia from the United States and Western Europe and within East Asia from Japan to China (but the shifts are not yet completed).

In the following charts, East Asian and Chinese GDP as percentages of world GDP are respectively presented. Both show very strong trends of growth over the past half century. In 1960, East Asian GDP, comprising of the GDPs of the 10 ASEAN countries, plus China (Mainland only),[7] Japan, and South Korea was just over 10% of world GDP. Today, East Asian economies account for approximately one-quarter of world GDP, comparable to the size of the U.S. economy and that of the Euro Zone. Similarly, China's Share of World GDP has grown—from 1% or less in 1960 to approximately 7% in 2009.

Chart 12.14. East Asian Share of World GDP, 1960–2009

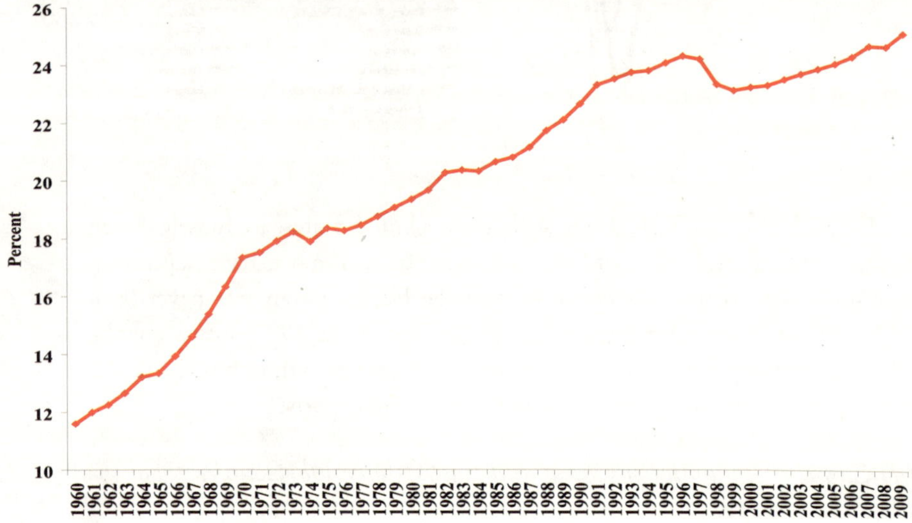

7 Only data on Mainland China is included, as data on 1960 GDP of Hong Kong and Macau are not readily available.

Chart 12.15. China's Share of World GDP, 1960–2009

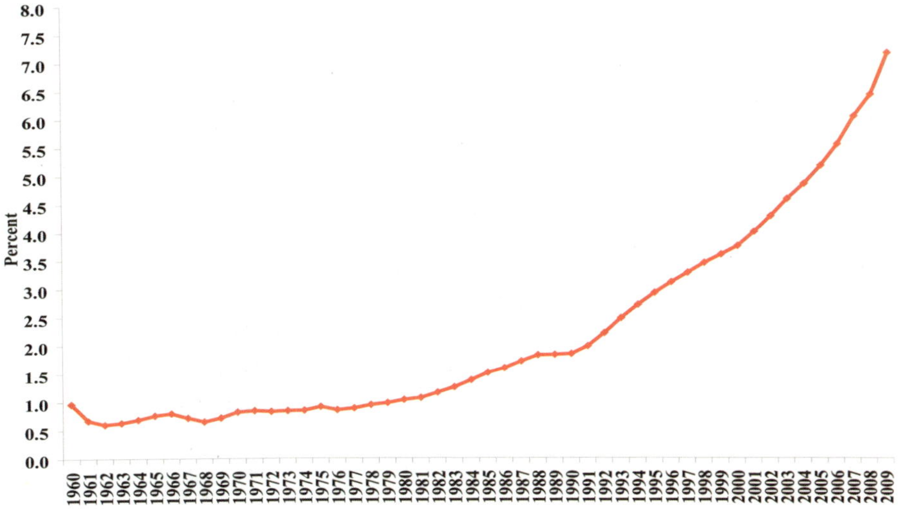

Given the current trends in rates of economic growth, East Asia will surpass the United States in terms of aggregate GDP, with China perhaps contributing the highest proportion of the total by 2015. This is what gives credence to the hypothesis of partial "de-coupling" of the world economies—that the Chinese and East Asian economies can continue to do reasonably well despite the current economic problems in the U.S. and elsewhere.[8] However, China, with its GDP accounting for only 7% of the world total, and East Asia (excluding Japan), are not large enough to turn around the entire world economy.

East Asian shares of world exports, imports, and international trade have also grown from approximately 10% in 1960 to 25% in 2009, paralleling the growth of the East Asian share of world GDP (see the following chart). Similarly, Chinese shares of world exports, imports and international trade have also grown. Chinese exports and imports have risen from approximately 1% of world exports and imports in 1960 to approximately 10% of world exports and imports in 2009.

---

8 It is important to note that the "de-coupling" works both ways. It is possible, under different circumstances, for the East Asian economies to perform poorly while the United States and European economies prosper, as, for example, during the 1997–1998 East Asian currency crisis.

Chart 12.16. The Rising Share of East Asian Trade in Total World Trade, 1960–2009

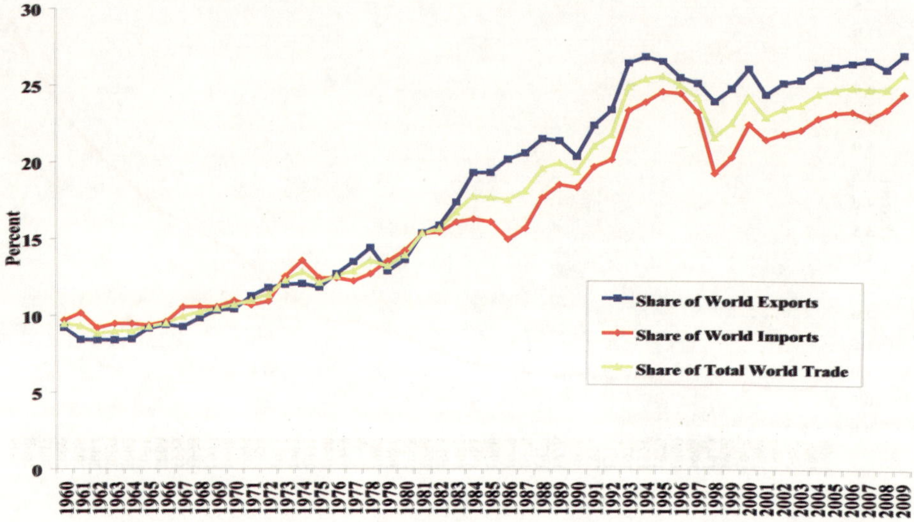

Chart 12.17. The Share of Chinese Trade in Total World Trade, 1950–2009

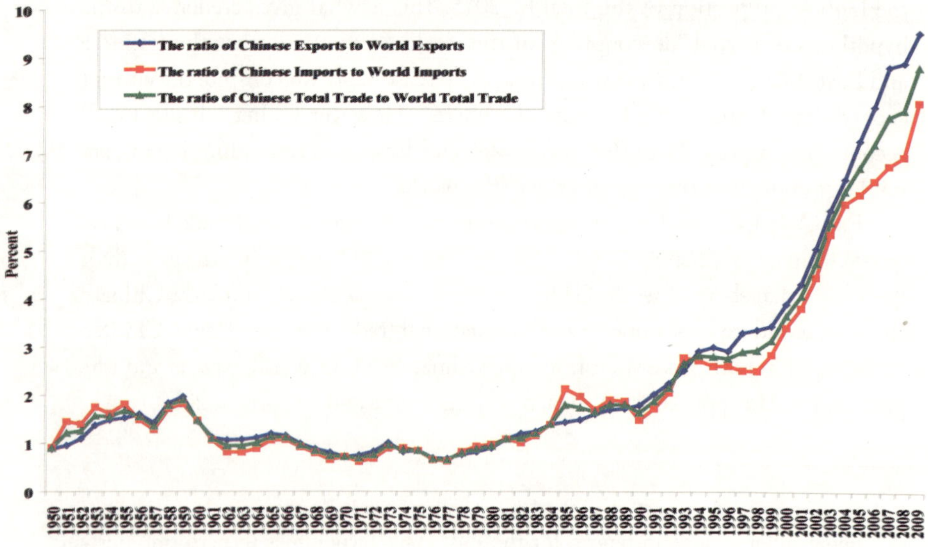

Chart 12.18. The Share of Chinese Trade in Total East Asian Trade, 1952–2009

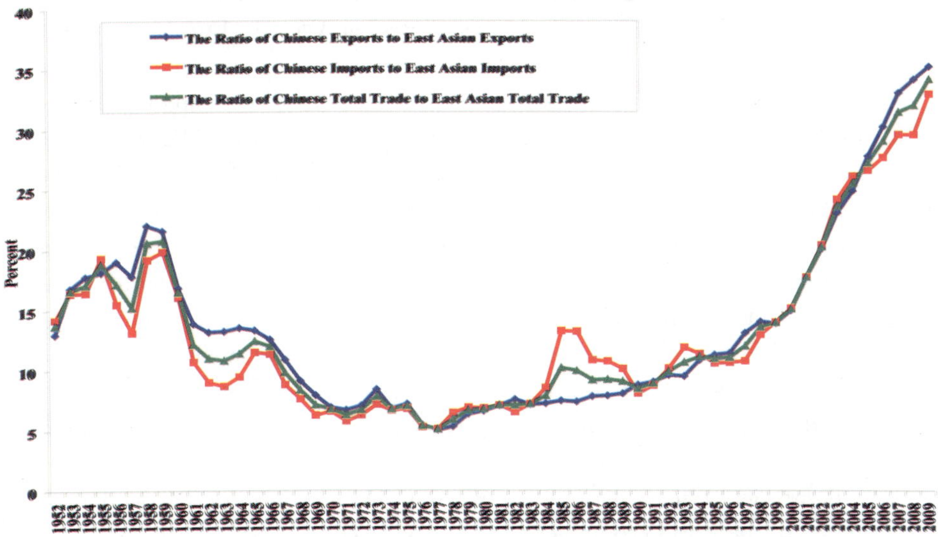

The emergence of the Chinese economy on the global market was the one most important new development during the past three decades. Today, China accounts for one-third of East Asian international trade. It has overtaken Japan to become both the largest exporting country and the largest importing country in East Asia. China is the most important export market for almost all East Asian economies and runs trade deficits vis-à-vis almost every other East Asian economy. Japan has become China's largest trading partner since the mid-1990s and China became Japan's largest source of imports in 2002. The recent pick-up in economic activities in Japan is due in no small part to the Chinese demand for Japanese exports.

Because of the rapid economic growth of China and the rest of East Asia outside of Japan, and the demand and supply that such economic growth has generated, the East Asian economies now trade more with one another than with economies outside of East Asia, including the United States. By the late 1990s, approximately half of East Asian trade is among East Asian economies (see the following charts). And while much of the East Asian trade consists of raw materials, components, and semi-finished goods that are further processed for exporting to developed economies ultimately, much of it has also found itself into the final demands of the East Asian domestic markets. This represents a sea change compared to, say, 30 years ago, when most of the East Asian trade was between East Asia and the United States and Western Europe, not within East Asia itself.

Interdependence of the East Asian economies has been rising rapidly over the years and East Asian dependence on the United States and Western Europe has declined. Interdependence of the East Asian economies will rise even further within the next five to ten years as East Asia becomes the only region in the world with a high rate of economic growth and as the ASEAN Free Trade Area as well as its variations (+1 [China]; + 3 [China, Japan and South Korea]) become increasingly realities. There is also the more recently concluded Indo-ASEAN Free Trade Agreement, which testifies to the possibility of significant World demand and supply growth outside of the United States and Europe.

It is this shifting economic centre of gravity and the rising interdependence of the East Asian economies, that in combination with the regional self-sufficiency in savings, give credence to the hypothesis of "partial de-coupling" of the world economies—that the Chinese and East Asian economies can continue to do reasonably well despite the current economic problems in the U.S. and elsewhere.

(5) Are Chinese Households Saving Too Much?

The high Chinese national savings rate, which has been around 40% since the early 1990s and has approached or even exceeded 50% in recent years, has also been blamed as a cause of the Chinese trade surplus and hence the global imbalances and ultimately the global financial crisis. A temporarily high national (and household) savings rate can be the result of the rapid growth of real GDP (and real household income)—it takes time for the growth of consumption to catch up to the growth of income.[9] However, a consistently high national savings rate also means, among other things, that the Chinese economy can finance all of its domestic investment needs from its own domestic savings alone, and does not have to depend on the more fickle foreign capital inflows (foreign direct investment or foreign portfolio investment) or foreign loans.

9 This possibility was suggested by Prof. David Hendry.

Chart 12.19. The Share of East Asian Exports Destined for East Asia

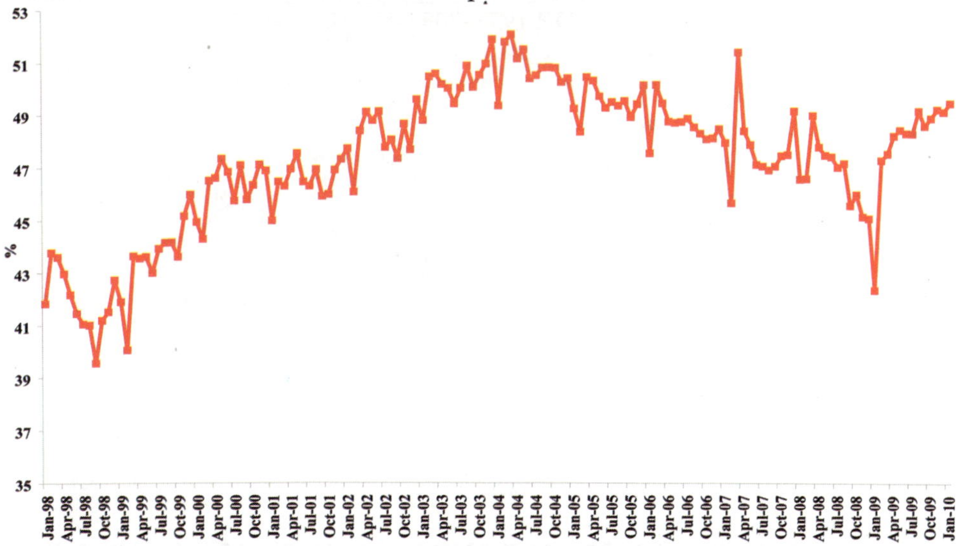

Chart 12.20. The Share of East Asian Imports Originated from East Asia

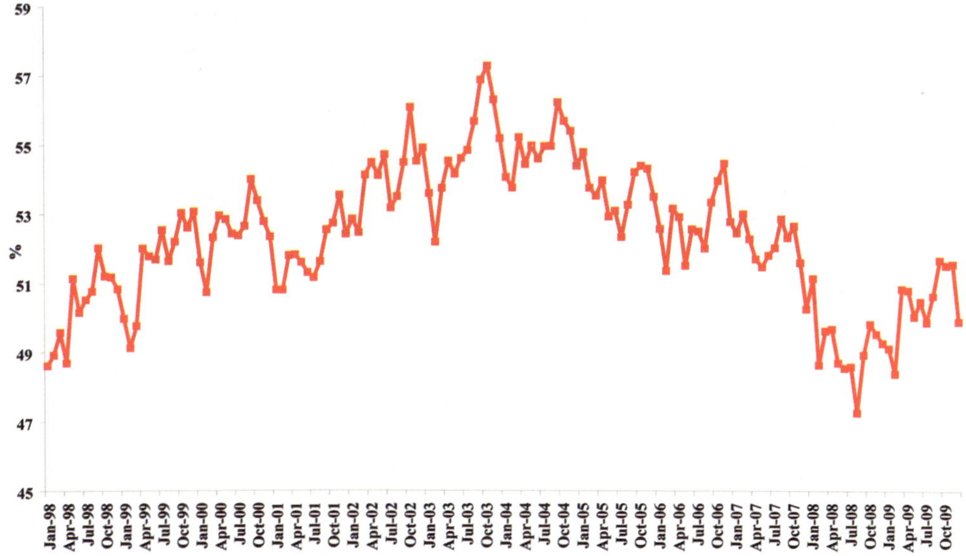

Chart 12.21. Chinese National Savings and Gross Domestic Investment as a Percent of GDP, 1952–2009

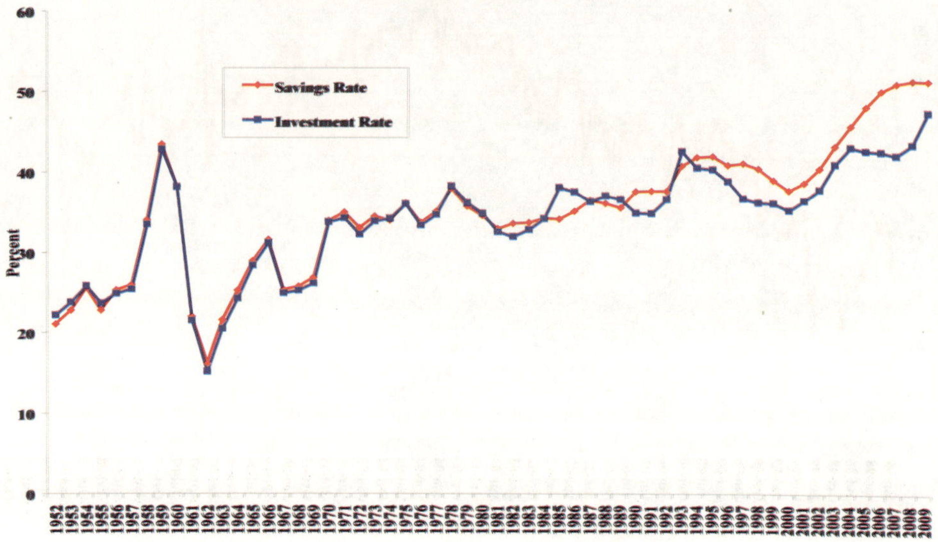

While the high, and some would say excessive,[10] Chinese national savings rate is well known, the equally high and excessive Chinese investment rate is not as well known. Chinese gross domestic investment as a percentage of GDP has been above 35% since the early 1990s and has exceeded 40% for quite a few years, since 2003. Such a high investment rate is significantly beyond the normal absorptive capacity of any economy and has resulted in over-investment and excess capacity in many industries, such as steel, cement, and glass. China both saves too much and invests too much. However, the excessive savings and excessive investment were in approximate balance and thus there was little or no excess savings to be exported, and hence no trade surplus, until 2005, when China began to have a trade surplus vis-à-vis the world. More recently, the Chinese trade surplus, which has been declining

10 Few economies, if any, have savings rates in excess of 30% and few have the capacity of absorbing gross domestic investment greater than 30% of their GDP productively each year.

continuously and significantly since 2007, even turned into a trade deficit in March 2010, reflecting the decline in export demand and the rise in domestic demand as a result of the Chinese economic stimulus programme and signalled a significant narrowing of its savings-investment gap.

The Chinese household savings rate, as distinct from the national savings rate, has been much lower, with the savings rate of the urban households approaching 30%. The savings behaviour of Chinese households on the mainland of China appears to be little different from those in Hong Kong and Taiwan at the same level of per capita household income, with an average savings rate of urban households of approximately 30%. Chinese household consumption has actually been growing quite rapidly, as indicated by the double-digit rates of growth of real retail sales, which are much higher than the rates of growth of real GDP or real household income.

Chart 12.22. Savings Rates of Chinese Urban and Rural Households

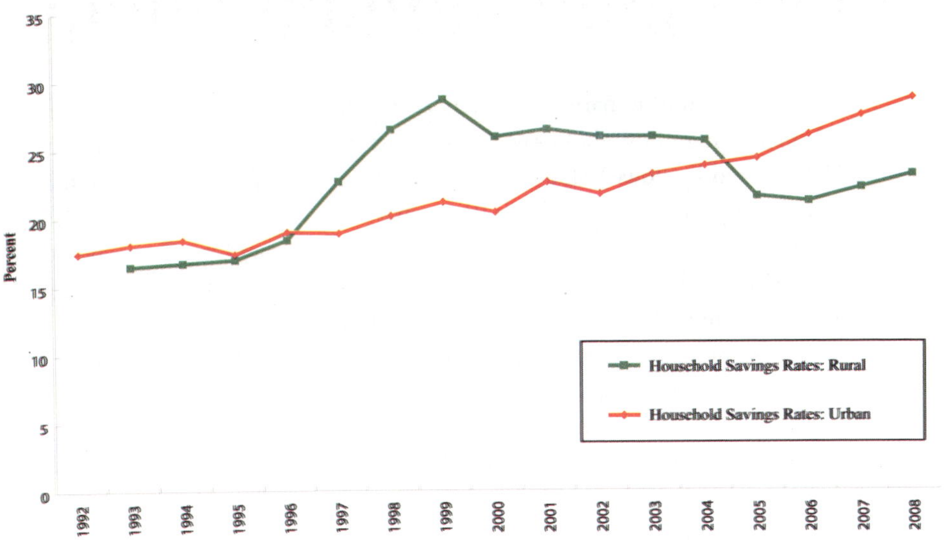

Chart 12.23. Monthly Rates of Growth of Chinese Real Retail Sales, Year-on-Year

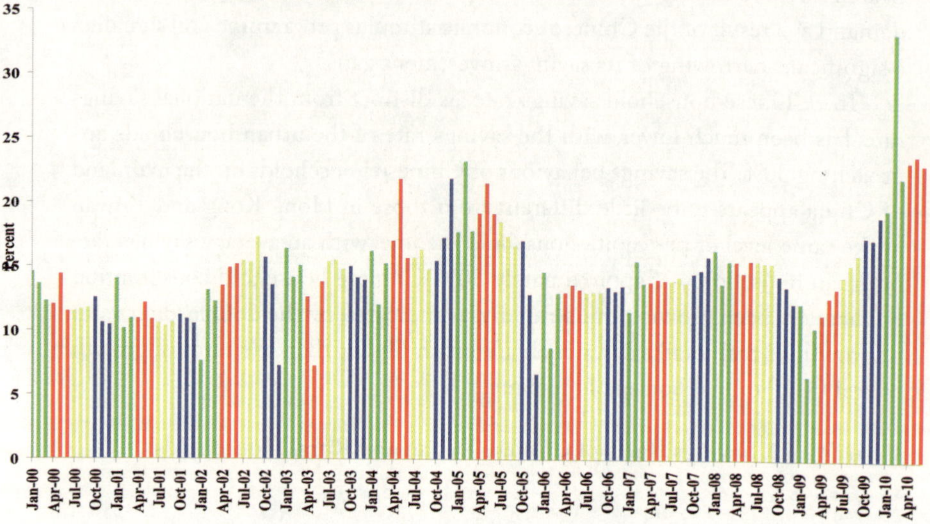

The high Chinese national savings rate of almost 50% is not due to an exceptionally high household savings rate, but to (1) the much lower share of GDP received by households as income (in particular, the share of labour is low in China, less than 50% of GDP, compared to approximately 70% in the developed economies of the West), and (2) the much higher Chinese corporate savings rates—Chinese enterprises typically reinvest almost all of their earnings and distribute little or no cash dividends to their shareholders.

Chinese household real consumption can increase significantly only with a significant increase in household real income, which in turn depends on either rising real wage rates, which are constrained by the abundance of surplus labour, or increasing distribution of cash dividends by Chinese enterprises to their shareholders, including the Chinese government. Improving the social safety net as well as increasing public financing of services such as education and health care may also help to raise Chinese real household consumption. However, as noted previously, the consumption-savings behaviour of Chinese households on the mainland of China is already quite similar to ethnic Chinese households in Hong Kong and Taiwan, both of which have reasonable social safety nets in place and substantial public financing of education and health care.

(6) Does the Chinese Economy Face Labour Shortages?

China, like Japan, Taiwan, and South Korea in their early stage of economic development, has an abundant supply of surplus labour. This means China can grow without being constrained by the supply of labour or by rising real wage rates of unskilled, entry-level labour over an extended period of time. Physical capital is very productive under conditions of surplus labour—as long as there is sufficient complementary domestic physical capital, the surplus labour can be transferred to the other two sectors enabling the economy to grow rapidly. This is exactly what the late Prof. W. Arthur Lewis (1954), Nobel Laureate in Economic Sciences, said in his famous paper on surplus labour more than 50 years ago.

The distribution of Chinese GDP by originating sector has become approximately: primary (agriculture), 10.6%; secondary (manufacturing, mining, and construction), 46.8%; and tertiary (services), 42.6%. But the bulk of the labour force, more than 40%, is still employed in the primary sector, waiting to be transferred to the other two sectors with higher productivity.

Chart 12.24. The Distribution of Chinese GDP by Sector since 1952

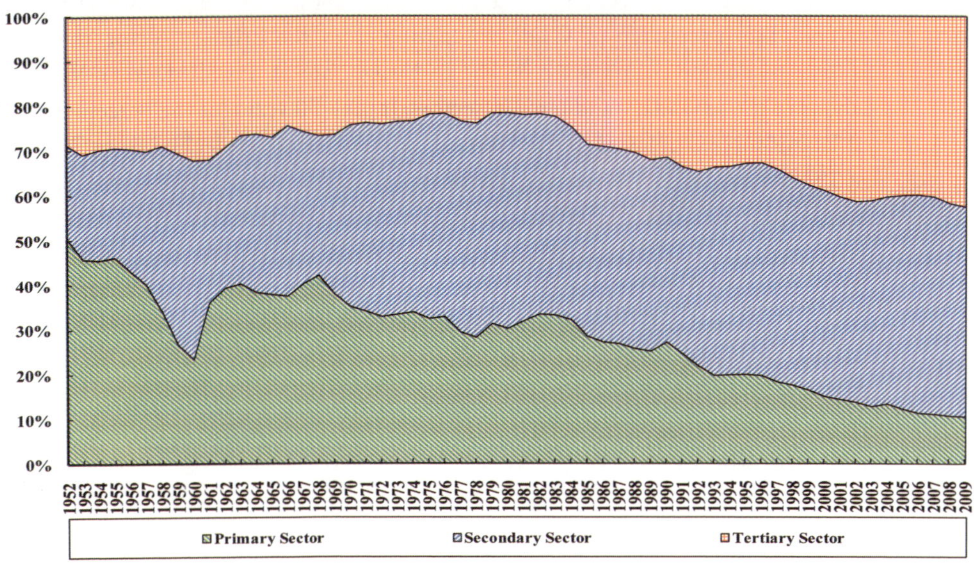

Chart 12.25. The Distribution of Chinese Employment by Sector since 1952

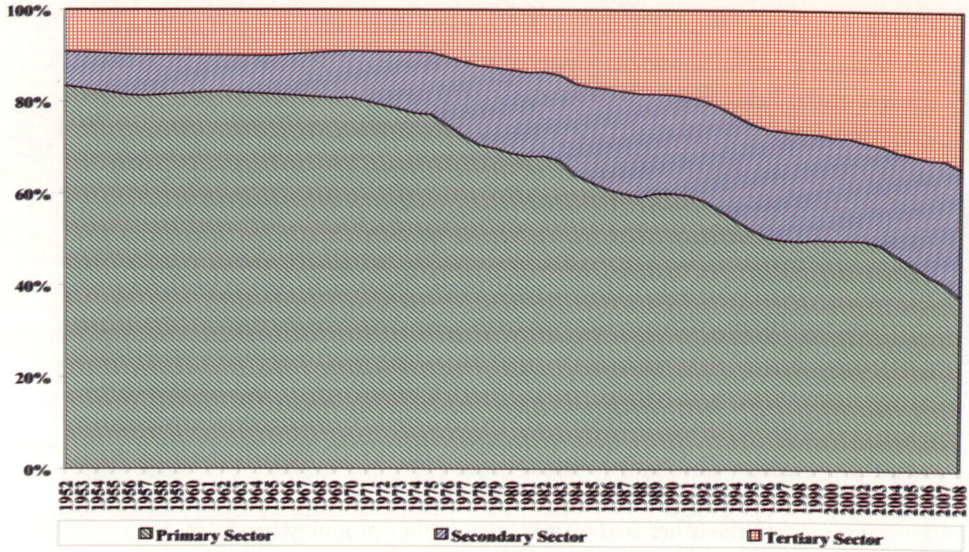

As long as the percentage of labour force employed in the primary sector exceeds the percentage of GDP originating from the primary sector, there is little or no upward pressure on the real wage rate of unskilled, entry-level labour in the secondary and tertiary sectors. It took 30 years for the percentage of labour force employed in the Chinese primary sector to decline from 70% in 1978 to its current 40%, at the rate of approximately 1% per year. It will take another 30 years for the percentage of labour force employed in the Chinese primary sector to decline from its current 40% to below 10%. By that time, 2040, it is expected that the primary sector will account for only approximately 5% of Chinese GDP. The Chinese economy will therefore continue to have surplus labour for another three decades or even longer. There will not be any shortage of unskilled, entry-level labour for a long time to come, even though there may be shortages of skilled or experienced labour in the secondary and tertiary sectors.

(7) Is Chinese Economic Power Comparable to That of the United States?

There is much talk that the world economy is now dominated by G-2 (Group of Two)—the United States and China. This is, however, very far from the truth. The United States accounts for more than 20% of world GDP, whereas China accounts for only 7% of world GDP. (East Asia, including China, accounts for approximately one-quarter of world GDP.) China by itself is not large enough by far to turn around the entire world economy. Moreover, Chinese GDP per capita is approximately US$3,700 in 2009 prices, compared to US$46,000 for the U.S.

Another measure of economic strength is the rate of technical progress—that is, the ability to produce more output with the same inputs (or equivalently, the rate of growth of total factor productivity). U.S. economic growth has been mostly driven by technical progress, whereas Chinese economic growth during the past 30 years has been mostly driven by the growth in the primary inputs—tangible capital and labour.

The U.S. lead in technical progress is attributable to its past and present investment in research and development (R&D). China has begun to invest in R&D in recent years. However, even though Chinese R&D expenditure has been rising rapidly, both in absolute value and as a percentage of GDP, it still lags far behind that of the U.S. by a whole order of magnitude.

Chart 12.26. China's R&D Expenditure and Its Share of Chinese GDP

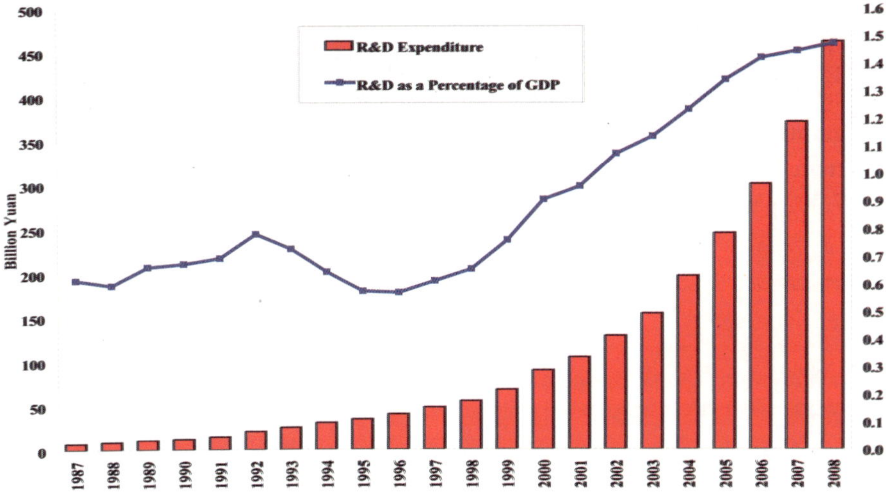

Chart 12.27. R&D Expenditures as a Ratio of GDP: G-7 Countries, Three East Asian Newly Industrialised Economies, and China

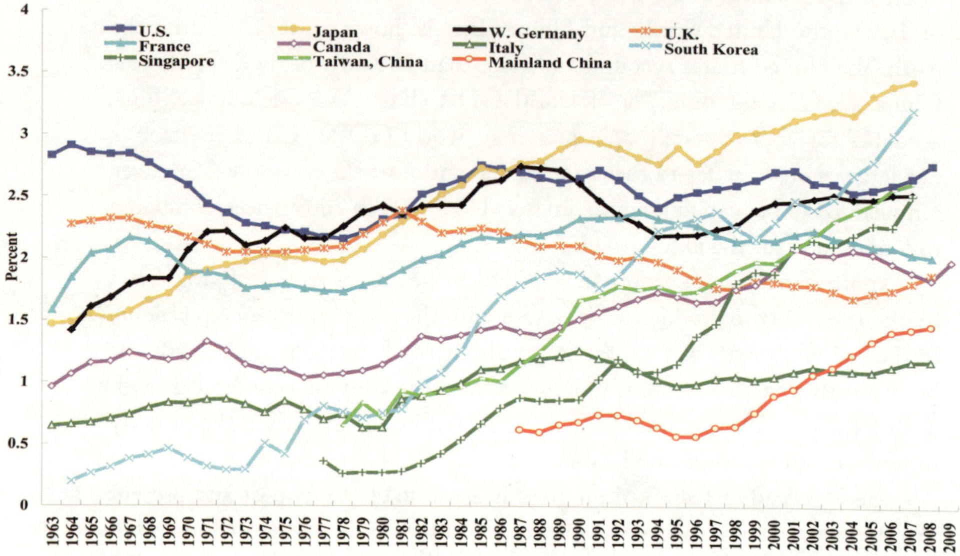

Sustained investment in R&D is essential to innovation. One indicator of national innovative ability is the number of patents created each year. In the following chart, the number of patents granted in the United States each year to the nationals of different countries, including the U.S., over time, is presented. The U.S. is the undisputed champion over the past 40 years, with close to 100,000 patents granted each year, followed by Japan. China has been catching up rapidly but still lags far behind, with approximately 1,000 patents granted each year. South Korea and Taiwan are still way ahead of China in terms of the number of patents granted in the U.S., averaging approximately 7,000 patents a year each.

Chart 12.28. Patents Granted in the U.S.: G-7 Countries, Four East Asian Newly Industrialised Economies, and China

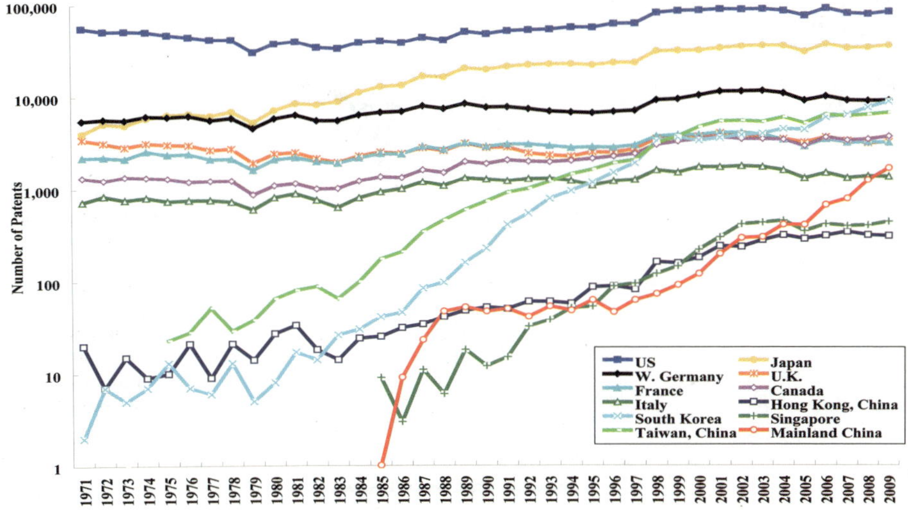

The stock of R&D capital, defined as the cumulative past investment in R&D less depreciation of 10% per year, can be shown to have a direct causal relationship to the number of patents granted (see the following chart, in which the number of patents granted is plotted against the R&D capital stock for each country and each year). Because China has had both a much lower R&D expenditure to GDP ratio and a much lower GDP than the United States, it will take more than a couple of decades before Chinese R&D capital can catch up to the level of U.S. R&D capital (and hence to the number of patents granted each year). China also lags behind the U.S. in terms of human capital even though China has had a long tradition of emphasis on education and learning. The talk about G-2 is simply pre-mature at this time.

Chart 12.29. Patents Granted in the U.S. and R&D Capital Stocks, Selected Economies

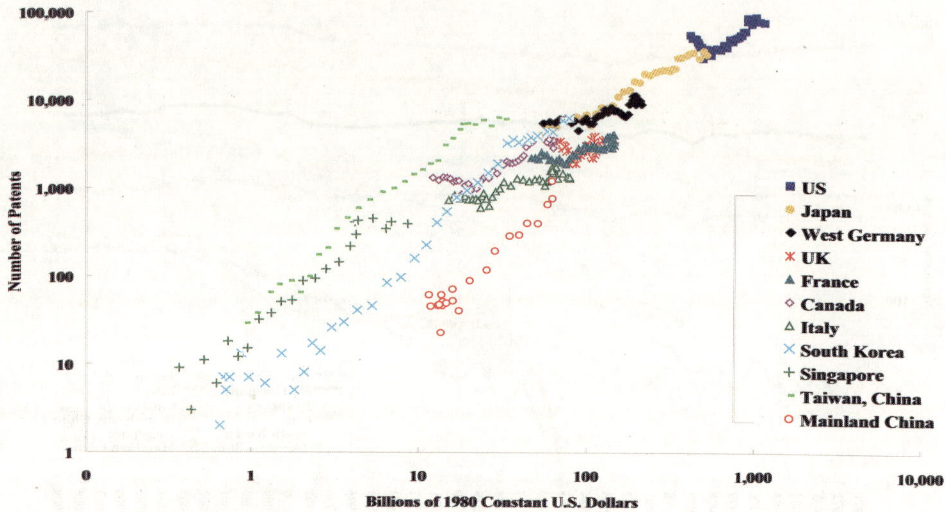

4. Concluding Remarks

(1) The renminbi (yuan) is not under-valued. There is little empirical evidence that the renminbi is under-valued except for the period between 2005 and 2008, during which the renminbi actually appreciated by more than 20%. If China is able to maintain an approximate balance of trade in goods and services combined under conditions of free trade (WTO conditions), its exchange rate should be neither under-valued nor over-valued, and no artificial adjustment should be necessary.

(2) Chinese trade surpluses did not cause the global imbalances. They simply occurred too late to be held responsible for the irrational exuberance in the United States and European economies.

(3) Chinese economic growth does not depend critically on exports. Chinese economic growth will be marginally, but not critically, affected by a large decline in its exports, as demonstrated by its experience in the past couple of years as well as during the 1997–1998 East Asian currency crisis. International trade will continue to be important, but not critical, to the growth of the Chinese economy.

(4) The economies of China and East Asia are partially de-coupled from the U.S. and Europe. Thus, China should be able to survive financial crises in, and effectively de-couple partially from, the European and U.S. economies. The Chinese economy should be able to continue growing at an average rate of 8% per annum for at least another couple of decades, driven by its own strong economic fundamentals and based on its own domestic internal demand.

(5) Chinese household savings rates are not too high—they are comparable to those of ethnically Chinese households in Hong Kong and Taiwan. It is the national savings rate that may have been too high. Chinese household consumption can increase significantly only with significant increases in Chinese household income.

(6) The Chinese economy will not face any labour shortages for at least three decades or more, until around 2040, when surplus labour will begin to disappear in the Chinese economy and the real wage rates of unskilled, entry-level labour will begin to rise.

(7) Chinese economic power will not be comparable to that of the United States for at least a couple of decades, perhaps even longer. Chinese GDP will probably catch up with U.S. GDP in approximately 20 years. It will probably take at least another 20 years, until the middle of this century, for Chinese per capita GDP to reach a level comparable to that of U.S. per capita GDP.

References

Chen, Xikang, Leonard K. Cheng, K. C. Fung, and Lawrence J. Lau. "The Estimation of Domestic Value-added and Employment Induced by Exports—An Application to Chinese Exports to the United States." In Yin-Wong Cheung and Kar-Yiu Wong, eds., *China and Asia: Economic and Financial Interactions*. New York: Routledge, 2009, pp. 64–82.

Lau, Lawrence J., Xikang Chen, C. Yang, Leonard K. Cheng, K. C. Fung, Sung Yun Wing, et. al. "Non-Competitive Input-Output Model and Its Application: An Examination of the China-U.S. Trade Surplus," *Social Sciences in China* 5 (2007), pp. 91–103 (in Chinese).

Lau, Lawrence J., Xikang Chen, Cuihong Yang, Leonard K. Cheng, Kwok-Chiu Fung, Yun-Wing Sung, et. al. "Input-Occupancy-Output Models of the Non-Competitive Type and Their Application—An Examination of the China-US Trade Surplus." *Social Sciences in China* 31, no. 1 (2010), pp. 35–54.

Lewis, W. Arthur. "Economic Development with Unlimited Supplies of Labour." *Manchester School of Economic and Social Studies* 22 (1954), pp. 139–191.

Section III

The Chinese Economy in the New Era

Commentary

The chapters included in Section III review the more recent developments and the future prospects of the Chinese economy. After the Chinese accession to the World Trade Organization (WTO) in 2001, the Chinese economy underwent a significant transformation, driven by the growth of net exports, which in turn enabled the massive movements of the surplus labour from the agricultural sector to the non-agricultural sector. However, by 2020, the export promotion strategy has basically run its course, and the Chinese economy is once again largely dependent on its own domestic aggregate demand. Actually, beginning in the 2010s, the external environment facing the Chinese economy has also begun to change. The China-U.S. strategic competition has become more intense—leading to wars on trade and technology, and restrictions on exports and investments. There have also been various attempts at economic de-globalisation, decoupling, and de-risking around the world.

However, as a large, continental economy just like the U.S., the Chinese economy is not significantly affected by external disturbances. The economic fundamentals of China still look favourable. Even though its population has begun to decline, the Chinese economy will not suffer from a labour shortage for at least a couple of decades. China continues to be committed to economic reform and opening to the world, policies it has followed since 1978.

The trade war between China and the U.S. began to brew in early 2018. Chapter 13 was written once again to show that while the real impacts would be negative for both countries, they would be relatively small and manageable, and there should be no need to panic. However, it also notes that the competition between China and the U.S. for economic and technological dominance in the world is likely to be a long-running affair. It is hoped that through developing greater mutual economic interdependence between the two countries, the potential conflicts between them can be mitigated. But some decoupling of the two economies seems inevitable. It concludes by emphasising the importance of keeping the China–U.S. economic relations win-win for both countries.[1]

Chapter 14, titled "Chinese Economy in the New Era," is forward-looking. It describes and projects what the Chinese economy is likely to look like in the "New Era",[2] between 2018 and 2050. What are the implications of economic growth with an emphasis on quality? The projections of the Chinese economy in this chapter are based on the then most recent data on the Chinese and U.S. economies. They project that the Chinese economy will reach parity with the U.S. economy in terms of aggregate real GDP sometime in 2031, but Chinese real GDP per capita will probably continue to lag behind that of the U.S. until the end of the 21st century. Similar projections have been presented in Chapter 5 of Section I as well as Chapter 16 below. These projections are all slightly different, reflecting the different dates, price bases, and exchange rates on which they were made.[3] I have not attempted to revise the projections in any of these chapters, but a revised set of projections based on the most recent data is presented in the Conclusion.

Domestically, China has shifted its emphasis from the quantity of growth to the quality of growth through the expansion of the supply of public goods. Chapter 15, titled "Public Goods Provision and Chinese Economic Development," reviews the progress that China has made in education, the environment, public health, and poverty alleviation. It was based on a lecture presented in the China Centre Seminar Series at Jesus College, Cambridge, the United Kingdom, on May 5, 2022. However, the provision of public goods such as clean air and water or mass transit frequently results in negative value-added at market prices and will therefore reduce rather than enhance the rate

1 Chapter 13 has subsequently been expanded into a book, Lau (2019).

2 "New Era" is a term introduced by President Xi Jinping of the People's Republic of China, referring to the period beginning in 2018.

3 It should be noted that the projected date on which the real GDP of the Chinese economy reaches parity with that of the U.S. is also sensitive to the renminbi-U.S. dollar exchange rate.

of growth of GDP as conventionally measured. The overall economic outlook remains positive, even though the emphasis on the quality of growth may reduce the future rate of growth of Chinese real GDP marginally.

In Chapter 16,[4] titled "The Prospects for the Chinese Economy in 2023 and Beyond," there is a projection, based on 2021 prices and exchange rates, that the Chinese real GDP will reach parity with the U.S. real GDP in 2030. However, the projected year of parity is sensitive to the renminbi-U.S. dollar exchange rate. As the renminbi has devalued relative to the U.S. dollar since 2021, a revised set of projections of Chinese and U.S. real GDPs and their rates of growth, based on 2022 prices and exchange rate is presented in the Conclusion. They represent my best guesses of the future of the Chinese economy at the present time.

References

Lau, Lawrence J. *The China-U.S. Trade War and Future Economic Relations*. Hong Kong: The Chinese University of Hong Kong Press, 2019.

———. "The Prospects for the Chinese Economy in 2023 and Beyond." *China-U.S. Focus*, January 24, 2003, https://www.chinausfocus.com/finance-economy/the-prospects-for-the-chinese-economy-in-2023-and-beyond.

---

4 Lau (2023).

Chapter 13.

The Sky is Not Falling! —The China-U.S. Trade War (2018)*

1. Introduction

As of October 2018, almost half of United States imports from China are subject to new U.S. tariffs at various rates, mostly at 10% until the end of 2018, when the rates will be raised to 25%. These tariff rates will prove to be prohibitive for most, if not all, of the U.S. imports from China subject to them. What are the impacts of the on-going China-U.S. trade war on the Chinese economy? Assuming that U.S. imports from China will be reduced by one half, the initial direct real impact on the Chinese economy may be estimated at a loss of 0.43% of Chinese GDP. If indirect effects are included, the full real impact may be estimated at a maximum loss of 1.12% of Chinese GDP. These estimated impacts are relatively small and quite manageable, especially for an economy expected to grow at an average annual rate of 6.5%—a reduction of 1.12% still leaves 5.38%, a very respectable rate of growth. There is a possibility that the scope of the U.S. tariffs may be expanded to cover all U.S. imports from China, in which case the full negative economic impact will be doubled to 2.24% of Chinese GDP, but still leaving an expected rate of growth in excess of 4%. Moreover, other sources of additional aggregate demand are likely to be mobilised by China in response to mitigate the decline in the rate of growth. There is no need to panic. The sky is not falling!

In 1997, at the height of the East Asian Currency Crisis, I wrote an essay titled "The Sky Isn't Falling!", explaining why the Chinese economy should be able to manage, and in particular, why the renminbi should not be devalued at that time.[1] Indeed, the sky did not fall, the renminbi did not devalue, and the

---

* This chapter was originally published as "The Sky Is Not Falling!," *Economic and Political Studies* 7, no. 2 (June 2019), pp. 122–147.

1 See Lau (1998), reprinted as Chapter 8 in this volume.

Chinese economy wound up with a real rate of growth of approximately 8%. Since then, I have written under the same title a couple of times, immediately after the collapse of the Lehman Brothers in the United States in September of 2008,[2] and also after the bursting of the Chinese stock market bubble and the unexpected devaluation of the renminbi in 2015.[3] With the advent of the trade war between China and the U.S., I feel that it is time to write yet another essay under this same title—"The Sky Is Not Falling!".

It should be noted that the China-U.S. trade war, at least for the time being, affects only the trade in goods between the two countries. The overall impacts of the trade war on both economies will certainly be negative, but relatively small and manageable, and perhaps proportionately more serious for China than for the U.S. This is because Chinese exports to the U.S. are much greater than U.S. exports to China, and hence China has much more at risk, and at the same time China has a smaller aggregate GDP and a very much lower per capita GDP.

The proximate cause of the current China-U.S. trade war is the large and persistent U.S.-China trade deficit in goods and services. The U.S.-China bilateral trade deficit was considered by the U.S. to be the result of unfair trade practices on the part of China. There are also other U.S. economic grievances not directly related to trade as well.[4] However, there exist significant differences in the official Chinese and U.S. estimates of the magnitude of the bilateral trade deficit itself. For 2017, the U.S. estimate of the trade deficit for goods only is US$375 billion, whereas the Chinese estimate is only US$274 billion. The large discrepancy is due to many factors, such as differences in the valuation of exports and imports, differences in the treatment of re-exports through third countries and regions, and whether trade in services, in which the U.S. enjoys a large annual surplus on the order of US$50 billion, is included. After making all the appropriate adjustments, a more accurate estimate is approximately US$300 billion, still a very large number.[5]

---

2 Lau (2008).

3 Lau (2015).

4 See the discussion in Lau (2019), Chapter 13.

5 See the analysis in Chen et. al. (2018).

U.S. President Donald Trump wishes to reduce the U.S.-China trade deficit by US$100 billion. He proposed to accomplish this objective by imposing tariffs on up to US$250 billion worth of U.S. imports from China[6] (and if necessary on an additional US$267 billion worth of U.S. imports from China, thus practically covering all imports from China). Whether this can be done in a manner consistent with the World Trade Organization (WTO) rules is not so clear, and China, like the European Union and other countries subject to new U.S. tariffs, have filed complaints with the WTO. However, these complaints are unlikely to resolve the disputes. Predictably, China retaliated with new tariffs on Chinese imports from the U.S. totalling US$110 billion,[7] at various rates but mostly at 10%. Under the new tariffs, Chinese exports to the U.S. will most certainly fall, as will U.S. exports to China. However, just as increased voluntary trade between two trading-partner countries raises the aggregate welfare in both countries, an involuntary decrease in the trade between them lowers the aggregate welfare in both countries. It will be lose-lose for both countries.

An alternative way to measure the bilateral trade surplus or deficit is in terms of the domestic value-add that the respective exports generate in the exporting country. The domestic value-added content of a good to be exported is the GDP generated by its manufacture, relative to its export value, which represents its real contribution to the domestic economy. For example, the Apple iPhone is finally assembled in China, with components, parts and technology from all over the world. The export value of an iPhone is approximately US$500.[8] The domestic value-added of its Chinese manufacturer, Foxconn,

---

6 The U.S. tariffs were imposed on Chinese imports in three separate batches: a first on US$34 billion in July 2018, a second on US$16 billion in August 2018 and a third on US$200 billion in September 2018. Imports of consumer goods such as cell phones, garments and shoes are at the time of publication not subject to U.S. tariffs.

7 The Chinese retaliatory tariffs were also imposed on U.S. imports in three separate batches: a first on US$34 billion in July 2018, a second on US$16 billion in August 2018 and a third on US$60 billion in September 2018. Approximately US$40 billion of U.S. imports, including large aircrafts, integrated circuits and semiconductors are at the time of publication not subject to Chinese tariffs.

8 This is the wholesale value, not the retail value.

may be estimated at US$15. Thus, the domestic value-added content is 3% (=15/500). The average domestic value-added content of Chinese exports to the U.S. is approximately 25%.[9] The average domestic value-added content of U.S. exports to China is approximately 50%,[10] a ratio of two to one compared to the Chinese value-added content. Thus, the U.S.-China trade deficit, if measured in terms of domestic value-added, may be estimated at approximately US$150 billion in 2017.[11] This contrasts with the U.S. official estimate for the trade deficit in goods only of US$375 billion in gross value terms. However, even US$150 billion is a large number. An efficient way to close this trade gap is for China to import from the U.S. goods that it needs but with close to 100% U.S. domestic value-added contents, such as oil and gas, agricultural commodities (meat and grains), and services, so an additional US$150 billion worth of exports in gross-value terms from the U.S., perhaps slightly higher, should suffice. The U.S. definitely has the capacity to increase its supply of these goods, and China has high and rising demands for these goods, so such an increase in the trade between the two countries should be completely feasible, but will take a little time to develop and implement.[12]

However, the trade war itself may also do damage to the longer-term economic relations between the two countries. For example, it may affect the future rate of growth of the trade in services[13] between the two countries, in which the U.S. has a persistent, large and growing surplus, estimated to be US$54 billion by China and US$40 billion by the U.S. for 2017.[14] Education and tourism constitute a significant part of U.S. exports to China. Yet it has been reported that the U.S. government considered a blanket ban on all Chinese student visas. If implemented, it would reduce the U.S. surplus in trade in services by US$18 billion.[15] The trade war may also affect the flow of direct as well as portfolio investment between the two countries.

---

9 Chen and Wang (2016), Tables 2.2 and 2.4.

10 Ibid., Tables 2.6 and 2.8.

11 See Chen et al. (2018).

12 See Lau (2018a).

13 Exports of services from the U.S. have an almost 100% domestic value-added content.

14 See Chen et al. (2018).

15 *Financial Times*, 3 October 2018, p. 1.

In part 2, the immediate impacts of the new U.S. tariffs on the Chinese economy are discussed. In part 3, the real impacts on the Chinese economy are analysed and compared with the real impacts on the U.S. economy. In part 4, the longer-term forces behind the China-U.S. trade war are considered. In part 5, the promotion of greater mutual economic interdependence is proposed as a means of arresting the deterioration in China-U.S. relations. Some brief concluding remarks, to the effect that the real economic impacts of the trade war, while negative, are quite manageable for both China and the U.S., are made in part 6.

2. The Immediate Impacts

The immediate impact of the current trade war was psychological and fell mostly on the Chinese financial markets. As a result of the trade war, uncertainty has increased worldwide. Expectations have turned negative. Confidence of firms and households has slipped. Consumption and investment have been partially put on hold.

Stock markets abhor uncertainty. Any uncertainty will lead to a decline. The Chinese stock markets—Shanghai and Shenzhen, and even Hong Kong—have taken a direct hit from the start of the trade war (see Chart 14.1). The Shenzhen Stock Exchange has seen its average stock price decline by almost 25% since the beginning of 2018. Similarly, the average price level of the Shanghai Stock Exchange has declined 15%. The MSCI China Index has declined 13%. Hong Kong overall has declined almost 10%, but Mainland Chinese enterprises listed there have declined by somewhat less. In contrast, the S&P 500 has gained approximately 10% since the beginning of 2018. However, not all of the declines in the Chinese stock markets can or should be attributed to the trade war. The actual and expected increases in the rate of interest in the U.S. by the U.S. Federal Reserve Board also had a role in the falling prices of assets and exchange rates vis-a-vis the U.S. dollar in emerging markets.[16]

16 However, this does not explain why the S&P 500 Index kept hitting new highs—perhaps this is another round of "irrational exuberance."

Chart 13.1. The Chinese, Hong Kong and U.S. Stock Market Indices, January to October 2018

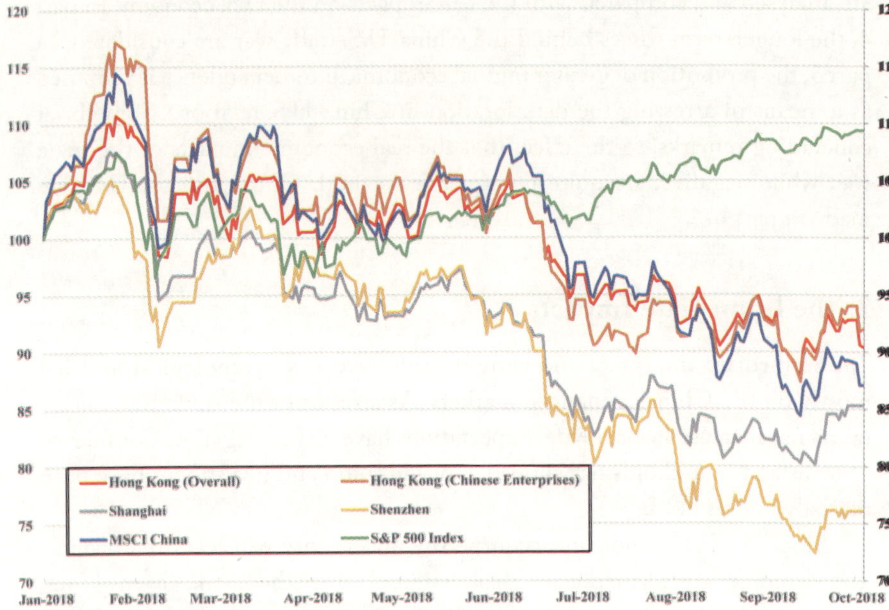

Source: Bloomberg.

However, the performance of the Shanghai and Shenzhen stock markets is not a reliable barometer of the state of the Chinese economy. Rather, it is a measure of the degree of "irrational exuberance," to use a phrase coined by Dr. Alan Greenspan, the former Chairman of the U.S. Federal Reserve Board, or the opposite, "irrational gloom." This is because the Mainland Chinese stock exchanges are dominated by individual investors, most of whom are only looking for quick profits through frequent trading. The average holding period of individual Chinese common stock investors is less than 20 trading days and that of institutional investors is between 30 and 40 trading days.[17] Since the trade war looks like it will last for a while, certainly until after the mid-term elections in the U.S. on 6 November 2018, and perhaps even much longer, most Mainland Chinese investors have elected to bail out and stay on the sidelines for now.

---

17 This is according to a report by the Capital Market Research Institute of the Shanghai Stock Exchange based on the transactions of all Chinese investors in 2016.

Similarly, the renminbi exchange rate has also been negatively affected, but also in part because of the actual and expected increases in the U.S. rate of interest. In Chart 13.2, an index of the renminbi central parity rate, the rate set by the People's Bank of China (the central bank of China) at the beginning of each daily trading session of the onshore renminbi, is compared to the China Foreign Exchange Trade System (CFETS) Index, an index of the changes in the value of a Chinese trade-weighted basket of currencies,[18] for the period since 2015.[19] While there was wide divergence between the two indexes at the beginning, they began to move in tandem with each other in the second half of 2017. More recently, while the renminbi has devalued vis-a-vis the super-strong U.S. dollar by approximately 9% since the end of January 2018, the average absolute deviation of the central parity rate from the CFETS Index has not widened beyond 1.7% (see Chart 13.3).

Chart 13.2. The Renminbi Central Parity Exchange Rate and the CFETS Index since 2015 (31 Dec. 2014 = 100)

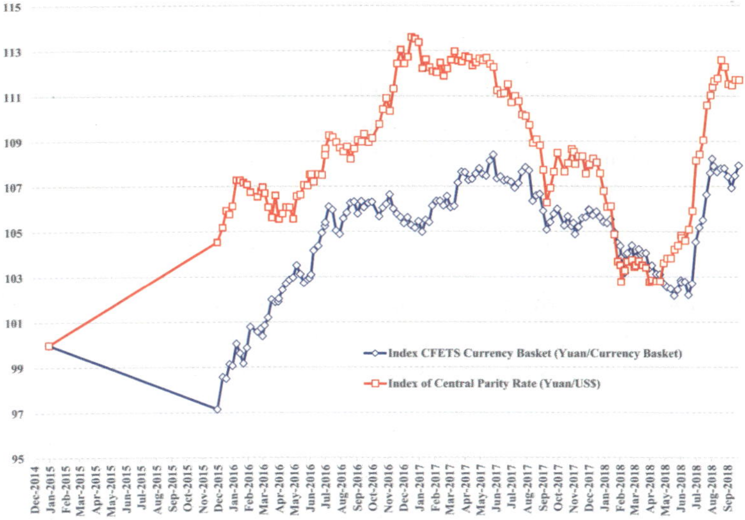

Source: China Foreign Exchange Trade System.

18 The U.S. dollar had a weight of 26.4% before 2017. On 1 January 2017, the weights of the different currencies were adjusted in accordance with changes in the trade shares of the respective countries and regions. The U.S. dollar currently has a weight of 22.4%.

19 Note that the offshore renminbi exchange rates may be different from the onshore renminbi exchange rates because capital controls still exist in China.

Chart 13.3, which compares the movements of the renminbi central parity rate and the CFETS Index since year-end 2017, shows that the central parity rate has devalued approximately 5% with respect to the U.S. dollar (and 9% since the start of the trade war at the end of January 2018), in part also because of the actual and expected increases in the U.S. rate of interest, quite apart from the trade war. However, relative to the CFETS Index, the central parity rate has only devalued by 2.2%. A useful way of looking at the CFETS Index is that it measures the average change of the exchange rates of the currencies of China's trading-partner countries and regions relative to the renminbi. So, if the percentage change of the renminbi central parity rate is the same as that of the CFETS Index, it means that the renminbi exchange rate is unchanged relative to the weighted average of the currencies of China's trading-partner countries, even though the renminbi may have appreciated or devalued vis-a-vis a specific currency such as the U.S. dollar. Actually, there is no compelling reason for the renminbi to follow the U.S. dollar, which implies that the renminbi will appreciate or devalue with respect to other currencies precisely as the U.S. dollar. When the U.S. dollar is super-strong, for the renminbi to follow the U.S. dollar effectively amounts to Chinese exporters raising their prices to the importers of all other countries, which does not necessarily make sense. If the renminbi exchange rate follows the CFETS Index, it amounts to keeping the renminbi exchange rate approximately constant for the average trading-partner country of China.

Another implication of the renminbi exchange rate following the CFETS Index is that the average purchasing power of the renminbi overseas will be preserved, that is, kept approximately constant. If the U.S. dollar is super-strong, U.S. goods will become more expensive, but the goods of other countries will become cheaper, so that the Chinese consumers of imported goods are on average no worse off. Moreover, by following the CFETS Index, the renminbi exchange rate will have a lower volatility than the U.S. dollar exchange rate because it will move, in general, in the same direction as the U.S. dollar but by a smaller amount. This means when the U.S. dollar appreciates with respect to other currencies, the renminbi will devalue relative to the U.S. dollar, and when the U.S. dollar devalues with respect to other currencies, the renminbi will appreciate relative to the U.S. dollar. The renminbi exchange rate will be less volatile than the U.S. dollar exchange rate.

Chart 13.3. The Renminbi Central Parity Exchange Rate and the CFETS Index (29 Dec. 2017=100)

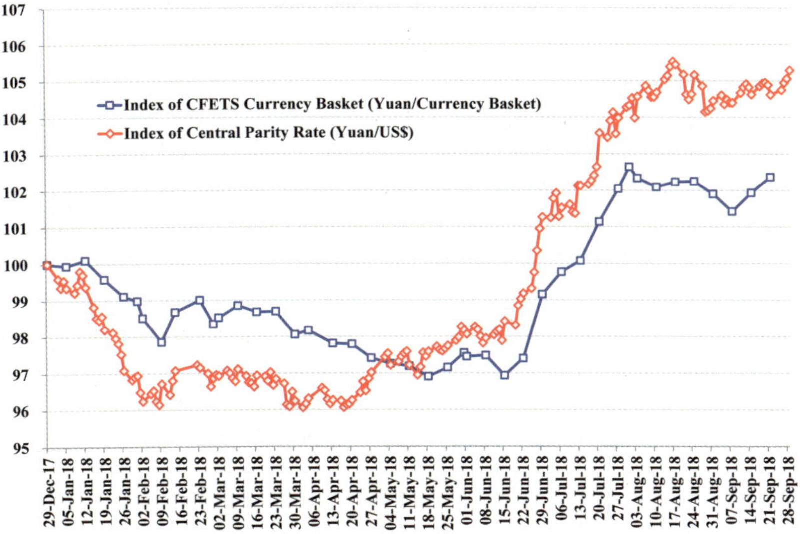

Source: China Foreign Exchange Trade System.

Despite widespread expectations that the renminbi will be devalued significantly in response to the trade war, it is actually quite unlikely. The new U.S. tariffs on Chinese exports of goods are prohibitive and a moderate devaluation of the renminbi accomplishes nothing except to make the renminbi less desirable domestically and internationally as a medium of exchange and a store of value. For a large economy such as China's, with a relatively low degree of export dependence (see Charts 13.7 and 13.8 below), devaluation is never a useful strategy. It is also not necessary for the renminbi to devalue. The Chinese current-account will remain in balance, even if Chinese exports to the U.S. decline by one half.[20] The Chinese wage rate in the private sector is still downward flexible, so that economic adjustments can occur without having to tinker with the exchange rate. It is in China's interests to maintain a relatively stable renminbi exchange rate so that its own citizens will continue

20 See the discussions in part 3 below.

to want to hold the renminbi as a store of value. It is also the only way for the internationalisation of the renminbi to become a reality eventually.

The people who will really be affected immediately by the U.S. tariffs are the actual U.S. users of Chinese goods, consumers as well as producers, because they are the ones who will have to pay the higher prices as a result of the new tariffs. Since the Chinese imports arriving at U.S. ports have already been paid for by the U.S. importers, the cost of the tariffs will have to be passed on to the actual users in the U.S. to the extent possible. However, it has been announced by the Office of the U.S. Trade Representative that exemptions from the new tariffs for a year may be granted to U.S. importers upon application on a product-by-product basis. At the same time, it has also been reported that very few exemptions have been approved. So it is really not clear how things will end up at this time. The new tariffs have also kicked in on the Chinese side, although there is no similar exemption for Chinese importers of U.S. goods. In this case, China has simply been reacting to the U.S. moves, in a reciprocal but measured manner.

3. The Real Impacts

The new U.S. tariffs range at various rates for the first batch of US$34 billion of Chinese imports into the U.S., and are 25% ad valorem for the second batch of US$16 billion and 10% for the third batch of US$200 billion (to be raised to 25% on 1 January 2019). These rates will prove to be prohibitive for most of the goods imported from China as neither the Chinese exporters nor the U.S. importers have the kind of profit margins that can allow them to absorb the cost of these tariffs and alternative sources of supplies are possible. Thus, the new tariffs, if fully implemented, will effectively lead to a complete halt of Chinese exports to the U.S. of goods that are subject to them, resulting in a potential reduction of U.S. imports of goods from China of up to US$250 billion on an "arrival valuation" or equivalently "cost, insurance and freight" (c.i.f.) basis. This translates into a reduction of Chinese exports to the U.S. of approximately US$225 billion on a "departure valuation" or equivalently "free on board" (f.o.b.) basis.[21] What will be the real impacts of such a reduction in exports on the Chinese economy?

---

21 The reduction of U.S. imports from China of US$250 billion on a c.i.f. basis translates into approximately US$227 (=250 x 10/11) billion on an f.o.b., Chinese ports, basis. We shall use the rounded-off number of US$225 billion.

First of all, China, as a large continental economy with a huge domestic market, like the United States, has a relatively low export dependence, and has always been relatively immune to external disturbances. During the past two decades, the rates of growth of Chinese exports and imports have fluctuated like those of all other Asian economies, large and small. Chart 13.4 presents the quarterly rates of growth of exports of selected Asian economies and Chart 13.5 presents the quarterly rates of growth of imports of the same selected Asian economies. The red lines in both charts, representing the Chinese quarterly rates of growth of exports and imports respectively, fluctuate like those of all the other Asian economies. However, the quarterly rate of growth of Chinese real GDP, represented by a red line in Chart 13.6, has remained positive and relatively stable compared to those of all the other Asian economies, including Japan.

Chart 13.4. Quarterly Rates of Growth of Exports of Goods: Selected Asian Economies

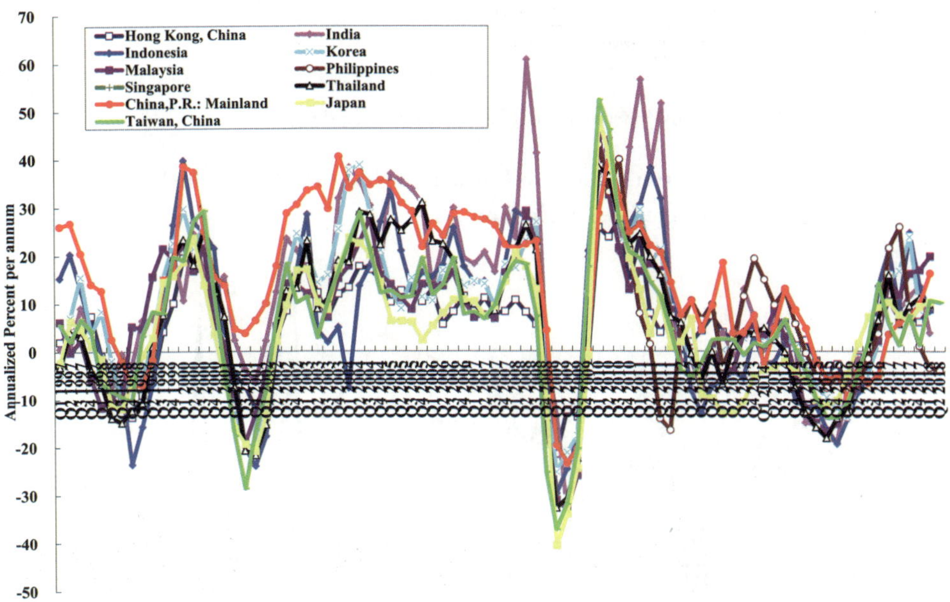

Source: International Monetary Fund, *International Financial Statistics*.

Chart 13.5. Quarterly Rates of Growth of Imports of Goods: Selected Asian Economies

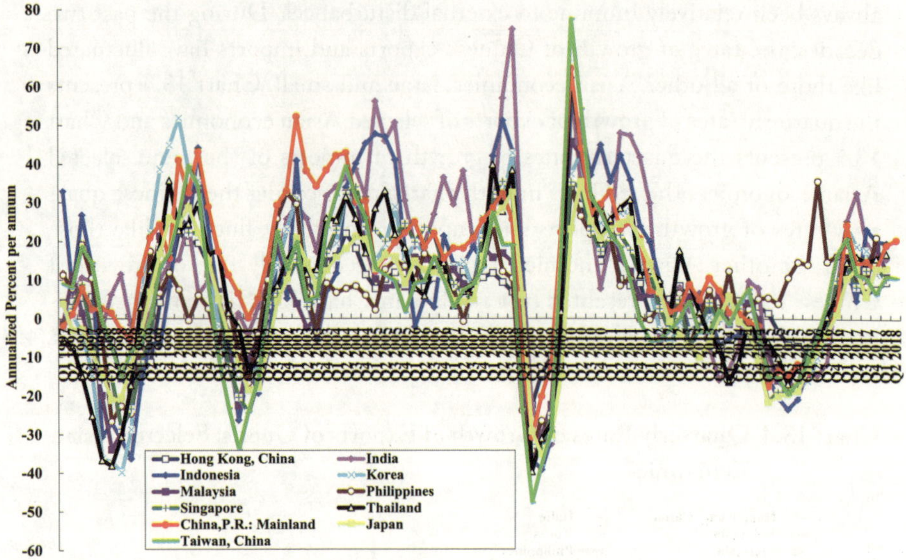

Source: International Monetary Fund, *International Financial Statistics*.

Chart 13.6. Quarterly Rates of Growth of Real GDP, Year-on-Year: Selected Asian Economies

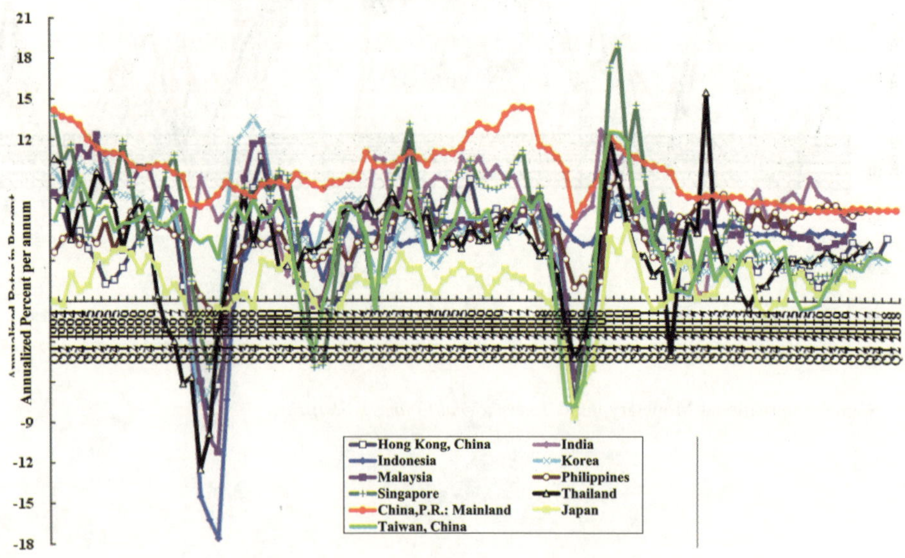

Source: International Monetary Fund, *International Financial Statistics*.

Moreover, Chinese dependence on exports has been declining over the past decade. The value of Chinese exports of goods and services to the world as a share of Chinese GDP has fallen from a peak of 35.3% in 2006 to 19.8% in 2017 (see the red line in Chart 13.7). Similarly, the share of exports of goods and services to the U.S. in Chinese GDP has also fallen by more than half, from a peak of 7.6% in 2006 to 3.5% in 2017 (see the red line in Chart 13.8). For goods alone, Chinese exports to the world and the U.S. were 18.1% and 3.4% of Chinese GDP in 2017 respectively (see the blue lines in Charts 13.7 and 13.8).

Chart 13.7. Chinese Exports of Goods and Services and Goods Only as a Percent of GDP

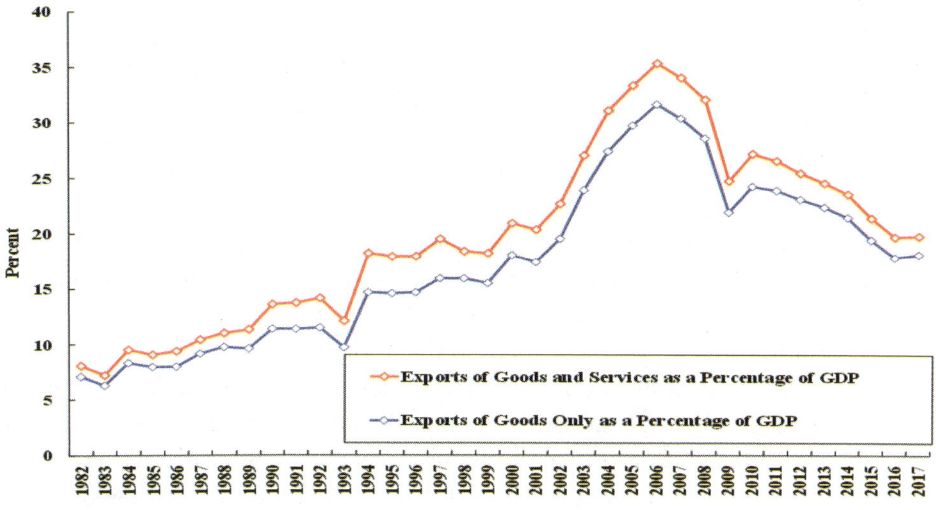

Source: State Administration of Foreign Exchange, the People's Republic of China.

Chart 13.8. Chinese Exports of Goods and Services and Goods Only to the U.S. as a Percent of Chinese GDP

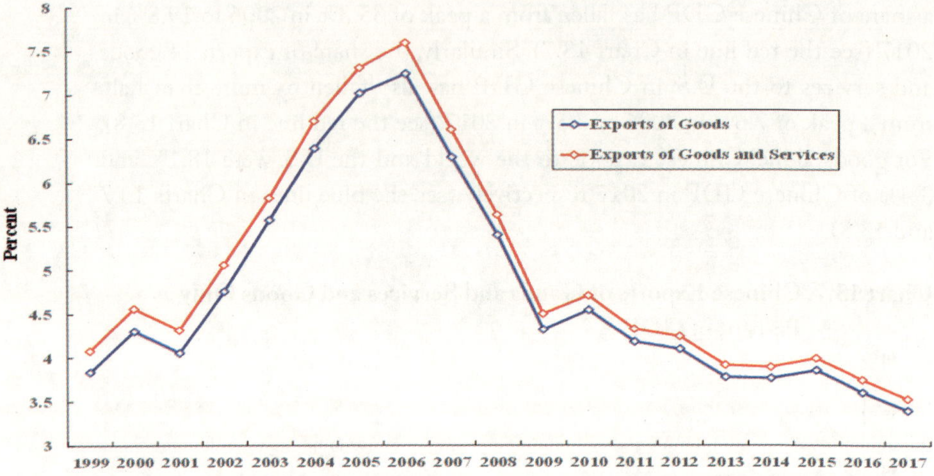

Sources: National Bureau of Statistics of China, U.S. Bureau of Economic Analysis.

During this same period, the rates of growth of Chinese exports of goods to the world (represented by the red columns in Chart 13.9) and to the U.S. (represented by the blue columns in Chart 13.9) have also declined significantly. Chinese exports of goods to the world grew at an average annual rate of 22.6% in the decade 1998–2007, but slowed to only 7.9% in the following decade, 2008–2017, in part because of the 2008–2009 global financial crisis and the subsequent European sovereign debt crisis. Similarly, exports to the U.S. grew at 22% per annum in the decade 1998–2007, but slowed to less than 7% per annum in the most recent decade. The most important engine of Chinese economic growth today is no longer exports but its domestic demand, driven by its household consumption (especially that of the rapidly growing middle class), infrastructural investments, and public goods consumption such as environmental preservation, protection and restoration, education, health care and elderly care.

Chart 13.9. The Rates of Growth of Chinese Exports of Goods to the World and to the U.S. (Percent per annum)

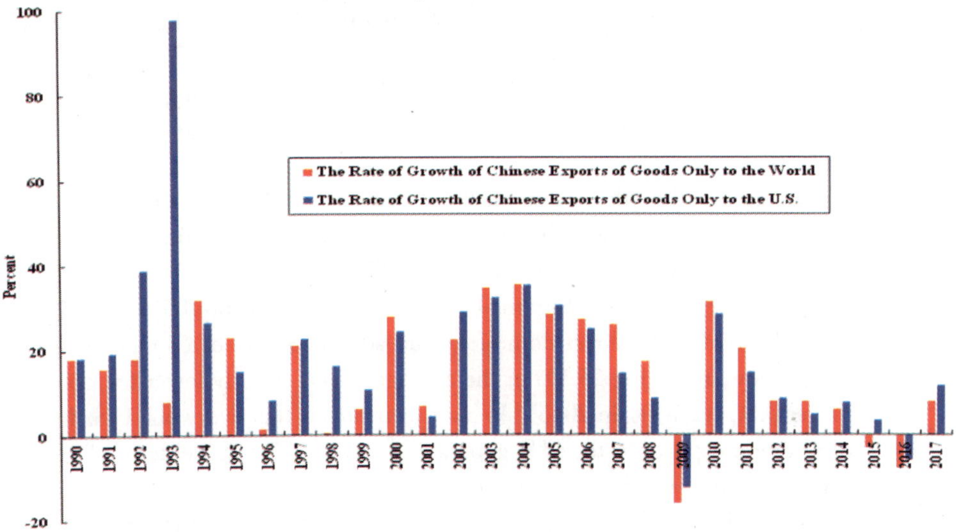

Source: National Bureau of Statistics of China.

Total Chinese exports of goods to the U.S. in 2017, on an f.o.b. basis, was US$430 billion according to the National Bureau of Statistics of China, or 3.4% of the 2017 Chinese GDP.[22] At present, new U.S. tariffs are levied on US$250 billion worth of U.S. imports of goods from China. This is approximately equivalent to US$225 billion of Chinese exports of goods to the U.S. on an f.o.b. basis, or approximately half of total Chinese exports of goods to the

22 This is not the place to discuss or reconcile the discrepancy between Chinese and U.S. official data. However, if we add a 10% c.i.f. adjustment to the reported Chinese exports to the U.S. f.o.b. of US$430 billion, U.S. imports from China would amount to US$473 billion, which is not that far apart from the U.S. official data on imports of good from China in 2017 of US$506 billion. The remaining discrepancy can be mostly attributed to re-exports through a third country or region like Hong Kong.

U.S. in 2017.[23] Assuming that half of all Chinese exports of goods to the U.S. will be halted because of the prohibitive new tariffs, total Chinese exports of goods to the world, which was US$2.28 trillion in 2017 according to Chinese official statistics, will fall by 9.9%. As a comparison, in the aftermath of the collapse of Lehman Brothers in 2008, total Chinese exports of goods declined by 16% in 2009, and the Chinese economy still managed to grow 8.7% in real terms that year.

What would be the real impacts of such a fall in Chinese exports due to the new U.S. tariffs on the Chinese real GDP? As the total Chinese exports of goods to the U.S. was 3.4% of Chinese GDP in 2017, the decline of one half of Chinese exports of goods to the U.S. would amount to only 1.7% (=3.4/2) of GDP. Moreover, the direct domestic value-added content of Chinese exports is quite low, averaging 25.5% in the aggregate, and slightly lower for exports to the U.S., at 24.8%, in 2015.[24] What this means is that every one U.S. dollar of Chinese exports to the U.S. generates less than 25 U.S. cents of Chinese GDP.[25] In contrast, the direct domestic value-added content of U.S. exports of goods to China may be estimated at 50.8% in 2015, slightly more than twice the domestic value-added content of Chinese exports to the U.S.[26] Therefore, the maximum loss in Chinese GDP in the first instance, assuming that half of the exports to the U.S. is completely halted, may be estimated at 0.43% (=1.7 x 0.25), a tolerable level, especially for an economy growing at an average annual real rate of 6.5% and with a per capita GDP of US$9,137 in 2017, which is way above the subsistence level.

Thus, even if all Chinese exports to the U.S. subject to the new tariffs are halted and in addition are not re-directed elsewhere, the initial reduction in the domestic value-added (GDP) caused directly is less than 0.5%. In the

---

23 Strictly speaking, half of US$430 billion is US$215 billion. However, it is well known that Chinese official data on exports do not include re-exports through a third country or region such as Hong Kong, so US$225 billion may be a reasonable estimate of one half of Chinese exports of goods to the U.S. on an f.o.b. basis. See footnote 22 above.

24 Chen and Wang (2016), Tables 2.2 and 2.4.

25 While the domestic value-added content of Chinese exports may have risen since 2015, the increase is not believed to be significant.

26 Chen and Wang (2016), Tables 2.6 and 2.8.

subsequent period, the reductions in the intermediate input demands of the Chinese economy caused by the reduction of exports will cause further reductions in the intermediate input demands, accompanied by further reductions in the domestic value-added. This is the indirect second-round effect. These further reductions in the intermediate input demands will in turn cause further reductions of the intermediate input demands as well as domestic value-added (GDP), as the third-, fourth- and higher-round effects kick in, but with the effects becoming successively smaller with each higher round. The total effect on domestic value-added (GDP), taking into account all the rounds, may be estimated at 66% of the value of the reduced exports.[27] This implies ultimately a total loss in Chinese GDP of 1.12% (=1.7 x 0.66). In absolute terms, this amounts to US$137 billion in 2017 prices compared to a Chinese GDP of US$12.2 trillion in 2017. A reduction of 1.12% from an expected annual growth rate of 6.5% leaves 5.38%, still a very respectable rate compared to the average of 3.7% for the world as a whole in 2018, as forecast recently by the International Monetary Fund.

In order to mitigate the negative economic impacts of the trade war, the Chinese government can try to increase aggregate demand on the margin by increasing its investments in basic infrastructure and R&D, and in the provision of public goods, such as environmental preservation, protection and restoration (blue skies, green mountains and turquoise waters) and education, health care and elderly care. With all the existing excess production capacities in China, supply is not a constraint—as long as there is demand, there will be supply.

However, even though the real impacts on the Chinese economy in the aggregate are relatively small, they can be more significant for specific individual municipalities, provinces and regions, especially those oriented towards exports. Guangdong, which includes Shenzhen, is the largest exporting province/municipality/autonomous region in China, accounting for more than 16% of total Chinese exports, followed by Shanghai and then Zhejiang. Guangdong exports of goods to the world and to the U.S. were respectively 49.9% and 8.7% of its GDP in 2017, much higher than the respective national averages of 18.1% and 3.4%.

---

27 Ibid., Table 2.4.

Within the province of Guangdong, the municipality of Shenzhen has had the highest exports to GDP ratio. In 1990, Shenzhen exports amounted to almost 250% of its GDP (see the blue line in Chart 13.10). Over the years, its export share has declined to 73.7% in 2017, with the share of exports to the U.S. at 11.3%, more than three times the national average of 3.4% and higher than the provincial average of 9.6% (see the red line in Chart 13.10). If there is any devastating economic damage from the trade war, we should find it in Shenzhen. Assuming that the domestic value-added content of Shenzhen exports to the U.S. is the same as that of Chinese exports to the U.S. as a whole, that is, 25%, the maximum loss in Shenzhen GDP in the first instance—assuming that half of its exports to the U.S. is completely halted—may be estimated at 1.41% (=11.3/2 x 0.25). Such a decline in GDP is manageable for Shenzhen, as the real rate of growth of its GDP was 8.8% and its GDP per capita was US$27,123 in 2017.[28] Taking into account the indirect, that is, second-, third-, fourth- and higher-round effects of the reduction of exports from Shenzhen, the total loss of real GDP of Shenzhen may be estimated at 3.7% (=11.3/2 x 0.66). This will represent a significant slowdown for the Shenzhen economy.

Even then, the Shenzhen economy will still be growing at an annual rate of 5.1%, higher than the average rate of growth of the world economy of 3.7% as forecast recently by the International Monetary Fund, and that of neighbouring Hong Kong, projected to be around 4.0%. And the relatively high GDP per capita of Shenzhen will help it to weather the trade war. However, if all Chinese exports to the U.S. were halted, it would imply a reduction in the rate of growth of Shenzhen of 7.4% (=11.3 x 0.66), leaving Shenzhen with an anaemic but still positive annual rate of growth of 1.4%. The recently announced Guangdong-Hong Kong-Macau Greater Bay Area Initiative, which involves 11 cities in the Pearl River Delta region, amongst which are Hong Kong and Shenzhen, should provide some economic stimulus to mitigate the impacts of the trade war to the region.

---

28 See the Annual Economic Report of Shenzhen, retrieved from http://www.sztj.gov.cn/xxgk/zfxxgkml/tjsj/tjgb/201804/t20180416_11765330.htm.

Chart 13.10. Exports of Goods to the World and the U.S. as a Percent of GDP: Shenzhen

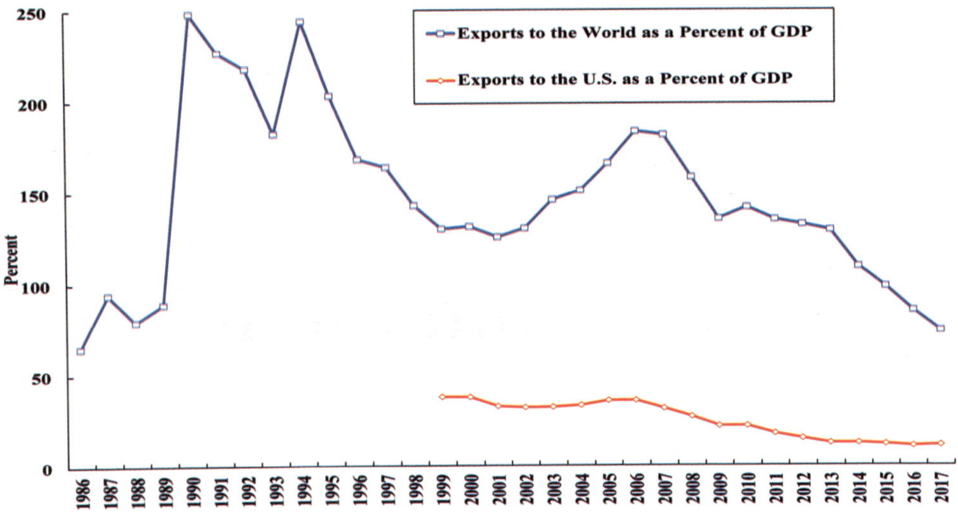

Source: Statistics Bureau of Shenzhen Municipality, China.

Even with a fall in Chinese exports of goods to the U.S. by a half, amounting to 1.7% of Chinese GDP, the total Chinese trade in goods and services, which had a surplus with the world equal to 1.71% of GDP in 2017, will still remain in balance, without taking into account any potential reduction of Chinese imports from the U.S. (see Chart 13.11). Thus, there should be little pressure for the renminbi to devalue as a result of the new U.S. tariffs from balance of payments considerations. In fact, it is probably in the best interests of the Chinese economy to maintain a relatively stable renminbi exchange rate.

Chart 13.11. Chinese Trade Surplus in Goods and Services as a Percent of GDP

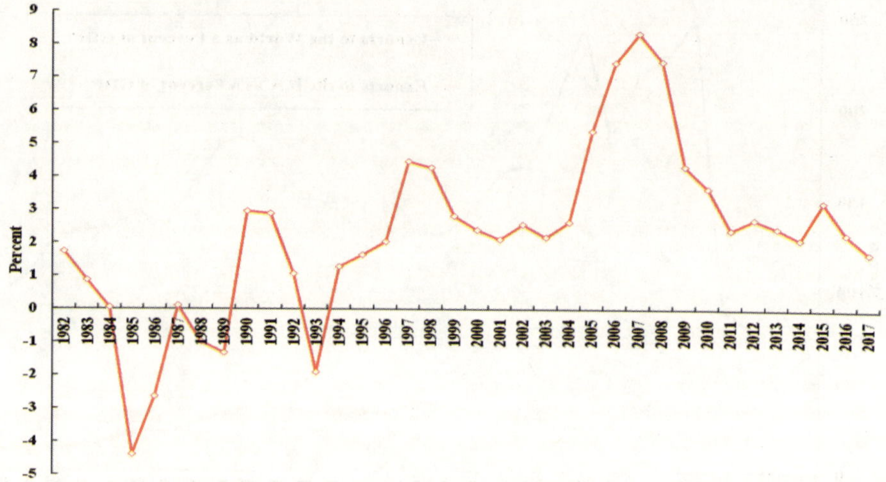

Sources: National Bureau of Statistics of China and State Administration of Foreign Exchange, the People's Republic of China.

There is a possibility that the scope of the U.S. tariffs may be expanded to cover all U.S. imports from China, in which case the full negative economic impact will be doubled to 2.24% of Chinese GDP, but still leaving the Chinese economy an expected rate of growth in excess of 4%. If this happens, it is likely that the Chinese government will undertake an economic stimulus programme focused on investments in basic infrastructure and public goods provision to mitigate the negative impacts of the trade war.

In the longer run, assuming that the tariffs continue on both sides, the U.S. importers will begin to replace Chinese imports by imports from other Asian countries such as Vietnam, Cambodia and Bangladesh, and eventually perhaps even North Korea. That is why the new tariffs against China may not lower the overall U.S. trade deficit with the world. The history of the U.S. apparel trade provides an interesting example. Between 1989 and 2017, the share of Hong Kong, Taiwan and South Korea combined in U.S. apparel imports declined from 36.9% to 1.7%, replaced by the share of Chinese imports, which rose from 11.7% to 36.6% (see Chart 13.12). With new tariffs on apparel imports from China, the Chinese share will fall sharply, to be replaced by imports from Vietnam, Cambodia, Indonesia and Bangladesh. The total U.S. apparel imports may remain more or less the same. But this shift in the sourcing of imports away from China has already been occurring since 2010, because of the rise in labour costs in China and the appreciation of the renminbi. This is similar to the earlier shift of the sources of U.S. imports of apparel from Hong Kong, South Korea and Taiwan to Mainland China. The new U.S. tariffs will accelerate this process. The ASEAN and South Asian countries may benefit, but it is really hard to predict by how much because the supply chains today are so internationalised. However, it is unlikely, in most cases, that the tariffs will stimulate new employment-generating domestic production in the U.S.[29]

Chart 13.12. The Distribution of U.S. Apparel Imports by Countries of Origin, 1989–2017

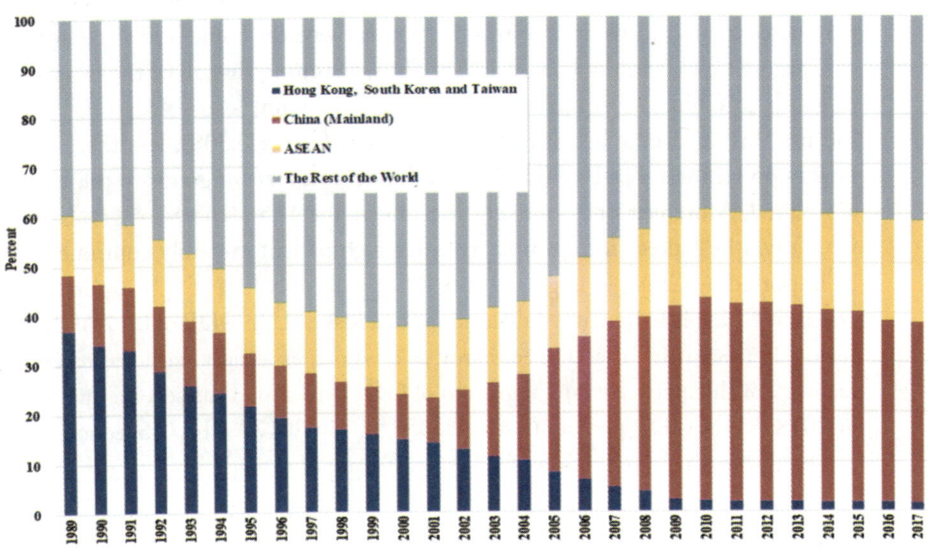

Source: Lau and Tang (2018), Chart 3.

29 While it may be possible to bring some production back to the U.S., it will be mostly through the use of automation and industrial robots, generating little actual new employment.

The Real Impacts on the U.S. Economy

China has responded to the trade war by imposing new tariffs on US$110 billion of imports from the U.S., at a rate of 25% for the first batch of US$50 billion and 10% for the second batch of US$60 billion. What are the economic impacts of these tariffs on the U.S.? The dependence of the U.S., a large continental economy with a huge domestic market in terms of purchasing power, on exports is even lower than that of China. U.S. exports of goods and services combined as a share of its GDP was 12.1% in 2017 (see Chart 13.13). Its exports of goods alone as a share of its GDP was only 8.0%. The shares of U.S. exports of goods and services and goods alone to China in U.S. GDP was 0.97% and 0.67% respectively in 2017 (see Chart 13.14), much lower than Chinese exports to the world and to the U.S. as shares of Chinese GDP.

The direct domestic value-added content of U.S. exports of goods to China may be estimated to be 50.8% in 2015, about twice the value-added content of Chinese exports to the U.S. of 25%.[30] Thus, assuming that all of the exports of goods to China are completely halted, the maximum loss in U.S. GDP in the first instance may be estimated at 0.34% (=0.67 x 0.508), less than the impact on Chinese GDP of 0.85% if all Chinese exports of goods to the U.S. are halted. Moreover, it is unlikely that all of the U.S. exports of goods to China will be halted; for example, computer chips will probably continue to be imported by China in large quantities. Suppose only half of U.S. exports of goods to China is halted, it would amount to a loss of U.S. GDP of 0.17%. This is not significant for the U.S. economy as a whole, especially with the recent recovery of the quarterly rate of growth of GDP to 4.2% in the second quarter of 2018.[31] U.S. GDP per capita was US$59,518 in 2017.[32] The U.S. economy can easily weather a reduction of 0.17% in its rate of growth.

---

30 See Chen and Wang (2016), Tables 2.6 and 2.8.

31 See https://www.bea.gov/news/2018/gross-domestic-product-2nd-quarter-2018-third-estimate-corporate-profits-2nd-quarter-2018.

32 This is calculated by dividing official U.S. GDP of 2017 by official U.S. mid-year population of 2017.

Chart 13.13. U.S. Exports of Goods and Services, and Goods Only, to the World as a Percent of GDP

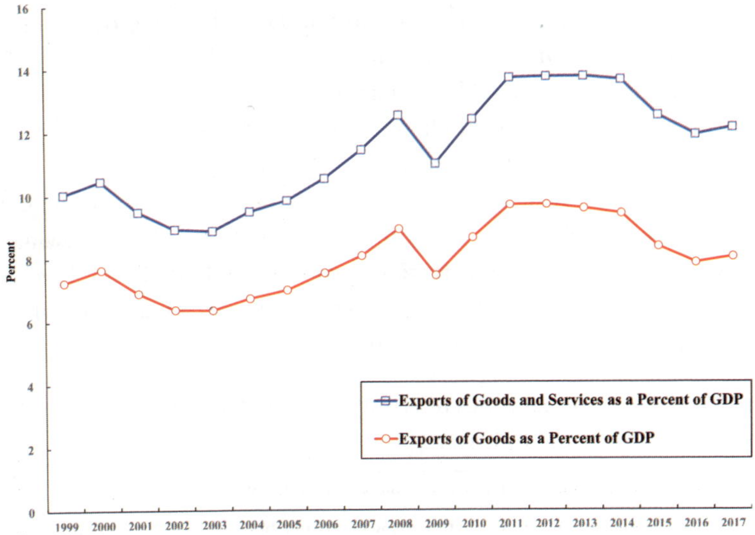

Sources: U.S. Bureau of Economic Analysis and U.S. Census Bureau.

Chart 13.14. U.S. Exports of Goods and Services, and Goods Only, to China as a Percent of U.S. GDP

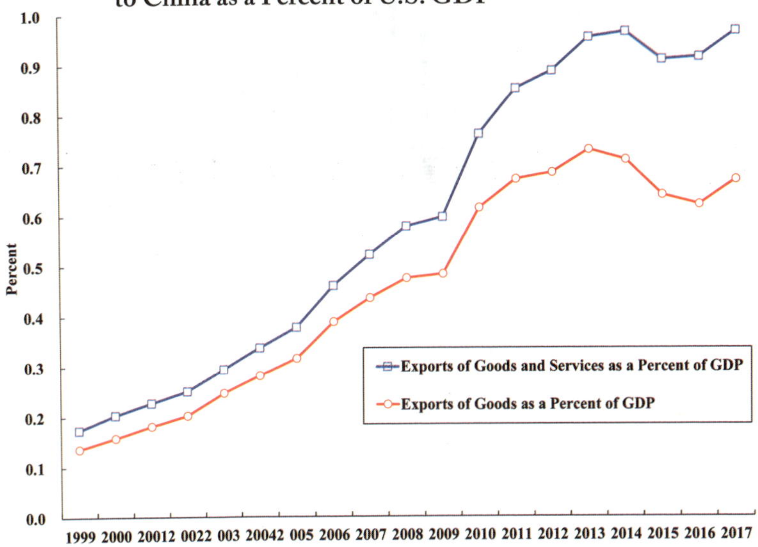

Sources: U.S. Bureau of Economic Analysis and U.S. Census Bureau.

With the indirect—that is, second-, third-, fourth- and higher-round effects of the reduction of U.S. exports of goods kicking in—the total domestic value-added (GDP) affected increases to 88.7% of the value of the reduced exports.[33] This implies ultimately a total loss in U.S. GDP of 0.30% (=0.67/2 x 0.887), assuming that half of U.S. exports to China will be halted. In absolute terms, this amounts to US$58 billion (0.30 x 19.4 trillion) in 2017 prices, less than half of the estimated Chinese loss in GDP of US$137 billion.

However, this is actually not a particularly opportune time for the U.S. to have a trade war with China. U.S. exports to China have been growing at a much higher rate than U.S. exports to the world (see Chart 13.15). This means that the huge and growing Chinese market can become a major growth point for U.S. exports if it is not interrupted by the trade war.

Chart 13.15. The Annual Rates of Growth of U.S. Exports of Goods to the World and to China

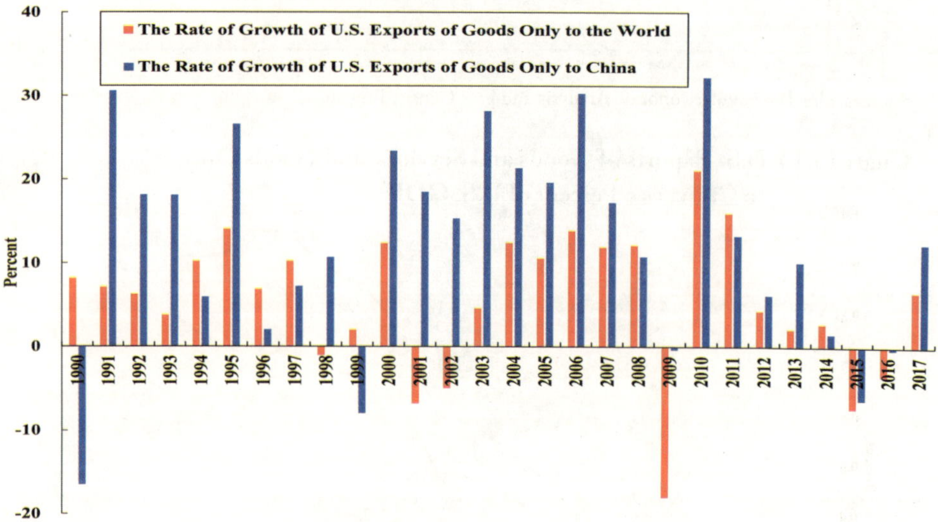

Sources: U.S. Bureau of Economic Analysis and U.S. Census Bureau.

33 See Chen and Wang (2016), Tables 2.6 and 2.8.

Imposing tariffs on Chinese exports to the U.S. is unlikely to do the trick of eliminating the U.S.-China trade deficit because of the possibility of retaliation by China, which would reduce U.S. exports to China at the same time. The problem with a trade war is that there are no real winners—both countries lose because the feasible consumption choices open to each of them are artificially restricted and reduced. Exporters in both countries will be hurt because of the reduction in their exports, and importers in both countries will see their businesses decline. And the consumers and producers who rely on imported goods and inputs in both countries will have to pay higher prices. A serious trade war, however short in duration, is disruptive in the sense that it introduces a great deal of uncertainty in future trade and investment decisions. Moreover, if agreements can be easily overturned and treaties can be readily broken, long-term trade agreements will have little credibility or usefulness. The most likely net outcome of these new country-specific tariffs is the substitution of imports from China by imports from other countries on the part of U.S. importers, and similarly by the Chinese importers. Thus, while the U.S. trade deficit with China falls, its trade deficits with other countries rise. The overall U.S. trade deficit with the world will not be significantly altered, and neither GDP nor employment in the U.S. will increase much.

Unfortunately, the trade war is not likely to end soon, certainly not before the U.S. mid-term elections to be held on 6 November 2018. The real concern is that the trade war itself may do damage to the longer-term relations between China and the U.S.

4. Longer-Term Developments

It is important to realise that there are two significant long-term developments simultaneously in play in China-U.S. relations here. The first has to do with the competition between major world powers for economic and technological dominance, and the second has to do with the rise of populist, isolationist and protectionist sentiments in the world and in particular in the U.S.

Competition for Economic and Technological Dominance

First, one of the principal causes of the current trade war between China and the United States is actually not trade itself, but the potential competition between China and the U.S. for economic and technological dominance. This competition, whether explicit or implicit, and whether intentional or not, did not begin with President Donald Trump and is not going away even after President Trump leaves office. The "pivot to Asia" and the Trans-Pacific Partnership (TPP), both policies supposedly meant to contain China, were initiated under President Barack Obama (but seemingly abandoned by President Trump). Comparison between China and the U.S., and hence implicit competition between the two major world powers, is probably unavoidable. However, such competition can potentially lead to constructive and positive, as well as destructive and negative, outcomes. For example, the competition on building the fastest super-computer in the world has already resulted in both countries producing better and faster super-computers. The champion in 2018 is the IBM Summit, a U.S. super-computer, which beat the Sunway TaihuLight, the champion in 2016 and 2017, a Chinese super-computer that was built entirely with indigenously designed chips. This is not unlike the launch of the Sputnik I satellite by the Soviet Union back in 1957, which spurred the development of science and technology in the U.S.

However, the targets of competition must be chosen carefully. There is of course no point in China and the U.S. competing in terms of total population. In fact, even China has long ago resigned to ceding the top position in population in the world to India in the mid-2030s. In terms of aggregate GDP, China went from only 20% of the U.S. GDP in 2000 to two-thirds in 2017. It is only a matter of time before the Chinese GDP catches up with the U.S. GDP, given its much larger population and much higher rate of growth, probably in the 2030s. However, in terms of GDP per capita, China is still way behind, with US$9,137 compared to almost US$60,000 for the U.S. in 2017. My own projections suggest that it will probably take until the end of the 21st century before Chinese GDP per capita approaches the U.S. level, if it does at all. In terms of the number of nuclear-armed warheads, the U.S. is way ahead by at least an order of magnitude in total and even more in per capita terms. This is not a competition that China should wish to join. However, a race to find an effective cure for cancer or Alzheimer's disease would be worthwhile for both countries and indeed for all humankind.

The competition for technological dominance has bred grievances on the part of the U.S. on intellectual property rights protection, forced transfer of technology, and cyber-theft. (Note that none of these grievances have much to do with trade per se.) Intellectual property rights protection in China has actually been vastly improved since special intellectual property courts were set up in Beijing, Shanghai and Guangzhou in 2014.[34] Economically meaningful fines have begun to be levied on violators of intellectual property rights in China. It is considered a fundamental property right for an individual or a firm to protect the core knowledge or technology. This was certainly the case in the old days in China—masters would withhold their core competence from most apprentices except their own direct lineal male descendants. As the Chinese begin to innovate on their own (China now grants the largest annual number of invention patents in the world), they themselves will demand that intellectual property rights protection be strengthened in China, and this will apply to all, not only the Chinese, patent holders. This evolution in intellectual property rights protection is no different from the past experiences of Japan and Taiwan.

Forced technology transfer has to do with the Chinese requirements for foreign direct investors in certain industries to take Chinese enterprises as equal joint-venture partners. It is perfectly understandable that General Motors does not want to share trade secrets with Ford Motors, or any other actual or potential competitor. However, the sharing of technology in a joint-venture is a voluntary one. The foreign direct investor will have to weigh the benefits of having a local joint-venture partner versus the costs. In any case, the technology used in the current manufacturing process is probably already on the way to becoming obsolete. What is more valuable is the next-generation technology that has yet to be implemented. This is what the foreign direct investor can still maintain as its own in its home factories and labouratories. This issue has now become mostly moot, as joint-ventures are no longer required of foreign direct investors by the Chinese government in many industries. For example, in the automobile manufacturing industry, Tesla has been able to establish a wholly-owned subsidiary in Shanghai to manufacture electric cars;

34 In fact, the Ministry of Commerce of the People's Republic of China revealed that Chinese enterprises paid almost US$30 billion in intellectual property royalties to U.S. companies in 2017 (*Financial Times*, 16 July 2018, p. 4). However, part of these payments may show up as service income received by Ireland or Netherlands subsidiaries of U.S. companies, instead of the U.S. companies themselves.

and even though it is now possible for General Motors to buy out its Chinese joint-venture partner, it has indicated that it does not intend to do so; and the German automobile manufacturer BMW has also announced that it will pay US$4.1 billion to buy from Brilliance China Automotive Holding Limited, its Chinese joint-venture partner, sufficient shares to give it super-majority (75%) control of its Chinese operation.[35] There are also significant liberalisation measures in the financial sector, including allowing foreign life insurance companies to have majority control and to even own 100% of their ventures in China in a year or so. These latest moves on the part of China, and the new, much shortened negative list on foreign direct investment in China, should go a long way towards eliminating the issue of forced technology transfer.

Finally, cyber-theft is an issue that requires the cooperation of both governments to solve. The solution should be a vigorous prosecution of the criminal perpetrators on both sides. I believe instances of state-sanctioned commercial cyber-theft are rare, even though state-sponsored espionage is a game played by everyone. However, one cannot rule out free-lancers being engaged and financed by private individuals and firms, and they need to be identified and prosecuted to the fullest extent possible.

Trade in high-technology products and in technology itself, including cross-border investment in high-technology firms, will probably remain problematic as long as there are considerations of both technological competition and national security. The U.S. government has long restricted the exports of high-technology products to China. It has also discouraged the use of Huawei servers and cell phones in the U.S. For the same national security reasons, the Chinese government may also eventually decide that it is risky to rely on U.S. high-technology products. It is interesting to note that mobile telephones, including Apple iPhones, are at the present time exempted from the list of Chinese export products subject to the new U.S. tariffs. The potential mutual standoff is likely to lead to de facto protection in both countries, to the benefit of their respective domestic monopolistic producers. But it will also encourage and incentivise indigenous technological development in China. China is in the process of acceding to the WTO Agreement on Government Procurement

35 "BMW Makes US$4.1b Push for Control in China's Car Market." Bloomberg, 11 October 2018.

(GPA), which would allow foreign enterprises to bid for Chinese government procurement contracts. It is uncertain whether Chinese accession to the GPA would benefit U.S. enterprises, but it is a further step in the opening of the Chinese economy and should at least improve the overall atmosphere.

The Rise of Populism, Isolationism, and Protectionism

Second, the rise of populist, isolationist and protectionist sentiments in the U.S. and elsewhere in the world will also have significant impacts on international trade and investment (and migration too). President Donald Trump did not create these sentiments, but he has been able to tap into them and exploited them very effectively. The root cause is that while economic globalisation (and innovation) have benefitted all countries in the world, including both China and the U.S., the economic benefits have not been widely shared within each country, resulting in the emergence of losers. In principle, there is sufficient overall gain to be shared so that no one needs to lose, but the free market alone cannot and will not make it happen. Thus, there are people who have been left behind and whose well-being has not improved for the past two, three or even four decades. In the meantime, the income distribution has become more unequal in every country. The abnormally low rate of interest during the past decade did not help. The losers believe that the government and the elite establishment have failed them and they are eager to try something else, anything. It is easy to lay the blame on globalisation—in other words, on the foreigners—and become isolationist and protectionist.

In addition, it is natural and instinctive for any individual to entertain the feeling of "us" versus "them." Most people believe that all deals are zero-sum, that is, "more for them is less for us, and vice versa." It is therefore a revelation to many that voluntary trade between two countries benefits both—that is, it is in fact win-win. Unfortunately, it will take a while before the public at large realises that protectionism is a lose-lose proposition. The eventual solution has to be some form of redistribution within each country—taxing the winners to compensate the losers so that everyone wins.

President Donald Trump believes that every deal is zero sum—one country's gain must be another country's loss. Moreover, he also believes that the U.S. can achieve much better trade deals by negotiating bilaterally with each single country, taking full advantage of the size and power of the

U.S., including the fact that the U.S. dollar has to be used as an international medium of exchange by almost every country. President Trump would like to modify the existing distribution of gains from trade between the U.S. and its trading-partner countries by making full use of the relative bargaining power of the U.S. and he believes that this would work the best in a bilateral rather than multilateral context.[36]

5. The Promotion of Greater Mutual Economic Interdependence

A better way to narrow the U.S. trade deficit with China is for the U.S. to increase its exports of goods and services to China, especially newly created goods and services, for example, by producing and exporting meat (beef, pork and poultry) instead of feed grains (corn and soybeans) to China, and exporting the newly developed liquefied natural gas from Alaska and shale oil and gas from the continental U.S. Chinese demands for food and energy will continue to be high and rising for many years. These U.S. exports will lead to genuine increases in GDP and employment in the U.S. because they will consist of new production rather than simple re-direction of existing production. They will also enhance economic well-being in both China and the U.S.[37] However, for both potential U.S. producers and Chinese importers, long-term contracts with credible enforcement mechanisms are necessary in order that both supplies in the U.S. and demands in China are forthcoming and sustained. Another fast-growing component of U.S. exports of services to China that has huge potential for further expansion is education and tourism. The expenditures of Chinese students (currently totalling 350,000, not including the many teenagers enrolled in the summer and winter camps) and tourists in the U.S. have been rising rapidly. Moreover, their presence in the U.S. can enhance the understanding between the Chinese and American peoples and improve long-term ties. U.S. students and tourists in China can also play the same role.

Through these trade transactions and cultural and educational exchanges, it is possible to promote a degree of economic interdependence between the

36 More simply put, a large country does not have to be a price-taker internationally.
37 See the discussion in Lau (2018a).

two countries. China can become the largest customer of U.S. energy, food and educational services exports and the U.S. can become China's most important supplier in these areas. A further area of significant potential win-win collabouration is the deployment of the excess Chinese savings in the U.S. for the financing of the renovation and upgrading of U.S. basic infrastructure[38] and the augmentation of the equity capital of U.S. corporations,[39] especially as Chinese households begin to diversify their wealth portfolios overseas.

One of President Trump's grievances is that the U.S. has not benefitted enough from China-U.S. economic relations, while China has reaped most of the benefits. However, it is difficult to assess which country has benefitted more. Clearly both countries have benefitted. China has been able to lift 600 million of its citizens out of poverty, initially through the vast expansion of export-oriented light-manufacturing jobs in the coastal provinces. The U.S. consumers have benefitted from two decades of low prices for their consumer goods because of imports from China. Research shows that had the share of U.S. imports from China remained at 1994 levels, the U.S. Consumer Price Index would have been 27% higher in 2017, or approximately one percentage point higher annually.[40] The lowered rate of inflation has helped to enable a lower rate of interest in the U.S. It has also helped to reduce the living expenses of middle– and low-income households in the U.S. The reduced price of non-oil consumer goods in the U.S. has resulted in an estimated average annual savings for U.S. consumers of US$623 billion between 1994 and 2016, approximately 12% of the average annual U.S. non-oil consumer expenditure during the same period.[41]

Whether the U.S.-China trade deficit is a benefit or a cost to the U.S. is not as clear-cut as it may seem. The cumulative U.S.-China trade deficit from 1999 to 2017 amounted to US$2.6 trillion (US$220 billion in 2017)

---

38 This can be done through Chinese purchases of long-term project bonds. The Committee on Foreign Investment in the United States (CFIUS) should not have to worry about these portfolio investments. In any case, the infrastructure projects are located in the U.S. and under the control and management of U.S. entities.

39 This can take the form of Chinese Depositary Receipts (CDRs) issued by U.S. corporations and traded on the Chinese stock exchanges.

40 See Lau and Tang (2018).

41 Ibid.

according to Chinese official data. The traditional mercantilist view is that China has greatly benefitted at the expense of the U.S. However, the modern financial view is that the U.S. has greatly benefitted all these years because all it has managed to trade are pieces of paper that it can print at will (U.S. dollars and U.S. Treasury bonds) at almost zero marginal cost in exchange for real goods and services from China. China has kept most of the pieces of paper in its official foreign exchange reserves, approximately US$3 trillion at year-end 2017.[42] It is a tremendous U.S. advantage that no other country has! The U.S. has been able to do so because of the U.S. dollar's position as the only major international medium of exchange and store of value (this is the seigneurage earned by the U.S.).

Additional benefits for the U.S. include the profits of U.S. corporations earned by their operations in China, such as General Motors and Walmart. The sales of Apple iPhones in China (since they are finally assembled within China) are not considered U.S. exports to China, but the bulk of the profits accrues to Apple. These U.S. corporations are clearly the beneficiaries of China-U.S. economic exchanges. Their profits will show up as "factor income from abroad" in U.S. national income accounts if they are repatriated to the U.S. However, if the profits are not repatriated to the U.S., but are credited to subsidiaries of these corporations in third countries such as Ireland and the Netherlands, they will show up as incomes for the third countries instead. Similarly, royalties and license fees paid to U.S. corporations such as Apple and Qualcomm are considered U.S. exports of services. However, such payments to their third-country subsidiaries are no longer U.S. exports of services, but the exports of services to China from these third countries. The official statistics on bilateral trade in services probably understate the true level of U.S. exports of services to China because of the use of these subsidiaries in third-country tax havens by U.S. corporations to receive payments of royalties and license fees. Finally, there are also potential opportunities for China and the U.S. to cooperate on initiatives of global interest, such as the prevention of climate change, space exploration, and development of a common and universal 5G standard.

---

42 As of mid-2018, Chinese official foreign exchange reserves included more than US$1.3 trillion of U.S. Treasury and Agency securities. See http://ticdata.treasury.gov/Publish/slt3d.txt and http://ticdata.treasury.gov/Publish/slt1d.txt.

Both countries can win. The successful conclusion of the Paris Agreement in 2015 is an excellent example of what China and the U.S. can accomplish if they cooperate and work together.

6. Concluding Remarks

When will the current trade war end? Since the current trade war is lose-lose, it is in the interests of both China and the U.S. to try to end it soon. Thus, it should and will end eventually, but probably not before the mid-term elections in the U.S. on 6 November 2018. The U.S. President will need to be able to declare victory in the trade war[43] and China will need to maintain that it has not capitulated to U.S. pressure.

Domestically, the Chinese government should ensure that the workers affected by the trade war are adequately supported with subsistence allowance and retraining grants. Moreover, it should also increase aggregate demand on the margin through additional infrastructural investments, and public goods consumption such as environmental preservation, protection and restoration, education, health care and elderly care.

More generally, it is important that all losers from economic globalisation and innovation in China be adequately compensated. Everyone should be able to share in the gains from economic globalisation and innovation. Thus far, even though the distribution of income in China has become much more unequal in recent years, complaints are relatively few as yet because everyone has gained significantly, albeit to varying degrees, from the policies of economic reform and opening that started in 1978. However, as light manufacturing jobs begin to move away from China to South and Southeast Asia, rising domestic discontent can be expected in the absence of an adequate social safety net, satisfactory public goods provision, and an effective redistributive policy.

Our analysis shows that while the real impacts of the trade war on both the Chinese and U.S. economies are definitely negative, they are relatively

43 It is possible to do so on the basis of the recent Chinese liberalisation of the rules on direct investment, the shortened Chinese negative list on direct investment, strengthened enforcement of intellectual property rights by China, and any new long-term trade deals that have been agreed and signed.

small and certainly manageable by both countries. The annual losses in GDP as a result of the trade war may be estimated to be US$137 billion for China and US$58 billion for the U.S. in 2017 prices. Compared to their respective GDPs of US$12.2 trillion and US$19.4 trillion in 2017, these are relatively small numbers for both economies, especially for the U.S. Even the Chinese economy, with its much lower GDP per capita, can readily weather the impacts of the trade war. There is no need to panic. The sky is not falling!

However, there are also longer-term underlying forces at work in China-U.S. relations. The competition between China and the U.S., whether friendly or unfriendly, can be assumed to be an on-going and long-term one. To reduce the probability of an armed conflict between China and the U.S. down the road, both countries should promote greater mutual economic interdependence, to make their relations win-win, so that a war between them would be unthinkable, just as another war between France and Germany is not possible today.

It is difficult to predict how things will end up. China and the rest of the world, except possibly the U.S., will probably continue to uphold the current multilateral trading system under the WTO. After all, they have all benefitted and will continue to benefit from it. This is actually the time for China to continue opening its economy to both international trade and investment, both inbound and outbound. It can lower tariffs unilaterally to all countries not engaged in a trade war with China. It should understand that international trade and cross-border direct investment are always win-win, and that competition, both domestic and international, improves efficiency and encourages innovation. It should therefore try to be as inclusive as possible in terms of its international economic relations.

It is important for China's economic relations with the rest of the world, in particular with the European Union, Japan, the ASEAN and Russia, to be carefully managed going forward. However, China-U.S. relations are concerned with more than just economics, and must be even more carefully managed in the future.

References

Chen, Xikang, Lawrence J. Lau, Junjie Tang, and Yanyan Xiong. "New and Revised Estimates of the China-U.S. Trade Balance." Working Paper, Lau Chor Tak

Institute of Global Economics and Finance, The Chinese University of Hong Kong, October 2018.

Chen, Xikang, and Huijuan Wang. *Touru zhanyong chanchu jishu* 投入佔用產出技術 (Input-output-occupancy techniques). Beijing: Kexue chubanshe (Scientific Publishing Co.), 2016.

Lau, Lawrence J. "The Sky Isn't Falling." *ICBC Economic Review* no. 305 (September–October 1998), pp. 1–12; translated into Chinese as "Tian ta bu xia lai 天塌不下來," *Jingji shehui tizhi bijiao* 經濟社會體制比較 no. 4 (June 1998), pp. 6–9.

———. "The Sky is Not Falling on China's Economy." *China Daily*, 30 September 2015.

———. "A Better Alternative to a Trade War." *China and the World: Ancient and Modern Silk Road* 1, no. 2 (2018), pp. 1–13.

———. *The China-U.S. Trade War and Future Economic Relations*. Hong Kong: The Chinese University Press, 2019.

Lau, Lawrence J., and Junjie Tang. "The Impact of U.S. Imports from China on U.S. Consumer Prices and Expenditures." Working Paper No. 66, Lau Chor Tak Institute of Global Economics and Finance, The Chinese University of Hong Kong, April 2018.

Chapter 14.

Chinese Economy in the New Era*

1. Introduction

The New Era

What is the meaning of the "new era"? The new era refers specifically to present-day China. Three distinct eras may be distinguished in the history of the People's Republic of China since its establishment in 1949:

(1) 1949–1978, the Mao Zedong Era, during which the People's Republic of China was established and consolidated;

(2) 1979–2012, the Deng Xiaoping Era,[1] during which economic reform was undertaken and the Chinese economy was opened to the world; and

(3) 2013–present, the Xi Jinping Era, during which China was transformed from a moderately well-off to a modernised, strong and wealthy nation.

Today, China is already the second largest economy in the world. At its current average annual rate of growth of approximately 6%, it is expected to catch up with and overtake the U.S. to become the world's largest economy

---

* This chapter was originally published in *Pacific Economic Review* 24, no. 2 (May 2019), pp. 187–207. The author wishes to thank Prof. Albert E. Dien, Mrs. Ayesha Macpherson Lau and Prof. Yanyan Xiong for their insightful comments and suggestions, and Mr. Junjie Tang and Mr. Ting-Hin Yan for their able research assistance. The author retains sole responsibility for all remaining errors.

1 While Deng Xiaoping passed away in 1997, this era can still be referred to as the Deng Era, because his policies of reform and opening were continued, and the two senior leaders that followed Deng, Jiang Zemin and Hu Jintao, were both chosen by him.

some time before 2035. Nevertheless, even then, Chinese real GDP per capita, at a projected US$20,000 in 2017 prices, will still be less than one-quarter of the projected then U.S. real GDP per capita.

In the new era, the principal driving force of the economy is the contradiction between "unbalanced and inadequate development" of the economy and "the people's ever-growing need for a better life." The economic tasks in the "new era" are aimed at enabling the economy to better serve the people's needs. Thus, the Chinese government will undertake to deepen reform, widen opening, and enhance quality. It is also expected to share prosperity and reduce risks to the economy. The Deng Era was one in which some of the people would become wealthy first. In the Xi Era, all people will become wealthy together. In the Thirteenth Five-Year (2016–2020) Plan, the only mandatory targets have to do with the preservation, protection and restoration of the environment and the alleviation and elimination of poverty. In the Xi Era, the economic policies will be people-centric. A modern socialist market economy with Chinese characteristics will be established under the leadership and stewardship of the Communist Party of China.

The Chinese Economy in 2017

We begin with a brief review of the Chinese economy in 2017. The rate of growth of real GDP was 6.9%, its first year-on-year increase since 2011 (See Chart 14.1). (The rate of growth of real GDP in the first quarter of 2018 was 6.8%). This signals the end of the vertical portion and the beginning of the horizontal portion of the "L-shaped" recovery. The monthly rates of growth of the real value-added of the Chinese industrial sector also confirm that the rates of growth of the economy have stabilised and are no longer declining (see Chart 14.2). The rate of growth of the consumer price index (CPI) was 1.6% compared to 2% in 2016. In contrast, the producer price index (PPI) increased by 6.3%, the first increase in years, indicating that the reduction of excess production capacities had begun to have some success.

Chart 14.1. Quarterly Rates of Growth of Chinese Real GDP, Year-on-Year (Percent)

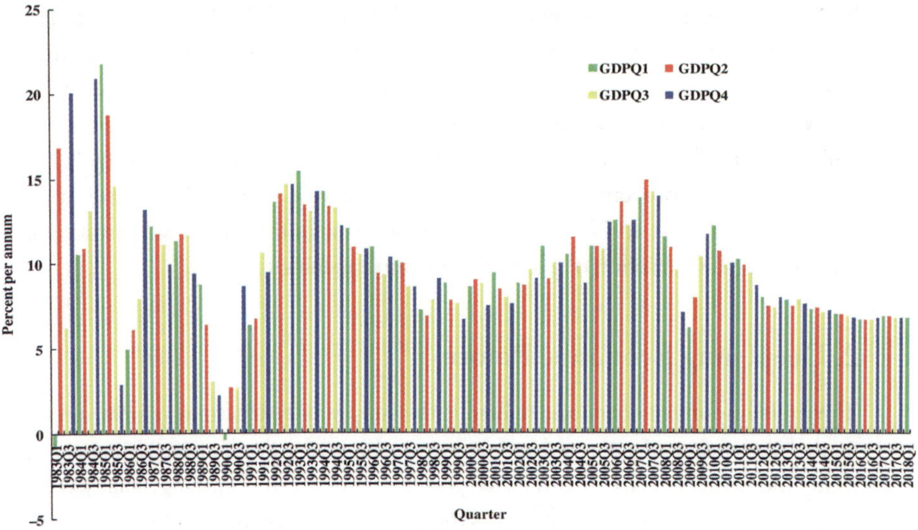

Source: National Bureau of Statistics of China (available from http://data.stats.gov.cn/easyquery.htm?cn=B01).

Chart 14.2. The Monthly Rates of Growth of Real Value-Added of Chinese Industry, Year-on-Year (Percent)

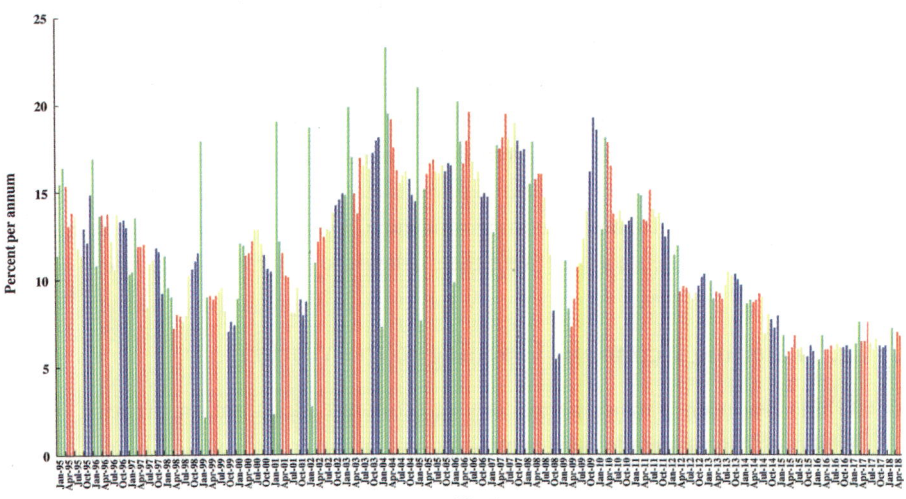

Source: National Bureau of Statistics of China (available from http://data.stats.gov.cn/easyquery.htm?cn=A01 and http://www.stats.gov.cn/tjsj/zxfb/201806/t20180614_1604530.html).

In 2017, employment increased by more than 13 million. The urban unemployment rate at year-end was 4.98%. The disposable income per capita increased by 7.3%, more than the growth of real GDP and real GDP per capita. The renminbi exchange rate remained stable. The level of official foreign exchange reserves was little changed, amounting to US$3.14 trillion at year-end 2017, equivalent to almost one and a half years' worth of annual imports (US$2.21 trillion in 2017). The energy consumed per unit of real GDP declined by 3.7%, indicating an improvement in the quality of growth. The capacity utilisation rate in industry rose to 77%, reflecting the progress in the supply side structural reform and the reduction of excess production capacities.

2. Deepening Economic Reform

The most important economic reform is the supply side structural reform, aimed at the prevention of new and reduction of old excess production capacities in many industries (steel, cement, plate glass, aluminium, shipbuilding, solar panels and coal mining) and the rationalisation of the so-called "zombie enterprises." The reform is also aimed at enabling the market to play the decisive role. However, this requires changes in the key performance indicators of local party and government officials, away from the exclusive emphasis on the growth of real GDP and employment. It also requires cooperation and collabouration across local governments. In particular, it requires the central government to step up to vigorously prevent protectionism at the local level. In principle, Chinese local governments cannot impose any restrictions on the inflow and outflow of goods and services to and from their jurisdictions. In reality, they use their power of permit issuance to practice de facto local protectionism, which is totally illegal according to Chinese law. The central government must also formulate, enact and use anti-trust laws to intervene to prevent monopolistic or oligopolistic practices and keep the markets competitive if the market is to play the decisive role.

3. Widening Economic Opening to the World

China has been a major beneficiary of economic globalisation. At least 600 million Chinese people have been lifted out of poverty through Chinese economic reform and opening since 1978 (see the discussion in part 5 below). A study of Chinese history indicated that the closing of the borders in the

Ming and Qing dynasties (and in the early years of the People's Republic of China) was in retrospect a huge mistake. China failed to take advantage of its then comparative advantages. (Of course, the forced imports of opium by Great Britain in the 19th century was another issue.) Japan's opening to the world since the Meiji Restoration of 1868 enabled its rapid development into a modern nation. China was left far behind. Isolationism and protectionism have repeatedly proved to be failed ideas.

Today, 40 years after the beginning of economic reform and opening up, China is already the most important trading partner of many countries and regions (see Table 14.1). However, Chinese exports comprise only a relatively small percentage, less than 15%, of Chinese GDP, similar to other large economies such as the U.S., Japan and India (see Chart 14.3). What this means is that while Chinese exports and imports may experience large fluctuations as in many other economies, its GDP remains relatively stable, in contrast to the other smaller economies (see Chart 14.4–14.6). In other words, the Chinese economy today is not too vulnerable to external disturbances, including those possibly caused by a trade war.

Table 14.1. The Ranks of China as Trading Partner of Asia-Pacific Countries/Regions and Vice Versa, 2017

Country/Region	China Rank as Trading Partner of Country/Region	Rank of Country/Region as Trading Partner of China
Australia	1	7
Brunei	4	125
Cambodia	1	63
Hong Kong	1	3
Indonesia	1	17
Japan	1	2
Korea	1	4
Laos	2	85
Macau	1	81
Malaysia	1	9
Myanmar	1	44
New Zealand	1	41
Philippines	1	20
Singapore	1	14
Taiwan	1	5
Thailand	1	13
U.K.	3	15
U.S.	1	1
Vietnam	1	8

Chart 14.3. Exports of Goods and Services as a Share of GDP in Selected Economies

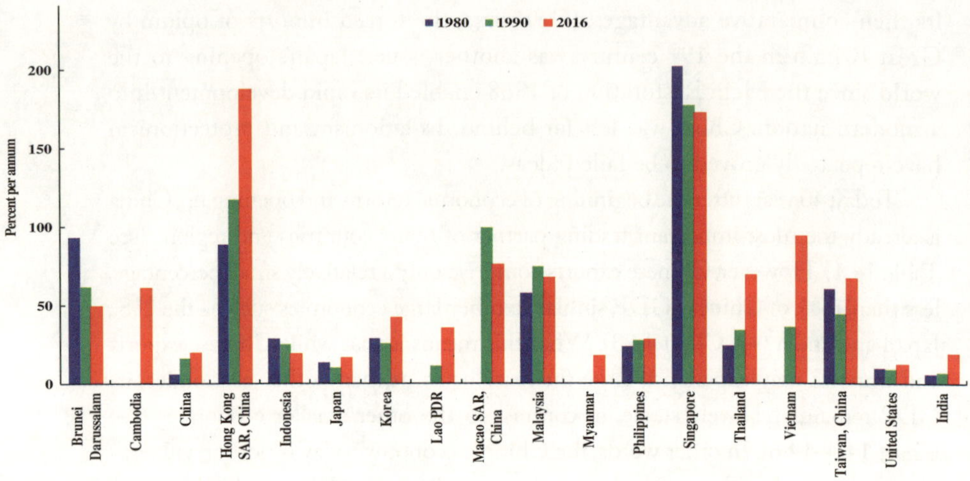

Source: World Development Indicators, The World Bank; Data for Taiwan, China are from https://eng.stat.gov.tw/mp.asp?mp=5.

Chart 14.4. Quarterly Rates of Growth of Exports of Goods: Selected Asian Economies

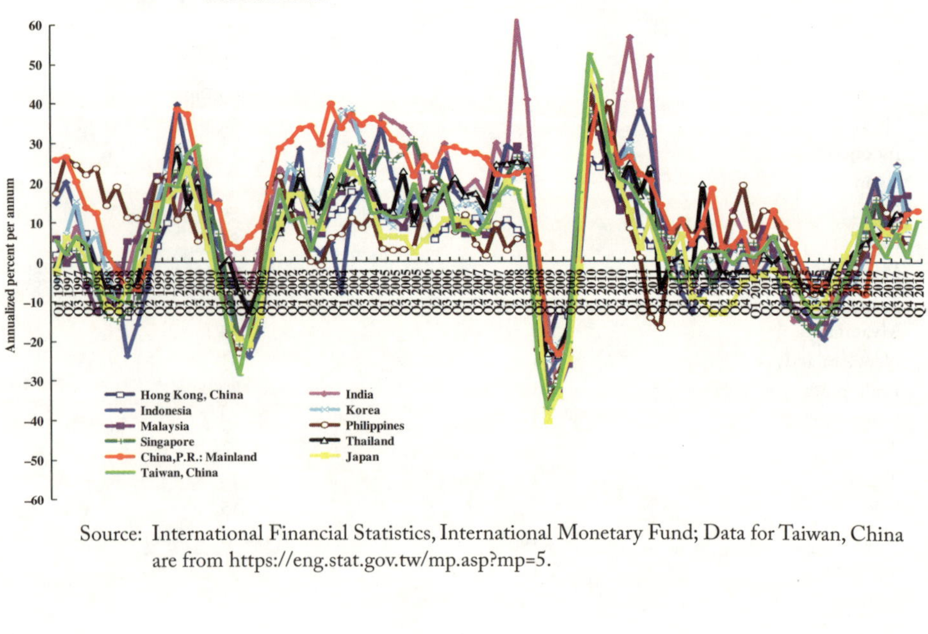

Source: International Financial Statistics, International Monetary Fund; Data for Taiwan, China are from https://eng.stat.gov.tw/mp.asp?mp=5.

Chart 14.5. Quarterly Rates of Growth of Imports of Goods: Selected Asian Economies

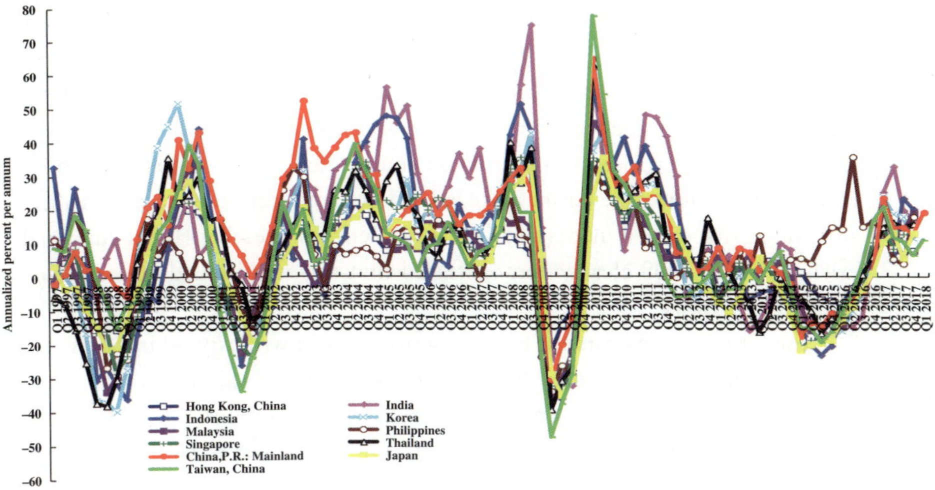

Source: International Financial Statistics, International Monetary Fund; Data for Taiwan, China are from https://eng.stat.gov.tw/mp.asp?mp=5.

Chart 14.6. Quarterly Rates of Growth of Real GDP, Year-on-Year: Selected Asian Economies

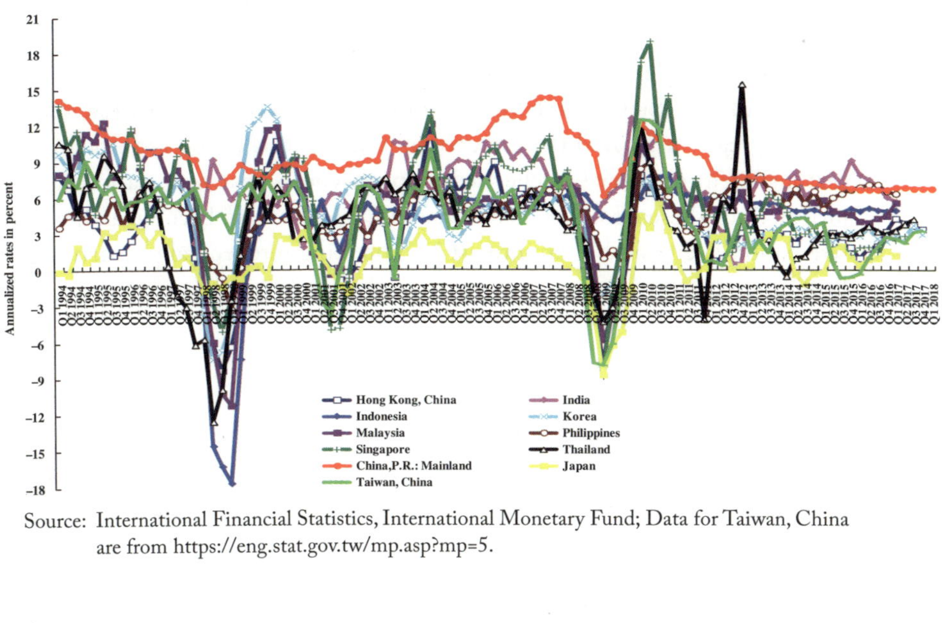

Source: International Financial Statistics, International Monetary Fund; Data for Taiwan, China are from https://eng.stat.gov.tw/mp.asp?mp=5.

Opening its economy wider serves Chinese interests. With a national savings rate exceeding 40%, China continues to have substantial excess national savings. China wishes to continue to benefit from technology transfer, which has begun to be more two-way. Competition from foreign firms can exert pressure on Chinese enterprises in Chinese markets and help to prevent the emergence of monopolies and quasi-monopolies, thus making Chinese enterprises more efficient, more quality-conscious, and more competitive. However, China, like all other large economies, can readily survive on its own if necessary. The experience since the global financial crisis of 2007–2008 clearly demonstrated that this was indeed the case (see Chart 14.4–14.6).

The Chinese government has announced that it will expand imports and reduce tariffs (e.g., on automobiles). Customs revenue is already a very small percentage of the total revenue of the central government. Many Chinese manufacturing enterprises are already among the largest in the world. They are no longer "infants" that need protection from imports. China aims to balance its international trade in goods and services and not to maintain a surplus. China will also continue to liberalise the rules for foreign direct investment into China and improve the investment environment, including allowing majority- and wholly-owned foreign enterprises in both financial and manufacturing sectors (e.g., insurance, securities brokerage, and automobile manufacturing). This will make the complaints about "forced technology transfer" moot as foreign direct investors no longer need to take local partners if they do not wish to do so. China has in the last few years already greatly improved the protection of intellectual property through its establishment of special intellectual property courts that have nation-wide jurisdiction. These efforts will continue as China has also become an inventive nation itself and has an interest in protecting intellectual property and facilitating innovation.

4. Enhancing the Quality of Growth

The focus of the Chinese economy going forward will be on the quality of growth rather than the quantity of growth. It means growth with an emphasis on environmental protection and preservation, and the restoration of green mountains, blue skies and clear waters in China. It also means growth that is innovation-driven rather than input-driven. It means more competitive markets through the regulation of monopolies and quasi-monopolies and the use of anti-trust laws. It means growth with an emphasis on product safety, especially in food and drugs. It also means growth with a more equitable distribution (and redistribution) of income, through the alleviation of poverty and the provision of public goods (including, in addition to the environment, education, health care and elderly care) and reform of the wage determination mechanism. The problem of the status of long-term migrant workers in the urban areas will also have a permanent solution through the revision of household registration rules.

Increasing Energy Efficiency

One measure of energy efficiency is the energy used per unit real GDP. In Chart 14.7, we compare the energy-GDP ratios of China, Japan and the United States in terms of million joules per unit real GDP in 2010 U.S. dollars.[2] It is clear that China has been improving its energy efficiency over time, which implies that overall carbon emission per unit real GDP is being steadily reduced. However, China still has significant room to improve, compared to Japan and the U.S. By 2020, the Chinese economy will still use more energy per unit GDP than both the U.S. and Japan (although part of this is due to the higher shares of the service sector, which uses much less energy, in the GDPs of Japan and the U.S.). However, China is committed to an absolute reduction of its carbon emissions around 2030, in accordance with the 2016 Paris Climate Agreement, and should continue to make progress beyond 2020.

2 The joule is a unit of energy and is equal to 0.000948 of the more familiar BTU (British Thermal Unit).

Chart 14.7. Final Energy Consumption/GDP Ratio for China, Japan, and the U.S. (million joules/2010 US$)

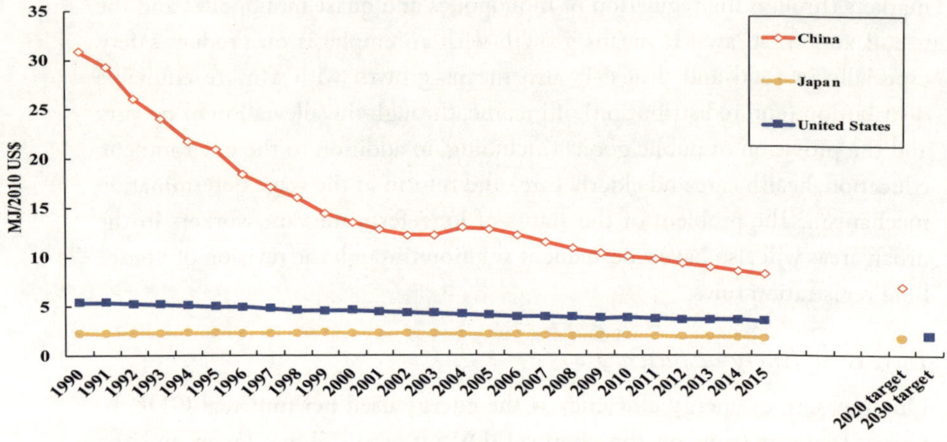

Reduction of Pollution

Another measure of the quality of economic growth is the quantity of PM 2.5 particles in the air of major urban centres. In Chart 14.8, we present the incidence of PM 2.5 particles in Beijing between 2013 and 2018. Here we can see from the data the gradual improvement in air quality in Beijing. It still has a considerable way to go. However, as the quality of air has become a mandatory key performance indicator in the Thirteenth Five-Year Plan, it will likely continue to improve over time, not only in Beijing, but in all major urban centres.

Promoting Innovation

Investment in intangible capital (human capital and Research and Development [R&D] capital) is indispensable for innovation. The annual expenditures on R&D as percentages of GDP are presented for selected economies in Chart 14.8, which shows that the U.S. has consistently invested a relatively high percentage of its GDP in R&D, averaging 2.5% since 1963. Even though the East Asian economies, including Mainland China, have lagged behind, they have been catching up fast, with the exception of Hong Kong. China is expected to reach its R&D expenditure target of 2.5%

Chart 14.8. The Incidence of PM 2.5 in Beijing: Daily Data from 2013M2 to 2018M4

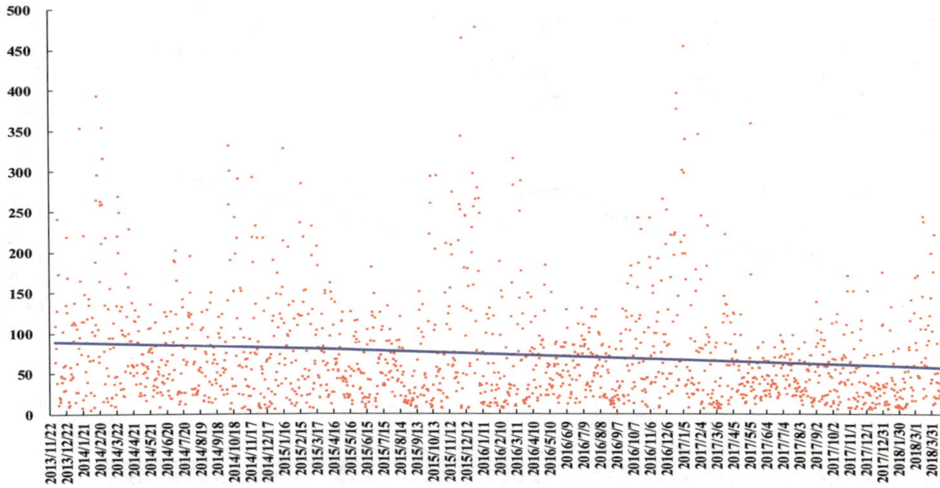

Source: www.aqistudy.cn (available from https://www.aqistudy.cn/historydata/monthdata.php?city=%E5%8C%97%E4%BA%AC)

of GDP in 2020, approximately the same as the average U.S. share in the past. However, it will still be below the expected or targeted levels of the European countries, Japan and South Korea.

One indicator of the potential for innovation is the number of patents granted each year. In Chart 14.9, the number of patents granted in the United States each year to the nationals of different countries, including the U.S. itself, over time is presented. The U.S. is the undisputed champion over the past 40 years, with 140,969 patents granted in 2015, followed by Japan, with 52,409. (Since these are patents granted in the U.S., the U.S. may have a home advantage; however, for all the other countries and regions, the comparison across them should be fair.) The number of patents granted to Mainland Chinese applicants each year has increased from the single-digit levels prior to the mid-1980s to 8,166 in 2015. The economies of South Korea and Taiwan, granted 17,924 and 11,690 U.S. patents respectively in 2015, were far ahead of Mainland China. In contrast, the number of U.S. patents granted to Hong Kong residents was only 601 in 2015.

Chart 14.9. R&D Expenditures as a Share of GDP and Their Target Levels for 2020: Selected Economies

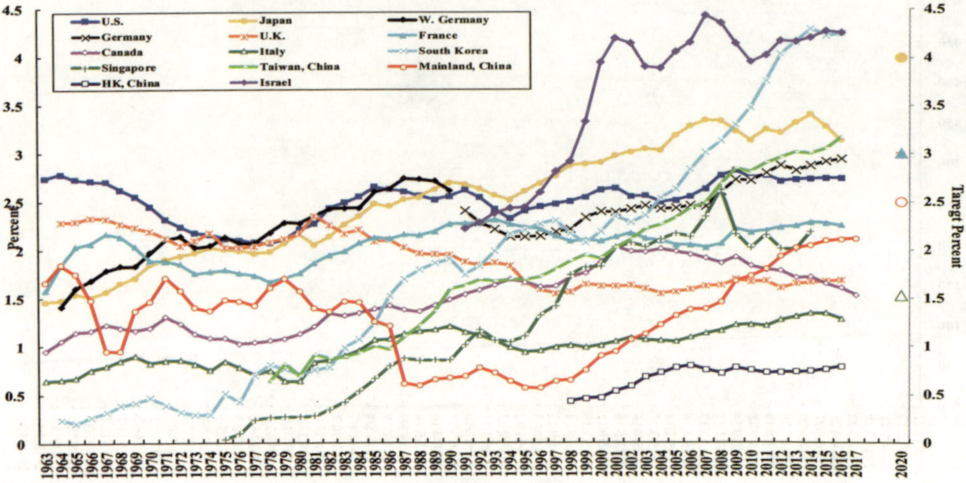

Source: Lau and Xiong (2018).

Chart 14.10. Patents Granted in the U.S.: Selected Economies

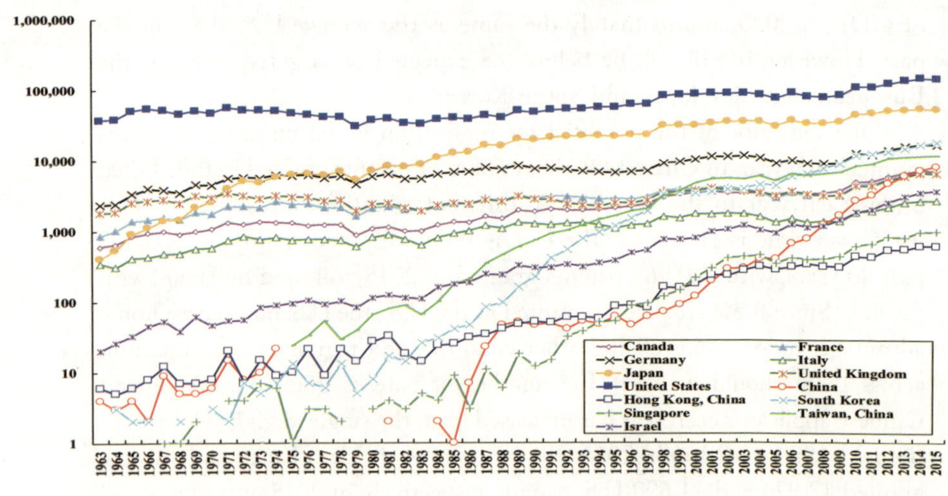

Source: Lau and Xiong (2018).

The R&D capital stock, defined as the cumulative past real expenditures on R&D less depreciation of 10% per year, is a useful indicator of innovative capacity. R&D expenditure should quite properly be treated as investment since R&D efforts generally take years to yield any positive results. The R&D capital stock can be shown to have a direct and positive causal relationship with the number of patents granted (see Chart 14.10, in which the annual number of U.S. patents granted is plotted against the R&D capital stock of that year for each selected economy). Chart 14.10 shows clearly that the higher the stock of R&D capital of an economy, the higher is the number of patents granted to it by the U.S.

However, in order for breakthrough discovery or invention to be made, there must be significant investment in basic research. Basic research is by definition patient and long-term research. The rate of return on basic research, at any reasonable discount rate, will be low. It must therefore be financed by either the government or non-profit institutions, and not by for-profit firms. The atomic and hydrogen bombs, nuclear reactors, the internet, packets transmission technology and the browser are all outcomes of basic research done many years ago, often with government support. However, Chinese investment in basic research has remained low relative to the other major countries (see Chart 14.11). China has been devoting only 5% of its R&D expenditures to basic research, compared to the more than 15% of the U.S. and the more than 10% of Germany, Israel, Japan and Russia. China must increase its expenditure on basic research if it aspires to be a global leader in science and technology.

Chart 14.11. U.S. Patents Granted and R&D Capital Stocks: Selected Economies

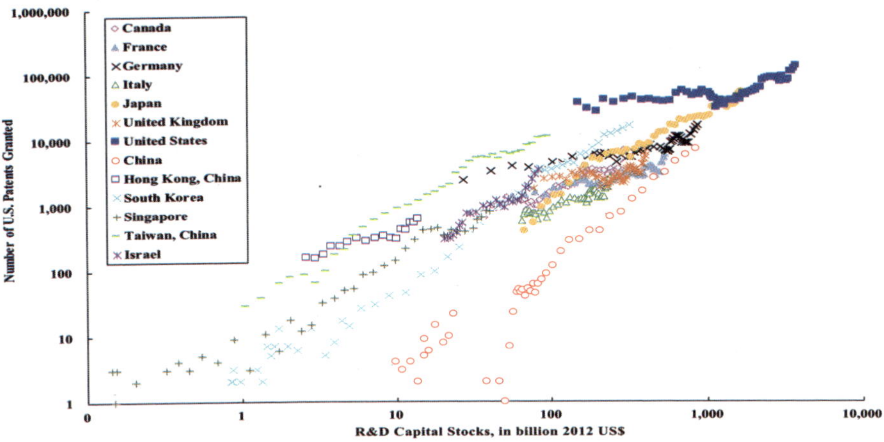

Source: Lau and Xiong (2018).

Chart 14.12. Basic Research Expenditure as a Share of Total R&D Expenditure: Selected Economies

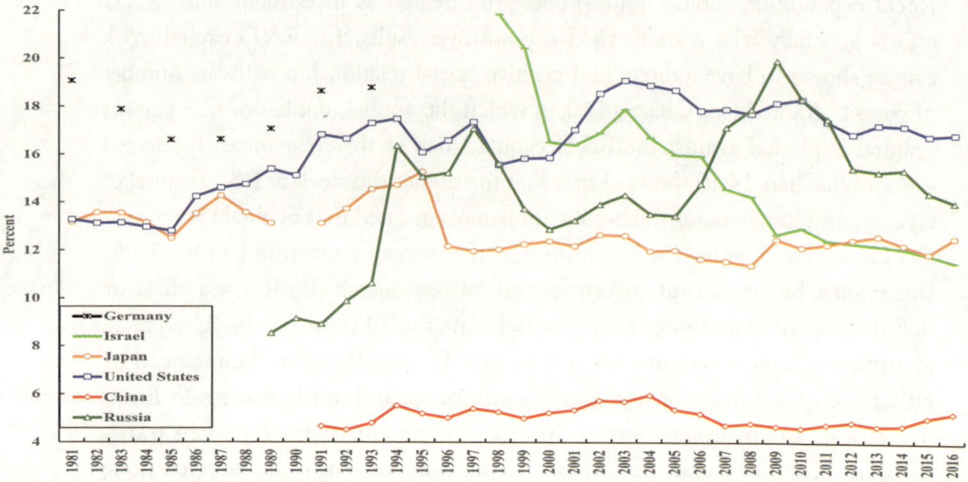

Source: Lau and Xiong (2018).

5. Sharing of Prosperity

The distribution of income in the Chinese economy is a separate issue altogether. It is interesting to note that both China before the economic reform and Taiwan until the 1990s had one of the most egalitarian distributions of household income in the world, despite very different economic systems. The Scandinavian countries, which also have different political and economic systems, have always had relatively egalitarian distributions of income. During the past couple of decades, the global distribution of income has become more egalitarian at the same time that, within each economy, the distribution of income has become more unequal. This is the combined result of economic globalisation and technological innovation, which tend to create both winners and losers in each economy, increasing the income of certain special groups relative to the others.

While economic globalisation increases the welfare of every country and region in the aggregate, it creates both winners and losers in each economy in the process. The winners will be the exporters and the consumers and users of imports in every economy. The losers will be the domestic industries disrupted by the exports and the imports and their workers. Similarly, technological innovation favours the educated and the highly skilled but not the uneducated and low-skill labour. Moreover, the market system itself cannot and does not compensate the losers from either economic globalisation or technological innovation. Thus, in both cases, the income distribution tends to become more unequal. The Chinese economy is no exception. However, because almost everyone in China has become much better off as a result of the economic reform begun in 1978, there is not the anger or frustration among the (relative) "losers" from globalisation or technological innovation as in the United States or Europe.

In Chart 14.13, the Gini coefficients of the Chinese economy are presented. The Gini coefficient is a measure of the degree of inequality of the income distribution—it takes the value zero for perfect equality, that is, everyone has the same income, and the value 1 for perfect inequality, that is, one person has all the income. A value of 0.5 is considered high. A rising Gini coefficient is an inevitable result of "letting some of the people become wealthy first." The two-time series of Gini coefficients are not really comparable. The Gini coefficient based on GDP per capita attempts to measure the distribution of income on a regional basis. The Gini coefficient based on disposable income per capita attempts to measure the distribution of income with household level data. However, regardless of whichever series is used, the overall picture is one in which the distribution of income improved after the beginning of economic reform until 1990 and then it began to worsen significantly until 2003, when it stabilised and started to improve again gradually. It is clear that the distribution of income has become considerably more unequal over time.[3] But perhaps this represents the high point of the inverted U-shape hypothesis of Simon Kuznets.[4]

---

3 The Chinese distribution of income is probably still not as unequal as that of Hong Kong or India.

4 See Kuznets (1955). For more discussion on the distribution of income in China, see Zhao (2018).

Chart 14.13. The Gini Coefficients of the Chinese Distribution of Income, 1978–2016

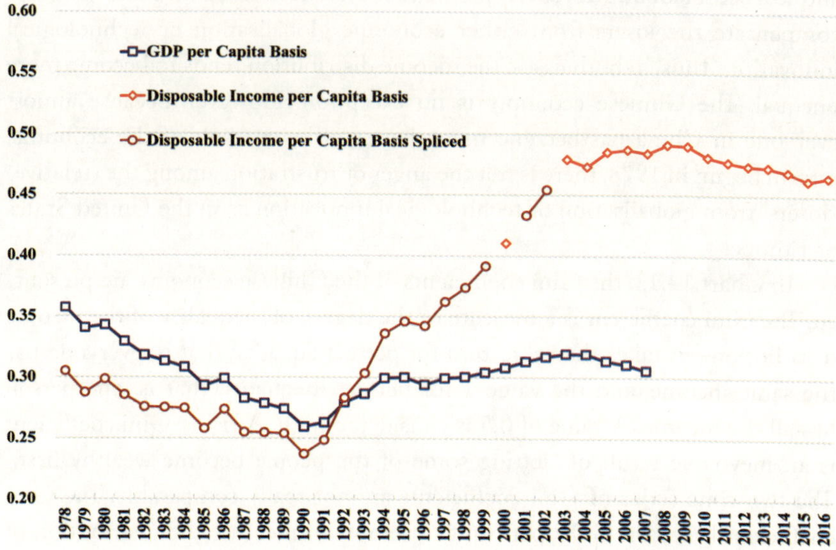

Sources: GDP per capita calculated on a regional basis, *China Development Report*, 2009, p. 349; disposable income per capita basis, 2000 data from Institute of Research, National Bureau of Statistics of the People's Republic of China, *Zhongguo Quanmian Jianshe Xiaokang Shehui Jincheng Tongji Jiance Baogao* (2001), 19 December 2011; 2003–2016 data from China Yearbook of Household Survey, 2011–2017; disposable income per capita basis spliced, calculated by the author.[5]

The Chinese labour share of GDP as well as its household share of GDP have been consistently significantly lower than those in other economies, developed and developing. It has hovered around 50% whereas in most other economies it is between 60 and 70%. There is significant room for China to increase its labour share of GDP. One effective way to do so without changing entry-level wages is to raise the wage-seniority profile, that is, to accelerate the wage increases due to seniority in the early years of an employee's career but

5 The spliced series is obtained by regressing the data on the Gini coefficient for the disposable income per capita on the data on the Gini coefficient on GDP per capita for the overlapping data years.

maintain the same level of the terminal wage rate. This will enable the rate of growth of average wages to rise above the rate of growth of GDP for a couple of decades, which should eventually result in a higher share of household consumption in GDP more similar to other economies. Excess national savings will fall and the Chinese trade surplus will eventually disappear.

In Chart 14.14, we present the poverty headcount rates of China according to different standards adopted in 1978, 2008, and 2010 respectively. The 1978 standard of poverty classified households with a disposable income of below 100 yuan per person per year in 1978 prices as living in poverty. The 2008 standard provided for a disposable household income of below 1,196 yuan per person per year in 2008 prices. The 2010 standard, which is still the current standard, is the highest, classifying those households with a disposable income below 2,300 yuan per person per year in 2010 prices, or approximately US$1 per person per day at the 2010 exchange rate, as living in poverty.[6] Irrespective of which standard is used, the poverty headcount rate has been declining continuously since the economic reform began in 1978. If we apply the 2010 standard of poverty, over 95% of the Chinese population was below the poverty line in 1978. Today that share is below 5%, which means almost 1.3 billion Chinese people have been lifted out of poverty! It is expected that by 2020, poverty according to the 2010 standard will have been completely eradicated.

6. Reducing Systemic Risks

The major risk to the Chinese economy is the potential systemic failure in the financial sector. The failure of a large enterprise may lead to the failure of its creditors, contractors and suppliers, with significant spillover effects, especially if the degree of leverage of the enterprise is high. At year-end 2016, the total debt of all kinds to GDP ratio was 247% in China. It was believed to be more or less the same at year-end 2017. However, the central government debt to GDP ratio was below 20% at year-end 2017, compared to almost 100% for the U.S. and 250% for Japan. At year-end 2017, official local government

---

6 See the discussions on the National Bureau of Statistics of the People's Republic of China website: http://www.stats.gov.cn/tjzs/cjwtjd/201308/t20130829_74325.html, accessed 14 May 2018.

Chart 14.14. Poverty Headcount Rates of China, 1978–2017

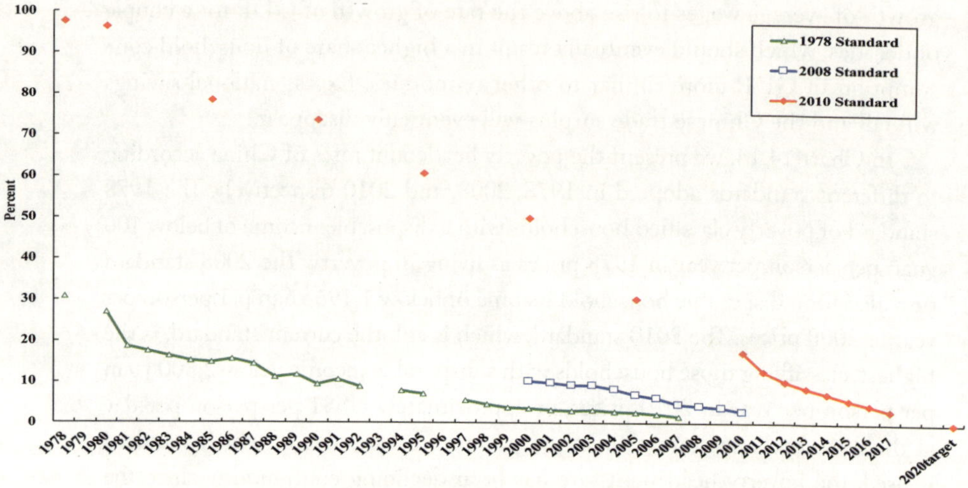

Sources: Poverty headcount rates are from the National Bureau of Statistics of China (available from http://www.stats.gov.cn/tjsj/ndsj/2017/indexch.htm); 2020 target is from the State Council of the People's Republic of China (available from http://www.gov.cn/zhengce/content/2016-12/02/content_5142197.htm).

debt was 16.47 trillion yuan and total local government liability was estimated to be around 31 trillion yuan, or not quite 40% of a Chinese GDP of 82.7 trillion yuan. The rest of the Chinese debt consists mostly of enterprise debt and household debt, for which the central government does not provide a guarantee and has no responsibility for repayment. There is a widely held but false assumption in the West that the state-owned enterprises will be bailed out by the Chinese government. However, this assumption has very little factual basis because it is tantamount to having the shareholders bail out a failing firm, which no investor in the West will expect in general. The bankruptcy of Guangdong International Trust and Investment Corporation (GITIC), a Chinese state-owned enterprise, in 1999 is an example.

In the third quarter of 2017, publicly listed Chinese enterprises had an average debt to assets ratio of 60% or a debt to equity ratio of approximately 150%, which is on the high side. But enterprises, unlike the government, had net assets (positive net worth). Moreover, almost all of the public debt and the great majority of the enterprise and household debts are denominated in renminbi and held by Chinese nationals. So any problem should be quite manageable, especially given the high national savings rate of China in the mid-forties. Nevertheless, shadow banking, financial derivatives, and internet-related financial fraud can create significant problems if not adequately monitored and regulated.

7. Toward a Modern Socialist Market Economy with Chinese Characteristics

Continuity of Governance

One common feature of the early development stages of the East Asian economies is that they were all characterised by continuous one-party rule, beginning with the Liberal Democratic Party in Japan, the British colonial government in Hong Kong, the Kuomintang (Nationalist Party) in Taiwan, President Park Chung-Hee in South Korea, Prime Minister Lee Kuan Yew and his People's Action Party of Singapore, the National Front (Barisan Nasional and its predecessor the Alliance) led by the United Malaysian Native Organisation (UMNO) in Malaysia, and then the Communist parties of China and Vietnam. The advantages of continuous one-party rule are:

(1) It is possible to plan long-term, without regard to the election cycle, so that there is no need to settle for only short-term outcomes (basic infrastructure, so critical in the early development stage, can only be provided by a government with a long-term perspective);

(2) There is consistency, continuity and predictability in economic plans and policies; and

(3) The households and enterprises can share a common long-term vision and common expectations about the future, facilitating investment planning and coordination.

Of course, this is not to say that there are no disadvantages to continuous one-party rule. Many countries governed by long-term dictatorships are among the poorest in the world. But when one-party rule works well, it is better and more efficient than any other system.

President Xi Jinping wants to strengthen the Communist Party of China (CPC) so that it can provide the leadership for achieving the tasks of the New Era. It is his intention to ensure the faithful implementation and execution of the policies adopted by the CPC under his leadership in a sustained manner. The party cadres should be transformed into a dedicated and incorruptible "priesthood," so that the CPC can not only continue to survive but also thrive for many more decades. Ultimately, all party cadres should be incorruptible not only because they are deterred by potential punishment, and not only because the operating system prevents them from becoming corrupt, but also because they genuinely do not wish to be corrupt. This has to involve a fundamental change in their basic values (and a revival of the basic behavioural norms and virtues that used to characterise the meritocratic scholar-official class of previous dynasties): that is, propriety (*li*), righteousness (*yi*), integrity (*lian*), and sense of shame (*chi*). Above all, they should not be motivated by personal gains. This is one sense of "socialism with Chinese characteristics."

Under both the capitalist and the socialist market systems, there is an agency problem in the sense that the managers of the enterprises may not act in the best interests of the owners (shareholders) of the enterprises. Instead, they often act in their own best interests. This is the moral hazard. However, if the managers themselves can become more public-spirited and less self-centred, then the probability that their interests and those of the owners are more aligned is enhanced. Corruption is the result of an agent pursuing his or her own interests rather than those of the principal.

8. Projections of the Future

Long-Term Forecasts of the Chinese and the U.S. Economies

We present some projections of the Chinese and U.S. real GDP during the New Era and beyond. It is assumed that the Chinese economy will continue to grow around 6% per annum for a few more years, declining gradually to between 5% and 6%, and that the U.S. economy will grow at an average rate of 3% per annum between now and 2050. It may be thought that the Chinese economy will be unable to sustain an average annual rate of growth of between 5% and 6% for such a long time, as experience shows that the rate of growth of an economy declines as its real GDP per capita rises. While this is decidedly true, given the still relatively low level of real GDP per capita in China, and the low level of its capital per unit labour, such a rate of growth should still be possible for at least several decades (see Chart 14.15, in which the experiences of China, Japan and the U.S. are compared). Chart 14.15 shows that both Japan and the U.S. were able to maintain relatively high rates of growth of above 5% even when their real GDPs per capita were around US$30,000. Our projections below show that Chinese real GDP per capita would only reach US$20,000 in 2017 prices sometime after 2030, so that the Chinese economy could likely continue to grow at these relatively high rates beyond 2040. In addition, there is still and will continue to be significant surplus labour in the Chinese economy. In 2016, the share of employment in the primary sector was around 30%, whereas the share of GDP originating from the primary sector was already below 10% (see Charts 14.16 and 14.17). It will take at least a couple of decades for the share of Chinese employment in the primary sector to decline to the share of GDP originating from the primary sector. Thus, this surplus labour should provide an additional source of continuing Chinese economic growth.

Chart 14.15. Real GDP Growth Rate (%) vs. Level of Real GDP per Capita (Thousand 2017 US$): China, Japan, and the U.S.

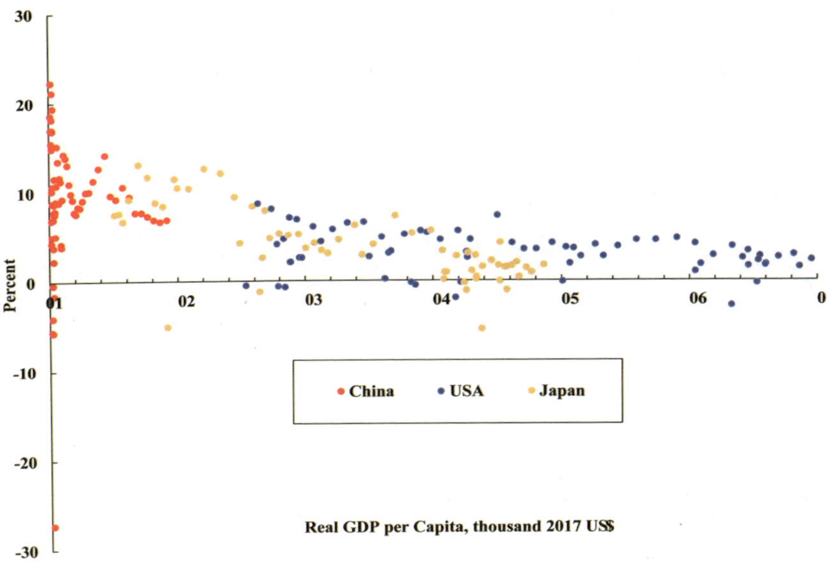

Sources: US data are from U.S. Bureau of Economic Analysis; Chinese data are from National Bureau of Statistics of China; Japanese data are from International Monetary Fund, *International Financial Statistics*.

Chart 14.16. The Distribution of Chinese GDP by Sector since 1952

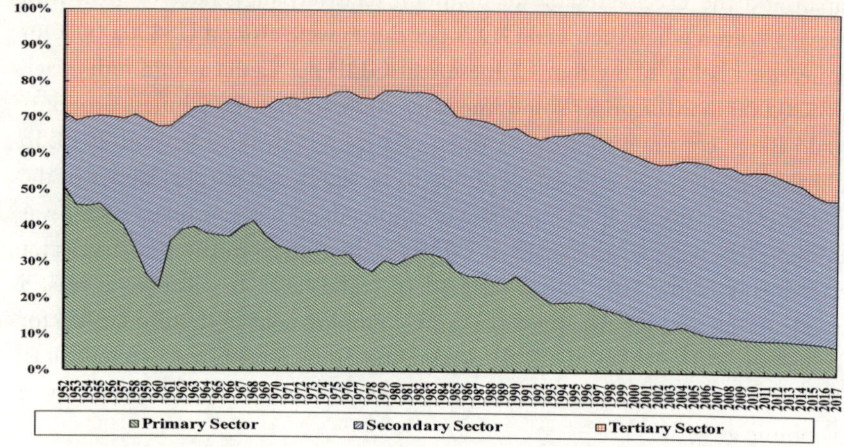

Source: Data from 1952 to 1977 are based on "China Compendium of Statistics 1949–2008" (National Bureau of Statistics of China, 2010); data for the year 1978 and thereafter are from National Bureau of Statistics of China (available from http://data.stats.gov.cn/easyquery.htm?cn=C01).

Chart 14.17. The Distribution of Chinese Employment by Sector since 1952

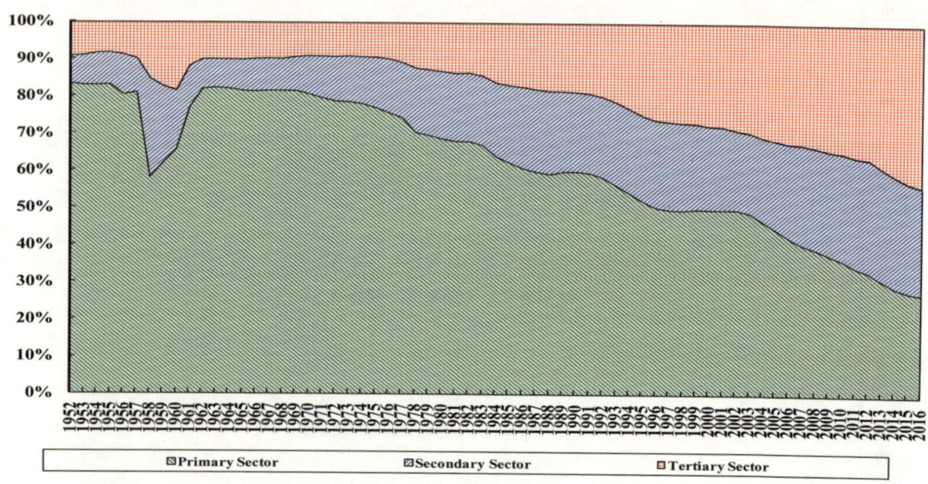

Source: Data from 1952 to 1977 are based on "China Compendium of Statistics 1949–2008" (National Bureau of Statistics of China, 2010); data for the year 1978 and thereafter are from National Bureau of Statistics of China (Available from http://data.stats.gov.cn/easyquery.htm?cn=C01).

In his work report to the Nineteenth National Congress of the Communist Party of China, President Xi Jinping identified three Chinese development milestones at 2020, 2035 and 2050. The first milestone is to become a moderately well off society by 2020. Our projections (see Chart 14.18) show that by 2020, Chinese real GDP per capita (in 2017 prices) will exceed US$10,898, compared to US$63,703 for the U.S. The second milestone is to become a modern and prosperous nation by 2035. Our projections show that by 2031, Chinese real GDP will surpass U.S. real GDP (US$29.4 trillion versus US$29.3 trillion respectively), making China the largest economy in the world (see Chart 14.19). However, in terms of real GDP per capita, China will still lag behind significantly, with US$20,009 compared to US$82,502 for the U.S. (Thus, the Chinese economy should still be in a 5% growth phase.) The third milestone is to become a strong and wealthy nation by 2050. According to our projections, by 2050, Chinese real GDP will reach US$82.6 trillion compared to US$51.4 trillion for the U.S. In terms of real GDP per capita, China will reach US$52,870, slightly less than the current level of U.S real GDP per capita, still significantly below the US$134,071 of the U.S. It will not be until the end of the 21st century that the Chinese real GDP per capita can reach parity with the U.S. real GDP per capita, given that the Chinese population is approximately four times that of the U.S.

Chart 14.18. Actual and Projected Chinese and U.S. Real GDP per Capita and Their Rates of Growth (Thousand 2017 US$)

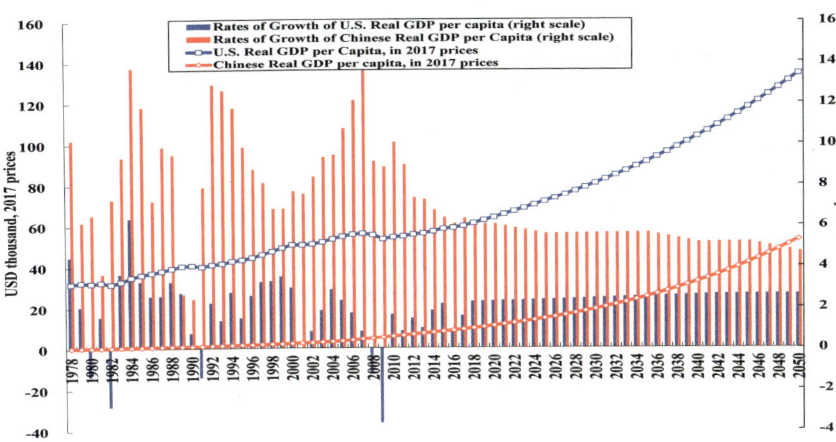

Chart 14.19. Actual and Projected Levels and Growth Rates of Chinese and U.S. Real GDP (Trillion 2017 US$)

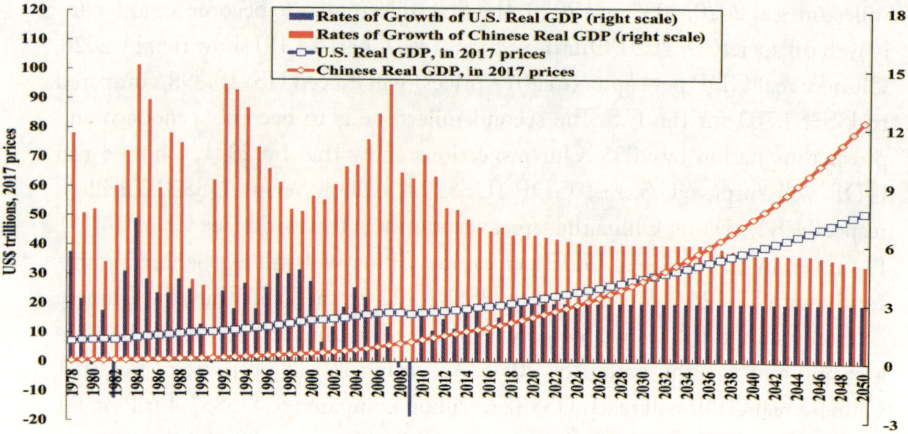

9. Concluding Remarks

The New Era will be transformative for the Chinese economy. China will join the ranks of developed economies of the world. It will be more innovation-driven than inputs-driven. It will be more quality-motivated than quantity-motivated. It will be more household consumption-driven than investment driven. The New Era will restore green mountains, blue skies and clear waters in China. There will be greater real income equality and an improved social safety net, assuring shared prosperity for all in the New Era!

References

Kuznets, Simon. "Economic Growth and Income Inequality." *American Economic Review* 45, no. 1 (1955): pp. 1–28.

Lau, Lawrence J., and Yanyan Xiong. "Are There Laws of Innovation." Working Paper, Lau Chor Tak Institute of Global Economics and Finance, The Chinese University of Hong Kong, 2018.

Zhao, Litao. "High Inequality Levelling Off in China." EAI Background Brief No. 1346, East Asian Institute, National University of Singapore, 26 April 2018.

Chapter 15.

Public Goods Provision and Chinese Economic Development*

1. Introduction

We set the stage with a brief review of the Chinese economic record since 1949, followed by a discussion of the Chinese economic fundamentals.

The Growth of Chinese Real GDP and Real GDP per Capita, 1949–2021

Between 1949 and 2021, the Chinese real GDP has grown from 329 billion yuan (US$51.55 billion) to 114.4 trillion yuan (US$17.94 trillion), in 2021 prices, an almost 350-fold increase (see Chart 15.1). During the same period, the Chinese real GDP per capita has grown more than 130-fold, from 607 yuan (US$95.2) to 80,962 yuan (US$12,699), in 2021 prices (see Chart 15.2).

Despite significant fluctuations and volatility of the rates of growth during the two decades from the late 1950s to the late 1970s, which are clearly apparent in both Charts 15.1 and 15.2, the average annual rates of growth

---

* This chapter was originally published in *China and the World: Ancient and Modern Silk Road* 5, no. 01n4 (2022). It is based on a lecture presented in the China Centre Seminar Series, Jesus College, Cambridge, U.K. on May 5, 2022. The author wishes to thank Prof. Peter Nolan for his invitation to present this lecture and for the insightful comments from him and the participants in the Seminar. He is also most grateful to Mrs. Ayesha Macpherson Lau and Prof. Yanyan Xiong for their advice and comments on earlier drafts, and to Ms. Sophia Lok for her able research assistance. However, all remaining errors are the sole responsibility of the author.

of real GDP and real GDP per capita for the entire period from 1949 to 2021 are, respectively, 8.47% and 7.03%, a truly remarkable and historically unprecedented achievement over a period of more than seven decades. We can attribute this success largely to the economic reform and opening-up to the world undertaken in 1978, as well as to the long-time horizon of the Chinese economic policy-makers and their single-minded focus on economic growth from 1978 onwards. With a long enough planning horizon, one can afford to undertake investment in development-leading infrastructure, i.e., infrastructure the demand for which has not yet materialised but can be created by the supply itself, infrastructure that may take a long time to pay off.

Chart 15.1. Chinese Real GDP and Its Annual Rate of Growth: 1949–2021

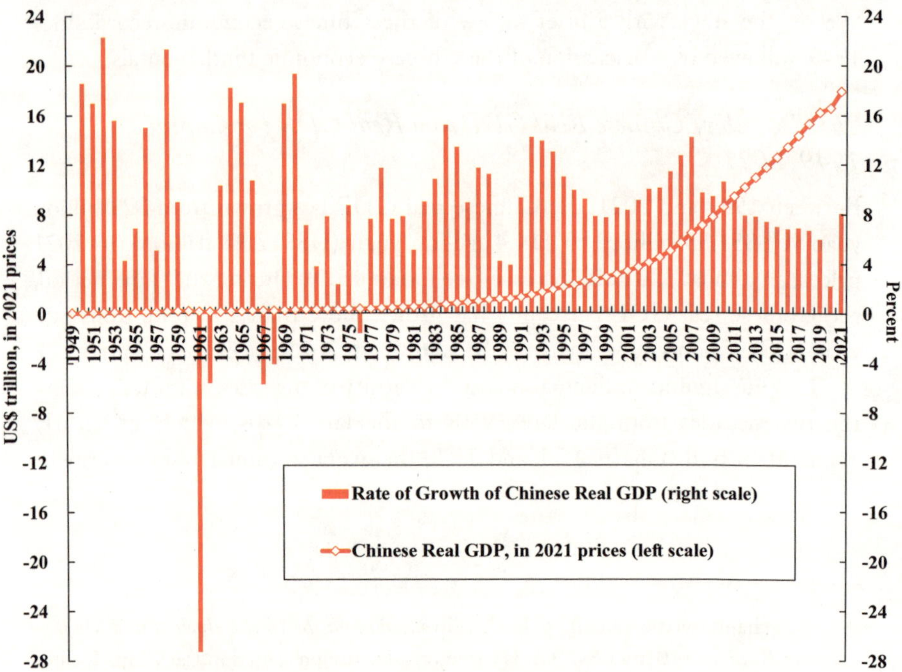

Source: Rates of growth of real GDP from 1950 to 1952 are from the National Bureau of Statistics of China (1959). Chinese GDP and its rate of growth from 1952 to 2021 are from the online statistical database of the National Bureau of Statistics of China (https://data.stats.gov.cn/easyquery.htm?cn=C01).

Chart 15.2. Chinese Real GDP per Capita and Its Rate of Growth: 1949–2021

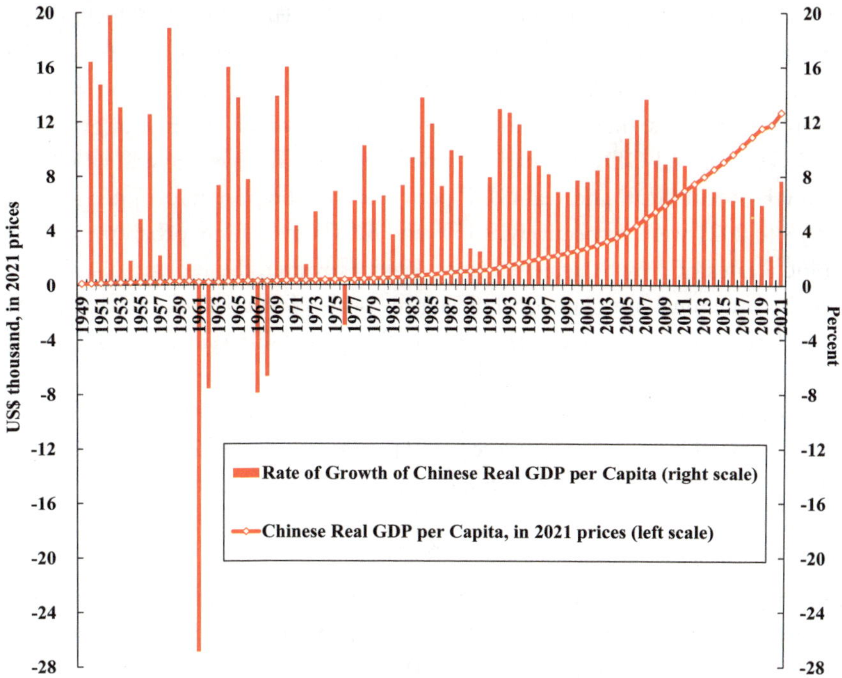

Source: Rates of growth from 1950 to 1952 are from the National Bureau of Statistics of China (1959). Chinese real GDP and its rate of growth from 1952 to 2021, and Chinese population from 1949 to 2021 are from the online statistical database of the National Bureau of Statistics of China (https://data.stats.gov.cn/easyquery.htm?cn=C01).

If we consider the 30-year period 1949–1978, before the beginning of Chinese economic reform and opening-up, the average annual rates of growth of real GDP and real GDP per capita were, respectively, 8.01% and 5.85%. This economic performance, due, in part, to the rapid recovery in the rehabilitation period of 1949–1952, was really quite respectable by itself. The Chinese First Five-Year Plan (1953–1957) was also a success. The years of significant negative economic growth in the pre-reform period occurred during the Great Famine of 1959–1961 (in the aftermath of the Great Leap Forward of 1958) and the Great Proletarian Cultural Revolution of 1966–1967.

Between 1978, the beginning of the Chinese economic reform and opening-up, and 2021, the Chinese real GDP has grown more than 40-fold, from 2.65 trillion yuan (US$415 billion) to 114.4 trillion yuan (US$17.94 trillion), in 2021 prices, and the real GDP per capita has grown almost 30-fold, from 2,749 yuan (US$431.2) to 80,962 yuan (US$12,699). During this period of more than four decades, there was not one single year in which the rate of growth of real GDP or real GDP per capita turned negative. The average annual rates of growth of real GDP and real GDP per capita for the post-reform period from 1978 to 2021 were, respectively, 9.15% and 8.18%, even higher than the average annual rates of growth achieved since 1949. However, the income distribution did become much more unequal during the post-reform period. But despite the significant rise in the value of the Gini coefficient in China since the mid-1980s, the welfare of all Chinese people has also improved significantly.

The Chinese GDP of US$17.94 trillion in 2021 was 78% of the U.S. GDP of US$23 trillion, but the Chinese GDP per capita of US$12,699 remained far behind, at only 18.4% of the U.S. GDP per capita of US$68,971.

The Chinese Economic Fundamentals

We now turn to consider the Chinese economic fundamentals. Are there sufficient primary inputs of production—capital and labour—to continue to support Chinese economic growth? The Chinese national savings rate has remained high, currently at approximately 45%, certainly the highest in the world amongst major economies. This means that the investment rate can also remain high, even in the absence of inflows of foreign direct investment or foreign loans. However, the recent Chinese demographic developments appear unfavorable—its population is ageing rapidly, with almost zero growth. But, as will be explained below, the labour supply problems are basically manageable.

Indigenous innovation has also been occurring in many areas, e.g., the 5G communication, the BeiDou Navigation Satellite System, high-speed trains, quantum communication, super-computers, and ultra-high-voltage transmission of electricity. In time, innovation or technical progress should also become an important source of economic growth.

The Chinese national savings rate rose from 21.1% in 1952 to 36.8% in 1979 and 45.7% in 2020 (see Chart 15.3). It will remain high and provide the necessary resources for additional investment in fixed assets, including infrastructure, human capital, research and development (R&D), and the

Chart 15.3. Chinese National Savings and Gross Domestic Investment as Shares of GDP

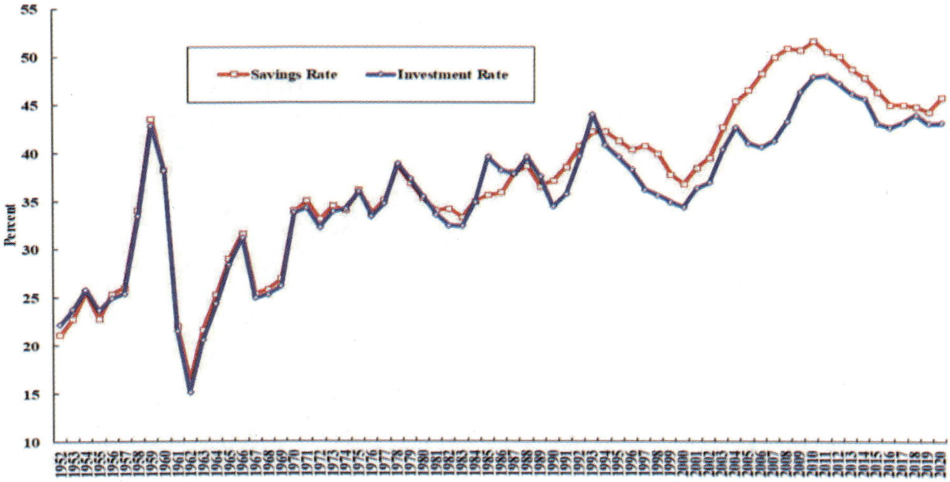

Source: National Bureau of Statistics of China (https://data.stats.gov.cn/easyquery.htm?cn=C01).

provision of public goods such as education, healthcare, environmental preservation, protection, and restoration, elderly care, and poverty alleviation. Household consumption will rise as the household income continues to rise and more and more households join the ranks of the middle class. However, as shares of GDP, household consumption as well as total consumption (including government consumption) have been on a downward trend for the past 60 years. As of 2020, they were, respectively, less than 40% and 60% of GDP (see Chart 15.4). Left on their own, they are probably not sufficient to shore up the aggregate demand needed for the economy to continue its growth.

The Chinese crude death rate declined from 2% in 1949 to 0.72% in 2021, with the exception of the period of the Great Famine (1959–1961), reflecting the improvements of the economic and public health conditions in China. The Chinese crude birth rate also declined from 3.60% in 1949 to 0.75% in 2021, barely above the crude death rate (see Chart 15.5). This was due, in part, to the legacy of the "one-child" policy, which was implemented in 1980 and discontinued in 2016, as well as to the rising educational level of women and urbanisation.

Chart 15.4. Chinese Total Final and Household Consumptions as a Percent of Its GDP

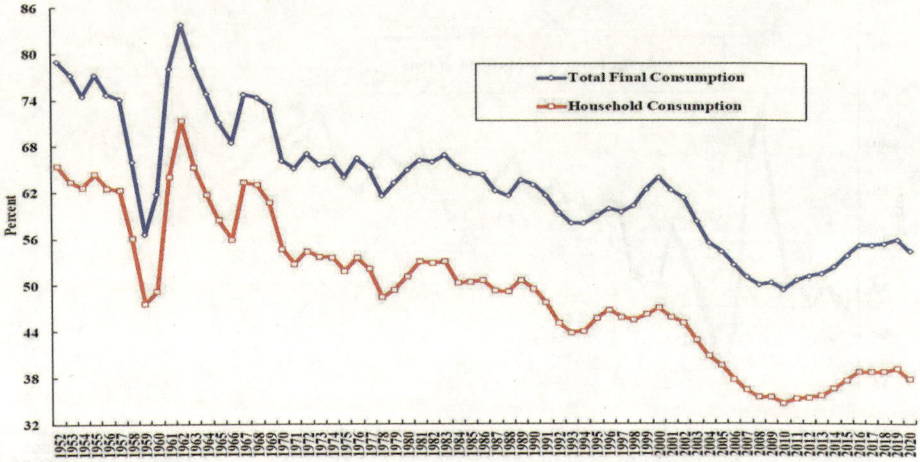

Source: National Bureau of Statistics of China (https://data.stats.gov.cn/easyquery.htm?cn=C01).

While the net rate of growth of the total population, the difference between the crude birth and death rates, has been approaching zero (see Chart 15.5), and may even turn negative soon, it is unlikely to result in a serious shortage of labour as yet. The demand for labour can be satisfied through continued urbanisation, i.e., by the movement of surplus labour from the rural to the urban areas. Despite the claim that the "Lewis Turning Point" has arrived in China, there still exists substantial surplus labour. The primary (agriculture) sector, which generated only 7.3% of GDP in 2020, but accounted for 23.6% of the total employment in 2020, is still in a position to supply labour to the secondary (manufacturing, mining, and construction) and tertiary (services) sectors without affecting its output (see Charts 15.6 and 15.7).

Chart 15.5. The Crude Birth Rate and Death Rate (Numbers per Thousand)

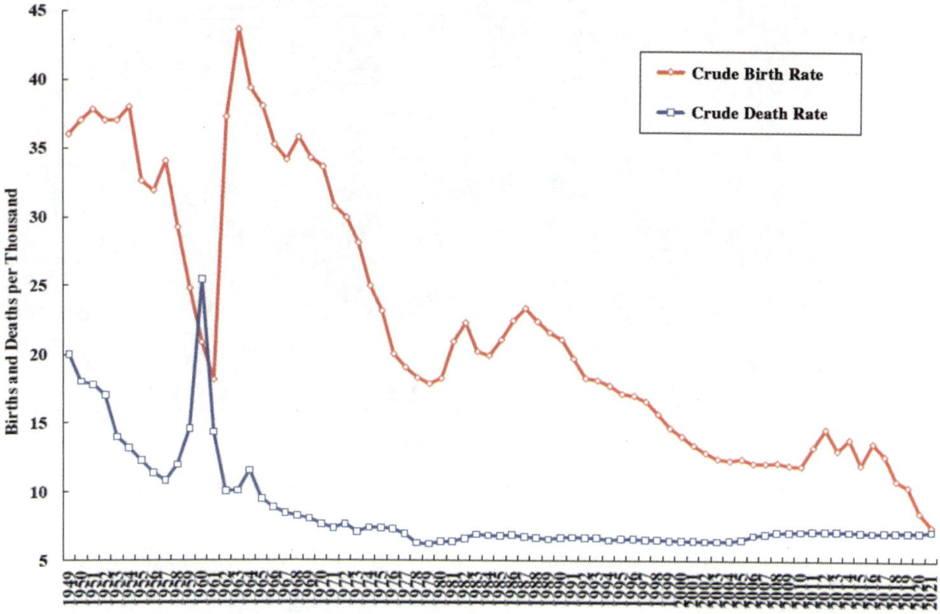

Source: National Bureau of Statistics of China (https://data.stats.gov.cn/easyquery.htm?cn=C01).

Chart 15.6. The Distribution of Chinese GDP by Sector since 1952

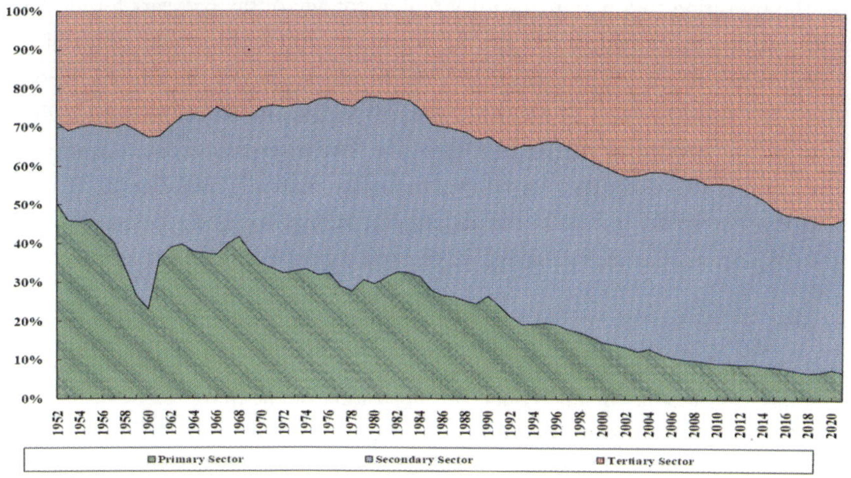

Source: National Bureau of Statistics of China (https://data.stats.gov.cn/easyquery.htm?cn=C01).

Chart 15.7. The Distribution of Chinese Employment by Sector since 1952

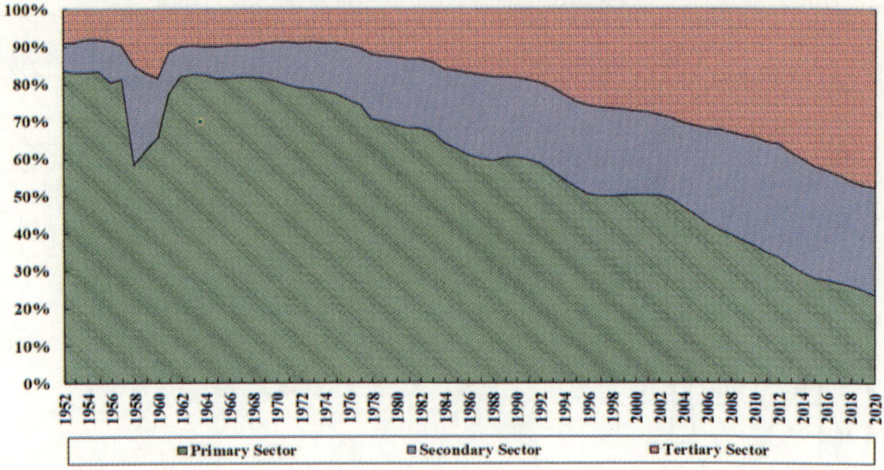

Source: National Bureau of Statistics of China (https://data.stats.gov.cn/easyquery.htm?cn=C01).

In addition, the mandatory retirement ages, which have officially remained at 55 years for women and 60 years for men, an anachronism inherited from the early 1950s, when life expectancy was in the low sixties, are ready for a change. The gradual raising of the mandatory retirement ages, given the current life expectancy at birth of more than 77 years, should help augment the labour force. In the transition to a new mandatory retirement age of say 65 years for all, one can make the retirement at 55 years for women and 60 years for men optional, so that no one's rights will be abridged.[1] Moreover, the quality of the Chinese labour force has also improved significantly through various investments in education and public health over the past decades. The "efficiency-equivalent" quantity of the labour force continues to grow even though numerically the labour force may no longer be growing. Finally, the adoption of automation and robotics through the application of artificial intelligence can also enhance the effective labour force.

---

1 Opposition to raising the mandatory retirement age also comes from those awaiting to succeed their supervisors. This opposition can be mitigated by instituting term limits for executive positions. For example, a medical doctor is allowed to serve as the head of a hospital for only two terms but can remain as a clinician at the hospital afterwards until the new mandatory retirement age is reached.

The elimination of restrictions on the number of children and the possible lowering of the marriage-eligible ages should also help increase the Chinese birth rate gradually, but it will take a couple of decades before there will be a noticeable impact on the labour force.

With a large population and hence a large domestic market, China also enjoys economies of scale from both production and marketing, learning-by-doing (i.e., efficiency improvement resulting from repetitive production of the same good, such as high-speed trains), and the advantage of longer upper tails in the ability distribution because of the size of its population. Moreover, as a large continental economy, the domestic Chinese economy is largely unaffected by external disturbances, similar to the U.S. Thus, while the Chinese rates of growth of exports and imports fluctuate like other East Asian economies, the rate of growth of its real GDP has remained relatively stable.

2. The Definition of a Public Good

In economics, a public good is usually defined as a product or service that is openly available to be enjoyed by all members of a society. The *Encyclopaedia Britannica* defines a public good to be a product or service that is non-excludable and non-depletable (or "non-rivalrous"). Examples of such public goods include law enforcement, national defense, a stable local currency, and clean air and water. The elimination of a public bad, such as air pollution, is also a public good. The definition of a "public good" used in this article is slightly generalised to include potentially rivalrous goods, such as a seat on a train, so long as it is non-excludable *ex ante*. (The supply of a public good may have capacity constraints so some form of rationing, whether by price or otherwise, may be necessary.) Basic education is a public good that is generally non-rivalrous; whereas, mass transit is a public good that can at times be rivalrous. The National Health Service in the United Kingdom is a public good, even though there may have to be rationing through waiting for some treatments.

Typically, these goods and services are administered and/or provided by the central or local governments and paid for collectively through taxation. Public goods are unlikely to be supplied in sufficient quantities to satisfy potential demand through the free market because they are frequently "money-losers." Public goods provision may therefore require taxes, subsidies, or even direct government intervention. A public good often faces the "free-rider" problem, i.e., someone who is happy to enjoy the good or service, but will try to avoid bearing the cost. Food is normally a private good, but the provision of food security is a public good. Personal insurance is a private good. But a social safety net is a public good, as is the alleviation of poverty. Infrastructure is a (local) public good. Goods that generate externalities, e.g., mandatory basic education, and the simplification of Chinese characters—goods that provide a benefit for the society as a whole, are public goods.

3. The Possible Roles of Public Goods

China has done a relatively good job in the provision of public goods to its people, as will be shown below. The provision of these public goods has in turn enhanced the real rate of growth of the Chinese economy in various ways.

Public goods provision mandates both capital and current expenditures and hence increases aggregate demand. They include, e.g., fire and police protection, environmental preservation, protection, and restoration, and the maintenance of blue skies, green mountains, and turquoise waters. These current expenditures can become part of an important component of the aggregate demand for government consumption. The capital expenditures such as those on infrastructure (communication, transportation, and power), and the building of schools, hospitals, and charging stations for electric cars, can also become a part of an important component of the aggregate demand for fixed-asset investment.

Moreover, the provision of many public goods such as education, public health, and basic research can also be considered intangible investments even though they are often expensed on a current basis. A stable currency (money) in terms of purchasing power, is also a public good. The regulation of the markets so that they remain competitive and free of monopolistic influences is also a public good. Finally, maintaining public confidence and creating positive expectations of the future are also important public goods.

4. Public Goods Provision as Intangible Investment (I): Education, Public Health, and R&D

Public Goods Provision as Intangible Investment: Literacy

Traditionally, for at least a couple of millennia, the Chinese people have always valued education highly, in large part because it was one of the very few channels for upward social mobility. In the social hierarchy of old China, up to the early 20th century, scholars were on the very top, followed by farmers, and then by labourers, with the merchants at the very bottom. Being wealthy alone did not improve social status or earn respect.

Chart 15.8. The Literacy Rate (Percent)

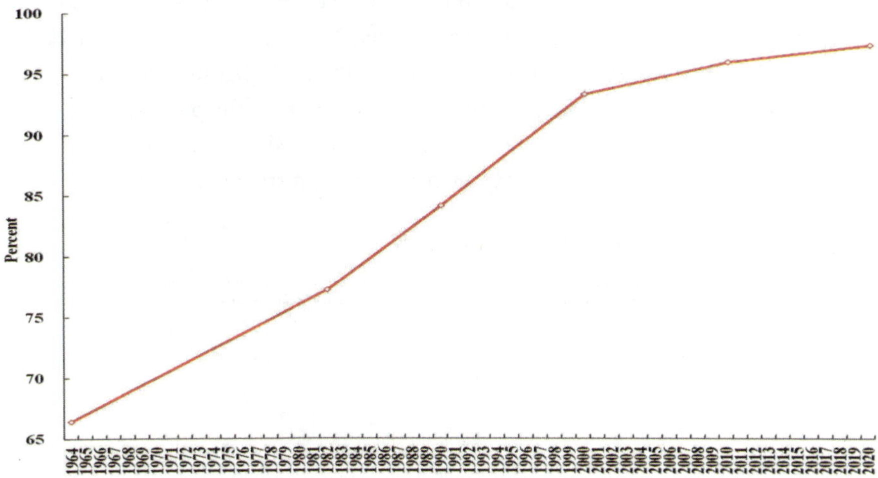

Source: China Statistical Yearbook 2021.

More generally, literacy and the promotion of Putonghua (commonly spoken Chinese) are clearly public goods because they enable all Chinese people to communicate with one another in both speech and writing. The literacy rate, which must have been way below 50% in 1949, increased from 66.4% in 1964 to 97.3% in 2020 (see Chart 15.8), thanks in part to the simplification of the Chinese characters undertaken in the 1950s and codified in 1964. The simplification has been subject to much criticism, some quite justifiable, but it did reduce the number of years of schooling required for an average person to be able to read a newspaper from eight to four years, a major accomplishment.

Public Goods Provision as Intangible Investment: Educational Attainments

Mandatory nine-year education for all was introduced in China in 1986. Today, most young people have had at least 12 years of education, even though senior secondary education is still not yet mandatory at this time.

The proportions of people with only primary education (the yellow line) or junior secondary education (the blue line) have already peaked and begun to decline (see Chart 15.9). The tertiary enrolment rate of graduates of senior secondary schools was 24.6% in 1989 and rose to 94.5% in 2016. This means almost everyone who wishes to attend a tertiary educational institution is now able to do so. (However, the proportion of the population aged 18–22 years that were enrolled in tertiary education institutions in 2021 was only 57.8%, because not everyone in that age cohort had completed senior secondary school.) The proportion of the total population with tertiary education (the red line), which was only 0.42% in 1964, rose to 17% in 2021, and is expected to increase further with time.[2]

Chart 15.9. Educational Attainment Rates

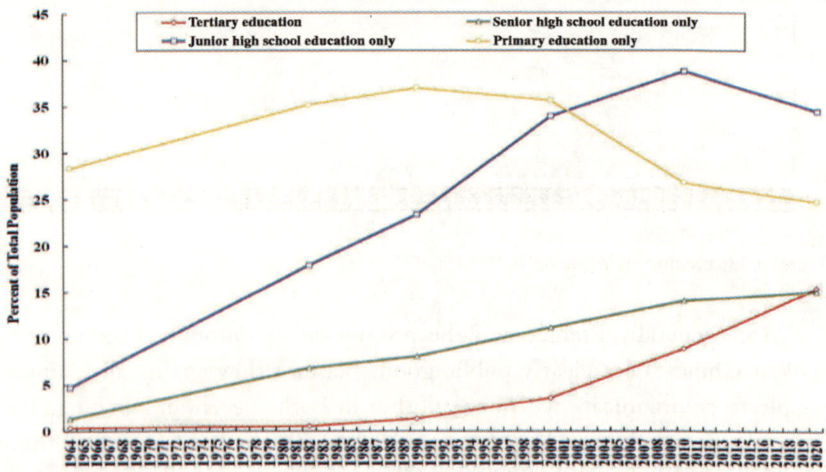

Source: China Statistical Yearbook 2021.

2 The 2021 figures are based on an announcement by the Ministry of Education on May 17, 2022.

Public Goods Provision as Intangible Investment: Public Health

Much improvement has also occurred in healthcare and public hygiene in China. As mentioned above, the population mortality rate declined by more than half from 2% in 1949 to 0.72% in 2021. Life expectancy at birth, which was only 35 years in 1949 and 67.8 years in 1981, grew to 77.3 years in 2019 (see Chart 15.10), compared to 72.6 years for the world as a whole. Life expectancy at age 60 was 20.21 years in 2020.

Chart 15.10. The Life Expectancy at Birth (Years)

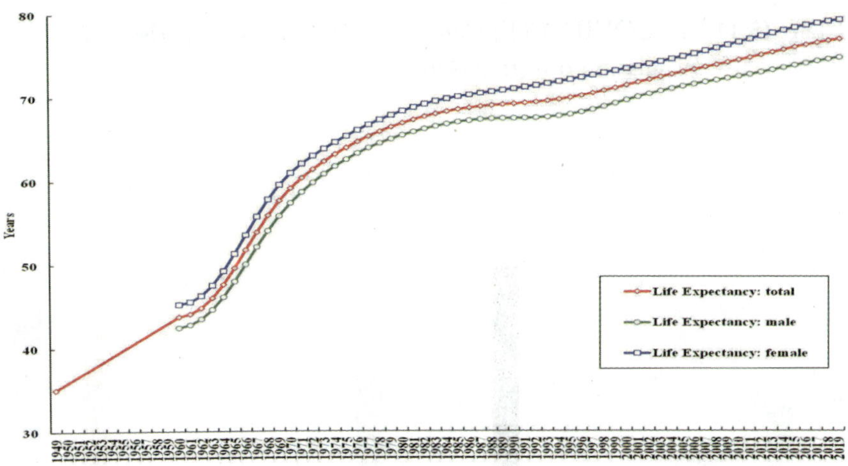

Source: Data from 1960 to 2019 are from the World Development Indicators. Data in 1949 are from http://www.nhc.gov.cn/xcs/zllkrm/201909/c5b349de3ede49db971c9ec9520cb5a9.shtml.

The COVID-19 epidemic first broke out in China in Wuhan, Hubei, in December 2019. However, it was soon successfully contained through a blockade of the city of Wuhan and the province of Hubei, and a complete lockdown in Hubei. Through rapid testing, isolation, and quarantine of the infected, and timely treatment, the epidemic was brought under control by the end of March 2020.[3]

3 See also the discussions in Lau and Xiong (2021b).

In early 2022, there were once again surges of the epidemic in different parts of China—Shanghai, Shenzhen, Jilin, Guangdong, and Beijing—due to the omicron variant. However, as of April 22, 2022, Mainland China still had the lowest per-capita cumulative infection rate and the lowest per-capita cumulative death rate from the COVID-19 epidemic among the Group-of-Seven (G-7) and the BRICS countries (see Charts 15.11 and 15.12).[4] There was a significant loss of Chinese GDP in 2020 that could be attributed to the epidemic, to the tune of approximately 4%. This was partially compensated by the recovery growth of 8.1% in 2021.

Chart 15.11. The COVID-19 Epidemic: International Comparison of Population Infection Rates

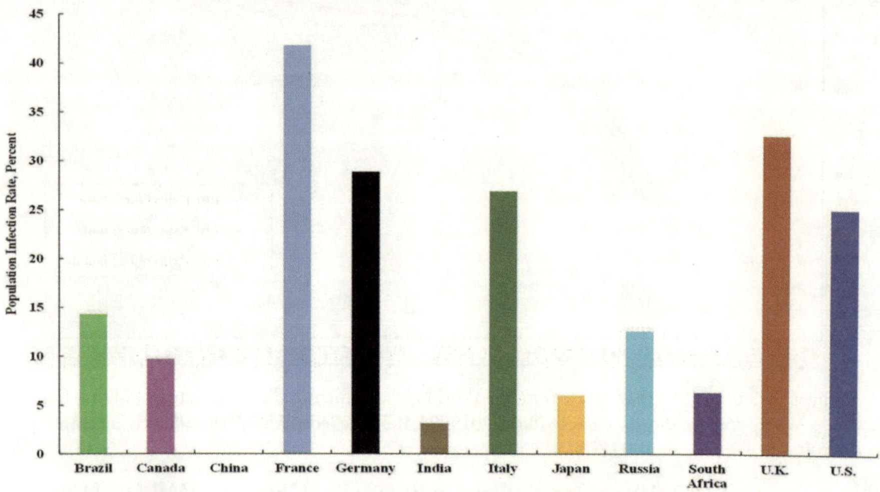

Source: Worldometer, https://www.worldometers.info/coronavirus/.

4 Earlier versions of these figures can be found in Lau and Xiong (2021a).

Chart 15.12. The COVID-19 Epidemic: International Comparison of Population Mortality Rates

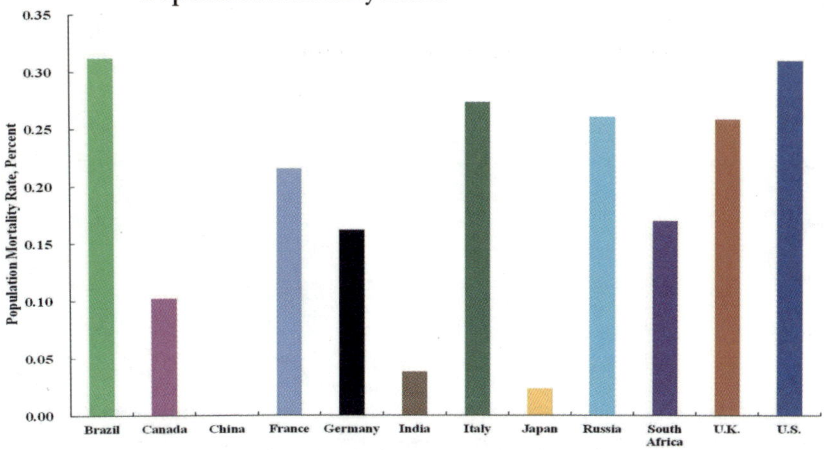

Source: Worldometer, https://www.worldometers.info/coronavirus/.

The management of the COVID-19 epidemic in China must be considered quite successful. As of April 22, 2022, the COVID-19 epidemic infected 180,982 persons (excluding imported cases) and resulted in 4,686 deaths on the Mainland, with a quarter of the world's population. By comparison, the rest of the world had, on the same date, a cumulative total of more than 508 million (508,526,800) infected cases and more than 6.2 million (6,235,952) fatalities. The recent surges in COVID-19 cases in China appeared to have come under control. The potential reduction in 2022 GDP due to the COVID-19 epidemic may be estimated to be between 0.5% and 1%.

Public Goods Provision as Intangible Investment: Innovation

China has been increasing its investment in R&D, which reached 2.44% of GDP in 2021. Since 2014, it has also strengthened the intellectual property rights protection significantly by establishing special intellectual property courts with sole nationwide jurisdiction on such matters. The numbers of patents awarded to Chinese discoverers and inventors by, respectively, the United States Patent and Trademark Office (USPTO; blue line), the European Patent Office (EPO; black line), and the China National Intellectual Property Administration (CNIPA; red line) have all been increasing by leaps and bounds in recent years (see Chart 15.13). China is now the recipient of the largest number of patent grants in the world from these three patent offices combined.

Chart 15.13. Chinese Patent Grants Awarded by USPTO, EPO, and CNIPA

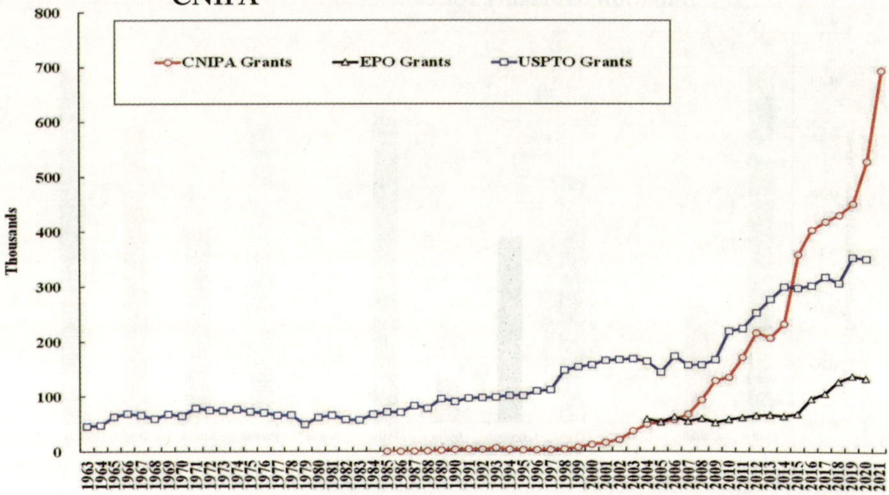

Source: Data on the CNIPA patent grants are taken from the China Statistical Yearbook, various issues. Data on the EPO patent grants are taken from the EPO website. Data on the USPTO patent grants are taken from Table A5.2 in Lau and Xiong (2022).

Chart 15.14. Innovation: The Number of Scientific and Engineering Articles Published

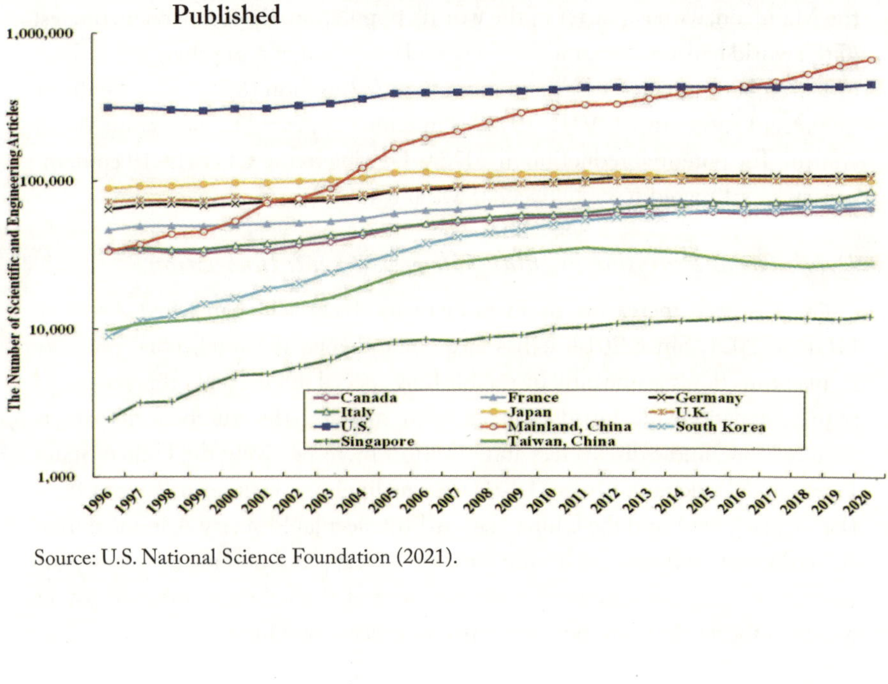

Source: U.S. National Science Foundation (2021).

Another possible measure of the quantity of innovation output is the number of scientific and engineering articles published. The total number of scientific and engineering scholarly articles published in international professional journals by Mainland Chinese authors exceeded that by U.S. authors in 2016 (see Chart 15.14). Chinese authors now collectively publish the largest number of such articles in the world.

However, what should count more is not the total number of published articles, but the total number of citations received by the published articles. The number of top-10% most-cited scientific articles by the Chinese authors overtook that by U.S. authors in 2019, according to a Japanese study. A recent study published in the journal *Scientometrics* shows that China and the U.S. were neck and neck in the number of top-1% most-cited scientific articles in 2019 (see Charts 15.15 and 15.16). China trailed the U.S. and the European Union countries for many years.

Chart 15.15. The Number of Top-1% Most-Cited Articles

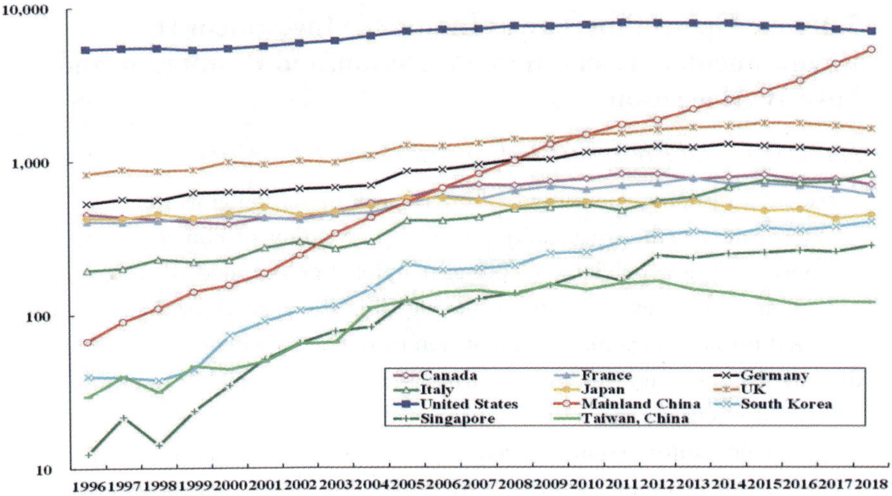

Source: National Center for Science and Engineering Statistics; Science-Metrix; Elsevier's Scopus, an abstract and citation database, accessed May 2021.

Chart 15.16. Innovation: The Number of Top-1% Most-Cited Articles

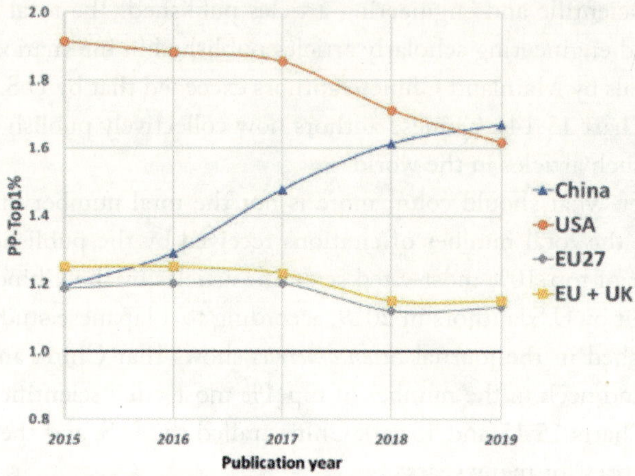

Source: Wagner, Zhang, and Leydesdorff (2022).

5. Public Goods Provision as Intangible Investment II: Environmental Preservation, Protection, and Restoration and Poverty Alleviation

Environmental Preservation, Protection, and Restoration

President Xi Jinping committed China to peak its carbon emissions by 2030 and to achieve carbon neutrality by 2060. Prevention of climate change is not only a Chinese public good, but also a global public good. The objectives of carbon peaking by 2030 and achieving carbon neutrality by 2060 will be achieved through, e.g., massive expansion of renewable energy, including hydro, massive solar, and wind power farms, and potentially nuclear fusion, as the sources of electricity generation, replacing the fossil fuels; ultra-high-voltage long-distance transmission of electricity from the West to the East; replacement of fossil-fuel vehicles with electric and hydrogen vehicles; substitution of air travel by high-speed rail travel domestically; and large-scale reforestation.

Carbon dioxide emissions have basically plateaued in China since the early 2010s, after a period of rapid increase (see Charts 15.17–15.19). The emissions have been growing very slowly in the past few years. If the current trends continue, it is entirely feasible that the emissions will peak before 2030 and fall to zero by 2060.

The energy intensity, defined as the primary energy consumed per unit real GDP, has been declining over time in China (see Chart 15.20).[5] This is due to a number of factors: energy conservation efforts both public and private as a result of prices, taxes, and regulatory requirements; technological improvements, e.g., higher efficiency and lower transmission losses; and the relative contraction of the energy-intensive secondary (manufacturing, mining, and construction) sector and the relative expansion of the much-less-energy-intensive tertiary (services) sector.

Chart 15.17. Total Carbon Dioxide Emissions in China, 1960–2018: World Development Indicators Data (billion metric tons)

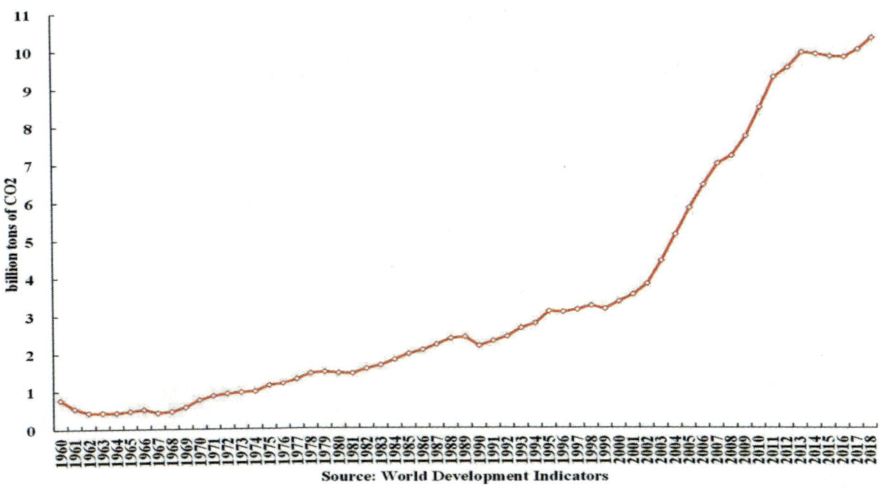

Source: World Development Indicators.

5 The energy consumed per unit GDP declined by a further 2.7% between 2020 and 2021. However, the energy intensity of China is still approximately 1.5 times the global average.

Chart 15.18. Total Carbon Dioxide Emissions, 1994–2019: Chinese Data

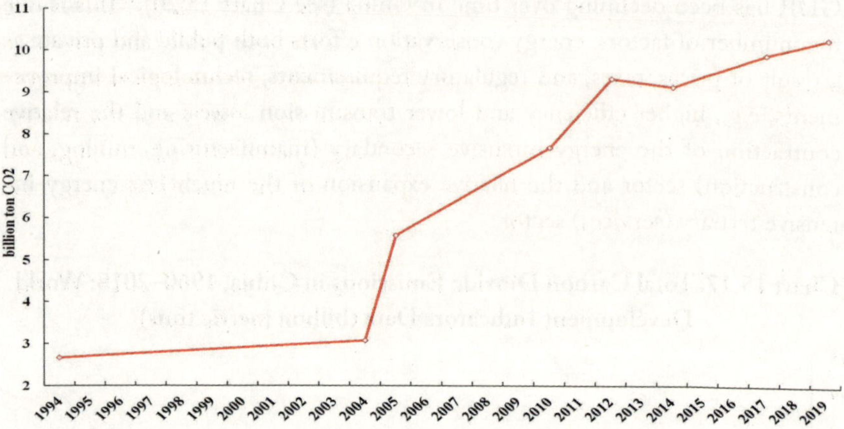

Source: Che (2021); Ministry of Ecology and Environment of the People's Republic of China (2004, 2018a, 2018b).

Chart 15.19. Daily Chinese Carbon Dioxide Emissions, 1 January 2019 to 31 December 2021

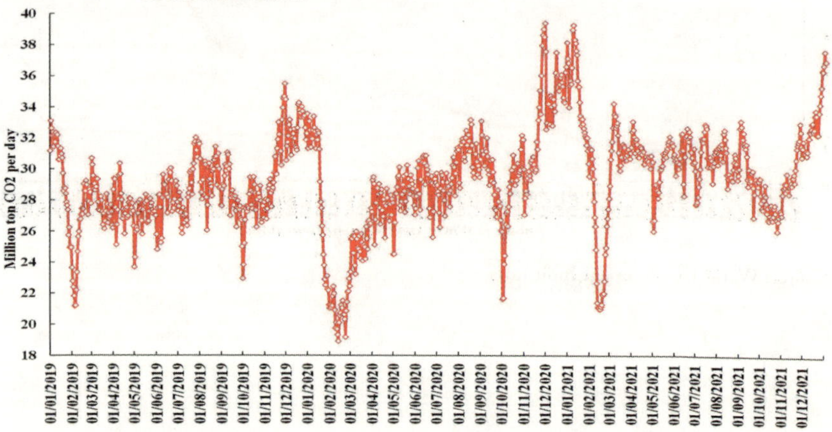

Source: Carbon Monitor, https://www.carbonmonitor.org.cn/user/.

Chart 15.20. Chinese Energy Intensity: Primary Energy Consumed per Unit Real GDP, 1980–2019

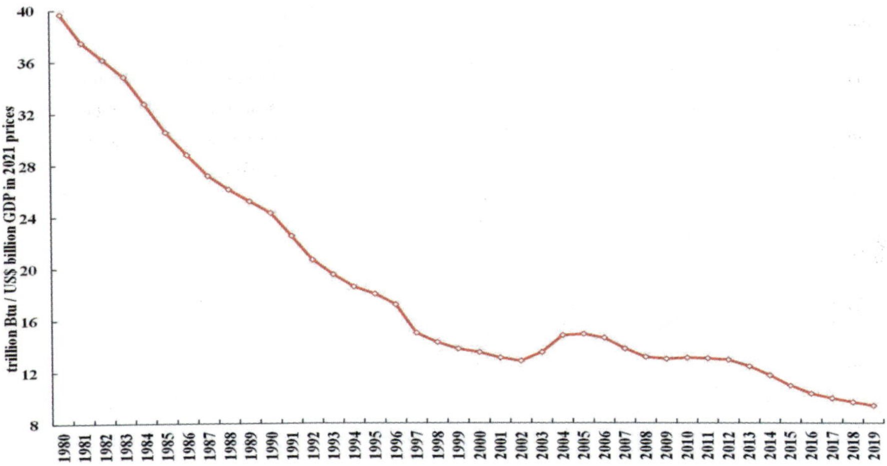

Source: U.S. Energy Information Administration.

The quality of air in major Chinese urban centers has improved significantly. Fine particulate matter 2.5 (PM2.5) is an air pollutant that reduces visibility and causes the air to appear hazy when its level is high. It is also a concern for people's health. China implemented the new ambient air quality standard (GB3095-2012) in 2013. The levels of PM2.5 in the air of 31 major Chinese cities have been declining since. The actual levels of PM2.5 of seven major cities—Beijing, Chongqing, Guangzhou, Nanjing, Shanghai, Shenzhen, and Tianjin—between 2013 and 2020 are shown in Chart 15.21. A comparison of a PM2.5 map of China in 2015 and 2021 is presented in Chart 15.22 (blue is good and red is bad). The improvement over time is clearly apparent.

The Huang He (Yellow River), the second longest river in China, used to be very polluted and full of fine sediments, and would flood easily. Its water is now in the process of being cleared up through the planting of vegetation in the upstream regions of the River. The vegetation holds the top soil in place and prevents it from being blown into the river by the winds. The River is expected to clear up within the next decade.

Chart 15.21. The Levels of PM2.5 in the Air of Major Chinese Cities, in Microgram per Cubic Meter

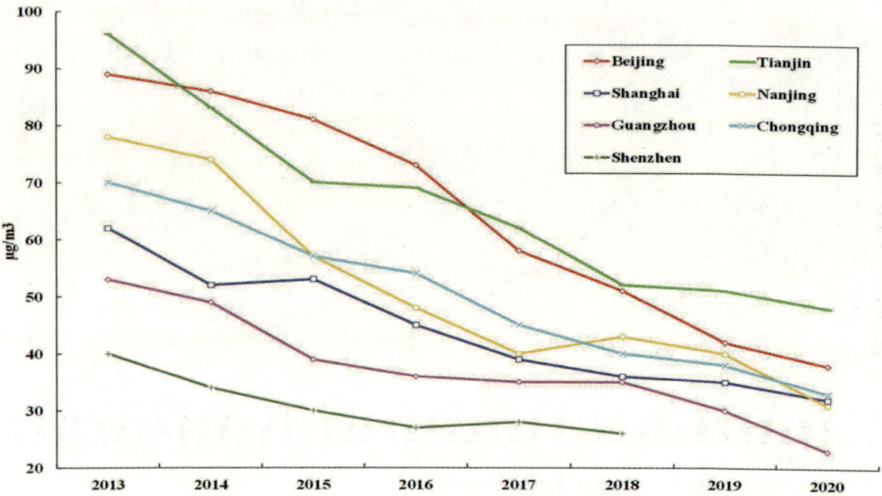

Source: China Statistical Yearbook, various issues.

Chart 15.22. The Levels of PM2.5 in the Air: A Comparison of 2015 and 2021

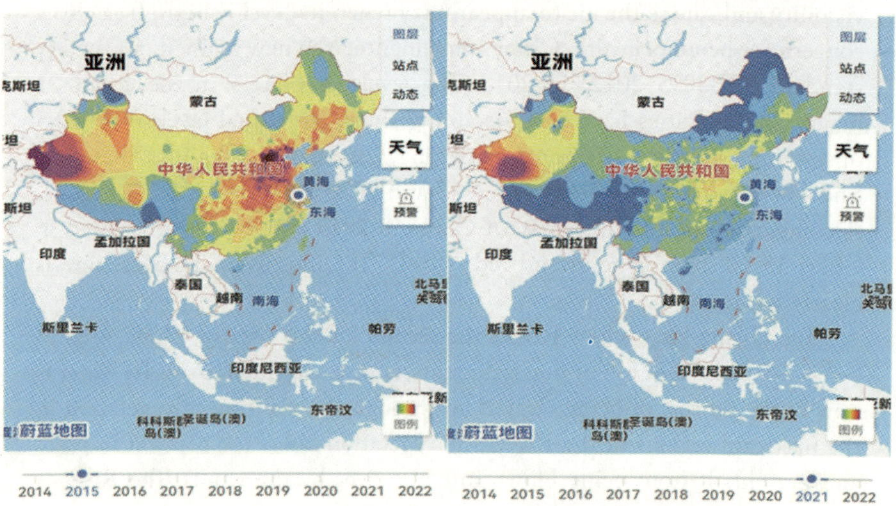

Source: The Institute of Public and Environmental Affairs, http://www.ipe.org.cn.

Poverty Alleviation

China has been the most successful in the eradication of chronic extreme poverty. The Chinese poverty standard, adopted in 2010, defines a family to be in poverty if its annual per-capita income is below 2,300 yuan in 2010 prices. This is equivalent to approximately 3,054 yuan in 2021 prices (US$479). In 1978, before the beginning of the economic reform and opening-up, the poverty rate according to this standard was a whopping 97.5%! By the end of 2020 it reached zero (see Chart 15.23). Granted that this is still a rather low level of annual income per capita, but it is slightly more than US$1.30 per person per day, higher than the United Nations' standard of US$1 a day. We should emphasize that this is a permanent eradication of extreme poverty, rather than a one-off relief. The formerly extremely poor are now able to provide a decent living for themselves in a sustainable manner.

Chart 15.23. The Eradication of Extreme Poverty: The Share of Population under the 2010 Poverty Line

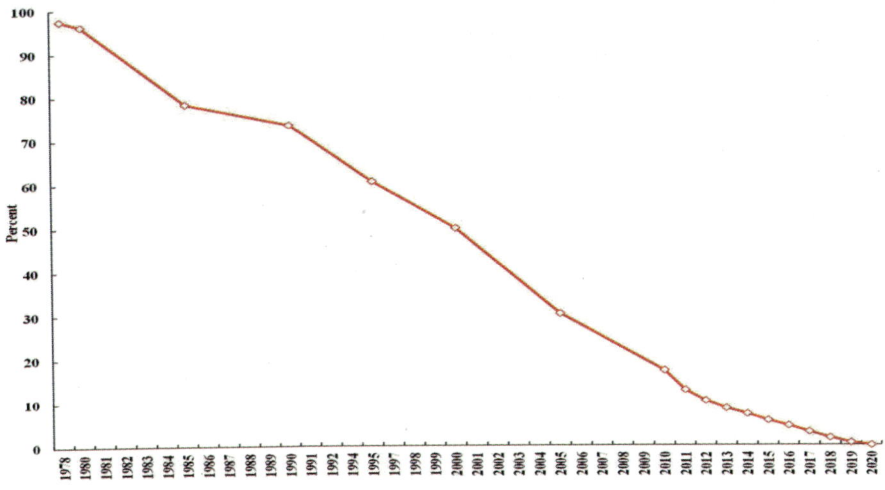

Source: China Statistical Abstract (National Bureau of Statistics of China, 2020).

However, despite significant progress in the alleviation of poverty in China, the degree of income inequality in China has increased significantly since 1983 (see Chart 15.24). According to the National Bureau of Statistics of China (NBSC), the Gini coefficient for China stood at 0.47 in 2020, compared to 0.49 for the U.S. Historically, the Chinese Gini coefficient fell from 0.56 in 1953 to 0.28, its lowest point, in 1983, a tremendous improvement, according to the data compiled by the United Nations. It then turned around and rose to a peak of 0.45 (0.49 according to NBSC) in 2008. It has since declined to 0.43 (0.47 according to NBSC) in 2019.

This is a very high level of income inequality, but consistent with Mr. Deng Xiaoping's policy of letting some people get rich first. It is now time to let other people get rich too. This is the reason for the "Common Prosperity" policy.

Chart 15.24. The Evolution of the Chinese Gini Coefficient over Time

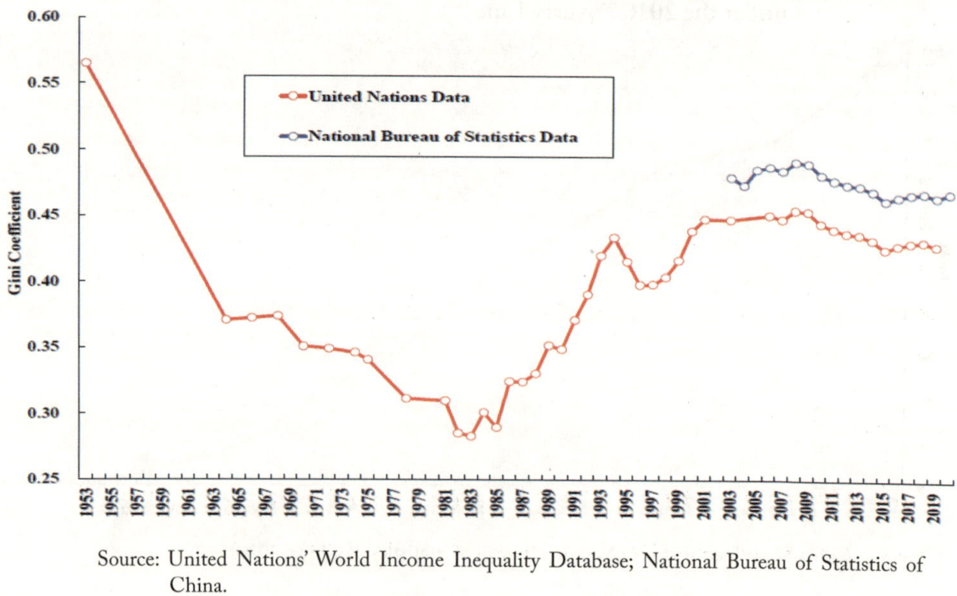

Source: United Nations' World Income Inequality Database; National Bureau of Statistics of China.

6. Public Goods Provision through Infrastructural Investment

In the short run, all increases in government expenditures have the same macroeconomic effects on both the GDP and employment. However, in the long run, increases in real fixed-asset investments augment the real capital stock and increase the real GDP, whereas increases in consumption due to increases in disposable income through, e.g., tax cuts and transfer payments, generate no direct lasting benefits. Infrastructural investment, which is often needed for the provision of public goods, can generate benefits that can be widely shared in the economy even though they cannot be fully captured or internalised by the projects themselves.

Historically, in China, the Great Wall, built in the Qin Dynasty (221–206 BC), was an infrastructure for national defense, and the Grand Canal, constructed in the Sui Dynasty (581–618 AD), was an infrastructure for the transportation of grains. Over the past few millennia, there were numerous water conservancy projects for irrigation and flood control. These were all government-financed and often depended on conscripted labour.

Infrastructural investment includes investment in communication, transportation, and power. Infrastructural investment is complementary to non-infrastructural fixed-asset investment because it can enhance the latter's rate of return. (Think of how a new highway can enhance and facilitate the expansion of trade among the enterprises located *en route*.) The existence of appropriate infrastructure can make the markets even more efficient (the "visible hand" working with the "invisible hand").

In addition, many infrastructural investments are "development-leading" investments, with their supplies creating their own demands, as opposed to "development-lagging" investments, i.e., investments that are undertaken only when the demands already exist. "Development-leading" infrastructural investments can generate significant externalities and enhance the returns of other fixed-asset investments both public and private.

Real fixed-asset investment, including real infrastructural investment, grew rapidly in China between 2008 and 2017, partly as a response to the Global Financial Crisis of 2008 (see Chart 15.25). Since 2017, their rates of growth have considerably moderated. Infrastructural investment is a major component of fixed-asset investment. The share of infrastructural investment in total fixed-asset investment ranged between a low of 30% and a high of 40%

between 2003 and 2021, with an average of 35.8%. Infrastructural investment in communication and transportation has also helped to make the Chinese economy a single unified market, realising the huge benefits of its economies of scale. However, infrastructural investment frequently generates benefits known as externalities that cannot be captured by the investment itself and hence must be financed or subsidised by the government. On April 26, 2022, in a meeting of the Central Committee for Financial and Economic Affairs, President Xi Jinping called for "all-out efforts to strengthen infrastructure construction" in the country.

Chart 15.25. Real Fixed-Asset Investment and Real Infrastructural Investment (2019 Prices)

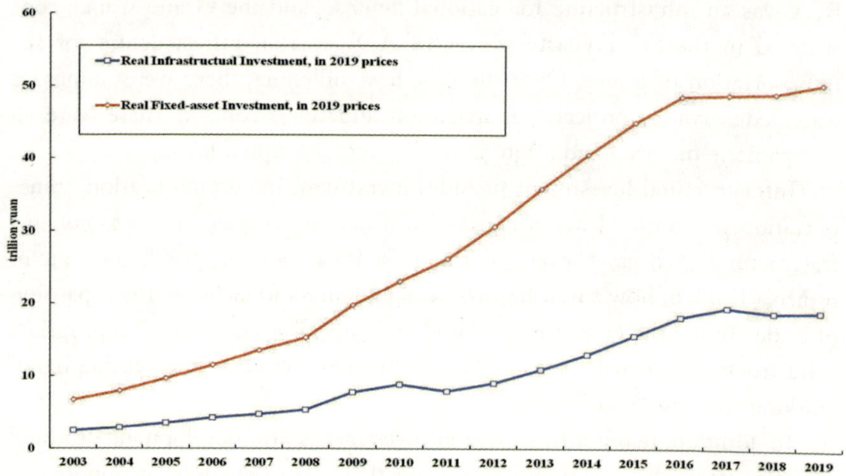

Source: Author's calculations from the data published in the China Yearbook of Social Statistics 2020.

7. Public Goods Provision as Aggregate Demands for Consumption and Fixed-Asset Investment

The Components of Chinese Aggregate Demand

The share of household consumption in aggregate demand (GDP) has been declining over time, from a peak of almost 71% in 1962 to less than 38% in 2020 (see Chart 15.4). Gross domestic investment, which includes real fixed-asset investment, has become the most important source of aggregate demand since 2004 (see Chart 15.26). It was just below 43% in 2020. The share of government consumption, which includes most public goods consumption, has been increasing slowly and gradually from 13.5% in 1952 to just below 17% in 2020. There is a great deal of room for both government investment and government consumption to grow through increased public goods provision. Net exports will continue to decline in relative importance as a component of Chinese aggregate demand, given the Chinese objective of balanced international trade.

The share of household consumption in household disposable income has also been declining over time, from over 90% in 1988 to 68.6% in 2021 (see Chart 15.27). Moreover, as China becomes increasingly urbanised, the share of household consumption in household disposable income is likely to decline further, since urban households have a higher propensity to save than rural households. In 2021, the shares of household consumption in disposable income were, respectively, 84.1% for rural households and 63.9% for urban households. Between 1949 and 2021, the share of rural population fell from almost 90% to slightly more than 35% (see Chart 15.28). Thus, increases in household disposable income alone are not likely to be sufficient to increase household consumption significantly as a component of aggregate demand. Increases in fixed-asset investments and government consumption are needed. This is where public goods provision can make an important contribution.

Chart 15.26. The Percentage Distribution of the Sources of Aggregate Demand

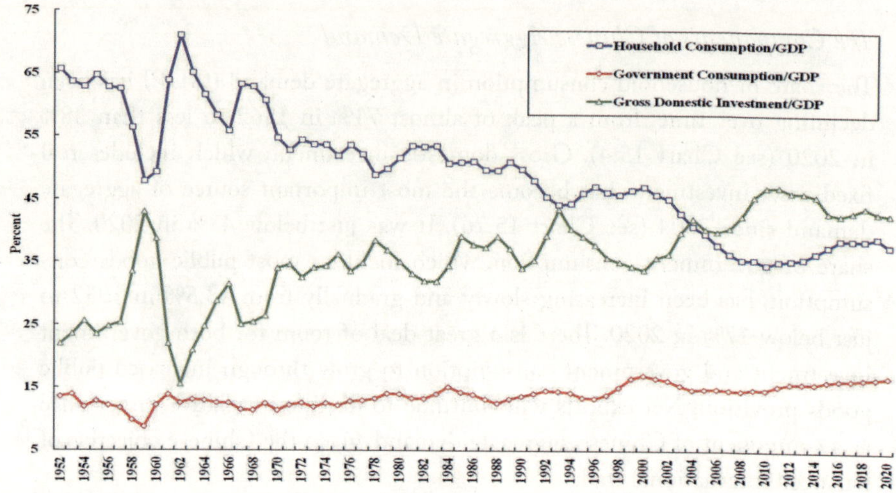

Source: National Bureau of Statistics of China (https://data.stats.gov.cn/easyquery.htm?cn=C01).

Chart 15.27. Household Consumption as a Share of Household Disposable Income

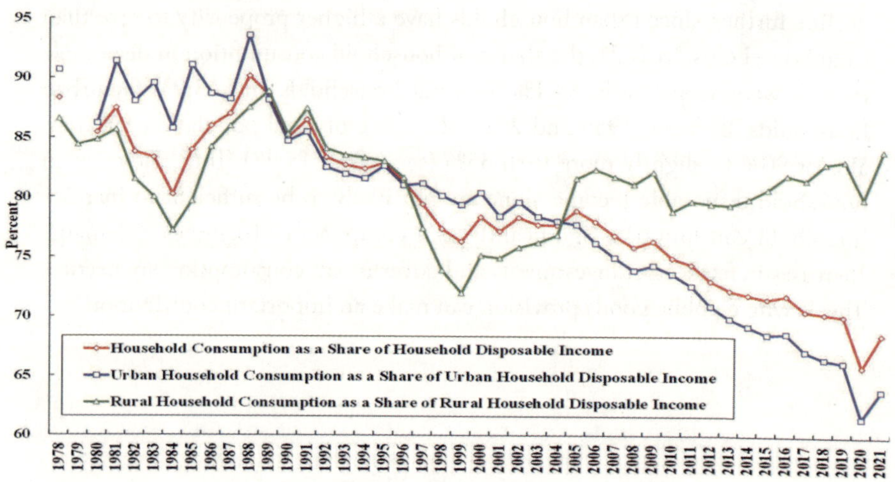

Source: National Bureau of Statistics of China (https://data.stats.gov.cn/easyquery.htm?cn=C01).

Chart 15.28. The Distribution of Chinese Population between Rural and Urban

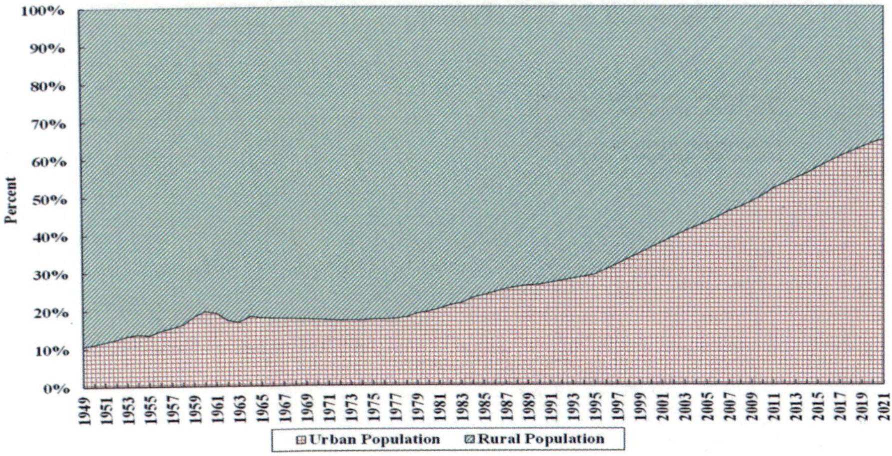

Source: National Bureau of Statistics of China (https://data.stats.gov.cn/easyquery.htm?cn=C01).

The Dual-Circulation Economic Development Strategy

The Chinese economy will pursue a dual-circulation development strategy with a domestic circulation and an international circulation complementing each other, but with the domestic circulation playing the primary role, which is to be expected for large continental economies like China (and also the U.S.). The Chinese economy is no longer export-driven. It aims to have balanced international trade. It will be domestic-demand-driven—by household consumption, gross domestic investment, and public goods consumption. The adoption of a dual-circulation strategy by China is evidence of its recognition that total self-sufficiency is not a viable alternative and of its continuing commitment to an open economy and to economic globalisation.

The Chinese ratio of international circulation to domestic circulation was below 10% before 1981, when it began to rise. It reached a peak of almost 70% in 2006, but then declined to 35% by 2020 (see Chart 15.29). The U.S.'s ratio was around 20% between 1980 and 2000 and rose to a peak of 30% in 2011, but then declined to 23% by 2020. It is expected that the ratios for both countries will be declining some more over time and eventually reach similar levels. A possible de-coupling of the Chinese and U.S. economies will increase the importance of domestic circulation for China. Public goods provision can become a major source of increase in domestic aggregate demand for both consumption and investment going forward.

Chart 15.29. International Circulation as a Ratio of Domestic Circulation: China and the U.S. (Percent)

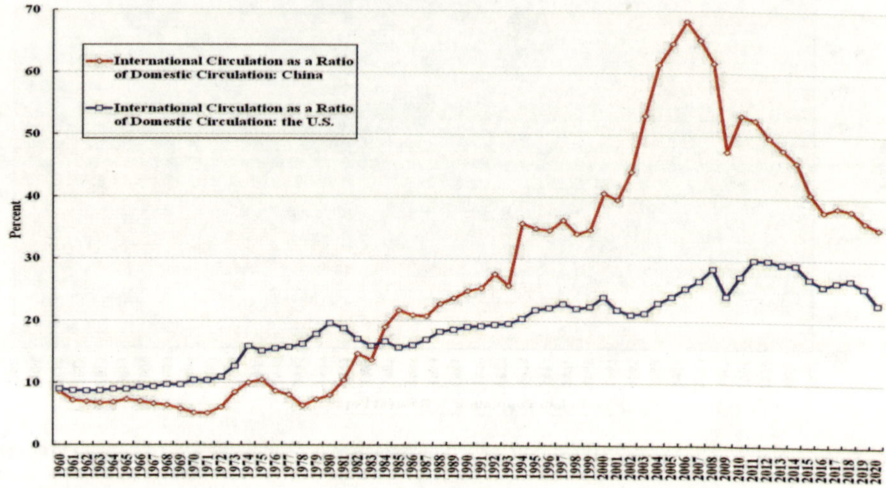

Source: National Bureau of Statistics of China (https://data.stats.gov.cn/easyquery.htm?cn=C01); U.S. Bureau of Economic Analysis (https://apps.bea.gov/itable/index.cfm).

What Public Goods Will Be Provided?

What are some of the public goods that need to be provided in the next decade or decades that require significant capital and current expenditures? The following is a possible list:

(1) Prevention of climate change: This will require both infrastructural and non-infrastructural fixed-asset investments—the replacement of fossil-fuel-based infrastructure and equipment, carbon sequestration, and research on nuclear fusion.
(2) Environmental preservation, protection, and restoration.
(3) Common prosperity: alleviation of poverty in accordance with a new 2030 standard.
(4) A free and free-standing public text (including email), voice, and video communication system that is respectful of personal data privacy.
(5) The construction and operation of pre-schools, schools, and universities, hospitals, and elderly care homes.

(6) The construction and operation of public rental housing in urban areas.
(7) Outer space exploration.

8. The Financing of Public Goods Provision

One problem of public goods provision is that most of the activities do not generate positive value-added at market prices. For example, cleaning up air pollution is costly but does not generate any net revenue and hence does not create any net positive GDP; providing mass transit improves the environment, reduces traffic congestion, and enhances welfare, but often cannot break even on its own. Thus, increasing public goods provision is likely to result in a reduction of the rate of growth of conventionally measured real GDP even as it enhances social welfare (unless and until China adopts a "green GDP" as a metric).

How can public goods provision be financed? In general, it has to be subsidised by the government. Public goods can be financed through general revenue, project bonds, user fees, or specific taxes such as a carbon tax. One potential source of government revenue that can be tapped by China is the accumulated undistributed earnings of state-owned enterprises (SOEs) and their parents. Publicly listed SOEs should be required to pay annual cash dividends to their shareholders, including their state-owned parent companies. These funds will eventually end up in the State Treasury to help finance the budget deficit, if any. General revenue can also be increased through a reform of both individual and enterprise taxation and through enhanced tax compliance and enforcement. For example, Chinese income taxation is supposed to be "worldwide," just like that of the U.S., but the income of Chinese individuals from foreign sources is currently effectively not taxed.

9. Concluding Remarks

The economic development of China since the establishment of the People's Republic is characterised by not only quantitative growth, but also significant improvements in the "quality" of growth. Most of the improvements in quality have been brought about through the provision of more and better public goods. Provision of public goods such as education, public health, elderly care, environmental preservation, protection, and restoration, basic research, infrastructure, social safety net, and alleviation of poverty has been vastly expanded over the past seven decades, with significant positive results. The provision of public goods has also raised the potential GDP of the Chinese economy through its effects on increasing the aggregate demand, the real capital stock, the productivity of the labour force, and the rate of return on other fixed-asset investments. For example, the improvements in the quality of the Chinese labour force have greatly enhanced its productivity.

Public goods are by their very nature mostly "local," and their provision is consistent with the Chinese "dual-circulation development strategy," which has its primary focus on domestic circulation. The provision of public goods also constitutes a form of redistribution in kind, e.g., clean air and water, which can be enjoyed by everyone, and hence also directly advances the goal of "common prosperity." Finally, increasing the provision of public goods can be a significant source of growth of the domestic aggregate demand for both consumption and investment, over and above what increases in household consumption alone are able to provide. Maintaining an adequate growth of domestic aggregate demand is essential for continued Chinese economic prosperity. However, the provision of public goods frequently results in negative value-added at market prices, and will therefore reduce, rather than enhance, the rate of growth of measured GDP. This is one reason the targeted rate of growth of the Chinese economy in 2022 has been set at a relatively low level of 5.5%, the lowest in more than four decades. Despite significant increase in the degree of income inequality in China, as measured by the Gini coefficient, the welfare of all Chinese people has improved significantly since 1978 as a result of its economic reform and opening-up to the world.

References

Che, Haigang. *Almanac of China's Economy, 2020.* Beijing: Almanac of China's Economy Press, 2021.

Lau, Lawrence J., and Yanyan Xiong. "An International Comparison of the COVID-19 Experiences of the Group-of-Seven and the BRICS Countries." *China and the World: Ancient and Modern Silk Road* 4, no. 4 (December 2021a), pp. 1–21, doi: 10.1142/S2591729321500164.

Lau, Lawrence J., and Yanyan Xiong. *The COVID-19 Epidemic in China.* Singapore: World Scientific Publishing Company, 2021b.

Lau, Lawrence J., and Yanyan Xiong. *Are There Laws of Innovation?* Singapore: World Scientific Publishing Company, 2022.

Ministry of Ecology and Environment of the People's Republic of China. *The People's Republic of China Initial National Communication on Climate Change.* Beijing: China Planning Press, 2004. https://www.mee.gov.cn/ywgz/ydqhbh/wsqtkz/201904/P020190419524224387926.pdf.

Ministry of Ecology and Environment of the People's Republic of China. "Second Biennial Update Report on Climate Change of the People's Republic of China." Beijing: National Development and Reform Commission (NDRC), 2018a. https://www.mee.gov.cn/ywgz/ydqhbh/wsqtkz/201907/P020190701765971866571.pdf.

Ministry of Ecology and Environment of the People's Republic of China. "The Third National Communication on Climate Change of the People's Republic of China." Beijing: NCCC, 2018b. https://www.mee.gov.cn/ywgz/ydqhbh/wsqtkz/201907/P020190701762678052438.pdf.

National Bureau of Statistics of China. *Great Decade: Statistics on the Achievements of Economic and Cultural Construction of the People's Republic of China.* Beijing: People's Publishing House, 1959.

National Bureau of Statistics of China. *China Statistical Abstract.* Beijing: China Statistics Press, 2020.

National Bureau of Statistics of China. *China Statistical Yearbook*, various issues. Beijing: China Statistics Press.

U.S. National Science Foundation. "Table SPBS-2: S&E Articles in all S&E Fields, Fractional Count, by Region, Country, or Economy: 1996–2020." Publications Output: U.S. Trends and International Comparisons, 2021. https://ncses.nsf.gov/pubs/nsb20214/data.

Wagner, Caroline S., Lin Zhang, and Loet Leydesdorff. "A Discussion of Measuring the Top-1% Most-Highly Cited Publications: Quality and Impact of Chinese Papers." *Scientometrics* 127 (2022), pp. 1825–1839, doi: 10.1007/s11192-022-04291-z.

Chapter 16.

The Prospects for the Chinese Economy in 2023 and Beyond*

2022 was not a good year for the Chinese economy. In 2022, the COVID-19 epidemic, which started in December 2019, caused significant economic disruptions in the second quarter, especially in Shanghai, resulting in a real rate of growth for the Mainland economy of only 3.0% for the year as a whole. This is the second lowest annual rate since economic reform and opening began in 1978,[1] and only slightly more than half of the original target rate of 5.5%. Moreover, the crude birth rate, which has been declining, fell to 6.77 per thousand, below the crude death rate, 7.37 per thousand, for the first time since 1960 (see Chart 16.1).[2] The total population declined by 850,000 to 1.411 billion. In the near term, it is unlikely that the Chinese crude birth rate will rise significantly. China is likely to be replaced by India as the most populous nation in the world in 2023.

---

* This chapter was originally published in *China-US Focus*, January 24, 2003, https://www.chinausfocus.com/finance-economy/the-prospects-for-the-chinese-economy-in-2023-and-beyond.

1 The lowest was the 2.2% of 2020. The third lowest was the 3.9% of 1990.

2 It should, however, be recognised that the COVID-19 epidemic and the resulting control measures have also contributed to falls in the crude birth rate as well as marriage rates and to a rise in the crude death rates since early 2020. The rate of growth of the total population is expected to recover to a certain extent now that the epidemic has come under control.

Chart 16.1. The Crude Birth and Death Rates of Mainland China

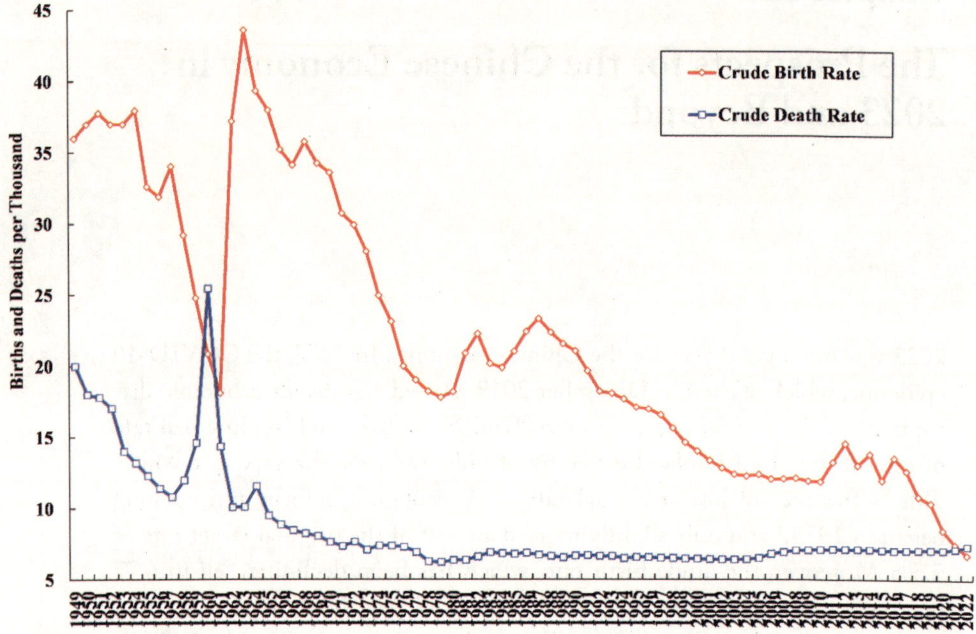

However, 2022 was not all negative. Despite the COVID-19 epidemic, the Russia-Ukraine conflict, and the threat of a worldwide economic recession, total Chinese exports and imports of goods increased 7.7% to exceed 42 trillion Yuan (US$6.0 trillion at the 2022 year-end exchange rate of 6.986 Yuan per U.S. Dollar) for the first time and China remains the largest trading nation in goods in the world. The declining total population does have one advantage—it implies that the Chinese real GDP per capita will rise at a rate faster than the Chinese real GDP.

2023 can turn out to be significantly different. First, given that the lethality of the current COVID-19 virus variant has declined significantly, the Mainland has been undergoing a rapid transition from a strict "Dynamic Zero" policy to an essentially "Living with the Virus" policy. Such a transition may be economically disruptive in the short term, as hundreds of millions of people become infected within a relatively short period of time, but it does accelerate considerably the return to normalcy. As of this writing, some unverified reports suggested that perhaps close to 1 billion persons out of a total population of 1.4 billion on the Mainland may have been infected in some way by the COVID-19 virus, effectively approaching "herd immunity", but the fatality rate has remained extremely low. Hopefully the transition and recovery will have been completed before the end of the first quarter of 2023.

Second, 2023 is also the first year of a complete transition of the executive branch of the Chinese Government in March, which occurs once every five years. The new administration is ready to launch new initiatives to restart and restore the economy. The focus of the Government will clearly be on economic development—the Mainland GDP per capita in 2022, US$12,270,[3] was only one fifth of the GDP per capita of the U.S. and ranked approximately eightieth among all economies in the world. China has its work cut out to continue to improve the livelihood of the Chinese people. The repeated affirmation of a socialist market economy with Chinese characteristics by various Chinese Government leaders should dispel any anxiety that China would return to a centrally-planned economic system. It cannot and will not. The purpose of the Mainland anti-monopoly and anti-trust laws is actually to promote and ensure the efficiency of the competitive market system, similar to that in the U.S. and the European Union. It should be viewed as an attempt to strengthen the market system rather than the opposite. Of course, China also wants to avoid the emergence of a plutocracy on the Mainland, under which moneyed interests control the politics.

According to the report on the Economic Work Conference held in mid-December, the private sector will continue to enjoy support from the Government in the same way as the state-owned sector, and property rights will continue to be protected. "Common Prosperity (*gongfu*)", as advocated by President Xi Jinping, should not be misinterpreted as "Equalised Prosperity (*junfu*)". It simply means that the time has come for people who have not yet become rich to have the opportunity to also become rich. In fact, in the same week during which "Common Prosperity" was first introduced, the brand-new Beijing Stock Exchange was established to enable small and medium private enterprises to raise equity capital for their businesses. It is not something that would have been undertaken by a government intent on discouraging private enterprises.

3 At 2022 year-end market exchange rate.

1. The Chinese Economic Fundamentals

Are there enough primary factors, capital, and labour, in the Chinese economy to enable it to continue to grow? The Chinese national savings rate, currently at approximately 45 percent, the highest in the world amongst major economies, should be amply sufficient to support a high domestic investment rate, even in the absence of inflows of foreign direct investment.[4] There is no shortage of supply of capital.

Current Chinese demographic developments do appear unfavorable—its total population is ageing rapidly and has begun to fall (which is, in part, the legacy of the "one-child" policy which was in place between 1980 and 2015). However, the labour supply problem is basically manageable. The demand for labour can be satisfied by continued urbanisation, that is, by the movement of surplus labour from the rural to the urban areas. There still exists substantial surplus labour—the primary (agricultural) sector generated only 7.3% of GDP but accounted for 22.9% of total employment in 2021. In addition, the gradual raising of the mandatory retirement ages, which have officially remained at 50 for women[5] and 60 for men, a practice inherited from the early 1950s, when life expectancy was in the low sixties, should help greatly. Chinese life expectancy at birth, which was only 35 years in 1949 and 67.8 years in 1981, grew to 77.9 years in 2020 (compared to 72.3 years for the world as a whole). Life expectancy at age 60 was 20.21 years in 2020. In 2022, there were some 70 million persons in China between the ages of 60 and 65, who could be mobilised into the labour force if the mandatory retirement ages are extended. In the report on the Economic Work Conference, mention is made of the possibility of extending the retirement ages. In addition, the recent elimination of restrictions on the number of children per married couple and the possible lowering of the marriage-eligible ages should also help to increase the Chinese birth rate gradually, but it will take a couple of decades before they have a noticeable impact on the labour force. Despite the alarm bells set off by the

---

4 Foreign direct investment, which accounted for approximately 15% of the gross domestic investment on the Mainland at its peak in 1994, accounts for only slightly more than 2%, including "round-tripped" investment, today.

5 However, if a woman is a cadre (*ganbu*), she does not have to retire until 55.

decline in total population, China is still very far from suffering a serious chronic shortage of labour.

Moreover, the quality of the Chinese labour force has improved significantly through various investments in education and public health. For example, the proportion of the total population with tertiary education increased from 0.6% in 1982 to over 15% in 2020, a huge improvement. The "efficiency-equivalent" quantity of the labour force continues to grow even though in strictly numerical terms the labour force is no longer growing.

Investment in research and development (R&D) is critical to innovation. China's expenditure on R&D in 2022 was 2.55% of its GDP.[6] Indigenous innovation has been occurring in many areas, for example: 5G communication, the BeiDou Navigation Satellite System, high-speed trains, quantum communication, super-computers, and ultra-high-voltage transmission of electricity. China also enjoys significant economies of scale, learning-by-doing (that is, efficiency improvement resulting from repetitive production of the same good, such as high-speed trains), and the advantage of longer upper tails in its ability distribution because of the size of its population.

2. The Major Uncertainties

However, even as the COVID-19 epidemic has become "normalised", the Chinese economy is still faced with significant uncertainties. A first uncertainty is the possibility of a global economic recession, affecting Europe and North America. A pause in the Russia-Ukraine conflict should help. Fortunately, the Mainland economy is no longer dependent on exports—with the main driver of its growth being domestic demand. Moreover, as a large continental economy like the U.S., the domestic Chinese economy is largely unaffected by external disturbances. Thus, while the Chinese rates of growth of exports and imports fluctuate like other East Asian economies, the rate of growth of its real GDP has remained relatively stable.

A second uncertainty is the China-U.S. strategic competition, which is likely to be the new normal for the coming decade, with continuing "wars" in trade, investment, and technology. Some de-coupling of the Chinese and U.S.

---

6 http://www.stats.gov.cn/tjsj/sjjd/202301/t20230119_1892374.html.

economies is inevitable under these circumstances, but the economic impacts on both economies will be relatively marginal. The continuing U.S. tariffs on imports from China have had only a small effect on the Chinese economy. Export controls on U.S. high-technology hardware and software can indeed slow down some sectors in the Chinese economy to a certain extent, but not really essential Chinese projects related to its national security, such as the manufacturing of super-computers, for which cost per se is not an important consideration. Chinese super-computers today can be built entirely with domestically produced components.

However, the China-U.S. strategic competition is not likely to result in a hot war because the resulting casualties and losses will be unthinkably enormous on both sides. There will be no winners, only losers. I remain optimistic that rationality will prevail and there will not be a hot war, just as the former Soviet Union and the U.S. managed to avoid a war in the last Century despite their intense rivalry.

A third uncertainty is a long-term one and has to do with the demographic developments. In the short and medium terms, the problems of a potential labour shortage can be mitigated, as discussed above. However, in the longer term, it is in Chinese national interests to try to achieve a net reproduction rate of one, that is, to maintain an essentially stable population. This requires an increase in the crude birth rate to over 7 per thousand in the long run. I believe this is feasible but cannot predict when it will be achieved.

3. Is There Sufficient Aggregate Demand?

The real question for the Mainland economy is whether there will be sufficient aggregate demand. China is a surplus economy, with not only surplus labour, but also surplus capital, as well as surplus productive capacity. As long as there is demand, there will be supply. The Chinese economy today is mostly driven by internal demand--household consumption, public goods consumption, and gross fixed investment--with gross fixed investment being the most important. However, investment demand is mostly driven by expectations about the future. And expectations, if credible, can be self-fulfilling. This is where the Chinese Government has to exercise leadership and try to change public expectations by its concrete actions, as was done through the 1992 "Southern Tour" of the late Mr. Deng Xiaoping,[7] and the 2008 economic stimulus package of 4 trillion Yuan in the aftermath of the Global Financial Crisis.[8] Monetary policy alone will be insufficient: as is well known, one can pull on a string, but one cannot push on a string. I believe there will be a major effort on the part of the Government to increase aggregate demand directly through gross fixed investment and transform expectations in the coming year.

Two major components of gross fixed investment are infrastructural and real estate investments. Infrastructural investments are needed on climate change, environmental preservation, protection and restoration, and communication, transportation and power. Other infrastructural investment can also include the construction of schools, universities, hospitals, and elderly care homes, especially in the less developed parts of China. Real estate investments may be impacted by the massive failure or insolvency of some of the real estate developers, which will in turn affect the construction and building materials sectors of the Chinese economy. However, the demand for residential real estate investments can be supported by not only owner-occupied housing but also by rental housing. The Chinese Government can promote rental housing under corporate or other institutional ownership as a viable alternative to owner-occupied housing, thus maintaining the demands for housing and hence for the construction and building material sectors. The ultimate total residential housing demand is of course the same, but there can be a different equilibrium between renting and owning.[9]

4. Forecasts of the Real Rate of Chinese Economic Growth in 2023[10]

For 2023, the Chinese Academy of Social Sciences has made a forecast of 5.1% real growth. The Chinese Academy of Sciences has issued a forecast of

---

7 The "Southern Tour" was followed by five years of double-digit real rates of growth.

8 This was followed by five years of average annual real rate of growth of 9.4%.

9 In some German cities, for example, up to 40 percent of the residents may be renters.

10 These forecasts have been collected from different reports in the press at various times. They may have been updated by the different organisations since.

growth of around 6%. From multilateral institutions, there are the forecasts of 4.3% by the World Bank, 4.4% by the International Monetary Fund, 4.6% by the Organisation for Economic Cooperation and Development (OECD), and 5.2% by the European Union. Nikkei Asia and Economic Intelligence Unit (EIU), both research institutions, said respectively that growth would be 4.7% and 5.2%. Among investment banks, J.P. Morgan predicted 4.3%, Goldman Sachs, 4.5%, both BNP Paribas and ING 5%, and Morgan Stanley, 5.4%. In summary, the minimum forecast is 4.3% and the maximum forecast is 6%, with a median of 5% and a mean of 4.9%.

Another source of information consists of the announced 2023 target growth rates of the 31 provinces, municipalities and autonomous regions of Mainland China.[11] These target growth rates range between a low of around 4% for Tianjin and a high of around 9.5% for Hainan, followed by Tibet (around 8%), and Jiangxi and Xinjiang (both around 7%). There are four provinces and regions with a target growth rate of around 6.5%, Chongqing at over 6%, and Gansu and Henan at 6%. Then follow nine provinces and regions with target growth rate of around 6%. Three of the four economically most important provinces, Guangdong, Jiangsu, Shandong and Zhejiang, which together account for almost 35% of Chinese GDP, have a target growth rate of above 5%, with Jiangsu at around 5%. Only two municipalities, Beijing and Tianjin, have a target growth rate below 5%, with Beijing at above 4.5% and Tianjin at around 4%.

Since the provinces, municipalities, and regions are of different sizes, the unweighted arithmetic mean of their target GDP growth rates is of little use. The median provincial target growth rate is around 6%. A provincial GDP-weighted average of the target growth rates yields 5.64%.[12] All of this suggests that the national target rate of growth is most certainly going to be above 5%, and possibly close to 6%, especially considering that nine of the provinces and municipalities have committed to try to exceed their respective target growth rates.[13]

---

11 These provincial, municipal and regional target growth rates are taken from www.Chinanews.com.

12 The provincial GDP weights of 2020 are used for this calculation.

13 These provinces and municipalities include Beijing, Chongqing, Guangdong, Jiangxi, Liaoning, Shandong, Shanghai, Sichuan, and Zhejiang.

5. Economic Growth Beyond 2023

The Chinese economy will be growing faster than those of North America and Europe in the next ten years even though all of them will be slowing down to varying degrees. It is an empirical regularity that as the real GDP per capita of an economy rises, its real rate of growth falls. Thus, the Chinese economy cannot continue to grow at a real rate of over 9% per annum as it did between 1978 and 2018, but its real GDP per capita, around US$12,270, is still in a range that allows its economy to grow at an average annual real rate of approximately 6% for at least another decade. In Chart 16.2, we have plotted the real rates of economic growth of China (in red), Japan (in yellow), and the U.S. (in blue), against their respective real GDPs per capita. It is clear that with a real GDP per capita below US$20,000, an economy can still grow at an average annual real rate of approximately 6% and the Chinese economy will be operating within that range over the coming decade.

Chart 16.2. The Rate of Growth of Real GDP versus Real GDP per Capita, China, Japan, and the U.S.

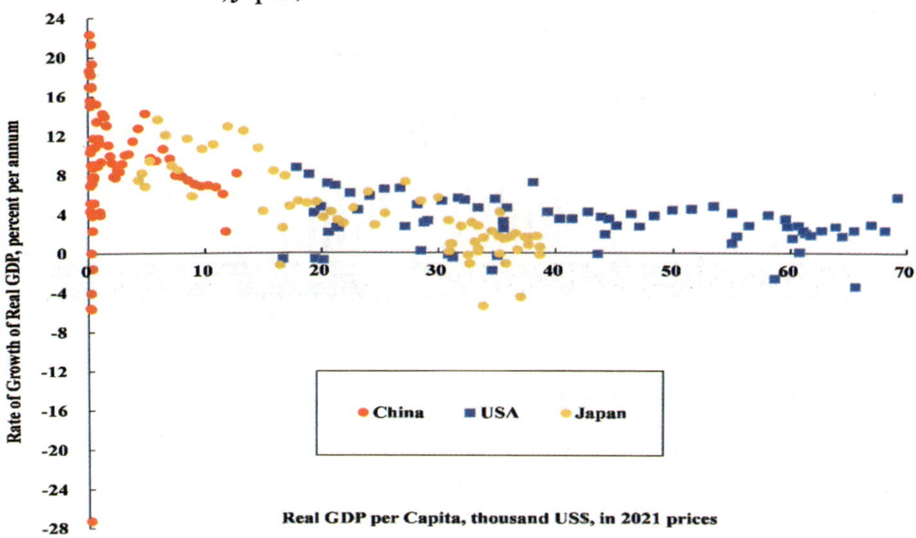

My own forecast is that by 2030, the real GDP of Mainland China at market prices will reach parity with that of the U.S., at approximately US$29.5 trillion, in 2021 prices (see Chart 16.3). Even then, Chinese real GDP per capita will still be less than 30 percent of the then U.S. real GDP per capita.

Chart 16.3. Actual and Projected Real GDP of China and the U.S. (2021 Prices) and Their Respective Rates of Growth

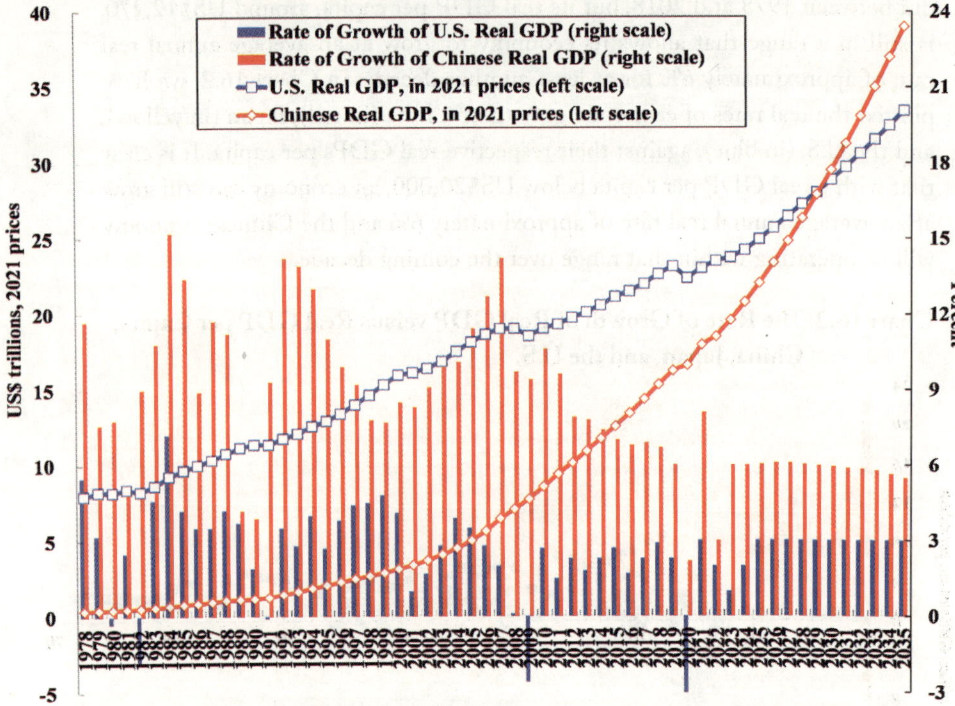

6. Concluding Remarks

Given the facts and uncertainties above, my personal forecast for the Chinese economy in 2023 is a 6% real rate of growth, based on my optimistic belief that there will be a rapid turn-around in public expectations, led by the Government. And for the coming decade, the average annual real rate of Chinese economic growth is likely to lie between 5.5% and 6%.

Conclusion

While the Chinese economy is unique and exceptional in many ways, its development experience can be explained and attributed conventionally, as we have done in the Introduction and Sections I through III. As Chapter 4 shows, the growth in Chinese output may be mostly attributed to the growth of Chinese inputs, and the most important source of growth turns out to be the accumulation of tangible or physical capital, that is, structures and equipment, accounting for 55.7 percent. The growth of labour accounted for 9.7 percent. Economies of scale, the initial economic inefficiency prior to the economic reform, and technical progress accounted for 14.0, 12.7, and 8.0 percent, respectively. It cannot therefore be said to be a miracle. Is it unexpected? Yes. Is it miraculous? Not quite. It was the combined outcome of the economic reform and opening to the world in 1978 and the pragmatic strategies and policies undertaken by generations of able and wise leaders.

The Chinese economy has grown rapidly during the past four and a half decades at an average annual rate of over 9 percent. It is projected to continue growing at average annual rates of between 5 and 6 percent for at least a couple more decades. Chinese economic growth is sustained and sustainable, even though it has begun to slow, and is therefore definitely also not a bubble.

As shown in Chapter 6, the Chinese development experience also shares many commonalities with those of other East Asian economies, in terms of initial endowments (or lack thereof), initial conditions (such as the existence of surplus agricultural labour), cultural characteristics (high savings rates, industriousness, and high value for education), economic strategies and policies (export promotion, investment in basic infrastructure, and maintenance of macroeconomic stability), and the predictability, stability, and long-term orientation of government policies that result from continuous single-party rule during the early stages of economic development.

However, there are also some characteristics that are unique to the Chinese economy. The initial economic slack in the economy resulting from its legacy as a centrally-planned economy was an advantage that most other East Asian economies did not have. The economies of scale and the benefits of "learning by doing," which result from the size of its economy, including its population, are also not found elsewhere, except for India and possibly Indonesia. However, it is much more costly for Indonesia, being an extensive archipelago, to achieve connectivity within the entire country to be able to realise its economies of scale.[1] The large size of the Chinese economy and hence its domestic market also reduces its degree of dependence on international trade and helps to insulate it from the impacts of external disturbances. Its large geographical footprint also implies that there is adequate diversity in terms of climate and natural resources so that overall, it can be more self-sufficient and less vulnerable than it otherwise may be.[2]

The Chinese economy also has the advantage of relative backwardness. It has been able to learn from the experiences of successes and failures of other economies and to leapfrog and bypass stages of development (e.g., the telex machine, the VHS videotape player, the fixed landline telephone, and the personal checking bank account are all mostly unknown in China). It is also possible for the Chinese economy to have creation without destruction (e.g., the cellphone does not have to compete with the fixed landline phone; online virtual stores like Taobao do not have to destroy brick and mortar bookstores that do not exist in the first place; internet payment services such as Alipay and WeChat Pay serve the needs of a population with no prior personal checking bank accounts). Thus, the adoption of innovation in China has lower costs and higher net benefits than in other more mature economies.

Finally, the Chinese model for economic reform, which can enable a smooth economic transition from a centrally-planned to a market economy, while at the same time allow the existing government to retain political control and preserve social stability, has been adopted, and its success has been replicated to varying degrees in the formerly centrally-planned economies of Vietnam, Cambodia, and the Lao People's Democratic Republic. The replicability of the Chinese economic development experience elsewhere proves that the Chinese economy is neither a miracle nor a bubble.

---

1 Although 60 percent of the Indonesian population resides on the island of Java.

2 It is, however, not self-sufficient in either oil or natural gas.

However, this also means that the Chinese economy is not exempt from economic laws. It is an empirical regularity that as the real GDP per capita of an economy rises, the real rate of growth of its measured GDP will decline. This is demonstrated in Chart 0.6, in which the annual real rates of economic growth of China (red), Japan (yellow), and the U.S. (blue) are plotted against their respective real GDPs per capita. It is clear that there is a negative relationship between the rate of growth of real GDP and the level of real GDP per capita. There are a variety of reasons why this is the case. One important reason is that many of the benefits of economic development, such as increased leisure and reduced work hours, blue skies, green hills, and clear water, enhanced educational opportunities and life expectancy, do not command positive market prices and are therefore not adequately reflected in a conventionally measured GDP.

Chart 0.6. Rate of Growth of Real GDP versus Real GDP per Capita: Mainland China, Japan, and the U.S.

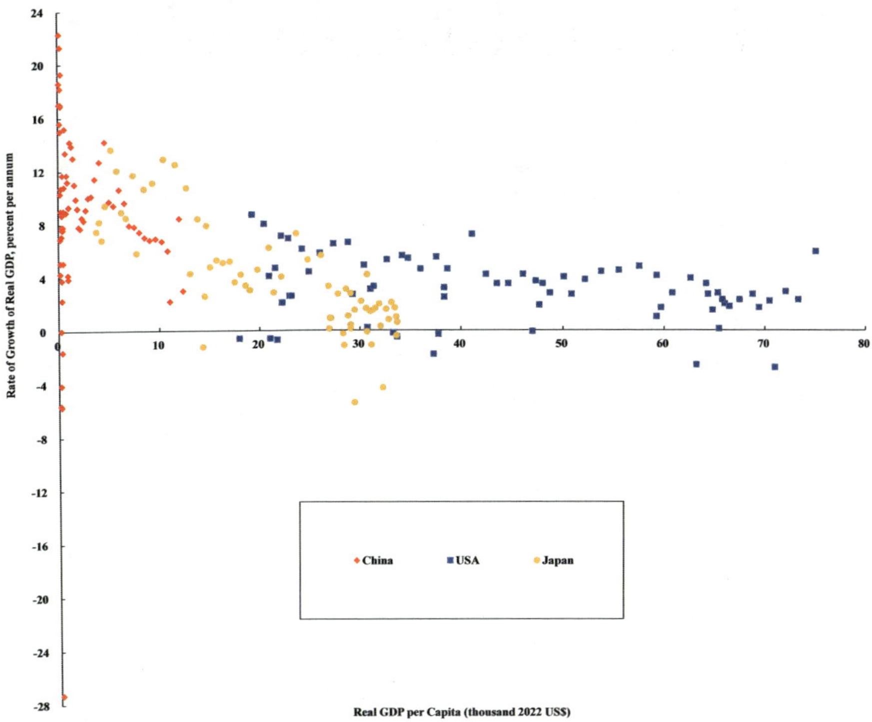

Sources: Chinese data are from the National Bureau of Statistics of China; Japanese data are from the published Statistics of the Japanese Government; and U.S. data are from the U.S. Bureau of Economic Analysis. They are converted into 2022 prices and at 2022 exchange rates by the author.

Chart 0.7. Actual and Projected Chinese and U.S. Real GDPs and Their Rates of Growth (Trillion 2022 US$ and percent)

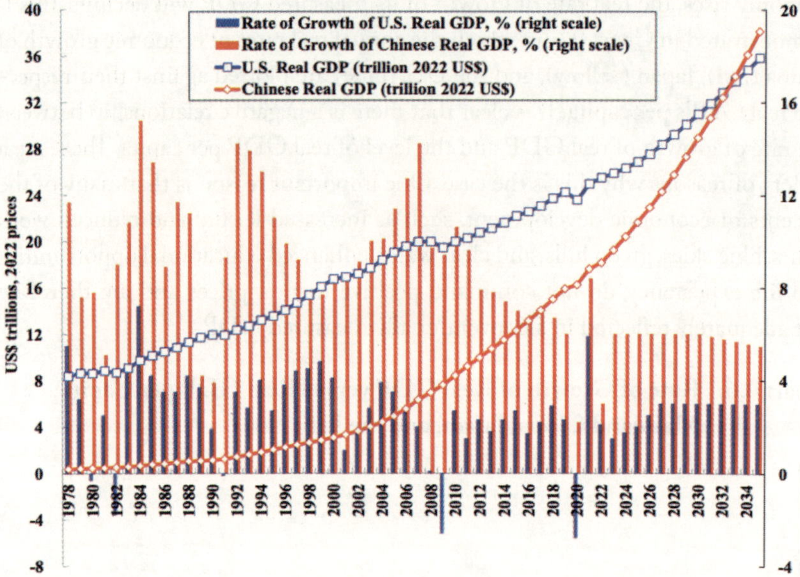

Sources: Chinese data are from the National Bureau of Statistics of China and U.S. data are from the U.S. Bureau of Economic Analysis. They are converted into 2022 prices and at 2022 exchange rate by the author. The projections are made by the author.

However, we note that China, with a GDP per capita of US$12,309 in 2022, is currently still in the range that permitted average annual rates of growth much higher than 6 percent for both Japan and the U.S. in their respective earlier periods. The real GDP per capita of the U.S. was US$76,414 in 2022, with its economy operating within a range of an average annual rate of growth of around 3 percent. This is the justification for our optimistic assumption of an average real rate of growth for the Chinese economy of between 5 and 6 percent over the next decade or two.

Our revised set of projections of the future levels of Chinese and U.S. real GDPs and their rates of growth, based on the most recent data, are presented in Chart 0.7. The underlying assumptions are that the Chinese real GDP will continue to grow at an average annual rate between 5 and 6 percent and that the U.S. real GDP will grow at an average annual rate of 3 percent, similar to its experience in the past few decades. The projections show that in 2033, the Chinese real GDP, in 2022 prices and exchange rate, will reach US$34.2 trillion, slightly surpassing the U.S. real GDP of US$33.8 trillion. These projections represent our best guesses at this time. However, the Chinese real GDP per capita in 2033 will be less than a quarter of the U.S. real GDP per capita and will lag behind that of the U.S. at least until the end of this century.